GOVERNMENT JOBS IN AMERICA

U.S. State, City & Federal Jobs & Careers
With Job Titles, Salaries & Pension Estimates
Why You Want One, What Jobs Are Available, How to Get One

By The Editors of Government Job News

A Partnerships for Community Publication
561 Hudson Street, Suite 23
New York, N.Y. 10014

Copyright: 2009

Publisher: Louis R. VanArsdale

By The Editors of Government Job News

Technical Editor: Jessica Li

Cover Design: Cheryl Klinginsmith

Layout & Design: Pierre Studios

GOVERNMENT JOBS IN AMERICA
U.S. State, City & Federal Jobs & Careers
With Job Titles, Salaries & Pension Estimates
Why You Want One, What Jobs Are Available, How to Get One

By The Editors of Government Job News

A Partnerships for Community Publication
561 Hudson Street, Suite 23
New York, N.Y. 10014

Copyright 2009

Printed in the United States of America

ISBN: 1-933639-57-1

Publisher: Louis R. VanArsdale
Technical Editor: Jessica Li
Cover Design: Cheryl Klinginsmith
Layout & Design: Pierre Studios

Table Of Contents

Chapter One
Introduction to Government Jobs in America 10

Introduction 10
Government Jobs in America 13

    ■ Good News – Government Keep Hiring As Demand Grows
    ■ Why 'Outsourcing' May Lose Its Power as a Scare Word
    ■ More Managing - Jobs Changing in Nature
    ■ Career & Hiring Choices for Employer & Employee Expand
    ■ New Workforce Model Presenting Opportunities for Part-Time,
       Contracting, & High-Paid In-House Expertise For Jobs
    ■ A Higher Educated Workforce
    ■ Experience Is an Acceptable Substitute for Education
    ■ No Test Required
    ■ Jobs with Government Are Lively Stable, Secure, and Well-Paid
    ■ Lucrative Jobs
    ■ Internships as Front Door to Hiring
    ■ Core Skills Include Business-Process Understanding
    ■ Critical Thinking Communication
    ■ Drawing Graduates from Various College Degree Programs & Majors
    ■ Government Attracting & Retaining Experienced Workers
    ■ Climate Favorable for Entry Level & Experienced

Chapter Two
Government Jobs in America
U.S. Federal – State - City Jobs
Why You Want One - How to Get One 22

Why You Want One – How to Get One 22
    ■ 10 Good Reasons to Get a Job in Government
    ■ The Best Pensions
    ■ Financial Facts
    ■ Benefits in Brief

The New Face of Government 26
    ■ The New Civil Service & Public Unionism 26
       The New Face of Civil Service 28
       Public Unionism for Jobs
    ■ Government Goes High Tech 32
       A New Government Workforce 32
       Modified Processes 33
       Re-Engineering Government & e-Government

     Major Service Delivery Models & Methods 35

     Technology in Fire, Police, EMS, 911 36

     What Government Jobs Look Like Today 39

   ◼ New Areas of Work 39
       Information Technology
       Homeland Security
       Environmental Protection

Chapter Three

What Jobs Are Available with U.S. Federal–State-City Government **41**

What Jobs Are Available 41
   ◼ Identifying Your Job Title 41

U.S. Federal Government Jobs
   ◼ Federal Government Hiring for U.S. Government Federal Agencies 43
      Hiring for 15 Executive Agencies & 101 Other Federal Agencies (Chart I)
      Competitive Hiring & Civil Service in U.S. Federal Government Based on Qualifications
      No Written Civil Service Exam Required for IT Jobs
      Knowledge – Skills – Abilities (KSAs) - Requirements
      Federal Government Job Group, Job Title & Salary Grade Pay
      General Services Salary Table – Grades 1-15 (Appendix A)

   ◼ Job Titles - Salaries & Pension Rates in U.S. Federal Government 43
      5-Year Salary Projections - Pension Estimates (Chart II)

   ◼ Factors in Determining Job Title Classification & Pay Grade (Appendix B) 43
      Knowledge Factors
      Competency Factors in Specialties
      Supervisory Factors
      Judgment Factors
      Nature of Assignment Factors
      Scope of Contacts – Purpose of Contacts

   ◼ Sample Job Announcements (U.S. Federal) (Appendix C) 44
      Criminal Investigator
      Contract Specialist
      Environmental Engineer/Environmental Scientist/Life Scientist
      Information Technology Specialist
      Transportation Security Officer (TSO) (DHS) (Screening)

   ◼ Positions in Senior Executive Service (SES) 44
   ◼ Recruitment of Interns through the Federal Career Intern Program 44

   ◼ Jobs for People with Disabilities 45
   ◼ Veteran's Preference - Jobs for Veterans 45

■ The Job Package- U.S. Federal Government 46

■ U.S. Postal Service Jobs - Job Titles - Salaries (Chart V) 49
   Corporate
   Mail Carrier & Service Jobs

U.S. State & City Government Jobs **52**
■ U.S. State & Municipal Government Hiring 52

■ Job Titles - Salaries & Pension Rates in U.S. States & Cities 53
   5-Year Salary Projections - Pension Estimates (Chart III)

■ Sample Job Descriptions – U.S. States & City Government (Appendix E) 53
■ The Job Package - U.S. State & Municipal Government 54

Chapter Four
Completing the Application & Hiring Process
U.S. Federal–State-City Government **59**

Federal Employment Process
■ Learning about Job Announcements in U.S. Federal Government Agencies 59
   Search the Official Federal Government Website Portal
   Locate Jobs Posted at Local Offices of Federal Agencies
   Locate Jobs Posted with Direct Hiring Authority and by Excepted Agencies (Appendix F)
   Locate Entry Level Administrative Jobs (Administrative Careers with America -ACWA),
   Outstanding Scholar Program, and Student Employment Programs
   Search Supplemental Job Announcements - Search Career One Stop Centers and
   America's Job Bank

■ Sample Job Announcements (U.S. Federal) (Appendix C) 62
   Criminal Investigator
   Contract Specialist
   Environmental Engineer/Environmental Scientist/Life Scientist
   Information Technology Specialist
   Transportation Security Officer (TSO) (DHS) (Screening)

■ Completing a Federal Employment Application 62
   Submitting a Federal Style Resume (by using the Resume Creator at
   USAJOBS.gov or other method), AND/OR 62
   Completing a Standard Form OF-612 (Appendix G) 63
   Customizing the Response to the Job Announcement 63
   Completing a Standard OPM Form 1203, Form C, Supplemental Qualifications Statement
   Preparing a Knowledge, Skills, Abilities (KSA) Statement (Appendix B) 64

■ Model Knowledge, Skills, Abilities Statements for Job Announcements (KSAs)
(U.S. Federal) (Appendix B)
  Information Technology Specialist

■ The Interview 65
Preparing
Asking for the Salary & Step Level You Want

U.S. State & City Government Employment Process 67
■ Learning about and Applying for a Provisional Job in State
  or Municipal Government
  Search State & City Government Websites - Job Application Websites
  Locate Jobs Posted at the U.S. State or Municipal Government
  Personnel Department Offices
  Locate Jobs Posted by Visiting Local Offices of individual Agencies in
   U.S. State & Municipal Government
  Locate Provisional Jobs Advertised in local newspaper business sections
  Search Supplemental Job Announcements at Career One Stop Centers
  –and America's Job Bank

■ Applying for a Posted or Advertised Provisional Position 68
■ Completing a U.S. State or City Employment Application 69
■ Obtaining a Civil Service Exam Application 69
  Filing the Application during an Open Filing Period
  The Civil Service Exam 70
  Ranking by Score 70
  Certified Civil Service Lists Created for the Job Titles 71
  Job Hiring Pools 71
  Types of Employment Status 72

■ Sample Job Announcements (U.S. States & City) (Appendix E) 72

■ The Interview 72
Preparing
 Asking for the Salary & Level You Want

Chapter Five
New Areas of Work
U.S. Federal – State - City **75**

Information Technology 75
- ■ Information Technology Jobs in Government
- ■ IT Job Titles in Government (U.S. Federal Government & U.S. States & Cities) (Chart IV)
- ■ Special Career Programs
- ■ Sample IT Job Descriptions & Qualifications (Appendix C & E)

Homeland Security 88
- ■ Homeland Security Jobs in Government (U.S. Federal Government)
- ■ Homeland Security Job Titles
- ■ Special Career Programs
- ■ Sample Job Announcements/Qualifications (Appendix C)

Environmental Protection - Green America Jobs 92
- ■ Environmental Protection Jobs in Government (U.S. Federal Government & U.S. States & Cities)
- ■ Environmental Protection Job Titles
- ■ Special Career Programs
- ■ Sample Job Announcements/Qualifications (Appendix C)

CHARTS 96
- ■ **CHART I:** Federal Government Hiring for U.S. Government Federal Agencies 96
  15 Executive Agencies
  101 Other Federal Agencies
- ■ **CHART II:** Job Titles - Salaries 98
  5-Year Salary Projections & Pension Estimates in U.S. Federal Government
- ■ **CHART III** Job Titles - Salaries 133
  5-Year Salary Projections & Pension Estimates in U.S. State & Municipal Government

ARIZONA
AZ-Phoenix
CALIFORNIA
COLORADO
CO-Denver
District of Columbia
FLORIDA
FL-Miami
IOWA
IL-Chicago

MARYLAND
NEW JERSEY
NV-Las Vegas
NY-New York City
TEXAS
VIRGINIA
WA-Seattle

- ■ **CHART IV:** Information Technology Skill Sets & Job Titles 235
- ■ **CHART V: U.S. Postal Service Jobs** - Job Titles - Salaries 237

■ APPENDICES 241

■ APPENDIX A: U.S. Federal Government General Service Salary Schedule 241
Grades GS-1-GS-15 (Steps 1-9)

■ APPENDIX B: U.S. Federal Government 242
Definitions of Factors Determining Job Title Classification & Pay Grade

■ APPENDIX C: U.S. Federal Government 244
Sample Job Announcements/Qualifications
Contract Specialist
Criminal Investigator
Environmental Engineer/Environmental Scientist/Life Scientist
Information Technology Specialist
Transportation Security Officer (TSO) (DHS) (Screening)

■ APPENDIX D: U.S. Federal Government, Application for Employment-
Model Knowledge, Skills, Abilities (KSAs) Statement 254

■ APPENDIX E: U.S. States & Major Cities 259
Sample Job Descriptions & Qualification Requirements

■ APPENDIX F: Locate Jobs at Direct Hire Authorities & Excepted Agencies through
Excepted Agency Personnel Departments 261

■ APPENDIX G: U.S. Federal Government, Application for Employment, Form 612
(Required) 263

■ BIBLIOGRAPHY 265

■ INDEX 268

Chapter One
Introduction
Government Jobs in America

Introduction

Chapter One: We are now in a global economy with shifts in industries and markets. A government job with job permanence over a 25-year career, a higher class of salaries , and built-in pension may be the right choice for you.

A new government workforce has taken shape because of computers in Federal, State and Municipal government. The workforce is *leaner* and *greener*. It is characterized by a reduction of clerical level jobs, the creation of a new class of employees with higher salaries, the creation of new Civil Service titles to cover new emerging jobs, and the incorporation of technology into all phases of government operations and business processes. The composition of the American workforce is changing; the nature of tech work is changing.

Government Keeps Hiring As Demand Grows. Career & Hiring Choices for Employer & Employee Expand. A New Workforce Model Presents Opportunities for Part-Time, Contracting, & High-Paid In-House Expertise. Jobs with Government Are Lively Stable, Secure, and Well-Paid. Jobs Are Changing in Nature-More Managing. Government Hiring Staff from Third-Party Providers. Experience Is an Acceptable Substitute for Education. Core Skills Include Business-Process Understanding – Critical Thinking – Communication. Government Is Attracting & Retaining Experienced Workers. The Climate is Favorable for Entry Level & Experienced- Professional, Administrative & Trade. Government Jobs are Lucrative. Professional, Administrative & Trade-Technical & 'Non-Technical' Jobs Are Available.

Chapter Two:

Why You Want One - How to Get One, indicates the reasons why a government job is a sound career choice in today's global economy. With shifting markets, mergers and re-organizations, a government job is one of the best long term career choices. It is a sound career choice for economic reasons, as well as for reasons of career interest. To support this outlook, you will learn how the government workforce has taken a new shape in the U.S., becoming a *leaner & greener* workforce, with a new class of employees with higher salaries. Public Unions, Civil Service Commissions and Agency

Good News.

Government keeps hiring as demand grows.

More Managing.

Personnel Departments have created new job titles to fill the need for a workforce in emerging technologies. A re-cap of major developments in the computer revolution and technology in government demonstrates the exciting developments surrounding most every government job in America today.

'The New Face of Government' describes **The New Civil Service & Public Unionism for Emerging Jobs**, outlining the seminal role of the Civil Service in ensuring a qualified workforce. It explains how Civil Service Commissions, Personnel Departments and Public Unions have defined new job titles and work to fulfill staffing requirements for emerging jobs in government.

'Who is Qualified' demonstrates how, in today's market, there are opportunities in government for most people who want a government job in America. Experience is an acceptable substitute for education in almost all cases. There are professional, administrative and trade technical and 'non-technical' jobs in government.

A new picture exists for job qualifications. People applying may submit an Experience and Education Resume for many jobs. Many jobs DO NOT REQUIRE taking a Multiple Choice Exam.

'Government Goes High Tech' takes you inside government. It shows how the shape and nature government have changed because of technology. Technology has made the "re-engineering of government" possible. It has modified the shape and nature of the workforce. It has modified business processes and government processes. These changes affect processes and jobs.

Chapter Three:
What Jobs Are Available – Federal-State-City, presents information on actual jobs and job titles, in the U.S. Federal government, in U.S. State governments for U.S. States, and in Municipal government for the major U.S. cities.

Salary & Pension Charts are presented for Job Titles in the U.S. Federal Government, and in 22 representative U.S. States & Cities.

A Salary Profile and Salary Projection, for each job title, indicates current and estimated 5-Year salary projection for the job title. Projections are based on a survey of real raises over 5 years. Further, the Chart includes a 20-25-30 year Pension Projection

The Job Package describes what benefits you can expect to receive with your Federal, State or City government job.

Chapter Four:
Completing the Application & Hiring Process-U.S. Federal-State-City, outlines the basic application and hiring process for U.S. Federal, State and City jobs. It explains in detail: Learning about Actual Job Announcements, Completing the Application, Taking a Civil Service Exam (or writing an Experience and Education Exam Paper if it is required); and the Federal, State and City Hiring Process.

Chapter Five: New Areas of Work.
 Exciting new developments have created new areas of work in government. New job titles and qualifications are explained for these exciting new areas of work in Chapter Five.

Information Technology
Homeland Security-Law Enforcement-Security
Enviornmental Protection

Government Jobs in America

Good News – Government Keeps Hiring As Demand Grows

There is good news for U.S. jobseekers. There will continue to be an abundance of government jobs in America for jobseekers throughout the decade. There will be expanding U.S. opportunities for those trained in fields such as health, environment, security, technology, project management, technical support and IT administration. Jobs will continue to develop in all 50 U.S. States (BLS, 2007).

Why 'Outsourcing' May Lose Its Power as a Scare Word

The fears of jobs migrating overseas far outweigh the reality. According to a new study by the ACMC released March 2006, the United States continues to increase the value of the work it is performing with its jobs in the national and global economy. The U.S. will be better off identifying the high-growth, high-value opportunities that lie ahead, rather than trying to hang on to work that's been commoditized by technology and the global dispersion of knowledge to low-cost countries. Therefore, U.S. jobs will continue to increase (Levy and Murnane, 2004).

Jobs requiring teamwork, expert communication, and critical thinking—such as troubleshooting, making decisions, developing systems that are business-driven, and building and maintaining nfrastructures will not be outsourced overseas. Government agencies and departments continue to discover greater efficiency and more competitive operations through investment in information technolgoy. Therefore, there will be continued growing demand for emerging technologies as underserved fields such as health care, e-commerce, taxation and finance, social services, buildings and construction, and certain services make greater investment in technology. Jobs in government using new technologies will continue to increase.

More Managing –Jobs Changing in Nature

Managers' ranks, Specialists and senior positions are swelling. People who once were line staff now take on managing outsourcers or work in small teams that include information technology and business-unit peers. As information technology becomes ingrained in every aspect of an enterprise, more people are needed to manage the flow and integration of information.

With thousands of baby boomers retiring from the work force each day, the brain drain will prompt government to hire for a new set of jobs. Hands-on managers will handle projects that may be require work with third-party vendors, information technology infrastructure or enterprise, technical support, or requiring you to be an overall enterprise player.

The successful management of new with older jobs will require managers with experience in both. New government employees will be asked to work with core inside staff and partnership with third-pary vendors. Third-party vendors and outsourcing contracts and staff need to be managed within government by government staff and managers.

Career & Hiring Choices for Employer & Employee Expand

Government agencies have a choice in who they will hire from and how they will hire to fill their jobs. They may hire from Service Providers, or Staffing Firms, to supplement a core staff. They may hire to build and maintain an In-house Staff or to have outside contractors develop and deploy their projects. Government agencies and departments will fill the needs of hiring a workforce to fill emerging jobs.

Experts may be paid a lot to come in and jumpstart a project. In-house staff may work with the contractors and consultants, in a seamless way. Often management and planning staff will monitor work progress and contracts. In-house staff will take over and shepherd the project through to deployment or use the procedures or equipment on a regular basis.

Entry-level jobs are often filled by people hired in-house to supplement and expand the knowledge base, to bring skills from recent education, and ability to learn to grow with the organization in their skills, and learn from the experts who may stay or who may move on.

Where the cost of keeping contractors or consultants on board full time is not deemed cost effective, or essential to the primary business of a government agency, a contractor may be asked to develop and maintain a system or provide a service.

Today government agencies have a choice. Many of them will use a combination of personnel strategies. For projects where expertise does not exist in-house, agencies will rely on contractors for staff and support. Often staff from service providers will develop and turn over a project to in-house staff, training them along the way. The service provider may carry an ongoing maintenance agreement that requires maintenance of a turnkey system, thus insuring the service provider of continued work. Thus there is a play of contract, contract-to-permanent, and permanent employment opportunities.

A New Workforce Model Presents Opportunities for Part-Time, Contracting and High-Paid In-House Expertise

As 77 million baby boomers retire over the next decade, the U.S. work force will not produce enough qualified workers to replace all of them. The boomer retirement trend will force government agencies to rethink and adapt from their traditional work forces, which are likely comprised primarily of full-time employees from executive leadership all the way down to line-level workers.

American government agencies will need to restructure their staffing models. Because the generation of new employees place a high premium on the work-life balance, often more than did previous generations, they appreciate the flexibility offered by part-time, job sharing, outsourcing and contracting opportunities.

In order to operate and grow in tomorrow's economy, government will need to shift to a new work-force model that is comprised of a smaller group of full-time employees who perform core business functions.

Highly specialized Non-core competencies may be contracted out to qualified third-party vendor partners or part-time contract workers. A generation of new employees will have a prime opportunity to fill these roles as well as work together.

While contracting for niche talent is hardly a new concept, it will become common in the post-boomer workplace. As top talent becomes scarcer due to a shrinking national work force, it will also become more expensive.

Your expertise will be highly paid, whether working as an employee for a third-party vendor, or for core in-house and managerial government jobs. With the law of supply and demand, American government will be competing for a smaller supply of trained experts in specialized fields and new areas. This will be a prime opportunity for top talent to get top dollar and for new people to enter the field. These jobs will require an understanding of the industry, business processing knowledge, people and project management skills, technical know-how, and skill sets.

A Higher Educated Workforce

Personnel Departments in government look to candidates with higher education, with their proven ability to learn. Since many new fields such as environment, energy, information technology and security have only recently graduated college students with majors in these areas, many people moved into new fields with degrees in English, Liberal Arts, Math, Engineering, and Business. With their abilities to think critically and research, new staff learned new fields, state-of-the art practices, best of breed products, software packages, performed systems analyses, and built new procedures, methods applications, and information technology infrastructures and systems.

In their book, <u>The New Division of Labor: How Computers are Creating the Next Job Market</u>, Frank Levy and Richard Murnane describe how the increased use of computers corresponds to an increased demand for a higher skilled workforce. (Levy and Murnane, 2004, 3-34) "Expert thinking" is required to know a technology, a product, a process, and to interpret data or situations and solve problems. "Critical reasoning" is required to understand how the parts fit together and to assess what needs to be done. "Complex communication skills" are required to communicate with vendors, clients, and team members within the organization. Rapid technology change raises the value of verbal and quantitative literacy.

"This dynamic, repeated in many workplaces, has contributed to the extraordinary growth over the past twenty-give years in the earnings gap between college graduates and high school graduates. In 1979, the average thirty-year old man with a bachelor's degree earned just 17 percent more than a thirty-year old man with a high school diploma. Today, the equivalent college to high school wage gap exceeds 50 percent, and the gap for women is larger. Employers judge that college graduates are more likely than high school graduates to have the skills needed to do the jobs requiring expert thinking and complex communication....These skills include the ability to bring facts to bear in problem-solving, the ability to judge when one problem-solving strategy is not working and another should be tried, and the ability to engage in complex communication with others" (Levy and Murnane, 2004, 3-34).

Computers are creating jobs and modifying jobs even as they destroy jobs. Since the 1970's, government agencies that have invested heavily in computers have shifted their workforces away from high school graduates and upward toward college graduates. (Levy and Murnane, 2004, 3-34).

Clerical jobs have been reduced. Clerical functions such as timekeeping and payroll are now automated. Computers now substitute for and complement some work. Computers also take over various rules-based operations, where the operation can be automated. Middle manager and supervisory positions have been redefined, because the need to maintain an army of clerks has disappeared.

However, the new fields and new technologies open doors. They require a higher skilled workforce that can bring "expert thinking" and "complex communication skills" to the job. A proportionately smaller and higher paid class of employee, a "new division of labor", has been created in U.S. Federal, State and Municipal government, to research, develop, implement and maintain new procedures, infrastructure and systems. In addition, managers and analysts are required to re-engineer government processes in all agencies and departments to a service delivery model utilizing the emerging technologies.

Experience Is an Acceptable Substitute for Education

Because demand exceeds supply, jobs are available to people with experience, as an acceptable substitute for formal education, in almost all cases.

Government jobs require teamwork, expert communication, and critical thinking—troubleshooting, making decisions, developing systems that are business-driven, and building and maintaining physical and computer infrastructures at all levels of government. These government jobs will be required throughout the decade and beyond. Because demand exceeds supply, government jobs are available to people with experience, as an acceptable substitute for formal education, in almost all cases.

Government jobs allow experience to substitute for formal college education in nearly all cases. Because of high demand, many jobseekers are moving into government by bringing experience, vendor-sponsored training or vendor product certifications. Because knowledge and application and new technologies are changing so rapidly, it is difficult for college students to learn all applications of knowledge, products or new technologies. College students will bring principles and a mind-set capable of life-long learning to their jobs. They will bring their educational success to their careers.

Government jobs will also continue to go to people with a specific degree major and education. These new hires will bring their educational success to their careers. Jobs will also go to people who bring experience as an acceptable substitute for formal college training.

No Test Required

Increasingly, government jobs require NO TEST. Experience & Education Resumes and Knowledge, Skills & Abilities (KSA) Statements made by the candidate-applicant, permit the agency and departmenr reviewers and interviewers to assess the candidate's qualifications, prior to interview. Government jobs allow experience to substitute for formal college education in nearly all cases.

Jobs with Government Are Lively Stable, Secure, and Well-Paid

Public Unions, Civil Service Commissions and Agency Personnel Departments have created new job titles to fill the need for a workforce in new fields and emerging technologies.

Government careers are one of the most lucrative careers today. While minimum wage in the U.S. is around $7. per hour, most government jobs in median salary ranges pay an annual $16.-$35. per hour, with an additional 33% vacation, and health care benefit package, making the job package equivalent to $21.-47. per hour. Most government pensions pay 1.5-2% of highest final salary, or average of last three year's salary, times number of years worked. These pensions provide government employees an uninterrupted lifelong income after retirement, close to half of the final year's salary. The pension benefits are paid in addition to Social Security benefits. Tax deferred savings programs also allow government employees to save during their working years, tax deferred, to pay taxes on their savings when they retire.

Government jobs exist in all 50 U.S. States and most major U.S. Cities, in all government agencies and departments. The Average Raise per Year for Job Titles, according to the Partnerships for Community Survey, is 2.25%, with a cumulative 5-Year Raise of 11.25%, and a Compounded Raise of 11.75%. In addition, many U.S. States and Major Cities have Service in Job and Service in Title Longevity Increases, at 5 years, and at 10 years. These Longevity Increases, once earned, continue to be compounded as part of the Salary, and paid over the career of the employee. The Average Retirement Pension Percentage among the 50 U.S. States and Major U.S. Cities, found in the Survey, was found to be between 1.5%-2% (highest salary or average of 3-years highest salary times number of years worked times 1.50% to 2.0% (Partnerships for Community, 2007.)

Lucrative Jobs

Using the figures gathered in the Survey, a starting salary of $55,000 in a job, and a 2.25% raise per year yields an 11.75% compounded raise over 5 years (or $61,475.). The 20-Year Retirement Pension for a career employee at a starting salary of $55,000 (without Longevity added in) is an estimated $27,369 per year. The 25-Year Retirement Pension for a career employee at $55,000 (without Longevity) is estimated at $45,876 per year. The 30-year Retirement Pension for a career employee at $55,000 (without Longevity added in) is estimated at $61,530 per year (Partnerships for Cummunity Survey). The Career Pension is in addition to Social Security Benefits. The Estimated Pension amount is in today's dollars.

Students have always poured into the most lucrative and promising careers. As salaries continue to be generously met by employers seeking to meet demand, college students will see the wisdom of that 4-year degree. A government job in America is a viable long-term career path. A four-year degree will yield the graduate over 85% more in higher wages during his or her lifetime, than that earned by the high school graduate. Good jobs in the U.S. will not go offshore to foreign workers at very low wages. Whether someone qualifies for a job through a college degree or through on the job experience, the salaries are lucrative.

Information on actual jobs and job titles, defined by and for the Federal government, all 50 U.S. States, and major U.S. Cities shows what job titles exist to fill continued job placement. A Salary Profile and Salary Projection indicates current salary for the job title, based on 5-year average raise per year. Analysis includes a 5-year salary projection, based on 5-year average raise recorded. Analysis also includes a 20-25-30 year Pension Projection based on the current salary and that State or Municipality's' formula for determining pension. Job Titles shown represent the majority of job titles in U.S. Federal, State and Municipal government agencies. The Job Titles are those as published by the U.S. Federal Government and by the U.S. States and Cities.

Internships as Front Door to Hiring

Nothing can cement a government career start quite like a good internship. Internships are a front door to hiring. Major companies, local businesses, and government agencies will take Interns with academic or computer-based training education. Typically, they will take on the Intern for 6 months to a year and assign them to an area and mentor employee. Internships can be key to getting the kind of business and industry understanding that business leaders say entry-level people often lack.

The Intern will be hired by the business or government agency. Some prospective professionals have an Internship every summer they are in school. This adds up to 3 or 4 Internships, paid or unpaid, with experience in 3-4 different companies. The staffer will have the Internship experience to put on a resume, and the references.

Government agencies often attend Job Fairs. Prospective professionals may work for government agencies while pursuing their education, seek Internships, and parlay that work into full time desirable employment.

Core Skills Include Business-Process Understanding – Critical Thinking – Communication

The core skills for U.S. jobseekers building a career are technical skills, as well as business skills. Professionals with business skills and excellent communication skills will be highly prized. The business and soft skills play key role in a job. The soft skills, such as oral and written communication, team working, critical/analytical thinking, problem solving, and adaptability, are cardinal. Business skills, such as project management, customer relations, needs analysis, and understanding of business-driven decisions and value cost-benefit analysis come into high play.

As Frank Levy and Richard Murnane indicate in The New Division of Labor: How Computers are Creating the Next Job Market (Levy and Murnane, 2006), while the lower-end rules-based virtual jobs may be outsourced overseas, jobs requiring critical thinking, pattern recognition, and symptom analysis, will not be outsourced overseas. All jobs requiring troubleshooting, making decisions, developing systems that are business-driven, and building and maintaining infrastructures require hands-on critical thinking and teamwork (Levy and Murnane, 2006). These jobs will never be outsourced overseas.

Professionals moving into government need to acquire more knowledge of the business side of processes in order to advance their careers. Technical aptitude will always be a prerequisite for entry into the IT profession, but business skills account for five of the top 10 critical skills that organizations will require for their in-house staffs over the next three years.

The need to acquire business knowledge in addition to technical proficiency has been a recurring theme for IT solution providers during the past few years, and it's especially true for those who buy technology solutions.

A successful government career requires working well individually and as a team member, embracing knowledge about emerging technologies, demonstrating troubleshooting ability, and the ability to work to facilitate the core functions and services of government.

Professional education is one corner stone. A technical postsecondary education is strongly recommended. A four-year degree makes a professional highly qualified. Postgraduate degree programs qualify an applicant to negotiate for a higher pay level.

Drawing Graduates
from Various College Degree Programs & Majors

English, Math, Computer Science, Business Administration, Management Information Systems, Public Administration, and other college degree programs and majors are suitable B.A. and M.A. majors to meet an education requirement for most government jobs. While a degree, associate tegree, technical college degree or certification is desirable, it is not necessary to have a degree or major to get a government job. Applicants are usually credited as meeting the education requirement with a high school diploma and/or 4-year college degree. Job requirements may give additional credit for a specific college major, a certain number of courses in a technical skill, or post graduate work. As an acceptable substitute for the formal education requirement, a certain amount of experience is specified in the open competitive test filing or job announcement.

Government Agencies
Attracting & Retaining Experienced Workers

By 2015, nearly one in three workers in the United States will be over the age of 50 (BLS, 2006). As the relative proportion of younger workers declines, attracting and retaining experienced and reliable workers will become a core business strategy for all employers. There are good opportunities in government for experienced employees to get new computer jobs, to change agencies, or to change divisions and obtain job upgrade promotions.

Climate Favorable for Entry Level & Experienced Personnel

There will be more government jobs available than supply over the next decade. Demand will be exceeding supply, for several reasons. An aging workforce is retiring, making it an optimum time for entry-level people to move into Entry level jobs. Entry-level jobs are available, as well as advanced positions. There are good opportunities in government for experienced employees to get new jobs, to change agencies, or to change divisions and obtain job upgrade promotions.

Chapter Two
Government Jobs in America
U.S. Federal – State - City
Why You Want One - How to Get One

Why You Want One – How to Get One

To put the U.S. job market into perspective, we are now in a Global Economy. This creates shifts in industries and markets. As industries compete and as markets open and fold, downsizing, outsourcing and restructuring are common. A Government Job in America may be a good choice for you -- if you want to move with your area and industry for a steady career, and work in delivering the promise of a new government throughout the United States.

The individual with education or experience and skills who wants to work in the government endeavor in an organization has excellent employment opportunities and choices. You may work as 1) Contract labor, 2) Contract Labor-hired to a Permanent Position; 3) Full time Employee in business or industry, or 4) Full Time Employee in City, State or Federal Government.

Only the last choice, Full Time Employee in City, State or Federal Government, is an employment choice without the risks and upsets commonly caused by corporate downsizing, outsourcing and restructuring.

Contract Labor is hired on an as "needed basis" by a hiring agent for a company or government agency. The employee will be placed for a fixed term at an hourly rate. This type of work is often good for 1) the person entering the field, 2) the person wanting to see many types of work situations before settling down, 3) the person who wants to work in the Information Technology Professional Services sector on a regular and continuing basis (Info Tech Employment, 2007).

Contract Labor hired to Permanent employment often results 1) when an employer wants to hire an employee full time or 2) when an employer no longer wants to or is unable to (due to changes in hiring policy) pay the employee on a consultant basis and must move the employee to full time status.

Full Time Employment at a Business or Industry occurs as businesses and industries rely increasingly on specialists in the industry or the vendor's products, on information technology, to create a data center or infrastructure, and hire staff to handle the technology or other specialized needs of the organization. Almost all businesses and industries have need for employees. Jobs are easily found. However, the nature of business and industry

We are now in a global economy with shifts in industries and markets.
A government job with job permanence over a 25-year career, a higher class of salaries, and built-in pension may be the right choice for you.

22

is often unstable for the individual employee. Downsizing, Outsourcing, Obsolescence and Restructuring often spell the "DOOR" for the individual employee.

Full Time, Permanent Employment in Government – U.S. Federal-City or State – adds a new word to the mix. *"Permanent"* generally means that once an employee is hired competitively and passes a probationary performance period; they are considered a Career Employee. They will be permitted to perform their job, or a similar job in another agency should there be a restructuring, for the lifetime of their career. (This is not the place for explaining the nature of the Career Civil Service in Federal-State and City governments. See the References provided in the bibliography for more information).   A 'Full Time Permanent Employment in Government' will not suffer the same effects of downsizing and outsourcing as a non-permanent government employee, and is not subject to the same downsizing, outsourcing, and restructuring as in business or industry. The Full Time Permanent Employee in Government will not lose his/her job under most circumstances.

Top 10 Reasons To Get a Government Job

1. In almost all cases, **Experience is an acceptable substitute for Education** in obtaining the government job.

2. The **Career Ladder for the job career growth series of jobs allows you to move from position to position, agency to agency, department to department to achieve Promotion and Advancement**

3. Over the long run, **you will probably make more money with a government job than with private employment** with its expected periods of unemployment and transition.

4. Government jobs offer **on-the-job training. A**s government transitions to new procedures, methods, equipment and software, agencies provide training for its career employees

5. City, State, and Federal jobs typically offer, on average, a 2.25%- -3.5% raise **per year.** This raise may not seem a lot. However, these raises are **compounded**. They can be **counted on** by permanent employees. A "Survey of IT Jobs in U.S. States & Major U.S. Cities 2007-2008" conducted by Partnerships for CommunityInfo Tech Employment shows that most U.S. States and Major Cities offer an Average Raise per Year for Job Titles, according to the Survey, is 2.25%, with a cumulative 5-Year Raise of 11.25%, and a Compounded Raise of 11.75% (Partnerships for Community, Survey, 2008.   In addition, many States and Major Cities have Service in Job and Service in Title Longevity Increases, at 5 years, and at 10 years. These Longevity Increases, once earned, continue to be compounded as part of the Salary, and paid over the career of the employee. Over the course of a career history, these raises and longevity in title increases add up. A government employee, whose job skills will be enhanced with training along the road, will experience an equal or better salary than an

employee in private business. The government employee will not lose
income due to unemployment. The government employee will not have
to accept a job at a lower wage in a job transition, lose a job due to
outdated skills, or suffer layoffs due to downsizing or restructuring.

6. Government Jobs come with a **built-in pension** that the Employer
pays for. The **Pension** is equivalent in most cases to ½ salary or 50% of final
3 year salary average, times number of years of employment.

The Average Retirement Pension Percentage among the 50 U.S. States and
Major U.S. Cities, found in the Survey, was found to be between 1.5%-2% .
Using the figures gathered in the Pension Survey, a starting
salary of $55,000 in a job, a 2.25% raise per year yields an 11.75% compounded
raise over 5 years (or $61,475.). The 20-Year Retirement Pension for a career
employee at a starting salary of $55,000 (without Longevity added in) is an
estimated $27,369. The 25-Year Retirement Pension for a career employee at $
55,000 (without Longevity) is estimated at $45,876. The 30-year Retirement
Pension for a career employee at $55,000 (without Longevity added in) is
estimated at $61,530. The Career Pension is in addition to Social Security
Benefits. The Estimated Pension amount is in today's dollars.

7. **Learning on the job and training comes with the territory**. You will
supplement your skills and move with your field or industry as you work with
others in the endeavor.

8.   While the wait on a list call may seem long, tedious and time wasted,
in reality it is time well spent. **Good employment is on the other end of a
list call wait**.

9. **Health and Medical Benefits** continue to be a part of government jobs.
It is estimated that the Health and Medical Benefits package for you and
your family, on average, supplements your salary by 33%.

 In other words, if you were to pay for your health and medical benefits
out of pocket, it would cost you an additional 33% of your salary. Or, to
put it another way, your salary is, in effect, worth 33% more than base
salary because your employer, the government agency, is paying for your
benefits. A $55,000 salary is in effect worth $55,000 x 33% ($18,150) or
$73,150. Health & Benefit Coverage is available for you and your family.

10. **Paid Vacation Time & Sick Time** continues to be equal to or higher than
that provided in private industry.

The Best Pensions

Financial facts

To put the U.S. job market and your career into further perspective, here are some further facts.   Your career and personal finances will benefit greatly over a 25 year work history by fewer or zero bouts of unemployment. Your career and personal finances can suffer greatly over a 25 year career life, by any bouts of unemployment.

You will benefit from a Health and Benefits package offered by a government employer. Most companies will stop offering significant benefits packages because they won't be able to afford them.

That means a government salary is, in effect, increased by 25-35%, the value of the health and benefits package paid by the government employer. It means, to the contrary, a salary in private industry, is decreased by as much as 25-35% because the employee will have to spend an additional 25-35% of salary out of their own pocket for health coverage for the employee and his or her family.

Your career as a government employee will provide an employer-sponsored and paid Pension. Employer-sponsored and paid for Pension Plans in private business and industry have almost all disappeared in the past 50 years. They have been replaced by 401K plans, where the employee saves their own money, and in some, not all cases, the employer makes a partial match to the funds.

The Government paid-for **Pension Benefit Payout can be equal to half the final average salary**, of the employee's final three work years. In recent years, many government paid-for Pension Plans have stopped requiring the employee to make a contribution to their pension from out of their annual salary. (For more Pension Benefit Projections for Job Titles in Government, see Chapter Three & Charts II & III).

Benefits in Brief
These are the Benefits in Brief, discussed in greater detail in Chapter Three in the Section, The Job Package.
- **Pay**
- **Permanence**
- **Annual Raises**
- **Longevity Increases**
- **Pension Plan**
- **Security**
- **Union Representation**
- **Health & Benefits Package**
- **Vacation**
- **Sick Days**
- **Flex Time**
- **Long Term & Short Term Disability**
- **Career Ladder**
- **Training and Career Development**

The New Face of Government

The New Civil Service and Public Unionism for Jobs

Beginning in the 1980's, a new Civil Service took shape. Dramatic downsizing in U.S. Federal, State, and City government, from peak 1960's workforce levels, occurred. Business-process engineering reshaped government departments, job functions, and titles, focusing services on business processes. Productivity gains brought about by technology reshaped workforce levels and government processes.

The new Civil Service retains its seminal historic purpose – to provide a workforce hired by merit rather than by personal patronage. It continues to ensure the entrance of qualified workers for new industries into government.

Yet the face of the Civil Service, especially for the new employee, has changed. The Civil Service is *leaner* and *greener*. It is characterized by a reduction of clerical level jobs, the creation of a new class of employees with higher salaries, the creation of new Civil Service titles to cover new fields including emerging technology jobs; and the incorporation of technology into all phases of government operations and business processes.

Civil service designates the body of people employed in the civil administration of governments. It excludes elected officials, as well as the military, and encompasses the vast bulk of those who see to the daily functioning of the public sector, from the municipal level to the national level. In recent times, the term Civil Service has come to mean not just the strata of officials who administer government, but a set of standards by which they are selected: it reflects the idea that government functions best when it is staffed based on merit and not political patronage. Most civil servants throughout the world today are chosen based on examinations or experience and education papers as a substitute for multiple choice examinations (AFSCME, CWA Local 1180, 2006).

Example: *New York Civil Service Law*

In New York State, the merit system of Civil Service is enshrined in the State Constitution. Article V, section 6 of the Constitution states:

Appointments and promotions in the civil service of the State and all of the civil divisions thereof, including cities and villages, shall be made according to merit and fitness to be ascertained, as far as practicable, by examination which, as far as practicable, shall be competitive.

The state's Civil Service Law implements this mandate of the State Constitution. It applies to state as well as municipal employment. Municipalities each have their own rules to implement the state Civil Service Law. In New York City, those rules are set by the New

York City Civil Service Commission, and administered by the <u>Department of Citywide Administrative Services (DCAS)</u> (AFSCME, CWA Local 1180, 2006).

Civil Service and Civil Service Employees

The bulk of Civil Service employees work in Civil Service titles subject to examinations in respective States and Cities (or Experience and Education summary papers as a substitute for exam). The Federal Government requires an Application that will be graded to see if a candidate meets the job requirements; the best candidate based on this review, will be offered a job interview.

In almost all cases, experience is an acceptable substitute for formal education for Civil Service jobs. The opportunity to describe experience and education is provided on all job and exam or experience and education applications

The Union Locals of the State, City or Federal government represent both workers who are "permanent," i.e., who have passed the Civil Service test for the title they are serving in, and workers who are "provisional," i.e., who have not passed the civil service test for the title they are serving in and were appointed provisionally to their job.

When a Civil Service exam or qualification by experience and education paper is given, the exam or qualification requirements are reviewed and graded. People who pass and have the requirements are certified as Qualified and placed on a Certified List. Once the list is established afterwards, City or State agencies hire from it. The list consists of all those who passed the test, ranked by their scores. Civil Service Law in most U.S. States and Cities requires agencies to utilize the list when they are hiring for that title, and requires them to consider the top three scorers remaining on this list; this is known as the "one-in-three rule." Once a list is established, it remains in effect for one year, and can be extended for up to three additional years. (For more information, see Completing the Application & Hiring Process.)

Provisional employees have no tenure rights. They may be initially appointed to their jobs if there is no list in effect at the time, but when a list is established following a test, agencies are required to hire from the list, and provisionals may lose their jobs as permanent civil servants are hired off the list.

There are two types of exams: "promotional exams" are open to those who hold a permanent Civil Service title in the same promotional line (e.g., someone who has a Clerical Associate title would be eligible to take the Principal Administrative Associate promotional exam); while "open competitive exams" are open to anyone regardless of civil service title (there are still educational and other requirements). Local Unions urge eligible provisional members to take a promotional exam for the title in which they are serving as soon as possible. They urge those without any Civil Service title to take an open competitive exam for the Civil Service title in direct line for promotion into their Local Union title. <u>Department of Citywide Administrative Services (DCAS)</u> (AFSCME, CWA Local 1180, 2006). (For more information, see Completing the Application & Hiring Process.)

The New Civil Service

The first use of examinations to select civil officials was in China during the Han dynasty (206 B.C.E. - 220 C.E.). In the west, the selection of civil administrators based on merit did not begin until the rise of national states replaced the feudal order. In the mid-17th century, Prussia instituted a Civil Service on a competitive basis. Similar reforms followed in France, where they became the basis for the Napoleonic reforms at the beginning of the 19th century.

In the United States, as early as 1853 Congress set to fight the forces of corruption, waste and ineptness in hiring by setting a salary scale for four types of clerks in the Washington offices of the Treasury, War, Navy and Department of the Interior, and required major departments to establish examining boards to hold "pass examinations" for applicants. In 1868, during Andrew Johnson's administration, a joint committee of Congress recommended the introduction of competitive examinations and other reforms. The first Civil Service Commission was established by Congress in 1871, authorizing the President to regulate the "admission of persons into the Civil Service. A board quickly adopted rules classifying all positions according to the duties to be performed and grades for purposes of promotion, setting up competitive examinations. In 1882 The U.S. Civil Service Commission was formed.   The first civil service reform association was formed in New York City in 1877, and in 1883 New York City and Brooklyn became the first cities in the nation to adopt Civil Service regulations. The national civil service movement was inspired by the New York examples, and the 1883 Pendleton Act reestablished a federal Civil Service Commission, and this one lasted (Liston, 1967).

The Civil Service was started nationally in the Theodore Roosevelt era. He insisted that exams be practical and test the actual duties performed. The Retirement Act of 1920 and the Classification Act of 1923 established the principle of equal pay for equal work. In 1938 President Roosevelt issued two executive orders stating that all positions which were not excepted by law from the competitive service were in the competitive service. The second order established Divisions of Personnel in the executive departments and agencies. The sense of security and well being Civil Servants enjoy today is largely due to the gains made by unions in the post depression years through WWII. (Liston, 1967, 38).   By 1950, 45 States had Civil Service systems to hire for State and City jobs.

Public Employee Unionism expanded membership of Civil Servants in the 1950's. The American Federation of State, County and Municipal Employees (AFSCME), the American Federation of Teachers (AFT), and other unions of firefighters, policemen, nurses, civil servants and post office workers swelled the ranks of the public employee unions from under 400,000 in 1955 to over 4 million by the early 1970's.

AFSCME, a union for small groups of technical and professional workers, became one of the AFL/CIO's largest affiliates. It grew into a union of gray and new white collar workers, encompassing industrial trades, social service workers, clerical workers, and the class of information technology workers (Zieger, 1994, 164).

Public Unionism for New Job Titles

The breakthrough of Public Employee Unionism into the 1960's prepared a climate ripe for the representation of new job titles in new fields and emerging technology workers by the public unions in the 1970's, 1980's, and 1990's.

As Personnel Departments identified new workforce demands and created job titles and classifications in the 1970s-1990's, the AFSCME/AFL/CIO unions spread their wings to represent the workers in the titles. The various Civil Service Commissions, Departments of Personnel and Public Employee Unions worked to incorporate new job titles and examinations into the government Civil Service.

Ensuring a Qualified Workforce for New Technologies
Civil Service Job Titles for New Jobs

The role of labor is essential in the operation of government. As new needs develop, business and government need to hire new staff. In business, companies hire competitively by advertising job openings, searching college placement and employment offices and hiring companies specializing in the field to provide them the expert staff they need.   In government, labor is hired either open competitively through the Civil Service exam process, or contractually by hiring subcontractors to provide the expert labor.

Since the mid-1970's, the need for an emerging technologies workforce has changed the landscape of State, Municipal and Federal U.S. government. New workforce needs have necessitated new job titles, job classifications, on-the-job education, training, hiring, and pay scales.

Developing New Job Titles for Emerging Technologies

First generation technology workers often worked under non-technology job titles. During the 1980's, Federal, State, and City Personnel and Administrative Services Departments created task forces to create job titles and job descriptions that would ensure the movement of qualified workers into jobs needed for the future. The job descriptions could neither be too specific, as related to a specific hardware or software, nor too generic, because that would leave the door open to people with no training or experience. In Information Technology, often training to operate specific hardware and software was required. To accommodate this, Certification, Education and Experience requirements, with particular vendor products, were included in many job descriptions. These jobs titles have been expanded and refined, as new needs have been identified and new job titles required.

The sense of security and well being Civil Servants enjoy today is largely due to the gains made by Public Unions in the post depression years through WWII. (Liston, 1967, 38). Affluent workers and stable unions characterized the 1950's and 1960's. (Zieger, 1994, 164).

"Aggressive organizing by such unions as the American Federation of State, City & Municipal Employees (AFSCME), the American Federation of Teachers (AFT), and other unions of firefighters, policemen, nurses, civil servants, and postal employees...swelled union membership among government workers from under 400,000 in 1955 to over 4 million by the early 1970's," according to Robert Zieger in <u>American Workers, American Unions</u>. Public sector unionism grew through through the 1960's and 1970's. While the microchip revolution permitted private sector corporate employers to relocate in low-wage non-union countries like Malaysia, the Carribean, China and India, one of the biggest buyers of the new microchip equipment was government – spending money on a new trained workforce to use the equipment. Despite problems for unions in the private sector in the 1980's and 1990's, unions in the public sector continued to provide the stable workforce the Federal, State and Local governments needed." (Zieger, 1994).

Between 1950 and 1980, the prosperity and growth of gross national product led to "big government", both in terms of the payrolls of federal, state and local governments, and the programs and constituents government supported in a new welfare state. By the 1980's the cost of this government to the American taxpayer was deemed too high.

New technology enabled Federal, State and Municipal government to "downsize," to trim payrolls. It enabled Federal, State and Municipal governments to reduce the cost of social programs with legislated "welfare reform." Welfare reform coincided with new technologies. New technologies were used by State and Local social services agencies to develop job opportunity databases in conjunction with American businesses. Information technology systems continue to be used by social service workers to identify job opportunities for welfare clients and to help them schedule interviews and start to work.

The stable unions maintained their stability in government through these years. They supported reduction of workforce through the attrition of older workers. They furthered the "re-engineering of government" by developing of new Civil Service job titles and salary bases with Departments of Personnel to accommodate a new class of technological workers.

The breakthrough in public employee unionism from the 1950's and 1960's laid the ground to benefit the new class of educated and skilled professionals.

Growth in membership by representing these new titles balanced losses in union membership brought about by reduction of payrolls elsewhere. The unions continue to serve as a channel for economic gain and equality of treatment among minorities, immigrants and highly educated and skilled professionals. Collective bargaining and coverage of information technology professionals has created a high standard of living, rather than a substandard living, for a new class of educated and skilled technology professionals. Personnel Departments identified new workforce demands and created job titles and classifications in the 1980s-1990's. New Civil Service job titles, with union representation, are an ardent reminder to government workers or Americans that we too will share in the fruits of the capitalistic system, and the productivity gains brought by technology.

Organized labor's achievements to organize the workforce in new fields, new titles and emerging technologies can be seen in:

☐ the creation of Union Locals to represent new jobs titles and fields,
☐ the creation and definition of job titles to reflect the new skills required for these new jobs,
☐ the creation of experience and education exams to determine the qualifications of job candidates, and
☐ workplace safety and security guidelines and measures for workers who operate high tech equipment.

While the zeal in organized labor of the 1930's and 1940's waned during the 1960's and 1970's, when there was more job security and less limitation to obtaining a job, the concerns of that zeal have been raised again with the current generation.

International outsourcing, corporate mergers, and reorganizations are driving up the desirability of government jobs with union protection and benefits. More people want good government jobs. The high cost of union negotiated government job benefits makes the nature of union-management negotiations as much "about the money" as it was prior to WWII.

Labor and Management today are locking heads on sticking points such as who pays what share of medical benefits, salaries, benefits for new employees, and other tradeoffs that would reduce the union benefit package and reduce the cost of pensions.

In the 1990's, as an alternative to all-Union Civil Service staff with information technology staff reaping full benefits and paid pensions, many Federal, State and Local governments brought in consultants. The injunction in many State and City administrations was to "jump start" new technology applications and build infrastructure and applications fast with expert trained staff, and to build a core trained information technology workforce in Civil Service.

Management now has a choice of hiring options: they can hire contract, contract-to-permanent, or full time permanent for an in-house staff, and use a combination of all three employment methods. Government jobs have grown, those filled by third-party providers and those filled through Competitive Civil Service for a Career Civil Service workforce. The benefits to the jobseeker of these job hiring choices have been and will continue to be considerable.

Government Goes High Tech
The New Government Workforce

Between 1950 and 1980, the prosperity and growth of gross national product led to "big government", both in terms of the payrolls of Federal, State and local governments, and the programs and constituents government supported in a new welfare state. By the 1980's the cost of this government to the American taxpayer was deemed too high.

New technology enabled Federal, State and Municipal government to "downsize," to trim payrolls. It enabled Federal, State and Municipal governments to reduce the cost of social programs with legislated "welfare reform." Welfare reform coincided with new technologies. New technologies were used by State and Local social services agencies to develop job opportunity databases in conjunction with American businesses. Information technology systems continue to be used by social service workers to identify job opportunities for welfare clients and to help them schedule interviews and start to work.

Beginning in the 1980's, dramatic downsizing in U.S. Federal, State, and City government, from peak 1960's workforce levels, occurred. Business-process engineering reshaped government departments, job functions, and titles, focusing services on business processes. Productivity gains brought about by the technology itself reshaped workforce levels and government processes.

The changing shape of government coincided with the computer revolution and was facilitated by it. Technology helped government re-engineer and re-shape itself. Government helped technology come into the fabric of government and business processes.

Downsizing & Change in Shape
Changing Pay Scales & Education Requirements

A new government workforce has taken shape because of computers in Federal, State and Municipal government. The workforce is *leaner* and *greener*. It is characterized by a reduction of clerical level jobs, the creation of a new class of employees with higher salaries, the creation of new Civil Service titles to cover new fields and computer and emerging technology jobs; and the incorporation of technology into all phases of government operations and business processes.

As the need for clerical workers has disappeared, as well as the need for middle managers to manage staff, salaries have been redirected to tech job workers. Pay Scales have changed. Savings from reduction of workforce and downsizing have been rolled into new fields and computer tech job salaries.

Staffing Requirements for Government

The staffing directions in government are driven by workforce requirements. They reflect the trends that drive hiring by corporations and IT service providers. (For more information, see Chapter III, Section II, The New Face of Government, for a full description of these forces that drive hiring.)

New Players - New Partnerships

Application of business principles to e-government has brought with it the cost-saving techniques of relying on expertise by hiring third-party vendors rather than retaining an in-house staff. Challenges involve 1) defining responsibilities that cannot go to third party vendors, 2) utilizing the available hiring strategies for building and retaining specialized staff; 3) assessing projects on the basis of development and maintenance needs and determining staffing requirements accordingly (Richardson, 2004, x; 200-217; Franzel and Coursey, 2004, 63-77).

Modified Processes
Re-Engineering Government & E-Government

New technology enabled Federal, State and Municipal government to "downsize," to trim payrolls by capitalizing on the productivity gains offered by automation and technology. Throughout the 1970's office automation created productivity gains in government.

In the 1980's with the possibilities afforded by LANS, WANS, the Internet, and the co-joining of electronic data processing and computer communications technologies, a digital government became possible to further automate government processes.

"Electronic government or E-government, can be defined as the 'use of technology, particularly web-based Internet applications, to enhance the access to and delivery of government information and service to citizens, business partners, employees, other agencies and government entities (McClure, 2000) The "Promise of e-Government" is described by David Garson as an attempt "to bring the e-business model into the public sector." (Garson, 1999). To bring about the promise, "reinventing government" and "reengineering government" has become central and co-creative.

In 1993, Vice President Al Gore's National Performance Review (NPR), he emphasized the need of 1) making government more business-like, including more reliance on markets and public-private technology, 2) using technology to replace existing processes, and 3)achieving cost-savings by shrinking the overall size of government. (Fletcher, 1999). In 1997 Vice President Al Gore coined the term "information superhighway." Re-engineering government departments to improve productivity involves modifying processes: 1) delivering services using digital government; 2) cost saving using online processes with the realignment of staffing, and 3) creating a new class of employee to develop and maintain technology systems.

The Functions of Technology in Government
E-Government - Digital Government

In <u>*The Tools of Government*</u> Christopher Hood (1983) explained the functions of government as:

- ☐ **Node** – being in the middle of an information or social network
- ☐ **Treasure** – being the holder and distributor of social and monetary goods
- ☐ **Authority** – being the administrator of Laws; possessing Legal and Official power;
- ☐ **Organization** – a group of people with skills to deliver and administer the resources of government.

Technology is used in government in parallel ways as:

- ☐ **Information Node** - to deliver and gather information
- ☐ **Governance Tool** - to implement policy and uphold the law by data processing/decision-processing systems,
- ☐ **Treasure Tool** - to distribute goods and services, including monies and goods, electronically
- ☐ **Organizational Tool** – to facilitate the delivery of services within the organization (Margetts, 1999).

New technologies are used in:

- ☐ **E-Governance** - to sustain policies and regulatory systems and administer   goods and services based on the Law
- ☐ **E-Management** - to use information, the information technology infrastructure, and IT processes to enhance the management of government
- ☐ **e-Democracy** - to interact with citizens in support of the democratic process
- ☐ **E-Commerce** - to conduct the business of government with citizens, business partners, vendors and other government agencies using information technology (Richardson, 1999, 214)

Further, the use of technology in government delivers goods and services:
- ☐ **Government to Citizen**
- ☐ **Government to Business**
- ☐ **Government to Government** (Margetts, 1999).

Digital Government's Major Service Delivery Models & Methods

The Web Portal Model – Internet & Intranets

The web portal model is being used as a technology framework in the U.S. Federal government to carry out the electronic government strategies set forth in the President's Management Agenda of 2002. A portal is a doorway for users to access the web. The web portal model has been adopted by many Federal, State and City agencies. It is used for the delivery of services to U.S. citizens, to provide interactions with business, and to conduct business between other government agencies.

USAJOBS www.USAjobs.gov; www.irs.gov; www.nsf.gov and other portal sites all follow the portal model of delivering services and information to citizens (Fletcher, 2004, 52-86; Franzel, 2004, 69-77.) Today, all 50 U.S. States and most U.S. Cities have web portals as a single point of entry to State and City information and services.

Intranets are used within government agencies and departments to provide a private network for the exchange of data and information within the organization, closed to the public.

The Internet and the World Wide Web (WWW), electronic mail, file transfer, and on-line interactive processing permitting interoffice, local, national and global communications, e-commerce, and electronic data processing, in interactive real time.

Data Processing Applications

Data Processing Applications handle the processing of information. From large mainframe computers, to mid-range computers, to PC workstations, data processing applications gather information, legacy systems

Relational Databases & Data Warehouse

Today in E-Commerce and E-Government, information databases, client-customer-citizen databases, and service-product databases, function at a speed and detail due to the relational database model and query languages. Relational databases allow analysts in government to specify the relations they want to exist between pieces of data and the processes and functions they want to perform with the data.

Office Automation Applications

Office Automation applications handle business applications easily and locally, with the use of office automation software, such as Microsoft WORD, Excel, Access, PowerPoint, Microsoft Outlook, and Graphics software such as Quark xPress and Adobe Acrobat, InDesign, Photoshop, and other software products.

E-Procurement

The Internet is a tool for the procurement process used for 1) issuing bids, 2) publishing RFI's and RFPs; 3) reporting on contracts, 4) registration of vendors, 5) publishing service and product pricing schedules; 5) verification about vendor compliance on work laws, scofflaws and tax delinquencies; 6) electronic payment.

E-Commerce

E-Commerce, or the transacting of business electronically, between government and citizen, government and business and government and business, characterizes many software applications. When citizens e-File their IRS Tax Return, this is e-Commerce. When the U.S. Federal Government issues a refund and deposits in a citizen's Bank Account, this is e-Commerce.

Major e-Commerce systems include the U.S. Internal Revenue Service Tax Collection & Refund Systems, the U.S. Social Security Administration systems; State and City Property Tax and other Revenue Collection Systems, State and City Vendor Payment Systems, Social Service Benefits Systems; all Electronic File Transfer payment systems.

Geographic Information Systems

"GIS uses information and communication technology tools to store, analyze, query, manipulate, distribute and display data that has been spatially-referenced using addresses, political and administrative boundaries, or earth bound coordinate systems. GIS is used in a broad range of public sector applications, including, for example, land use and urban growth planning, legislative redistricting, crime tracking and law enforcement, benchmarking human services, emergency management, environmental monitoring, and public information services" (O'Looney, 2000, Gant & Ijams, 2004, 249.)

Technology in Fire, Police, EMS, 911

The Fire, Police, Fire, EMS and 911 Departments are determined to leverage the best technologies available in the war on crime and in delivery of emergency services for citizens. The tools encompass a broad spectrum of applications. They include resources designed to train the best officers in the country and tools to identify the perpetrators of crime, the locations of or problems, and the dispatch of services.

Mobile Data Terminals
800MHz Trunked Radio System
Advanced Mobile Operations Simulator
Computer Aided Dispatch System
Driving Emulation System
Firearms TrainingSystem (FATS)
Preliminary Arraignment System (PARS)
GIS Crime Mapping
DNA Laboratory
Forensic ScienceLaboratory
Chemistry (Drug)Laboratory
Police 9-1-1 System

800MHz Trunked Radio System

The Federal Communications Commission (FCC) has determined that trunking will be the radio standard into the 21st century because it uses the radio spectrum more efficiently and allows more users onto the airwaves. Since field units infrequently transmit at the same time and most police transmissions are relatively short, frequency sharing can create more on-air time. Because trunked systems are handled by computer, Police departments can quickly "create" an additional channel to handle a hostage situation or change channel assignments to allow public works or other city agencies to communicate on the police channel during natural disasters. "Dispatch Monthly Magazine."

Advanced Mobile Operations Simulator (AMOS)

The Advanced Mobile Operations Simulator (A.M.O.S.) is a fully interactive one person Driving Simulator that utilizes five monitors to provide a realistic 225-degree view of the road. This provides a view that encompasses the driver's full peripheral vision. The scenarios dictate that the student operates in both patrol and emergency vehicle operations (E.V.O.), The A.M.O.S. provides immediate feedback to the officers regarding their strengths and weakness (Philadelphia Police Department).

Computer Aided Dispatch System

A Computer Aided Dispatch (CAD) is a system of processing telephone calls from the public and the dispatches to police vehicles. The CAD computer system is has a completely redundant back-up protocol to ensure 99% reliability. It is the most sophisticated computer-operated dispatching system of any large police department.

Driving Simulation System

A multi-position semi-interactive driving simulation system helps to develop and refine basic driving skills in numerous circumstances and in various traffic situations, road conditions and emergencies. Drivers respond to real life simulated judgment, decision making and crash avoidance skills. Using multiple simulator stations, instructors can train and evaluate multiple drivers simultaneously. Crash avoidance teaches students to react appropriately, including stopping distance and speed.

Firearms Training Simulator (F.A.T.S.)

A Firearms Training Simualator is an advanced firearms simulator that features system operated weapons that actually recoil and give shot sounds. Use of verbal commands and use of available cover/concealment is expected of the trainee. Once the scenario begins, the trainee is expected to behave as they would if this were an actual encounter. The camera mounted on the front of the unit records the trainees shots fired (FATS® Virtual Training Solutions Company).

Preliminary Arraignment System (PARS)

A Preliminary Arraignment System (PARS) is designed to capture all arrest information that pertains to individuals charged with a crime. It is based upon client server technology and is configured into a wide area network that services every police installation that processes prisoners. A PARS is connected to the District Attorney's Office, which uses the system to aid in the arraignment process.

DNA Laboratory, Forensic Science Laboratory, Chemistry Laboratory

A DNA Identification Laboratory utilizes state-of-the-art techniques to identify and compare biological stains like blood, semen, hairs, to samples from known individuals to assist in numerous investigations and prosecutions, especially with sexual assault.

A Forensic Science Laboratory, commonly referred to as a "Crime Lab", is responsible for analysis of all physical evidence, other than controlled substances or firearms, related to crimes of violence and property, in three categories: (1) Trace evidence, like paint, fibers, gunshot residue; (2) Biological evidence - blood, semen, hairs and (3) Miscellaneous evidence - footwear impressions, arsons.

A Chemistry Laboratory, often referred to as the "Drug Lab", conducts chemical analysis of evidence confiscated during criminal investigations. Street drugs, prescription drugs and chemically engineered designer drugs are identified; clandestine laboratory crime scene processing and any other types of chemical consultation services are provided.

911 Call Taking & Dispatch Systems

U.S. State, County and City government use sophisticated 911 systems to receive calls, identificy location of calls, assign calls priority status, route calls to dispatchers. These 911 systems use a variety of sophisticated telecommunications equipment, Geographic Positioning System (GIS) equipment, Interactive Voice Response (IVR) equipment, databases, and radio dispatch equipment. 911 Systems employ trained Call Takers, and employees in Fire Dispatch Rooms, Police Dispathc Rooms, Emergency Management System Dispatch Rooms, and others to operate and utilize systems, and information technology and telecommunications staff to build and maintain infrastructure.

What New Government Jobs Look Like

While it would be difficult to give a uniform picture of a job in government, there are some characteristics that define jobs. Jobs will involve:

☐ **Unique Agency & Department Missions**
☐ **Information Technology Functions**
☐ Delivery of Services
☐ **Research & Planning into Business Processes**
☐ **Research & Planning into Emerging Technologies**
☐ **Building Systems**
☐ **Building & Maintaining Databases**
☐ **Building & Maintaining Internet and Intranet Website Portals**
☐ **New Players & Partnerships with Third-Party Vendors & Staff**
☐ **Maintaining Systems**
☐ **Building Physical and Electronic Infrastructure**
☐ **Maintaining Physical and Electronic Infrastructure**
☐ **Procurement & Management Analysis**
☐ **Management of Contractors & Vendors**
☐ **Constant Work**

New Areas of Work

New areas of work exist in these exciting areas.
See Chapter Five:

Information Technology
Homeland Security-Law Enforcement-Security
Enviornmental Protection

Chapter Three
What Jobs Are Available
U.S. Federal - U.S. States & Cities

Identifying Your Job Title (Chart II)

1. **Identify Job Titles that are in your Field**
2. **Identify Job Titles that Support your Field, Program Area, Industry or Interest**
3. **Identify Entry-Level, Mid Career and Upper Level Job Titles**

U.S. Federal Government Jobs

Federal Government Hiring for U.S. Government Federal Agencies

The Federal Government hires for 15 Executive Agencies & 101 Other Federal Agencies (Chart I). The range of jobs required by these agencies is wide. The number of jobs required is in the thousands. (USOPM, Executive Agencies)

Competitive Hiring & Civil Service in U.S. Federal Government Based on Qualifications

The U.S. Federal Government hires staff competitively, based on the best qualifications, hiring the best qualified candidate who applies for the job. "Competitive" means hiring the best candidate with the best qualifications for the job.

No Written Civil Service Exam Required for Most Jobs

There is No Written (Multiple Choice or Essay) Civil Service Exam required for most jobs. The job reviewer will review the candidate's work experience and education and qualifications for the particular job, based on a review of the candidate's information, submitted on the Form 612 (Appendix G) Job Application or Resume, and the Form C. The "Competitive" appointment is made, and the candidate hired, on the basis of Experience and Education.

To plan a career path in government, examine the Job Titles, Salaries, 5-Year Projected Salaries and Pension Estimates, shown in Charts II & II.

Knowledge – Skills – Abilities (KSAs) Requirements

Each Job Announcement designates the requirements for the job. In U.S. Federal job announcements, these requirements are called Knowledge, Skills, and Abilities (KSAs) that are required. These are the minimum requirements. Since the job reviewer will select the "best" qualified candidate, a job applicant should list as much applicable education and work experience as possible, to achieve a higher rank than another candidate.

To learn how the Job Title in the Job Announcement you are responding to has been classified, consult the "Job Family Position Classification Standard GS Group" (USOPM, 2003). You may search the government website www.opm.gov for the Classification Standard specifications for every GS group number. In the Search box, simply put the GS number, i.e. GS-2200. This document will tell you what the qualifications are for each job in the job group and its salary grade on the career ladder.

Consult the "Introduction to the Position Classifications Standard" (USOPM, Position Classifications, 1995,) and "The Classifier's Handbook (USOPM, Classifier's Handbook, 1991) to understand further the instructions to the classifiers and reviewers for determining job title salary grading and reviewing candidate qualifications.

To learn how to provide additional pages to your Resume, with your Knowledge, Skills & Abilities see **Chapter V: Completing the Application & Hiring Process, and Appendix H: Knowledge, Skills, Abilities (KSAs) Formatting & Factors Response.**

Federal Government Job Group, Job Title & Salary Grade Pay System

When a position is needed, the Classifier assigns the position a Job Group, Job Title, and Salary Pay Grade, based on the job standards and qualifications required.

The Grade Pay will correspond to the U.S. Federal Government General Schedule of Annual Rates by Grade and Step. The U.S. Federal Government General Services Salary Table published below shows the GS Salary Grades 1-15, with their corresponding Salaries, and the Steps 1-10 for each Grade. Steps 1-10 are achieved by promotions based on experience and performance.

General Services Salary Table – Salary Grades 1-15
[See Appendix A: General Services Salary Table]

Factors in Determining Job Title Classification & Pay Grade

Federal Jobs are given job title and pay grades based on several factors:

☐ Knowledge Factors in Determining Job Grade & Salary
☐ Competency Factors in Determining Job Grade & Salary
☐ Supervisory Factors
☐ Judgment Factors
☐ Nature of Assignment Factors
☐ Scope of Contacts – Purpose of Contacts

Each Job Announcement lists Job Requirements. When you are preparing your Resume for a specific Job Announcement, refer to Appendix C: Definitions of Factors Determining Job Title Classification & Pay Grade to understand how you may write your Resume to reflect how your experience fulfills these Factors and Requirements of the job. (See Appendix C: Definitions of Factors Determining Job Title Classification & Pay Grade).

Job Titles - Salaries - 5-Year Projected Salaries - Pension Estimates in U.S. Federal Government

Chart II

To Estimate a Career Path for Yourself:

1. Identify Job Titles that are in your Field
2. Identify Job Titles that Support your Field, Program Area, Industry or Interest
3. Identify Entry-Level, Mid Career and Upper Level Job Titles

4. Identify Job Announcements
5. Apply for and receive the Job
6. Work hard to achieve a completely Satisfactory Job Performance each year, based on Tasks & Standards for your Job. You will receive an In-Service Step Increase.
7.. Consider applying for new Job Announcements for Jobs at a Higher Salary in a New Job Title

8. Estimate your Salary & Pension based on In-Service Step Level Increases, Promotions, Job Title changes, and Years in Service.

Sample Job Announcements - U.S. Federal Government

Contract Specialist
Criminal Investigator
Environmental Engineer/Environmental Scientist/Life Scientist
Information Technology Specialist
Transportation Security Officer (TSO) (DHS) (Screener)

See Appendix D for Sample Job Announcements in the above Job Titles

All Current Job Announcements will be found at http://www.USAJOBS.gov, the official U.S. Federal Job Web Portal.
Appendix C: Sample Job Announcements - U.S. Federal Government.

Positions in Senior Executive Service (SES)

Members of the Senior Executive Service serve in the key positions just below the top Presidential appointees., providing the major link between these appointees and the rest of the Federal work force in approximately 75 Federal agencies (USAOPM, 2006).

SES jobs are announced on http://www.USAJOBS.gov. The SES pay range has a minimum rate of basic pay equal to 120 percent of the rate for GS-15, step 1, and the maximum rate of basic pay is equal to the rate for level III of the Executive Schedule (USAOPM, 2006).

Recruitment of Interns through The Federal Career Intern Program

The Federal Career Intern Program is designed to help agencies recruit and attract exceptional individuals into a variety of occupations. It is intended for positions at grade levels GS-5, 7, and 9. In general, individuals are appointed to a 2-year internship. Upon successful completion of the internships, the interns may be eligible for permanent placement within an agency. Individuals interested in Career Intern opportunities must contact specific agencies directly (http://www.opm.gov/careerintern/.)

Jobs for People with Disabilities

U.S. Federal government agencies provide reasonable accommodation to applicants with disabilities. For additional information on the employment of people with disabilities within the Federal Government, please visit the Office of Personnel Management Web site: www.opm.gov/disability

The Office of Personnel Management (OPM) has established special appointing authorities for people with disabilities. EPA has the authority to use a special appointing authority to hire a qualified person with a disability for vacant positions. These special appointing authorities include:

5 CFR 213.3102(ll) for hiring readers, interpreters and personal assistants. This excepted authority is used to appoint readers, interpreters and personal assistants for employees with severe disabilities.
5 CFR 213.3102(t) for hiring people with mental retardation. This excepted authority is used to appoint persons with cognitive disabilities (mental retardation). They may qualify for conversion to permanent status after 2 years of satisfactory service.
5 CFR 213.3102(u) for hiring people with severe physical disabilities. This excepted authority is used to appoint persons with severe physical disabilities who have demonstrated satisfactory performance through a temporary appointment, or have been certified as likely to succeed in performing the duties of the job. After 2 years of satisfactory service, they may qualify for conversion to permanent status.

Veteran's Preference - Jobs for Veterans

Veterans meeting the criteria for preference and who are found eligible (achieve a score of 70 or higher either by a written examination or an evaluation of their experience and education) have 5 or 10 points added to their numerical ratings depending on the nature of their preference.

For scientific and professional positions in grade GS-9 or higher, names of all eligibles are listed in order of ratings, augmented by veteran preference, if any. For all other positions, the names of 10-point preference eligibles who have a compensable, service-connected disability of 10 percent or more are placed ahead of the names of all other eligibles on a given register.

When applying for Federal jobs, eligible veterans should claim preference on their application or resume.

Applicants claiming 10-point preference must complete form SF-15, Application for 10-Point Veteran Preference. The SF-15 is available online at: http://www.opm.gov/forms/pdf_fill/SF15.pdf .

The Job Package - U.S. Federal Government

Pay

A Federal job provides equal to or better pay than in the private sector, over the long term. There are no disruptions in employment, caused by private merger, downsizing or reorganization. Base pay factors could include performance-based pay, competency-based pay, geographic locality pay, structural and market adjustments, longevity pay, skills-based pay and other factors (USAOPM, Primer, 2006.) The Pay Benefit Package includes 13 Paid Holidays, 13 Paid Sick Days, between 13-26 Paid Annual Leave Days, and a Health Benefit Package that is equivalent to 33% salary. This is like adding an additional 1/3 on to your paycheck.

Permanence

A Career Service Federal employee will achieve job permanence after a probationary period, usually of one year, in the job title, and a successful performance evaluation. The Civil Service Merit System provides for a one-year Probationary Period, during which the employee's performance is evaluated to determine if it is satisfactory and permits Permanent Appointment. There are strict procedures and guidelines for severance from Federal employment service. An employee is entitled to Union Representation in any action toward severance. (USAOPM, Glossary, 2006).

Annual Raises

Annual Raises in Federal Career Service are typically 2.1%, 10.4% 5-Year cumulative, and 10.75% compounded over 5 years.

Longevity Increases

The Longevity-Competency and Performance-Based System makes pay increases on a regular basis based on a performance system .

Pension Plan

The Federal Employment Retirement System (FERS) is based on a 3-part benefit structure, allowing for:

☐ *Social Security Benefits*

☐ *Pension Benefits –Basic Benefit Plan*

   Average 3-Years Highest Salary X Creditable Service X 1%

☐ *Thrift Savings Program & Deferred Compensation Plan*

   Your agency will set up a Thrift Savings Plan account for you and will automatically contribute an amount equal to 1% of your basic pay each pay period. These Agency Automatic (1%) Contributions are not taken out of your salary, and your agency makes these contributions whether or not you contribute your own money to the TSP.

Vacation Days – Annual Leave

Annual Leave is used for vacations, rest and relaxation, and personal business or emergencies. New full-time employees earn 4 hours of annual leave each 2 week pay period (13 Days per year). When you have 3 years of service this increases to 6 hours every 2 weeks (19.5 Days per year) , and at 15 years it increases to 8 hours every 2 weeks (26 Days per year).

Paid Holidays

☐ **New Year's Day**
☐ **Birthday of Martin Luther King, Jr.**
☐ **Washington's Birthday**
☐ **Memorial Day**
☐ **Independence Day**
☐ **Labor Day**
☐ **Columbus Day**
☐ **Veterans Day**
☐ **Thanksgiving Day**
☐ **Christmas Day**

Sick Leave

Federal Employees accrue 4 hours sick leave every two weeks, or 13 days of Sick Leave per year. You can accrue this leave without limit.

☐ *Different Ways to Use Sick Leave*

    Sick Leave for Family Care or Bereavement

    Sick Leave for Adoption

    12 Weeks of Paid or Leave without Pay Sick Leave for Family Care

    Interaction with 13 days of Sick Leave for Family Care/Bereavement Purposes

    The Family and Medical Leave Act (FMLA)

    Interaction of Sick Leave for Family Care With the Family and Medical Leave Act

    Leave Transfer And Leave Bank Programs

    Interaction of Sick Leave for Family Care With the Leave Sharing Program

    Leave for Childbirth;   Leave for Adoption

    Sick Leave for Family Care or Bereavement

Student Loan Repayment Program

The Federal student loan repayment program permits agencies to repay Federally insured student loans as a recruitment or retention incentive for candidates.

Health & Benefits Package

☐ **Federal Employees Health Benefits Program (Over 350 Plans)**

    Individual Health Benefits

    Family health benefits

    Medical Health Plan

    Major Medical & Hospitalization

☐ **Prescription Plan**

Career Ladder - Advancement

☐ **Advancement in Job Title Grades (Steps I-IV)**

    Federal Employees may achieve normal advancement through successful Performance Evaluation, and advance within Job Title Series, from Steps 1-9 on the GS Pay Schedule, at a rate of 1-2 Step Increases per year.

☐ **Advancement through Promotion (Grades I-IV)**

    Federal Employees may advance through Promotions by achieving exceptional Performance Evaluations, and advance within Job Title Series, from Steps 1-9 on the GS Pay Schedule, at a rate of 1-3 Step Increases per year.

☐ **Advancement through Changing Positions within a Department, Agency, or Between Agencies. Federal Employees may achieve career advancement by changing positions within a Department or Agency, or between Federal Agencies.**

Multiple Employment Opportunities

☐ **Transfers within an Agency or Department**

☐ **Transfers between Agencies**

Training and Career Development

☐ **Intergovernmental Personnel Act Mobility Program**

    The Intergovernmental Personnel Act Mobility Program provides for the temporary assignment of personnel between the Federal Government and state and local governments, colleges and universities, Indian tribal governments, federally funded research and development centers, and other eligible organizations

☐ **Detail and Transfer of Federal Employees to International Organizations**

☐ **The Executives in Residence Program: Executives in Residence (EIR)**

☐ **Leadership & Knowledge Management Programs**

☐ **Individual Learning accounts (ILA)**

□ *Individual Development Plans (IDP)*
□ *Candidate Development Programs for Senior Executive Service -Senior Executive Service (SES) Candidate Development Programs (CDP's)*
□ *Career Transition Resources- Federal employees gain access to over 1 million jobs through Career One Stop in addition to other career transition resources .*

Union Representation

Federal employees are entitled to full Union Representation in contracts, negotiations, disputes and settlements, or unfair labor practice complaints .

Union Benefits

□ *Major Medical Supplemental Health Benefits*
□ *Educational Assistance*
□ *Career Development Assistance*
□ *Supplemental Life Insurance Policies*
□ *Legal Representation at Hearings & Other Legal Support*

Long Term Care Insurance & Flexible Savings Account

The Federal Long Term Care Insurance Program (FLTCIP) helps cover long term care costs. Premium conversion uses Federal tax rules to let employees deduct their share of health insurance premiums from their taxable income, thereby reducing their taxes. John Hancock and MetLife provide this insurance, under a company called Long Term Care Partners, LLC to administer the Program.

The Federal Flexible Spending Account Program

The Federal Flexible Spending Account (FSA) Program lets the employee set aside pre-tax money to pay for health and dependent care expenses. The result can be a discount of 20% to more than 40% on services routinely paid for out-of-pocket.
□ *Health Care Flexible Spending Account (HCFSA)*
The maximum annual amount that can be allotted for the HCFSA is $5,000. Covers eligible health care expenses not reimbursed by your FEHB Plan, or any other medical, dental, or vision care plan you or your dependents may have. The minimum annual amount is $250.
□ *Dependent Care Flexible Spending Account (DCFSA)*
Covers eligible dependent care expenses incurred so you, or your spouse, if married, can work, look for work, or attend school full-time.

Federal Life Insurance Program

The Federal Employees' Group Life Insurance Program is the largest group life nsurance program in the world, covering over 4 million Federal employees and retirees, as well as many of their family members. FEGLI provides group term life insurance. The cost of Basic insurance is shared between you and the Government. You pay 2/3 of the total cost and the Government pays 1/3. Your age does not affect the cost of Basic insurance.

Survivor Benefits

If you die while you are a Federal employee, payments will be made in a particular order set by law from:
□ *Life Insurance (FEGLI)*
□ *Unpaid Salary*
□ *Thrift Savings Plan funds*
□ *Retirement Lump Sum*

U.S. Postal Service Jobs

The United States Postal Service (USPS) is an independent establishment of the executive branch of the United States government (see 39 U.S.C. § 201) responsible for providing postal service in the U.S. The Postal Reorganization Act signed by President Richard Nixon on August 12, 1970, replaced the cabinet-level Post Office Department with the independent United States Postal Service. The Act took effect on July 1, 1971.

The U.S. Postal Service

- ☐ Employs nearly 700,000 career employees.
- ☐ Processes and delivers more than 213 billion pieces of mail — letters, cards, ads, bills, payments and packages — every year.
- ☐ Delivers mail to more than 300 million people at 146 million homes, businesses and PO Boxes in every state, city and town, and in Puerto Rico, Guam, the American Virgin Islands and American Samoa.
- ☐ Adds 1.8 million new addresses each year to our delivery network — equivalent to the number of addresses in a city the size of Chicago.
- ☐ Serves more than 9 million customers daily at nearly 37,000 Post Offices.
- ☐ Has annual operating revenue of nearly $73 billion.
- ☐ Is the second-largest employer in the United States.

- ☐ Pays nearly $2 billion in employee salaries and benefits every two weeks.
- ☐ Does not receive tax dollars for operations. Is a self-supporting agency, using the revenue from the sale of postage and products to pay expenses.
- ☐ Handles more than 46 percent of the world's card and letter mail volume — delivering more mail to more addresses to a larger geographical area than any other post in the world.
- ☐ Moves mail using planes, trains, trucks, cars, boats, ferries, helicopters, bicycles, hovercrafts, subways and even mules.
- ☐ Operates the largest civilian vehicle fleet in the world with more than 216,000 vehicles driving more than 1.2 billion miles each year and using nearly 121 million gallons of fuel.
- ☐ Issues nearly 900,000 money orders per day.
- ☐ Operates Automated Postal Centers (APCs), self-service kiosks that provide customers with access to the most frequently purchased postal products and services.

"Neither snow nor rain nor heat nor gloom of night stays these couriers from the swift completion of their appointed rounds."
These words, inscribed at the top of the James A. Farley building in New York City, are considered to be the motto of the Postal Service. In fact, it isn't a motto at all. The phrase is the translation of an ancient Greek work of Herodotus describing the Persian system of mounted carriers, c. 500 B.C.

Jobs with the U.S. Postal Service are available in two categories: Mail Processing Jobs and Corporate Jobs. Mail Processing Jobs require an exam; application to take an exam can be made online at http://www.usps.gov. Corporate jobs require submitting a Resume. Information about Mail Processing Jobs and Corporate Jobs can be found at the USPS.gov website (http://www.usps.gov). The USPS.gov website lists exams being given, procedures for making online applications, and job descriptions.

Major Postal Unions at a Glance - Salary Rates

Four public unions represent all the employees in the U.S. Postal Service:

The American Postal Workers Union (APWU) (http://www.apwu.org) is the largest postal union, representing more than 260,000 USPS career employees primarily in the Clerk, Maintenance and Motor Vehicle Services crafts.

The National Association of Letter Carriers (NALC), (http://www.nalc.org) the second largest postal union, represents about 222,000 career employees. NALC members deliver mail to residences and businesses on city delivery routes.

National Rural Letter Carriers' Association (NRLCA) (http://www.nrlca.org) career and part-time relief workers deliver mail to residences and businesses on rural delivery routes.

The National Postal Mail Handlers Union (NPMHU), (http://www.npmhu.org) a division of the Laborers' International Union of North America, represents nearly 58,000 career employees engaged in the bulk transfer, loading and unloading of mail.

Note	APWU	Note	NALC	Note	NRLCA	Note	NPMHU	Note
Represents	260,049	1	222,132	1	128,028	1	57,894	1
Full-time	221,069	1	193,660	1	66,725	1	52,880	1
Part-time	38,980	1	28,472	1	61,303	1,2	5,014	1
Maximum salary without premium or overtime pay	$59,749	3	$51,021	3	$47,404	3,7	$48,521	3
Minimum salary without premium or overtime pay	$29,557	3	$38,527	3	$36,424	3	$28,516	3
Average annual salary without premium or overtime pay	$48,316	4	$47,911	4,6	$45,280	4	$45,044	4
Average hourly rate without benefits premium or overtime pay	$23.35	5	$23.22	5,6	$21.77	5	$21.80	5
Average hourly rate with benefits premium and overtime pay	$37.91	5	$37.44	5,6	$34.02	5	$36.65	5

Notes: As of September 2007
1. From USPS PP 20-07 ORPES.
2. Part-time count for NRLCA includes long-term "non-career" employees while non-career categories are not included in counts for other unions.
3. Salary schedules as of Sept. 30, 2007.
4. Calculated from distribution of employees and salary schedule.
5. From USPS National Payroll Hours Summary (NPHS) PP20-07.
6. NALC September NPHS numbers, plus estimate of the impact of the November 2006 wage increase.
7. This salary is the 40-hour evaluated route salary. There are routes evaluated at more hours that have higher salaries.

Detailed information, provided by these unions at their websites, explains the salary, hiring and promotion provisions, and retirement and pension systems offered to USPS employees. USPS employees typically receive between 1.2% and 2% raise per year, or an average of 1.7% raise over five years.

U.S. Postal Service Employees are covered by either the Civil Service Retirement System (CSRS) or Federal Employment Retirement System (FERS) provisions and benefits offered to Federal Civil Service Employees.

Job Titles - Salaries - 5-Year Projected Salaries - Pension Estimates in U.S. Postal Service

Chart V

U.S. State & City Government Jobs

U.S. State & Municipal Government Hiring
for State & City Agencies & Departments

Jobs exist in all 50 U.S. States and most major U.S. City government agencies and departments. U.S. States and major U.S. Cities hire staff for most of their government departments and agencies. Agencies and Departments that are found in most U.S. States and Cities include

Board of Elections	Housing Authority
Buildings, Department of	Human Resources Administration – Social Services
City Clerk	Information Technology and Telecommunications,
State & City Employees' Retirement System	Investigation, Department of
Civil Service Commission	Management and Budget, Office of
Consumer Affairs, Department of	Mayor's Office
Correction, Department of	Parks and Recreation, Department of
Cultural Affairs, Department of	Payroll Administration, Office of
Economic Development Corporation	Personnel, Department of
Education, Department of	Police Department
Emergency Management, Office of	Probation, Department of
Environmental Protection, Department of	Records, Department of
Finance, Department of	Sanitation, Department of
Fire Department	Transportation, Department of

The Salaries for Job Titles in State and City government are higher than for many trade, labor and administrative titles. The Average Raise per Year for Job Titles, according to the Partnerships for Community Survey, is 2.25%, with a cumulative 5-Year Raise of 11.25%, and a Compounded Raise of 11.75%. In addition, many States and Major Cities have Service in Job and Service in Title Longevity Increases, at 5 years, and at 10 years. These Longevity Increases, once earned, continue to be compounded as part of the Salary, and paid over the career of the employee. The Average Retirement Pension Percentage among the 50 U.S. States and Major U.S. Cities, found in the Survey, was found to be 1.5% (Partnerships for Community).

Using the figures gathered in the Survey, a starting salary of $55,000 in an Information Technology job, a 2.25% raise per year yields an 11.75% compounded raise over 5 years (or $61,475.). The 20-Year Retirement Pension for a career employee at a starting salary of $55,000 (without Longevity added in) is an estimated $27,369 per year. The 25-Year Retirement Pension for a career employee at $55,000 (without Longevity) is estimated at $45,876 per year. The 30-year Retirement Pension for a career employee at $55,000 (without Longevity added in) is estimated at $61,530 per year. The Career Pension is in addition to Social Security Benefits. The Estimated Pension amount is in today's dollars. The Job Titles – Salaries – Salary Projections and Estimated Pensions are listed in the Charts below for representative U.S. States and Major Cities., based on published current Salaries, published by each of the U.S. States and Cities (U.S. Government, Freedom of Information Act).

Job Titles - Salaries - 5-Year Salary Projections
Estimated Pension in U.S. States & Municipalities

Chart III

To Estimate a Career Path for Yourself:

1. Identify Job Titles that are in your Field
2. Identify Job Titles that Support your Field, Program Area, Industry or Interest
3. Identify Entry-Level, Mid Career and Upper Level Job Titles

4. Identify Job Announcements
5. Apply for and receive the Job
6. Work hard to achieve a completely Satisfactory Job Performance each year, based on Tasks & Standards for your Job. You will receive an In-Service Step Increase.
7.. Consider applying for new Job Announcements for Jobs at a Higher Salary in a New Job Title

8. Estimate your Salary & Pension based on In-Service Step Level Increases, Promotions, Job Title changes, and Years in Service.

Sample Job Descriptions
U.S. States & City Government (Appendix C)

If you are seeking a position, you may read Job Descriptions to understand the job qualifications and levels of experience required. These Job Descriptions are found on the State and City, Personnel Department and Employment websites. Job Descriptions may also be obtained by sending an e-mail to the Contact person identified at the Personnel Website. We have provided Sample Job Descriptions for some of the main job titles, published by U.S. States and major cities. (**Appendix C**).

The Job Package – Benefits
U.S. State & City Government

Pay

A U.S. State or Municipal government job provides equal or better pay than in the private sector, over the long term. There are no disruptions in employment, caused by private merger, downsizing or reorganization. Base pay factors could include performance-based pay, competency-based pay, schedule differential pay, longevity pay, and other factors. The Pay Benefit Package includes 11 Paid Holidays, 13 Paid Sick Days, between 13-26 Paid Annual Leave Days, and a Health Benefit Package that is equivalent to 33% salary. This is like adding an additional 1/3 on to your paycheck.

Permanence

A U.S. State or Municipal employee will achieve job permanence after a probationary period in the job title, usually of one year, and a successful performance evaluation. The Civil Service Merit System provides for a one-year Probationary Period, during which the employee's performance is evaluated to determine if it is satisfactory and permits Permanent Appointment. There are strict procedures and guidelines for severance from employment. An employee is entitled to Union Representation and Legal Representation during any severance action that might, in rare cases, be taken.

Annual Raises

Annual Raises in U.S. State and Municipal government typically average between 2.25%-3%, per year, 11.25%-15% 5-Year cumulative, and 11.75%-15.75% compounded over 5 years (Info Tech Employment, Survey, 2007.)

Longevity Increases

U.S. States and Municipal government have a variety of In Service and/or In Title Longevity Increases, ranging from No Increase, to as much as $3,000 In Service Longevity after 10 years In Service, and $3,000 after 5 Years In Title. These Longevity Increases are rolled into Base Pay and Compounded over time, in most cases (Info Tech Employment, Survey, 2007.)

Pension Plan

The Employee Retirement Systems for most U.S. States and Cities make provisions for:

☐ *Social Security Benefits*

U.S. State and Municipal career employees pay full social security taxes and receive full social security benefits.

☐ *Pension Benefits –Basic Benefit Plan*

Employees pay either zero or a small contribution to the Pension Plan, ranging from 0% - 6% of pay, for a determined number of years, based on the specific Union or Non-Union hiring contract the employee is hired under. The Retirement Formula for the Pension is, on average: Average 3-Years Highest Salary X Creditable Service X 1.5%-2.25% (depending on specific U.S. State or City. Some States and Cities have undefined Pension Plans based on employee contributions.) (Info Tech Employment, Survey, 2007.)

☐ *Pre-Tax Deferred Compensation Savings Program*
   Most U.S. State and Municipal government agencies offer a voluntary employee-
   funded retirement savings program, with choice of providers and investment options.
   You may defer a percentage of your base pay up to a specified amount, in before-tax
   dollars. Thus, you are paying less on your Income Taxes during the year you defer i
   income. Savings is taxed at the time of distribution.

☐ *After-Tax 401K or 401K Roth Retirement Savings Program*
   A voluntary 401K or 401K Roth Retirement Savings Program is also available for most
   U.S. State and City government employees. You may save to a 401K or 401 Roth with a
   choice of providers and investment options. Taxes are paid at the time of
   saving. However, no taxes are paid at the time of withdrawal.

Vacation Days – Annual Leave

Annual Leave is used for vacations, rest and relaxation, and personal
business or emergencies. While U.S. State and Municipal Labor-
Management contracts vary from State-to-State and City-to-City, most
new full-time employees earn 4 hours of annual leave each 2 week pay
period (13 Days per year). When you have 3 years of service this often
increases to 6 hours every 2 weeks (19.5 Days per year) , and at 15 years it
often increases to 8 hours every 2 weeks (26 Days per year).

Paid Holidays

☐ **New Year's Day**
☐ **Birthday of Martin Luther King, Jr.**
☐ **Washington's Birthday (or President's Day)**
☐ **Memorial Day**
☐ **Independence Day**
☐ **Labor Day**
☐ **Columbus Day**
☐ **Election Day**
☐ **Veterans Day**
☐ **Thanksgiving Day**
☐ **Christmas Day**

Sick Leave

Most U.S. State and Municipal employees accrue 4 hours sick leave every
two weeks, or 13 days of Sick Leave per year. You can accrue this leave
without limit.

☐ **Different Ways to Use Sick Leave**
   ☐ **Sick Leave for Family Care or Bereavement**
   ☐ **Sick Leave for Adoption**

☐ **The Family and Medical Leave Act (FMLA)**
☐ **Interaction of Sick Leave for Family Care With the Family and Medical Leave Act**
☐ **Leave Transfer And Leave Bank Programs**
☐ **Interaction of Sick Leave for Family Care With the Leave Sharing Program**
☐ **Leave for Childbirth**
☐ **Leave for Adoption**
☐ **Sick Leave for Family Care or Bereavement**

Health & Benefits Package Health Care

Comprehensive Health Care coverage is available to U.S. State and City government employees and eligible dependents. Cost for coverage varies for each State or City, from No Cost to a specified bi-weekly fee, or maximum out of pocket expense per contract, per benefit year. Choices of Health Care Coverage Plans are offered. Health Care Coverage includes Doctor-Provider Coverage and Hospital Coverage. Employees may also choose to pay for uncovered Health Care Expenses out of a Medical Spending Account, that establishes their own pre-tax account to pay for medical or dental expenses for the employee and their dependents.

☐ *Individual Health Benefits*
☐ *Family health benefits*
☐ *Medical Health Plan*
☐ *Major Medical & Hospitalization*

Career Ladder -Advancement

☐ *Advancement in Job Title Levels (not Automatic in most cases)*
   U.S. State and Municipal employees in certain titles, may advance to the next level of the title, based on performance or duties performed.
☐ *Advancement through Promotional Exams or Provisional Promotion*
   U.S. State and Municipal employees may achieve Promotion either through successful completion of a Promotional Civil Service Exam and appointment by an Agency, or by Provisional Promotion to a higher job titles or level by an Agency or Department.
☐ *Advancement through Changing Positions within a Department, Agency, or Between*
   AgenciesU.S. State and Municipal employees may achieve career advancement by changing
   positions within a Department or Agency, or between Federal Agencies, either by Transfer to a Higher Job Title or by taking a Civil Service Exam and achieving successful appointment, or applying for an achieving Provisional Appointment in the same of higher title with higher pay.

Multiple Employment Opportunities

☐ *Transfers within an Agency or Department*
   U.S. State and Municipal employees may apply for any job opening within an Agency or Department and seek to obtain the position through competitive qualification.
☐ **Transfers between Agencies**
   U.S. State and Municipal employees may apply for any job opening within an Agency or Department and seek to obtain the position through competitive qualification. This provides employees with an optimum opportunity to advance by bringing acquired skills and experience to a new job.

Training and Career Development

The Training and Career Development programs vary from State-to-State and City-to-City. They often include these types of training and career development:

☐ *Equal Opportunity Employment Opportunity Training*
☐ *On-Site Training*
☐ *Computer-Based Training from Learning Libraries*
☐ *Instructor-Led Courses*
☐ *Off Site Training*
☐ *Vendor Product Specific Training*

Union Representation

U.S. State and Municipal employees are entitled to full Union Representation in contracts, negotiations, disputes and settlements, or unfair labor practice complaints.

Union Benefits

Union Benefits vary from State-to-State and City-to-City. They often include these types of benefits:

☐ *Eyeglasses – VDT Glasses*
☐ *Major Medical Supplemental Health Benefits*
☐ *Educational Assistance*
☐ *Civil Service Exam Preparation Assistance*
☐ *Supplemental Life Insurance Policies*
☐ *Legal Representation at Hearings & Other Legal Support*
☐ *Prescription Plans and/or Dental Plans (varies by Union)*

Other Benefits

U.S. State and Municipal employees receive these other types of Benefits, which may vary from State-to-State and City-to-City.

☐ *Medical Spending Conversion Health Benefits Buy-Out Waiver Program*
☐ *Medical Spending Plan Premium Pre-Tax Conversion*
☐ *Health Care Flexible Spending Accounts*
☐ *Dependent Care Flexible Spending Account Program*
☐ *College Pre-Tax Savings Program*
☐ *Long Term Care Insurance*
☐ *Long-Term Disability Insurance*
☐ *Life Insurance*
☐ *Survivor Benefits*

Chapter Four
Completing the Application and Hiring Process
U.S. Federal – State - City

Federal Employment Process

Learning about Job Announcements
with U.S. Federal Government Agencies

There are several ways to find all the job announcements for current available Federal jobs in Information Technology

1. **Search the Official Federal Government Website Portal –**
   http://www.USAJOBS.gov
2. **Locate Jobs Posted at Local Offices of Federal Agencies by contacting regional Federal Executive Boards for Agency Local Office & Personnel Department Listings**
3. **Locate Jobs Posted with Direct Hiring Authority and by Excepted Agencies (See Appendix F) by directly contacting these Agency Personnel Departments & searching** http://www.USAJOBS.gov
4. **Locate Entry Level Administrative Jobs (Administrative Careers with America -ACWA), Outstanding Scholar Program, and Student Employment - Search** http://www.opm.gov/qualifications/SEC-V/sec-v.asp; http://www.opm.gov/employ/luevano-archive.asp#Outstanding; http://www.studentjobs.gov;
5. **Apply for the Information Technology Exchange Program (ITEP). Visit** http://www.opm.gov **for more details about the program.**
6. **Search Supplemental Job Announcements - Search Career One Stop Centers -** http://www.careeronestop.org; **and America's Job Bank** http://www.ajb.org/

1. Official Federal Government Jobs Website Portal
http://www.USAJOBS.gov

Your Career in the U.S. Government Starts at the Official Federal Government Job Website Portal! USAJOBS is provided at no cost and offers information on 20,545 U.S. government job opportunities worldwide. USAJOBS.gov is the official job site of the United Stated Federal Government. You may search job announcements by Job Category, Job Location, and Job Salary Grade. You may also request E-Mail notifications about jobs in your job categories, locations and salary grades. For representative, sample job Announcements from USAJOBS.gov, see Appendix D.

2. Locate Jobs Posted at Local Offices of Federal Agencies by contacting regional Federal Executive Boards for Agency Local Office & Personnel Department Listings

Federal Executive Boards, located in each U.S. Region maintain a list of all
Federal Agency Regional & Local Offices. Contact your
regional Federal Executive Board for Agency local offices in your region.
Contact or visit these Local Office Personnel Departments for Job
Announcements **http://www.feb.gov**.

3. Locate Jobs Posted with Direct Hiring Authority and by Excepted Agencies (See Appendix F) by directly contacting these Agency Personnel Departments & searching http://www.USAJOBS.gov

While the traditional method to enter Federal service is by appointment through the competitive examining process, (Competitive Appointment Job Announcements are announced on USAJOBS.gov), Agencies may also appoint candidates directly to jobs. When an agency has a severe shortage of candidates or has a critical hiring need, direct hire provides a quick way to hire individuals into the Competitive Civil Service (GS-15 and below or equivalent) in permanent or nonpermanent positions. Direct hire allows the agency to attract a larger pool of candidates by advertising job openings. Jobseekers may go to USAJOBS.gov to see many Direct Hire positions. Jobseekers may also go to individual Agency websites to identify direct hire job openings, that may or may not be posted on USAJOBS.gov.

Information Technology Management (Information Security),
GS-2210, GS-9 and above, jobs at all locations, are Direct Hire jobs.

Excepted Service Positions, Senior Executive Positions, and Appointments
Authorized by Statute, the "excepted service", consists of all positions in
Excepted Service Agencies (See Appendix G). This includes the Executive
Branch, the President, the Library of Congress, the Federal Bureau of
Investigation and other agencies.

To locate Jobs posted with Direct Hire Excepted Agencies, search the list of
Excepted Agencies provided in Appendix G and search the Agency's individual
website employment page. You may also contact the Personnel Departments
of Excepted Agencies for Posted Job Announcements. Appendix G provides
website and personnel department contact information for Excepted Agencies.

4. Locate Entry Level Administrative Jobs (Administrative Careers with America (ACWA), Outstanding Scholar Program, and Student Employment Jobs-Search http://www.opm.gov/qualifications/SEC-V/sec-v.asp;http://www.opm.gov/employ/luevano-archive.asp#Outstanding; http://www.studentjobs.gov;

For Entry-Level Administrative Jobs (GS 5-GS-7) (with or without information technology skills), the Federal Government offers the *Administrative Careers with America Program (ACWA)*. Over 150 Federal Job occupations are eligible for ACWA appointments, whereby candidates will complete scannable questionnaires detailing their qualifications and experience. The U.S. Office of Personnel Management grades the questionnaires and provides Federal Agencies with a list of the best qualified candidates. For some positions, a written exam may be given by the hiring Agency. For a list of titles where a written and performance test may be given, see http://www.opm.gov/qualifications/.

Through the *Outstanding Scholar Program*, Agencies may appoint those college graduates from accredited schools who obtained a grade point average of 3.5 or higher on a 4.0 scale for all undergraduate courses completed toward a baccalaureate degree. They may also appoint those who stand in the upper 10% of a baccalaureate graduating class, or of a major university subdivision such as a College of Arts and Sciences. These appointments may be made without going through an examination procedure for jobs at grades GS-5 and GS-7 in covered occupations. To learn more about appointment through the Outstanding Scholar Program, see http://www.opm.gov/employ/luevano-archive.asp#Outstanding.

Student Job opportunities are available for students who are working towards a diploma, certificate, or degree. The *Student Temporary Employment Program (STEP)* and the *Student Career Experience Program (SCEP)* provide training and a means for students to achieve a career conditional appointment. To learn more about these appointment opportunities, see http://www.studentjobs.gov. The *Presidential Management Internship Program* (http://www.opm.gov/fedregis/1995/60r11017.pdf) offers professional, entry-level positions to graduate students, leading to a permanent career position.

Plus, at http://www.studentjobs.gov you will find information for students on:
Apprenticeships
Cooperative Programs
Fellowships
Grants
Internships
Scholarships

5. Apply for the U.S. Federal Government Information Technology Exchange Program (ITEP) The ITEP is a new and exciting professional development opportunity. If you are already employed in IT in the private sector, or if you are currently employed in IT in a federal agency, you may be eligible to participate. This program allows exceptional performers from the Federal and private IT sectors to participate in temporary assignments of three (3) months to 1 year, in the other sector. ITEP promotes the interchange of IT workers to develop, supplement, and modernize IT skills to expand the long term conpetencies of the Federal IT workforce. While Federal agencies have a strong interest in the areas of Enterprise Architecture, Solutions Architecture, IT Project Management, and IT Security, ITEP Exchange opportrnities can exist in all IT disciplines. Please visit http://www.opm.gov for more details about the program.

The following federal agencies are participating in this program. To contact the ITEP representative for jobs for IT professionals from the Private Sector for this program with these listed Agencies, visit http://www.usajobs.opm.gov/itep.asp.

**DEPARTMENT OF COMMERCE
DEPARTMENT OF DEFENSE
DEPARTMENT OF HEALTH AND HUMAN SERVICES
DEPARTMENT OF HOMELAND SECURITY (DHS)
DEPARTMENT OF JUSTICE (DOJ)**

**DEPARTMENT OF THE TREASURY
ENVIRONMENTAL PROTECTION AGENCY
FEDERAL BUREAU OF INVESTIGATION
OFFICE OF PERSONNEL MANAGEMENT (OPM)**

To view ITEP opportunities in the private sector for existing Federal employees, visit http://www.actgov.org/ITEP.

5. Search Supplemental Job Announcements - Search Career One Stop Centers – http://www.careeronestop.org; **and America's Job Bank –** http://www.ajb.org/

CareerOneStop is an integrated suite of national web sites that help businesses, job seekers, students, and workforce professionals find employment and career resources. *CareerOneStop*, sponsored by the U.S. Department of Labor, includes three core products:

America's Career InfoNet (http://www.CareerInfoNet.org) provides national, state and local career information and labor market data using unique career tools, career reports, videos, a career resource library and other innovative web-based tools.

America's Job Bank (http://www.ajb.org) is the nation's largest online labor exchange. Businesses post job listings, create customized job orders, and search resumes. Job seekers post resumes and search for jobs that fit their career goals. A companion web site, *Department of Defense Job Search* (http://dod.jobsearch.org), is a career resource for businesses and military personnel transitioning to civilian careers to match work opportunities.

America's Service Locator (http://www.ServiceLocator.org) maps customers to a range of local services including workforce centers, unemployment benefits, job training, education opportunities, and other workforce services.

Sample Job Announcements/Qualifications (U.S. Federal) (Appendix C)

Information Technology Specialist
Criminal Investigator
Transportation Security Officer (TSO) (DHS) (Screener)
Contract Specialist
Environmental Engineer/Environmental Scientist/Life Scientist

Completing a Federal Employment Application OF-612 to Obtain a Federal Job

Responding to the Job Announcement comes after locating the position(s) you want to apply for. Responding to a Federal Job Announcement involves:

1. **Submitting a Federal Style Resume (by using the Resume Creator at USAJOBS.gov or other method), AND/OR**
2. **Completing a Standard Form OF-612 (Appendix G)**
3. **Customizing the Response to the Job Announcement**
4. **Completing a Standard OPM Form 1203, Form C, Supplemental Qualifications Statement (SQS),**
5. **Preparing a Knowledge, Skills, Abilities (KSA) Statement (Appendix B)**

It is Required that you Mail, Fax, or Electronically Submit your Standard Form OF-612, Form C, and KSAs. You may also submit a Federal Style Resume by preparing one with the Resume Creator at USAJOBS.gov and submitting it electronically at http://www.USAJOBS.gov, in addition to Mailing, Faxing or Electronically Submitting the OF-612, Form C, and KSAs

1. Submitting a Federal Style Resume, using the Resume Creator at http://www.USAJOBS.gov

It is recommended that you use the Resume Creator at http://www.USAJOBS.gov. It provides the format the Federal Government expects to see in a resume, and will help you structure your resume. It is important to structure your Federal Resume and your KSAs to 1) respond to the specific Job Announcement, and 2) to clearly identify where your experience and education fill the specific requirements and demonstrate the specific experience and skills being asked for. Your Resume may be examined by someone who is not the hiring manager. Therefore, your Resume must read clearly and present the best possible case for why you are the right fit for the job announcement and what is being asked for. More on structuring and customizing your Resume will be found in the section on Customizing the Response.

2. Completing a Standard Form OF-612 (See Appendix G)

The Standard OF-612 may be downloaded and printed from http://www.opm.gov/forms/pdf_fill/of612.pdf. The downloadable form may be filled in electronically online. You may Print the Form or Save the Form. Section C, Additional Work Experience pages, will need to be copied or duplicated, so you may fill your work experience that will take more space than the section on the form for Additional Work Experience provides. You need to Mail, Faxing or Electronically Submitting the OF-612, Form C, and KSAs. You will find a copy of OF-612 in Appendix G.

3. Customizing the Response to the Job Announcement

Your Response, in the Federal Resume, OF-612, and the KSAs Statement should mirror the words of the specific Job Announcement. Where the Job Announcement asks for the candidate to perform named task and duty, your response will indicate how and where you performed named task and duty. For example "Performed [Name Task & Duty] in this position, in this assignment, in this context, with these competencies and knowledge, skills, and abilities, with this degree of supervision or supervisory control, with this degree of difficulty, calling on this type of special knowledge or contacts with others (See Factors determining Salary Grade, Appendix C.)

In Responding to each Named Task or Duty required of the job, indicate how & where you previously performed or demonstrated the:

[Named Knowledge, Competencies or Specialties]
[Named degree of Supervisory control or Minimal Supervision Authority]
[Named Degree of Difficulty]
[Named Degree of Judgment called for]
[Named Special Knowledge (i.e. of Equipment, Software, Procedures, Legislation)]
[Named Nature of Assignment]
[Named Scope of Contacts]

Your Response should directly respond to the Requirements specified in the Job Announcement. Essentially, it is responding to 1) **Factors** and 2) **Factor Levels** used to determine the job classification and create the job announcement (Appendix C.)

In addition, your response should indicate, where you began on the job, what you had to learn, who you had to work with, what level of competency you achieved, what results you achieved, and the significance of the project, task or duty for the project, mission or employer. These "extra mile" responses will indicate to the reviewer that you are detail oriented, attuned to your working team environment, keen to your part in the organization and its purpose or mission, a life-long learner, and capable of handling complex thinking.

4. Completing a Standard OPM Form 1203, Form C, Supplemental Qualifications Statement (SQS)

The Job Announcement will indicate whether you need to fill out this form.

You may fill it out and submit it either electronically at http://www.USAJOBS.gov, or by downloading it, filling out the form, printing it, and mailing or Faxing the Form C.

If you choose to complete the Form C, Supplemental Qualifications Statement (SQS) online, go to http://www.USAJOBS.gov. Click on *Online Application*. Click on *Complete Online Supplemental Qualifications Statement*. Enter the Control Number of the Job Announcement to start filling out the form.

If you choose to download, fill out, print and send the Form C, it may be downloaded from http://www.opm.gov/forms/pdf_fill/OPM1203fx.pdf. It is a Scannable Occupational Questionnaire, where you answer occupational questions, and the answers are used by reviewers to assess your qualifications and rank them. The downloadable form may be filled in electronically online. You may Print the Form or Save the Form and Mail or Fax it before the Closing Date of the Job Announcement.

5. Preparing a Knowledge, Skills, Abilities (KSA) Statement

A Knowledge, Skills, Abilities (KSA) Statement is your opportunity to review and structure your Response to the Job Announcement to demonstrate that you qualify for the 1) **GS Salary Grade or Grades** indicated in the Job Announcement (if the job Grade is between GS-11-GS13, for example), and that you qualify for the 2) **Job Announcement Job Title Requirements and Factor Levels. (Appendix B).**

While a KSA Statement may tell a Reviewer about your Job History, it is designed to clarify to the Reviewer how your qualifications meet the job requirements in a particular Salary Grading Structure and Job Title Structure.

To learn how your Job Announcement has been classified and created, refer to the manual for "Introduction to the Position Classifications Standards" and "The Classifier's Handbook" for Information Technology Job Groups (USOPM, GS-2200, 2001, 2003; http://www.opm.gov/FEDCLASS/gs2200a.pdf). This document will tell you how the job classification has been determined, and what is expected to meet the requirements. When the Classifier classified the position, they wrote the Job Announcement with certain expectations in mind. They expect someone to fill the position with the qualifications specified in the Job Announcement for the specified **Salary Grade** and for the **Job Title Requirements and Factor Levels.**

These requirements include:

Knowledge
Competencies
Supervisory Background
Degree of Difficulty
Degree of Judgment
Special Knowledge (i.e. of Equipment, Software, Procedures, Legislation)]
Nature of Assignment
Scope of Contacts

Therefore, to write your KSA Statement, you need to indicate the Knowledge, Skills Abilities that you have demonstrated in previous experience that now qualify you for the **Salary Grade**, and for the **Job Title Requirements and Factor Levels** specified in the Job Announcement.

To demonstrate how a KSA Statement is written, we have prepared a KSA Statement that responds to the Job Announcement for Information Technology Specialist Job Announcement shown in Appendix C. Note how the KSA Statement answers, point for point, the qualifications required, named in the Job Announcement, by matching the KSA Statements (Appendix D) with the Job Announcements (Appendix C).

After Completing the Application you will receive a Notice of Rating or Notice of Results within 2-4 weeks by mail or e-Mail.

The Interview

Preparing for the Interview
Preparing for the Interview involves 1) Learning about the Agency and its Mission, and 2) Preparing a Verbal Portrait of Yourself.

Learning about the Agency

Read the Agency's website. What is the Agency's Mission. What are the Agency's primary Information Technology applications, related to its Mission. Call or ask for the Agency's Mission Statement, and the individual Department's Mission Statement. Familiarize yourself with the individual Department where the job will be performed.

Preparing a Verbal Portrait of Yourself

To prepare a Verbal Portrait of Yourself, indicate in a few verbal sentences, who you are, what your major experience and focus has been, main skills, strengths, why you are interested in this Job Announcement, and why you are a good fit. Your emphasis should be on what you bring to this position, rather than on your previous employers. Preparing a Verbal Portrait, will help you structure strengths, work ethics, skills, and abilities. It will prepare you to bring a clear focus to the Interview.

The Interview

A good Interview is a discussion or dialog. You are expected to ask questions, to clarify what the Job and Job Context is about. Questions to ask may focus in these areas:

The Agency or Department
1.   What are the Agency's Major Missions
2.   What are the Agency's Major Functions
3.   What are the Agency's Major Business Applications
4.   What are the Agency's Major Information Technology Applications
5.   What are the Agency's Major & Auxiliary Computer Platforms
6.   What is the scope of the Agency's IT/IS work

The Job Required
1.   What will I be doing
2.   Who will I be reporting to
3.   Who will I be working with
4.   What knowledge, skills, abilities will I be using the most
5.   Questions-Discussion about the Specific Job

The Job Employment Status
1.   What is the Employment Status of this Position (i.e. Competitive, Direct Hire, Non-Competitive, Senior Executive Service, Wage Grade, other)
2.   Salary Discussion
3.   What is the next step in the Interview process
4.   What is the Interviewer's Name, Telephone, e-Mail

Asking for the Salary & Level You Want
Ask the interviewer to MATCH the salary you are earning, during the Interview, and before accepting the job. Take a current Pay Stub to show the interviewer your current salary. Leave a Copy of your current Pay Stub with the interviewer. The Interviewer may need to conclude the Interview and check with Personnel before offering you a Salary.

You can also ask for a salary increase above and beyond your current salary. Government employers are often authorized to give at least a 10-15% salary increase above the candidate's current salary. They are also normally authorized to give a 10-15% salary increase for candidates who are changing jobs within government.

Point out evidence that supports your request for a higher salary, or salary above Step 1 or Level I, including higher education, grades, certifications, additional course work, shortages of skilled applicants in your field, technical or systems specialties and experience, and supervisory or team leader work.

The U.S. State & City Employment Process

Learning about and Applying for a Provisional Job in State or Municipal Government

1. State & City Government Websites - Job Application Websites

There are several ways to find all the job announcements for current available State and City jobs in Information Technology

2. Search the Official U.S. State & Municipal Government Website Portals –http://www.50States.com; or Search State or City on http://www.google.com

Each U.S. State and Municipality has an official website portal. Your Career in U.S. State or City Government Starts at the Official State and Municipal Job Website Portals! An easy way to locate the official State or City website is to search for State of [Name State] or City of [Name City] on http://www.google.com. Or, you may use the website http://www.50states.com to click on the State or City, and go to its official website. Once you have gone to the official website, search for employment or job or personnel department links. These links will take you to job postings.

3. Locate Jobs Posted at the U.S. State or Municipal Government Personnel Department Website Portals or Personnel Offices

At the Official Website Portal for each U.S. State and Municipality, you will find links to individual State or City Agencies and Departments. Click on these individual Agencies and Departments; **search for** *employment or job or personnel department links.* **These links will take you to job postings.**

4. Locate Jobs Posted by Visiting Local Offices of individual Agencies in U.S. State & Municipal Government and reviewing jobs posted on the Job Bulletin Boards

One of the best ways to locate U.S. State and Municipal Government jobs is to visit the local office of the State Employment Services, State Personnel Department, City Personnel Department or Human Resources Department, or State or City Agency or Department Personnel Department where you want to work. Often, the most recent and most needed jobs are immediately posted by these departments on their Job Bulletin Boards. It is advised you contact the department by telephone before visiting, to find out the address, if they have a job bulletin board, and if you as a private citizen (rather than government employee) will have the required access to visit the location, office and job bulletin board.

5. Read about Advertised U.S. State or Municipal Government Provisional Jobs announced in local newspaper help wanted or business sections

Information Technology jobs, Managerial jobs and other professional jobs are often advertised in local newspaper help wanted or business sections. These are usually positions that are required immediately. They will customarily be filled on a Provisional basis. The employee will be hired and given a Provisional Appointment. The employee will work until the position is no longer required. The employee will be given the opportunity to take a Civil Service Exam for the position when the exam is given. Often, a Provisional Appointment will result in a full-time, permanent Career Competitive Appointment.

6. Search Supplemental Job Announcements -
Search Career One Stop Centers – http://www.careeronestop.org;
and America's Job Bank – http://www.ajb.org/
CareerOneStop is an integrated suite of national web sites that help businesses, job seekers, students, and workforce professionals find employment and career resources. *CareerOneStop*, sponsored by the U.S. Department of Labor, includes three core products:
America's Career InfoNet (http://www.CareerInfoNet.org) provides national, state and local career information and labor market data using unique career tools, career reports, videos, a career resource library and other innovative web-based tools.
America's Job Bank (http://www.ajb.org) is the nation's largest online labor exchange. Businesses post job listings, create customized job orders, and search resumes. Job seekers post resumes and search for jobs that fit their career goals. A companion web site, *Department of Defense Job Search* (http://dod.jobsearch.org), is a career resource for businesses and military personnel transitioning to civilian careers to match work opportunities.
America's Service Locator (http://www.ServiceLocator.org) maps customers to a range of local services including workforce centers, unemployment benefits, job training, education opportunities, and other workforce services.

Applying for a Posted or Advertised Provisional Position

When you locate a Posted or Advertised Provisional Position you want to apply for, the Announcement will state the application requirements. Typically, the application requires submitting a **Resume.** The same guidelines apply for preparing a Resume for U.S. State or Municipal government employment, as for Federal Employment. Your Resume and Skills Statement should mirror the words of the specific Job Announcement. Where the Job Announcement asks for the candidate to perform named task and duty, your response will indicate how and where you performed named task and duty. For example "Performed [Name Task & Duty] in this position, in this assignment, in this context, with these competencies and knowledge, skills, and abilities, with this degree of supervision or supervisory control, with this degree of difficulty, calling on this type of special knowledge or contacts with others.

While the term KSA or Knowledge, Skills, Abilities Statement is not used in U.S. State and Municipal government, a similar **Skills Statement**, in direct response to the Job Announcement, often known as an Experience and Education Paper or Test, is often required. An Experience and Education Paper can be a valuable statement to send with the Resume. The Reviewer can easily discern why you meet the requirements of the job position.

Completing a U.S. State or City Employment Application to Obtain a Competitive Civil Service Information Technology Job Title

Most employment in U.S. State and City government comes by way of Civil Service Open Competitive (or Promotional) Exam and Appointment. A jobseeker makes an application to take a Civil Service Exam for a specific Job Title (or to fill out the Experience & Education Paper that will serve as an Exam).

After applications are reviewed and scored for the Job Title, and candidates Ranked, a Certified Civil Service List is created for the Job Title. Agencies and Departments then use the list to Call, Interview, and Hire candidates.

Candidates are called for Interview from the Certified List by list rank number. They are interviewed from a Civil Service Pool, during which 3 candidates are interviewed at a time, and an Agency must hire one of the three (or may hire more where there are more positions), before going on to interview the next three candidates.

A candidate may accept or decline a position offered. If a jobseeker declines the job, they may be restored to the Certified List for the Job Title, and will be called for another Civil Service Pool and round of interviews.

Certified Lists of Candidates may be in effect for one to three years, or until all the candidates have been hired and the list is exhausted. Certified Lists may contain a few or many certified qualified candidates. Open Competitive Exam Filings for a Job Title may be open for candidates to apply, from once a year to once every few years.

Obtaining a Civil Service Exam Application

To obtain a *Civil Service Exam Application* and *Schedule of Open Exam Filings*, go to the U.S. State or Municipal government website portal. Click on the *Personnel Department* or *Employment or Jobs link. Search Schedule of Exams or Schedule of Open Exam Filings. You may also call the telephone number for the Personnel Department and ask for a Schedule of Open Exam Filings and When [Named Job Title] Exam will have an open filing.*

Filing the Application during an Open Filing Period
After you determine when the Application should be filed, and will be accepted, you are ready to fill out the Application or Application for Exam.

The Civil *Service Exam*

The Civil Service Exam (or Experience and Education Paper) is a way of assessing your qualifications, as related to the Job Requirements for the Job Title. An *Experience & Education Application Form* is often a Substitute for Civil Service Exam for IT Job Titles in many cases. There are no multiple choice or essay exams for many IT titles in most States and Cities.

Filling out the Application Form (and/or Experience and Education Paper) for the Job Title is critical in receiving a high enough score to be certified to a Civil Service List. You are demonstrating your qualifications to perform the duties, tasks and responsibilities of the Job Title, as specified in the published Job Title Description. There are several key points in filling out the Application:

☐ **List all your Education**, indicating dates and number of months and years attended, and diplomas, certifications, or credits received. List Academic, Vendor and Employer Education and Training.

☐ **List all your Experience**, indicating dates and number of months and years for each position, assignment, specialty, project. These must meet the Experience and/or Education Requirements specified for the Job Title.

☐ **Respond to the Job Title Requirements.** Your Application and Experience and Education Paper should mirror the words of the specific Job Announcement. Where the Job Title Requirements ask for the candidate to demonstrate that they performed named task and duty, your response will indicate how and where you performed named task and duty. For example "Performed [Name Task & Duty] in this position, in this assignment, in this context, with these competencies and knowledge, skills, and abilities, with this degree of supervision or supervisory control, with this degree of difficulty, calling on this type of special knowledge or contacts with others."

☐ **Ask for Veteran's Preference points, if this applies.**

Ranking by Score

A Certified Civil Service List of Qualified Candidates for the Job Title will be created from 6 months to 1 year from the time you make your application. Your application will be graded and given points based on the degree to which you meet the qualifications. You will be ranked along with other candidates who applied. After a Certified Civil Services List for Job Title is created, you will be notified of your List Number. You will be called to a Job Hiring Pool based on your list number. While the process may seem slow, career employment is a valuable and honorable achievement.

Certified Civil Service Lists Created for the Job Titles

As State and City agency personnel departments need staff in the job title, they use the Certified Civil Service Job Title List and request a Civil Service Pool be formed of candidates to hire from.

Job Hiring Pools - U.S. State & City Civil Service

Candidates are called for Interview from the Certified List by list rank number. They are interviewed from a Civil Service Pool, during which 3 candidates are interviewed at a time, and an Agency must hire one of the three (or may hire more where there are more positions), before going on to interview the next three candidates. A candidate may accept or decline a position offered. If a jobseeker declines the job, they may be restored to the Certified List for the Job Title, and will be called for another Civil Service Pool and round of interviews. Certified Lists of Candidates may be in effect for one to three years, or until all the candidates have been hired and the list is exhausted. Certified Lists may contain a few or many certified qualified candidates. Open Competitive Exam Filings for a Job Title may be open for candidates to apply, from once a year to once every few years.

Types of Employment Status

Your job and hiring status may be classified as:
- ☐ **Competitive Permanent**
- ☐ **Competitive Provisional**
- ☐ **Non-Competitive**
- ☐ **Labor**
- ☐ **Exempt**

A **permanent** employee is someone who has been appointed from a civil service list in a **competitive** class job title. The employee has taken and passed a competitive civil service exam for the job title. After being hired, the employee must complete a probationary period (typically one year). If performance during this probationary period is satisfactory, the employee will be appointed permanent status.

A **provisional** employee is someone who has been hired prior to the establishment of a civil service list for his/her job title in a **competitive, non-competitive exempt or labor** class job title, or because there is no civil service job title list. A provisional employee may be terminated any time, because services are no longer required, because a civil service list for the job title has been established and the provisional employee's name does not appear on the list or is too low on the list to be reached, or because of poor performance. Most provisional employees will take and pass the civil service exams to secure their position career path.

An employee in a **non-competitive** class job title may be hired because the position has been classified as non-competitive due to its unique nature, and is appointed on the basis of educational background and or experience, and is not required to take a civil service examination.

The non-competitive position may be eliminated and the employee may no longer be required.

An employee in an **exempt** class works at the executive level, in an administrative position reporting to a commissioner level or executive level officer. An exempt class position. The exempt class position may be eliminated and the employee may no longer be required.

An employee in a **labor** job class works in one of the trade titles, not otherwise classified as competitive or non-competitive.

Employees **pay status** may be per annum (full-time whose salary is determined on an annual basis, eligible for longevity in title and longevity in service pay), or per diem (full time or part time whose salary is determined and paid by the hour only for the hours worked.) (The City of New York, 2006; AFSCME, CWA Local 1180, 2006).

Sample Job Descriptions & Qualification Requirements (U.S. States & Cities) (Appendix C)

The Interview/List Call Interview

Preparing
A good Interview is a discussion or dialog. You are expected to ask questions, to clarify what the Job and Job Context is about. Questions to ask may focus in these areas:

The Agency or Department
1.   What are the Agency's Major Missions
2.   What are the Agency's Major Functions
3.   What are the Agency's Major Business Applications
4.   What are the Agency's Major Information Technology Applications
5.   What are the Agency's Major & Auxiliary Computer Platforms
6.   What is the scope of the Agency's IT/IS work

The Job Required
1.   What will I be doing
2.   Who will I be reporting to
3.   Who will I be working with
4.   What knowledge, skills, abilities will I be using the most
5.   Questions-Discussion about the Specific Job

The Job Employment Status

1. What is the Employment Status of this Position (i.e. Competitive, Direct Hire, Non-Competitive, Senior Executive Service, Wage Grade, other)
2. Salary Discussion
3. What is the next step in the Interview process
4. What is the Interviewer's Name, Telephone, e-Mail

Asking for the Salary & Level You Want

Ask the interviewer to MATCH the salary you are earning, during the Interview, and before accepting the job. Take a current Pay Stub to show the interviewer your current salary. Leave a Copy of your current Pay Stub with the interviewer. The Interviewer may need to conclude the Interview and check with Personnel before offering you a Salary.

You can also ask for a salary increase above and beyond your current salary. Government employers are often authorized to give at least a 10-15% salary increase above the candidate's current salary. They are also normally authorized to give a 10-15% salary increase for candidates who are changing jobs within government.

Point out evidence that supports your request for a higher salary, or salary above Step1 or Level I, including higher education, grades, certifications, additional course work, shortages of skilled applicants in your field, technical or systems specialties and experience, and supervisory or team leader work.

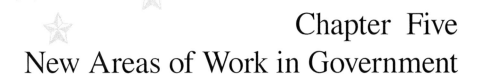

Chapter Five
New Areas of Work in Government

Information Technology

Information Technology Jobs in Government

A true information technology infrastructure is in place today for use by business and government, creating new levels of productivity 1) in the storage and dissemination of information, 2) in the management and use of information to govern, and 3) in the dispersal and collection of the government 'treasure', monies, revenues, taxes, food stamps, social services, other tangible and non-tangible public services (Margetts, 1999, 3-20). Developments in the technology create the need for a new workforce creating new IT jobs in government.

Mainframe-Minicomputer-Personal Computer
Local Area Networks-Wide-Area Networks

The personal computer, with local storage power and connectivity potential over LANS and WANS to larger mainframe and minicomputer processors, has changed the office and electronic data processing landscape. Private and public telecommunications networks played an important role in this development (Margetts, 1999, 2). High-speed telecommunications with packet switching makes digital networks possible. Within organizations, digital computer networks started to serve as the opportunity for Voice Over IP where telephone data could ride on top of computer networks.

Network Computing - The Internet – World Wide Web -- e-Mail

The Internet has grows through the 1980's and 1990's to take its central place today in national and global communications. The Internet, capitalizing on a loose confederation of inter-connected computer networks being built by organizations, government, and businesses (with servers residing at the location of the individual user or organization), permits government agencies to put information they want to transmit to the public on web servers to make it available to the public over the Internet. With the Internet and the World Wide Web (WWW), electronic mail, file transfer, and on-line interactive processing became possible for the first time, permitting national and global communications, e-commerce, and electronic data processing, in interactive real time.

Relational Databases – Data Warehouse

Today in E-Commerce and E-Government, information databases, client-customer-citizen databases, and service-product databases, function at a speed and detail due to the relational database model and query languages. Relational databases allow analysts in government to specify the relations they want to exist between pieces of data and the processes and functions they want to perform with the data.

Cryptography- Data Security-Information Privacy

Government agencies are stewards of Information Privacy and Data Security as essential components of the computer revolution. (Anderson, 2001; Kirschbaum, 2006).

Multi-Platform – Cross Platform Resource Sharing Operating Systems
Sun Solaris, Unix, Linux

Client-server technologies, coupled with LAN and WAN networks are the success story of the 21st Century. These Unix-based operating systems allow government users to:

- ☐ easily share printers and files across any network
- ☐ break down barriers between platforms to make resource sharing easy
- ☐ provide Windows file and print services
- ☐ integrate web and hosting services
- ☐ painlessly manage network access
- ☐ develop enterprise applications
- ☐ manage storage

Multi Platform & Component Programming Software - JAVA Software

Java, JavaScript, Visual Basic Programming Software

Java and Java Script allow other possibilities for government computing. These programming languages and scripts have created new possibilities in the computer industry when client-server technology mounted, creating the need for Java, Java Script and Visual Basic Programmers able to do Graphical User Interface (GUI) interfaces and direct to web scripting, in order to:

- ☐ Write software on one platform and run it on another.
- ☐ Create programs to run within a web browser.
- ☐ Develop server-side applications for online forums, stores, polls, processing HTML forms, and more.
- ☐ Write applications for cell phones, two-way pagers, and other consumer devices. (Sun Microsystems 2006)

Government programmers may now use Sun Microsystem's Java application development product, with knowledge of the JavaScript programming language to script direct to web. Java Programming JavaScript also utilize related Web development scripting languages, such as HTML, CGI, Perl, CSS, ASP, and PHP. In addition, Java and JavaScript programming interfaces with Macromedia Flash, DREAMWEAVER, Adobe Photoshop.

Speech Recognition-Interactive Voice Response Software

Speech recognition technologies allow government to improve productivity and increase ease of use for the public in a wide variety of computer-telephony applications.. Voice recognition or speech recognition technology is used increasingly with Interactive Voice Response (IVR) computer-telephone systems to speed caller transactions and provide information from relational databases.

Computer Graphics –
Geographic Information Systems (GIS)

Computer graphics enable scientific visualizations, computer-aided design programs, biomedical imaging, geographic information systems (GIS), art and publishing graphics, and computer animation.

Geographic Information Systems (GIS)

Geographic Information Systems (GIS) combine computer graphics capabilities and relational database capabilities to create, store, analyze and manage spatial data and associated attributes. Geographic Positioning Systems are being developed for voice-over IP telephony to be able to identify the location of incoming calls for emergency services. GPS devices integrated with everyday objects (Cell phones, PDA's, Laptops) will facilitate other government services.

GIS work includes:
☐ Data Capture: the most common method of data creation is
   digitization)
☐ Data Representation: GIS data represents real world objects (roads, l
   and use, elevation) as discrete objects (a house) and continuous fields
☐ Relating information from different sources
☐ Data manipulation Projections, coordinate systems and registration
☐ Spatial analysis with GIS
☐ Data modeling: A rainfall contour map
☐ Topological modeling
☐ Data output and cartography: the design and production of maps, or
   visual representations of spatial data.
☐ Data Analysis, Problem Solving & Interpretation

GIS Specialists are required by industry and government. GIS Specialists are required for:

☐ Sustainable Development - Zoning - Urban Planning
☐ Natural Resources - Parks & Recreation
☐ Natural Resources - Environmental Protection
☐ Real Estate - Taxation & Revenue
☐ Safety & Security - Defense and Homeland Security
☐ Public Health – Disease Control & Departments of Health
☐ Crime Mapping - Police

Managing Technology in Government

Players - Departments - Information Stakeholders

Managing Technology in Government involves many players and departments. It creates jobs both within information technology departments and within program area departments. There are clear divisions of responsibility across agencies and departments. All players or stakeholders in government need to understand where management responsibility lies – for governance, for service identification and implementation, for service delivery, and for information technology systems and services to departments.

Typically, agencies and departments are responsible for programmatic duties. Human Services Agencies, for example, are responsible for following the Law to deliver social services mandated by Federal, State and Municipal Law, and for creating the processes for the delivery of services. The program areas within Human Services, for example, – child welfare, medical assistance, income support, emergency assistance, job training and placement –identify the programs to carry out their responsibilities in these areas. They establish the processes, and when required, they work with information technology department to program the processes, create data processing applications, and operate the information technology systems required.

IT departments, either within departments and agencies, within Federal government, States and Cities, are responsible for the digital storage, processing and archiving of information and the computer systems and infrastructure that are necessary to carry out e-government processes. Information Technology departments also provide services to programmatic areas in helping design and program information technology systems required.

Technology in government cuts across departments and agencies. IT jobs can be in departments that are directly responsible for collecting information and implementing services, known commonly as Program Areas. Or, government jobs in technology can be in management information systems department, department of information technology departments, or computer centers, responsible for the digital storage, processing and archiving of information and the computer systems and infrastructure that is necessary to carry out e-government processes.

Types of Jobs - Technical and Non-Technical 'Tech' Jobs

IT Procurement - IT Training Jobs - Project Management - IT Security Jobs

There are many types of technology jobs – technical and non-technical. Electronic data processing, programming, information technology, IT, management information systems and telecommunications all refer to departments and activities related to technology. Other departments and Program Areas in Federal, State and City government, besides the Information Technology Departments, also have technology jobs, both technical and non-technical.(Info Tech Employment, 2007).

Information technology has become so integral to American business and government that it has created new occupations to provide auxiliary support to the IT infrastructure and endeavor.

IT Procurement Jobs have grown up to manage the creation of RFPs (Requests for Proposals), Bid Analysis, Purchase and Maintenance Contracts, Personnel Contracting and the management of contracts. These jobs require special knowledge of the IT industry and the procurement field. People may enter an IT procurement job from another department and learn-as-you-go. Or they may be hired as a computer programmer or systems engineer to facilitate the procurement function for the hardware and software requirements. Computer Project managers often manage IT procurement contracts for staff and services. There is usually continuous communication between staff holding IT procurement jobs and technical staff delineating hardware and software contracts and outlining staffing needs.

IT Training Jobs exist both within an organization and with the numerous information technology training suppliers. Companies and government agencies contract for information technology training on new software and hardware or train trainers in Civil Service titles to train staff. They may also contract for on-site or off-site information technology training for their employees. People may enter an information technology training job with a liberal arts or other degree or with hands-on business or training experience. IT trainers who work for a software or hardware vendor will be expected to know their product. IT trainers who train on software use will expand their tech jobs horizons by knowing may software products used in the workplace. Information technology training will be an integral part of any organization's employee development program. Both specialized information technology training and generic information technology training will ensure a modern organization where employees are conversant with software and the ability to handle information.

IT Project Management jobs, utilizing project management software such as Microsoft Project, Crystal Reports, Network Associates Magic, and Visio, are required in many departments. They are especially integral to the IT and Telecommunications departments of an organization. Project managers and systems analysts using project management software create project plans outlining system development life cycles and timelines. They gather statistics of call centers, tech support centers and organization

IT center server configurations. IT project management jobs usually do not require a degree in computer science. They require project management software skills, an ability to understand the parts of an organization and IT operation, and good communication skills.

IT Security jobs may fall under the web development group of an organization, under the telecommunications department, or in tech support. Information technology security jobs may reside in a separate security department responsible for facility and data security. IT service providers and outsourcers often hire IT staff to do security planning for their clients. Outsourcers may perform the access control function for their clients. Access control managers and access control specialists carry out access control functions for computer users, workgroups, and applications. Security specialist jobs exist for network engineers to establish secure network connections, decide on proxy servers to control content, and to determine firewall requirements. Systems analysts jobs are required to determine security requirements for safe electronic file transmissions, electronic file payment systems, HIPPA data release requirements and e-commerce systems.

While some tech jobs are clearly "technical" in nature, requiring math experience, there are so many non-technical tech jobs that no one should consider themselves out of the running for information technology employment. Skills are transferable from one agency to another and from one business process to another.

☐ **Information Technology Job Skill Sets (Chart IV)**

Employers increasingly want a bundle of skill sets. The Skills Set chart will help you think about your abilities and present your array for your Federal Knowledge, Skills and Abilities Statement, or for a State or City Experience & Education Paper, Resume or Application Form.

"Tech Job Titles – Tech Skill Sets", in the Charts Section of this book, is an excellent chart, put together by the editors of Information Technology *Jobs in America*, to show you an array of current tech job titles covering all aspects of technology within an organization.

☐ **Information Technology Generic Job Titles (Chart IV)**

Chart IV shows major Information Technology Job Titles, in addition to the skill sets that may be desirable to bring to the job. The Top 8 Fastest Growing Jobs between now and 2015, according to the U.S. Bureau of Labor Statistics (BLS, 2009) are:

> ☐ **Computer software engineers, applications**
>
> ☐ **Computer support specialists**
>
> ☐ **Computer software engineers, systems software**
>
> ☐ **Network and computer systems administrators**
>
> ☐ **Network systems and data communications analysts**
>
> ☐ **Desktop publishers**
>
> ☐ **Database administrators**
>
> ☐ **Computer systems analysts**

Information Technology Job Titles in Government (U.S. Federal & U.S. States & Cities) (Charts II, III, IV)

IT Job Titles - Salaries & Pension Rates in U.S. Federal Government

The GS series Information Technology job group provides job title classifications and occupational guidance for positions that manage, supervise, lead, administer, develop, deliver, and support the job group.

The Grade Pay will correspond to the U.S. Federal Government General Schedule of Annual Rates by Grade and Step. The U.S. Federal Government General Services Salary Table published below shows the GS Salary Grades 1-15, with their corresponding Salaries, and the Steps 1-10 for each Grade. Steps 1-10 are achieved by promotions based on experience and performance.

General Services Salary Table – Salary Grades 1-15
[See Appendix A: General Services Salary Table]

Information Technology Main Job Titles

The Job Group is called Information Technology Management. The Job Title series has two main job titles, with Supervisory and Team Leader levels, and 10 Competency Specialties. The Information Technology Job Group replaces an earlier job group known as **Computer Specialist GS-0334 and Telecommunications GS-0391.** Computer

☐ *Information Technology Manager*

Work that involves directly managing information technology projects to provide a unique service or product. The title also applies to supervisory project manager positions evaluated under the General Schedule Supervisory Guide.

☐ *Information Technology Specialist or IT Specialist*

Work that involves developing, delivering, and supporting IT systems and services is Information Technology Specialist or IT Specialist. Use the parenthetical specialty titles defined below with the basic title to further identify the duties and responsibilities performed and the special knowledge and skills needed. The Job Title Classification may have any combination of two parenthetical specialty titles in official position titles; e.g., Information Technology Specialist (Applications Software/Systems Analysis), where the two specialties are of significant importance to the position.

☐ *Information Technology Supervisory and Leader Job Positions*
Further, IT Job Titles may be classified as **"Supervisory"** or **"Team Leader"**
positions.

☐ *Information Technology Management Series Grades GS-5-GS-15 (*GS-11-GS-15)*

The Information Technology Management Job Title Series offers salaries from GS-5 – GS-15. However, a Survey of the IT Job Announcements on the http://www.USAJOBS.gov website over a 1-month period by Info Tech Employment indicates that most IT jobs in the IT Jobs Series listed offer a salary between GS-11 and GS-15 (*Info Tech Employment, IT Federal Jobs Survey). Each Job Announcement states the Job Salary Grade for the Title. Salary grades are negotiable at the time of hiring. Higher education and greater job experience will be considered to apply a higher Salary Grade.

Supervisory Positions may be assigned a Grade-Level Increase. Leader Positions may be assigned one or more Grade-Level Increases based on a points assessment of the work required. Supervisory Positions may earn a 1-Grade Level Increase per year. Team Leader positions may earn a 1-3 Grade Level Increases per year.

Experience and Performance in U.S. Federal Government employment lead to Salary Grade & Step Promotions. Step Promotions may be earned over the course of a career. No more than one Step Promotion may be earned in a single year for most job titles. See the GS Salary Schedule (Appendix A) for the Step increase rate amounts.

The IT Job Titles 5-Year Salary Projections Chart (Chart IV) calculates salary projections and estimated pensions based on some assumptions for the Step increase rate amounts over the course of a career.

☐ *Information Technology Ten (10) Specialties – Job Descriptions*

An **IT Project Manager** job or **Information Technology Specialist (IT Specialist)** job may be defined with these ten (10) specialties. A job announcement and classification may call on up to two (2) of these Core Competency specialties in the job description. A general description of the relationships among the specialties is presented below:

- **Policy and Planning (PLCPLN)** – develop, implement, and ensure compliance with plans, policies, standards, infrastructures, and architectures that establish the framework for the management of all IT programs.
- **Security (INFOSEC)** – plan, develop, implement, and maintain programs, polices, and procedures to protect the integrity and confidentiality of systems, networks, and data.
- **Systems Analysis (SYSANALYSIS)** – consult with customers to refine functional requirements and translate functional requirements into technical specifications.
- **Applications Software (APPSW)** – translate technical specifications into programming specifications; develop, customize, or acquire applications software programs; and test, debug, and maintain software programs.
- **Operating Systems (OS)** – install, configure, and maintain the operating systems environment including systems servers and operating systems software on which applications programs run.

- **Network Services (NETWORK)** – test, install, configure, and maintain networks including hardware (servers, hubs, bridges, switches, and routers) and software that permit the sharing and transmission of information.
- **Data Management (DATAMGT)** – develop and administer databases used to store and retrieve data and develop standards for the handling of data.
- **Internet (INET)** – provide services that permit the publication and transmission of information about agency programs to internal and external audiences using the Internet.
- **Systems Administration (SYSADMIN)** – install, configure, troubleshoot, and maintain hardware and software to ensure the availability and functionality of systems.
- **Customer Support (CUSTSPT)** – provide technical support to customers who need advice, assistance, and training in applying hardware and software systems.

(See Appendix B: Competencies Required for Federal IT Job Specialties)

☐ *Other Job Groups with Computer-Related, Technology-Related Job Titles Requiring Information Technology Knowledge*

Other Job Groups in U.S. Federal Government have computer-related, technology-related job titles. When seeking a career in U.S. Federal Government, your information technology knowledge, skills, and abilities might apply and qualify you for a job in one of the following job titles. The following list of job titles provides examples of situations where the work may involve the application of related knowledge and skills, but not to the extent that it may warrant classification to IT job family. These job titles exist in other job groups.

These other job groups will look favorably on your computer-related, technology-related skills and experience. It is important to look for job announcements on http://www. USAJOBS.gov, in these Other Job Groups as well at the IT Job Group. Simply search on the job group and you will find job announcements and job descriptions for the available jobs in the group. The General Services Salary Grade possibilities for each of the groups or titles is listed in Parentheses, (i.e. GS-3-GS-9 means that job titles in this group may have a salary from GS-3 to GS-9).

GS-0335, Computer Clerk & Assistant (GS-3-GS-9)
Work involves IT support or services functions. Work requires a practical knowledge of IT systems, workflow, and controls rather than the broad and in depth knowledge of IT principles, concepts, and methods characteristic of positions covered by this standard

GS-0332, Computer Operation (GS-3-GS-9)
Work involves operating or supervising the operation of computer systems, including the operation of peripheral equipment. Work requires knowledge of functions and features of computer systems and skill in reading, interpreting, and correctly responding to information transmitted through computer systems.

GS-0391, Telecommunications (GS-5-GS-11)

Work involves acquisition, technical acceptance, installation, testing, modification, or r
eplacement of telecommunications equipment, services, and systems. Work requires
paramount knowledge of:
• the operational and performance characteristics of telecommunications equipment;
• the relationships among component parts of telecommunications systems; and
• telecommunications equipment interoperability and compatibility characteristics; as
  well as an understanding of basic electronics theories and operating principles. Work
  in this series also typically requires knowledge of IT concepts that is secondary to the
  paramount knowledge requirements described above.

GS-0854, Computer Engineering (GS-5-GS-15)

Work involves professional knowledge of fundamentals and principles of computer
engineering; computer hardware, systems, software, and computer systems
architecture and integration; and mathematics as the paramount requirement.

GS-1550, Computer Science (GS 5-GS-15)

Work involves professional knowledge of theoretical foundations of computer science;
specialized knowledge of design characteristics, limitations, and potential applications
of information systems; and knowledge of relevant mathematical and statistical
sciences.

GS-0300, Clerical, and Office Services Group, such as:
GS-0303, Miscellaneous Clerk and Assistant
GS-0318, Secretary (GS-2-GS-13)

Work involves skill in the use of personal computers and knowledge of specialized
and/or general office software applications, e.g., desktop publishing, to provide
administrative support.

GS-0200, Subject Area Computer Work, i.e. Human Resources Management Group (GS-1-GS-15)

Work involves knowledge of e.g., human resources management, even when performing IT
assignments.

GS-2010, Inventory Management (GS-9-GS-11)

GS-1300P, Professional Work in the Physical Sciences Group, (GS-5-GS-15)

Work involves professional knowledge of mathematics, engineering, physics, or
related fields as the paramount requirement even when performing IT assignments.

GS-0500, Accounting and Budget Group, (GS-2-GS-9)

Work involves designing new automated financial accounting systems or developing
modifications to existing systems. Work requires knowledge of application of
accounting theories, concepts, principles, and standards as the paramount
requirement.

GS-0343, Management and Program Analysis, (GS-5-GS-9)

Work involves substantive knowledge of agency programs and activities; agency
mission, policies, and objectives; management principles and processes; and analytical
and evaluative methods as they relate to the evaluation of government programs and
operations.

GS-0080, Security Administration, (GS-5-GS-15)

Work involves knowledge of security concepts, methods, practices, and procedures as the paramount requirement in developing, evaluating, maintaining, and/or operating systems, policies, devices, procedures, and methods used for safeguarding information, property, personnel, operations, and materials.

GS-1811, Criminal Investigating, (GS-5-GS-13)

Work involves knowledge of investigative techniques, rules of evidence, Federal laws and statutes, and criminal laws as the paramount requirement in planning and conducting investigations of computer and Internet related crimes.

GS-1410, Librarian, (GS-9-GS-14)

Work involves professional knowledge of the theories, principles, and techniques of library science as the paramount requirement in the collection, organization, preservation, and retrieval of recorded knowledge.

GS-1412, Technical Information Services, (GS-9-GS-14)

Work involves knowledge of one or more scientific, engineering, technical, or other fields and practical knowledge of techniques for organizing, accessing, or disseminating information as the paramount requirements in developing, coordinating, processing, and transmitting specialized information.

GS-1084, Visual Information, (GS-7-GS-12)

Work involves communicating information through visual means that requires knowledge of the principles of visual design and the ability to present subject matter i nformation in a visual form that will convey the intended message to, or have the desired effect on, the intended audience.

Appropriate Subject-Matter Series (GS-1-GS-15)

Work involves preparing and updating subject-matter information on an organization's Web site that requires knowledge of subject-matter programs and processes and knowledge of basic Web site development techniques rather than knowledge of IT principles, concepts, and methods as the paramount requirement.

GS-1910, Quality Assurance, (GS-5-GS-15)

Work involves knowledge of quality assurance methods, principles and practices as the paramount requirement in assuring the quality of products acquired and used by the Federal Government, including software used in manufacturing, maintenance, and operational applications.

GS-2600, Electronic Equipment Installation and Maintenance, (GS-5-GS-15 or Wage Grade)

Work involves operating computerized analytical test and diagnostic equipment to install, test, troubleshoot, maintain, and repair electronic equipment that requires knowledge of the operational capabilities and limitations of electronic equipment and systems and skill in the use of computerized testing and diagnostic equipment.
U.S. State and Municipal employees may apply for any job opening within an Agency or

Special Career Programs

Information Technology Positions in Senior Executive Service (SES)

Members of the Senior Executive Service serve in the key positions just below the top Presidential appointees. SES members are the major link between these appointees and the rest of the Federal work force. They operate and oversee nearly every government activity in approximately 75 Federal agencies (USAOPM, 2006).

There are continuous opportunities for qualified Information Technology professionals to take key positions in the Senior Executive Service. Many governmental functions and departments rely keenly on information technology systems. Therefore, managing key information technology systems becomes a key responsibility in many Senior Executive Service positions. Jobs in information technology are also announced on http://www.USAJOBS.gov. The SES pay range has a minimum rate of basic pay equal to 120 percent of the rate for GS-15, step 1, and the maximum rate of basic pay is equal to the rate for level III of the Executive Schedule (USAOPM, 2006).

U.S. Federal Government
Information Technology Exchange Program (ITEP)
for Federal & Private Sector IT Employees

The ITEP is a new and exciting professional development opportunity. If you are already employed in IT in the private sector, or if you are currently employed in IT in a federal agency, you may be eligible to participate. This program allows exceptional performers from the Federal and private IT sectors to participate in temporary assignments of three (3) months to 1 year, in the other sector. ITEP promotes the interchange of IT workers to develop, supplement, and modernize IT skills to expand the long term competencies of the Federal IT workforce. While Federal agencies have a strong interest in the areas of Enterprise Architecture, Solutions Architecture, IT Project Management, and IT Security, ITEP exchange opportunities can exist in all IT disciplines. Please visit, http://www.opm.gov for more details about the program.

The following Federal agencies are participating in this program. To contact the ITEP representative for jobs for IT professionals from the Private Sector for this program with these listed Agencies, visit http://www.usajobs.opm.gov/itep.asp

> **DEPARTMENT OF COMMERCE**
> **DEPARTMENT OF DEFENSE**
> **DEPARTMENT OF HEALTH AND HUMAN SERVICES**
> **DEPARTMENT OF HOMELAND SECURITY (DHS)**
> **DEPARTMENT OF JUSTICE (DOJ)**
> **DEPARTMENT OF THE TREASURY**
> **ENVIRONMENTAL PROTECTION AGENCY**
> **FEDERAL BUREAU OF INVESTIGATION**
> **OFFICE OF PERSONNEL MANAGEMENT (OPM)**

To view ITEP opportunities in the private sector for existing Federal employees, visit http://www.actgov.org/ITEP.

Recruitment of IT Interns through
The Federal Career Intern Program

The Federal Career Intern Program is designed to help agencies recruit and attract exceptional individuals into a variety of occupations. It is intended for positions at grade levels GS-5, 7, and 9. In general, individuals are appointed to a 2-year internship. Upon successful completion of the internships, the interns may be eligible for permanent placement within an agency. Individuals interested in Career Intern opportunities must contact specific agencies directly (http://www.opm.gov/careerintern/.)

Sample Information Technology Job Announcements
Descriptions & Qualifications (Appendix C & E)

Homeland Security

Homeland Security Jobs in Government (U.S. Federal)

The Department of Homeland Security, created by the National Strategy for Homeland Security and the Homeland Security Act of 2002, provides the unifying core of functions for the vast national network of organizations and institutions involved in efforts to secure our nation. Homeland Security employees help secure our borders, airports, seaports and waterways; research and develop the latest security technologies; respond to natural disasters or terrorists assaults; and analyze intelligence reports. The Department's Components provide various functions, employing individuals to carry out these functions.

Homeland Security Department Components

The Office of the Secretary hires employees to work in multiple offices contributing to the overall Homeland Security mission.

The Directorate for National Protection and Programs works to advance the Department's risk-reduction mission. Reducing risk requires an integrated approach that encompasses both physical and virtual threats and their associated human elements. The Directorate for National Protection and Programs hires employees to work to advance the Department's risk-reduction mission. Reducing risk requires an integrated approach that encompasses both physical and virtual threats and their associated human elements.

The Directorate for Science and Technology is the primary research and development arm of the Department. It provides federal, state and local officials with the technology and capabilities to protect the homeland. The Directorate for Science and Technology (S&T) hires employees to plan, fund, and manage top-flight research and development programs in almost all technical fields to ensure that our Nation's Federal, State, and local responders have the scientific resources and technological capabilities that they need to protect our homeland.

The Directorate for Management is responsible for Department budgets and appropriations, expenditure of funds, accounting and finance, procurement; human resources, information technology systems, facilities and equipment, and the identification and tracking of performance measurements. The Directorate for Management hires employees to work in one of a variety of critical areas, from human resources and administration to budgeting, procurement and IT, making certain the right resources and systems are in place for the agency's mission.

The Office of Policy is the primary policy formulation and coordination component for the Department of Homeland Security. It provides a centralized, coordinated focus to the development of Department-wide, long-range planning to protect the United States.

The Office of Health Affairs coordinates all medical activities of the Department of Homeland Security to ensure appropriate preparation for and response to incidents having medical significance.

The Office of Intelligence and Analysis is responsible for using information and intelligence from multiple sources to identify and assess current and future threats to the United States. The Office of Intelligence and Analysis hires employees to use information and intelligence gathered from multiple sources to identify and assess current and future threats to the United States.

The Office of Intelligence and Analysis is responsible for using information and intelligence from multiple sources to identify and assess current and future threats to the United States. The Office of Intelligence and Analysis hires employees to use information and intelligence gathered from multiple sources to identify and assess current and future threats to the United States.

The Office of Inspector General hires employees to work side-by-side with special agents, attorneys, engineers, and IT experts to prevent and detect fraud, waste, and abuse in Homeland Security programs and operations.

The Office of Operations Coordination is responsible for monitoring the security of the United States on a daily basis and coordinating activities within the Department and with governors, Homeland Security Advisors, law enforcement partners, and critical infrastructure operators in all 50 states and more than 50 major urban areas nationwide.

The Federal Law Enforcement Training Center (http://www.fletc.gov) provides career-long training to law enforcement professionals to help them fulfill their responsibilities safely and proficiently. Federal Law Enforcement Training Center (FLETC) employees develop the skills, knowledge, and professionalism of law enforcers from 80+ Federal agencies in this unique inter-agency training organization.

The Domestic Nuclear Detection Office works to enhance the nuclear detection efforts of federal, state, territorial, tribal, and local governments, and the private sector and to ensure a coordinated response to such threats.

The Transportation Security Administration (TSA) (http://www.tsa.gov) protects the nation's transportation systems to ensure freedom of movement for people and commerce. U.S. Transportation Security Administration (TSA) employees help secure our transportation infrastructure from future terrorist acts in intelligence, regulation enforcement and inspection positions. (Sample Job Announcement, Transportation Security Officer (TSO) (Screener), Appendix C.)

United States Customs and Border Protection (CBP) (http://www.cbp.gov) is responsible for protecting our nation's borders in order to prevent terrorists and terrorist weapons from entering the United States, while facilitating the flow of legitimate trade and travel. U.S. Customs and Border Protection (CBP) employees prevent terrorists and terrorist weapons from entering the United States while facilitating the flow of legitimate trade and travel.

United States Citizenship and Immigration Services (http://www.ucsis.gov) is responsible for the administration of immigration and naturalization adjudication functions and establishing immigration services policies and priorities. U.S. Citizenship and Immigration Services (USCIS) employees are responsible for adjudicating and processing the host of applications and forms necessary to ensure the immigration of people and their families to the United States, from initial stages through their transition, to permanent residence, and finally to citizenship.

Homeland Security, is responsible for identifying and shutting down vulnerabilities in the nation's border, economic, transportation and infrastructure security. The U.S. Immigration and Customs Enforcement (ICE) hires employees to enforce immigration and customs laws, safeguard U.S. commercial aviation, and protect Federal facilities.

The United States Coast Guard (http://www.uscg.mil) protects the public, the environment, and U.S. economic interests—in the nation's ports and waterways, along the coast, on international waters, or in any maritime region as required to support national security. The U.S. Coast Guard hires civilian employees to work together with military personnel to save lives, enforce the law, operate ports and waterways, and protect the environment.

United States Immigration and Customs Enforcement (ICE), (http://www.ice.gov) the largest investigative arm of the Department of The Federal Emergency Management (FEMA) (http://www.fema.gov) prepares the nation for hazards, manages Federal response and recovery efforts following any national incident, and administers the National Flood Insurance Program. The Federal Emergency Management Agency (FEMA) hires employees to prevent losses from disasters wherever possible, and assist when they do happen.

The United States Secret Service (http://www.secretservice.gov) protects the President and other high-level officials and investigates counterfeiting and other financial crimes, including financial institution fraud, identity theft, computer fraud; and computer-based attacks on our nation's financial, banking, and telecommunications infrastructure. The U.S. Secret Service - employees have the dual missions of protecting our nation's leaders, and criminal investigation involving law enforcement, security, information technology, communications, administration, intelligence, forensics, and other specialized fields.

Special Career Programs

Acquisition Professional Career Program for Contract Specialists

The Acquisition Professional Career Program for Contract Specialists, at the Department of Homeland Security, invites candidate to apply to be part of a team that procures goods and services annually in support of the Department's mission, such as IT hardware and software, boats, aircraft. Appointees will receive over 400 hours of technical training leading to the federally recognized certification in Contracting, plus more than 100 hours of leadership-specific training.

Starting at the GS-05 or GS-07 grade level, employees are appointed to three one-year rotational assignments through component organizations to provide an opportunity to gain a broader perspective of the Department. This experience will enhance background and comprehension of the contracting career field, and prepare employees for an extended career within the federal government once you complete the program. Upon successful completion of the program, employees will be placed into a permanent full time position with promotion potential up to a GS-13.

The following are Department of Homeland Security component organizations with contracting opportunities:
US Secret Service (USSS)
US Coast Guard (USCG)
Customs & Border Protection (CBP)
Federal Emergency Management Agency (FEMA)
Immigrations & Customs Enforcement (ICE)
Transportation Security Administration (TSA)
Federal Law Enforcement Training Center (FLETC)
Department of Homeland Security HQ Office of Procurement Operations

How to Apply
Send your resume, transcripts (if available), and any questions via email to
acquisitioncandidates@dhs.gov.
Please identify that you were referred from the "DHS Acquisition Careers" website.
All Department of Homeland Security jobs require U.S. citizenship and most require successful completion of a background investigation.

Legal Career
Employment Opportunities with the Office of the General Counsel

Attorneys from the Office of the General Counsel and its major components play major roles in crafting, developing, and defending policies relating to many of the most important issues facing the nation today, including counterterrorism, immigration and border security, emergency response and recovery, and countless other matters.

Vacancies in the Office of the General Counsel are posted directly on the U.S. Office of Personnel Management's USAJOBS Web site, a comprehensive listing of employment opportunities within the government.

Honors Program

The Office of the General Counsel Honors Program is the Department's preferred recruitment program for entry-level attorneys. The Office of the General Counsel seeks to recruit outstanding graduates each year to join for a two-year rotational assignment through various components of the Department. Honors attorneys who achieve satisfactory performance ratings will ordinarily be offered permanent full-time positions, depending on the Department's needs and availability of funding at that time.

How to Apply

Candidates interested in the Honors Attorney Program should submit a resume, cover letter, and a current law school transcript to OGCstaffing@dhs.gov. Address further questions to Jeffery Reily, Chief of OGC Management Division, at 202-282-9352.

Summer Law Intern Program

The Office of the General Counsel runs a competitive recruitment program for compensated summer internships. Selection for employment is based on many elements of a candidate's background including academic achievement, law review or moot court experience, legal aid and clinical experience, and summer or part-time legal employment.

Applications are solicited annually beginning in January through USAJOBS.

Volunteer Legal Intern/Extern Program

The Office of the General Counsel accepts volunteer interns and externs during the academic year. These positions are without compensation but are highly sought after because of the responsibility and experience they offer. Applications may be made at any time by sending a cover letter, resume, and writing sample to OGCStaffing@dhs.gov

Contact: OGCStaffing@dhs.gov

Sample Job Announcements/Qualifications (Appendix C)

Contract Specialist
Criminal Investigator
Transportation Security Officer (TSO) (Screener)

Environmental Protection - Green Jobs

Environmental Protection Jobs in Government

Environmental Protection cuts across government agencies and departments, providing essential essential protection to the environment ane ecology of the U.S. and services to U.S. citizens. These are some of the areas Environmental Protection is responsible for:

☐ **Air**
   Acid Rain, Climate Change, Vehicle Emissions...

☐ **Cleanup**
   Brownfields, Superfund, Corrective Action...

☐ **Compliance & Enforcement**
   Complaints, Compliance Assistance...

☐ **Economics**
   Cost Sharing, Grants, Financing...

☐ **Ecosystems**
   Wetlands, Watersheds, Endangered Species...

☐ **Emergencies**

☐ **Environmental Protection Agency**
   Mission, Jobs, Regulatory Role, History...

☐ **Environmental Technology**

☐ **Government**
   Federal Facilities, Federal/State Cooperation, Tribal Government...

☐ **Human Health**
   Children's Health, Aging Initiative, School Environments...

☐ **Industry**
   Small Businesses, Permits, Reporting...

☐ **International Cooperation**
   Border Issues, Treaties and Agreements...

☐ **Pesticides**
   Labeling, Registration, Food Safety...

☐ **Pollutants/Toxics**
   Lead, Dioxins, Asbestos, Mercury...

☐ **Pollution Prevention**

☐ **Recycling, Conservation, Fuel Economy...**

☐ **Radiation and Radioactivity**

☐ **Treatment & Control**
   Treatment Technologies, Pollution Control..

☐ **Wastes**
   Hazardous Wastes, Landfills, Household Waste...

☐ **Water**
   Wastewater, Drinking Water, Ground Water...

Environmental Protection Job Titles

U.S. Federal Agencies, State and City Departments and Agencies seek people with business, scientific, and technical education and experience to fill a wide variety of positions in many departments to study the environment, monitor it, and provide services in protecting the environment of the U.S. for its residents and for future generations.

These Departments and Agencies in U.S. Federal, State and City government have jobs in environmental protection functions:

- **Buildings, Department of**
- **City Planning, Department of**
- **Commerce, Department of**
- **Defense, Department of**
- **Economic Development Corporation**
- **Emergency Management, Office of**
- **Environmental Protection, Department of**
- **Fire Department**
- **General Services (Real Estate)**
- **Homeland Security, Department of**
- **Housing Authority**
- **Parks & Recreation, Department of**
- **Ports of Authority**
- **Sanitation, Department of**
- **Transportation, Department of**

Special Career Programs

Student Opportunities

Numerous opportunities are available within the U.S. Federal Environmental Protection Agency (http://www.epa.gov) for students to gain vital career experience while contributing to the mission of protecting human health and safeguarding the environment. Internships, fellowships and other opportunities are available in Washington, DC, laboratories, and at regional EPA locations nationwide.

Fellowships
National Network for Environmental Management Studies
Science to Achieve Results (STAR) Graduate Fellowships
Greater Research Opportunities (GRO) Graduate Fellowships
Greater Research Opportunities (GRO) Undergraduate Fellowships
Public Health Fellowships
American Association for the Advancement of Science (AAAS) Fellowships

Student Programs
Student Career Experience Program (SCEP)
OECA Student Career Experience Program
Student Environmental Associate Program and Diversity Initiative
Student Temporary Employment Program (STEP)
Student Summer Employment Opportunities
Tribal Lands Environmental Science Scholarship Program
Resident Research Associate Program
Office of General Counsel (OG) Honors Fellowship Program

Other Student Opportunities
http://www.epa.gov/careers/stuopp.htmlOpportunities for College Graduates

EPA Intern Program (EIP)

This is an entry-level, full-time employment and career development program. You must be a U.S. citizen and have a bachelor's degree. You should also have:
leadership potential
teamwork skills
a commitment to a career in public service
interest in environmental issues
solid communications skills, and
academic accomplishment and/or relevant work experience.

The objective of the program is to help Interns develop their potential for future advancement within EPA. When these positions are available, they are advertised at EPA at USAJobs. Applications are completed online with supplemental materials mailed to addresses noted in the application packages. For further information on the EPA Intern Program, visit http://www.epa.gov/ohr/eip.html.

Presidential Management Fellows Program (PMFP)

This program provides a special means of entry into the federal service for recipients of graduate degrees. Career development is emphasized and you will be exposed to a variety of work assignments. This program is managed by the U.S. Office of Personnel Management. An application can be obtained from your graduate school or placement office. To obtain more information on this program, visit http://www.pmf.opm.gov/ or call OPM at (202) 606-2525.

Office of Research and Development Post Doctoral Program

EPA's Office of Research and Development (ORD) seeks candidates to fill four-year, post-doctoral research positions. Positions focus on the exposure and effects of environmental contaminants on human health and the environment. The preferred candidate will have earned a Ph.D. within the last five years or will have it awarded prior to their Federal employment start date.

The duty station will be based on the particular disciplinary focus of the candidate and the overall requirements of the program. Applicants must be United States citizens or permanent residents. Only in the absence of qualified U.S. citizens will permanent residents who are citizens of countries specified as exceptions to the appropriations act ban on paying non-U.S. citizens be considered. For more information, see: http://www.epa.gov/ord/htm/jobs_ord.htm or contact Ms. Dorothy Carr at carr.dorothy@epa.gov

The Senior Environmental Employment (SEE) Program

The Senior Environmental Employment (SEE) Program provides an opportunity for retired and unemployed older Americans age 55 and over to share their expertise with the Environmental Protection Agency (EPA). Administered by EPA, cooperating organizations recruit qualified candidates to work in positions in Washington, DC, laboratories nationwide and in regional offices. Regional offices are located in Boston, MA; New York, NY; Philadelphia, PA; Atlanta, GA; Chicago, IL; Dallas, TX; Kansas City, KS; Denver, CO; San Francisco, CA; and Seattle, WA. Their salary, benefits, vacation and sick leave, and any personnel actions or issues are administered by the grantee organization. Their productivity is monitored by a Federal employee.

Types of SEE Program enrollment positions include:

• clerical (non-typing) - messenger, receptionist, file clerk, and copy machine

• clerical (typing) - clerk-typist, secretarial support, and administrative

• technical - such as physical science technician, grant specialist, writer-editor, technical researcher, and technical writer; and

• professional - such as: engineer, scientist and accountant.

Sample Environmental Protection Job Announcements Descriptions & Qualifications (Appendix C)

Contract Specialist
Criminal Investigator
Environmental Scientist/Engironmental Engineers/Life Scientist

CHART I: U.S. FEDERAL EXECUTIVE

Executive Office of the President (EOP)

White House

Office of Management and Budget (OMB)

United States Trade Representative (USTR)

Executive Agencies

Department of Agriculture (USDA)

Agricultural Research Service

Animal & Plant Health Inspection Service

Economic Research Service

Farm Service Agency

Forest Service

National Agricultural Library

Natural Resources Conservation Service

Rural Development

Department of Commerce (DOC)

Bureau of the Census

Bureau of Economic Analysis (BEA)

STAT-USA Database

FEDWorld

International Trade Administration (ITA)

National Institute of Standards & Technology (NIST)

National Marine Fisheries Service (NMFS)

National Oceanic & Atmospheric Administration (NOAA)

National Ocean Service

National Technical Information Service (NTIS)

National Telecommunications & Information Administration

National Weather Service

Patent and Trademark Office Database

Department of Defense (DOD)

Department of Education

Educational Resources Information Center (ERIC)

Clearinghouses

National Library of Education (NLE)

Other Federal Government Internet Educational Resources

Department of Energy

Environment, Safety and Health (ES&H)

Federal Energy Regulatory Commission

Los Alamos National Laboratory

Office of Science

Southwestern Power Administration

INDEPENDENT AGENCIES

Advisory Council on Historic Preservation (ACHP)

American Battle Monuments Commission

Central Intelligence Agency (CIA)

Commodity Futures Trading Commission (CFTC)

Consumer Product Safety Commission (CPSC)

Corporation for National Service

Environmental Protection Agency (EPA)

Equal Employment Opportunity Commission (EEOC)

Farm Credit Administration (FCA)

Federal Communications Commission (FCC)

Federal Deposit Insurance Corporation (FDIC)

Federal Election Commission (FEC)

Federal Energy Regulatory Commission (FERC)

Federal Labor Relations Authority (FLRA)

Federal Maritime Commission

Federal Reserve System, Board of Governors of the Federal Reserve

Federal Retirement Thrift Investment Board (FRTIB)

Federal Trade Commission (FTC)

General Services Administration (GSA)

Federal Consumer Information Center (Pueblo, CO)

Institute of Museum and Library Services (IMLS)

International Boundary and Water Commission

International Broadcasting Bureau (IBB)

Merit Systems Protection Board (MSPB)

National Aeronautics and Space Administration (NASA)

National Archives and Records Administration (NARA)

National Capital Planning Commission (NCPC)

National Commission on Libraries and Information Science (NCLIS)

National Council on Disability

National Credit Union Administration (NCUA)

National Endowment for the Arts (NEA)

National Endowment for the Humanities (NEH)

National Indian Gaming Commission (NIGC)

National Labor Relations Board (NLRB)

National Mediation Board (NMB)

National Railroad Passenger Corporation (AMTRAK)

National Science Foundation (NSF) Board

National Transportation Safety Board (NTSB)

Nuclear Regulatory Commission (NRC)

Department of Health and Human Services (HHS)	US Nuclear Waste Technical Review Board (NWTRB)
HHS Agencies	Occupational Safety and Health Administration (OSHA)
National Institutes of Health (NIH)	Office of Federal Housing Enterprise Oversight (OFHEO)
National Library of Medicine (NLM)	Office of Personnel Management (OPM)
Department Homeland Security (DHS)	Overseas Private Investment Corporation (OPIC)
Customs & Border Protection	Peace Corps
Coast Guard	Pension Benefit Guaranty Corporation
Federal Emergency Management Agency (FEMA)	Postal Rate Commission
Federal Law Enforcement Training Center	Railroad Retirement Board (RRB)
Secret Service	Securities and Exchange Commission (SEC)
US Citizenship and Immigration Services	Selective Service System (SSS)
U.S. Intelligence Community (Jobs)	Small Business Administration (SBA)
Department of Housing and Urban Development (HUD)	Social Security Administration (SSA)
Government National Mortgage Association (Ginnie Mae)	Tennessee Valley Authority (TVA)
Office of Healthy Homes and Lead Hazard Control	Thrift Savings Plan (TSP)
Office of Public and Indian Housing (PIH)	United States Agency for International Development (USAID)
Department of the Interior (DOI)	United States Arms Control and Disarmament Agency (ACDA)
Bureau of Indian Affairs	United States International Trade Commission (USITC)
Bureau of Land Management	Dataweb (Import/export data)
Bureau of Reclamation	United States Office of Government Ethics (OGE)
Fish and Wildlife Service	United States Postal Service (USPS)
Geological Survey	United States Trade and Development Agency
Minerals Management Service	Voice of America (VOA)

Chart II - U.S. Federal - Job Titles - Salaries - Pensior

Chart II: U.S. Federal Job Titles & Salaries
5-Year Salary Projections & Pension Estimates

LEGEND:

U.S. Federal Job Titles shown here represent all the job titles used by U.S. Federal agencies and departments. *Salary is provided, starting with minimum salary published for the Median Grade in the Grade Range for a title For example, if the Grade Range for a title is GS 5-13, the median starting salary, eliminating the lowest Grade and the highest Grade, would be GS 9. This means a job candidate would be likely to find jobs they qualified for in the middle of the Grade Range. While there are Federal job announcements listed within the full Grade Range, many new hires will try to position themselves around the Median Salary Grade, or Grade 9, in this case scenario.

The Salary median (minimum) and maximum amounts are projected estimates, based on actual base publishec salaries, from base year in the U.S. Federal GS Schedule, plus the estimated raise percentage. The raise percentage used is based on a 5-year average of actual published raises for the U.S. Federal Government from over the most recent 5 years (USAOPM, GS Pay Schedule, 2006.).

** Cumulative 5-Year Raise Estimate, is based on 5-Year Average Raise Estimate, as determined from actual published raise figures from over the most recent 5 years. Compounded 5-Year Raise Estimate (not shown) is greater than Cumulative 5-Year Raise Estimate.

***Estimated Pension at 20-Years, 25-Years, and 30-Years is based on the Pension Formula for the U.S. Federal Government 3 part plan: 1) The Basic Benefit annual pension of Average of 3 Highest Years Salaries times Pension Percentage 1.1% times Number of Years. The Pension Benefit is based on a fixed formula. 2) Social Security Benefits are paid in addition to The Basic Plan Benefits. 3) The Thrift Savings Plan pays an Automatic Agency Contribution of 1% of base salary per year. Employees may make additional contributions to the Thrift Savings Plan; contributions will be matched by the Agency at a rate of $1.00 for $1.00 for the first 3% of base salary contributed, and $.50 for $1.00 for the second 2% of base salary contributed (USAOPM, FERS, 2006.)

****Retirement Benefit from Agency Thrift Savings Plan. The Retirement Benefit calculated here from The Thrif Savings Plan is calculated as 1% of base salary minimum or maximum per year, plus an estimated 4.5% estimated Interest accrued per year on the 1%. Employees may choose to save their Thrift Savings in any of a variety of investment savings vehicles; interest rates may vary. This calculation shown for demonstration purposes is made without any additional Employee Contributions (USAOPM, TSP, 2006.)

*****Senior Executive Service: The SES pay range has a minimum rate of basic pay equal to 120 percent of the rate for GS-15, step 1, and the maximum rate of basic pay is equal to the rate for level III of the Executive Schedule. For any agency certified as having a performance appraisal system, the maximum rate of basic pay will be the rate for level II of the Executive Schedule (USAOPM, SES, 2006.)

Disclaimer: The Salary & Pension performance data featured is based on past performance, which is no guarantee of future results. Current Salary & Pension may be higher or lower than the performance data quoted.

REFERENCEs:
U.S. Federal Government, Office of Personnel Management, Federal Employee Retirement System 2006, http://www.opm.gov/forms/pdfimage/RI90-1.pdf
U.S. Federal Government, Office of Personnel Administration, GS Pay Schedule, 2006, http://www.opm.gov/oca/06tables/pdf/gs.pdf; http://www.opm.gov/oca/06tables/indexGS.asp.
U.S. Federal Government, Office of Personnel Administration, Senior Executive Service, 2006, http://www.opm.gov/oca/06tables/pdf/es.pdf http://www.opm.gov/ses.
U.S. Federal Government, Office of Personnel Administration, Thrift Savings Plan, 2006, http://www.opm.gov/

Chart II - U.S. Federal - Job Titles - Salaries - Pension Estimates

Biological Sciences

U.S. Federal Government Agencies	GS Grade Range:	GS Grade Median	2010 Median Grade Min Salary (STEP 1)	2010 Maximum Grade Salary (STEP 1)	2011 Median Grade Min Salary (STEP 2)	2011 Maximum Grade Salary (STEP 2)	2012 Median Grade Min Salary (STEP 3)	2012 Maximum Grade Salary (STEP 3)	2013 Median Grade Min Salary (STEP 4)	2013 Maximum Grade Salary (STEP 4)	10-Year Cumulative Raise Percentage (1.96%) + Step Increase Percentage (1.7%)	20-Year Annual Pension Benefit Estimate (Min.)	20-Year Annual Pension Benefit Estimate (Max.)	25-Year Annual Pension Benefit Estimate (Min.)	25-Year Annual Pension Benefit Estimate (Max.)	30-Year Annual Pension Benefit Estimate (Min.)	30-Year Annual Pension Benefit Estimate (Max.)	Agency Automatic Contributions 1% Thrift Savings Plan 20 Year Savings Plus 4.5% Interest (Min)	Agency Automatic Contributions 1% Thrift Savings Plan 20 Year Savings Plus 4.5% Interest (Max)	Agency Automatic Contributions 1% Thrift Savings Plan 25 Year Savings Plus 4.5% Interest (Min)	Agency Automatic Contributions 1% Thrift Savings Plan 25 Year Savings Plus 4.5% Interest (Max)	Agency Automatic Contributions 1% Thrift Savings Plan 30 Year Savings Plus 4.5% Interest (Min)	Agency Automatic Contributions 1% Thrift Savings Plan 30 Year Savings Plus 4.5% Interest (Max)
General Biological Science Series																							
Agricultural Biotechnology Advisor	GS-5-GS-13	9	38,824	66,951	39,738	69,339	40,667	71,767	40,667	71,767	37%	10,289	19,297	12,973	24,413	15,567	29,295	9,465	17,161	11,929	21,800	13,988	25,738
Agricultural Development Officer	GS-5-GS-13	9	38,824	66,951	39,738	69,339	40,667	71,767	40,667	71,767	37%	10,289	19,297	12,973	24,413	15,567	29,295	9,465	17,161	11,929	21,800	13,988	25,738
Biological Scientist	GS-5-GS-13	9	38,824	66,951	39,738	69,339	40,667	71,767	40,667	71,767	37%	10,289	19,297	12,973	24,413	15,567	29,295	9,465	17,161	11,929	21,800	13,988	25,738
Interdisciplinary – General Biological Scientist	GS-5-GS-13	9	38,824	66,951	39,738	69,339	40,667	71,767	40,667	71,767	37%	10,289	19,297	12,973	24,413	15,567	29,295	9,465	17,161	11,929	21,800	13,988	25,738
Lead Interdisciplinary Scientist	GS-5-GS-13	9	38,824	66,951	39,738	69,339	40,667	71,767	40,667	71,767	37%	10,289	19,297	12,973	24,413	15,567	29,295	9,465	17,161	11,929	21,800	13,988	25,738
Natural Resources Specialist (Recreation)	GS-5-GS-13	9	38,824	66,951	39,738	69,339	40,667	71,767	40,667	71,767	37%	10,289	19,297	12,973	24,413	15,567	29,295	9,465	17,161	11,929	21,800	13,988	25,738
Supervisory Wildland Fire Operations Specialist (FOS)	GS-5-GS-13	9	38,824	66,951	39,738	69,339	40,667	71,767	40,667	71,767	37%	10,289	19,297	12,973	24,413	15,567	29,295	9,465	17,161	11,929	21,800	13,988	25,738
Microbiology Series																							
Microbiologist	GS-5-GS-13	9	38,824	66,951	39,738	69,339	40,667	71,767	40,667	71,767	37%	10,289	19,297	12,973	24,413	15,567	29,295	9,465	17,161	11,929	21,800	13,988	25,738
Supervisory positions	GS-5-GS-13	9	38,824	66,951	39,738	69,339	40,667	71,767	40,667	71,767	37%	10,289	19,297	12,973	24,413	15,567	29,295	9,465	17,161	11,929	21,800	13,988	25,738
Biological Science Technician Series**																							
Biological Science Lab Technician	GS-5-GS-13	9	38,824	66,951	39,738	69,339	40,667	71,767	40,667	71,767	37%	10,289	19,297	12,973	24,413	15,567	29,295	9,465	17,161	11,929	21,800	13,988	25,738
Biological Science Technician (Plants)	GS-5-GS-13	9	38,824	66,951	39,738	69,339	40,667	71,767	40,667	71,767	37%	10,289	19,297	12,973	24,413	15,567	29,295	9,465	17,161	11,929	21,800	13,988	25,738
Biological Science Laboratory Technician	GS-5-GS-13	9	38,824	66,951	39,738	69,339	40,667	71,767	40,667	71,767	37%	10,289	19,297	12,973	24,413	15,567	29,295	9,465	17,161	11,929	21,800	13,988	25,738
Forestry Technician Series																							
Forestry Aid	GS-3-GS-4	9	38,824	22,902	39,551	23,718	40,291	24,548	40,291	24,548	37%	9,933	6,600	12,505	8,349	15,006	10,019	9,272	5,870	11,648	7,456	13,618	8,803
Forestry Technician	GS-3-GS-4	9	38,824	22,902	39,551	23,718	40,291	24,548	40,291	24,548	37%	9,933	6,600	12,505	8,349	15,006	10,019	9,272	5,870	11,648	7,456	13,618	8,803
Lead Forestry Technician	GS-3-GS-4	9	38,824	22,902	39,551	23,718	40,291	24,548	40,291	24,548	37%	9,933	6,600	12,505	8,349	15,006	10,019	9,272	5,870	11,648	7,456	13,618	8,803
Supervisory Forestry Technician	GS-3-GS-4	9	38,824	22,902	39,551	23,718	40,291	24,548	40,291	24,548	37%	9,933	6,600	12,505	8,349	15,006	10,019	9,272	5,870	11,648	7,456	13,618	8,803
Soil Science Series																							
Soil Scientist	GS-5-GS-13	9	38,824	66,951	39,738	69,339	40,667	71,767	40,667	71,767	37%	10,289	19,297	12,973	24,413	15,567	29,295	9,465	17,161	11,929	21,800	13,988	25,738
Supervisory Soil Scientist	GS-5-GS-13	9	38,824	66,951	39,738	69,339	40,667	71,767	40,667	71,767	37%	10,289	19,297	12,973	24,413	15,567	29,295	9,465	17,161	11,929	21,800	13,988	25,738
Agronomy Series																							
Research Agronomist.	GS-5-GS-13	9	38,824	66,951	39,738	69,339	40,667	71,767	40,667	71,767	37%	10,289	19,297	12,973	24,413	15,567	29,295	9,465	17,161	11,929	21,800	13,988	25,738
Management Agronomist.	GS-5-GS-13	9	38,824	66,951	39,738	69,339	40,667	71,767	40,667	71,767	37%	10,289	19,297	12,973	24,413	15,567	29,295	9,465	17,161	11,929	21,800	13,988	25,738
Conservation Agronomist.	GS-5-GS-13	9	38,824	66,951	39,738	69,339	40,667	71,767	40,667	71,767	37%	10,289	19,297	12,973	24,413	15,567	29,295	9,465	17,161	11,929	21,800	13,988	25,738
Wildlife Refuge Management Series																							
Refuge Program Specialist	GS-9-GS-15	9	38,824	93,063	40,208	96,387	41,616	99,767	41,616	99,767	37%	11,189	26,832	14,156	33,946	16,987	40,735	9,951	23,859	12,641	30,309	14,925	35,786
Refuge Manager	GS-9-GS-15	9	38,824	93,063	40,208	96,387	41,616	99,767	41,616	99,767	37%	11,189	26,832	14,156	33,946	16,987	40,735	9,951	23,859	12,641	30,309	14,925	35,786

Chart II - U.S. Federal - Job Titles - Salaries - Pension Estimates

U.S. Federal Government Agencies	GS Grade Range:	GS Grade Median	2010 Median Grade Min Salary (STEP 1)	2010 Maximum Grade Salary (STEP 1)	2011 Median Grade Min Salary (STEP 2)	2011 Maximum Grade Salary (STEP 2)	2012 Median Grade Min Salary (STEP 3)	2012 Maximum Grade Salary (STEP 3)	2013 Median Grade Min Salary (STEP 4)	2013 Maximum Grade Salary (STEP 4)	10-Year Cumulative Raise Percentage (1.96%) + Step Increase Percentage (1.7%)	20-Year Annual Pension Benefit Estimate (Min.)	20-Year Annual Pension Benefit Estimate (Max.)	25-Year Annual Pension Benefit Estimate (Min.)	25-Year Annual Pension Benefit Estimate (Max.)	30-Year Annual Pension Benefit Estimate (Min.)	30-Year Annual Pension Benefit Estimate (Max.)	Agency Automatic Contributions 1% Thrift Savings Plan 20 Year Savings Plus 4.5% Interest (Min)	Agency Automatic Contributions 1% Thrift Savings Plan 20 Year Savings Plus 4.5% Interest (Max)	Agency Automatic Contributions 1% Thrift Savings Plan 25 Year Savings Plus 4.5% Interest (Min)	Agency Automatic Contributions 1% Thrift Savings Plan 25 Year Savings Plus 4.5% Interest (Max)	Agency Automatic Contributions 1% Thrift Savings Plan 30 Year Savings Plus 4.5% Interest (Min)	Agency Automatic Contributions 1% Thrift Savings Plan 30 Year Savings Plus 4.5% Interest (Max)
Supervisory Refuge Program Specialist	GS-9 GS-15	9	38,824	93,063	40,208	96,387	41,616	99,767	41,616	99,767	37%	11,189	26,832	14,156	33,946	16,987	40,735	9,951	23,859	12,641	30,309	14,925	35,786

Budget_ Industry _ Procurement

U.S. Federal Government Agencies	GS Grade Range:	GS Grade Median	2010 Median Grade Min Salary (STEP 1)	2010 Maximum Grade Salary (STEP 1)	2011 Median Grade Min Salary (STEP 2)	2011 Maximum Grade Salary (STEP 2)	2012 Median Grade Min Salary (STEP 3)	2012 Maximum Grade Salary (STEP 3)	2013 Median Grade Min Salary (STEP 4)	2013 Maximum Grade Salary (STEP 4)	10-Year Cumulative Raise Percentage (1.96%) + Step Increase Percentage (1.7%)	20-Year Annual Pension Benefit Estimate (Min.)	20-Year Annual Pension Benefit Estimate (Max.)	25-Year Annual Pension Benefit Estimate (Min.)	25-Year Annual Pension Benefit Estimate (Max.)	30-Year Annual Pension Benefit Estimate (Min.)	30-Year Annual Pension Benefit Estimate (Max.)	Agency Automatic Contributions 1% Thrift Savings Plan 20 Year Savings Plus 4.5% Interest (Min)	Agency Automatic Contributions 1% Thrift Savings Plan 20 Year Savings Plus 4.5% Interest (Max)	Agency Automatic Contributions 1% Thrift Savings Plan 25 Year Savings Plus 4.5% Interest (Min)	Agency Automatic Contributions 1% Thrift Savings Plan 25 Year Savings Plus 4.5% Interest (Max)	Agency Automatic Contributions 1% Thrift Savings Plan 30 Year Savings Plus 4.5% Interest (Min)	Agency Automatic Contributions 1% Thrift Savings Plan 30 Year Savings Plus 4.5% Interest (Max)
Economist Series																							
economy	GS-5 GS-15	9	38,824	93,063	39,738	96,387	40,667	99,767	40,667	99,767	37%	10,289	26,832	12,973	33,946	15,567	40,735	9,465	23,859	11,929	30,309	13,988	35,786
Economist	GS-5 GS-15	9	38,824	93,063	39,738	96,387	40,667	99,767	40,667	122,669	37%	10,289	31,871	12,973	40,244	15,567	48,293	9,465	27,928	11,929	35,574	13,988	42,248
Financial Economist	GS-5 GS-15	9	38,824	93,063	39,738	96,387	40,667	99,767	87,641	122,669	37%	20,623	31,871	25,891	40,244	31,069	48,293	17,809	27,928	22,729	35,574	27,242	42,248
Labor Economist	GS-5 GS-15	9	38,824	93,063	39,738	96,387	40,667	99,767	87,641	122,669	37%	20,623	31,871	25,891	40,244	31,069	48,293	17,809	27,928	22,729	35,574	27,242	42,248
Regional Economist	GS-5 GS-15	9	38,824	93,063	39,738	96,387	40,667	99,767	40,667	122,669	37%	10,289	31,871	12,973	40,244	15,567	48,293	9,465	27,928	11,929	35,574	13,988	42,248
Industry Economist	GS-5 GS-15	9	38,824	93,063	39,738	96,387	40,667	99,767	40,667	122,669	37%	10,289	31,871	12,973	40,244	15,567	48,293	9,465	27,928	11,929	35,574	13,988	42,248
Agricultural Economist	GS-5 GS-15	9	38,824	93,063	39,738	96,387	40,667	99,767	63,569	99,767	37%	15,327	26,832	19,271	33,946	23,125	40,735	13,533	23,859	17,195	30,309	20,450	35,786
Accounting Series																							
Accountant	GS-5 GS-15	10	42,755	93,063	43,669	96,387	44,598	99,767	67,500	122,669	37%	16,192	31,871	20,352	40,244	24,422	48,293	14,396	27,928	18,263	35,574	21,683	42,248
Supervisory Accountant	GS-5 GS-15	10	42,755	93,063	43,669	96,387	44,598	99,767	67,500	99,767	37%	16,192	26,832	20,352	33,946	24,422	40,735	14,396	23,859	18,263	30,309	21,683	35,786
Systems Accountant	GS-5 GS-15	10	42,755	93,063	43,669	96,387	44,598	99,767	44,598	99,767	37%	11,154	26,832	14,054	33,946	16,864	40,735	10,327	23,859	12,997	30,309	15,221	35,786
Supervisory Systems Accountant	GS-5 GS-15	10	42,755	93,063	43,669	96,387	44,598	99,767	44,598	134,918	37%	11,154	34,565	14,054	43,612	16,864	52,335	10,327	30,104	12,997	38,390	15,221	45,704
Staff Accountant	GS-5 GS-15	10	42,755	93,063	43,669	96,387	44,598	99,767	67,500	134,918	37%	16,192	34,565	20,352	43,612	24,422	52,335	14,396	30,104	18,263	38,390	21,683	45,704
Supervisory Staff Accountant	GS-5 GS-15	10	42,755	93,063	43,669	96,387	44,598	99,767	67,500	134,918	37%	16,192	34,565	20,352	43,612	24,422	52,335	14,396	30,104	18,263	38,390	21,683	45,704
Accounting Officer	GS-5 GS-15	10	42,755	93,063	43,669	96,387	44,598	99,767	44,598	99,767	37%	11,154	26,832	14,054	33,946	16,864	40,735	10,327	23,859	12,997	30,309	15,221	35,786
Auditing Series																							
Auditor	GS-5 GS-15	10	42,755	93,063	43,669	96,387	44,598	99,767	79,749	146,741	37%	18,887	37,166	23,720	46,864	28,464	56,236	16,572	32,204	21,079	41,108	25,139	49,040
Supervisory Auditor	GS-5 GS-15	10	42,755	93,063	43,669	96,387	44,598	99,767	79,749	99,767	37%	18,887	26,832	23,720	33,946	28,464	40,735	16,572	23,859	21,079	30,309	25,139	35,786
Internal Revenue Agent Series																							
Internal Revenue Agent	GS-9 GS-15	10	42,755	93,063	44,139	96,387	45,547	99,767	92,521	146,741	37%	22,388	37,166	28,155	46,864	33,785	56,236	19,159	32,204	24,508	41,108	29,411	49,040
Supervisory Internal Revenue Agent	GS-9 GS-15	10	42,755	93,063	44,139	96,387	45,547	99,767	92,521	146,741	37%	22,388	37,166	28,155	46,864	33,785	56,236	19,159	32,204	24,508	41,108	29,411	49,040
Budget Analysis Series																							
Budget Analyst	GS-5 GS-15	10	42,755	93,063	43,669	96,387	44,598	99,767	91,572	146,741	37%	21,488	37,166	26,972	46,864	32,366	56,236	18,672	32,204	23,797	41,108	28,475	49,040

Chart II - U.S. Federal - Job Titles - Salaries - Pension Estimates

U.S. Federal Government Agencies	GS Grade Range	GS Grade Median	2010 Median Grade Min Salary (STEP 1)	2010 Maximum Grade Salary (STEP 1)	2011 Median Grade Min Salary (STEP 2)	2011 Maximum Grade Salary (STEP 2)	2012 Median Grade Min Salary (STEP 3)	2012 Maximum Grade Salary (STEP 3)	2013 Median Grade Min Salary (STEP 4)	2013 Maximum Grade Salary (STEP 4)	10-Year Cumulative Raise Percentage (1.96%) + Step Increase Percentage (1.7%)	20-Year Annual Pension Benefit Estimate (Min.)	20-Year Annual Pension Benefit Estimate (Max.)	25-Year Annual Pension Benefit Estimate (Min.)	25-Year Annual Pension Benefit Estimate (Max.)	30-Year Annual Pension Benefit Estimate (Min.)	30-Year Annual Pension Benefit Estimate (Max.)	Agency Automatic Contributions 1% Thrift Savings Plan 20 Year Savings Plus 4.5% Interest (Min)	Agency Automatic Contributions 1% Thrift Savings Plan 20 Year Savings Plus 4.5% Interest (Max)	Agency Automatic Contributions 1% Thrift Savings Plan 25 Year Savings Plus 4.5% Interest (Min)	Agency Automatic Contributions 1% Thrift Savings Plan 25 Year Savings Plus 4.5% Interest (Max)	Agency Automatic Contributions 1% Thrift Savings Plan 30 Year Savings Plus 4.5% Interest (Min)	Agency Automatic Contributions 1% Thrift Savings Plan 30 Year Savings Plus 4.5% Interest (Max)
Budget Officer	GS-5-GS-15	10	42,755	93,063	43,669	96,387	44,598	99,767	91,572	146,741	37%	21,488	37,166	26,972	46,864	32,366	56,236	18,672	32,204	23,797	41,108	28,475	49,040
Budget Examiner	GS-5-GS-15	10	42,755	93,063	43,669	96,387	44,598	99,767	91,572	146,741	37%	21,488	37,166	26,972	46,864	32,366	56,236	18,672	32,204	23,797	41,108	28,475	49,040

Industrial Property Management Series

U.S. Federal Government Agencies	GS Grade Range	GS Grade Median	2010 Min	2010 Max	2011 Min	2011 Max	2012 Min	2012 Max	2013 Min	2013 Max	10-Yr %	20-Yr Min	20-Yr Max	25-Yr Min	25-Yr Max	30-Yr Min	30-Yr Max	TSP 20 Min	TSP 20 Max	TSP 25 Min	TSP 25 Max	TSP 30 Min	TSP 30 Max
Industrial Property Management Specialist	GS-5-GS-12		5-12	25,623	56,301	25,623	56,301	25,623	56,301	25,623	56,301	26,537	58,309	27,466	60,351	74,440	95,502	74,440	95,502	75,417	97,650	75,417	97,650
Industrial Property Management Specialist	GS-5-GS-12		5-12	25,623	56,301	25,623	56,301	25,623	56,301	25,623	56,301	26,537	58,309	27,466	60,351	74,440	95,502	74,440	95,502	75,417	97,650	75,417	97,650
Industrial Property Clearance Specialist	GS-5-GS-12		5-12	25,623	56,301	25,623	56,301	25,623	56,301	25,623	56,301	26,537	58,309	27,466	60,351	74,440	95,502	74,440	95,502	75,417	97,650	75,417	97,650
Supervisory Industrial Property Mgmt Spec	GS-5-GS-12	8	5-12	25,623	56,301	25,623	56,301	25,623	56,301	25,623	56,301	26,537	58,309	27,466	60,351	74,440	95,502	74,440	95,502	75,417	97,650	75,417	97,650
Supervisory Industrial Property Mgmt Spec	GS-5-GS-12	8	5-12	25,623	56,301	25,623	56,301	25,623	56,301	25,623	56,301	26,537	58,309	27,466	60,351	27,466	95,502	27,466	95,502	28,443	97,650	28,443	97,650
Industrial Property Management Officer	GS-5-GS-12	8	5-12	25,623	56,301	25,623	56,301	25,623	56,301	25,623	56,301	26,537	58,309	27,466	60,351	27,466	60,351	27,466	60,351	28,443	62,499	28,443	62,499
Industrial Property Clearance Specialist	GS-5-GS-12	8	5-12	25,623	56,301	25,623	56,301	25,623	56,301	25,623	56,301	26,537	58,309	27,466	60,351	62,617	60,351	62,617	60,351	63,594	62,499	63,594	62,499

Property Disposal Series

U.S. Federal Government Agencies	GS Grade Range	GS Grade Median	2010 Min	2010 Max	2011 Min	2011 Max	2012 Min	2012 Max	2013 Min	2013 Max	10-Yr %	20-Yr Min	20-Yr Max	25-Yr Min	25-Yr Max	30-Yr Min	30-Yr Max	TSP 20 Min	TSP 20 Max	TSP 25 Min	TSP 25 Max	TSP 30 Min	TSP 30 Max
Property Disposal Specialist	GS-9-GS-13	11	46,974	66,951	48,358	69,339	49,766	71,767	84,917	118,741	37%	20,716	29,631	26,063	37,330	31,276	44,796	17,984	25,506	22,936	32,599	27,398	38,992
Property Disposal Officer	GS-9-GS-13	11	46,974	66,951	48,358	69,339	49,766	71,767	49,766	118,741	37%	12,982	29,631	16,397	37,330	19,676	44,796	11,740	25,506	14,855	32,599	17,480	38,992

Procurement Clerical and Technician Series

U.S. Federal Government Agencies	GS Grade Range	GS Grade Median	2010 Min	2010 Max	2011 Min	2011 Max	2012 Min	2012 Max	2013 Min	2013 Max	10-Yr %	20-Yr Min	20-Yr Max	25-Yr Min	25-Yr Max	30-Yr Min	30-Yr Max	TSP 20 Min	TSP 20 Max	TSP 25 Min	TSP 25 Max	TSP 30 Min	TSP 30 Max
Procurement Clerk	GS-1-GS-7	4	22,902	31,740	22,902	32,872	22,902	34,023	69,876	34,023	37%	15,373	9,148	19,216	11,573	23,059	13,888	13,371	8,136	17,022	10,335	20,433	12,202
Procurement Technician	GS-1-GS-7	4	22,902	31,740	22,902	32,872	22,902	34,023	69,876	34,023	37%	15,373	9,148	19,216	11,573	23,059	13,888	13,371	8,136	17,022	10,335	20,433	12,202
Lead Procurement Clerk	GS-1-GS-7	4	22,902	31,740	22,902	32,872	22,902	34,023	69,876	34,023	37%	15,373	9,148	19,216	11,573	23,059	13,888	13,371	8,136	17,022	10,335	20,433	12,202
Lead Procurement Technician	GS-1-GS-7	4	22,902	31,740	22,902	32,872	22,902	34,023	22,902	34,023	37%	5,038	9,148	6,298	11,573	7,558	13,888	5,026	8,136	6,222	10,335	7,180	12,202
Supervisory Procurement Technician	GS-1-GS-7	4	22,902	31,740	22,902	32,872	22,902	34,023	22,902	34,023	37%	5,038	9,148	6,298	11,573	7,558	13,888	5,026	8,136	6,222	10,335	7,180	12,202

Property Disposal Clerical and Technician Series

U.S. Federal Government Agencies	GS Grade Range	GS Grade Median	2010 Min	2010 Max	2011 Min	2011 Max	2012 Min	2012 Max	2013 Min	2013 Max	10-Yr %	20-Yr Min	20-Yr Max	25-Yr Min	25-Yr Max	30-Yr Min	30-Yr Max	TSP 20 Min	TSP 20 Max	TSP 25 Min	TSP 25 Max	TSP 30 Min	TSP 30 Max
Property Disposal Clerk	GS-3-GS-7	4	22,902	31,740	23,629	32,872	24,369	34,023	24,369	34,023	37%	6,430	9,148	8,126	11,573	9,752	13,888	5,778	8,136	7,322	10,335	8,627	12,202
Property Disposal Technician	GS-3-GS-7	4	22,902	31,740	23,629	32,872	24,369	34,023	24,369	34,023	37%	6,430	9,148	8,126	11,573	9,752	13,888	5,778	8,136	7,322	10,335	8,627	12,202

Financial Analysis Series

U.S. Federal Government Agencies	GS Grade Range	GS Grade Median	2010 Min	2010 Max	2011 Min	2011 Max	2012 Min	2012 Max	2013 Min	2013 Max	10-Yr %	20-Yr Min	20-Yr Max	25-Yr Min	25-Yr Max	30-Yr Min	30-Yr Max	TSP 20 Min	TSP 20 Max	TSP 25 Min	TSP 25 Max	TSP 30 Min	TSP 30 Max
Financial Assistant	GS-5-GS-12	8	35,151	56,301	36,065	58,309	36,994	60,351	36,994	60,351	37%	9,481	16,227	11,963	20,529	14,355	24,635	8,659	14,431	10,931	18,332	12,837	21,644
Financial Analyst	GS-5-GS-12	8	35,151	56,301	36,065	58,309	36,994	60,351	36,994	60,351	37%	9,481	16,227	11,963	20,529	14,355	24,635	8,659	14,431	10,931	18,332	12,837	21,644
Supervisory Financial Analyst	GS-5-GS-12	8	35,151	56,301	36,065	58,309	36,994	60,351	36,994	60,351	37%	9,481	16,227	11,963	20,529	14,355	24,635	8,659	14,431	10,931	18,332	12,837	21,644

Internal Revenue Officer Series

U.S. Federal Government Agencies	GS Grade Range	GS Grade Median	2010 Min	2010 Max	2011 Min	2011 Max	2012 Min	2012 Max	2013 Min	2013 Max	10-Yr %	20-Yr Min	20-Yr Max	25-Yr Min	25-Yr Max	30-Yr Min	30-Yr Max	TSP 20 Min	TSP 20 Max	TSP 25 Min	TSP 25 Max	TSP 30 Min	TSP 30 Max
Revenue Officer	GS-9-GS-13	11	46,974	66,951	48,358	69,339	49,766	71,767	49,766	71,767	37%	12,982	19,297	16,397	24,413	19,676	29,295	11,740	17,161	14,855	21,800	17,480	25,738
Supervisory Revenue Officer	GS-9-GS-13	11	46,974	66,951	48,358	69,339	49,766	71,767	49,766	71,767	37%	12,982	19,297	16,397	24,413	19,676	29,295	11,740	17,161	14,855	21,800	17,480	25,738

Realty Series

U.S. Federal Government Agencies	GS Grade Range	GS Grade Median	2010 Min	2010 Max	2011 Min	2011 Max	2012 Min	2012 Max	2013 Min	2013 Max	10-Yr %	20-Yr Min	20-Yr Max	25-Yr Min	25-Yr Max	30-Yr Min	30-Yr Max	TSP 20 Min	TSP 20 Max	TSP 25 Min	TSP 25 Max	TSP 30 Min	TSP 30 Max
Realty Specialist	GS-9-GS-14	11	46,974	79,115	48,358	81,936	49,766	84,805	49,766	84,805	37%	12,982	22,802	16,397	28,847	19,676	34,616	11,740	20,279	14,855	25,760	17,480	30,414

Chart II - U.S. Federal - Job Titles - Salaries - Pension Estimates

U.S. Federal Government Agencies	GS Grade Range	GS Grade Median	2010 Median Grade Min Salary (STEP 1)	2010 Maximum Grade Salary (STEP 1)	2011 Median Grade Min Salary (STEP 2)	2011 Maximum Grade Salary (STEP 2)	2012 Median Grade Min Salary (STEP 3)	2012 Maximum Grade Salary (STEP 3)	2013 Median Grade Min Salary (STEP 4)	2013 Maximum Grade Salary (STEP 4)	10-Year Cumulative Raise Percentage + Step Increase Percentage (1.96%) (1.7%)	20-Year Annual Pension Benefit Estimate (Min.)	20-Year Annual Pension Benefit Estimate (Max.)	25-Year Annual Pension Benefit Estimate (Min.)	25-Year Annual Pension Benefit Estimate (Max.)	30-Year Annual Pension Benefit Estimate (Min.)	30-Year Annual Pension Benefit Estimate (Max.)	Agency Automatic Contributions 1% Thrift Savings Plan 20 Year Savings Plus 4.5% Interest (Min)	Agency Automatic Contributions 1% Thrift Savings Plan 20 Year Savings Plus 4.5% Interest (Max)	Agency Automatic Contributions 1% Thrift Savings Plan 25 Year Savings Plus 4.5% Interest (Min)	Agency Automatic Contributions 1% Thrift Savings Plan 25 Year Savings Plus 4.5% Interest (Max)	Agency Automatic Contributions 1% Thrift Savings Plan 30 Year Savings Plus 4.5% Interest (Min)	Agency Automatic Contribution 1% Thrift Plan 3... (Max)
Supervisory Realty Specialist	GS-9-GS-14	11	46,974	79,115	48,358	81,936	49,766	84,805	49,766	84,805	37%	12,982	22,802	16,397	28,847	19,676	34,616	11,740	20,279	14,855	25,760	17,480	30,41
Realty Officer	GS-9-GS-14	11	46,974	79,115	48,358	81,936	49,766	84,805	49,766	84,805	37%	12,982	22,802	16,397	28,847	19,676	34,616	11,740	20,279	14,855	25,760	17,480	30,41

Appraising Series

U.S. Federal Government Agencies	GS Grade Range	GS Grade Median	2010 Median (STEP 1)	2010 Max (STEP 1)	2011 Median (STEP 2)	2011 Max (STEP 2)	2012 Median (STEP 3)	2012 Max (STEP 3)	2013 Median (STEP 4)	2013 Max (STEP 4)	10-Yr %	20-Yr Min	20-Yr Max	25-Yr Min	25-Yr Max	30-Yr Min	30-Yr Max	20 Yr Min	20 Yr Max	25 Yr Min	25 Yr Max	30 Yr Min	30 Yr Max
Appraiser	GS-9-GS-14	11	46,974	79,115	48,358	81,936	49,766	84,805	49,766	84,805	37%	12,982	22,802	16,397	28,847	19,676	34,616	11,740	20,279	14,855	25,760	17,480	30,41
Review Appraiser	GS-9-GS-14	11	46,974	79,115	48,358	81,936	49,766	84,805	49,766	84,805	37%	12,982	22,802	16,397	28,847	19,676	34,616	11,740	20,279	14,855	25,760	17,480	30,41
Chief Appraiser	GS-9-GS-14	11	46,974	79,115	48,358	81,936	49,766	84,805	49,766	84,805	37%	12,982	22,802	16,397	28,847	19,676	34,616	11,740	20,279	14,855	25,760	17,480	30,41

Housing Management Series

U.S. Federal Government Agencies	GS Grade Range	GS Grade Median	2010 Median (STEP 1)	2010 Max (STEP 1)	2011 Median (STEP 2)	2011 Max (STEP 2)	2012 Median (STEP 3)	2012 Max (STEP 3)	2013 Median (STEP 4)	2013 Max (STEP 4)	10-Yr %	20-Yr Min	20-Yr Max	25-Yr Min	25-Yr Max	30-Yr Min	30-Yr Max	20 Yr Min	20 Yr Max	25 Yr Min	25 Yr Max	30 Yr Min	30 Yr Max
Housing Manager	GS-5-GS-13	8	35,151	66,951	36,065	69,339	36,994	71,767	36,994	71,767	37%	9,481	19,297	11,963	24,413	14,355	29,295	8,659	17,161	10,931	21,800	12,837	25,73
Housing Management Assistant	GS-5-GS-13	8	35,151	66,951	36,065	69,339	36,994	71,767	36,994	71,767	37%	9,481	19,297	11,963	24,413	14,355	29,295	8,659	17,161	10,931	21,800	12,837	25,73
Housing Management Specialist	GS-5-GS-13	8	35,151	66,951	36,065	69,339	36,994	71,767	36,994	71,767	37%	9,481	19,297	11,963	24,413	14,355	29,295	8,659	17,161	10,931	21,800	12,837	25,73
Housing Management Assistant	GS-5-GS-13	8	35,151	66,951	36,065	69,339	36,994	71,767	36,994	71,767	37%	9,481	19,297	11,963	24,413	14,355	29,295	8,659	17,161	10,931	21,800	12,837	25,73

Building Management Series

U.S. Federal Government Agencies	GS Grade Range	GS Grade Median	2010 Median (STEP 1)	2010 Max (STEP 1)	2011 Median (STEP 2)	2011 Max (STEP 2)	2012 Median (STEP 3)	2012 Max (STEP 3)	2013 Median (STEP 4)	2013 Max (STEP 4)	10-Yr %	20-Yr Min	20-Yr Max	25-Yr Min	25-Yr Max	30-Yr Min	30-Yr Max	20 Yr Min	20 Yr Max	25 Yr Min	25 Yr Max	30 Yr Min	30 Yr Max
Building Manager	GS-9-GS-13	11	46,974	66,951	48,358	69,339	49,766	71,767	49,766	71,767	37%	12,982	19,297	16,397	24,413	19,676	29,295	11,740	17,161	14,855	21,800	17,480	25,73
Building Management Specialist	GS-9-GS-13	11	46,974	66,951	48,358	69,339	49,766	71,767	49,766	71,767	37%	12,982	19,297	16,397	24,413	19,676	29,295	11,740	17,161	14,855	21,800	17,480	25,73
Building Management Officer	GS-9-GS-13	11	46,974	66,951	48,358	69,339	49,766	71,767	49,766	71,767	37%	12,982	19,297	16,397	24,413	19,676	29,295	11,740	17,161	14,855	21,800	17,480	25,73
Supervisory Building Management Specialist	GS-9-GS-13	11	46,974	66,951	48,358	69,339	49,766	71,767	49,766	71,767	37%	12,982	19,297	16,397	24,413	19,676	29,295	11,740	17,161	14,855	21,800	17,480	25,73

Copyright_Patent_Trademark

U.S. Federal Government Agencies	GS Grade Range	GS Grade Median	2010 Median Grade Min Salary (STEP 1)	2010 Maximum Grade Salary (STEP 1)	2011 Median Grade Min Salary (STEP 2)	2011 Maximum Grade Salary (STEP 2)	2012 Median Grade Min Salary (STEP 3)	2012 Maximum Grade Salary (STEP 3)	2013 Median Grade Min Salary (STEP 4)	2013 Maximum Grade Salary (STEP 4)	10-Year Cumulative Raise Percentage + Step Increase Percentage (1.96%) (1.7%)	20-Year Annual Pension Benefit Estimate (Min.)	20-Year Annual Pension Benefit Estimate (Max.)	25-Year Annual Pension Benefit Estimate (Min.)	25-Year Annual Pension Benefit Estimate (Max.)	30-Year Annual Pension Benefit Estimate (Min.)	30-Year Annual Pension Benefit Estimate (Max.)	Agency Automatic Contributions 1% Thrift Savings Plan 20 Year Savings Plus 4.5% Interest (Min)	Agency Automatic Contributions 1% Thrift Savings Plan 20 Year Savings Plus 4.5% Interest (Max)	Agency Automatic Contributions 1% Thrift Savings Plan 25 Year Savings Plus 4.5% Interest (Min)	Agency Automatic Contributions 1% Thrift Savings Plan 25 Year Savings Plus 4.5% Interest (Max)	Agency Automatic Contributions 1% Thrift Savings Plan 30 Year Savings Plus 4.5% Interest (Min)	Agency Auto Contri- bution 1% Thrift Saving... (Max)

Patent Adviser Series

U.S. Federal Government Agencies	GS Grade Range	GS Grade Median	2010 Median (STEP 1)	2010 Max (STEP 1)	2011 Median (STEP 2)	2011 Max (STEP 2)	2012 Median (STEP 3)	2012 Max (STEP 3)	2013 Median (STEP 4)	2013 Max (STEP 4)	10-Yr %	20-Yr Min	20-Yr Max	25-Yr Min	25-Yr Max	30-Yr Min	30-Yr Max	20 Yr Min	20 Yr Max	25 Yr Min	25 Yr Max	30 Yr Min	30 Yr Max
Patent Adviser	GS-5-GS-14	8	35,151	79,115	36,065	81,936	36,994	84,805	36,994	84,805	37%	9,481	22,802	11,963	28,847	14,355	34,616	8,659	20,279	10,931	25,760	12,837	30,41
Supervisory	GS-5-GS-14	8	35,151	79,115	36,065	81,936	36,994	84,805	36,994	84,805	37%	9,481	22,802	11,963	28,847	14,355	34,616	8,659	20,279	10,931	25,760	12,837	30,41
Electrical engineering	GS-5-GS-14	8	35,151	79,115	36,065	81,936	36,994	84,805	36,994	84,805	37%	9,481	22,802	11,963	28,847	14,355	34,616	8,659	20,279	10,931	25,760	12,837	30,41

Patent Attorney Series

U.S. Federal Government Agencies	GS Grade Range	GS Grade Median	2010 Median (STEP 1)	2010 Max (STEP 1)	2011 Median (STEP 2)	2011 Max (STEP 2)	2012 Median (STEP 3)	2012 Max (STEP 3)	2013 Median (STEP 4)	2013 Max (STEP 4)	10-Yr %	20-Yr Min	20-Yr Max	25-Yr Min	25-Yr Max	30-Yr Min	30-Yr Max	20 Yr Min	20 Yr Max	25 Yr Min	25 Yr Max	30 Yr Min	30 Yr Max
Patent Attorney	GS-15	15	93,063	93,063	96,387	96,387	99,767	99,767	99,767	99,767	37%	26,832	26,832	33,946	33,946	40,735	40,735	23,859	23,859	30,309	30,309	35,786	35,78

Design Patent Examining Series

U.S. Federal Government Agencies	GS Grade Range	GS Grade Median	2010 Median (STEP 1)	2010 Max (STEP 1)	2011 Median (STEP 2)	2011 Max (STEP 2)	2012 Median (STEP 3)	2012 Max (STEP 3)	2013 Median (STEP 4)	2013 Max (STEP 4)	10-Yr %	20-Yr Min	20-Yr Max	25-Yr Min	25-Yr Max	30-Yr Min	30-Yr Max	20 Yr Min	20 Yr Max	25 Yr Min	25 Yr Max	30 Yr Min	30 Yr Max
Supervisory	GS-5-GS-13	8	35,151	66,951	36,065	69,339	36,994	71,767	36,994	71,767	37%	9,481	19,297	11,963	24,413	14,355	29,295	8,659	17,161	10,931	21,800	12,837	25,73
Supervisory Design Patent Examiner	GS-5-GS-13	8	35,151	66,951	36,065	69,339	36,994	71,767	36,994	71,767	37%	9,481	19,297	11,963	24,413	14,355	29,295	8,659	17,161	10,931	21,800	12,837	25,73

Chart II - U.S. Federal - Job Titles - Salaries - Pension Estimates

Education

U.S. Federal Government Agencies	GS Grade Range:	GS Grade Median	2010 Median Grade Min Salary (STEP 1)	2010 Maxi- mum Grade Salary (STEP 1)	2011 Median Grade Min Salary (STEP 2)	2011 Maxi- mum Grade Salary (STEP 2)	2012 Median Grade Min Salary (STEP 3)	2012 Maxi- mum Grade Salary (STEP 3)	2013 Median Grade Min Salary (STEP 4)	2013 Maxi- mum Grade Salary (STEP 4)	10-Year Cumu- lative Raise Per- centage (1.96%) + Step In- crease Per- centage (1.7%)	20-Year Annual Pension Ben- efit Es- timate (Min.)	20-Year Annual Pension Ben- efit Es- timate (Max.)	25-Year Annual Pension Ben- efit Es- timate (Min.)	25-Year Annual Pension Ben- efit Es- timate (Max.)	30-Year Annual Pension Ben- efit Es- timate (Min.)	30-Year Annual Pension Ben- efit Es- timate (Max.)	Agency Auto- matic Contri- butions 1% Thrift Savings Plan 20 Year Plus 4.5% Interest (Min)	Agency Auto- matic Contri- butions 1% Thrift Savings Plan 20 Year Plus 4.5% Interest (Max)	Agency Auto- matic Contri- butions 1% Thrift Savings Plan 25 Year Plus 4.5% Interest (Min)	Agency Auto- matic Contri- butions 1% Thrift Savings Plan 25 Year Plus 4.5% Interest (Max)	Agency Auto- matic Contri- butions 1% Thrift Savings Plan 30 Year Plus 4.5% Interest (Min)	Agency Auto- matic Contri- butions 1% Thrift Savings Plan 30 Year Plus 4.5% Interest (Max)
Education and Training Technician Series																							
Educational Aid	GS-5-GS-15	9	38,824	93,063	39,738	96,387	40,667	99,767	40,667	99,767	37%	10,289	26,832	12,973	33,946	15,567	40,735	9,465	23,859	11,929	30,309	13,988	35,786
Educational Technician and Training Technician	GS-5-GS-15	9	38,824	93,063	39,738	96,387	40,667	99,767	40,667	99,767	37%	10,289	26,832	12,973	33,946	15,567	40,735	9,465	23,859	11,929	30,309	13,988	35,786
Supervisory Educational Technician and Supv	GS-5-GS-15	9	38,824	93,063	39,738	96,387	40,667	99,767	40,667	99,767	37%	10,289	26,832	12,973	33,946	15,567	40,735	9,465	23,859	11,929	30,309	13,988	35,786
Education and Vocational Training Series																							
Teacher	GS-5-GS-14	8	35,151	79,115	36,065	81,936	36,994	84,805	36,994	84,805	37%	9,481	22,802	11,963	28,847	14,355	34,616	8,659	20,279	10,931	25,760	12,837	30,414
Teacher Supervisor	GS-5-GS-14	8	35,151	79,115	36,065	81,936	36,994	84,805	36,994	84,805	37%	9,481	22,802	11,963	28,847	14,355	34,616	8,659	20,279	10,931	25,760	12,837	30,414
Principal	GS-5-GS-14	8	35,151	79,115	36,065	81,936	36,994	84,805	36,994	84,805	37%	9,481	22,802	11,963	28,847	14,355	34,616	8,659	20,279	10,931	25,760	12,837	30,414
Assistant Principal	GS-5-GS-14	8	35,151	79,115	36,065	81,936	36,994	84,805	36,994	84,805	37%	9,481	22,802	11,963	28,847	14,355	34,616	8,659	20,279	10,931	25,760	12,837	30,414
Education Program Administrator	GS-5-GS-14	8	35,151	79,115	36,065	81,936	36,994	84,805	36,994	84,805	37%	9,481	22,802	11,963	28,847	14,355	34,616	8,659	20,279	10,931	25,760	12,837	30,414
Education Program Series																							
Education Program Specialist	GS-5-GS-15	9	38,824	93,063	39,738	96,387	40,667	99,767	40,667	99,767	37%	10,289	26,832	12,973	33,946	15,567	40,735	9,465	23,859	11,929	30,309	13,988	35,786
Supervisory Education Program Specialist	GS-5-GS-15	9	38,824	93,063	39,738	96,387	40,667	99,767	40,667	99,767	37%	10,289	26,832	12,973	33,946	15,567	40,735	9,465	23,859	11,929	30,309	13,988	35,786
Education Research Series																							
Education Research Analyst	GS-11-GS-15	12	56,301	93,063	57,976	96,387	59,680	99,767	59,680	99,767	37%	15,591	26,832	19,693	33,946	23,632	40,735	14,087	23,859	17,829	30,309	20,983	35,786
Supervisory Education Research Analyst	GS-11-GS-15	12	56,301	93,063	57,976	96,387	59,680	99,767	59,680	99,767	37%	15,591	26,832	19,693	33,946	23,632	40,735	14,087	23,859	17,829	30,309	20,983	35,786

Chart II - U.S. Federal - Job Titles - Salaries - Pension Estimates

Engineering _ Architecture

U.S. Federal Government Agencies	GS Grade Range:	GS Grade Median	2010 Median Grade Min Salary (STEP 1)	2010 Maximum Grade Salary (STEP 1)	2011 Median Grade Min Salary (STEP 2)	2011 Maximum Grade Salary (STEP 2)	2012 Median Grade Min Salary (STEP 3)	2012 Maximum Grade Salary (STEP 3)	2013 Median Grade Min Salary (STEP 4)	2013 Maximum Grade Salary (STEP 4)	10-Year Cumulative Raise Percentage (1.96%) + Step Increase Percentage (1.7%)	20-Year Annual Pension Benefit Estimate (Min.)	20-Year Annual Pension Benefit Estimate (Max.)	25-Year Annual Pension Benefit Estimate (Min.)	25-Year Annual Pension Benefit Estimate (Max.)	30-Year Annual Pension Benefit Estimate (Min.)	30-Year Annual Pension Benefit Estimate (Max.)	Agency Automatic Contributions 1% Thrift Savings Plan 20 Year Savings Plus 4.5% Interest (Min)	Agency Automatic Contributions 1% Thrift Savings Plan 20 Year Savings Plus 4.5% Interest (Max)	Agency Automatic Contributions 1% Thrift Savings Plan 25 Year Savings Plus 4.5% Interest (Min)	Agency Automatic Contributions 1% Thrift Savings Plan 25 Year Savings Plus 4.5% Interest (Max)	Agency Automatic Contributions 1% Thrift Savings Plan 30 Year Savings Plus 4.5% Interest (Min)	Agency Automatic Contributions 1% Thrift Savings Plan 30 Year Savings Plus 4.5% Interest (Max)
Engineering Technician Series																							
Supervisory Positions	GS-1-GS-11	5	25,623	46,974	25,623	48,649	25,623	50,353	72,597	85,504	37%	15,971	21,272	19,964	26,795	23,957	32,154	13,968	18,285	17,761	23,376	21,287	27,976
Landscape Architecture Series																							
Supervisory Landscape Architect"	GS-5-GS-14	9	38,824	79,115	39,738	81,936	40,667	84,805	40,667	84,805	37%	10,289	22,802	12,973	28,847	15,567	34,616	9,465	20,279	11,929	25,760	13,988	30,414
Architecture Series																							
General ScheduleSupervisory Guide	GS-9-GS-14	11	46,974	79,115	48,358	81,936	49,766	84,805	84,917	119,956	37%	20,716	30,535	26,063	38,513	31,276	46,216	17,984	26,523	22,936	33,841	27,398	40,331
Construction Control Series																							
Construction Inspection Aid	GS-2-GS-9	5	25,623	38,824	26,350	40,208	27,090	41,616	27,090	76,767	37%	7,029	18,923	8,875	23,822	10,650	28,587	6,375	16,196	8,061	20,722	9,480	24,843
Construction Inspector	GS-2-GS-9	5	25,623	38,824	26,350	40,208	27,090	41,616	62,241	76,767	37%	14,762	18,923	18,541	23,822	22,249	28,587	12,620	16,196	16,143	20,722	19,398	24,843
Construction Representative	GS-2-GS-9	5	25,623	38,824	26,350	40,208	27,090	41,616	62,241	41,616	37%	14,762	11,189	18,541	14,156	22,249	16,987	12,620	9,951	16,143	12,641	19,398	14,925
Civil Engineering Series																							
Surveying Aid	GS-1-GS-8	3	20,401	35,151	20,401	36,405	20,401	37,680	55,552	37,680	37%	12,221	10,132	15,277	12,818	18,332	15,381	10,722	9,010	13,624	11,446	16,314	13,514
Surveying Technician	GS-1-GS-8	3	20,401	35,151	20,401	36,405	20,401	37,680	55,552	37,680	37%	12,221	10,132	15,277	12,818	18,332	15,381	10,722	9,010	13,624	11,446	16,314	13,514
Supervisory Surveying Technician	GS-1-GS-8	3	20,401	35,151	20,401	36,405	20,401	37,680	20,401	37,680	37%	4,488	10,132	5,610	12,818	6,732	15,381	4,477	9,010	5,543	11,446	6,396	13,514
Engineering Drafting Series																							
Engineering Draftsman	GS-1-GS-7	3	20,401	31,740	20,401	32,872	20,401	34,023	20,401	34,023	37%	4,488	9,148	5,610	11,573	6,732	13,888	4,477	8,136	5,543	10,335	6,396	12,202
Supervisory Engineering Draftsman	GS-1-GS-7	3	20,401	31,740	20,401	32,872	20,401	34,023	20,401	34,023	37%	4,488	9,148	5,610	11,573	6,732	13,888	4,477	8,136	5,543	10,335	6,396	12,202
Environmental Engineering Series																							
Supervisory Environmental Engineer	GS-5-GS-15	9	38,824	93,063	39,738	96,387	40,667	99,767	40,667	99,767	37%	10,289	26,832	12,973	33,946	15,567	40,735	9,465	23,859	11,929	30,309	13,988	35,786
Construction Analyst Series																							
Construction Analyst	GS-5-GS-12	7	31,740	56,301	32,654	58,309	33,583	60,351	33,583	60,351	37%	8,730	16,227	11,025	20,529	13,230	24,635	7,910	14,431	10,005	18,332	11,768	21,644
Supervisory Construction Analyst	GS-5-GS-12	7	31,740	56,301	32,654	58,309	33,583	60,351	33,583	60,351	37%	8,730	16,227	11,025	20,529	13,230	24,635	7,910	14,431	10,005	18,332	11,768	21,644
Mechanical Engineering Series																							
Supervisory Mechanical Engineer	GS-5-GS-15	9	38,824	93,063	39,738	96,387	40,667	99,767	40,667	99,767	37%	10,289	26,832	12,973	33,946	15,567	40,735	9,465	23,859	11,929	30,309	13,988	35,786
Electronics Technician Series																							
Electronics Technician	GS-4-GS-11	7	31,740	46,974	32,556	48,649	33,386	50,353	33,386	50,353	37%	8,544	13,539	10,780	17,128	12,936	20,554	7,809	12,041	9,858	15,295	11,574	18,059
Supervisory Electronics Technician	GS-4-GS-11	7	31,740	46,974	32,556	48,649	33,386	50,353	33,386	50,353	37%	8,544	13,539	10,780	17,128	12,936	20,554	7,809	12,041	9,858	15,295	11,574	18,059
Naval Architecture Series																							
Naval Architect	GS-9-GS-15	11	46,974	93,063	48,358	96,387	49,766	99,767	49,766	99,767	37%	12,982	26,832	16,397	33,946	19,676	40,735	11,740	23,859	14,855	30,309	17,480	35,786
Naval Architecture	GS-9-GS-15	11	46,974	93,063	48,358	96,387	49,766	99,767	49,766	99,767	37%	12,982	26,832	16,397	33,946	19,676	40,735	11,740	23,859	14,855	30,309	17,480	35,786
Supervisory Classes	GS-9-GS-15	11	46,974	93,063	48,358	96,387	49,766	99,767	49,766	99,767	37%	12,982	26,832	16,397	33,946	19,676	40,735	11,740	23,859	14,855	30,309	17,480	35,786

Mining Engineering Series

Chart II - U.S. Federal - Job Titles - Salaries - Pension Estimates

U.S. Federal Government Agencies	GS Grade Range	GS Grade Median	2010 Median Grade Min Salary (STEP 1)	2010 Maximum Grade Salary (STEP 1)	2011 Median Grade Min Salary (STEP 2)	2011 Maximum Grade Salary (STEP 2)	2012 Median Grade Min Salary (STEP 3)	2012 Maximum Grade Salary (STEP 3)	2013 Median Grade Min Salary (STEP 4)	2013 Maximum Grade Salary (STEP 4)	10-Year Cumulative Raise Percentage (1.96%) + Step Increase Percentage (1.7%)	20-Year Annual Pension Benefit Estimate (Min.)	20-Year Annual Pension Benefit Estimate (Max.)	25-Year Annual Pension Benefit Estimate (Min.)	25-Year Annual Pension Benefit Estimate (Max.)	30-Year Annual Pension Benefit Estimate (Min.)	30-Year Annual Pension Benefit Estimate (Max.)	Agency Automatic Contributions 1% Thrift Savings Plan 20 Year Savings Plus 4.5% Interest (Min)	Agency Automatic Contributions 1% Thrift Savings Plan 20 Year Savings Plus 4.5% Interest (Max)	Agency Automatic Contributions 1% Thrift Savings Plan 25 Year Savings Plus 4.5% Interest (Min)	Agency Automatic Contributions 1% Thrift Savings Plan 25 Year Savings Plus 4.5% Interest (Max)	Agency Automatic Contributions 1% Thrift Savings Plan 30 Year Savings Plus 4.5% Interest (Min)	Agency Automatic Contributions 1% Thrift Savings Plan 30 Year Savings Plus 4.5% Interest (Max)
Mining Engineer	GS-5-GS-12	8	35,151	56,301	36,065	58,309	36,994	60,351	36,994	60,351	37%	9,481	16,227	11,963	20,529	14,355	24,635	8,659	14,431	10,931	18,332	12,837	21,644
Supervisory	GS-5-GS-12	8	35,151	56,301	36,065	58,309	36,994	60,351	36,994	60,351	37%	9,481	16,227	11,963	20,529	14,355	24,635	8,659	14,431	10,931	18,332	12,837	21,644
Mining Engineer	GS-5-GS-12	8	35,151	56,301	36,065	58,309	36,994	60,351	36,994	60,351	37%	9,481	16,227	11,963	20,529	14,355	24,635	8,659	14,431	10,931	18,332	12,837	21,644
Agricultural Engineering Series																							
Agricultural Engineer	GS-5-GS-12	8	35,151	56,301	36,065	58,309	36,994	60,351	36,994	60,351	37%	9,481	16,227	11,963	20,529	14,355	24,635	8,659	14,431	10,931	18,332	12,837	21,644
Supervisory Agricultural Engineer.	GS-5-GS-12	8	35,151	56,301	36,065	58,309	36,994	60,351	36,994	60,351	37%	9,481	16,227	11,963	20,529	14,355	24,635	8,659	14,431	10,931	18,332	12,837	21,644
Chemical Engineering Series																							
Chemical Engineer	GS-5-GS-13	8	35,151	66,951	36,065	69,339	36,994	71,767	36,994	71,767	37%	9,481	19,297	11,963	24,413	14,355	29,295	8,659	17,161	10,931	21,800	12,837	25,738
Supervisory Chemical Engineer	GS-5-GS-13	8	35,151	66,951	36,065	69,339	36,994	71,767	36,994	71,767	37%	9,481	19,297	11,963	24,413	14,355	29,295	8,659	17,161	10,931	21,800	12,837	25,738

Equipment_ Facilities _ Service

U.S. Federal Government Agencies	GS Grade Range	GS Grade Median	2010 Median Grade Min Salary (STEP 1)	2010 Maximum Grade Salary (STEP 1)	2011 Median Grade Min Salary (STEP 2)	2011 Maximum Grade Salary (STEP 2)	2012 Median Grade Min Salary (STEP 3)	2012 Maximum Grade Salary (STEP 3)	2013 Median Grade Min Salary (STEP 4)	2013 Maximum Grade Salary (STEP 4)	10-Year Cumulative Raise Percentage (1.96%) + Step Increase Percentage (1.7%)	20-Year Annual Pension Benefit Estimate (Min.)	20-Year Annual Pension Benefit Estimate (Max.)	25-Year Annual Pension Benefit Estimate (Min.)	25-Year Annual Pension Benefit Estimate (Max.)	30-Year Annual Pension Benefit Estimate (Min.)	30-Year Annual Pension Benefit Estimate (Max.)	Agency Automatic Contributions 1% Thrift Savings Plan 20 Year Savings Plus 4.5% Interest (Min)	Agency Automatic Contributions 1% Thrift Savings Plan 20 Year Savings Plus 4.5% Interest (Max)	Agency Automatic Contributions 1% Thrift Savings Plan 25 Year Savings Plus 4.5% Interest (Min)	Agency Automatic Contributions 1% Thrift Savings Plan 25 Year Savings Plus 4.5% Interest (Max)	Agency Automatic Contributions 1% Thrift Savings Plan 30 Year Savings Plus 4.5% Interest (Min)	Agency Automatic Contributions 1% Thrift Savings Plan 30 Year Savings Plus 4.5% Interest (Max)
Realty Series																							
Realty Specialist	GS-9-GS-14	10	42,755	79,115	44,139	81,936	45,547	84,805	45,547	84,805	37%	12,054	22,802	15,237	28,847	18,284	34,616	10,814	20,279	13,709	25,760	16,157	30,414
Supervisory Realty Specialist	GS-9-GS-14	10	42,755	79,115	44,139	81,936	45,547	84,805	45,547	84,805	37%	12,054	22,802	15,237	28,847	18,284	34,616	10,814	20,279	13,709	25,760	16,157	30,414
Realty Officer	GS-9-GS-14	10	42,755	79,115	44,139	81,936	45,547	84,805	45,547	84,805	37%	12,054	22,802	15,237	28,847	18,284	34,616	10,814	20,279	13,709	25,760	16,157	30,414
Facility Management Series																							
Facility Manager	GS-11-GS-12	11	46,974	56,301	48,649	58,309	50,353	60,351	50,353	60,351	37%	13,539	16,227	17,128	20,529	20,554	24,635	12,041	14,431	15,295	18,332	18,059	21,644
Facility Management Officer	GS-11-GS-12	11	46,974	56,301	48,649	58,309	50,353	60,351	50,353	60,351	37%	13,539	16,227	17,128	20,529	20,554	24,635	12,041	14,431	15,295	18,332	18,059	21,644
Facility Management Specialist	GS-11-GS-12	11	46,974	56,301	48,649	58,309	50,353	60,351	50,353	60,351	37%	13,539	16,227	17,128	20,529	20,554	24,635	12,041	14,431	15,295	18,332	18,059	21,644
Equipment Specialist Series																							
Equipment Specialist	GS-9-GS-12	10	42,755	56,301	44,139	58,309	45,547	60,351	45,547	60,351	37%	12,054	16,227	15,237	20,529	18,284	24,635	10,814	14,431	13,709	18,332	16,157	21,644
Specializations	GS-9-GS-12	10	42,755	56,301	44,139	58,309	45,547	60,351	45,547	60,351	37%	12,054	16,227	15,237	20,529	18,284	24,635	10,814	14,431	13,709	18,332	16,157	21,644

Chart II - U.S. Federal - Job Titles - Salaries - Pension Estimates

Human Resources

U.S. Federal Government Agencies	GS Grade Range	GS Grade Median	2010 Median Grade Min Salary (STEP 1)	2010 Maximum Grade Salary (STEP 1)	2011 Median Grade Min Salary (STEP 2)	2011 Maximum Grade Salary (STEP 2)	2012 Median Grade Min Salary (STEP 3)	2012 Maximum Grade Salary (STEP 3)	2013 Median Grade Min Salary (STEP 4)	2013 Maximum Grade Salary (STEP 4)	10-Year Cumulative Raise Percentage (1.96%) + Step Increase Percentage (1.7%)	20-Year Annual Pension Benefit Estimate (Min.)	20-Year Annual Pension Benefit Estimate (Max.)	25-Year Annual Pension Benefit Estimate (Min.)	25-Year Annual Pension Benefit Estimate (Max.)	30-Year Annual Pension Benefit Estimate (Min.)	30-Year Annual Pension Benefit Estimate (Max.)	Agency Automatic Contributions 1% Thrift Savings Plan 20 Year Savings Plus 4.5% Interest (Min)	Agency Automatic Contributions 1% Thrift Savings Plan 20 Year Savings Plus 4.5% Interest (Max)	Agency Automatic Contributions 1% Thrift Savings Plan 25 Year Savings Plus 4.5% Interest (Min)	Agency Automatic Contributions 1% Thrift Savings Plan 25 Year Savings Plus 4.5% Interest (Max)	Agency Automatic Contributions 1% Thrift Savings Plan 30 Year Savings Plus 4.5% Interest (Min)	Agency Automatic Contributions 1% Thrift Savings Plan 30 Year Savings Plus 4.5% Interest (Max)
Unemployment Insurance Series																							
Unemployment Insurance Program Specialist	GS-9-GS-13	11	46,974	66,951	48,358	69,339	49,766	71,767	49,766	71,767	37%	12,982	19,297	16,397	24,413	19,676	29,295	11,740	17,161	14,855	21,800	17,480	25,73
Manpower Development Series																							
Manpower Development Specialist	GS-5-GS-13	8	35,151	66,951	36,065	69,339	36,994	71,767	72,145	128,068	37%	17,214	31,683	21,629	39,895	25,955	47,874	14,903	27,163	19,013	34,743	22,755	41,62
Supervisory Manpower Development Specialist	GS-5-GS-13	8	35,151	66,951	36,065	69,339	36,994	71,767	36,994	128,068	37%	9,481	31,683	11,963	39,895	14,355	47,874	8,659	27,163	10,931	34,743	12,837	41,62
Civil Rights Analysis Series																							
Civil Rights Analyst	GS-5-GS-15	9	38,824	93,063	39,738	96,387	40,667	99,767	96,968	156,068	37%	22,675	39,218	28,455	49,429	34,147	59,314	19,466	33,861	24,873	43,253	29,874	51,67
Supervisory	GS-5-GS-15	9	38,824	93,063	39,738	96,387	40,667	99,767	96,968	99,767	37%	22,675	26,832	28,455	33,946	34,147	40,735	19,466	23,859	24,873	30,309	29,874	35,78
Human Resources Management Series																							
Personnel Officer	GS-9-GS-15	13	66,951	93,063	68,335	96,387	69,743	99,767	126,044	125,390	37%	29,764	32,469	37,373	40,992	44,848	49,191	26,126	28,411	33,227	36,200	39,628	43,01
Assistant Personnel Officer	GS-9-GS-15	13	66,951	93,063	68,335	96,387	69,743	99,767	126,044	99,767	37%	29,764	26,832	37,373	33,946	44,848	40,735	26,126	23,859	33,227	30,309	39,628	35,78
Human Resources Specialist	GS-9-GS-15	13	66,951	93,063	68,335	96,387	69,743	99,767	69,743	99,767	37%	17,377	26,832	21,891	33,946	26,269	40,735	16,124	23,859	20,283	30,309	23,743	35,78
Supervisory Human Resources Specialist	GS-9-GS-15	13	66,951	93,063	68,335	96,387	69,743	99,767	69,743	99,767	37%	17,377	26,832	21,891	33,946	26,269	40,735	16,124	23,859	20,283	30,309	23,743	35,78
Human Resources Assistance Series																							
Staffing Clerk	GS-4-GS-9	6	28,562	38,824	29,378	40,208	30,208	41,616	30,208	41,616	37%	7,845	11,189	9,906	14,156	11,887	16,987	7,112	9,951	8,994	12,641	10,578	14,92
Personnel Actions Clerk	GS-4-GS-9	6	28,562	38,824	29,378	40,208	30,208	41,616	30,208	41,616	37%	7,845	11,189	9,906	14,156	11,887	16,987	7,112	9,951	8,994	12,641	10,578	14,92
Classification Assistant	GS-4-GS-9	6	28,562	38,824	29,378	40,208	30,208	41,616	30,208	41,616	37%	7,845	11,189	9,906	14,156	11,887	16,987	7,112	9,951	8,994	12,641	10,578	14,92
Employee Development Assistant	GS-4-GS-9	6	28,562	38,824	29,378	40,208	30,208	41,616	30,208	41,616	37%	7,845	11,189	9,906	14,156	11,887	16,987	7,112	9,951	8,994	12,641	10,578	14,92
Employee Relations Assistant	GS-4-GS-9	6	28,562	38,824	29,378	40,208	30,208	41,616	30,208	41,616	37%	7,845	11,189	9,906	14,156	11,887	16,987	7,112	9,951	8,994	12,641	10,578	14,92
Labor Relations Assistant	GS-4-GS-9	6	28,562	38,824	29,378	40,208	30,208	41,616	30,208	41,616	37%	7,845	11,189	9,906	14,156	11,887	16,987	7,112	9,951	8,994	12,641	10,578	14,92
Staffing Assistant	GS-4-GS-9	6	28,562	38,824	29,378	40,208	30,208	41,616	30,208	41,616	37%	7,845	11,189	9,906	14,156	11,887	16,987	7,112	9,951	8,994	12,641	10,578	14,92
Lead	GS-4-GS-9	6	28,562	38,824	29,378	40,208	30,208	41,616	30,208	41,616	37%	7,845	11,189	9,906	14,156	11,887	16,987	7,112	9,951	8,994	12,641	10,578	14,92
Supervisory	GS-4-GS-9	6	28,562	38,824	29,378	40,208	30,208	41,616	30,208	41,616	37%	7,845	11,189	9,906	14,156	11,887	16,987	7,112	9,951	8,994	12,641	10,578	14,92
Personnel Clerk	GS-4-GS-9	6	28,562	38,824	29,378	40,208	30,208	41,616	30,208	41,616	37%	7,845	11,189	9,906	14,156	11,887	16,987	7,112	9,951	8,994	12,641	10,578	14,92
Mediation Series																							
Mediator	GS-11-GS-14	11-14	46,974	79,115	46,974	79,115	46,974	79,115	46,974	79,115		48,649	81,936	50,353	84,805	50,353	84,805	50,353	84,805	52,145	87,823	52,145	87,82
Supervisory	GS-11-GS-14	11-14	46,974	79,115	46,974	79,115	46,974	79,115	46,974	79,115		48,649	81,936	50,353	84,805	50,353	84,805	50,353	84,805	52,145	87,823	52,145	87,82
Apprenticeship and Training Series																							
Apprenticeship	GS-11-GS-13	11-13	46,974	66,951	46,974	66,951	46,974	66,951	46,974	66,951		48,649	69,339	50,353	71,767	50,353	71,767	50,353	71,767	52,145	74,321	52,145	74,32
Training	GS-11-GS-13	11-13	46,974	66,951	46,974	66,951	46,974	66,951	46,974	66,951		48,649	69,339	50,353	71,767	50,353	71,767	50,353	71,767	52,145	74,321	52,145	74,32

Chart II - U.S. Federal - Job Titles - Salaries - Pension Estimates

U.S. Federal Government Agencies	GS Grade Range:	GS Grade Median	2010 Median Grade Min Salary (STEP 1)	2010 Maximum Grade Salary (STEP 1)	2011 Median Grade Salary (STEP 2)	2011 Maximum Grade Salary (STEP 2)	2012 Median Grade Salary (STEP 3)	2012 Maximum Grade Salary (STEP 3)	2013 Median Grade Min Salary (STEP 4)	2013 Maximum Grade Salary (STEP 4)	10-Year Cumulative Raise Percentage (1.96%) + Step Increase Percentage (1.7%)	20-Year Annual Pension Benefit Estimate (Min.)	20-Year Annual Pension Benefit Estimate (Max.)	25-Year Annual Pension Benefit Estimate (Min.)	25-Year Annual Pension Benefit Estimate (Max.)	30-Year Annual Pension Benefit Estimate (Min.)	30-Year Annual Pension Benefit Estimate (Max.)	Agency Automatic Contributions 1% Thrift Savings Plan 20 Year Plus 4.5% Interest (Min)	Agency Automatic Contributions 1% Thrift Savings Plan 20 Year Plus 4.5% Interest (Max)	Agency Automatic Contributions 1% Thrift Savings Plan 25 Year Plus 4.5% Interest (Min)	Agency Automatic Contributions 1% Thrift Savings Plan 25 Year Plus 4.5% Interest (Max)	Agency Automatic Contributions 1% Thrift Savings Plan 30 Year Plus 4.5% Interest (Min)	Agency Automatic Contributions 1% Thrift Savings Plan 30 Year Plus 4.5% Interest (Max)
Representative	GS-11-GS-13		11-13	46,974	66,951	46,974	66,951	46,974	66,951	46,974	66,951	48,649	69,339	50,353	71,767	50,353	71,767	50,353	71,767	52,145	74,321	52,145	74,321
Supervisory	GS-11-GS-13		11-13	46,974	66,951	46,974	66,951	46,974	66,951	46,974	66,951	48,649	69,339	50,353	71,767	50,353	71,767	50,353	71,767	52,145	74,321	52,145	74,321

Labor Management Relations Examining Series

U.S. Federal Government Agencies	GS Grade Range:	GS Grade Median	2010 STEP1 Min	2010 STEP1 Max	2011 STEP2 Med	2011 STEP2 Max	2012 STEP3 Med	2012 STEP3 Max	2013 STEP4 Med	2013 STEP4 Max	10-Year %	20Yr Min	20Yr Max	25Yr Min	25Yr Max	30Yr Min	30Yr Max	TSP20 Min	TSP20 Max	TSP25 Min	TSP25 Max	TSP30 Min	TSP30 Max
Labor Management Relations Examiner.	GS-5-GS-13	8	35,151	66,951	36,065	69,339	36,994	71,767	36,994	71,767	37%	9,481	19,297	11,963	24,413	14,355	29,295	8,659	17,161	10,931	21,800	12,837	25,738
Supervisory	GS-5-GS-13	8	35,151	66,951	36,065	69,339	36,994	71,767	36,994	71,767	37%	9,481	19,297	11,963	24,413	14,355	29,295	8,659	17,161	10,931	21,800	12,837	25,738

Wage and Hour Compliance Series

Title	Range	Med	2010Min	2010Max	2011Med	2011Max	2012Med	2012Max	2013Med	2013Max	%	20Min	20Max	25Min	25Max	30Min	30Max	T20Min	T20Max	T25Min	T25Max	T30Min	T30Max
Wage and Hour Compliance Specialist	GS-11-GS-14	12	56,301	79,115	57,976	81,936	59,680	84,805	59,680	84,805	37%	15,591	22,802	19,693	28,847	23,632	34,616	14,087	20,279	17,829	25,760	20,983	30,414
Supervisory Wage and Hour Compliance Spec	GS-11-GS-14	12	56,301	79,115	57,976	81,936	59,680	84,805	59,680	84,805	37%	15,591	22,802	19,693	28,847	23,632	34,616	14,087	20,279	17,829	25,760	20,983	30,414
Equal Employment Opportunity Series*	GS-11-GS-14	12	56,301	79,115	57,976	81,936	59,680	84,805	59,680	84,805	37%	15,591	22,802	19,693	28,847	23,632	34,616	14,087	20,279	17,829	25,760	20,983	30,414
Equal Employment Specialist	GS-11-GS-14	12	56,301	79,115	57,976	81,936	59,680	84,805	59,680	84,805	37%	15,591	22,802	19,693	28,847	23,632	34,616	14,087	20,279	17,829	25,760	20,983	30,414
Supervisory	GS-11-GS-14	12	56,301	79,115	57,976	81,936	59,680	84,805	59,680	84,805	37%	15,591	22,802	19,693	28,847	23,632	34,616	14,087	20,279	17,829	25,760	20,983	30,414
Equal Employment Manager	GS-11-GS-14	12	56,301	79,115	57,976	81,936	59,680	84,805	59,680	84,805	37%	15,591	22,802	19,693	28,847	23,632	34,616	14,087	20,279	17,829	25,760	20,983	30,414
Organizational Titles	GS-11-GS-14	12	56,301	79,115	57,976	81,936	59,680	84,805	59,680	84,805	37%	15,591	22,802	19,693	28,847	23,632	34,616	14,087	20,279	17,829	25,760	20,983	30,414

Equal Opportunity Assistance Series

Title	Range	Med	2010Min	2010Max	2011Med	2011Max	2012Med	2012Max	2013Med	2013Max	%	20Min	20Max	25Min	25Max	30Min	30Max	T20Min	T20Max	T25Min	T25Max	T30Min	T30Max
General Schedule Leader Grade Eval Guide	GS-4-GS-6	5	25,623	28,562	26,439	29,580	27,269	30,616	27,269	30,616	37%	7,198	8,232	9,098	10,414	10,917	12,497	6,467	7,321	8,196	9,300	9,656	10,980
General Schedule Supervisory Guide	GS-4-GS-6	5	25,623	28,562	26,439	29,580	27,269	30,616	27,269	30,616	37%	7,198	8,232	9,098	10,414	10,917	12,497	6,467	7,321	8,196	9,300	9,656	10,980

Chart II - U.S. Federal - Job Titles - Salaries - Pension Estimates

Information_ Arts_ Pub Affairs

U.S. Federal Government Agencies	GS Grade Range	GS Grade Median	2010 Median Grade Min Salary (STEP 1)	2010 Maximum Grade Salary (STEP 1)	2011 Median Grade Min Salary (STEP 2)	2011 Maximum Grade Salary (STEP 2)	2012 Median Grade Min Salary (STEP 3)	2012 Maximum Grade Salary (STEP 3)	2013 Median Grade Min Salary (STEP 4)	2013 Maximum Grade Salary (STEP 4)	10-Year Cumulative Raise Percentage (1.96%) + Step Increase Percentage (1.7%)	20-Year Annual Pension Benefit Estimate (Min.)	20-Year Annual Pension Benefit Estimate (Max.)	25-Year Annual Pension Benefit Estimate (Min.)	25-Year Annual Pension Benefit Estimate (Max.)	30-Year Annual Pension Benefit Estimate (Min.)	30-Year Annual Pension Benefit Estimate (Max.)	Agency Automatic Contributions 1% Thrift Savings Plan 20 Year Savings Plus 4.5% Interest (Min)	Agency Automatic Contributions 1% Thrift Savings Plan 20 Year Savings Plus 4.5% Interest (Max)	Agency Automatic Contributions 1% Thrift Savings Plan 25 Year Savings Plus 4.5% Interest (Min)	Agency Automatic Contributions 1% Thrift Savings Plan 25 Year Savings Plus 4.5% Interest (Max)	Agency Automatic Contributions 1% Thrift Savings Plan 30 Year Savings Plus 4.5% Interest (Min)	Agency Automatic Contributions 1% Thrift Savings Plan 30 Year Savings Plus 4.5% Interest (Max)
Museum Curator Series																							
Museum Curator	GS-5-GS-9	7	31,740	38,824	32,654	40,208	33,583	41,616	68,734	41,616	37%	16,464	11,189	20,691	14,156	24,829	16,987	14,155	9,951	18,086	12,641	21,685	14,925
Staff Curator	GS-5-GS-9	7	31,740	38,824	32,654	40,208	33,583	41,616	68,734	41,616	37%	16,464	11,189	20,691	14,156	24,829	16,987	14,155	9,951	18,086	12,641	21,685	14,925
Museum Specialist and Technician Series																							
Supervisory	GS-2-GS-12	5	25,623	56,301	26,350	58,309	27,090	60,351	27,090	60,351	37%	7,029	16,227	8,875	20,529	10,650	24,635	6,375	14,431	8,061	18,332	9,480	21,644
Trainee Specialist	GS-2-GS-12	5	25,623	56,301	26,350	58,309	27,090	60,351	27,090	60,351	37%	7,029	16,227	8,875	20,529	10,650	24,635	6,375	14,431	8,061	18,332	9,480	21,644
Assistant	GS-2-GS-12	5	25,623	56,301	26,350	58,309	27,090	60,351	27,090	60,351	37%	7,029	16,227	8,875	20,529	10,650	24,635	6,375	14,431	8,061	18,332	9,480	21,644
Office Drafting Series																							
Office Draftsman	GS-2-GS-5	3	20,401	25,623	21,128	26,537	21,868	27,466	21,868	27,466	37%	5,880	7,385	7,439	9,342	8,926	11,211	5,229	6,568	6,642	8,343	7,843	9,850
Supervisory Office Draftsman	GS-2-GS-5	3	20,401	25,623	21,128	26,537	21,868	27,466	21,868	27,466	37%	5,880	7,385	7,439	9,342	8,926	11,211	5,229	6,568	6,642	8,343	7,843	9,850
Audiovisual Production Series																							
Producer	GS-9-GS-13	10	42,755	66,951	44,139	69,339	45,547	71,767	45,547	71,767	37%	12,054	19,297	15,237	24,413	18,284	29,295	10,814	17,161	13,709	21,800	16,157	25,738
Director	GS-9-GS-13	10	42,755	66,951	44,139	69,339	45,547	71,767	45,547	71,767	37%	12,054	19,297	15,237	24,413	18,284	29,295	10,814	17,161	13,709	21,800	16,157	25,738
Producer-Director	GS-9-GS-13	10	42,755	66,951	44,139	69,339	45,547	71,767	45,547	71,767	37%	12,054	19,297	15,237	24,413	18,284	29,295	10,814	17,161	13,709	21,800	16,157	25,738
Editor	GS-9-GS-13	10	42,755	66,951	44,139	69,339	45,547	71,767	45,547	71,767	37%	12,054	19,297	15,237	24,413	18,284	29,295	10,814	17,161	13,709	21,800	16,157	25,738
Audiovisual Production Specialist	GS-9-GS-13	10	42,755	66,951	44,139	69,339	45,547	71,767	45,547	71,767	37%	12,054	19,297	15,237	24,413	18,284	29,295	10,814	17,161	13,709	21,800	16,157	25,738
Supervisory	GS-9-GS-13	10	42,755	66,951	44,139	69,339	45,547	71,767	45,547	71,767	37%	12,054	19,297	15,237	24,413	18,284	29,295	10,814	17,161	13,709	21,800	16,157	25,738
Writing and Editing Series																							
Writer	GS-7-GS-13	8	35,151	66,951	36,283	69,339	37,434	71,767	37,434	71,767	37%	9,898	19,297	12,511	24,413	15,013	29,295	8,884	17,161	11,261	21,800	13,271	25,738
Editor	GS-7-GS-13	8	35,151	66,951	36,283	69,339	37,434	71,767	37,434	71,767	37%	9,898	19,297	12,511	24,413	15,013	29,295	8,884	17,161	11,261	21,800	13,271	25,738
Writer-Editor	GS-7-GS-13	8	35,151	66,951	36,283	69,339	37,434	71,767	37,434	71,767	37%	9,898	19,297	12,511	24,413	15,013	29,295	8,884	17,161	11,261	21,800	13,271	25,738
Technical Writing and Editing Series																							
Technical Writer	GS-1-GS-13	5	25,623	66,951	25,623	69,339	25,623	71,767	25,623	71,767	37%	5,637	19,297	7,046	24,413	8,456	29,295	5,623	17,161	6,962	21,800	8,033	25,738
Technical Editor	GS-1-GS-13	5	25,623	66,951	25,623	69,339	25,623	71,767	25,623	71,767	37%	5,637	19,297	7,046	24,413	8,456	29,295	5,623	17,161	6,962	21,800	8,033	25,738
Technical Writer-Editor	GS-1-GS-13	5	25,623	66,951	25,623	69,339	25,623	71,767	25,623	71,767	37%	5,637	19,297	7,046	24,413	8,456	29,295	5,623	17,161	6,962	21,800	8,033	25,738
Supervisory	GS-1-GS-13	5	25,623	66,951	25,623	69,339	25,623	71,767	25,623	71,767	37%	5,637	19,297	7,046	24,413	8,456	29,295	5,623	17,161	6,962	21,800	8,033	25,738
Editorial Assistance Series																							
Editorial Clerk	GS-3-GS-7	4	22,902	31,740	23,629	32,872	24,369	34,023	24,369	34,023	37%	6,430	9,148	8,126	11,573	9,752	13,888	5,778	8,136	7,322	10,335	8,627	12,202
Editorial Assistant	GS-3-GS-7	4	22,902	31,740	23,629	32,872	24,369	34,023	24,369	34,023	37%	6,430	9,148	8,126	11,573	9,752	13,888	5,778	8,136	7,322	10,335	8,627	12,202
Supervisory Editorial Clerk	GS-3-GS-7	4	22,902	31,740	23,629	32,872	24,369	34,023	24,369	34,023	37%	6,430	9,148	8,126	11,573	9,752	13,888	5,778	8,136	7,322	10,335	8,627	12,202
Navigational Information Series																							
Aeronautical Information Specialist	GS-5-GS-12	8	35,151	56,301	36,065	58,309	36,994	60,351	36,994	60,351	37%	9,481	16,227	11,963	20,529	14,355	24,635	8,659	14,431	10,931	18,332	12,837	21,644

Chart II - U.S. Federal - Job Titles - Salaries - Pension Estimates

U.S. Federal Government Agencies	GS Grade Range:	GS Grade Median	2010 Median Grade Min Salary (STEP 1)	2010 Maximum Grade Salary (STEP 1)	2011 Median Grade Min Salary (STEP 2)	2011 Maximum Grade Salary (STEP 2)	2012 Median Grade Min Salary (STEP 3)	2012 Maximum Grade Salary (STEP 3)	2013 Median Grade Min Salary (STEP 4)	2013 Maximum Grade Salary (STEP 4)	10-Year Cumulative Raise Percentage (1.96%) + Step Increase Percentage (1.7%)	20-Year Annual Pension Benefit Estimate (Min.)	20-Year Annual Pension Benefit Estimate (Max.)	25-Year Annual Pension Benefit Estimate (Min.)	25-Year Annual Pension Benefit Estimate (Max.)	30-Year Annual Pension Benefit Estimate (Min.)	30-Year Annual Pension Benefit Estimate (Max.)	Agency Automatic Contributions 1% Thrift Savings Plan 20 Year Savings Plus 4.5% Interest (Min)	Agency Automatic Contributions 1% Thrift Savings Plan 20 Year Savings Plus 4.5% Interest (Max)	Agency Automatic Contributions 1% Thrift Savings Plan 25 Year Savings Plus 4.5% Interest (Min)	Agency Automatic Contributions 1% Thrift Savings Plan 25 Year Savings Plus 4.5% Interest (Max)	Agency Automatic Contributions 1% Thrift Savings Plan 30 Year Savings Plus 4.5% Interest (Min)	Agency Automatic Contributions 1% Thrift Savings Plan 30 Year Savings Plus 4.5% Interest (Max)
Marine Information Specialist	GS-5-GS-12	8	35,151	56,301	36,065	58,309	36,994	60,351	36,994	60,351	37%	9,481	16,227	11,963	20,529	14,355	24,635	8,659	14,431	10,931	18,332	12,837	21,644

Information Tech Group Jobs

U.S. Federal Government Agencies	GS Grade Range:	GS Grade Median	2010 Median Grade Min Salary (STEP 1)	2010 Maximum Grade Salary (STEP 1)	2011 Median Grade Min Salary (STEP 2)	2011 Maximum Grade Salary (STEP 2)	2012 Median Grade Min Salary (STEP 3)	2012 Maximum Grade Salary (STEP 3)	2013 Median Grade Min Salary (STEP 4)	2013 Maximum Grade Salary (STEP 4)	10-Year Cumulative Raise Percentage (1.96%) + Step Increase Percentage (1.7%)	20-Year Annual Pension Benefit Estimate (Min.)	20-Year Annual Pension Benefit Estimate (Max.)	25-Year Annual Pension Benefit Estimate (Min.)	25-Year Annual Pension Benefit Estimate (Max.)	30-Year Annual Pension Benefit Estimate (Min.)	30-Year Annual Pension Benefit Estimate (Max.)	Agency Automatic Contributions 1% Thrift Savings Plan 20 Year Savings Plus 4.5% Interest (Min)	Agency Automatic Contributions 1% Thrift Savings Plan 20 Year Savings Plus 4.5% Interest (Max)	Agency Automatic Contributions 1% Thrift Savings Plan 25 Year Savings Plus 4.5% Interest (Min)	Agency Automatic Contributions 1% Thrift Savings Plan 25 Year Savings Plus 4.5% Interest (Max)	Agency Automatic Contributions 1% Thrift Savings Plan 30 Year Savings Plus 4.5% Interest (Min)	Agency Automatic Contributions 1% Thrift Savings Plan 30 Year Savings Plus 4.5% Interest (Max)

Information Technology Group Jobs

Job Title	GS Grade Range	Median	2010 Min	2010 Max	2011 Min	2011 Max	2012 Min	2012 Max	2013 Min	2013 Max	10-Yr %	20-Yr Min	20-Yr Max	25-Yr Min	25-Yr Max	30-Yr Min	30-Yr Max	TSP 20 Min	TSP 20 Max	TSP 25 Min	TSP 25 Max	TSP 30 Min	TSP 30 Max
Information Technology Project Manager	GS-11-GS-15	12	56,301	93,063	57,976	96,387	59,680	99,767	59,680	99,767	37%	15,591	26,832	19,693	33,946	23,632	40,735	14,087	23,859	17,829	30,309	20,983	35,786
Information Technology Project Manager (Supervisor)	GS-11-GS-15	12	56,301	93,063	57,976	96,387	59,680	99,767	59,680	99,767	37%	15,591	26,832	19,693	33,946	23,632	40,735	14,087	23,859	17,829	30,309	20,983	35,786
Information Technology Project Manager (Team Leader)	GS-11-GS-15	12	56,301	93,063	57,976	96,387	59,680	99,767	59,680	99,767	37%	15,591	26,832	19,693	33,946	23,632	40,735	14,087	23,859	17,829	30,309	20,983	35,786
Information Technology Specialist	GS-11-GS-15	12	56,301	93,063	57,976	96,387	59,680	99,767	59,680	99,767	37%	15,591	26,832	19,693	33,946	23,632	40,735	14,087	23,859	17,829	30,309	20,983	35,786
Information Technology Specialist (Supervisor)	GS-11-GS-15	12	56,301	93,063	57,976	96,387	59,680	99,767	59,680	99,767	37%	15,591	26,832	19,693	33,946	23,632	40,735	14,087	23,859	17,829	30,309	20,983	35,786
Information Technology Specialist (Team Leader)	GS-11-GS-15	12	56,301	93,063	57,976	96,387	59,680	99,767	59,680	99,767	37%	15,591	26,832	19,693	33,946	23,632	40,735	14,087	23,859	17,829	30,309	20,983	35,786

Other Job Groups with IT-Computer-Technical Services Work

Job Title	GS Grade Range	Median	2010 Min	2010 Max	2011 Min	2011 Max	2012 Min	2012 Max	2013 Min	2013 Max	10-Yr %	20-Yr Min	20-Yr Max	25-Yr Min	25-Yr Max	30-Yr Min	30-Yr Max	TSP 20 Min	TSP 20 Max	TSP 25 Min	TSP 25 Max	TSP 30 Min	TSP 30 Max
Computer Engineering	GS-5-GS-15	9	38,824	93,063	39,738	96,387	40,667	99,767	40,667	99,767	37%	10,289	26,832	12,973	33,946	15,567	40,735	9,465	23,859	11,929	30,309	13,988	35,786
Computer Science	GS-5-GS-15	9	38,824	93,063	39,738	96,387	40,667	99,767	40,667	99,767	37%	10,289	26,832	12,973	33,946	15,567	40,735	9,465	23,859	11,929	30,309	13,988	35,786
Subject Area Computer Work, i.e. Human Resources	GS-1-GS-15	9	38,824	93,063	38,824	96,387	38,824	99,767	38,824	99,767	37%	8,541	26,832	10,677	33,946	12,812	40,735	8,520	23,859	10,548	30,309	12,171	35,786
Professional Work Physical Sciences Group	GS-5-GS-15	9	38,824	93,063	39,738	96,387	40,667	99,767	40,667	99,767	37%	10,289	26,832	12,973	33,946	15,567	40,735	9,465	23,859	11,929	30,309	13,988	35,786
Security Administration	GS-5-GS-15	9	38,824	93,063	39,738	96,387	40,667	99,767	40,667	99,767	37%	10,289	26,832	12,973	33,946	15,567	40,735	9,465	23,859	11,929	30,309	13,988	35,786
Subject Matter Series	GS-5-GS-15	9	38,824	93,063	39,738	96,387	40,667	99,767	40,667	99,767	37%	10,289	26,832	12,973	33,946	15,567	40,735	9,465	23,859	11,929	30,309	13,988	35,786
Quality Assurance	GS-5-GS-15	9	38,824	93,063	39,738	96,387	40,667	99,767	40,667	99,767	37%	10,289	26,832	12,973	33,946	15,567	40,735	9,465	23,859	11,929	30,309	13,988	35,786
Electronic Equipment Installation & Maintenance	GS-5-GS-15	9	38,824	93,063	39,738	96,387	40,667	99,767	40,667	99,767	37%	10,289	26,832	12,973	33,946	15,567	40,735	9,465	23,859	11,929	30,309	13,988	35,786
Telecommunications	GS-5-GS-15	9	38,824	93,063	39,738	96,387	40,667	99,767	40,667	99,767	37%	10,289	26,832	12,973	33,946	15,567	40,735	9,465	23,859	11,929	30,309	13,988	35,786
Management & Program Analysis	GS-5-GS-9	9	38,824	38,824	39,738	40,208	40,667	41,616	40,667	41,616	37%	10,289	11,189	12,973	14,156	15,567	16,987	9,465	9,951	11,929	12,641	13,988	14,925
Criminal Investigating	GS-5-GS-13	9	38,824	66,951	39,738	69,339	40,667	71,767	40,667	71,767	37%	10,289	19,297	12,973	24,413	15,567	29,295	9,465	17,161	11,929	21,800	13,988	25,738

Chart II - U.S. Federal - Job Titles - Salaries - Pension Estimates

U.S. Federal Government Agencies	GS Grade Range:	GS Grade Median	2010 Median Grade Min Salary (STEP 1)	2010 Maximum Grade Salary (STEP 1)	2011 Median Grade Min Salary (STEP 2)	2011 Maximum Grade Salary (STEP 2)	2012 Median Grade Min Salary (STEP 3)	2012 Maximum Grade Salary (STEP 3)	2013 Median Grade Min Salary (STEP 4)	2013 Maximum Grade Salary (STEP 4)	10-Year Cumulative Raise Percentage (1.96%) + Step Increase Percentage (1.7%)	20-Year Annual Pension Benefit Estimate (Min.)	20-Year Annual Pension Benefit Estimate (Max.)	25-Year Annual Pension Benefit Estimate (Min.)	25-Year Annual Pension Benefit Estimate (Max.)	30-Year Annual Pension Benefit Estimate (Min.)	30-Year Annual Pension Benefit Estimate (Max.)	Agency Automatic Contributions 1% Thrift Savings Plan 20 Year Savings Plus 4.5% Interest (Min)	Agency Automatic Contributions 1% Thrift Savings Plan 20 Year Savings Plus 4.5% Interest (Max)	Agency Automatic Contributions 1% Thrift Savings Plan 25 Year Savings Plus 4.5% Interest (Min)	Agency Automatic Contributions 1% Thrift Savings Plan 25 Year Savings Plus 4.5% Interest (Max)	Agency Automatic Contributions 1% Thrift Savings Plan 30 Year Savings Plus 4.5% Interest (Min)	Agency Automatic Contributions 1% Thrift Savings Plan 30 Year Savings Plus 4.5% Interest (Max)
Visual Information	GS-7-GS-12	9	38,824	56,301	39,956	58,309	41,107	60,351	41,107	60,351	37%	10,706	16,227	13,521	20,529	16,225	24,635	9,690	14,431	12,259	18,332	14,423	21,64

Other Job Groups with IT-Computer-Technical Services Work

U.S. Federal Government Agencies	GS Grade Range:	GS Grade Median	2010 STEP 1 Min	2010 STEP 1 Max	2011 STEP 2 Min	2011 STEP 2 Max	2012 STEP 3 Min	2012 STEP 3 Max	2013 STEP 4 Min	2013 STEP 4 Max	10-Yr %	20-Yr Min	20-Yr Max	25-Yr Min	25-Yr Max	30-Yr Min	30-Yr Max	20 Yr Min	20 Yr Max	25 Yr Min	25 Yr Max	30 Yr Min	30 Yr Max
Inventory Management	GS-9-GS-11	10	42,755	46,974	44,139	48,649	45,547	50,353	45,547	50,353	37%	12,054	13,539	15,237	17,128	18,284	20,554	10,814	12,041	13,709	15,295	16,157	18,05
Librarian	GS-9-GS-14	11	46,974	79,115	48,358	81,936	49,766	84,805	49,766	84,805	37%	12,982	22,802	16,397	28,847	19,676	34,616	11,740	20,279	14,855	25,760	17,480	30,41
Technical Information Services	GS-9-GS-14	11	46,974	79,115	48,358	81,936	49,766	84,805	49,766	84,805	37%	12,982	22,802	16,397	28,847	19,676	34,616	11,740	20,279	14,855	25,760	17,480	30,41

Other Job Groups with IT-Computer-Technical Services Work

U.S. Federal Government Agencies	GS Grade Range:	GS Grade Median	2010 STEP 1 Min	2010 STEP 1 Max	2011 STEP 2 Min	2011 STEP 2 Max	2012 STEP 3 Min	2012 STEP 3 Max	2013 STEP 4 Min	2013 STEP 4 Max	10-Yr %	20-Yr Min	20-Yr Max	25-Yr Min	25-Yr Max	30-Yr Min	30-Yr Max	20 Yr Min	20 Yr Max	25 Yr Min	25 Yr Max	30 Yr Min	30 Yr Max
Computer Clerk & Assistant	GS-3-GS-9	6	28,562	38,824	29,289	40,208	30,029	41,616	30,029	41,616	37%	7,675	11,189	9,683	14,156	11,619	16,987	7,020	9,951	8,860	12,641	10,401	14,92
Computer Operation	GS-3-GS-9	6	28,562	38,824	29,289	40,208	30,029	41,616	30,029	41,616	37%	7,675	11,189	9,683	14,156	11,619	16,987	7,020	9,951	8,860	12,641	10,401	14,92
Professional Work/ Administration Work Accounting & Budget	GS-2-GS-9	5	25,623	38,824	26,350	40,208	27,090	41,616	27,090	41,616	37%	7,029	11,189	8,875	14,156	10,650	16,987	6,375	9,951	8,061	12,641	9,480	14,92
Miscellaneous Clerk & Assistant	GS-1-GS-7	4	22,902	31,740	22,902	32,872	22,902	34,023	22,902	34,023	37%	5,038	9,148	6,298	11,573	7,558	13,888	5,026	8,136	6,222	10,335	7,180	12,20
Secretary	GS-2-GS-13	6	28,562	66,951	29,289	69,339	30,029	71,767	30,029	71,767	37%	7,675	19,297	9,683	24,413	11,619	29,295	7,020	17,161	8,860	21,800	10,401	25,73

Chart II - U.S. Federal - Job Titles - Salaries - Pension Estimates

Investigation _ Inspection

U.S. Federal Government Agencies	GS Grade Range	GS Grade Median	2010 Median Grade Min Salary (STEP 1)	2010 Maximum Grade Salary (STEP 1)	2011 Median Grade Salary (STEP 2)	2011 Maximum Grade Salary (STEP 2)	2012 Median Grade Salary (STEP 3)	2012 Maximum Grade Salary (STEP 3)	2013 Median Grade Salary (STEP 4)	2013 Maximum Grade Salary (STEP 4)	10-Year Cumulative Raise Percentage (1.96%) + Step Increase Percentage (1.7%)	20-Year Annual Pension Benefit Estimate (Min.)	20-Year Annual Pension Benefit Estimate (Max.)	25-Year Annual Pension Benefit Estimate (Min.)	25-Year Annual Pension Benefit Estimate (Max.)	30-Year Annual Pension Benefit Estimate (Min.)	30-Year Annual Pension Benefit Estimate (Max.)	Agency Automatic Contributions 1% Thrift Savings Plan 20 Year Savings Plus 4.5% Interest (Min)	Agency Automatic Contributions 1% Thrift Savings Plan 20 Year Savings Plus 4.5% Interest (Max)	Agency Automatic Contributions 1% Thrift Savings Plan 25 Year Savings Plus 4.5% Interest (Min)	Agency Automatic Contributions 1% Thrift Savings Plan 25 Year Savings Plus 4.5% Interest (Max)	Agency Automatic Contributions 1% Thrift Savings Plan 30 Year Savings Plus 4.5% Interest (Min)	Agency Automatic Contributions 1% Thrift Savings Plan 30 Year Savings Plus 4.5% Interest (Max)
Correctional Officer Series																							
Correctional Officer	GS-6-GS-9	7	31,740	38,824	32,758	40,208	33,794	41,616	33,794	41,616	37%	8,931	11,189	11,288	14,156	13,546	16,987	8,018	9,951	10,163	12,641	11,976	14,925
Supervisory Correctional Officer	GS-6-GS-9	7	31,740	38,824	32,758	40,208	33,794	41,616	72,618	73,356	37%	17,472	18,172	21,965	22,884	26,358	27,461	14,915	15,590	19,089	19,938	22,930	23,880
Fingerprint Identification Series																							
Fingerprint Examiner	GS-2-GS-12	7	31,740	56,301	32,467	58,309	33,207	60,351	33,207	60,351	37%	8,374	16,227	10,557	20,529	12,668	24,635	7,718	14,431	9,723	18,332	11,397	21,644
Fingerprint Specialist	GS-2-GS-12	7	31,740	56,301	32,467	58,309	33,207	60,351	33,207	92,091	37%	8,374	23,210	10,557	29,258	12,668	35,109	7,718	20,070	9,723	25,629	11,397	30,600
United States Marshal Series																							
United States Marshal	GS-5-GS-9	7	31,740	38,824	32,654	40,208	33,583	41,616	33,583	41,616	37%	8,730	11,189	11,025	14,156	13,230	16,987	7,910	9,951	10,005	12,641	11,768	14,925
Chief Deputy United States Marshal	GS-5-GS-9	7	31,740	38,824	32,654	40,208	33,583	41,616	33,583	41,616	37%	8,730	11,189	11,025	14,156	13,230	16,987	7,910	9,951	10,005	12,641	11,768	14,925
Supervisory Deputy United States Marshal	GS-5-GS-9	7	31,740	38,824	32,654	40,208	33,583	41,616	65,323	41,616	37%	15,713	11,189	19,753	14,156	23,704	16,987	13,549	9,951	17,302	12,641	20,723	14,925
Deputy United States Marshal	GS-5-GS-9	7	31,740	38,824	32,654	40,208	33,583	41,616	65,323	41,616	37%	15,713	11,189	19,753	14,156	23,704	16,987	13,549	9,951	17,302	12,641	20,723	14,925
Air Safety Investigating Series																							
Air Safety Investigator (Field)	GS-11-GS-14	12	56,301	79,115	57,976	81,936	59,680	84,805	59,680	84,805	37%	15,591	22,802	19,693	28,847	23,632	34,616	14,087	20,279	17,829	25,760	20,983	30,414
Air Safety Investigator (Airworthiness)	GS-11-GS-14	12	56,301	79,115	57,976	81,936	59,680	84,805	59,680	84,805	37%	15,591	22,802	19,693	28,847	23,632	34,616	14,087	20,279	17,829	25,760	20,983	30,414
Air Safety Investigator (Operations)	GS-11-GS-14	12	56,301	79,115	57,976	81,936	59,680	84,805	59,680	84,805	37%	15,591	22,802	19,693	28,847	23,632	34,616	14,087	20,279	17,829	25,760	20,983	30,414
Air Safety Investigator (Analysis)	GS-11-GS-14	12	56,301	79,115	57,976	81,936	59,680	84,805	59,680	84,805	37%	15,591	22,802	19,693	28,847	23,632	34,616	14,087	20,279	17,829	25,760	20,983	30,414
Air Safety Investigator (Hearing and Reports)	GS-11-GS-14	12	56,301	79,115	57,976	81,936	59,680	84,805	59,680	84,805	37%	15,591	22,802	19,693	28,847	23,632	34,616	14,087	20,279	17,829	25,760	20,983	30,414
Air Safety Specialist (Military)	GS-11-GS-14	12	56,301	79,115	57,976	81,936	59,680	84,805	59,680	84,805	37%	15,591	22,802	19,693	28,847	23,632	34,616	14,087	20,279	17,829	25,760	20,983	30,414
Air Safety Investigator (General)	GS-11-GS-14	12	56,301	79,115	57,976	81,936	59,680	84,805	59,680	84,805	37%	15,591	22,802	19,693	28,847	23,632	34,616	14,087	20,279	17,829	25,760	20,983	30,414
Immigration Inspection Series																							
Immigration Inspector	GS-5-GS-11	8	35,151	46,974	36,065	48,649	36,994	50,353	36,994	50,353	37%	9,481	13,539	11,963	17,128	14,355	20,554	8,659	12,041	10,931	15,295	12,837	18,059
Immigration Examiner	GS-5-GS-11	8	35,151	46,974	36,065	48,649	36,994	50,353	36,994	50,353	37%	9,481	13,539	11,963	17,128	14,355	20,554	8,659	12,041	10,931	15,295	12,837	18,059
Supervisory Immigration Inspector	GS-5-GS-11	8	35,151	46,974	36,065	48,649	36,994	50,353	36,994	50,353	37%	9,481	13,539	11,963	17,128	14,355	20,554	8,659	12,041	10,931	15,295	12,837	18,059
Immigration Examiner	GS-5-GS-11	8	35,151	46,974	36,065	48,649	36,994	50,353	36,994	50,353	37%	9,481	13,539	11,963	17,128	14,355	20,554	8,659	12,041	10,931	15,295	12,837	18,059
Mine Safety and Health Series																							
Mine Safety and Health Inspector	GS-5-GS-15	9	38,824	93,063	39,738	96,387	40,667	99,767	40,667	99,767	37%	10,289	26,832	12,973	33,946	15,567	40,735	9,465	23,859	11,929	30,309	13,988	35,786
Coal Mine Safety and Health Inspector	GS-5-GS-15	9	38,824	93,063	39,738	96,387	40,667	99,767	40,667	99,767	37%	10,289	26,832	12,973	33,946	15,567	40,735	9,465	23,859	11,929	30,309	13,988	35,786
Mine safety and Health Specialist	GS-5-GS-15	9	38,824	93,063	39,738	96,387	40,667	99,767	40,667	99,767	37%	10,289	26,832	12,973	33,946	15,567	40,735	9,465	23,859	11,929	30,309	13,988	35,786

Chart II - U.S. Federal - Job Titles - Salaries - Pension Estimates

U.S. Federal Government Agencies	GS Grade Range:	GS Grade Median	2010 Median Grade Min Salary (STEP 1)	2010 Maximum Grade Salary (STEP 1)	2011 Median Grade Min Salary (STEP 2)	2011 Maximum Grade Salary (STEP 2)	2012 Median Grade Min Salary (STEP 3)	2012 Maximum Grade Salary (STEP 3)	2013 Median Grade Min Salary (STEP 4)	2013 Maximum Grade Salary (STEP 4)	10-Year Cumulative Raise Percentage (1.96%) + Step Increase Percentage (1.7%)	20-Year Annual Pension Benefit Estimate (Min.)	20-Year Annual Pension Benefit Estimate (Max.)	25-Year Annual Pension Benefit Estimate (Min.)	25-Year Annual Pension Benefit Estimate (Max.)	30-Year Annual Pension Benefit Estimate (Min.)	30-Year Annual Pension Benefit Estimate (Max.)	Agency Automatic Contributions 1% Thrift Savings Plan 20 Year Savings Plus 4.5% Interest (Min)	Agency Automatic Contributions 1% Thrift Savings Plan 20 Year Savings Plus 4.5% Interest (Max)	Agency Automatic Contributions 1% Thrift Savings Plan 25 Year Savings Plus 4.5% Interest (Min)	Agency Automatic Contributions 1% Thrift Savings Plan 25 Year Savings Plus 4.5% Interest (Max)	Agency Automatic Contributions 1% Thrift Savings Plan 30 Year Savings Plus 4.5% Interest (Min)	Agency Automatic Contributions 1% Thrift Savings Plan 30 Year Savings Plus 4.5% Interest (Max)
Aviation Safety Series																							
Aviation Safety Inspectors	GS-5-GS-14	8	35,151	79,115	36,065	81,936	36,994	84,805	36,994	84,805	37%	9,481	22,802	11,963	28,847	14,355	34,616	8,659	20,279	10,931	25,760	12,837	30,414
Operation	GS-5-GS-14	8	35,151	79,115	36,065	81,936	36,994	84,805	36,994	84,805	37%	9,481	22,802	11,963	28,847	14,355	34,616	8,659	20,279	10,931	25,760	12,837	30,414
Alcohol, Tobacco and Firearms Inspection Series																							
Alcohol	GS-5-GS-11	9	38,824	46,974	39,738	48,649	40,667	50,353	40,667	50,353	37%	10,289	13,539	12,973	17,128	15,567	20,554	9,465	12,041	11,929	15,295	13,988	18,059
Tobacco	GS-5-GS-11	9	38,824	46,974	39,738	48,649	40,667	50,353	40,667	50,353	37%	10,289	13,539	12,973	17,128	15,567	20,554	9,465	12,041	11,929	15,295	13,988	18,059
Firearms Inspector	GS-5-GS-11	9	38,824	46,974	39,738	48,649	40,667	50,353	40,667	50,353	37%	10,289	13,539	12,973	17,128	15,567	20,554	9,465	12,041	11,929	15,295	13,988	18,059
Customs Patrol Officer Series																							
Customs Patrol Officer	GS-5-GS-11	7	31,740	46,974	32,654	48,649	33,583	50,353	33,583	50,353	37%	8,730	13,539	11,025	17,128	13,230	20,554	7,910	12,041	10,005	15,295	11,768	18,059
Supervisory Customs Patrol Officer	GS-5-GS-11	7	31,740	46,974	32,654	48,649	33,583	50,353	33,583	50,353	37%	8,730	13,539	11,025	17,128	13,230	20,554	7,910	12,041	10,005	15,295	11,768	18,059
Customs Inspection Series																							
Customs Inspector	GS-5-GS-11	7	31,740	46,974	32,654	48,649	33,583	50,353	33,583	50,353	37%	8,730	13,539	11,025	17,128	13,230	20,554	7,910	12,041	10,005	15,295	11,768	18,059
Supervisory Customs Inspector	GS-5-GS-11	7	31,740	46,974	32,654	48,649	33,583	50,353	33,583	50,353	37%	8,730	13,539	11,025	17,128	13,230	20,554	7,910	12,041	10,005	15,295	11,768	18,059

Chart II - U.S. Federal - Job Titles - Salaries - Pension Estimates

Legal _ Claims Examining

U.S. Federal Government Agencies	GS Grade Range:	GS Grade Median	2010 Median Grade Min Salary (STEP 1)	2010 Maximum Grade Salary (STEP 1)	2011 Median Grade Min Salary (STEP 2)	2011 Maximum Grade Salary (STEP 2)	2012 Median Grade Min Salary (STEP 3)	2012 Maximum Grade Salary (STEP 3)	2013 Median Grade Min Salary (STEP 4)	2013 Maximum Grade Salary (STEP 4)	10-Year Cumulative Raise Percentage (1.96%) + Step Increase Percentage (1.7%)	20-Year Annual Pension Benefit Estimate (Min.)	20-Year Annual Pension Benefit Estimate (Max.)	25-Year Annual Pension Benefit Estimate (Min.)	25-Year Annual Pension Benefit Estimate (Max.)	30-Year Annual Pension Benefit Estimate (Min.)	30-Year Annual Pension Benefit Estimate (Max.)	Agency Automatic Contributions 1% Thrift Savings Plan 20 Year Plus 4.5% Interest (Min)	Agency Automatic Contributions 1% Thrift Savings Plan 20 Year Plus 4.5% Interest (Max)	Agency Automatic Contributions 1% Thrift Savings Plan 25 Year Plus 4.5% Interest (Min)	Agency Automatic Contributions 1% Thrift Savings Plan 25 Year Plus 4.5% Interest (Max)	Agency Automatic Contributions 1% Thrift Savings Plan 30 Year Plus 4.5% Interest (Min)	Agency Automatic Contributions 1% Thrift Savings Plan 30 Year Plus 4.5% Interest (Max)
General Attorney Series																							
Functional titles	GS-7-GS-13	8	35,151	66,951	36,283	69,339	37,434	71,767	37,434	71,767	37%	9,898	19,297	12,511	24,413	15,013	29,295	8,884	17,161	11,261	21,800	13,271	25,738
Subject-matter titles	GS-7-GS-13	8	35,151	66,951	36,283	69,339	37,434	71,767	37,434	71,767	37%	9,898	19,297	12,511	24,413	15,013	29,295	8,884	17,161	11,261	21,800	13,271	25,738
Paralegal Specialist Series																							
Paralegal Specialist	GS-5-GS-11	7	31,740	46,974	32,654	48,649	33,583	50,353	33,583	50,353	37%	8,730	13,539	11,025	17,128	13,230	20,554	7,910	12,041	10,005	15,295	11,768	18,059
Supervisory	GS-5-GS-11	7	31,740	46,974	32,654	48,649	33,583	50,353	33,583	50,353	37%	8,730	13,539	11,025	17,128	13,230	20,554	7,910	12,041	10,005	15,295	11,768	18,059
Paralegal Specialist	GS-5-GS-11	7	31,740	46,974	32,654	48,649	33,583	50,353	33,583	50,353	37%	8,730	13,539	11,025	17,128	13,230	20,554	7,910	12,041	10,005	15,295	11,768	18,059
Contact Representative Series																							
Contact Representative	GS-4-GS-10	6	28,562	42,755	29,378	44,279	30,208	45,830	30,208	45,830	37%	7,845	12,322	9,906	15,589	11,887	18,707	7,112	10,959	8,994	13,921	10,578	16,436
Supervisory Contact Representative.	GS-4-GS-10	6	28,562	42,755	29,378	44,279	30,208	45,830	30,208	45,830	37%	7,845	12,322	9,906	15,589	11,887	18,707	7,112	10,959	8,994	13,921	10,578	16,436
Legal Instruments Examining Series																							
Legal Instruments Examiner	GS-6-GS-9	7	31,740	38,824	32,758	40,208	33,794	41,616	33,794	41,616	37%	8,931	11,189	11,288	14,156	13,546	16,987	8,018	9,951	10,163	12,641	11,976	14,925
Lead Legal Instruments Examiner	GS-6-GS-9	7	31,740	38,824	32,758	40,208	33,794	41,616	33,794	41,616	37%	8,931	11,189	11,288	14,156	13,546	16,987	8,018	9,951	10,163	12,641	11,976	14,925
Supervisory Legal Instruments Examiner	GS-6-GS-9	7	31,740	38,824	32,758	40,208	33,794	41,616	33,794	41,616	37%	8,931	11,189	11,288	14,156	13,546	16,987	8,018	9,951	10,163	12,641	11,976	14,925
Passport and Visa Examining Series																							
Passport Specialist	GS-7-GS-12	9	38,824	56,301	39,956	58,309	41,107	60,351	41,107	60,351	37%	10,706	16,227	13,521	20,529	16,225	24,635	9,690	14,431	12,259	18,332	14,423	21,644
Visa Specialist	GS-7-GS-12	9	38,824	56,301	39,956	58,309	41,107	60,351	41,107	60,351	37%	10,706	16,227	13,521	20,529	16,225	24,635	9,690	14,431	12,259	18,332	14,423	21,644
Supervisory Passport Specialist	GS-7-GS-12	9	38,824	56,301	39,956	58,309	41,107	60,351	41,107	60,351	37%	10,706	16,227	13,521	20,529	16,225	24,635	9,690	14,431	12,259	18,332	14,423	21,644
Workers' Compensation Claims Examining Series																							
Workers' Compensation Claims Examiner	GS-5-GS-12	7	31,740	56,301	32,654	58,309	33,583	60,351	33,583	60,351	37%	8,730	16,227	11,025	20,529	13,230	24,635	7,910	14,431	10,005	18,332	11,768	21,644
Supervisory Workers' Comp Claims Examiner	GS-5-GS-12	7	31,740	56,301	32,654	58,309	33,583	60,351	33,583	60,351	37%	8,730	16,227	11,025	20,529	13,230	24,635	7,910	14,431	10,005	18,332	11,768	21,644
Veterans Claims Examining Series																							
Supervisory	GS-5-GS-12	7	31,740	56,301	32,654	58,309	33,583	60,351	33,583	60,351	37%	8,730	16,227	11,025	20,529	13,230	24,635	7,910	14,431	10,005	18,332	11,768	21,644

Chart II - U.S. Federal - Job Titles - Salaries - Pension Estimates

Library _ Archives

U.S. Federal Government Agencies	GS Grade Range:	GS Grade Median	2010 Median Grade Min Salary (STEP 1)	2010 Maximum Grade Salary (STEP 1)	2011 Median Grade Min Salary (STEP 2)	2011 Maximum Grade Salary (STEP 2)	2012 Median Grade Min Salary (STEP 3)	2012 Maximum Grade Salary (STEP 3)	2013 Median Grade Min Salary (STEP 4)	2013 Maximum Grade Salary (STEP 4)	10-Year Cumulative Raise Percentage (1.96%) + Step Increase Percentage (1.7%)	20-Year Annual Pension Benefit Estimate (Min.)	20-Year Annual Pension Benefit Estimate (Max.)	25-Year Annual Pension Benefit Estimate (Min.)	25-Year Annual Pension Benefit Estimate (Max.)	30-Year Annual Pension Benefit Estimate (Min.)	30-Year Annual Pension Benefit Estimate (Max.)	Agency Automatic Contributions 1% Thrift Savings Plan 20 Year Savings Plus 4.5% Interest (Min)	Agency Automatic Contributions 1% Thrift Savings Plan 20 Year Savings Plus 4.5% Interest (Max)	Agency Automatic Contributions 1% Thrift Savings Plan 25 Year Savings Plus 4.5% Interest (Min)	Agency Automatic Contributions 1% Thrift Savings Plan 25 Year Savings Plus 4.5% Interest (Max)	Agency Automatic Contributions 1% Thrift Savings Plan 30 Year Savings Plus 4.5% Interest (Min)	Agency Automatic Contributions 1% Thrift Savings Plan 30 Year Savings Plus 4.5% Interest (Max)
History Series																							
Historian	GS-5-GS-14	8	35,151	79,115	36,065	81,936	36,994	84,805	36,994	84,805	37%	9,481	22,802	11,963	28,847	14,355	34,616	8,659	20,279	10,931	25,760	12,837	30,41
Supervisory	GS-5-GS-14	8	35,151	79,115	36,065	81,936	36,994	84,805	36,994	84,805	37%	9,481	22,802	11,963	28,847	14,355	34,616	8,659	20,279	10,931	25,760	12,837	30,41
Librarian Series																							
Librarian	GS-9-GS-14	11	46,974	79,115	48,358	81,936	49,766	84,805	49,766	84,805	37%	12,982	22,802	16,397	28,847	19,676	34,616	11,740	20,279	14,855	25,760	17,480	30,41
Supervisory Librarian	GS-9-GS-14	11	46,974	79,115	48,358	81,936	49,766	84,805	49,766	84,805	37%	12,982	22,802	16,397	28,847	19,676	34,616	11,740	20,279	14,855	25,760	17,480	30,41
Parenthetical Titles	GS-9-GS-14	11	46,974	79,115	48,358	81,936	49,766	84,805	49,766	84,805	37%	12,982	22,802	16,397	28,847	19,676	34,616	11,740	20,279	14,855	25,760	17,480	30,41
Archivist Series																							
Archivist	GS-5-GS-13	7	31,740	66,951	32,654	69,339	33,583	71,767	33,583	71,767	37%	8,730	19,297	11,025	24,413	13,230	29,295	7,910	17,161	10,005	21,800	11,768	25,73
Supervisory	GS-5-GS-13	7	31,740	66,951	32,654	69,339	33,583	71,767	33,583	71,767	37%	8,730	19,297	11,025	24,413	13,230	29,295	7,910	17,161	10,005	21,800	11,768	25,73
Library Technician Series																							
Library Aid	GS-3-GS-8	5	25,623	35,151	26,350	36,405	27,090	37,680	27,090	37,680	37%	7,029	10,132	8,875	12,818	10,650	15,381	6,375	9,010	8,061	11,446	9,480	13,51
Library Technician	GS-3-GS-8	5	25,623	35,151	26,350	36,405	27,090	37,680	27,090	37,680	37%	7,029	10,132	8,875	12,818	10,650	15,381	6,375	9,010	8,061	11,446	9,480	13,51
Lead Library Technician	GS-3-GS-8	5	25,623	35,151	26,350	36,405	27,090	37,680	27,090	37,680	37%	7,029	10,132	8,875	12,818	10,650	15,381	6,375	9,010	8,061	11,446	9,480	13,51
Supervisory Library Technician	GS-3-GS-8	5	25,623	35,151	26,350	36,405	27,090	37,680	27,090	37,680	37%	7,029	10,132	8,875	12,818	10,650	15,381	6,375	9,010	8,061	11,446	9,480	13,51
Technical Information Specialist Is the Title for All Nonsupervisory Positions in this Series																							
Parenthetical Titles	GS-9-GS-14	10	42,755	79,115	44,139	81,936	45,547	84,805	45,547	84,805	37%	12,054	22,802	15,237	28,847	18,284	34,616	10,814	20,279	13,709	25,760	16,157	30,41

Chart II - U.S. Federal - Job Titles - Salaries - Pension Estimates

Mgmt_Admin_ Clerical_Office

U.S. Federal Government Agencies	GS Grade Range:	GS Grade Median	2010 Median Grade Min Salary (STEP 1)	2010 Maximum Grade Salary (STEP 1)	2011 Median Grade Salary (STEP 2)	2011 Maximum Grade Salary (STEP 2)	2012 Median Grade Salary (STEP 3)	2012 Maximum Grade Salary (STEP 3)	2013 Median Grade Salary (STEP 4)	2013 Maximum Grade Salary (STEP 4)	10-Year Cumulative Raise Percentage (1.96%) + Step Increase Percentage (1.7%)	20-Year Annual Pension Benefit Estimate (Min.)	20-Year Annual Pension Benefit Estimate (Max.)	25-Year Annual Pension Benefit Estimate (Min.)	25-Year Annual Pension Benefit Estimate (Max.)	30-Year Annual Pension Benefit Estimate (Min.)	30-Year Annual Pension Benefit Estimate (Max.)	Agency Automatic Contributions 1% Thrift Savings Plan 20 Year Plus 4.5% Interest (Min)	Agency Automatic Contributions 1% Thrift Savings Plan 20 Year Plus 4.5% Interest (Max)	Agency Automatic Contributions 1% Thrift Savings Plan 25 Year Plus 4.5% Interest (Min)	Agency Automatic Contributions 1% Thrift Savings Plan 25 Year Plus 4.5% Interest (Max)	Agency Automatic Contributions 1% Thrift Savings Plan 30 Year Plus 4.5% Interest (Min)	Agency Automatic Contributions 1% Thrift Savings Plan 30 Year Plus 4.5% Interest (Max)
Information Receptionist Series *																							
Information Receptionist	GS-2-GS-4	3	20,401	22,902	21,128	23,718	21,868	24,548	21,868	24,548	37%	5,880	6,600	7,439	8,349	8,926	10,019	5,229	5,870	6,642	7,456	7,843	8,803
Supervisory Information Receptionist	GS-2-GS-4	3	20,401	22,902	21,128	23,718	21,868	24,548	21,868	24,548	37%	5,880	6,600	7,439	8,349	8,926	10,019	5,229	5,870	6,642	7,456	7,843	8,803
Mail and File Series *																							
Mail Clerk	GS-1-GS-4	2	18,698	22,902	18,698	23,718	18,698	24,548	47,260	50,171	37%	10,397	12,237	12,997	15,396	15,596	18,475	9,177	10,422	11,647	13,347	13,921	16,033
File Clerk	GS-1-GS-4	2	18,698	22,902	18,698	23,718	18,698	24,548	18,698	50,171	37%	4,114	12,237	5,142	15,396	6,170	18,475	4,103	10,422	5,080	13,347	5,862	16,033
Mail	GS-1-GS-4	2	18,698	22,902	18,698	23,718	18,698	24,548	18,698	50,171	37%	4,114	12,237	5,142	15,396	6,170	18,475	4,103	10,422	5,080	13,347	5,862	16,033
File Clerk	GS-1-GS-4	2	18,698	22,902	18,698	23,718	18,698	24,548	44,321	50,171	37%	9,751	12,237	12,188	15,396	14,626	18,475	8,655	10,422	10,971	13,347	13,091	16,033
Assistant	GS-1-GS-4	2	18,698	22,902	18,698	23,718	18,698	24,548	44,321	24,548	37%	9,751	6,600	12,188	8,349	14,626	10,019	8,655	5,870	10,971	7,456	13,091	8,803
Lead	GS-1-GS-4	2	18,698	22,902	18,698	23,718	18,698	24,548	44,321	24,548	37%	9,751	6,600	12,188	8,349	14,626	10,019	8,655	5,870	10,971	7,456	13,091	8,803
Correspondence Clerk Series																							
Clerk	GS-3-GS-5	4	22,902	25,623	23,629	26,537	24,369	27,466	49,992	27,466	37%	12,067	7,385	15,173	9,342	18,207	11,211	10,330	6,568	13,213	8,343	15,856	9,850
Lead Correspondence Clerk	GS-3-GS-5	4	22,902	25,623	23,629	26,537	24,369	27,466	24,369	27,466	37%	6,430	7,385	8,126	9,342	9,752	11,211	5,778	6,568	7,322	8,343	8,627	9,850
Correspondence Supervisor	GS-3-GS-5	4	22,902	25,623	23,629	26,537	24,369	27,466	24,369	47,867	37%	6,430	11,873	8,126	14,953	9,752	17,943	5,778	10,192	7,322	13,033	8,627	15,606
Typing	GS-3-GS-5	4	22,902	25,623	23,629	26,537	24,369	27,466	43,067	47,867	37%	10,544	11,873	13,268	14,953	15,922	17,943	9,100	10,192	11,621	13,033	13,902	15,606
Stenography	GS-3-GS-5	4	22,902	25,623	23,629	26,537	24,369	27,466	43,067	47,867	37%	10,544	11,873	13,268	14,953	15,922	17,943	9,100	10,192	11,621	13,033	13,902	15,606
Secretary Series																							
Secretary	GS-3-GS-9	5	25,623	38,824	26,350	40,208	27,090	41,616	47,491	67,239	37%	11,517	16,826	14,485	21,202	17,382	25,442	9,999	14,503	12,752	18,532	15,236	22,154
Supervisory Secretary	GS-3-GS-9	5	25,623	38,824	26,350	40,208	27,090	41,616	47,491	67,239	37%	11,517	16,826	14,485	21,202	17,382	25,442	9,999	14,503	12,752	18,532	15,236	22,154
Typing	GS-3-GS-9	5	25,623	38,824	26,350	40,208	27,090	41,616	47,491	67,239	37%	11,517	16,826	14,485	21,202	17,382	25,442	9,999	14,503	12,752	18,532	15,236	22,154
Stenography	GS-3-GS-9	5	25,623	38,824	26,350	40,208	27,090	41,616	27,090	41,616	37%	7,029	11,189	8,875	14,156	10,650	16,987	6,375	9,951	8,061	12,641	9,480	14,925
Clerk-Typist Series																							
Clerk-Typist	GS-1-GS-10	6	28,562	42,755	28,562	44,279	28,562	45,830	54,185	84,654	37%	11,921	20,864	14,901	26,266	17,881	31,519	10,820	17,856	13,651	22,846	16,184	27,390
Lead Clerk-Typist	GS-1-GS-10	6	28,562	42,755	28,562	44,279	28,562	45,830	54,185	45,830	37%	11,921	12,322	14,901	15,589	17,881	18,707	10,820	10,959	13,651	13,921	16,184	16,436
Supervisory Clerk-Typist	GS-1-GS-10	6	28,562	42,755	28,562	44,279	28,562	45,830	28,562	45,830	37%	6,284	12,322	7,855	15,589	9,425	18,707	6,268	10,959	7,760	13,921	8,954	16,436
Computer Operation Series																							
Computer Operator	GS-3-GS-9	5	25,623	38,824	26,350	40,208	27,090	41,616	65,914	41,616	37%	15,570	11,189	19,551	14,156	23,461	16,987	13,272	9,951	16,987	12,641	20,434	14,925
Lead Computer Operator.	GS-3-GS-9	5	25,623	38,824	26,350	40,208	27,090	41,616	27,090	41,616	37%	7,029	11,189	8,875	14,156	10,650	16,987	6,375	9,951	8,061	12,641	9,480	14,925
Supervisory Computer Operator.	GS-3-GS-9	5	25,623	38,824	26,350	40,208	27,090	41,616	27,090	41,616	37%	7,029	11,189	8,875	14,156	10,650	16,987	6,375	9,951	8,061	12,641	9,480	14,925
Computer Clerk and Assistant Series																							
Lead	GS-8-GS-9	8	35,151	38,824	36,405	40,208	37,680	41,616	37,680	41,616	37%	10,132	11,189	12,818	14,156	15,381	16,987	9,010	9,951	11,446	12,641	13,514	14,925

Chart II - U.S. Federal - Job Titles - Salaries - Pension Estimates

U.S. Federal Government Agencies	GS Grade Range	GS Grade Median	2010 Median Grade Min Salary (STEP 1)	2010 Maximum Grade Salary (STEP 1)	2011 Median Grade Min Salary (STEP 2)	2011 Maximum Grade Salary (STEP 2)	2012 Median Grade Min Salary (STEP 3)	2012 Maximum Grade Salary (STEP 3)	2013 Median Grade Min Salary (STEP 4)	2013 Maximum Grade Salary (STEP 4)	10-Year Cumulative Raise Percentage (1.96%) + Step Increase Percentage (1.7%)	20-Year Annual Pension Benefit Estimate (Min.)	20-Year Annual Pension Benefit Estimate (Max.)	25-Year Annual Pension Benefit Estimate (Min.)	25-Year Annual Pension Benefit Estimate (Max.)	30-Year Annual Pension Benefit Estimate (Min.)	30-Year Annual Pension Benefit Estimate (Max.)	Agency Automatic Contributions 1% Thrift Savings Plan 20 Year Savings Plus 4.5% Interest (Min)	Agency Automatic Contributions 1% Thrift Savings Plan 20 Year Savings Plus 4.5% Interest (Max)	Agency Automatic Contributions 1% Thrift Savings Plan 25 Year Savings Plus 4.5% Interest (Min)	Agency Automatic Contributions 1% Thrift Savings Plan 25 Year Savings Plus 4.5% Interest (Max)	Agency Automatic Contributions 1% Thrift Savings Plan 30 Year Savings Plus 4.5% Interest (Min)	Agency Automatic Contributions 1% Thrift Savings Plan 30 Year Savings Plus 4.5% Interest (Max)
Supervisory	GS-8-GS-9	8	35,151	38,824	36,405	40,208	37,680	41,616	37,680	41,616	37%	10,132	11,189	12,818	14,156	15,381	16,987	9,010	9,951	11,446	12,641	13,514	14,925
Management and Program Analysis Series																							
Management Analyst	GS-5-GS-7	6	28,562	31,740	29,476	32,872	30,405	34,023	30,405	34,023	37%	8,031	9,148	10,151	11,573	12,181	13,888	7,213	8,136	9,141	10,335	10,771	12,202
Program Analyst	GS-5-GS-7	6	28,562	31,740	29,476	32,872	30,405	34,023	30,405	34,023	37%	8,031	9,148	10,151	11,573	12,181	13,888	7,213	8,136	9,141	10,335	10,771	12,202
Management and Program Analyst	GS-5-GS-7	6	28,562	31,740	29,476	32,872	30,405	34,023	30,405	34,023	37%	8,031	9,148	10,151	11,573	12,181	13,888	7,213	8,136	9,141	10,335	10,771	12,202
Management and Program Clerical and Assistance Series																							
Management Clerk	GS-4-GS-7	5	25,623	31,740	26,439	32,872	27,269	34,023	27,269	34,023	37%	7,198	9,148	9,098	11,573	10,917	13,888	6,467	8,136	8,196	10,335	9,656	12,202
Management Assistant	GS-4-GS-7	5	25,623	31,740	26,439	32,872	27,269	34,023	27,269	34,023	37%	7,198	9,148	9,098	11,573	10,917	13,888	6,467	8,136	8,196	10,335	9,656	12,202
Program Clerk	GS-4-GS-7	5	25,623	31,740	26,439	32,872	27,269	34,023	27,269	34,023	37%	7,198	9,148	9,098	11,573	10,917	13,888	6,467	8,136	8,196	10,335	9,656	12,202
Program Assistant	GS-4-GS-7	5	25,623	31,740	26,439	32,872	27,269	34,023	27,269	34,023	37%	7,198	9,148	9,098	11,573	10,917	13,888	6,467	8,136	8,196	10,335	9,656	12,202
Management and Program Clerk	GS-4-GS-7	5	25,623	31,740	26,439	32,872	27,269	34,023	27,269	34,023	37%	7,198	9,148	9,098	11,573	10,917	13,888	6,467	8,136	8,196	10,335	9,656	12,202
Management and Program Assistant	GS-4-GS-7	5	25,623	31,740	26,439	32,872	27,269	34,023	27,269	34,023	37%	7,198	9,148	9,098	11,573	10,917	13,888	6,467	8,136	8,196	10,335	9,656	12,202
Data Transcriber Series																							
Data Transcriber	GS-1-GS-4	2	18,698	22,902	18,698	23,718	18,698	24,548	18,698	24,548	37%	4,114	6,600	5,142	8,349	6,170	10,019	4,103	5,870	5,080	7,456	5,862	8,803
Supervisory Data Transcriber	GS-1-GS-4	2	18,698	22,902	18,698	23,718	18,698	24,548	18,698	24,548	37%	4,114	6,600	5,142	8,349	6,170	10,019	4,103	5,870	5,080	7,456	5,862	8,803
Telephone Operating Series																							
Telephone Operator	GS-3-GS-4	3	20,401	22,902	21,128	23,718	21,868	24,548	21,868	24,548	37%	5,880	6,600	7,439	8,349	8,926	10,019	5,229	5,870	6,642	7,456	7,843	8,803
Lead Telephone Operator	GS-3-GS-4	3	20,401	22,902	21,128	23,718	21,868	24,548	21,868	24,548	37%	5,880	6,600	7,439	8,349	8,926	10,019	5,229	5,870	6,642	7,456	7,843	8,803
Supervisory Telephone Operator	GS-3-GS-4	3	20,401	22,902	21,128	23,718	21,868	24,548	21,868	24,548	37%	5,880	6,600	7,439	8,349	8,926	10,019	5,229	5,870	6,642	7,456	7,843	8,803
Telecommunications Processing Series																							
Telecommunications Equipment Operator	GS-5-GS-8	6	5-8	25,623	35,151	25,623	35,151	25,623	35,151	25,623	35,151	26,537	36,405	27,466	37,680	27,466	37,680	27,466	37,680	28,443	39,021	28,443	39,021
Lead Telecommunications Equipment Operator	GS-5-GS-8	6	5-8	25,623	35,151	25,623	35,151	25,623	35,151	25,623	35,151	26,537	36,405	27,466	37,680	27,466	37,680	27,466	37,680	28,443	39,021	28,443	39,021
Supervisory Telecommunications Equipment Operator	GS-5-GS-8	6	5-8	25,623	35,151	25,623	35,151	25,623	35,151	25,623	35,151	26,537	36,405	27,466	37,680	27,466	37,680	27,466	37,680	28,443	39,021	28,443	39,021
Telecommunications Series																							
Telecommunications Specialist	GS-5-GS-15	9	38,824	93,063	39,738	96,387	40,667	99,767	40,667	99,767														
Telecommunications Manager	GS-5-GS-15	9	38,824	93,063	39,738	96,387	40,667	99,767	40,667	99,767														

Chart II - U.S. Federal - Job Titles - Salaries - Pension Estimates

Mathematics _ Statistics

Operations Research Series

U.S. Federal Government Agencies	GS Grade Range:	GS Grade Median	2010 Median Grade Min Salary (STEP 1)	2010 Maximum Grade Salary (STEP 1)	2011 Median Grade Min Salary (STEP 2)	2011 Maximum Grade Salary (STEP 2)	2012 Median Grade Min Salary (STEP 3)	2012 Maximum Grade Salary (STEP 3)	2013 Median Grade Min Salary (STEP 4)	2013 Maximum Grade Salary (STEP 4)	10-Year Cumulative Raise Percentage (1.96%) + Step Increase Percentage (1.7%)	20-Year Annual Pension Benefit Estimate (Min.)	20-Year Annual Pension Benefit Estimate (Max.)	25-Year Annual Pension Benefit Estimate (Min.)	25-Year Annual Pension Benefit Estimate (Max.)	30-Year Annual Pension Benefit Estimate (Min.)	30-Year Annual Pension Benefit Estimate (Max.)	Agency Automatic Contributions 1% Thrift Savings Plan 20 Year Savings Plus 4.5% Interest (Min)	Agency Automatic Contributions 1% Thrift Savings Plan 20 Year Savings Plus 4.5% Interest (Max)	Agency Automatic Contributions 1% Thrift Savings Plan 25 Year Savings Plus 4.5% Interest (Min)	Agency Automatic Contributions 1% Thrift Savings Plan 25 Year Savings Plus 4.5% Interest (Max)	Agency Automatic Contributions 1% Thrift Savings Plan 30 Year Savings Plus 4.5% Interest (Min)	Agency Automatic Contributions 1% Thrift Savings Plan 30 Year Savings Plus 4.5% Interest (Max)
Operations Research Analyst	GS-1-GS-13	5	25,623	66,951	25,623	69,339	25,623	71,767	25,623	71,767	37%	5,637	19,297	7,046	24,413	8,456	29,295	5,623	17,161	6,962	21,800	8,033	25,738
Supervisory Operations Research Analyst	GS-1-GS-13	5	25,623	66,951	25,623	69,339	25,623	71,767	25,623	71,767	37%	5,637	19,297	7,046	24,413	8,456	29,295	5,623	17,161	6,962	21,800	8,033	25,738

Statistical Assistant Series

U.S. Federal Government Agencies	GS Grade Range:	GS Grade Median	2010 STEP 1 Min	2010 STEP 1 Max	2011 STEP 2 Min	2011 STEP 2 Max	2012 STEP 3 Min	2012 STEP 3 Max	2013 STEP 4 Min	2013 STEP 4 Max	10-Year	20-Yr Min	20-Yr Max	25-Yr Min	25-Yr Max	30-Yr Min	30-Yr Max	20 Yr Min	20 Yr Max	25 Yr Min	25 Yr Max	30 Yr Min	30 Yr Max
Statistical Clerk	GS-3-GS-9	5	25,623	38,824	26,350	40,208	27,090	41,616	27,090	41,616	37%	7,029	11,189	8,875	14,156	10,650	16,987	6,375	9,951	8,061	12,641	9,480	14,925
Statistical Assistant	GS-3-GS-9	5	25,623	38,824	26,350	40,208	27,090	41,616	27,090	41,616	37%	7,029	11,189	8,875	14,156	10,650	16,987	6,375	9,951	8,061	12,641	9,480	14,925

Sheet 15: Medical_ Dental_ Public Health

Medical Officer Series

U.S. Federal Government Agencies	GS Grade Range:	GS Grade Median	2010 Median Grade Min Salary (STEP 1)	2010 Maximum Grade Salary (STEP 1)	2011 Median Grade Min Salary (STEP 2)	2011 Maximum Grade Salary (STEP 2)	2012 Median Grade Min Salary (STEP 3)	2012 Maximum Grade Salary (STEP 3)	2013 Median Grade Min Salary (STEP 4)	2013 Maximum Grade Salary (STEP 4)	10-Year Cumulative Raise Percentage (1.96%) + Step Increase Percentage (1.7%)	20-Year Annual Pension Benefit Estimate (Min.)	20-Year Annual Pension Benefit Estimate (Max.)	25-Year Annual Pension Benefit Estimate (Min.)	25-Year Annual Pension Benefit Estimate (Max.)	30-Year Annual Pension Benefit Estimate (Min.)	30-Year Annual Pension Benefit Estimate (Max.)	Agency 20 Year Savings Plus 4.5% Interest (Min)	Agency 20 Year Savings Plus 4.5% Interest (Max)	Agency 25 Year Savings Plus 4.5% Interest (Min)	Agency 25 Year Savings Plus 4.5% Interest (Max)	Agency 30 Year Savings Plus 4.5% Interest (Min)	Agency 30 Year Savings Plus 4.5% Interest (Max)
Medical Officer	GS-12-GS-15	13	66,951	93,063	68,959	96,387	71,001	99,767	93,903	99,767	37%	23,609	26,832	29,756	33,946	35,707	40,735	20,837	23,859	26,491	30,309	31,445	35,786

Nurse Series

U.S. Federal Government Agencies	GS Grade Range:	GS Grade Median	2010 STEP 1 Min	2010 STEP 1 Max	2011 STEP 2 Min	2011 STEP 2 Max	2012 STEP 3 Min	2012 STEP 3 Max	2013 STEP 4 Min	2013 STEP 4 Max	10-Year	20-Yr Min	20-Yr Max	25-Yr Min	25-Yr Max	30-Yr Min	30-Yr Max	20 Yr Min	20 Yr Max	25 Yr Min	25 Yr Max	30 Yr Min	30 Yr Max
Nurse	GS-4-GS-12	8	35,151	56,301	35,967	58,309	36,797	60,351	59,699	60,351	37%	14,333	16,227	18,016	20,529	21,619	24,635	12,626	14,431	16,049	18,332	19,105	21,644
Clinical Nurse	GS-4-GS-12	8	35,151	56,301	35,967	58,309	36,797	60,351	36,797	60,351	37%	9,295	16,227	11,718	20,529	14,062	24,635	8,558	14,431	10,784	18,332	12,643	21,644
Community Health Nurse	GS-4-GS-12	8	35,151	56,301	35,967	58,309	36,797	60,351	36,797	76,981	37%	9,295	19,886	11,718	25,103	14,062	30,123	8,558	17,386	10,784	22,155	12,643	26,336
Occupational Health Nurse	GS-4-GS-12	8	35,151	56,301	35,967	58,309	36,797	60,351	55,495	76,981	37%	13,408	19,886	16,860	25,103	20,232	30,123	11,880	17,386	15,083	22,155	17,919	26,336
Operating Room Nurse	GS-4-GS-12	8	35,151	56,301	35,967	58,309	36,797	60,351	55,495	76,981	37%	13,408	19,886	16,860	25,103	20,232	30,123	11,880	17,386	15,083	22,155	17,919	26,336
Psychiatric Nurse	GS-4-GS-12	8	35,151	56,301	35,967	58,309	36,797	60,351	36,797	76,981	37%	9,295	19,886	11,718	25,103	14,062	30,123	8,558	17,386	10,784	22,155	12,643	26,336
Nurse Anesthetist	GS-4-GS-12	8	35,151	56,301	35,967	58,309	36,797	60,351	36,797	60,351	37%	9,295	16,227	11,718	20,529	14,062	24,635	8,558	14,431	10,784	18,332	12,643	21,644
Nurse Consultant	GS-4-GS-12	8	35,151	56,301	35,967	58,309	36,797	60,351	53,427	60,351	37%	12,953	16,227	16,291	20,529	19,549	24,635	11,512	14,431	14,608	18,332	17,336	21,644
Nurse Educator	GS-4-GS-12	8	35,151	56,301	35,967	58,309	36,797	60,351	53,427	88,913	37%	12,953	22,511	16,291	28,384	19,549	34,061	11,512	19,506	14,608	24,898	17,336	29,703
Nurse Midwife	GS-4-GS-12	8	35,151	56,301	35,967	58,309	36,797	60,351	53,427	88,913	37%	12,953	22,511	16,291	28,384	19,549	34,061	11,512	19,506	14,608	24,898	17,336	29,703
Nurse Practitioner	GS-4-GS-12	8	35,151	56,301	35,967	58,309	36,797	60,351	53,427	60,351	37%	12,953	16,227	16,291	20,529	19,549	24,635	11,512	14,431	14,608	18,332	17,336	21,644
Nurse Specialist	GS-4-GS-12	8	35,151	56,301	35,967	58,309	36,797	60,351	36,797	60,351	37%	9,295	16,227	11,718	20,529	14,062	24,635	8,558	14,431	10,784	18,332	12,643	21,644
Research Nurse	GS-4-GS-12	8	35,151	56,301	35,967	58,309	36,797	60,351	36,797	95,502	37%	9,295	23,961	11,718	30,196	14,062	36,235	8,558	20,676	10,784	26,413	12,643	31,562
Supervisory Positions	GS-4-GS-12	8	35,151	56,301	35,967	58,309	36,797	60,351	65,359	95,502	37%	15,578	23,961	19,572	30,196	23,487	36,235	13,632	20,676	17,351	26,413	20,702	31,562

Medical Supply Aide and Technician Series

Chart II - U.S. Federal - Job Titles - Salaries - Pension Estimates

U.S. Federal Government Agencies	GS Grade Range:	GS Grade Median	2010 Median Grade Min Salary (STEP 1)	2010 Maximum Grade Salary (STEP 1)	2011 Median Grade Min Salary (STEP 2)	2011 Maximum Grade Salary (STEP 2)	2012 Median Grade Min Salary (STEP 3)	2012 Maximum Grade Salary (STEP 3)	2013 Median Grade Min Salary (STEP 4)	2013 Maximum Grade Salary (STEP 4)	10-Year Cumulative Raise Percentage (1.96%) + Step Increase Percentage (1.7%)	20-Year Annual Pension Benefit Estimate (Min.)	20-Year Annual Pension Benefit Estimate (Max.)	25-Year Annual Pension Benefit Estimate (Min.)	25-Year Annual Pension Benefit Estimate (Max.)	30-Year Annual Pension Benefit Estimate (Min.)	30-Year Annual Pension Benefit Estimate (Max.)	Agency Automatic Contributions 1% Thrift Plan 20 Year Savings Plus 4.5% Interest (Min)	Agency Automatic Contributions 1% Thrift Plan 20 Year Savings Plus 4.5% Interest (Max)	Agency Automatic Contributions 1% Thrift Plan 25 Year Savings Plus 4.5% Interest (Min)	Agency Automatic Contributions 1% Thrift Plan 25 Year Savings Plus 4.5% Interest (Max)	Agency Automatic Contributions 1% Thrift Plan 30 Year Savings Plus 4.5% Interest (Min)	Agency Automatic Contribution 1% Thrift Plan (Max)
Medical Supply Aide	GS-2-GS-6	3	20,401	28,562	21,128	29,580	21,868	30,616	21,868	51,017	37%	5,880	12,720	7,439	16,024	8,926	19,229	5,229	10,945	6,642	13,990	7,843	16,73
Medical Supply Technician	GS-2-GS-6	3	20,401	28,562	21,128	29,580	21,868	30,616	57,019	51,017	37%	13,613	12,720	17,105	16,024	20,526	19,229	11,474	10,945	14,724	13,990	17,760	16,73

Dietitian and Nutritionist Series

U.S. Federal Government Agencies	GS Grade Range:	GS Grade Median	2010 Median Grade Min Salary (STEP 1)	2010 Maximum Grade Salary (STEP 1)	2011 Median Grade Min Salary (STEP 2)	2011 Maximum Grade Salary (STEP 2)	2012 Median Grade Min Salary (STEP 3)	2012 Maximum Grade Salary (STEP 3)	2013 Median Grade Min Salary (STEP 4)	2013 Maximum Grade Salary (STEP 4)	10-Year %	20-Yr (Min.)	20-Yr (Max.)	25-Yr (Min.)	25-Yr (Max.)	30-Yr (Min.)	30-Yr (Max.)	20Yr+4.5% (Min)	20Yr+4.5% (Max)	25Yr+4.5% (Min)	25Yr+4.5% (Max)	30Yr+4.5% (Min)	30Yr+4.5% (Max)
Dietitian	GS-5-GS-13	8	35,151	66,951	36,065	69,339	36,994	71,767	36,994	71,767	37%	9,481	19,297	11,963	24,413	14,355	29,295	8,659	17,161	10,931	21,800	12,837	25,73
Public Health Nutritionist	GS-5-GS-13	8	35,151	66,951	36,065	69,339	36,994	71,767	57,395	114,522	37%	13,969	28,703	17,573	36,170	21,087	43,404	12,283	24,757	15,622	31,629	18,593	37,80
Nutritionist	GS-5-GS-13	8	35,151	66,951	36,065	69,339	36,994	71,767	57,395	114,522	37%	13,969	28,703	17,573	36,170	21,087	43,404	12,283	24,757	15,622	31,629	18,593	37,80
Supervisory	GS-5-GS-13	8	35,151	66,951	36,065	69,339	36,994	71,767	57,395	114,522	37%	13,969	28,703	17,573	36,170	21,087	43,404	12,283	24,757	15,622	31,629	18,593	37,80

Occupational Therapist Series

Title	Range	Median	2010 Min	2010 Max	2011 Min	2011 Max	2012 Min	2012 Max	2013 Min	2013 Max	10-Yr	20(Min)	20(Max)	25(Min)	25(Max)	30(Min)	30(Max)	20T(Min)	20T(Max)	25T(Min)	25T(Max)	30T(Min)	30T(Max)
Occupational Therapist	GS-6-GS-13	9	38,824	66,951	39,842	69,339	40,878	71,767	83,633	71,767	37%	19,896	19,297	24,994	24,413	29,993	29,295	17,168	17,161	21,917	21,800	26,260	25,73
Supervisory Occupational Therapist	GS-6-GS-13	9	38,824	66,951	39,842	69,339	40,878	71,767	83,633	103,507	37%	19,896	26,280	24,994	33,141	29,993	39,769	17,168	22,800	21,917	29,097	26,260	34,69
Occupational Therapy Educator	GS-6-GS-13	9	38,824	66,951	39,842	69,339	40,878	71,767	83,633	103,507	37%	19,896	26,280	24,994	33,141	29,993	39,769	17,168	22,800	21,917	29,097	26,260	34,69

Rehabilitation Therapy Assistant Series

Title	Range	Median	2010 Min	2010 Max	2011 Min	2011 Max	2012 Min	2012 Max	2013 Min	2013 Max	10-Yr	20(Min)	20(Max)	25(Min)	25(Max)	30(Min)	30(Max)	20T(Min)	20T(Max)	25T(Min)	25T(Max)	30T(Min)	30T(Max)
Therapy Aid applies	GS-1-GS-6	4	22,902	28,562	22,902	29,580	22,902	30,616	22,902	30,616	37%	5,038	8,232	6,298	10,414	7,558	12,497	5,026	7,321	6,222	9,300	7,180	10,98
Occupational Therapy Assistant	GS-1-GS-6	4	22,902	28,562	22,902	29,580	22,902	30,616	54,642	59,178	37%	12,021	14,515	15,027	18,269	18,032	21,922	10,664	12,395	13,519	15,866	16,135	19,03
Physical Therapy Assistant	GS-1-GS-6	4	22,902	28,562	22,902	29,580	22,902	30,616	54,642	59,178	37%	12,021	14,515	15,027	18,269	18,032	21,922	10,664	12,395	13,519	15,866	16,135	19,03
Kinesiotherapy Assistant	GS-1-GS-6	4	22,902	28,562	22,902	29,580	22,902	30,616	54,642	59,178	37%	12,021	14,515	15,027	18,269	18,032	21,922	10,664	12,395	13,519	15,866	16,135	19,03
Manual Arts Therapy Assistant	GS-1-GS-6	4	22,902	28,562	22,902	29,580	22,902	30,616	22,902	59,178	37%	5,038	14,515	6,298	18,269	7,558	21,922	5,026	12,395	6,222	15,866	7,180	19,03
Educational Therapy Assistant	GS-1-GS-6	4	22,902	28,562	22,902	29,580	22,902	30,616	22,902	30,616	37%	5,038	8,232	6,298	10,414	7,558	12,497	5,026	7,321	6,222	9,300	7,180	10,98
Therapy Assistant	GS-1-GS-6	4	22,902	28,562	22,902	29,580	22,902	30,616	51,464	30,616	37%	11,322	8,232	14,153	10,414	16,983	12,497	10,100	7,321	12,789	9,300	15,239	10,98

Health Aid and Technician Series

Title	Range	Median	2010 Min	2010 Max	2011 Min	2011 Max	2012 Min	2012 Max	2013 Min	2013 Max	10-Yr	20(Min)	20(Max)	25(Min)	25(Max)	30(Min)	30(Max)	20T(Min)	20T(Max)	25T(Min)	25T(Max)	30T(Min)	30T(Max)
Health Aid	GS-1-GS-4	2	18,698	22,902	18,698	23,718	18,698	24,548	47,260	24,548	37%	10,397	6,600	12,997	8,349	15,596	10,019	9,177	5,870	11,647	7,456	13,921	8,80
Health Technician	GS-1-GS-4	2	18,698	22,902	18,698	23,718	18,698	24,548	18,698	24,548	37%	4,114	6,600	5,142	8,349	6,170	10,019	4,103	5,870	5,080	7,456	5,862	8,80

Pathology Technician Series

Title	Range	Median	2010 Min	2010 Max	2011 Min	2011 Max	2012 Min	2012 Max	2013 Min	2013 Max	10-Yr	20(Min)	20(Max)	25(Min)	25(Max)	30(Min)	30(Max)	20T(Min)	20T(Max)	25T(Min)	25T(Max)	30T(Min)	30T(Max)
Pathology Aid applies	GS-1-GS-7	4	1-7	16,630	31,740	16,630	31,740	16,630	31,740	16,630	31,740	16,630	32,872	16,630	34,023	63,604	34,023	63,604	34,023	63,604	35,234	63,604	35,23
Cytology Technician	GS-1-GS-7	4	1-7	16,630	31,740	16,630	31,740	16,630	31,740	16,630	31,740	16,630	32,872	16,630	34,023	16,630	62,585	16,630	62,585	16,630	63,796	16,630	63,79
Histopathology Technician	GS-1-GS-7	4	1-7	16,630	31,740	16,630	31,740	16,630	31,740	16,630	31,740	16,630	32,872	16,630	34,023	16,630	62,585	16,630	62,585	16,630	63,796	16,630	63,79
Pathology Technician	GS-1-GS-7	4	1-7	16,630	31,740	16,630	31,740	16,630	31,740	16,630	31,740	16,630	32,872	16,630	34,023	83,581	62,585	83,581	62,585	83,581	63,796	83,581	63,79

Medical Instrument Technician Series

Title	Range	Median	2010 Min	2010 Max	2011 Min	2011 Max	2012 Min	2012 Max	2013 Min	2013 Max	10-Yr	20(Min)	20(Max)	25(Min)	25(Max)	30(Min)	30(Max)	20T(Min)	20T(Max)	25T(Min)	25T(Max)	30T(Min)	30T(Max)
General Schedule Supervisory Guide	GS-4-GS-8	6	28,562	35,151	29,378	36,405	30,208	37,680	58,770	37,680	37%	14,129	10,132	17,761	12,818	21,313	15,381	12,186	9,010	15,560	11,446	18,636	13,51
Introduction to the Position Classification Standards	GS-4-GS-8	6	28,562	35,151	29,378	36,405	30,208	37,680	58,770	93,981	37%	14,129	22,518	17,761	28,300	21,313	33,960	12,186	19,012	15,560	24,389	18,636	29,3

Medical Technical Assistant Series

Chart II - U.S. Federal - Job Titles - Salaries - Pension Estimates

U.S. Federal Government Agencies	GS Grade Range:	GS Grade Median	2010 Median Grade Min Salary (STEP 1)	2010 Maximum Grade Salary (STEP 1)	2011 Median Grade Min Salary (STEP 2)	2011 Maximum Grade Salary (STEP 2)	2012 Median Grade Min Salary (STEP 3)	2012 Maximum Grade Salary (STEP 3)	2013 Median Grade Min Salary (STEP 4)	2013 Maximum Grade Salary (STEP 4)	10-Year Cumulative Raise Percentage (1.96%) + Step Increase Percentage (1.7%)	20-Year Annual Pension Benefit Estimate (Min.)	20-Year Annual Pension Benefit Estimate (Max.)	25-Year Annual Pension Benefit Estimate (Min.)	25-Year Annual Pension Benefit Estimate (Max.)	30-Year Annual Pension Benefit Estimate (Min.)	30-Year Annual Pension Benefit Estimate (Max.)	Agency Automatic Contributions 1% Thrift Plan 20 Year Savings Plus 4.5% Interest (Min)	Agency Automatic Contributions 1% Thrift Plan 20 Year Savings Plus 4.5% Interest (Max)	Agency Automatic Contributions 1% Thrift Plan 25 Year Savings Plus 4.5% Interest (Min)	Agency Automatic Contributions 1% Thrift Plan 25 Year Savings Plus 4.5% Interest (Max)	Agency Automatic Contributions 1% Thrift Plan 30 Year Savings Plus 4.5% Interest (Min)	Agency Automatic Contributions 1% Thrift Plan 30 Year Savings Plus 4.5% Interest (Max)
Part I, Medical Technical Assistant	GS-6-GS-12	8	35,151	56,301	36,169	58,309	37,205	60,351	37,205	80,752	37%	9,681	20,716	12,226	26,140	14,671	31,368	8,767	18,056	11,090	23,022	13,046	27,400
Part II, Chief Medical Technical Assistant	GS-6-GS-12	8	35,151	56,301	36,169	58,309	37,205	60,351	37,205	80,752	37%	9,681	20,716	12,226	26,140	14,671	31,368	8,767	18,056	11,090	23,022	13,046	27,400

Pharmacy Technician Series

U.S. Federal Government Agencies	GS Grade Range:	GS Grade Median	2010 Median	2010 Max	2011 Median	2011 Max	2012 Median	2012 Max	2013 Median	2013 Max	%	20Min	20Max	25Min	25Max	30Min	30Max	20Min	20Max	25Min	25Max	30Min	30Max
Pharmacy Aid	GS-1-GS-5	3	20,401	25,623	20,401	26,537	20,401	27,466	20,401	50,368	37%	4,488	12,423	5,610	15,640	6,732	18,769	4,477	10,636	5,543	13,608	6,396	16,312
Pharmacy Technician	GS-1-GS-5	3	20,401	25,623	20,401	26,537	20,401	27,466	40,802	50,368	37%	8,976	12,423	11,221	15,640	13,465	18,769	8,101	10,636	10,233	13,608	12,152	16,312
Supervisory Pharmacy Technician	GS-1-GS-5	3	20,401	25,623	20,401	26,537	20,401	27,466	40,802	27,466	37%	8,976	7,385	11,221	9,342	13,465	11,211	8,101	6,568	10,233	8,343	12,152	9,850

Optometrist Series

U.S. Federal Government Agencies	GS Grade Range:	GS Grade Median	2010 Median	2010 Max	2011 Median	2011 Max	2012 Median	2012 Max	2013 Median	2013 Max	%	20Min	20Max	25Min	25Max	30Min	30Max	20Min	20Max	25Min	25Max	30Min	30Max
Optometrist	GS-9-GS-12	10	42,755	56,301	44,139	58,309	45,547	60,351	68,449	95,502	37%	17,093	23,961	21,535	30,196	25,842	36,235	14,882	20,676	18,974	26,413	22,619	31,562
Optometrist	GS-9-GS-12	10	42,755	56,301	44,139	58,309	45,547	60,351	68,449	95,502	37%	17,093	23,961	21,535	30,196	25,842	36,235	14,882	20,676	18,974	26,413	22,619	31,562
Research Optometrist	GS-9-GS-12	10	42,755	56,301	44,139	58,309	45,547	60,351	45,547	60,351	37%	12,054	16,227	15,237	20,529	18,284	24,635	10,814	14,431	13,709	18,332	16,157	21,644
Optometrist	GS-9-GS-12	10	42,755	56,301	44,139	58,309	45,547	60,351	45,547	60,351	37%	12,054	16,227	15,237	20,529	18,284	24,635	10,814	14,431	13,709	18,332	16,157	21,644

Restoration Technician Series

U.S. Federal Government Agencies	GS Grade Range:	GS Grade Median	2010 Median	2010 Max	2011 Median	2011 Max	2012 Median	2012 Max	2013 Median	2013 Max	%	20Min	20Max	25Min	25Max	30Min	30Max	20Min	20Max	25Min	25Max	30Min	30Max
Ear inserts	GS-7-GS-11	8	7-11	31,740	46,974	31,740	46,974	31,740	46,974	31,740	46,974	32,872	48,649	34,023	50,353	69,174	89,177	69,174	89,177	70,385	90,969	70,385	90,969
Artificial eyes	GS-7-GS-11	8	7-11	31,740	46,974	31,740	46,974	31,740	46,974	31,740	46,974	32,872	48,649	34,023	50,353	34,023	89,177	34,023	89,177	35,234	90,969	35,234	90,969
Facial and body	GS-7-GS-11	8	7-11	31,740	46,974	31,740	46,974	31,740	46,974	31,740	46,974	32,872	48,649	34,023	50,353	34,023	50,353	34,023	50,353	35,234	52,145	35,234	52,145

Orthotist and Prosthetist Series

U.S. Federal Government Agencies	GS Grade Range:	GS Grade Median	2010 Median	2010 Max	2011 Median	2011 Max	2012 Median	2012 Max	2013 Median	2013 Max	%	20Min	20Max	25Min	25Max	30Min	30Max	20Min	20Max	25Min	25Max	30Min	30Max
Orthotic-Prosthetic Aid	GS-3-GS-9	6	28,562	38,824	29,289	40,208	30,029	41,616	68,853	76,767	37%	16,216	18,923	20,359	23,822	24,431	28,587	13,917	16,196	17,785	20,722	21,355	24,843
Orthotist	GS-3-GS-9	6	28,562	38,824	29,289	40,208	30,029	41,616	68,853	41,616	37%	16,216	11,189	20,359	14,156	24,431	16,987	13,917	9,951	17,785	12,641	21,355	14,925
Prosthetist	GS-3-GS-9	6	28,562	38,824	29,289	40,208	30,029	41,616	30,029	41,616	37%	7,675	11,189	9,683	14,156	11,619	16,987	7,020	9,951	8,860	12,641	10,401	14,925
Orthotist-Prosthetist	GS-3-GS-9	6	28,562	38,824	29,289	40,208	30,029	41,616	30,029	60,314	37%	7,675	15,303	9,683	19,298	11,619	23,157	7,020	13,273	8,860	16,940	10,401	20,200

Medical Records Administration Series

U.S. Federal Government Agencies	GS Grade Range:	GS Grade Median	2010 Median	2010 Max	2011 Median	2011 Max	2012 Median	2012 Max	2013 Median	2013 Max	%	20Min	20Max	25Min	25Max	30Min	30Max	20Min	20Max	25Min	25Max	30Min	30Max
Medical Records Administrator	GS-9-GS-14	11	46,974	79,115	48,358	81,936	49,766	84,805	49,766	103,503	37%	12,982	26,915	16,397	33,988	19,676	40,786	11,740	23,600	14,855	30,058	17,480	35,689
Medical Records Administration Specialist	GS-9-GS-14	11	46,974	79,115	48,358	81,936	49,766	84,805	49,766	84,805	37%	12,982	22,802	16,397	28,847	19,676	34,616	11,740	20,279	14,855	25,760	17,480	30,414

Health System Administration Series

U.S. Federal Government Agencies	GS Grade Range:	GS Grade Median	2010 Median	2010 Max	2011 Median	2011 Max	2012 Median	2012 Max	2013 Median	2013 Max	%	20Min	20Max	25Min	25Max	30Min	30Max	20Min	20Max	25Min	25Max	30Min	30Max
Health System Administrator	GS-12-GS-15	13	66,951	93,063	68,959	96,387	71,001	99,767	89,699	99,767	37%	22,684	26,832	28,600	33,946	34,320	40,735	20,090	23,859	25,524	30,309	30,259	35,786

Hospital Housekeeping Management Series

U.S. Federal Government Agencies	GS Grade Range:	GS Grade Median	2010 Median	2010 Max	2011 Median	2011 Max	2012 Median	2012 Max	2013 Median	2013 Max	%	20Min	20Max	25Min	25Max	30Min	30Max	20Min	20Max	25Min	25Max	30Min	30Max
Hospital Housekeeping Assistant	GS-5-GS-7	6	28,562	31,740	29,476	32,872	30,405	34,023	30,405	34,023	37%	8,031	9,148	10,151	11,573	12,181	13,888	7,213	8,136	9,141	10,335	10,771	12,202
Assistant Hospital Housekeeping Officer	GS-5-GS-7	6	28,562	31,740	29,476	32,872	30,405	34,023	30,405	34,023	37%	8,031	9,148	10,151	11,573	12,181	13,888	7,213	8,136	9,141	10,335	10,771	12,202
Hospital Housekeeping Officer	GS-5-GS-7	6	28,562	31,740	29,476	32,872	30,405	34,023	30,405	34,023	37%	8,031	9,148	10,151	11,573	12,181	13,888	7,213	8,136	9,141	10,335	10,771	12,202

Chart II - U.S. Federal - Job Titles - Salaries - Pension Estimates

U.S. Federal Government Agencies	GS Grade Range:	GS Grade Median	2010 Median Grade Min Salary (STEP 1)	2010 Maximum Grade Salary (STEP 1)	2011 Median Grade Min Salary (STEP 2)	2011 Maximum Grade Salary (STEP 2)	2012 Median Grade Min Salary (STEP 3)	2012 Maximum Grade Salary (STEP 3)	2013 Median Grade Min Salary (STEP 4)	2013 Maximum Grade Salary (STEP 4)	10-Year Cumulative Raise Percentage + Step Increase Percentage (1.96%) (1.7%)	20-Year Annual Pension Benefit Estimate (Min.)	20-Year Annual Pension Benefit Estimate (Max.)	25-Year Annual Pension Benefit Estimate (Min.)	25-Year Annual Pension Benefit Estimate (Max.)	30-Year Annual Pension Benefit Estimate (Min.)	30-Year Annual Pension Benefit Estimate (Max.)	Agency Automatic Contributions 1% Thrift Savings Plan 20 Year Plus 4.5% Interest (Min)	Agency Automatic Contributions 1% Thrift Savings Plan 20 Year Plus 4.5% Interest (Max)	Agency Automatic Contributions 1% Thrift Savings Plan 25 Year Plus 4.5% Interest (Min)	Agency Automatic Contributions 1% Thrift Savings Plan 25 Year Plus 4.5% Interest (Max)	Agency Automatic Contributions 1% Thrift Savings Plan 30 Year Plus 4.5% Interest (Min)	Agency Automatic Contributions 1% Thrift Savings Plan 30 Year Plus 4.5% Interest (Max)
Hospital Housekeeping Program Specialist	GS-5-GS-7	6	28,562	31,740	29,476	32,872	30,405	34,023	30,405	34,023	37%	8,031	9,148	10,151	11,573	12,181	13,888	7,213	8,136	9,141	10,335	10,771	12,202

Dental Officer Series

Dental Officer	GS-11-GS-14	12	56,301	79,115	57,976	81,936	59,680	84,805	59,680	84,805	37%	15,591	22,802	19,693	28,847	23,632	34,616	14,087	20,279	17,829	25,760	20,983	30,414

Dental Assistant Series

Dental Aid	GS-2-GS-6	3	20,401	28,562	21,128	29,580	21,868	30,616	21,868	30,616	37%	5,880	8,232	7,439	10,414	8,926	12,497	5,229	7,321	6,642	9,300	7,843	10,980
Dental Assistant	GS-2-GS-6	3	20,401	28,562	21,128	29,580	21,868	30,616	21,868	30,616	37%	5,880	8,232	7,439	10,414	8,926	12,497	5,229	7,321	6,642	9,300	7,843	10,980

Dental Laboratory Aid and Technician Series

Dental Laboratory Aid	GS-1-GS-9	4	22,902	38,824	22,902	40,208	22,902	41,616	22,902	41,616	37%	5,038	11,189	6,298	14,156	7,558	16,987	5,026	9,951	6,222	12,641	7,180	14,925
Dental Laboratory Technician	GS-1-GS-9	4	22,902	38,824	22,902	40,208	22,902	41,616	22,902	41,616	37%	5,038	11,189	6,298	14,156	7,558	16,987	5,026	9,951	6,222	12,641	7,180	14,925

Public Health Program Specialist Series

Public Health Advisor	GS-5-GS-13	8	35,151	66,951	36,065	69,339	36,994	71,767	36,994	71,767	37%	9,481	19,297	11,963	24,413	14,355	29,295	8,659	17,161	10,931	21,800	12,837	25,738
Public Health, Analyst	GS-5-GS-13	8	35,151	66,951	36,065	69,339	36,994	71,767	36,994	71,767	37%	9,481	19,297	11,963	24,413	14,355	29,295	8,659	17,161	10,931	21,800	12,837	25,738
Supervisory Positions	GS-5-GS-13	8	35,151	66,951	36,065	69,339	36,994	71,767	36,994	71,767	37%	9,481	19,297	11,963	24,413	14,355	29,295	8,659	17,161	10,931	21,800	12,837	25,738

Sanitarian Series

Sanitarian	GS-5-GS-15	9	38,824	93,063	39,738	96,387	40,667	99,767	40,667	99,767	37%	10,289	26,832	12,973	33,946	15,567	40,735	9,465	23,859	11,929	30,309	13,988	35,786
Supervisory Sanitarian.	GS-5-GS-15	9	38,824	93,063	39,738	96,387	40,667	99,767	40,667	99,767	37%	10,289	26,832	12,973	33,946	15,567	40,735	9,465	23,859	11,929	30,309	13,988	35,786
Industrial Hygiene Series*	GS-5-GS-15	9	38,824	93,063	39,738	96,387	40,667	99,767	40,667	99,767	37%	10,289	26,832	12,973	33,946	15,567	40,735	9,465	23,859	11,929	30,309	13,988	35,786
General Schedule Supervisory Guide	GS-5-GS-15	9	38,824	93,063	39,738	96,387	40,667	99,767	40,667	99,767	37%	10,289	26,832	12,973	33,946	15,567	40,735	9,465	23,859	11,929	30,309	13,988	35,786

Consumer Safety Series

Consumer Safety Officer	GS-5-GS-13	8	35,151	66,951	36,065	69,339	36,994	71,767	36,994	71,767	37%	9,481	19,297	11,963	24,413	14,355	29,295	8,659	17,161	10,931	21,800	12,837	25,738
Supervisory Consumer Safety Officer	GS-5-GS-13	8	35,151	66,951	36,065	69,339	36,994	71,767	36,994	71,767	37%	9,481	19,297	11,963	24,413	14,355	29,295	8,659	17,161	10,931	21,800	12,837	25,738

Environmental Health Technician Series

Environmental Health Aid	GS-1-GS-4	2	18,698	22,902	18,698	23,718	18,698	24,548	18,698	24,548	37%	4,114	6,600	5,142	8,349	6,170	10,019	4,103	5,870	5,080	7,456	5,862	8,803
Environmental Health Technician	GS-1-GS-4	2	18,698	22,902	18,698	23,718	18,698	24,548	18,698	24,548	37%	4,114	6,600	5,142	8,349	6,170	10,019	4,103	5,870	5,080	7,456	5,862	8,803
Supervisory Environmental Health Aid	GS-1-GS-4	2	18,698	22,902	18,698	23,718	18,698	24,548	18,698	24,548	37%	4,114	6,600	5,142	8,349	6,170	10,019	4,103	5,870	5,080	7,456	5,862	8,803
Supervisory Environmental Health Technician	GS-1-GS-4	2	18,698	22,902	18,698	23,718	18,698	24,548	18,698	24,548	37%	4,114	6,600	5,142	8,349	6,170	10,019	4,103	5,870	5,080	7,456	5,862	8,803

Chart II - U.S. Federal - Job Titles - Salaries - Pension Estimates

Physical Sciences

U.S. Federal Government Agencies	GS Grade Range:	GS Grade Median	2010 Median Grade Min Salary (STEP 1)	2010 Maximum Grade Salary (STEP 1)	2011 Median Grade Min Salary (STEP 2)	2011 Maximum Grade Salary (STEP 2)	2012 Median Grade Min Salary (STEP 3)	2012 Maximum Grade Salary (STEP 3)	2013 Median Grade Min Salary (STEP 4)	2013 Maximum Grade Salary (STEP 4)	10-Year Cumulative Raise Percentage (1.96%) + Step Increase Percentage (1.7%)	20-Year Annual Pension Benefit Estimate (Min.)	20-Year Annual Pension Benefit Estimate (Max.)	25-Year Annual Pension Benefit Estimate (Min.)	25-Year Annual Pension Benefit Estimate (Max.)	30-Year Annual Pension Benefit Estimate (Min.)	30-Year Annual Pension Benefit Estimate (Max.)	Agency Automatic Contributions 1% Thrift Savings Plan 20 Year Savings Plus 4.5% Interest (Min)	Agency Automatic Contributions 1% Thrift Savings Plan 20 Year Savings Plus 4.5% Interest (Max)	Agency Automatic Contributions 1% Thrift Savings Plan 25 Year Savings Plus 4.5% Interest (Min)	Agency Automatic Contributions 1% Thrift Savings Plan 25 Year Savings Plus 4.5% Interest (Max)	Agency Automatic Contributions 1% Thrift Savings Plan 30 Year Savings Plus 4.5% Interest (Min)	Agency Automatic Contributions 1% Thrift Savings Plan 30 Year Savings Plus 4.5% Interest (Max)
Microbiology Series																							
Microbiologist	GS-5-GS-13	9	38,824	66,951	39,738	69,339	40,667	71,767	66,290	71,767	37%	15,926	19,297	20,019	24,413	24,023	29,295	14,016	17,161	17,820	21,800	21,218	25,738
Supervisory Positions	GS-5-GS-13	9	38,824	66,951	39,738	69,339	40,667	71,767	40,667	118,741	37%	10,289	29,631	12,973	37,330	15,567	44,796	9,465	25,506	11,929	32,599	13,988	38,992
Plant Protection Technician Series																							
Plant Protection Aid	GS-2-GS-7	4	2-7	18,698	31,740	18,698	31,740	18,698	31,740	18,698	31,740	19,425	32,872	20,165	34,023	20,165	59,646	20,165	59,646	20,943	60,857	20,943	60,857
Plant Protection Technician	GS-2-GS-7	4	2-7	18,698	31,740	18,698	31,740	18,698	31,740	18,698	31,740	19,425	32,872	20,165	34,023	20,165	59,646	20,165	59,646	20,943	60,857	20,943	60,857
Supervisory Plant Protection Technician	GS-2-GS-7	4	2-7	18,698	31,740	18,698	31,740	18,698	31,740	18,698	31,740	19,425	32,872	20,165	34,023	67,139	59,646	67,139	59,646	67,917	60,857	67,917	60,857
Supervisory Plant Protection Technician	GS-2-GS-7	4	2-7	18,698	31,740	18,698	31,740	18,698	31,740	18,698	31,740	19,425	32,872	20,165	34,023	20,165	34,023	20,165	34,023	20,943	35,234	20,943	35,234
Irrigation System Operation Series*	GS-2-GS-7	4	2-7	18,698	31,740	18,698	31,740	18,698	31,740	18,698	31,740	19,425	32,872	20,165	34,023	20,165	34,023	20,165	34,023	20,943	35,234	20,943	35,234
Irrigation System Operator	GS-2-GS-7	4	2-7	18,698	31,740	18,698	31,740	18,698	31,740	18,698	31,740	19,425	32,872	20,165	34,023	45,788	54,424	45,788	54,424	46,566	55,635	46,566	55,635
Irrigation System Manager	GS-2-GS-7	4	2-7	18,698	31,740	18,698	31,740	18,698	31,740	18,698	31,740	19,425	32,872	20,165	34,023	45,788	54,424	45,788	54,424	46,566	55,635	46,566	55,635
Forestry Technician Series																							
Forestry Aid	GS-3-GS-4	3	20,401	22,902	21,128	23,718	21,868	24,548	21,868	24,548	37%	5,880	6,600	7,439	8,349	8,926	10,019	5,229	5,870	6,642	7,456	7,843	8,803
Forestry Technician	GS-3-GS-4	3	20,401	22,902	21,128	23,718	21,868	24,548	42,269	44,949	37%	10,368	11,088	13,049	13,960	15,659	16,752	8,853	9,494	11,333	12,146	13,599	14,559
Lead Forestry Technician	GS-3-GS-4	3	20,401	22,902	21,128	23,718	21,868	24,548	42,269	44,949	37%	10,368	11,088	13,049	13,960	15,659	16,752	8,853	9,494	11,333	12,146	13,599	14,559
Supervisory Forestry Technician	GS-3-GS-4	3	20,401	22,902	21,128	23,718	21,868	24,548	42,269	24,548	37%	10,368	6,600	13,049	8,349	15,659	10,019	8,853	5,870	11,333	7,456	13,599	8,803
Soil Science Series																							
Soil Scientist	GS-5-GS-13	6	28,562	66,951	29,476	69,339	30,405	71,767	50,806	71,767	37%	12,520	19,297	15,761	24,413	18,913	29,295	10,837	17,161	13,831	21,800	16,527	25,738
Supervisory Soil Scientist	GS-5-GS-13	6	28,562	66,951	29,476	69,339	30,405	71,767	50,806	71,767	37%	12,520	19,297	15,761	24,413	18,913	29,295	10,837	17,161	13,831	21,800	16,527	25,738
Agronomy Series																							
Research Agronomist.	GS-5-GS-13	6	28,562	66,951	29,476	69,339	30,405	71,767	69,229	71,767	37%	16,573	19,297	20,827	24,413	24,993	29,295	14,110	17,161	18,067	21,800	21,726	25,738
Management Agronomist.	GS-5-GS-13	6	28,562	66,951	29,476	69,339	30,405	71,767	30,405	71,767	37%	8,031	19,297	10,151	24,413	12,181	29,295	7,213	17,161	9,141	21,800	10,771	25,738
Conservation Agronomist.	GS-5-GS-13	6	28,562	66,951	29,476	69,339	30,405	71,767	30,405	110,591	37%	8,031	27,838	10,151	35,089	12,181	42,107	7,213	24,058	9,141	30,725	10,771	36,693
Wildlife Refuge Management Series																							
Refuge Program Specialist	GS-9-GS-15	10	42,755	93,063	44,139	96,387	45,547	99,767	45,547	131,507	37%	12,054	33,815	15,237	42,674	18,284	51,209	10,814	29,498	13,709	37,606	16,157	44,742
Refuge Manager	GS-9-GS-15	10	42,755	93,063	44,139	96,387	45,547	99,767	45,547	131,507	37%	12,054	33,815	15,237	42,674	18,284	51,209	10,814	29,498	13,709	37,606	16,157	44,742
Supervisory Refuge Program Specialist	GS-9-GS-15	10	42,755	93,063	44,139	96,387	45,547	99,767	84,371	99,767	37%	20,595	26,832	25,913	33,946	31,096	40,735	17,711	23,859	22,635	30,309	27,111	35,786
Home Economics Series																							
Home Economist.	GS-5-GS-11	5-11	25,623	46,974	25,623	46,974	25,623	46,974	25,623	46,974	26,537	48,649	27,466	50,353	59,206	97,327	59,206	97,327	60,183	99,119	60,183	99,119
Supervisory	GS-5-GS-11	5-11	25,623	46,974	25,623	46,974	25,623	46,974	25,623	46,974	26,537	48,649	27,466	50,353	59,206	97,327	59,206	97,327	60,183	99,119	60,183	99,119
Engineering Technician Series																							

Chart II - U.S. Federal - Job Titles - Salaries - Pension Estimates

U.S. Federal Government Agencies	GS Grade Range:	GS Grade Median	2010 Median Grade Min Salary (STEP 1)	2010 Maximum Grade Salary (STEP 1)	2011 Median Grade Min Salary (STEP 2)	2011 Maximum Grade Salary (STEP 2)	2012 Median Grade Min Salary (STEP 3)	2012 Maximum Grade Salary (STEP 3)	2013 Median Grade Min Salary (STEP 4)	2013 Maximum Grade Salary (STEP 4)	10-Year Cumulative Raise Percentage (1.96%) + Step Increase Percentage (1.7%)	20-Year Annual Pension Benefit Estimate (Min.)	20-Year Annual Pension Benefit Estimate (Max.)	25-Year Annual Pension Benefit Estimate (Min.)	25-Year Annual Pension Benefit Estimate (Max.)	30-Year Annual Pension Benefit Estimate (Min.)	30-Year Annual Pension Benefit Estimate (Max.)	Agency Automatic Contributions 1% Thrift Savings Plan 20 Year Savings Plus 4.5% Interest (Min)	Agency Automatic Contributions 1% Thrift Savings Plan 20 Year Savings Plus 4.5% Interest (Max)	Agency Automatic Contributions 1% Thrift Savings Plan 25 Year Savings Plus 4.5% Interest (Min)	Agency Automatic Contributions 1% Thrift Savings Plan 25 Year Savings Plus 4.5% Interest (Max)	Agency Automatic Contributions 1% Thrift Savings Plan 30 Year Savings Plus 4.5% Interest (Min)	Agency Automatic Contribution 1% Thrift Plan 3 Year Savings Plus 4.5% Intere (Max)
Supervisory Positions	GS-1-GS-11	5	25,623	46,974	25,623	48,649	25,623	50,353	72,597	85,504	37%	15,971	21,272	19,964	26,795	23,957	32,154	13,968	18,285	17,761	23,376	21,287	27,97

Landscape Architecture Series

Supervisory Landscape Architect	GS-5-GS-14	9	38,824	79,115	39,738	81,936	40,667	84,805	40,667	84,805	37%	10,289	22,802	12,973	28,847	15,567	34,616	9,465	20,279	11,929	25,760	13,988	30,41

Architecture Series

General Schedule Supervisory Guide	GS-9-GS-14	11	46,974	79,115	48,358	81,936	49,766	84,805	84,917	119,956	37%	20,716	30,535	26,063	38,513	31,276	46,216	17,984	26,523	22,936	33,841	27,398	40,33

Construction Control Series

Construction Inspection Aid	GS-2-GS-9	5	25,623	38,824	26,350	40,208	27,090	41,616	27,090	76,767	37%	7,029	18,923	8,875	23,822	10,650	28,587	6,375	16,196	8,061	20,722	9,480	24,84
Construction Inspector	GS-2-GS-9	5	25,623	38,824	26,350	40,208	27,090	41,616	62,241	76,767	37%	14,762	18,923	18,541	23,822	22,249	28,587	12,620	16,196	16,143	20,722	19,398	24,84
Construction Representative	GS-2-GS-9	5	25,623	38,824	26,350	40,208	27,090	41,616	62,241	41,616	37%	14,762	11,189	18,541	14,156	22,249	16,987	12,620	9,951	16,143	12,641	19,398	14,92

Civil Engineering Series

Surveying Aid	GS-1-GS-8	3	20,401	35,151	20,401	36,405	20,401	37,680	55,552	37,680	37%	12,221	10,132	15,277	12,818	18,332	15,381	10,722	9,010	13,624	11,446	16,314	13,51
Surveying Technician	GS-1-GS-8	3	20,401	35,151	20,401	36,405	20,401	37,680	55,552	37,680	37%	12,221	10,132	15,277	12,818	18,332	15,381	10,722	9,010	13,624	11,446	16,314	13,51
Supervisory Surveying Technician	GS-1-GS-8	3	20,401	35,151	20,401	36,405	20,401	37,680	20,401	37,680	37%	4,488	10,132	5,610	12,818	6,732	15,381	4,477	9,010	5,543	11,446	6,396	13,51

Engineering Drafting Series

Engineering Draftsman	GS-1-GS-7	3	20,401	31,740	20,401	32,872	20,401	34,023	20,401	34,023	37%	4,488	9,148	5,610	11,573	6,732	13,888	4,477	8,136	5,543	10,335	6,396	12,20
Supervisory Engineering Draftsman	GS-1-GS-7	3	20,401	31,740	20,401	32,872	20,401	34,023	20,401	34,023	37%	4,488	9,148	5,610	11,573	6,732	13,888	4,477	8,136	5,543	10,335	6,396	12,20

Environmental Engineering Series

Supervisory Environmental Engineer	GS-5-GS-15	9	38,824	93,063	39,738	96,387	40,667	99,767	40,667	99,767	37%	10,289	26,832	12,973	33,946	15,567	40,735	9,465	23,859	11,929	30,309	13,988	35,78

Construction Analyst Series

Construction Analyst	GS-5-GS-12	7	31,740	56,301	32,654	58,309	33,583	60,351	33,583	60,351	37%	8,730	16,227	11,025	20,529	13,230	24,635	7,910	14,431	10,005	18,332	11,768	21,64
Supervisory Construction Analyst	GS-5-GS-12	7	31,740	56,301	32,654	58,309	33,583	60,351	33,583	60,351	37%	8,730	16,227	11,025	20,529	13,230	24,635	7,910	14,431	10,005	18,332	11,768	21,64

Mechanical Engineering Series

Supervisory Mechanical Engineer	GS-5-GS-15	9	38,824	93,063	39,738	96,387	40,667	99,767	40,667	99,767	37%	10,289	26,832	12,973	33,946	15,567	40,735	9,465	23,859	11,929	30,309	13,988	35,78

Electronics Technician Series

Electronics Technician	GS-4-GS-11	7	31,740	46,974	32,556	48,649	33,386	50,353	33,386	50,353	37%	8,544	13,539	10,780	17,128	12,936	20,554	7,809	12,041	9,858	15,295	11,574	18,05
Supervisory Electronics Technician	GS-4-GS-11	7	31,740	46,974	32,556	48,649	33,386	50,353	33,386	50,353	37%	8,544	13,539	10,780	17,128	12,936	20,554	7,809	12,041	9,858	15,295	11,574	18,05

Naval Architecture Series

Naval Architect	GS-9-GS-15	11	46,974	93,063	48,358	96,387	49,766	99,767	49,766	99,767	37%	12,982	26,832	16,397	33,946	19,676	40,735	11,740	23,859	14,855	30,309	17,480	35,78
Naval Architecture	GS-9-GS-15	11	46,974	93,063	48,358	96,387	49,766	99,767	49,766	99,767	37%	12,982	26,832	16,397	33,946	19,676	40,735	11,740	23,859	14,855	30,309	17,480	35,78
Supervisory Classes	GS-9-GS-15	11	46,974	93,063	48,358	96,387	49,766	99,767	49,766	99,767	37%	12,982	26,832	16,397	33,946	19,676	40,735	11,740	23,859	14,855	30,309	17,480	35,78

Chart II - U.S. Federal - Job Titles - Salaries - Pension Estimates

U.S. Federal Government Agencies	GS Grade Range:	GS Grade Median	2010 Median Grade Min Salary (STEP 1)	2010 Maximum Grade Salary (STEP 1)	2011 Median Grade Min Salary (STEP 2)	2011 Maximum Grade Salary (STEP 2)	2012 Median Grade Min Salary (STEP 3)	2012 Maximum Grade Salary (STEP 3)	2013 Median Grade Min Salary (STEP 4)	2013 Maximum Grade Salary (STEP 4)	10-Year Cumulative Raise Percentage (1.96%) + Step Increase Percentage (1.7%)	20-Year Annual Pension Benefit Estimate (Min.)	20-Year Annual Pension Benefit Estimate (Max.)	25-Year Annual Pension Benefit Estimate (Min.)	25-Year Annual Pension Benefit Estimate (Max.)	30-Year Annual Pension Benefit Estimate (Min.)	30-Year Annual Pension Benefit Estimate (Max.)	Agency Automatic Contributions 1% Thrift Savings Plan 20 Year Savings Plus 4.5% Interest (Min)	Agency Automatic Contributions 1% Thrift Savings Plan 20 Year Savings Plus 4.5% Interest (Max)	Agency Automatic Contributions 1% Thrift Savings Plan 25 Year Savings Plus 4.5% Interest (Min)	Agency Automatic Contributions 1% Thrift Savings Plan 25 Year Savings Plus 4.5% Interest (Max)	Agency Automatic Contributions 1% Thrift Savings Plan 30 Year Savings Plus 4.5% Interest (Min)	Agency Automatic Contributions 1% Thrift Savings Plan 30 Year Savings Plus 4.5% Interest (Max)
Mining Engineering Series																							
Mining Engineer	GS-5-GS-12	8	35,151	56,301	36,065	58,309	36,994	60,351	36,994	60,351	37%	9,481	16,227	11,963	20,529	14,355	24,635	8,659	14,431	10,931	18,332	12,837	21,644
Supervisory	GS-5-GS-12	8	35,151	56,301	36,065	58,309	36,994	60,351	36,994	60,351	37%	9,481	16,227	11,963	20,529	14,355	24,635	8,659	14,431	10,931	18,332	12,837	21,644
Mining Engineer.	GS-5-GS-12	8	35,151	56,301	36,065	58,309	36,994	60,351	36,994	60,351	37%	9,481	16,227	11,963	20,529	14,355	24,635	8,659	14,431	10,931	18,332	12,837	21,644
Agricultural Engineering Series																							
Agricultural Engineer	GS-5-GS-12	8	35,151	56,301	36,065	58,309	36,994	60,351	36,994	60,351	37%	9,481	16,227	11,963	20,529	14,355	24,635	8,659	14,431	10,931	18,332	12,837	21,644
Supervisory Agricultural Engineer.	GS-5-GS-12	8	35,151	56,301	36,065	58,309	36,994	60,351	36,994	60,351	37%	9,481	16,227	11,963	20,529	14,355	24,635	8,659	14,431	10,931	18,332	12,837	21,644
Chemical Engineering Series																							
Chemical Engineer	GS-5-GS-13	8	35,151	66,951	36,065	69,339	36,994	71,767	36,994	71,767	37%	9,481	19,297	11,963	24,413	14,355	29,295	8,659	17,161	10,931	21,800	12,837	25,738
Supervisory Chemical Engineer	GS-5-GS-13	8	35,151	66,951	36,065	69,339	36,994	71,767	36,994	71,767	37%	9,481	19,297	11,963	24,413	14,355	29,295	8,659	17,161	10,931	21,800	12,837	25,738

Quality Assurance _ Grading

U.S. Federal Government Agencies	GS Grade Range:	GS Grade Median	2010 Median Grade Min Salary (STEP 1)	2010 Maximum Grade Salary (STEP 1)	2011 Median Grade Min Salary (STEP 2)	2011 Maximum Grade Salary (STEP 2)	2012 Median Grade Min Salary (STEP 3)	2012 Maximum Grade Salary (STEP 3)	2013 Median Grade Min Salary (STEP 4)	2013 Maximum Grade Salary (STEP 4)	10-Year Cumulative Raise Percentage (1.96%) + Step Increase Percentage (1.7%)	20-Year Annual Pension Benefit Estimate (Min.)	20-Year Annual Pension Benefit Estimate (Max.)	25-Year Annual Pension Benefit Estimate (Min.)	25-Year Annual Pension Benefit Estimate (Max.)	30-Year Annual Pension Benefit Estimate (Min.)	30-Year Annual Pension Benefit Estimate (Max.)	Agency Automatic Contributions 1% Thrift Savings Plan 20 Year Savings Plus 4.5% Interest (Min)	Agency Automatic Contributions 1% Thrift Savings Plan 20 Year Savings Plus 4.5% Interest (Max)	Agency Automatic Contributions 1% Thrift Savings Plan 25 Year Savings Plus 4.5% Interest (Min)	Agency Automatic Contributions 1% Thrift Savings Plan 25 Year Savings Plus 4.5% Interest (Max)	Agency Automatic Contributions 1% Thrift Savings Plan 30 Year Savings Plus 4.5% Interest (Min)	Agency Automatic Contributions 1% Thrift Savings Plan 30 Year Savings Plus 4.5% Interest (Max)
Agricultural Commodity Grading Series																							
Agricultural Commodity Grader	GS-5-GS-11	7	31,740	46,974	32,654	48,649	33,583	50,353	33,583	50,353	37%	8,730	13,539	11,025	17,128	13,230	20,554	7,910	12,041	10,005	15,295	11,768	18,059
Supervisory Agricultural Commodity Grader	GS-5-GS-11	7	31,740	46,974	32,654	48,649	33,583	50,353	33,583	50,353	37%	8,730	13,539	11,025	17,128	13,230	20,554	7,910	12,041	10,005	15,295	11,768	18,059

Chart II - U.S. Federal - Job Titles - Salaries - Pension Estimates

Safety_Health_Resource Protect

U.S. Federal Government Agencies	GS Grade Range	GS Grade Median	2010 Median Grade Min Salary (STEP 1)	2010 Maximum Grade Salary (STEP 1)	2011 Median Grade Min Salary (STEP 2)	2011 Maximum Grade Salary (STEP 2)	2012 Median Grade Min Salary (STEP 3)	2012 Maximum Grade Salary (STEP 3)	2013 Median Grade Min Salary (STEP 4)	2013 Maximum Grade Salary (STEP 4)	10-Year Cumulative Raise Percentage (1.96%) + Step Increase Percentage (1.7%)	20-Year Annual Pension Benefit Estimate (Min.)	20-Year Annual Pension Benefit Estimate (Max.)	25-Year Annual Pension Benefit Estimate (Min.)	25-Year Annual Pension Benefit Estimate (Max.)	30-Year Annual Pension Benefit Estimate (Min.)	30-Year Annual Pension Benefit Estimate (Max.)	Agency Automatic Contributions 1% Thrift Savings Plan 20 Year Savings Plus 4.5% Interest (Min)	Agency Automatic Contributions 1% Thrift Savings Plan 20 Year Savings Plus 4.5% Interest (Max)	Agency Automatic Contributions 1% Thrift Savings Plan 25 Year Savings Plus 4.5% Interest (Min)	Agency Automatic Contributions 1% Thrift Savings Plan 25 Year Savings Plus 4.5% Interest (Max)	Agency Automatic Contributions 1% Thrift Savings Plan 30 Year Savings Plus 4.5% Interest (Min)	Agency Automatic Contributions 1% Thrift Savings Plan 30 Year Savings Plus 4.5% Interest (Max)
Safety and Occupational Health Management Series																							
Safety and Occupational Health Manager	GS-5-GS-15	9	38,824	93,063	39,738	96,387	40,667	99,767	87,641	120,168	37%	20,623	31,320	25,891	39,556	31,069	47,467	17,809	27,484	22,729	34,999	27,242	41,543
Safety and Occupational Health Specialist	GS-5-GS-15	9	38,824	93,063	39,738	96,387	40,667	99,767	40,667	120,168	37%	10,289	31,320	12,973	39,556	15,567	47,467	9,465	27,484	11,929	34,999	13,988	41,543
Supervisory Safety and Occupational Health Specialist	GS-5-GS-15	9	38,824	93,063	39,738	96,387	40,667	99,767	40,667	99,767	37%	10,289	26,832	12,973	33,946	15,567	40,735	9,465	23,859	11,929	30,309	13,988	35,786
Park Ranger Series																							
Park Manager	GS-3-GS-13	8	35,151	66,951	35,878	69,339	36,618	71,767	57,019	106,918	37%	13,613	27,030	17,105	34,079	20,526	40,895	12,090	23,406	15,340	29,881	18,223	35,656
Park Ranger	GS-3-GS-13	8	35,151	66,951	35,878	69,339	36,618	71,767	57,019	71,767	37%	13,613	19,297	17,105	24,413	20,526	29,295	12,090	17,161	15,340	21,800	18,223	25,738
Environmental Protection Specialist Series																							
Environmental Protection Specialist	GS-9-GS-14	11	46,974	79,115	48,358	81,936	49,766	84,805	84,917	123,629	37%	20,716	31,343	26,063	39,523	31,276	47,428	17,984	27,176	22,936	34,685	27,398	41,368
Supervisory Environmental Protection Specialist	GS-9-GS-14	11	46,974	79,115	48,358	81,936	49,766	84,805	84,917	123,629	37%	20,716	31,343	26,063	39,523	31,276	47,428	17,984	27,176	22,936	34,685	27,398	41,368
Security Administration Series																							
Personnel Security Specialist	GS-5-GS-15	9	38,824	93,063	39,738	96,387	40,667	99,767	79,491	134,918	37%	18,830	34,565	23,649	43,612	28,379	52,335	16,362	30,104	20,855	38,390	24,943	45,704
Physical Security Specialist	GS-5-GS-15	9	38,824	93,063	39,738	96,387	40,667	99,767	79,491	134,918	37%	18,830	34,565	23,649	43,612	28,379	52,335	16,362	30,104	20,855	38,390	24,943	45,704
Information Security Specialist	GS-5-GS-15	9	38,824	93,063	39,738	96,387	40,667	99,767	79,491	99,767	37%	18,830	26,832	23,649	33,946	28,379	40,735	16,362	23,859	20,855	30,309	24,943	35,786
Industrial Security Specialist	GS-5-GS-15	9	38,824	93,063	39,738	96,387	40,667	99,767	40,667	99,767	37%	10,289	26,832	12,973	33,946	15,567	40,735	9,465	23,859	11,929	30,309	13,988	35,786
Security Specialist	GS-5-GS-15	9	38,824	93,063	39,738	96,387	40,667	99,767	40,667	138,591	37%	10,289	35,373	12,973	44,622	15,567	53,547	9,465	30,757	11,929	39,235	13,988	46,741
Security Officer	GS-5-GS-15	9	38,824	93,063	39,738	96,387	40,667	99,767	75,818	138,591	37%	18,022	35,373	22,639	44,622	27,167	53,547	15,709	30,757	20,011	39,235	23,906	46,741
Supervisory	GS-5-GS-15	9	38,824	93,063	39,738	96,387	40,667	99,767	75,818	138,591	37%	18,022	35,373	22,639	44,622	27,167	53,547	15,709	30,757	20,011	39,235	23,906	46,741
Fire Protection and Prevention Series																							
Fire Chief	GS-3-GS-9	6	28,562	38,824	29,289	40,208	30,029	41,616	68,853	73,356	37%	16,216	18,172	20,359	22,884	24,431	27,461	13,917	15,590	17,785	19,938	21,355	23,880
Firefighter	GS-3-GS-9	6	28,562	38,824	29,289	40,208	30,029	41,616	68,853	73,356	37%	16,216	18,172	20,359	22,884	24,431	27,461	13,917	15,590	17,785	19,938	21,355	23,880
Fire Protection Inspector	GS-3-GS-9	6	28,562	38,824	29,289	40,208	30,029	41,616	68,853	41,616	37%	16,216	11,189	20,359	14,156	24,431	16,987	13,917	9,951	17,785	12,641	21,355	14,925
Fire Protection Specialist	GS-3-GS-9	6	28,562	38,824	29,289	40,208	30,029	41,616	30,029	41,616	37%	7,675	11,189	9,683	14,156	11,619	16,987	7,020	9,951	8,860	12,641	10,401	14,925
Guide Series																							
Park Guide	GS-4-GS-6	5	25,623	28,562	26,439	29,580	27,269	30,616	59,009	30,616	37%	14,181	8,232	17,826	10,414	21,391	12,497	12,106	7,321	15,493	9,300	18,612	10,980
Reclamation Guide	GS-4-GS-6	5	25,623	28,562	26,439	29,580	27,269	30,616	27,269	30,616	37%	7,198	8,232	9,098	10,414	10,917	12,497	6,467	7,321	8,196	9,300	9,656	10,980
Guide	GS-4-GS-6	5	25,623	28,562	26,439	29,580	27,269	30,616	27,269	30,616	37%	7,198	8,232	9,098	10,414	10,917	12,497	6,467	7,321	8,196	9,300	9,656	10,980
Geography Series																							
Geographer	GS-9-GS-15	11	46,974	93,063	48,358	96,387	49,766	99,767	49,766	99,767	37%	12,982	26,832	16,397	33,946	19,676	40,735	11,740	23,859	14,855	30,309	17,480	35,786
Supervisory Geographer	GS-9-GS-15	11	46,974	93,063	48,358	96,387	49,766	99,767	49,766	99,767	37%	12,982	26,832	16,397	33,946	19,676	40,735	11,740	23,859	14,855	30,309	17,480	35,786

Chart II - U.S. Federal - Job Titles - Salaries - Pension Estimates

U.S. Federal Government Agencies	GS Grade Range:	GS Grade Median	2010 Median Grade Min Salary (STEP 1)	2010 Maximum Grade Salary (STEP 1)	2011 Median Grade Min Salary (STEP 2)	2011 Maximum Grade Salary (STEP 2)	2012 Median Grade Min Salary (STEP 3)	2012 Maximum Grade Salary (STEP 3)	2013 Median Grade Min Salary (STEP 4)	2013 Maximum Grade Salary (STEP 4)	10-Year Cumulative Raise Percentage (1.96%) + Step Increase Percentage (1.7%)	20-Year Annual Pension Benefit Estimate (Min.)	20-Year Annual Pension Benefit Estimate (Max.)	25-Year Annual Pension Benefit Estimate (Min.)	25-Year Annual Pension Benefit Estimate (Max.)	30-Year Annual Pension Benefit Estimate (Min.)	30-Year Annual Pension Benefit Estimate (Max.)	Agency Automatic Contributions 1% Thrift Savings Plan 20 Year Plus 4.5% Interest (Min)	Agency Automatic Contributions 1% Thrift Savings Plan 20 Year Plus 4.5% Interest (Max)	Agency Automatic Contributions 1% Thrift Savings Plan 25 Year Plus 4.5% Interest (Min)	Agency Automatic Contributions 1% Thrift Savings Plan 25 Year Plus 4.5% Interest (Max)	Agency Automatic Contributions 1% Thrift Savings Plan 30 Year Plus 4.5% Interest (Min)	Agency Automatic Contributions 1% Thrift Savings Plan 30 Year Plus 4.5% Interest (Max)
Soil Conservation Series*	GS-9-GS-15	11	46,974	93,063	48,358	96,387	49,766	99,767	49,766	99,767	37%	12,982	26,832	16,397	33,946	19,676	40,735	11,740	23,859	14,855	30,309	17,480	35,786
Supervisory Soil Conservationist	GS-9-GS-15	11	46,974	93,063	48,358	96,387	49,766	99,767	49,766	99,767	37%	12,982	26,832	16,397	33,946	19,676	40,735	11,740	23,859	14,855	30,309	17,480	35,786
Forestry Technician Series																							
Forestry Aid	GS-3-GS-4	3	20,401	22,902	21,128	23,718	21,868	24,548	21,868	24,548	37%	5,880	6,600	7,439	8,349	8,926	10,019	5,229	5,870	6,642	7,456	7,843	8,803
Forestry Technician	GS-3-GS-4	3	20,401	22,902	21,128	23,718	21,868	24,548	21,868	24,548	37%	5,880	6,600	7,439	8,349	8,926	10,019	5,229	5,870	6,642	7,456	7,843	8,803
Lead Forestry Technician	GS-3-GS-4	3	20,401	22,902	21,128	23,718	21,868	24,548	21,868	24,548	37%	5,880	6,600	7,439	8,349	8,926	10,019	5,229	5,870	6,642	7,456	7,843	8,803
Supervisory Forestry Technician	GS-3-GS-4	3	20,401	22,902	21,128	23,718	21,868	24,548	21,868	24,548	37%	5,880	6,600	7,439	8,349	8,926	10,019	5,229	5,870	6,642	7,456	7,843	8,803
Consumer Safety Series																							
Consumer Safety Officer	GS-5-GS-13	8	35,151	66,951	36,065	69,339	36,994	71,767	36,994	71,767	37%	9,481	19,297	11,963	24,413	14,355	29,295	8,659	17,161	10,931	21,800	12,837	25,738
Supervisory Consumer Safety Officer	GS-5-GS-13	8	35,151	66,951	36,065	69,339	36,994	71,767	36,994	71,767	37%	9,481	19,297	11,963	24,413	14,355	29,295	8,659	17,161	10,931	21,800	12,837	25,738
Mine Safety and Health Series																							
Mine Safety and Health Inspector	GS-5-GS-15	9	38,824	93,063	39,738	96,387	40,667	99,767	40,667	99,767	37%	10,289	26,832	12,973	33,946	15,567	40,735	9,465	23,859	11,929	30,309	13,988	35,786
Coal Mine Safety and Health Inspector	GS-5-GS-15	9	38,824	93,063	39,738	96,387	40,667	99,767	40,667	99,767	37%	10,289	26,832	12,973	33,946	15,567	40,735	9,465	23,859	11,929	30,309	13,988	35,786
Mine safety and Health Specialist	GS-5-GS-15	9	38,824	93,063	39,738	96,387	40,667	99,767	40,667	99,767	37%	10,289	26,832	12,973	33,946	15,567	40,735	9,465	23,859	11,929	30,309	13,988	35,786
Aviation Safety Series																							
AviationSafety Inspectors	GS-5-GS-14	8	35,151	79,115	36,065	81,936	36,994	84,805	36,994	84,805	37%	9,481	22,802	11,963	28,847	14,355	34,616	8,659	20,279	10,931	25,760	12,837	30,414
Operation	GS-5-GS-14	8	35,151	79,115	36,065	81,936	36,994	84,805	36,994	84,805	37%	9,481	22,802	11,963	28,847	14,355	34,616	8,659	20,279	10,931	25,760	12,837	30,414
Alcohol, Tobacco and Firearms Inspection Series																							
Alcohol	GS-5-GS-11	9	38,824	46,974	39,738	48,649	40,667	50,353	40,667	50,353	37%	10,289	13,539	12,973	17,128	15,567	20,554	9,465	12,041	11,929	15,295	13,988	18,059
Tobacco	GS-5-GS-11	9	38,824	46,974	39,738	48,649	40,667	50,353	40,667	50,353	37%	10,289	13,539	12,973	17,128	15,567	20,554	9,465	12,041	11,929	15,295	13,988	18,059
Firearms Inspector	GS-5-GS-11	9	38,824	46,974	39,738	48,649	40,667	50,353	40,667	50,353	37%	10,289	13,539	12,973	17,128	15,567	20,554	9,465	12,041	11,929	15,295	13,988	18,059
Customs Patrol Officer Series																							
Customs Patrol Officer	GS-5-GS-11	7	31,740	46,974	32,654	48,649	33,583	50,353	33,583	50,353	37%	8,730	13,539	11,025	17,128	13,230	20,554	7,910	12,041	10,005	15,295	11,768	18,059
Supervisory Customs Patrol Officer	GS-5-GS-11	7	31,740	46,974	32,654	48,649	33,583	50,353	33,583	50,353	37%	8,730	13,539	11,025	17,128	13,230	20,554	7,910	12,041	10,005	15,295	11,768	18,059
Customs Inspection Series																							
Customs Inspector	GS-5-GS-11	7	31,740	46,974	32,654	48,649	33,583	50,353	33,583	50,353	37%	8,730	13,539	11,025	17,128	13,230	20,554	7,910	12,041	10,005	15,295	11,768	18,059
Supervisory Customs Inspector	GS-5-GS-11	7	31,740	46,974	32,654	48,649	33,583	50,353	33,583	50,353	37%	8,730	13,539	11,025	17,128	13,230	20,554	7,910	12,041	10,005	15,295	11,768	18,059

Chart II - U.S. Federal - Job Titles - Salaries - Pension Estimates

Social Sci_ Psych _ Welfare

U.S. Federal Government Agencies	GS Grade Range	GS Grade Median	2010 Median Grade Min Salary (STEP 1)	2010 Maximum Grade Salary (STEP 1)	2011 Median Grade Salary (STEP 2)	2011 Maximum Grade Salary (STEP 2)	2012 Median Grade Salary (STEP 3)	2012 Maximum Grade Salary (STEP 3)	2013 Median Grade Salary (STEP 4)	2013 Maximum Grade Salary (STEP 4)	10-Year Cumulative Raise Percentage (1.96%) + Step Increase Percentage (1.7%)	20-Year Annual Pension Benefit Estimate (Min.)	20-Year Annual Pension Benefit Estimate (Max.)	25-Year Annual Pension Benefit Estimate (Min.)	25-Year Annual Pension Benefit Estimate (Max.)	30-Year Annual Pension Benefit Estimate (Min.)	30-Year Annual Pension Benefit Estimate (Max.)	Agency Automatic Contributions Thrift Savings Plan 20 Year Plus 4.5% Interest (Min)	Agency Automatic Contributions Thrift Savings Plan 20 Year Plus 4.5% Interest (Max)	Agency Automatic Contributions Thrift Savings Plan 25 Year Plus 4.5% Interest (Min)	Agency Automatic Contributions Thrift Savings Plan 25 Year Plus 4.5% Interest (Max)	Agency Automatic Contributions Thrift Savings Plan 30 Year Plus 4.5% Interest (Min)	Agency Automatic Contributions Thrift Savings Plan 30 Year Plus 4.5% Interest (Max)
Intelligence Series																							
Intelligence Research Specialist	GS-5-GS-14	8	35,151	79,115	36,065	81,936	36,994	84,805	36,994	84,805	37%	9,481	22,802	11,963	28,847	14,355	34,616	8,659	20,279	10,931	25,760	12,837	30,41
Intelligence Operations Specialist	GS-5-GS-14	8	35,151	79,115	36,065	81,936	36,994	84,805	36,994	84,805	37%	9,481	22,802	11,963	28,847	14,355	34,616	8,659	20,279	10,931	25,760	12,837	30,41
Psychology Series																							
Psychologist	GS-5-GS-13	8	35,151	66,951	36,065	69,339	36,994	71,767	36,994	71,767	37%	9,481	19,297	11,963	24,413	14,355	29,295	8,659	17,161	10,931	21,800	12,837	25,73
Counseling Psychologist	GS-5-GS-13	8	35,151	66,951	36,065	69,339	36,994	71,767	36,994	71,767	37%	9,481	19,297	11,963	24,413	14,355	29,295	8,659	17,161	10,931	21,800	12,837	25,73
Clinical Psychologist	GS-5-GS-13	8	35,151	66,951	36,065	69,339	36,994	71,767	36,994	71,767	37%	9,481	19,297	11,963	24,413	14,355	29,295	8,659	17,161	10,931	21,800	12,837	25,73
Engineering Psychologist	GS-5-GS-13	8	35,151	66,951	36,065	69,339	36,994	71,767	36,994	71,767	37%	9,481	19,297	11,963	24,413	14,355	29,295	8,659	17,161	10,931	21,800	12,837	25,73
Personnel Psychologist	GS-5-GS-13	8	35,151	66,951	36,065	69,339	36,994	71,767	36,994	71,767	37%	9,481	19,297	11,963	24,413	14,355	29,295	8,659	17,161	10,931	21,800	12,837	25,73
Social Services Series																							
Social Service Representative	GS-5-GS-9	7	31,740	38,824	32,654	40,208	33,583	41,616	33,583	41,616	37%	8,730	11,189	11,025	14,156	13,230	16,987	7,910	9,951	10,005	12,641	11,768	14,92
Social Work Associate	GS-5-GS-9	7	31,740	38,824	32,654	40,208	33,583	41,616	33,583	41,616	37%	8,730	11,189	11,025	14,156	13,230	16,987	7,910	9,951	10,005	12,641	11,768	14,92
Recreation Specialist Series																							
Institutional	GS-5-GS-11	8	35,151	46,974	36,065	48,649	36,994	50,353	36,994	50,353	37%	9,481	13,539	11,963	17,128	14,355	20,554	8,659	12,041	10,931	15,295	12,837	18,05
Outdoor Activities	GS-5-GS-11	8	35,151	46,974	36,065	48,649	36,994	50,353	36,994	50,353	37%	9,481	13,539	11,963	17,128	14,355	20,554	8,659	12,041	10,931	15,295	12,837	18,05
Community Activities	GS-5-GS-11	8	35,151	46,974	36,065	48,649	36,994	50,353	36,994	50,353	37%	9,481	13,539	11,963	17,128	14,355	20,554	8,659	12,041	10,931	15,295	12,837	18,05
Senior Citizens Activities	GS-5-GS-11	8	35,151	46,974	36,065	48,649	36,994	50,353	36,994	50,353	37%	9,481	13,539	11,963	17,128	14,355	20,554	8,659	12,041	10,931	15,295	12,837	18,05
Youth activities	GS-5-GS-11	8	35,151	46,974	36,065	48,649	36,994	50,353	36,994	50,353	37%	9,481	13,539	11,963	17,128	14,355	20,554	8,659	12,041	10,931	15,295	12,837	18,05

Chart II - U.S. Federal - Job Titles - Salaries - Pension Estimates

Supply

U.S. Federal Government Agencies	GS Grade Range:	GS Grade Median	2010 Median Grade Min Salary (STEP 1)	2010 Maximum Grade Salary (STEP 1)	2011 Median Grade Min Salary (STEP 2)	2011 Maximum Grade Salary (STEP 2)	2012 Median Grade Min Salary (STEP 3)	2012 Maximum Grade Salary (STEP 3)	2013 Median Grade Min Salary (STEP 4)	2013 Maximum Grade Salary (STEP 4)	10-Year Cumulative Raise Percentage (1.96%) + Step Increase Percentage (1.7%)	20-Year Annual Pension Benefit Estimate (Min.)	20-Year Annual Pension Benefit Estimate (Max.)	25-Year Annual Pension Benefit Estimate (Min.)	25-Year Annual Pension Benefit Estimate (Max.)	30-Year Annual Pension Benefit Estimate (Min.)	30-Year Annual Pension Benefit Estimate (Max.)	Agency Automatic Contributions 1% Thrift Savings Plan 20 Year Savings Plus 4.5% Interest (Min)	Agency Automatic Contributions 1% Thrift Savings Plan 20 Year Savings Plus 4.5% Interest (Max)	Agency Automatic Contributions 1% Thrift Savings Plan 25 Year Savings Plus 4.5% Interest (Min)	Agency Automatic Contributions 1% Thrift Savings Plan 25 Year Savings Plus 4.5% Interest (Max)	Agency Automatic Contributions 1% Thrift Savings Plan 30 Year Savings Plus 4.5% Interest (Min)	Agency Automatic Contributions 1% Thrift Savings Plan 30 Year Savings Plus 4.5% Interest (Max)
Medical Supply Aide and Technician Series																							
Medical Supply Aide	GS-2-GS-6	3	20,401	28,562	21,128	29,580	21,868	30,616	21,868	59,178	37%	5,880	14,515	7,439	18,269	8,926	21,922	5,229	12,395	6,642	15,866	7,843	19,039
Medical Supply Technician	GS-2-GS-6	3	20,401	28,562	21,128	29,580	21,868	30,616	21,868	30,616	37%	5,880	8,232	7,439	10,414	8,926	12,497	5,229	7,321	6,642	9,300	7,843	10,980
Civil Engineering Series																							
Surveying Aid	GS-1-GS-8	3	20,401	35,151	20,401	36,405	20,401	37,680	48,963	37,680	37%	10,772	10,132	13,465	12,818	16,158	15,381	9,551	9,010	12,109	11,446	14,454	13,514
Surveying Technician	GS-1-GS-8	3	20,401	35,151	20,401	36,405	20,401	37,680	48,963	37,680	37%	10,772	10,132	13,465	12,818	16,158	15,381	9,551	9,010	12,109	11,446	14,454	13,514
Supervisory Surveying Technician	GS-1-GS-8	3	20,401	35,151	20,401	36,405	20,401	37,680	20,401	37,680	37%	4,488	10,132	5,610	12,818	6,732	15,381	4,477	9,010	5,543	11,446	6,396	13,514
Procurement Clerical and Technician Series																							
Procurement Clerk	GS-1-GS-7	3	20,401	31,740	20,401	32,872	20,401	34,023	20,401	34,023	37%	4,488	9,148	5,610	11,573	6,732	13,888	4,477	8,136	5,543	10,335	6,396	12,202
Procurement Technician	GS-1-GS-7	3	20,401	31,740	20,401	32,872	20,401	34,023	20,401	34,023	37%	4,488	9,148	5,610	11,573	6,732	13,888	4,477	8,136	5,543	10,335	6,396	12,202
Lead Procurement Clerk	GS-1-GS-7	3	20,401	31,740	20,401	32,872	20,401	34,023	20,401	34,023	37%	4,488	9,148	5,610	11,573	6,732	13,888	4,477	8,136	5,543	10,335	6,396	12,202
Lead Procurement Technician	GS-1-GS-7	3	20,401	31,740	20,401	32,872	20,401	34,023	20,401	34,023	37%	4,488	9,148	5,610	11,573	6,732	13,888	4,477	8,136	5,543	10,335	6,396	12,202
Supervisory Procurement Technician	GS-1-GS-7	3	20,401	31,740	20,401	32,872	20,401	34,023	20,401	34,023	37%	4,488	9,148	5,610	11,573	6,732	13,888	4,477	8,136	5,543	10,335	6,396	12,202
Property Disposal Clerical and Technician Series																							
Property Disposal Clerk	GS-3-GS-7	4	22,902	31,740	23,629	32,872	24,369	34,023	24,369	34,023	37%	6,430	9,148	8,126	11,573	9,752	13,888	5,778	8,136	7,322	10,335	8,627	12,202
Property Disposal Technician	GS-3-GS-7	4	22,902	31,740	23,629	32,872	24,369	34,023	24,369	34,023	37%	6,430	9,148	8,126	11,573	9,752	13,888	5,778	8,136	7,322	10,335	8,627	12,202
Production Control Series																							
Production Control Aide	GS-4-GS-12	9	38,824	56,301	39,640	58,309	40,470	60,351	40,470	60,351	37%	10,103	16,227	12,728	20,529	15,274	24,635	9,364	14,431	11,782	18,332	13,795	21,644
Production Controller	GS-4-GS-12	9	38,824	56,301	39,640	58,309	40,470	60,351	40,470	60,351	37%	10,103	16,227	12,728	20,529	15,274	24,635	9,364	14,431	11,782	18,332	13,795	21,644
Production Controller (specialty)	GS-4-GS-12	9	38,824	56,301	39,640	58,309	40,470	60,351	40,470	60,351	37%	10,103	16,227	12,728	20,529	15,274	24,635	9,364	14,431	11,782	18,332	13,795	21,644
Supply Program Management Series																							
Supply Management Officer	GS-9-GS-14	11	46,974	79,115	48,358	81,936	49,766	84,805	49,766	84,805	37%	12,982	22,802	16,397	28,847	19,676	34,616	11,740	20,279	14,855	25,760	17,480	30,414
Supply Management Specialist	GS-9-GS-14	11	46,974	79,115	48,358	81,936	49,766	84,805	49,766	84,805	37%	12,982	22,802	16,397	28,847	19,676	34,616	11,740	20,279	14,855	25,760	17,480	30,414
Supply Systems Analyst	GS-9-GS-14	11	46,974	79,115	48,358	81,936	49,766	84,805	49,766	84,805	37%	12,982	22,802	16,397	28,847	19,676	34,616	11,740	20,279	14,855	25,760	17,480	30,414
Supervisory Supply Management Specialist	GS-9-GS-14	11	46,974	79,115	48,358	81,936	49,766	84,805	49,766	84,805	37%	12,982	22,802	16,397	28,847	19,676	34,616	11,740	20,279	14,855	25,760	17,480	30,414
Supply Clerical and Technician Series																							
Leader	GS-3-GS-7	5	25,623	31,740	26,350	32,872	27,090	34,023	27,090	34,023	37%	7,029	9,148	8,875	11,573	10,650	13,888	6,375	8,136	8,061	10,335	9,480	12,202
Inventory Management Series**																							
Inventory Management Officer	GS-1-GS-13	6	28,562	66,951	28,562	69,339	28,562	71,767	28,562	71,767	37%	6,284	19,297	7,855	24,413	9,425	29,295	6,268	17,161	7,760	21,800	8,954	25,738

127

Chart II - U.S. Federal - Job Titles - Salaries - Pension Estimates

U.S. Federal Government Agencies	GS Grade Range:	GS Grade Median	2010 Median Grade Min Salary (STEP 1)	2010 Maximum Grade Salary (STEP 1)	2011 Median Grade Min Salary (STEP 2)	2011 Maximum Grade Salary (STEP 2)	2012 Median Grade Min Salary (STEP 3)	2012 Maximum Grade Salary (STEP 3)	2013 Median Grade Min Salary (STEP 4)	2013 Maximum Grade Salary (STEP 4)	10-Year Cumulative Raise Percentage (1.96%) + Step Increase Percentage (1.7%)	20-Year Annual Pension Benefit Estimate (Min.)	20-Year Annual Pension Benefit Estimate (Max.)	25-Year Annual Pension Benefit Estimate (Min.)	25-Year Annual Pension Benefit Estimate (Max.)	30-Year Annual Pension Benefit Estimate (Min.)	30-Year Annual Pension Benefit Estimate (Max.)	Agency Automatic Contributions 1% Thrift Savings Plan 20 Year Savings Plus 4.5% Interest (Min)	Agency Automatic Contributions 1% Thrift Savings Plan 20 Year Savings Plus 4.5% Interest (Max)	Agency Automatic Contributions 1% Thrift Savings Plan 25 Year Savings Plus 4.5% Interest (Min)	Agency Automatic Contributions 1% Thrift Savings Plan 25 Year Savings Plus 4.5% Interest (Max)	Agency Automatic Contributions 1% Thrift Savings Plan 30 Year Savings Plus 4.5% Interest (Min)	Agency Automatic Contributions 1% Thrift Savings Plan 30 Year Savings Plus 4.5% Interest (Max)
Inventory Management Specialist	GS-1-GS-13	6	28,562	66,951	28,562	69,339	28,562	71,767	28,562	71,767	37%	6,284	19,297	7,855	24,413	9,425	29,295	6,268	17,161	7,760	21,800	8,954	25,738
Supervisory Inventory Management Specialist	GS-1-GS-13	6	28,562	66,951	28,562	69,339	28,562	71,767	28,562	71,767	37%	6,284	19,297	7,855	24,413	9,425	29,295	6,268	17,161	7,760	21,800	8,954	25,738

Distribution Facilities and Storage Management Series

U.S. Federal Government Agencies	GS Grade Range:	GS Grade Median	2010 Median Grade Min Salary (STEP 1)	2010 Maximum Grade Salary (STEP 1)	2011 Median Grade Min Salary (STEP 2)	2011 Maximum Grade Salary (STEP 2)	2012 Median Grade Min Salary (STEP 3)	2012 Maximum Grade Salary (STEP 3)	2013 Median Grade Min Salary (STEP 4)	2013 Maximum Grade Salary (STEP 4)	10-Year Raise %	20-Yr Min	20-Yr Max	25-Yr Min	25-Yr Max	30-Yr Min	30-Yr Max	TSP 20 Min	TSP 20 Max	TSP 25 Min	TSP 25 Max	TSP 30 Min	TSP 30 Max
Distribution Facilities Specialist	GS-1-GS-13	6	28,562	66,951	28,562	69,339	28,562	71,767	28,562	71,767	37%	6,284	19,297	7,855	24,413	9,425	29,295	6,268	17,161	7,760	21,800	8,954	25,738
Storage Specialist	GS-1-GS-13	6	28,562	66,951	28,562	69,339	28,562	71,767	28,562	71,767	37%	6,284	19,297	7,855	24,413	9,425	29,295	6,268	17,161	7,760	21,800	8,954	25,738
Supervisory Distribution Facilities Specialist	GS-1-GS-13	6	28,562	66,951	28,562	69,339	28,562	71,767	28,562	71,767	37%	6,284	19,297	7,855	24,413	9,425	29,295	6,268	17,161	7,760	21,800	8,954	25,738
Distribution Facilities Manager	GS-1-GS-13	6	28,562	66,951	28,562	69,339	28,562	71,767	28,562	71,767	37%	6,284	19,297	7,855	24,413	9,425	29,295	6,268	17,161	7,760	21,800	8,954	25,738

Chart II - U.S. Federal - Job Titles - Salaries - Pension Estimates

rades _ Labor

U.S. Federal Government Agencies	GS Grade Range	GS Grade Median	2010 Median Grade Min Salary (STEP 1)	2010 Maximum Grade Salary (STEP 1)	2011 Median Grade Min Salary (STEP 2)	2011 Maximum Grade Salary (STEP 2)	2012 Median Grade Min Salary (STEP 3)	2012 Maximum Grade Salary (STEP 3)	2013 Median Grade Min Salary (STEP 4)	2013 Maximum Grade Salary (STEP 4)	10-Year Cumulative Raise Percentage (1.96%) + Step Increase Percentage (1.7%)	20-Year Annual Pension Benefit Estimate (Min.)	20-Year Annual Pension Benefit Estimate (Max.)	25-Year Annual Pension Benefit Estimate (Min.)	25-Year Annual Pension Benefit Estimate (Max.)	30-Year Annual Pension Benefit Estimate (Min.)	30-Year Annual Pension Benefit Estimate (Max.)	Agency Automatic Contributions 1% Thrift Savings Plan 20 Year Plus 4.5% Interest (Min)	Agency Automatic Contributions 1% Thrift Savings Plan 20 Year Plus 4.5% Interest (Max)	Agency Automatic Contributions 1% Thrift Savings Plan 25 Year Plus 4.5% Interest (Min)	Agency Automatic Contributions 1% Thrift Savings Plan 25 Year Plus 4.5% Interest (Max)	Agency Automatic Contributions 1% Thrift Savings Plan 30 Year Plus 4.5% Interest (Min)	Agency Automatic Contributions 1% Thrift Savings Plan 30 Year Plus 4.5% Interest (Max)
Security Administration Series																							
Personnel Security Specialist	GS-5- GS-15	9	38,824	93,063	39,738	96,387	40,667	99,767	40,667	99,767	37%	10,289	26,832	12,973	33,946	15,567	40,735	9,465	23,859	11,929	30,309	13,988	35,786
Physical Security Specialist	GS-5- GS-15	9	38,824	93,063	39,738	96,387	40,667	99,767	40,667	99,767	37%	10,289	26,832	12,973	33,946	15,567	40,735	9,465	23,859	11,929	30,309	13,988	35,786
Information Security Specialist	GS-5- GS-15	9	38,824	93,063	39,738	96,387	40,667	99,767	40,667	99,767	37%	10,289	26,832	12,973	33,946	15,567	40,735	9,465	23,859	11,929	30,309	13,988	35,786
Industrial Security Specialist	GS-5- GS-15	9	38,824	93,063	39,738	96,387	40,667	99,767	40,667	99,767	37%	10,289	26,832	12,973	33,946	15,567	40,735	9,465	23,859	11,929	30,309	13,988	35,786
Security Specialist	GS-5- GS-15	9	38,824	93,063	39,738	96,387	40,667	99,767	40,667	99,767	37%	10,289	26,832	12,973	33,946	15,567	40,735	9,465	23,859	11,929	30,309	13,988	35,786
Security Officer	GS-5- GS-15	9	38,824	93,063	39,738	96,387	40,667	99,767	40,667	99,767	37%	10,289	26,832	12,973	33,946	15,567	40,735	9,465	23,859	11,929	30,309	13,988	35,786
Supervisory	GS-5- GS-15	9	38,824	93,063	39,738	96,387	40,667	99,767	40,667	99,767	37%	10,289	26,832	12,973	33,946	15,567	40,735	9,465	23,859	11,929	30,309	13,988	35,786
Human Resources Management Series																							
Personnel Officer	GS-5- GS-13	8	35,151	66,951	36,065	69,339	36,994	71,767	36,994	71,767	37%	9,481	19,297	11,963	24,413	14,355	29,295	8,659	17,161	10,931	21,800	12,837	25,738
Assistant Personnel Officer	GS-5- GS-13	8	35,151	66,951	36,065	69,339	36,994	71,767	36,994	71,767	37%	9,481	19,297	11,963	24,413	14,355	29,295	8,659	17,161	10,931	21,800	12,837	25,738
Administrative Officer Series																							
Administrative Assistant	GS-5- GS-15	9	38,824	93,063	39,738	96,387	40,667	99,767	40,667	99,767	37%	10,289	26,832	12,973	33,946	15,567	40,735	9,465	23,859	11,929	30,309	13,988	35,786
Administrative Officer	GS-5- GS-15	9	38,824	93,063	39,738	96,387	40,667	99,767	40,667	99,767	37%	10,289	26,832	12,973	33,946	15,567	40,735	9,465	23,859	11,929	30,309	13,988	35,786
Management and Program Analysis Series																							
Management Analyst	GS-5- GS-7	6	28,562	31,740	29,476	32,872	30,405	34,023	30,405	34,023	37%	8,031	9,148	10,151	11,573	12,181	13,888	7,213	8,136	9,141	10,335	10,771	12,202
Program Analyst	GS-5- GS-7	6	28,562	31,740	29,476	32,872	30,405	34,023	30,405	34,023	37%	8,031	9,148	10,151	11,573	12,181	13,888	7,213	8,136	9,141	10,335	10,771	12,202
Management and Program Analyst	GS-5- GS-7	6	28,562	31,740	29,476	32,872	30,405	34,023	30,405	34,023	37%	8,031	9,148	10,151	11,573	12,181	13,888	7,213	8,136	9,141	10,335	10,771	12,202
Industrial Property Management Series																							
Industrial Property Management Specialist	GS-5- GS-12	6	28,562	56,301	29,476	58,309	30,405	60,351	30,405	60,351	37%	8,031	16,227	10,151	20,529	12,181	24,635	7,213	14,431	9,141	18,332	10,771	21,644
Industrial Property Clearance Specialist	GS-5- GS-12	6	28,562	56,301	29,476	58,309	30,405	60,351	30,405	60,351	37%	8,031	16,227	10,151	20,529	12,181	24,635	7,213	14,431	9,141	18,332	10,771	21,644
Supervisory Industrial Property Management Specialist	GS-5- GS-12	6	28,562	56,301	29,476	58,309	30,405	60,351	30,405	60,351	37%	8,031	16,227	10,151	20,529	12,181	24,635	7,213	14,431	9,141	18,332	10,771	21,644
Supervisory Industrial Property Clearance Specialist	GS-5- GS-12	6	28,562	56,301	29,476	58,309	30,405	60,351	30,405	60,351	37%	8,031	16,227	10,151	20,529	12,181	24,635	7,213	14,431	9,141	18,332	10,771	21,644
Industrial Property Management Officer	GS-5- GS-12	6	28,562	56,301	29,476	58,309	30,405	60,351	30,405	60,351	37%	8,031	16,227	10,151	20,529	12,181	24,635	7,213	14,431	9,141	18,332	10,771	21,644
Industrial Property Clearance Officer	GS-5- GS-12	6	28,562	56,301	29,476	58,309	30,405	60,351	30,405	60,351	37%	8,031	16,227	10,151	20,529	12,181	24,635	7,213	14,431	9,141	18,332	10,771	21,644

Chart II - U.S. Federal - Job Titles - Salaries - Pension Estimates

Transportation

U.S. Federal Government Agencies	GS Grade Range	GS Grade Median	2010 Median Grade Min Salary (STEP 1)	2010 Maximum Grade Salary (STEP 1)	2011 Median Grade Min Salary (STEP 2)	2011 Maximum Grade Salary (STEP 2)	2012 Median Grade Min Salary (STEP 3)	2012 Maximum Grade Salary (STEP 3)	2013 Median Grade Min Salary (STEP 4)	2013 Maximum Grade Salary (STEP 4)	10-Year Cumulative Raise Percentage (1.96%) + Step Increase Percentage (1.7%)	20-Year Annual Pension Benefit Estimate (Min.)	20-Year Annual Pension Benefit Estimate (Max.)	25-Year Annual Pension Benefit Estimate (Min.)	25-Year Annual Pension Benefit Estimate (Max.)	30-Year Annual Pension Benefit Estimate (Min.)	30-Year Annual Pension Benefit Estimate (Max.)	Agency Automatic Contributions 1% Thrift Savings Plan 20 Year Savings Plus 4.5% Interest (Min)	Agency Automatic Contributions 1% Thrift Savings Plan 20 Year Savings Plus 4.5% Interest (Max)	Agency Automatic Contributions 1% Thrift Savings Plan 25 Year Savings Plus 4.5% Interest (Min)	Agency Automatic Contributions 1% Thrift Savings Plan 25 Year Savings Plus 4.5% Interest (Max)	Agency Automatic Contributions 1% Thrift Savings Plan 30 Year Savings Plus 4.5% Interest (Min)	Agency Automatic Contribution 1% Thrift Saving Plan 3 Year Saving Plus 4.5% Intere (Max)
Transportation Clerk and Assistant Series																							
Transportation Clerk	GS-1-GS-7	3	20,401	31,740	20,401	32,872	20,401	34,023	52,141	80,997	37%	11,471	19,482	14,339	24,491	17,207	29,389	10,116	16,481	12,840	21,134	15,351	25,45
Transportation Assistant	GS-1-GS-7	3	20,401	31,740	20,401	32,872	20,401	34,023	52,141	80,997	37%	11,471	19,482	14,339	24,491	17,207	29,389	10,116	16,481	12,840	21,134	15,351	25,45
Lead Transportation Clerk	GS-1-GS-7	3	20,401	31,740	20,401	32,872	20,401	34,023	20,401	80,997	37%	4,488	19,482	5,610	24,491	6,732	29,389	4,477	16,481	5,543	21,134	6,396	25,45
Lead Transportation Assistant	GS-1-GS-7	3	20,401	31,740	20,401	32,872	20,401	34,023	20,401	80,997	37%	4,488	19,482	5,610	24,491	6,732	29,389	4,477	16,481	5,543	21,134	6,396	25,45
Supervisory Transportation Assistant	GS-1-GS-7	3	20,401	31,740	20,401	32,872	20,401	34,023	67,375	80,997	37%	14,823	19,482	18,528	24,491	22,234	29,389	12,822	16,481	16,342	21,134	19,649	25,45
Transportation Industry Analysis Series																							
Transportation Industry Analyst	GS-5-GS-12	7	31,740	56,301	32,654	58,309	33,583	60,351	80,557	60,351	37%	19,065	16,227	23,942	20,529	28,731	24,635	16,255	14,431	20,804	18,332	25,021	21,64
Supervisory Transportation Industry Analyst	GS-5-GS-12	7	31,740	56,301	32,654	58,309	33,583	60,351	80,557	60,351	37%	19,065	16,227	23,942	20,529	28,731	24,635	16,255	14,431	20,804	18,332	25,021	21,64
Transportation Industry Analysis Officer	GS-5-GS-12	7	31,740	56,301	32,654	58,309	33,583	60,351	80,557	95,502	37%	19,065	23,961	23,942	30,196	28,731	36,235	16,255	20,676	20,804	26,413	25,021	31,56
Railroad Safety Series																							
Railroad Safety Inspector	GS-5-GS-15	9	38,824	93,063	39,738	96,387	40,667	99,767	40,667	134,918	37%	10,289	34,565	12,973	43,612	15,567	52,335	9,465	30,104	11,929	38,390	13,988	45,70
Railroad Accident Investigator	GS-5-GS-15	9	38,824	93,063	39,738	96,387	40,667	99,767	40,667	134,918	37%	10,289	34,565	12,973	43,612	15,567	52,335	9,465	30,104	11,929	38,390	13,988	45,70
Railroad Safety Specialist	GS-5-GS-15	9	38,824	93,063	39,738	96,387	40,667	99,767	75,818	99,767	37%	18,022	26,832	22,639	33,946	27,167	40,735	15,709	23,859	20,011	30,309	23,906	35,78
Highway Safety Series																							
Highway Safety Specialist	GS-5-GS-15	9	38,824	93,063	39,738	96,387	40,667	99,767	75,818	99,767	37%	18,022	26,832	22,639	33,946	27,167	40,735	15,709	23,859	20,011	30,309	23,906	35,78
Traffic Management Series																							
Traffic Management Specialist	GS-9-GS-14	8	35,151	79,115	36,535	81,936	37,943	84,805	37,943	84,805	37%	10,381	22,802	13,146	28,847	15,775	34,616	9,145	20,279	11,643	25,760	13,773	30,41
Supervisory Traffic Management Specialist	GS-9-GS-14	8	35,151	79,115	36,535	81,936	37,943	84,805	37,943	84,805	37%	10,381	22,802	13,146	28,847	15,775	34,616	9,145	20,279	11,643	25,760	13,773	30,41
Traffic Manager	GS-9-GS-14	8	35,151	79,115	36,535	81,936	37,943	84,805	37,943	84,805	37%	10,381	22,802	13,146	28,847	15,775	34,616	9,145	20,279	11,643	25,760	13,773	30,41
Cargo Scheduling Series																							
Cargo Scheduler	GS-5-GS-14	8	35,151	79,115	36,065	81,936	36,994	84,805	36,994	84,805	37%	9,481	22,802	11,963	28,847	14,355	34,616	8,659	20,279	10,931	25,760	12,837	30,41
Air Traffic Control Series*	GS-5-GS-14	8	35,151	79,115	36,065	81,936	36,994	84,805	36,994	84,805	37%	9,481	22,802	11,963	28,847	14,355	34,616	8,659	20,279	10,931	25,760	12,837	30,41
Air Traffic Control Specialist	GS-5-GS-14	8	35,151	79,115	36,065	81,936	36,994	84,805	36,994	84,805	37%	9,481	22,802	11,963	28,847	14,355	34,616	8,659	20,279	10,931	25,760	12,837	30,41
Supervisory Air Traffic Control Specialist	GS-5-GS-14	8	35,151	79,115	36,065	81,936	36,994	84,805	36,994	84,805	37%	9,481	22,802	11,963	28,847	14,355	34,616	8,659	20,279	10,931	25,760	12,837	30,41
Air Traffic Assistance Series																							
Air Traffic Assistant	GS-5-GS-15	9	38,824	93,063	39,738	96,387	40,667	99,767	40,667	99,767	37%	10,289	26,832	12,973	33,946	15,567	40,735	9,465	23,859	11,929	30,309	13,988	35,78
Supervisory Air Traffic Assistant	GS-5-GS-15	9	38,824	93,063	39,738	96,387	40,667	99,767	40,667	99,767	37%	10,289	26,832	12,973	33,946	15,567	40,735	9,465	23,859	11,929	30,309	13,988	35,78
Lead Air Traffic Assistant	GS-5-GS-15	9	38,824	93,063	39,738	96,387	40,667	99,767	40,667	99,767	37%	10,289	26,832	12,973	33,946	15,567	40,735	9,465	23,859	11,929	30,309	13,988	35,78
Marine Cargo Series																							

Chart II - U.S. Federal - Job Titles - Salaries - Pension Estimates

U.S. Federal Government Agencies	GS Grade Range:	GS Grade Median	2010 Median Grade Min Salary (STEP 1)	2010 Maximum Grade Salary (STEP 1)	2011 Median Grade Min Salary (STEP 2)	2011 Maximum Grade Salary (STEP 2)	2012 Median Grade Min Salary (STEP 3)	2012 Maximum Grade Salary (STEP 3)	2013 Median Grade Min Salary (STEP 4)	2013 Maximum Grade Salary (STEP 4)	10-Year Cumulative Raise Percentage (1.96%) + Step Increase Percentage (1.7%)	20-Year Annual Pension Benefit Estimate (Min.)	20-Year Annual Pension Benefit Estimate (Max.)	25-Year Annual Pension Benefit Estimate (Min.)	25-Year Annual Pension Benefit Estimate (Max.)	30-Year Annual Pension Benefit Estimate (Min.)	30-Year Annual Pension Benefit Estimate (Max.)	Agency Automatic Contributions 1% Thrift Savings Plan 20 Year Plus 4.5% Interest (Min)	Agency Automatic Contributions 1% Thrift Savings Plan 20 Year Plus 4.5% Interest (Max)	Agency Automatic Contributions 1% Thrift Savings Plan 25 Year Plus 4.5% Interest (Min)	Agency Automatic Contributions 1% Thrift Savings Plan 25 Year Plus 4.5% Interest (Max)	Agency Automatic Contributions 1% Thrift Savings Plan 30 Year Plus 4.5% Interest (Min)	Agency Automatic Contributions 1% Thrift Savings Plan 30 Year Plus 4.5% Interest (Max)
Marine Cargo Assistant	GS-5-GS-11	7	31,740	46,974	32,654	48,649	33,583	50,353	33,583	50,353	37%	8,730	13,539	11,025	17,128	13,230	20,554	7,910	12,041	10,005	15,295	11,768	18,059
Marine Cargo Specialist	GS-5-GS-11	7	31,740	46,974	32,654	48,649	33,583	50,353	33,583	50,353	37%	8,730	13,539	11,025	17,128	13,230	20,554	7,910	12,041	10,005	15,295	11,768	18,059
Supervisory Marine Cargo Specialist	GS-5-GS-11	7	31,740	46,974	32,654	48,649	33,583	50,353	33,583	50,353	37%	8,730	13,539	11,025	17,128	13,230	20,554	7,910	12,041	10,005	15,295	11,768	18,059
Aircraft Operation Series																							
Airplane Pilot	GS-9-GS-14	11	46,974	79,115	48,358	81,936	49,766	84,805	49,766	84,805	37%	12,982	22,802	16,397	28,847	19,676	34,616	11,740	20,279	14,855	25,760	17,480	30,414
Helicopter Pilot	GS-9-GS-14	11	46,974	79,115	48,358	81,936	49,766	84,805	49,766	84,805	37%	12,982	22,802	16,397	28,847	19,676	34,616	11,740	20,279	14,855	25,760	17,480	30,414
Aircraft Pilot	GS-9-GS-14	11	46,974	79,115	48,358	81,936	49,766	84,805	49,766	84,805	37%	12,982	22,802	16,397	28,847	19,676	34,616	11,740	20,279	14,855	25,760	17,480	30,414
Airplane Flight Instructor	GS-9-GS-14	11	46,974	79,115	48,358	81,936	49,766	84,805	49,766	84,805	37%	12,982	22,802	16,397	28,847	19,676	34,616	11,740	20,279	14,855	25,760	17,480	30,414
Airspace Systems Inspection Flight Instructor	GS-9-GS-14	11	46,974	79,115	48,358	81,936	49,766	84,805	49,766	84,805	37%	12,982	22,802	16,397	28,847	19,676	34,616	11,740	20,279	14,855	25,760	17,480	30,414
Test Pilot Flight Instructor	GS-9-GS-14	11	46,974	79,115	48,358	81,936	49,766	84,805	49,766	84,805	37%	12,982	22,802	16,397	28,847	19,676	34,616	11,740	20,279	14,855	25,760	17,480	30,414
Recruitment of Air Reserve Technicians Through Competitive Examination	GS-9-GS-14	11	46,974	79,115	48,358	81,936	49,766	84,805	49,766	84,805	37%	12,982	22,802	16,397	28,847	19,676	34,616	11,740	20,279	14,855	25,760	17,480	30,414
Supervisory	GS-9-GS-14	11	46,974	79,115	48,358	81,936	49,766	84,805	49,766	84,805	37%	12,982	22,802	16,397	28,847	19,676	34,616	11,740	20,279	14,855	25,760	17,480	30,414
Aircrew Technician Series																							
Flight Engineer	GS-7-GS-9	8	35,151	38,824	36,283	40,208	37,434	41,616	37,434	41,616	37%	9,898	11,189	12,511	14,156	15,013	16,987	8,884	9,951	11,261	12,641	13,271	14,925
Aerial Refueling Technician	GS-7-GS-9	8	35,151	38,824	36,283	40,208	37,434	41,616	37,434	41,616	37%	9,898	11,189	12,511	14,156	15,013	16,987	8,884	9,951	11,261	12,641	13,271	14,925
Aircraft Loadmaster	GS-7-GS-9	8	35,151	38,824	36,283	40,208	37,434	41,616	37,434	41,616	37%	9,898	11,189	12,511	14,156	15,013	16,987	8,884	9,951	11,261	12,641	13,271	14,925
Recruitment of Air Reserve Technicians Through Competitive Examination	GS-7-GS-9	8	35,151	38,824	36,283	40,208	37,434	41,616	37,434	41,616	37%	9,898	11,189	12,511	14,156	15,013	16,987	8,884	9,951	11,261	12,641	13,271	14,925
Supervisory	GS-7-GS-9	8	35,151	38,824	36,283	40,208	37,434	41,616	37,434	41,616	37%	9,898	11,189	12,511	14,156	15,013	16,987	8,884	9,951	11,261	12,641	13,271	14,925

Chart II - U.S. Federal - Job Titles - Salaries - Pension Estimates

Sheet 23: Veterinary Med Science

U.S. Federal Government Agencies	GS Grade Range	GS Grade Median	2010 Median Grade Min Salary (STEP 1)	2010 Maximum Grade Salary (STEP 1)	2011 Median Grade Min Salary (STEP 2)	2011 Maximum Grade Salary (STEP 2)	2012 Median Grade Min Salary (STEP 3)	2012 Maximum Grade Salary (STEP 3)	2013 Median Grade Min Salary (STEP 4)	2013 Maximum Grade Salary (STEP 4)	10-Year Cumulative Raise Percentage (1.96%) + Step Increase Percentage (1.7%)	20-Year Annual Pension Benefit Estimate (Min.)	20-Year Annual Pension Benefit Estimate (Max.)	25-Year Annual Pension Benefit Estimate (Min.)	25-Year Annual Pension Benefit Estimate (Max.)	30-Year Annual Pension Benefit Estimate (Min.)	30-Year Annual Pension Benefit Estimate (Max.)	Agency Automatic Contributions 1% Thrift Savings Plan 20 Year Savings Plus 4.5% Interest (Min)	Agency Automatic Contributions 1% Thrift Savings Plan 20 Year Savings Plus 4.5% Interest (Max)	Agency Automatic Contributions 1% Thrift Savings Plan 25 Year Savings Plus 4.5% Interest (Min)	Agency Automatic Contributions 1% Thrift Savings Plan 25 Year Savings Plus 4.5% Interest (Max)	Agency Automatic Contributions 1% Thrift Savings Plan 30 Year Savings Plus 4.5% Interest (Min)	Agency Automatic Contributions 1% Thrift Savings Plan 30 Year Savings Plus 4.5% Interest (Max)
Veterinary Medical Science Series																							
Veterinary Medical Officer	GS-5-GS-15	9	38,824	93,063	39,738	96,387	40,667	99,767	40,667	99,767	37%	10,289	26,832	12,973	33,946	15,567	40,735	9,465	23,859	11,929	30,309	13,988	35,786
Supervisors and Leaders	GS-5-GS-15	9	38,824	93,063	39,738	96,387	40,667	99,767	40,667	99,767	37%	10,289	26,832	12,973	33,946	15,567	40,735	9,465	23,859	11,929	30,309	13,988	35,786
Animal Health Technician Series*																							
Animal Health Aid	GS-3-GS-4	3	20,401	22,902	21,128	23,718	21,868	24,548	21,868	24,548	37%	5,880	6,600	7,439	8,349	8,926	10,019	5,229	5,870	6,642	7,456	7,843	8,803
Animal Care Inspector	GS-3-GS-4	3	20,401	22,902	21,128	23,718	21,868	24,548	21,868	24,548	37%	5,880	6,600	7,439	8,349	8,926	10,019	5,229	5,870	6,642	7,456	7,843	8,803
Animal Health Technician	GS-3-GS-4	3	20,401	22,902	21,128	23,718	21,868	24,548	21,868	24,548	37%	5,880	6,600	7,439	8,349	8,926	10,019	5,229	5,870	6,642	7,456	7,843	8,803
Work Leader Positions	GS-3-GS-4	3	20,401	22,902	21,128	23,718	21,868	24,548	21,868	24,548	37%	5,880	6,600	7,439	8,349	8,926	10,019	5,229	5,870	6,642	7,456	7,843	8,803
Supervisory Positions	GS-3-GS-4	3	20,401	22,902	21,128	23,718	21,868	24,548	21,868	24,548	37%	5,880	6,600	7,439	8,349	8,926	10,019	5,229	5,870	6,642	7,456	7,843	8,803

Veterinary Med Science

U.S. Federal Government Agencies	GS Grade Range	GS Grade Median	2010 Min	2010 Max	2011 Min	2011 Max	2012 Min	2012 Max	2013 Min	2013 Max	10-Yr %	20-Yr Min	20-Yr Max	25-Yr Min	25-Yr Max	30-Yr Min	30-Yr Max	TSP 20 Min	TSP 20 Max	TSP 25 Min	TSP 25 Max	TSP 30 Min	TSP 30 Max
Veterinary Medical Science Series																							
Veterinary Medical Officer	GS-5-GS-15	9	38,824	93,063	39,738	96,387	40,667	99,767	40,667	99,767	37%	10,289	26,832	12,973	33,946	15,567	40,735	9,465	23,859	11,929	30,309	13,988	35,786
Supervisors and Leaders	GS-5-GS-15	9	38,824	93,063	39,738	96,387	40,667	99,767	40,667	99,767	37%	10,289	26,832	12,973	33,946	15,567	40,735	9,465	23,859	11,929	30,309	13,988	35,786
Animal Health Technician Series*																							
Animal Health Aid	GS-3-GS-4	3	20,401	22,902	21,128	23,718	21,868	24,548	21,868	24,548	37%	5,880	6,600	7,439	8,349	8,926	10,019	5,229	5,870	6,642	7,456	7,843	8,803
Animal Care Inspector	GS-3-GS-4	3	20,401	22,902	21,128	23,718	21,868	24,548	21,868	24,548	37%	5,880	6,600	7,439	8,349	8,926	10,019	5,229	5,870	6,642	7,456	7,843	8,803
Animal Health Technician	GS-3-GS-4	3	20,401	22,902	21,128	23,718	21,868	24,548	21,868	24,548	37%	5,880	6,600	7,439	8,349	8,926	10,019	5,229	5,870	6,642	7,456	7,843	8,803
Work Leader Positions	GS-3-GS-4	3	20,401	22,902	21,128	23,718	21,868	24,548	21,868	24,548	37%	5,880	6,600	7,439	8,349	8,926	10,019	5,229	5,870	6,642	7,456	7,843	8,803
Supervisory Positions	GS-3-GS-4	3	20,401	22,902	21,128	23,718	21,868	24,548	21,868	24,548	37%	5,880	6,600	7,439	8,349	8,926	10,019	5,229	5,870	6,642	7,456	7,843	8,803

Chart II - U.S. Federal - Job Titles - Salaries - Pension Estimates

Chart II - U.S. Federal - Job Titles - Salaries - Pension Estimates

Chart III: U.S. States & Cities, Job Titles & Salaries
5-Year Salary Projections & Pension Estimates

LEGEND:

Job titles shown here represent a sampling of all job titles used by the U.S. State & City agencies and departments.

*Salary minimum and maximum amounts are projected estimates, based on actual base published salaries, from base year in the U.S. Federal GS Schedule, plus the estimated raise percentage. The raise percentage used is based on a 5-year average of actual published raises for the U.S. Federal Government from over the most recent 5 years (USAOPM, GS Pay Schedule, 2006.).

** Cumulative 5-Year Raise Estimate, is based on 5-Year Average Raise Estimate, as determined from actual published raise figures from over the most recent 5 years. Compounded 5-Year Raise Estimate (not shown) is greater than Cumulative 5-Year Raise Estimate.

***Estimated Pension at 20-Years, 25-Years, and 30-Years is based on the Pension Formula for the U.S. Federal Government 3 part plan: 1) The Basic Benefit annual pension of Average of 3 Highest Years Salaries times Pension Percentage 1.1% times Number of Years. The Pension Benefit is based on a fixed formula. 2) Social Security Benefits are paid in addition to The Basic Plan Benefits. 3) The Thrift Savings Plan pays an Automatic Agency Contribution of 1% of base salary per year. Employees may make additional contributions to the Thrift Savings Plan; contributions will be matched by the Agency at a rate of $1.00 for $1.00 for the first 3% of base salary contributed, and $.50 for $1.00 for the second 2% of base salary contributed (USAOPM, FERS, 2006.)

****Retirement Benefit from Agency Thrift Savings Plan. The Retirement Benefit calculated here from The Thrift Savings Plan is calculated as 1% of base salary minimum or maximum per year, plus an estimated 4.5% estimated Interest accrued per year on the 1%. Employees may choose to save their Thrift Savings in any of a variety of investment savings vehicles; interest rates may vary. This calculation shown for demonstration purposes is made without any additional Employee Contributions (USAOPM, TSP, 2006.)

*****Senior Executive Service: The SES pay range has a minimum rate of basic pay equal to 120 percent of the rate for GS-15, step 1, and the maximum rate of basic pay is equal to the rate for level III of the Executive Schedule. For any agency certified as having a performance appraisal system, the maximum rate of basic pay will be the rate for level II of the Executive Schedule (USAOPM, SES, 2006.)

Disclaimer: The Salary & Pension performance data featured is based on past performance, which is no guarantee of future results. Current Salary & Pension may be higher or lower than the performance data quoted.

REFERENCEs:
U.S. Federal Government, Office of Personnel Management, Federal Employee Retirement System 2006, http://www.opm.gov/forms/pdfimage/RI90-1.pdf

U.S. Federal Government, Office of Personnel Administration, GS Pay Schedule, 2006, http://www.opm.gov/oca/06tables/pdf/gs.pdf;   http://www.opm.gov/oca/06tables/indexGS.asp.

U.S. Federal Government, Office of Personnel Administration, Senior Executive Service, 2006, http://www.opm.gov/oca/06tables/pdf/es.pdf   http://www.opm.gov/ses.

U.S. Federal Government, Office of Personnel Administration, Thrift Savings Plan, 2006, http://www.opm.gov/benefits/correction/faq/Thrift.htm

Chart III - U.S. States & Cities - Job Titles - Salaries - Pension Estimates

Arizona	2010 (Min)	2010 (Max)	2011 (Min)	2011 (Max)	2012 (Min)	2012 (Max)	2013 (Min)	2013 (Max)	2014 (Min)	2014 (Max)	5-Year Average % Raise	5-Year Cumulative Raise Estimate**	20-Year Annual Pension Benefit Estimate (Min.)***	20-Year Annual Pension Benefit Estimate (Max.)	25-Year Annual Pension Benefit Estimate (Min.)	25-Year Annual Pension Benefit Estimate (Max.)	30-Year Annual Pension Benefit Estimate (Min.)	30-Year Annual Pension Benefit Estimate (Max.)
Accountant I-V	39,466	87,782	40,374	89,801	41,302	91,866	42,252	93,979	43,224	96,141	2.30%	11.50%	24,983	55,569	35,803	79,636	50,325	111,936
Admv Asst I-III	28,147	54,281	28,794	55,529	29,456	56,807	30,134	58,113	30,827	59,450	2.30%	11.50%	17,818	34,362	25,535	49,244	35,892	69,217
Admv Secy I-III	26,716	44,173	27,330	45,189	27,959	46,228	28,602	47,292	29,260	48,379	2.30%	11.50%	16,912	27,963	24,236	40,074	34,067	56,328
Admv Supp Spv I-III	30,026	54,281	30,716	55,529	31,423	56,807	32,146	58,113	32,885	59,450	2.30%	11.50%	19,007	34,362	27,239	49,244	38,288	69,217
Admv Svc Officer I-V	44,514	95,431	45,538	97,626	46,585	99,871	47,657	102,168	48,753	104,518	2.30%	11.50%	28,179	60,411	40,383	86,575	56,763	121,690
Agric Inspr I-IV	26,889	54,281	27,508	55,529	28,140	56,807	28,788	58,113	29,450	59,450	2.30%	11.50%	17,022	34,362	24,394	49,244	34,288	69,217
Atty I-IV	16,526	142,815	16,906	146,100	17,295	149,460	17,693	152,898	18,100	156,414	2.30%	11.50%	10,462	90,407	14,992	129,561	21,073	182,113
Bldg Maint Tech I-III	23,975	46,828	24,526	47,905	25,090	49,007	25,667	50,134	26,258	51,287	2.30%	11.50%	15,177	29,644	21,750	42,482	30,572	59,713
Budg Ctrl Dvmt Officer I-II	46,607	74,646	47,679	76,363	48,775	78,119	49,897	79,916	51,045	81,754	2.30%	11.50%	29,504	47,254	42,282	67,719	59,431	95,186
Budg Ctrl Dvmt Spct I-III	40,522	74,646	41,454	76,363	42,407	78,119	43,383	79,916	44,380	81,754	2.30%	11.50%	25,652	47,254	36,761	67,719	51,672	95,186
Buyer I-IV	27,937	74,646	28,579	76,363	29,237	78,119	29,909	79,916	30,597	81,754	2.30%	11.50%	17,685	47,254	25,344	67,719	35,624	95,186
Capitol Police Captain	52,568	87,782	53,777	89,801	55,014	91,866	56,279	93,979	57,574	96,141	2.30%	11.50%	33,277	55,569	47,689	79,636	67,033	111,936
Capitol Police Lieutenant	50,186	80,805	51,341	82,663	52,522	84,565	53,730	86,510	54,965	88,499	2.30%	11.50%	31,770	51,153	45,529	73,306	63,996	103,040
Capitol Police Officer I-II	39,090	68,663	39,989	70,242	40,909	71,857	41,850	73,510	42,812	75,201	2.30%	11.50%	24,745	43,466	35,462	62,291	49,846	87,556
Capitol Police Sergeant	47,928	74,646	49,031	76,363	50,158	78,119	51,312	79,916	52,492	81,754	2.30%	11.50%	30,340	47,254	43,481	67,719	61,117	95,186
Carpenter	31,849	50,793	32,581	51,961	33,331	53,156	34,097	54,379	34,881	55,630	2.30%	11.50%	20,161	32,154	28,893	46,079	40,612	64,770
Child Protv Svc Prg Spct	46,302	79,490	47,367	81,318	48,456	83,188	49,571	85,102	50,711	87,059	2.30%	11.50%	29,311	50,320	42,005	72,113	59,043	101,363
Child Protv Svc Spct I-II	36,485	67,397	37,324	68,947	38,182	70,532	39,060	72,155	39,959	73,814	2.30%	11.50%	23,096	42,664	33,099	61,142	46,524	85,942
Child Protv Svcs Spct III	42,555	73,219	43,534	74,903	44,535	76,625	45,560	78,388	46,608	80,191	2.30%	11.50%	26,939	46,350	38,606	66,424	54,265	93,366
Civil Rgts Cmplnc Officer I-III	31,770	74,646	32,501	76,363	33,249	78,119	34,013	79,916	34,796	81,754	2.30%	11.50%	20,112	47,254	28,822	67,719	40,512	95,186
Class/Comp Analyst Sr	50,434	68,663	51,594	70,242	52,780	71,857	53,994	73,510	55,236	75,201	2.30%	11.50%	31,926	43,466	45,753	62,291	64,311	87,556
Clerical Aide	16,962	16,962	17,352	17,352	17,751	17,751	18,159	18,160	18,577	18,577	2.30%	11.50%	10,737	10,738	15,388	15,388	21,629	21,630
Clerical Asst	19,346	30,872	19,790	31,582	20,246	32,309	20,711	33,052	21,188	33,812	2.30%	11.50%	12,246	19,543	17,550	28,007	24,669	39,367
Clerk Typist I-III	21,367	37,297	21,859	38,155	22,361	39,032	22,876	39,930	23,402	40,848	2.30%	11.50%	13,526	23,610	19,384	33,836	27,247	47,560
Clms Spct I-II	25,399	46,828	25,983	47,905	26,581	49,007	27,192	50,134	27,818	51,287	2.30%	11.50%	16,079	29,644	23,042	42,482	32,388	59,713
Clms Spct Spv	31,770	54,281	32,501	55,529	33,249	56,806	34,013	58,113	34,796	59,450	2.30%	11.50%	20,112	34,362	28,822	49,243	40,512	69,217
Cmpr Asstd Mass Aprasl Spct I-II	48,268	80,805	49,378	82,663	50,514	84,565	51,676	86,510	52,864	88,499	2.30%	11.50%	30,555	51,153	43,788	73,306	61,549	103,040
Cnsmr Svc Spct I-II	39,565	58,164	40,475	59,502	41,406	60,871	42,358	62,271	43,332	63,703	2.30%	11.50%	25,046	36,820	35,893	52,767	50,452	74,169
Collcn Spv I-III	44,854	74,646	45,886	76,363	46,941	78,119	48,021	79,916	49,125	81,754	2.30%	11.50%	28,394	47,254	40,691	67,719	57,196	95,186
Comucb Disease Invstgr I-II	25,399	46,828	25,983	47,905	26,581	49,007	27,192	50,134	27,818	51,287	2.30%	11.50%	16,079	29,644	23,042	42,482	32,388	59,713
Contracts Mgt Spct I-III	34,073	68,663	34,856	70,242	35,658	71,857	36,478	73,510	37,317	75,201	2.30%	11.50%	21,569	43,466	30,910	62,291	43,448	87,556
Contracts Mgt Spv I-II	47,643	80,805	48,739	82,663	49,860	84,565	51,007	86,510	52,180	88,499	2.30%	11.50%	30,160	51,153	43,222	73,306	60,753	103,040
Cook II-III	22,598	39,500	23,117	40,409	23,649	41,338	24,193	42,289	24,750	43,262	2.30%	11.50%	14,305	25,005	20,501	35,835	28,816	50,369
Corrl Chaplain I-II	32,064	62,388	32,802	63,823	33,556	65,291	34,328	66,793	35,118	68,329	2.30%	11.50%	20,298	39,494	29,089	56,599	40,887	79,555
Corrl Food Svc Mgr I-III	36,619	74,646	37,461	76,363	38,323	78,119	39,204	79,916	40,106	81,754	2.30%	11.50%	23,181	47,254	33,221	67,719	46,695	95,186
Corrl Food Svc Spv I-II	30,358	54,281	31,057	55,529	31,771	56,806	32,502	58,113	33,249	59,450	2.30%	11.50%	19,218	34,362	27,541	49,243	38,712	69,217
Corrl Inds Prodc Spct	31,770	54,281	32,501	55,529	33,249	56,806	34,013	58,113	34,796	59,450	2.30%	11.50%	20,112	34,362	28,822	49,243	40,512	69,217
Corrl Officer I-IV	34,922	70,175	35,725	71,789	36,547	73,440	37,388	75,129	38,247	76,857	2.30%	11.50%	22,107	44,423	31,681	63,662	44,531	89,484
Corrl Rcds Clerk I-II	22,598	39,500	23,117	40,409	23,649	41,338	24,193	42,289	24,750	43,262	2.30%	11.50%	14,305	25,005	20,501	35,835	28,816	50,369

Chart III - U.S. States & Cities - Job Titles - Salaries - Pension Estimates

Arizona	2010 (Min)	2010 (Max)	2011 (Min)	2011 (Max)	2012 (Min)	2012 (Max)	2013 (Min)	2013 (Max)	2014 (Min)	2014 (Max)	5-Year Average % Raise	5-Year Cumulative Raise Estimate**	20-Year Annual Pension Benefit Estimate (Min.)***	20-Year Annual Pension Benefit Estimate (Max.)	25-Year Annual Pension Benefit Estimate (Min.)	25-Year Annual Pension Benefit Estimate (Max.)	30-Year Annual Pension Benefit Estimate (Min.)	30-Year Annual Pension Benefit Estimate (Max.)
Corrl Rcds Spv I-II	28,084	50,793	28,730	51,961	29,391	53,156	30,067	54,379	30,758	55,630	2.30%	11.50%	17,778	32,154	25,478	46,079	35,812	64,770
Corrl Rcds Tech I-II	26,520	44,173	27,130	45,189	27,754	46,229	28,392	47,292	29,045	48,380	2.30%	11.50%	16,788	27,963	24,059	40,074	33,817	56,328
Corrl Rn Spv I-II	39,483	69,839	40,391	71,445	41,320	73,088	42,270	74,769	43,242	76,489	2.30%	11.50%	24,994	44,210	35,819	63,357	50,347	89,056
Corrl Sergeant	44,420	65,902	45,441	67,418	46,486	68,969	47,555	70,555	48,649	72,178	2.30%	11.50%	28,119	41,719	40,297	59,786	56,642	84,036
Cps Case Aide I-II	26,701	48,805	27,315	49,928	27,943	51,076	28,586	52,251	29,243	53,453	2.30%	11.50%	16,903	30,896	24,223	44,276	34,048	62,235
Cse Officer I-II	29,693	58,164	30,375	59,502	31,074	60,871	31,789	62,271	32,520	63,703	2.30%	11.50%	18,796	36,820	26,937	52,767	37,863	74,169
Cse Prg Mgr II	47,357	80,805	48,446	82,663	49,561	84,565	50,700	86,510	51,867	88,499	2.30%	11.50%	29,979	51,153	42,962	73,306	60,388	103,040
Cse Tech I-II	22,598	41,789	23,117	42,750	23,649	43,734	24,193	44,740	24,750	45,769	2.30%	11.50%	14,305	26,454	20,501	37,911	28,816	53,288
Cse Unit Spv I-II	39,407	68,663	40,313	70,242	41,240	71,857	42,189	73,510	43,159	75,201	2.30%	11.50%	24,946	43,466	35,750	62,291	50,250	87,556
Cust Svc Rep I-III	25,399	50,793	25,983	51,961	26,581	53,156	27,192	54,379	27,818	55,630	2.30%	11.50%	16,079	32,154	23,042	46,079	32,388	64,770
Custodial Crew Spv I-II	25,399	44,173	25,983	45,189	26,581	46,229	27,192	47,292	27,818	48,380	2.30%	11.50%	16,079	27,963	23,042	40,074	32,388	56,328
Custodial Worker I-II	20,387	35,425	20,856	36,240	21,336	37,073	21,826	37,926	22,328	38,798	2.30%	11.50%	12,906	22,425	18,495	32,137	25,997	45,172
Data Entry Oper II-IV	23,483	37,297	24,023	38,155	24,575	39,032	25,140	39,930	25,719	40,848	2.30%	11.50%	14,865	23,610	21,303	33,836	29,944	47,560
Data Entry Spv I-II	30,199	50,793	30,894	51,961	31,605	53,156	32,331	54,379	33,075	55,630	2.30%	11.50%	19,117	32,154	27,397	46,079	38,509	64,770
Disab Evalr I-V	38,515	80,805	39,401	82,663	40,308	84,565	41,235	86,510	42,183	88,499	2.30%	11.50%	24,382	51,153	34,941	73,306	49,114	103,040
Dispatcher I-II	29,505	44,173	30,184	45,189	30,878	46,229	31,589	47,292	32,315	48,380	2.30%	11.50%	18,678	27,963	26,767	40,074	37,624	56,328
Dpty Fire Marshall I-II	34,073	68,663	34,856	70,242	35,658	71,857	36,478	73,510	37,317	75,201	2.30%	11.50%	21,569	43,466	30,910	62,291	43,448	87,556
Drug Inspr I-II	49,462	128,216	50,599	131,165	51,763	134,182	52,953	137,268	54,171	140,425	2.30%	11.50%	31,311	81,165	44,871	116,317	63,072	163,496
Duplg Eqp Oper I-III	22,598	46,828	23,117	47,905	23,649	49,007	24,193	50,134	24,750	51,287	2.30%	11.50%	14,305	29,644	20,501	42,482	28,816	59,713
Duplg Svs Spv I-III	29,693	62,388	30,375	63,823	31,074	65,291	31,789	66,793	32,520	68,329	2.30%	11.50%	18,796	39,494	26,937	56,599	37,863	79,555
Econ Security Dist Prg Mgr I-II	43,790	80,805	44,797	82,663	45,828	84,565	46,882	86,510	47,960	88,499	2.30%	11.50%	27,721	51,153	39,726	73,306	55,840	103,040
Economist I-III	35,595	80,805	36,414	82,663	37,251	84,565	38,108	86,510	38,984	88,499	2.30%	11.50%	22,533	51,153	32,292	73,306	45,389	103,040
Educ Prg Spct	43,790	74,646	44,797	76,363	45,828	78,119	46,882	79,916	47,960	81,754	2.30%	11.50%	27,721	47,254	39,726	67,719	55,840	95,186
Electr Tech II-III	32,643	50,793	33,394	51,961	34,162	53,156	34,947	54,379	35,751	55,630	2.30%	11.50%	20,664	32,154	29,613	46,079	41,625	64,770
Electrician	36,791	54,281	37,637	55,529	38,503	56,806	39,388	58,113	40,294	59,450	2.30%	11.50%	23,290	34,362	33,376	49,243	46,914	69,217
Elevator Inspr	43,790	74,646	44,797	76,363	45,828	78,119	46,882	79,916	47,960	81,754	2.30%	11.50%	27,721	47,254	39,726	67,719	55,840	95,186
Emer Response Spct	50,035	68,663	51,186	70,242	52,363	71,857	53,567	73,510	54,799	75,201	2.30%	11.50%	31,674	43,466	45,391	62,291	63,802	87,556
Empmt Cnslr II-III	29,693	54,281	30,375	55,529	31,074	56,806	31,789	58,113	32,520	59,450	2.30%	11.50%	18,796	34,362	26,937	49,243	37,863	69,217
Engrg Plans Tech I-III	32,541	58,164	33,290	59,502	34,055	60,871	34,839	62,271	35,640	63,703	2.30%	11.50%	20,600	36,820	29,521	52,767	41,495	74,169
Envmtl Engr	54,936	80,805	56,199	82,663	57,492	84,565	58,814	86,510	60,167	88,499	2.30%	11.50%	34,776	51,153	49,838	73,306	70,052	103,040
Envmtl Engr Spct	52,417	74,646	53,622	76,363	54,856	78,119	56,117	79,916	57,408	81,754	2.30%	11.50%	33,182	47,254	47,552	67,719	66,840	95,186
Envmtl Hlth Spct I-II	33,556	62,388	34,328	63,823	35,118	65,291	35,925	66,793	36,752	68,329	2.30%	11.50%	21,242	39,494	30,442	56,599	42,790	79,555
Envmtl Instmt Tech II	34,445	50,793	35,237	51,961	36,048	53,156	36,877	54,379	37,725	55,630	2.30%	11.50%	21,805	32,154	31,248	46,079	43,923	64,770
Envmtl Prg Spct	42,294	68,663	43,266	70,242	44,262	71,857	45,280	73,510	46,321	75,201	2.30%	11.50%	26,773	43,466	38,369	62,291	53,931	87,556
Envmtl Prg Spv	49,726	80,805	50,870	82,663	52,040	84,565	53,237	86,510	54,462	88,499	2.30%	11.50%	31,479	51,153	45,112	73,306	63,409	103,040
Epidmog Spct I-II	34,073	68,663	34,856	70,242	35,658	71,857	36,478	73,510	37,317	75,201	2.30%	11.50%	21,569	43,466	30,910	62,291	43,448	87,556
Eqp Oper I-III	27,309	54,281	27,937	55,529	28,579	56,806	29,236	58,113	29,909	59,450	2.30%	11.50%	17,287	34,362	24,774	49,243	34,823	69,217
Equal Opportunity Spct I	27,937	46,828	28,579	47,905	29,237	49,007	29,909	50,134	30,597	51,287	2.30%	11.50%	17,685	29,644	25,344	42,482	35,624	59,713
Equal Oprty Spct II-III	41,788	62,388	42,749	63,823	43,732	65,291	44,738	66,793	45,767	68,329	2.30%	11.50%	26,453	39,494	37,910	56,599	53,287	79,555
Examiner Tech I-II	27,395	41,789	28,025	42,750	28,670	43,734	29,329	44,740	30,004	45,769	2.30%	11.50%	17,342	26,454	24,853	37,911	34,933	53,288
Exec Cons I-III	40,320	95,431	41,247	97,626	42,196	99,871	43,166	102,168	44,159	104,518	2.30%	11.50%	25,524	60,411	36,578	86,574	51,414	121,690
Exec Secy I-II	31,110	50,793	31,826	51,961	32,558	53,156	33,307	54,379	34,073	55,630	2.30%	11.50%	19,694	32,154	28,223	46,079	39,671	64,770
Exec Staff Asst	40,320	68,663	41,247	70,242	42,196	71,857	43,166	73,510	44,159	75,201	2.30%	11.50%	25,524	43,466	36,578	62,291	51,414	87,556
Fin Cons I-II	36,619	74,646	37,461	76,363	38,323	78,119	39,204	79,916	40,106	81,754	2.30%	11.50%	23,181	47,254	33,221	67,719	46,695	95,186
Fin Invstg Auditor II	43,790	74,646	44,797	76,363	45,828	78,119	46,882	79,916	47,960	81,754	2.30%	11.50%	27,721	47,254	39,726	67,719	55,840	95,186

Chart III - U.S. States & Cities - Job Titles - Salaries - Pension Estimates

Arizona	2010 (Min)	2010 (Max)	2011 (Min)	2011 (Max)	2012 (Min)	2012 (Max)	2013 (Min)	2013 (Max)	2014 (Min)	2014 (Max)	5-Year Average % Raise	5-Year Cumulative Raise Estimate**	20-Year Annual Pension Benefit Estimate (Min.)***	20-Year Annual Pension Benefit Estimate (Max.)	25-Year Annual Pension Benefit Estimate (Min.)	25-Year Annual Pension Benefit Estimate (Max.)	30-Year Annual Pension Benefit Estimate (Min.)	30-Year Annual Pension Benefit Estimate (Max.)
Fis Svs Mgr I-III	40,320	80,805	41,247	82,663	42,196	84,565	43,166	86,510	44,159	88,499	2.30%	11.50%	25,524	51,153	36,578	73,306	51,414	103,040
Fis Svs Spct I-V	29,621	62,388	30,303	63,823	31,000	65,291	31,713	66,793	32,442	68,329	2.30%	11.50%	18,751	39,494	26,872	56,599	37,772	79,555
Food Svc Mgr I-II	34,073	68,663	34,856	70,242	35,658	71,857	36,478	73,510	37,317	75,201	2.30%	11.50%	21,569	43,466	30,910	62,291	43,448	87,556
Food Svc Worker II-III	19,346	33,970	19,790	34,752	20,246	35,551	20,711	36,369	21,188	37,205	2.30%	11.50%	12,246	21,505	17,550	30,818	24,669	43,318
Geologist I-II	34,941	68,663	35,744	70,242	36,566	71,857	37,407	73,510	38,268	75,201	2.30%	11.50%	22,119	43,466	31,698	62,291	44,555	87,556
Graphic Designer I-III	38,278	44,173	39,158	45,189	40,059	46,229	40,980	47,292	41,923	48,380	2.30%	11.50%	24,231	27,963	34,725	40,074	48,810	56,328
Grounds Spv I-II	34,464	50,793	35,256	51,961	36,067	53,156	36,897	54,379	37,745	55,630	2.30%	11.50%	21,817	32,154	31,265	46,079	43,947	64,770
Groundskeeper I-II	25,154	39,500	25,733	40,409	26,325	41,338	26,930	42,289	27,550	43,262	2.30%	11.50%	15,924	25,005	22,820	35,835	32,076	50,369
Hab Spv I-II	27,937	54,281	28,579	55,529	29,237	56,806	29,909	58,113	30,597	59,450	2.30%	11.50%	17,685	34,362	25,344	49,243	35,624	69,217
Hab Svc Prg Mgr I-II	43,790	80,805	44,797	82,663	45,828	84,565	46,882	86,510	47,960	88,499	2.30%	11.50%	27,721	51,153	39,726	73,306	55,840	103,040
Hab Tech II-III	23,284	41,789	23,820	42,750	24,367	43,734	24,928	44,740	25,501	45,769	2.30%	11.50%	14,740	26,454	21,123	37,911	29,691	53,288
Hazrd Mats Spct I	31,770	54,281	32,501	55,529	33,249	56,806	34,013	58,113	34,796	59,450	2.30%	11.50%	20,112	34,362	28,822	49,243	40,512	69,217
Hearing Officer II-IV	40,320	95,431	41,247	97,626	42,196	99,871	43,166	102,168	44,159	104,518	2.30%	11.50%	25,524	60,411	36,578	86,574	51,414	121,690
Hlth Care Facs Insp Spct	36,619	62,388	37,461	63,823	38,323	65,291	39,204	66,793	40,106	68,329	2.30%	11.50%	23,181	39,494	33,221	56,599	46,695	79,555
Hlth Educator I-II	31,770	62,388	32,501	63,823	33,249	65,291	34,013	66,793	34,796	68,329	2.30%	11.50%	20,112	39,494	28,822	56,599	40,512	79,555
Hlth Prg Mgr I-III	48,162	80,805	49,270	82,663	50,403	84,565	51,563	86,510	52,749	88,499	2.30%	11.50%	30,489	51,153	43,693	73,306	61,415	103,040
Hlth Svc Cmty Prg Rep I-II	38,335	68,663	39,217	70,242	40,119	71,857	41,042	73,510	41,986	75,201	2.30%	11.50%	24,268	43,466	34,778	62,291	48,884	87,556
Housekeeper Spv I	27,470	44,173	28,102	45,189	28,748	46,229	29,409	47,292	30,086	48,380	2.30%	11.50%	17,390	27,963	24,921	40,074	35,029	56,328
Hum/S Prg Dvmt Spct	41,141	68,663	42,087	70,242	43,055	71,857	44,046	73,510	45,059	75,201	2.30%	11.50%	26,044	43,466	37,323	62,291	52,462	87,556
Hum/S Spct I-III	29,593	58,164	30,273	59,502	30,969	60,871	31,682	62,271	32,410	63,703	2.30%	11.50%	18,733	36,820	26,846	52,767	37,735	74,169
Hum/S Worker I-II	24,548	39,500	25,112	40,409	25,690	41,338	26,281	42,289	26,885	43,262	2.30%	11.50%	15,539	25,005	22,269	35,835	31,302	50,369
Hwy Maint Tech I-III	29,621	58,164	30,303	59,502	31,000	60,871	31,713	62,271	32,442	63,703	2.30%	11.50%	18,751	36,820	26,872	52,767	37,772	74,169
Hwy Sign Fabricator I-II	26,040	59,243	26,639	60,606	27,251	62,000	27,878	63,426	28,519	64,885	2.30%	11.50%	16,484	37,503	23,623	53,745	33,205	75,545
Hydrologist I-IV	34,941	87,782	35,744	89,801	36,566	91,866	37,407	93,979	38,268	96,141	2.30%	11.50%	22,119	55,569	31,698	79,636	44,555	111,936
Ind Hygienist II-III	40,320	80,805	41,247	82,663	42,196	84,565	43,166	86,510	44,159	88,499	2.30%	11.50%	25,524	51,153	36,578	73,306	51,414	103,040
Info Techngy Spct I-V	22,329	137,741	22,842	140,909	23,368	144,150	23,905	147,465	24,455	150,857	2.30%	11.50%	14,135	87,195	20,256	124,958	28,473	175,642
Ins Analyst	40,320	68,663	41,247	70,242	42,196	71,857	43,166	73,510	44,159	75,201	2.30%	11.50%	25,524	43,466	36,578	62,291	51,414	87,556
Ins Clms Spct	34,073	58,164	34,856	59,502	35,658	60,871	36,478	62,271	37,317	63,703	2.30%	11.50%	21,569	36,820	30,910	52,767	43,448	74,169
Instnl Chaplain I-II	31,770	62,388	32,501	63,823	33,249	65,291	34,013	66,793	34,796	68,329	2.30%	11.50%	20,112	39,494	28,822	56,599	40,512	79,555
Invgns Spv I-III	39,090	74,646	39,989	76,363	40,909	78,119	41,850	79,916	42,812	81,754	2.30%	11.50%	24,745	47,254	35,462	67,719	49,846	95,186
Invgtr I-III	27,937	58,164	28,579	59,502	29,237	60,871	29,909	62,271	30,597	63,703	2.30%	11.50%	17,685	36,820	25,344	52,767	35,624	74,169
Lab Eqp Main Tech I-II	31,849	58,164	32,581	59,502	33,331	60,871	34,097	62,271	34,881	63,703	2.30%	11.50%	20,161	36,820	28,893	52,767	40,612	74,169
Lab Tech I-III	28,494	50,793	29,149	51,961	29,820	53,156	30,505	54,379	31,207	55,630	2.30%	11.50%	18,038	32,154	25,849	46,079	36,334	64,770
Laborer	22,329	35,425	22,842	36,240	23,368	37,073	23,905	37,926	24,455	38,798	2.30%	11.50%	14,135	22,425	20,256	32,137	28,473	45,172
Land Dispos Proj Ldr I-III	42,302	80,805	43,275	82,663	44,271	84,565	45,289	86,510	46,330	88,499	2.30%	11.50%	26,779	51,153	38,376	73,306	53,942	103,040
Land Mgr I-III	43,790	87,782	44,797	89,801	45,828	91,866	46,882	93,979	47,960	96,141	2.30%	11.50%	27,721	55,569	39,726	79,636	55,840	111,936
Lgl Asst I-III	32,874	62,388	33,630	63,823	34,403	65,291	35,194	66,793	36,004	68,329	2.30%	11.50%	20,810	39,494	29,823	56,599	41,919	79,555
Lgl Secy I-II	31,110	50,793	31,826	51,961	32,558	53,156	33,307	54,379	34,073	55,630	2.30%	11.50%	19,694	32,154	28,223	46,079	39,671	64,770
Librn I-IV	36,619	74,646	37,461	76,363	38,323	78,119	39,204	79,916	40,106	81,754	2.30%	11.50%	23,181	47,254	33,221	67,719	46,695	95,186
Loan Officer I-III	36,619	80,805	37,461	82,663	38,323	84,565	39,204	86,510	40,106	88,499	2.30%	11.50%	23,181	51,153	33,221	73,306	46,695	103,040
Mail Clerk I-II	23,767	33,970	24,313	34,752	24,873	35,551	25,445	36,369	26,030	37,205	2.30%	11.50%	15,045	21,505	21,561	30,818	30,307	43,318
Manpower Spct II-VI	29,693	68,663	30,375	70,242	31,074	71,857	31,789	73,510	32,520	75,201	2.30%	11.50%	18,796	43,466	26,937	62,291	37,863	87,556
Med Cons I-II	79,244	216,411	81,067	221,389	82,931	226,481	84,839	231,690	86,790	237,019	2.30%	11.50%	50,164	136,996	71,890	196,328	101,049	275,960
Med Invgtr II	31,770	54,281	32,501	55,529	33,249	56,806	34,013	58,113	34,796	59,450	2.30%	11.50%	20,112	34,362	28,822	49,243	40,512	69,217

Chart III - U.S. States & Cities - Job Titles - Salaries - Pension Estimates

Arizona	2010 (Min)	2010 (Max)	2011 (Min)	2011 (Max)	2012 (Min)	2012 (Max)	2013 (Min)	2013 (Max)	2014 (Min)	2014 (Max)	5-Year Average % Raise	5-Year Cumulative Raise Estimate**	20-Year Annual Pension Benefit Estimate (Min.)***	20-Year Annual Pension Benefit Estimate (Max.)	25-Year Annual Pension Benefit Estimate (Min.)	25-Year Annual Pension Benefit Estimate (Max.)	30-Year Annual Pension Benefit Estimate (Min.)	30-Year Annual Pension Benefit Estimate (Max.)
Med Payments Recovery Spct	29,693	50,793	30,375	51,961	31,074	53,156	31,789	54,379	32,520	55,630	2.30%	11.50%	18,796	32,154	26,937	46,079	37,863	64,770
Med Rcds Librn I-II	30,996	62,388	31,709	63,823	32,438	65,291	33,184	66,793	33,947	68,329	2.30%	11.50%	19,621	39,494	28,119	56,599	39,525	79,555
Med Social Svc Rep II-III	34,073	62,388	34,856	63,823	35,658	65,291	36,478	66,793	37,317	68,329	2.30%	11.50%	21,569	39,494	30,910	56,599	43,448	79,555
Med Svcs Prg Review Spct	38,335	62,388	39,217	63,823	40,119	65,291	41,042	66,793	41,986	68,329	2.30%	11.50%	24,268	39,494	34,778	56,599	48,884	79,555
Med Technologist II	38,402	58,164	39,285	59,502	40,188	60,871	41,113	62,271	42,058	63,703	2.30%	11.50%	24,310	36,820	34,838	52,767	48,968	74,169
Member Svcs Spct I-II	22,598	41,789	23,117	42,750	23,649	43,734	24,193	44,740	24,750	45,769	2.30%	11.50%	14,305	26,454	20,501	37,911	28,816	53,288
Mental Hlth Prg Spct I-IV	25,399	62,388	25,983	63,823	26,581	65,291	27,192	66,793	27,818	68,329	2.30%	11.50%	16,079	39,494	23,042	56,599	32,388	79,555
Mental Hlth Therapist II	36,619	62,388	37,461	63,823	38,323	65,291	39,204	66,793	40,106	68,329	2.30%	11.50%	23,181	39,494	33,221	56,599	46,695	79,555
Mgt Analyst I-IV	31,770	74,646	32,501	76,363	33,249	78,119	34,013	79,916	34,796	81,754	2.30%	11.50%	20,112	47,254	28,822	67,719	40,512	95,186
Micofilm Tech I-II	21,367	33,970	21,859	34,752	22,361	35,551	22,876	36,369	23,402	37,205	2.30%	11.50%	13,526	21,505	19,384	30,818	27,247	43,318
Mine Inspr Dpty II-III	34,073	68,663	34,856	70,242	35,658	71,857	36,478	73,510	37,317	75,201	2.30%	11.50%	21,569	43,466	30,910	62,291	43,448	87,556
Mus Curator I-III	31,770	68,663	32,501	70,242	33,249	71,857	34,013	73,510	34,796	75,201	2.30%	11.50%	20,112	43,466	28,822	62,291	40,512	87,556
Mus Preparator I-II	31,770	62,388	32,501	63,823	33,249	65,291	34,013	66,793	34,796	68,329	2.30%	11.50%	20,112	39,494	28,822	56,599	40,512	79,555
Mvd Field Officer I-II	31,617	55,719	32,344	57,001	33,088	58,312	33,849	59,653	34,627	61,025	2.30%	11.50%	20,014	35,272	28,682	50,548	40,316	71,051
Natural Resrces Mgr I-III	40,880	68,663	41,820	70,242	42,782	71,857	43,766	73,510	44,773	75,201	2.30%	11.50%	25,878	43,466	37,086	62,291	52,129	87,556
Nurse I	32,209	51,969	32,950	53,165	33,708	54,388	34,483	55,638	35,276	56,918	2.30%	11.50%	20,390	32,899	29,220	47,147	41,072	66,270
Occupl Sfty Cons III-IV	36,619	74,646	37,461	76,363	38,323	78,119	39,204	79,916	40,106	81,754	2.30%	11.50%	23,181	47,254	33,221	67,719	46,695	95,186
Occupl Therapist III	43,790	74,646	44,797	76,363	45,828	78,119	46,882	79,916	47,960	81,754	2.30%	11.50%	27,721	47,254	39,726	67,719	55,840	95,186
Painter	31,849	50,793	32,581	51,961	33,331	53,156	34,097	54,379	34,881	55,630	2.30%	11.50%	20,161	32,154	28,893	46,079	40,612	64,770
Park Mgr I-III	41,334	74,646	42,285	76,363	43,257	78,119	44,252	79,916	45,270	81,754	2.30%	11.50%	26,166	47,254	37,498	67,719	52,708	95,186
Park Ranger I-III	27,937	39,500	28,579	40,409	29,237	41,338	29,909	42,289	30,597	43,262	2.30%	11.50%	17,685	25,005	25,344	35,835	35,624	50,369
Peronnel Asst I-II	22,598	44,173	23,117	45,189	23,649	46,229	24,193	47,292	24,750	48,380	2.30%	11.50%	14,305	27,963	20,501	40,074	28,816	56,328
Personnel Analyst I-III	31,770	68,663	32,501	70,242	33,249	71,857	34,013	73,510	34,796	75,201	2.30%	11.50%	20,112	43,466	28,822	62,291	40,512	87,556
Personnel Mgr I-III	44,721	87,782	45,749	89,801	46,801	91,866	47,878	93,979	48,979	96,141	2.30%	11.50%	28,310	55,569	40,570	79,636	57,026	111,936
Personnel Tech I-II	27,937	50,793	28,579	51,961	29,237	53,156	29,909	54,379	30,597	55,630	2.30%	11.50%	17,685	32,154	25,344	46,079	35,624	64,770
Pest Ctrl Inspns II	32,615	54,281	33,365	55,529	34,132	56,806	34,917	58,113	35,720	59,450	2.30%	11.50%	20,646	34,362	29,588	49,243	41,589	69,217
Physician II-IV	79,244	216,411	81,067	221,389	82,931	226,481	84,839	231,690	86,790	237,019	2.30%	11.50%	50,164	136,996	71,890	196,328	101,049	275,960
Pipeline Sfty Inspr I-III	40,320	87,782	41,247	89,801	42,196	91,866	43,166	93,979	44,159	96,141	2.30%	11.50%	25,524	55,569	36,578	79,636	51,414	111,936
Prg Proj Spct I-II	34,073	62,388	34,856	63,823	35,658	65,291	36,478	66,793	37,317	68,329	2.30%	11.50%	21,569	39,494	30,910	56,599	43,448	79,555
Prg Svc Evalr I-V	28,306	68,663	28,957	70,242	29,623	71,857	30,304	73,510	31,001	75,201	2.30%	11.50%	17,919	43,466	25,679	62,291	36,095	87,556
Prpty Appraiser I-IV	34,073	80,805	34,856	82,663	35,658	84,565	36,478	86,510	37,317	88,499	2.30%	11.50%	21,569	51,153	30,910	73,306	43,448	103,040
Prpty Examiner I	31,770	54,281	32,501	55,529	33,249	56,806	34,013	58,113	34,796	59,450	2.30%	11.50%	20,112	34,362	28,822	49,243	40,512	69,217
Psy Nurse I-II	36,063	113,903	36,892	116,523	37,741	119,203	38,609	121,945	39,497	124,749	2.30%	11.50%	22,829	72,105	32,716	103,333	45,986	145,245
Psychologist I-III	43,790	87,782	44,797	89,801	45,828	91,866	46,882	93,979	47,960	96,141	2.30%	11.50%	27,721	55,569	39,726	79,636	55,840	111,936
Psychology Assoc I-II	34,073	62,388	34,856	63,823	35,658	65,291	36,478	66,793	37,317	68,329	2.30%	11.50%	21,569	39,494	30,910	56,599	43,448	79,555
Pub Hlth Nurse I-II	36,619	74,646	37,461	76,363	38,323	78,119	39,204	79,916	40,106	81,754	2.30%	11.50%	23,181	47,254	33,221	67,719	46,695	95,186
Pub Hlth Sanitarian II	40,026	62,388	40,947	63,823	41,889	65,291	42,852	66,793	43,838	68,329	2.30%	11.50%	25,338	39,494	36,312	56,599	51,040	79,555
Pub Hlth Scientist I-III	34,073	80,805	34,856	82,663	35,658	84,565	36,478	86,510	37,317	88,499	2.30%	11.50%	21,569	51,153	30,910	73,306	43,448	103,040
Pub Info Officer I-IV	34,073	80,805	34,856	82,663	35,658	84,565	36,478	86,510	37,317	88,499	2.30%	11.50%	21,569	51,153	30,910	73,306	43,448	103,040
Pub Utils Analyst I-V	43,277	87,782	44,273	89,801	45,291	91,866	46,333	93,979	47,398	96,141	2.30%	11.50%	27,396	55,569	39,261	79,636	55,186	111,936
Pub Utils Cnsmr Analyst I-II	44,880	62,388	45,912	63,823	46,968	65,291	48,049	66,793	49,154	68,329	2.30%	11.50%	28,411	39,494	40,715	56,599	57,230	79,555
Purchasing Mgr I-II	43,826	80,805	44,834	82,663	45,865	84,565	46,920	86,510	47,999	88,499	2.30%	11.50%	27,744	51,153	39,759	73,306	55,885	103,040

Chart III - U.S. States & Cities - Job Titles - Salaries - Pension Estimates

Arizona	2010 (Min)	2010 (Max)	2011 (Min)	2011 (Max)	2012 (Min)	2012 (Max)	2013 (Min)	2013 (Max)	2014 (Min)	2014 (Max)	5-Year Average % Raise	5-Year Cumulative Raise Estimate**	20-Year Annual Pension Benefit Estimate (Min.)***	20-Year Annual Pension Benefit Estimate (Max.)	25-Year Annual Pension Benefit Estimate (Min.)	25-Year Annual Pension Benefit Estimate (Max.)	30-Year Annual Pension Benefit Estimate (Min.)	30-Year Annual Pension Benefit Estimate (Max.)
Racing Steward I-III	36,619	80,805	37,461	82,663	38,323	84,565	39,204	86,510	40,106	88,499	2.30%	11.50%	23,181	51,153	33,221	73,306	46,695	103,040
Radiological Technologist II-III	27,937	50,793	28,579	51,961	29,237	53,156	29,909	54,379	30,597	55,630	2.30%	11.50%	17,685	32,154	25,344	46,079	35,624	64,770
Railroad Sfty Inspr I-III	40,320	80,805	41,247	82,663	42,196	84,565	43,166	86,510	44,159	88,499	2.30%	11.50%	25,524	51,153	36,578	73,306	51,414	103,040
Real Estate Auditor II	31,770	54,281	32,501	55,529	33,249	56,806	34,013	58,113	34,796	59,450	2.30%	11.50%	20,112	34,362	28,822	49,243	40,512	69,217
Recreation Ldr I-II	20,387	35,425	20,856	36,240	21,336	37,073	21,826	37,926	22,328	38,798	2.30%	11.50%	12,906	22,425	18,495	32,137	25,997	45,172
Recreational Planner I-III	31,770	74,646	32,501	76,363	33,249	78,119	34,013	79,916	34,796	81,754	2.30%	11.50%	20,112	47,254	28,822	67,719	40,512	95,186
Recreational Therapist II-III	37,210	58,164	38,066	59,502	38,942	60,871	39,837	62,271	40,754	63,703	2.30%	11.50%	23,556	36,820	33,757	52,767	47,449	74,169
Rehab Instrl Svc Spct III	40,640	58,164	41,575	59,502	42,531	60,871	43,509	62,271	44,510	63,703	2.30%	11.50%	25,727	36,820	36,869	52,767	51,823	74,169
Rehab Svc Spct II-III	37,270	58,164	38,127	59,502	39,004	60,871	39,901	62,271	40,819	63,703	2.30%	11.50%	23,593	36,820	33,811	52,767	47,525	74,169
Research Stat Analyst I-IV	27,937	62,388	28,579	63,823	29,237	65,291	29,909	66,793	30,597	68,329	2.30%	11.50%	17,685	39,494	25,344	56,599	35,624	79,555
Residential Prg Spct I-III	27,937	62,388	28,579	63,823	29,237	65,291	29,909	66,793	30,597	68,329	2.30%	11.50%	17,685	39,494	25,344	56,599	35,624	79,555
Rev Ctrl Fis Svc Tech I-II	22,598	41,789	23,117	42,750	23,649	43,734	24,193	44,740	24,750	45,769	2.30%	11.50%	14,305	26,454	20,501	37,911	28,816	53,288
Revenue Auditor I-III	29,693	44,173	30,375	45,189	31,074	46,229	31,789	47,292	32,520	48,380	2.30%	11.50%	18,796	27,963	26,937	40,074	37,863	56,328
Revenue Field Auditor I-III	31,770	87,782	32,501	89,801	33,249	91,866	34,013	93,979	34,796	96,141	2.30%	11.50%	20,112	55,569	28,822	79,636	40,512	111,936
Risk Mgt Clms Adjtr I-II	44,569	68,663	45,594	70,242	46,643	71,857	47,716	73,510	48,813	75,201	2.30%	11.50%	28,214	43,466	40,433	62,291	56,833	87,556
Securities Spct III	47,357	80,805	48,446	82,663	49,561	84,565	50,700	86,510	51,867	88,499	2.30%	11.50%	29,979	51,153	42,962	73,306	60,388	103,040
Security Officer I-III	25,399	54,281	25,983	55,529	26,581	56,806	27,192	58,113	27,818	59,450	2.30%	11.50%	16,079	34,362	23,042	49,243	32,388	69,217
Secy	23,709	37,297	24,254	38,155	24,812	39,032	25,383	39,930	25,966	40,848	2.30%	11.50%	15,008	23,610	21,508	33,836	30,233	47,560
Social Svc Admr I-III	40,320	80,805	41,247	82,663	42,196	84,565	43,166	86,510	44,159	88,499	2.30%	11.50%	25,524	51,153	36,578	73,306	51,414	103,040
Solar Engrg Spct II	47,357	80,805	48,446	82,663	49,561	84,565	50,700	86,510	51,867	88,499	2.30%	11.50%	29,979	51,153	42,962	73,306	60,388	103,040
State Examiner I-II	25,399	46,828	25,983	47,905	26,581	49,007	27,192	50,134	27,818	51,287	2.30%	11.50%	16,079	29,644	23,042	42,482	32,388	59,713
State Hlth Physician I-II	34,073	68,663	34,856	70,242	35,658	71,857	36,478	73,510	37,317	75,201	2.30%	11.50%	21,569	43,466	30,910	62,291	43,448	87,556
Stwd Accountant I-III	39,466	39,000	40,374	39,897	41,302	40,814	42,252	41,753	43,224	42,713	2.30%	11.50%	24,983	24,688	35,803	35,380	50,325	49,731
Taxpayer Svc Tech II-III	27,160	46,828	27,785	47,905	28,424	49,007	29,077	50,134	29,746	51,287	2.30%	11.50%	17,193	29,644	24,639	42,482	34,633	59,713
Teacher Crtfn Spct I-II	38,292	62,388	39,172	63,823	40,073	65,291	40,995	66,793	41,938	68,329	2.30%	11.50%	24,240	39,494	34,738	56,599	48,828	79,555
Therapy Tech I-II	25,399	46,828	25,983	47,905	26,581	49,007	27,192	50,134	27,818	51,287	2.30%	11.50%	16,079	29,644	23,042	42,482	32,388	59,713
Title Examiner I-III	29,693	62,388	30,375	63,823	31,074	65,291	31,789	66,793	32,520	68,329	2.30%	11.50%	18,796	39,494	26,937	56,599	37,863	79,555
Tr Const Ops Tech I-II	36,361	69,805	37,197	71,410	38,052	73,053	38,928	74,733	39,823	76,452	2.30%	11.50%	23,018	44,189	32,986	63,327	46,366	89,013
Tr Const Tech I-IV	31,642	69,805	32,370	71,410	33,114	73,053	33,876	74,733	34,655	76,452	2.30%	11.50%	20,031	44,189	28,706	63,327	40,349	89,013
Tr Engrg Cmpr Apl Tech I-II	36,361	75,562	37,197	77,300	38,052	79,078	38,928	80,897	39,823	82,757	2.30%	11.50%	23,018	47,834	32,986	68,550	46,366	96,354
Tr Engrg Tech I-III	31,642	69,805	32,370	71,410	33,114	73,053	33,876	74,733	34,655	76,452	2.30%	11.50%	20,031	44,189	28,706	63,327	40,349	89,013
Tr Main Mgt Analyst I-II	36,361	69,805	37,197	71,410	38,052	73,053	38,928	74,733	39,823	76,452	2.30%	11.50%	23,018	44,189	32,986	63,327	46,366	89,013
Tr Mats Fld Crew Tech II-III	33,607	64,297	34,380	65,776	35,171	67,289	35,980	68,837	36,808	70,420	2.30%	11.50%	21,275	40,703	30,488	58,330	42,855	81,989
Traf Sig/Lit Ops Ut Mgr I-II	46,201	82,353	47,263	84,247	48,350	86,185	49,462	88,167	50,600	90,195	2.30%	11.50%	29,247	52,133	41,913	74,711	58,914	105,014
Traf Sig/Lit Tech I-II	31,642	64,297	32,370	65,776	33,114	67,289	33,876	68,837	34,655	70,420	2.30%	11.50%	20,031	40,703	28,706	58,330	40,349	81,989
Trng Officer I-III	39,324	74,646	40,229	76,363	41,154	78,119	42,100	79,916	43,069	81,754	2.30%	11.50%	24,894	47,254	35,675	67,719	50,145	95,186
Utils Audit	70,926	87,782	72,557	89,801	74,226	91,866	75,933	93,979	77,680	96,141	2.30%	11.50%	44,899	55,569	64,344	79,636	90,442	111,936
Utils Cons	54,133	74,646	55,378	76,363	56,651	78,119	57,954	79,916	59,287	81,754	2.30%	11.50%	34,268	47,254	49,109	67,719	69,028	95,186
Utils Engr	69,911	95,431	71,519	97,626	73,164	99,871	74,846	102,168	76,568	104,518	2.30%	11.50%	44,256	60,411	63,423	86,574	89,148	121,690

Chart III - U.S. States & Cities - Job Titles - Salaries - Pension Estimates

Arizona	2010 (Min)	2010 (Max)	2011 (Min)	2011 (Max)	2012 (Min)	2012 (Max)	2013 (Min)	2013 (Max)	2014 (Min)	2014 (Max)	5-Year Average % Raise	5-Year Cumulative Raise Estimate**	20-Year Annual Pension Benefit Estimate (Min.)***	20-Year Annual Pension Benefit Estimate (Max.)	25-Year Annual Pension Benefit Estimate (Min.)	25-Year Annual Pension Benefit Estimate (Max.)	30-Year Annual Pension Benefit Estimate (Min.)	30-Year Annual Pension Benefit Estimate (Max.)
ater Resrces Mgr I	52,499	87,782	53,706	89,801	54,942	91,866	56,205	93,979	57,498	96,141	2.30%	11.50%	33,234	55,569	47,627	79,636	66,945	111,936
ater Resrces Spct IV	40,178	80,805	41,102	82,663	42,047	84,565	43,014	86,510	44,003	88,499	2.30%	11.50%	25,434	51,153	36,449	73,306	51,233	103,040
ater Resrces ech I-II	29,188	46,828	29,859	47,905	30,546	49,007	31,248	50,134	31,967	51,287	2.30%	11.50%	18,477	29,644	26,479	42,482	37,219	59,713
elfare Staff Dvmt pct I	34,073	58,164	34,856	59,502	35,658	60,871	36,478	62,271	37,317	63,703	2.30%	11.50%	21,569	36,820	30,910	52,767	43,448	74,169
ildlife Law Efcmt oct	46,539	68,663	47,610	70,242	48,705	71,857	49,825	73,510	50,971	75,201	2.30%	11.50%	29,461	43,466	42,220	62,291	59,345	87,556
ildlife Spct I-III	34,395	68,663	35,186	70,242	35,995	71,857	36,823	73,510	37,670	75,201	2.30%	11.50%	21,773	43,466	31,203	62,291	43,859	87,556
krs Comp Ins Clms oct I-II	27,937	54,281	28,579	55,529	29,237	56,806	29,909	58,113	30,597	59,450	2.30%	11.50%	17,685	34,362	25,344	49,243	35,624	69,217
outh Corrs Officer II	33,796	62,310	34,573	63,743	35,368	65,209	36,182	66,709	37,014	68,243	2.30%	11.50%	21,394	39,444	30,659	56,527	43,095	79,455
outh Parole Officer III	36,617	68,609	37,460	70,187	38,321	71,801	39,203	73,453	40,104	75,142	2.30%	11.50%	23,180	43,432	33,219	62,242	46,693	87,488
outh Program fficer I-III	35,876	64,185	36,701	65,661	37,545	67,172	38,408	68,717	39,292	70,297	2.30%	11.50%	22,711	40,632	32,546	58,229	45,747	81,847

tp://az.gov

Chart III - U.S. States & Cities - Job Titles - Salaries - Pension Estimates

Arizona-Phoenix	2010 (Min)	2010 (Max)	2011 (Min)	2011 (Max)	2012 (Min)	2012 (Max)	2013 (Min)	2013 (Max)	2014 (Min)	2014 (Max)	5-Year Average % Raise	5-Year Cumulative Raise Estimate**	20-Year Annual Pension Benefit Estimate (Min.)***	20-Year Annual Pension Benefit Estimate (Max.)	25-Year Annual Pension Benefit Estimate (Min.)	25-Year Annual Pension Benefit Estimate (Max.)	30-Year Annual Pension Benefit Estimate (Min.)	30-Year Annual Pension Benefit Estimate (Max.)
Account Clerk I-III	27,041	53,216	27,663	54,440	28,299	55,692	28,950	56,973	29,616	58,283	2.30%	11.50%	17,118	33,688	24,532	48,277	34,482	67,859
Account Clerk Supervisor	38,681	57,612	39,571	58,937	40,481	60,293	41,412	61,679	42,364	63,098	2.30%	11.50%	24,487	36,471	35,091	52,265	49,325	73,465
Accountant I-IV	42,691	105,042	43,673	107,458	44,677	109,929	45,705	112,458	46,756	115,044	2.30%	11.50%	27,025	66,495	38,729	95,294	54,438	133,945
Admin Aide	37,634	54,628	38,500	55,884	39,385	57,169	40,291	58,484	41,218	59,829	2.30%	11.50%	23,824	34,581	34,141	49,558	47,990	69,659
Admin Asst I-III	45,015	115,293	46,050	117,945	47,109	120,657	48,193	123,433	49,301	126,272	2.30%	11.50%	28,496	72,985	40,837	104,593	57,401	147,018
Admin Secretary	38,681	57,612	39,571	58,937	40,481	60,293	41,412	61,679	42,364	63,098	2.30%	11.50%	24,487	36,471	35,091	52,265	49,325	73,465
Architect	70,438	105,042	72,058	107,458	73,716	109,929	75,411	112,458	77,145	115,044	2.30%	11.50%	44,590	66,495	63,901	95,294	89,820	133,945
Arts Specialist	52,236	77,978	53,437	79,771	54,666	81,606	55,923	83,483	57,210	85,403	2.30%	11.50%	33,067	49,363	47,388	70,741	66,609	99,434
Asst City Atty I-IV	57,612	140,192	58,937	143,416	60,293	146,715	61,679	150,089	63,098	153,541	2.30%	11.50%	36,471	88,747	52,265	127,182	73,465	178,768
Auto Parts Buyer	47,316	70,438	48,404	72,058	49,517	73,716	50,656	75,411	51,821	77,145	2.30%	11.50%	29,953	44,590	42,925	63,901	60,335	89,820
Auto Parts Clerk I-III	33,374	49,457	34,141	50,594	34,926	51,758	35,730	52,949	36,552	54,166	2.30%	11.50%	21,127	31,308	30,276	44,867	42,557	63,066
Aviation Supv I-III	38,681	86,043	39,571	88,022	40,481	90,046	41,412	92,117	42,364	94,236	2.30%	11.50%	24,487	54,468	35,091	78,058	49,325	109,719
Benefits Aide	37,634	56,017	38,500	57,306	39,385	58,624	40,291	59,972	41,218	61,352	2.30%	11.50%	23,824	35,461	34,141	50,819	47,990	71,431
Benefits Analyst I-II	45,015	86,043	46,050	88,022	47,109	90,046	48,193	92,117	49,301	94,236	2.30%	11.50%	28,496	54,468	40,837	78,058	57,401	109,719
Budget Analyst I-III	49,502	99,893	50,640	102,191	51,805	104,541	52,997	106,945	54,216	109,405	2.30%	11.50%	31,337	63,236	44,908	90,623	63,123	127,380
Building Equip Op I-II	51,644	67,043	52,832	68,585	54,047	70,162	55,290	71,776	56,562	73,427	2.30%	11.50%	32,693	42,441	46,851	60,821	65,855	85,491
Business Assistance Adm	76,794	121,056	78,560	123,840	80,367	126,689	82,215	129,603	84,106	132,583	2.30%	11.50%	48,613	76,633	69,667	109,822	97,925	154,366
Buyer	47,316	70,438	48,404	72,058	49,517	73,716	50,656	75,411	51,821	77,145	2.30%	11.50%	29,953	44,590	42,925	63,901	60,335	89,820
Buyer Aide	37,634	54,628	38,500	55,884	39,385	57,169	40,291	58,484	41,218	59,829	2.30%	11.50%	23,824	34,581	34,141	49,558	47,990	69,659
Case Work Services Coordinator	57,612	86,043	58,937	88,022	60,293	90,046	61,679	92,117	63,098	94,236	2.30%	11.50%	36,471	54,468	52,265	78,058	73,465	109,719
Casework Aide	28,316	41,028	28,967	41,972	29,633	42,937	30,315	43,925	31,012	44,935	2.30%	11.50%	17,925	25,972	25,688	37,221	36,107	52,318
Caseworker I-III	35,789	77,978	36,612	79,771	37,454	81,606	38,315	83,483	39,196	85,403	2.30%	11.50%	22,656	49,363	32,467	70,741	45,636	99,434
Chemist I-III	47,316	95,155	48,404	97,344	49,517	99,583	50,656	101,873	51,821	104,216	2.30%	11.50%	29,953	60,237	42,925	86,324	60,335	121,338
Chief Engineering Tech	47,452	69,641	48,543	71,243	49,660	72,881	50,802	74,557	51,970	76,272	2.30%	11.50%	30,039	44,085	43,048	63,178	60,509	88,804
Civil Engineer I-III	52,236	110,554	53,437	113,097	54,666	115,698	55,923	118,359	57,210	121,081	2.30%	11.50%	33,067	69,985	47,388	100,294	66,609	140,974
Civil Inspector I-III	47,452	80,302	48,543	82,149	49,660	84,038	50,802	85,971	51,970	87,948	2.30%	11.50%	30,039	50,834	43,048	72,849	60,509	102,398
Claims Adjuster I-II	45,015	77,978	46,050	79,771	47,109	81,606	48,193	83,483	49,301	85,403	2.30%	11.50%	28,496	49,363	40,837	70,741	57,401	99,434
Clerk I-III	23,601	47,316	24,144	48,404	24,699	49,517	25,267	50,656	25,848	51,821	2.30%	11.50%	14,940	29,953	21,411	42,925	30,095	60,335
Community Worker I-III	28,316	47,316	28,967	48,404	29,633	49,517	30,315	50,656	31,012	51,821	2.30%	11.50%	17,925	29,953	25,688	42,925	36,107	60,335
Computer Operations Specialist	52,236	77,978	53,437	79,771	54,666	81,606	55,923	83,483	57,210	85,403	2.30%	11.50%	33,067	49,363	47,388	70,741	66,609	99,434
Computer Production Scheduler	49,502	74,083	50,640	75,787	51,805	77,530	52,997	79,313	54,216	81,137	2.30%	11.50%	31,337	46,897	44,908	67,208	63,123	94,468
Computer Systems Librarian	32,622	47,452	33,373	48,543	34,140	49,660	34,925	50,802	35,729	51,970	2.30%	11.50%	20,651	30,039	29,595	43,048	41,599	60,509
Const Permit Spec I-II	52,145	88,298	53,344	90,329	54,571	92,406	55,826	94,532	57,110	96,706	2.30%	11.50%	33,009	55,896	47,305	80,104	66,493	112,594
Construction Drafting Tech	41,756	56,177	42,717	57,469	43,699	58,791	44,704	60,143	45,733	61,527	2.30%	11.50%	26,433	35,562	37,881	50,964	53,246	71,635
Construction Insp	38,864	51,644	39,758	52,832	40,672	54,047	41,608	55,290	42,565	56,562	2.30%	11.50%	24,602	32,693	35,257	46,851	49,558	65,855
Contracts Specialist I-II	45,015	95,155	46,050	97,344	47,109	99,583	48,193	101,873	49,301	104,216	2.30%	11.50%	28,496	60,237	40,837	86,324	57,401	121,338
Court/Legal Clerk I-III	28,316	54,855	28,967	56,117	29,633	57,408	30,315	58,728	31,012	60,079	2.30%	11.50%	17,925	34,725	25,688	49,765	36,107	69,950
Crime Lab Administrator	80,711	127,139	82,568	130,063	84,467	133,055	86,410	136,115	88,397	139,246	2.30%	11.50%	51,093	80,484	73,221	115,340	102,920	162,127
Crime Scene Specialist I-III	37,634	66,360	38,500	67,886	39,385	69,447	40,291	71,044	41,218	72,679	2.30%	11.50%	23,824	42,008	34,141	60,201	47,990	84,619
Custodial Supervisor I-II	34,922	57,612	35,725	58,937	36,547	60,293	37,388	61,679	38,248	63,098	2.30%	11.50%	22,107	36,471	31,681	52,265	44,532	73,465

Chart III - U.S. States & Cities - Job Titles - Salaries - Pension Estimates

Arizona-Phoenix	2010 (Min)	2010 (Max)	2011 (Min)	2011 (Max)	2012 (Min)	2012 (Max)	2013 (Min)	2013 (Max)	2014 (Min)	2014 (Max)	5-Year Average % Raise	5-Year Cumulative Raise Estimate**	20-Year Annual Pension Benefit Estimate (Min.)***	20-Year Annual Pension Benefit Estimate (Max.)	25-Year Annual Pension Benefit Estimate (Min.)	25-Year Annual Pension Benefit Estimate (Max.)	30-Year Annual Pension Benefit Estimate (Min.)	30-Year Annual Pension Benefit Estimate (Max.)
Custodial Worker I-II	28,908	40,345	29,573	41,273	30,253	42,222	30,949	43,193	31,661	44,186	2.30%	11.50%	18,300	25,540	26,226	36,601	36,863	51,446
Elections/Annexation Spec I-II	39,251	74,083	40,153	75,787	41,077	77,530	42,022	79,313	42,988	81,137	2.30%	11.50%	24,847	46,897	35,608	67,208	50,051	94,468
Electrical Inspector I-II	47,452	76,680	48,543	78,443	49,660	80,248	50,802	82,093	51,970	83,982	2.30%	11.50%	30,039	48,541	43,048	69,564	60,509	97,779
Electrical Plans Examiner I-II	52,145	84,151	53,344	86,087	54,571	88,067	55,826	90,092	57,110	92,165	2.30%	11.50%	33,009	53,271	47,305	76,342	66,493	107,307
Elevator Inspector I-II	47,452	76,680	48,543	78,443	49,660	80,248	50,802	82,093	51,970	83,982	2.30%	11.50%	30,039	48,541	43,048	69,564	60,509	97,779
Environmental Programs Asst	47,316	70,438	48,404	72,058	49,517	73,716	50,656	75,411	51,821	77,145	2.30%	11.50%	29,953	44,590	42,925	63,901	60,335	89,820
Environmental Programs Coord	74,083	110,554	75,787	113,097	77,530	115,698	79,313	118,359	81,137	121,081	2.30%	11.50%	46,897	69,985	67,208	100,294	94,468	140,974
Environmental Programs Spec	66,429	104,563	67,956	106,968	69,519	109,428	71,118	111,945	72,754	114,520	2.30%	11.50%	42,052	66,192	60,264	94,859	84,707	133,335
Equipment Op I-IV	31,505	52,897	32,230	54,114	32,971	55,358	33,729	56,632	34,505	57,934	2.30%	11.50%	19,944	33,486	28,581	47,988	40,174	67,452
Equipment Service Wkr I-II	30,936	43,443	31,647	44,442	32,375	45,464	33,120	46,510	33,881	47,580	2.30%	11.50%	19,583	27,501	28,065	39,411	39,448	55,397
Fire & Life Safety Prog Coord	54,855	81,873	56,117	83,756	57,408	85,683	58,728	87,654	60,079	89,670	2.30%	11.50%	34,725	51,829	49,765	74,275	69,950	104,402
Fire 911 Administrator	76,794	121,056	78,560	123,840	80,367	126,689	82,215	129,603	84,106	132,583	2.30%	11.50%	48,613	76,633	69,667	109,822	97,925	154,366
Fire Communications Coord	54,855	81,873	56,117	83,756	57,408	85,683	58,728	87,654	60,079	89,670	2.30%	11.50%	34,725	51,829	49,765	74,275	69,950	104,402
Fire Emergency Dispatcher	41,028	60,232	41,972	61,617	42,937	63,034	43,925	64,484	44,935	65,967	2.30%	11.50%	25,972	38,129	37,221	54,642	52,318	76,805
Fire Prevention Manager	67,043	99,893	68,585	102,191	70,162	104,541	71,776	106,945	73,427	109,405	2.30%	11.50%	42,441	63,236	60,821	90,623	85,491	127,380
Fire Prevention Spec I-II	47,452	84,151	48,543	86,087	49,660	88,067	50,802	90,092	51,970	92,165	2.30%	11.50%	30,039	53,271	43,048	76,342	60,509	107,307
Fire Prevention Supervisor	57,612	86,043	58,937	88,022	60,293	90,046	61,679	92,117	63,098	94,236	2.30%	11.50%	36,471	54,468	52,265	78,058	73,465	109,719
Fire Protection Engineer	67,043	99,893	68,585	102,191	70,162	104,541	71,776	106,945	73,427	109,405	2.30%	11.50%	42,441	63,236	60,821	90,623	85,491	127,380
Forensic Scientist I-IV	45,197	105,042	46,236	107,458	47,300	109,929	48,387	112,458	49,500	115,044	2.30%	11.50%	28,611	66,495	41,002	95,294	57,633	133,945
General Inspector I-II	47,452	76,680	48,543	78,443	49,660	80,248	50,802	82,093	51,970	83,982	2.30%	11.50%	30,039	48,541	43,048	69,564	60,509	97,779
GIS Coordinator	60,642	90,416	62,037	92,496	63,464	94,623	64,924	96,799	66,417	99,026	2.30%	11.50%	38,389	57,237	55,015	82,025	77,329	115,295
GIS Technician	45,197	66,360	46,236	67,886	47,300	69,447	48,387	71,044	49,500	72,679	2.30%	11.50%	28,611	42,008	41,002	60,201	57,633	84,619
Housing Inspector	39,251	57,384	40,153	58,704	41,077	60,054	42,022	61,435	42,988	62,848	2.30%	11.50%	24,847	36,326	35,608	52,059	50,051	73,174
Housing Investigator	38,681	57,612	39,571	58,937	40,481	60,293	41,412	61,679	42,364	63,098	2.30%	11.50%	24,487	36,471	35,091	52,265	49,325	73,465
Housing Manager	70,438	105,042	72,058	107,458	73,716	109,929	75,411	112,458	77,145	115,044	2.30%	11.50%	44,590	66,495	63,901	95,294	89,820	133,945
Housing Program Representative	32,622	47,452	33,373	48,543	34,140	49,660	34,925	50,802	35,729	51,970	2.30%	11.50%	20,651	30,039	29,595	43,048	41,599	60,509
Housing Rehabilitation Spec	47,452	69,641	48,543	71,243	49,660	72,881	50,802	74,557	51,970	76,272	2.30%	11.50%	30,039	44,085	43,048	63,178	60,509	88,804
Housing Supervisor	57,612	86,043	58,937	88,022	60,293	90,046	61,679	92,117	63,098	94,236	2.30%	11.50%	36,471	54,468	52,265	78,058	73,465	109,719
Human Services Center Supv	60,642	90,416	62,037	92,496	63,464	94,623	64,924	96,799	66,417	99,026	2.30%	11.50%	38,389	57,237	55,015	82,025	77,329	115,295
Human Services Planning Supv	63,718	95,155	65,183	97,344	66,683	99,583	68,216	101,873	69,785	104,216	2.30%	11.50%	40,336	60,237	57,805	86,324	81,251	121,338
Human Services Program Coord	63,718	95,155	65,183	97,344	66,683	99,583	68,216	101,873	69,785	104,216	2.30%	11.50%	40,336	60,237	57,805	86,324	81,251	121,338
Info Tech Analyst/ Prg I-III	57,612	105,042	58,937	107,458	60,293	109,929	61,679	112,458	63,098	115,044	2.30%	11.50%	36,471	66,495	52,265	95,294	73,465	133,945
Info Tech Project Manager	77,978	116,113	79,771	118,784	81,606	121,516	83,483	124,311	85,403	127,170	2.30%	11.50%	49,363	73,504	70,741	105,338	99,434	148,064
Info Tech Service Specialist	52,236	77,978	53,437	79,771	54,666	81,606	55,923	83,483	57,210	85,403	2.30%	11.50%	33,067	49,363	47,388	70,741	66,609	99,434
Info Tech Supervisor	54,855	81,873	56,117	83,756	57,408	85,683	58,728	87,654	60,079	89,670	2.30%	11.50%	34,725	51,829	49,765	74,275	69,950	104,402
Info Tech Trainee	41,028	60,232	41,972	61,617	42,937	63,034	43,925	64,484	44,935	65,967	2.30%	11.50%	25,972	38,129	37,221	54,642	52,318	76,805
Information Clerk	27,041	39,251	27,663	40,153	28,299	41,077	28,950	42,022	29,616	42,988	2.30%	11.50%	17,118	24,847	24,532	35,608	34,482	50,051

143

Chart III - U.S. States & Cities - Job Titles - Salaries - Pension Estimates

Arizona-Phoenix	2010 (Min)	2010 (Max)	2011 (Min)	2011 (Max)	2012 (Min)	2012 (Max)	2013 (Min)	2013 (Max)	2014 (Min)	2014 (Max)	5-Year Average % Raise	5-Year Cumulative Raise Estimate**	20-Year Annual Pension Benefit Estimate (Min.)***	20-Year Annual Pension Benefit Estimate (Max.)	25-Year Annual Pension Benefit Estimate (Min.)	25-Year Annual Pension Benefit Estimate (Max.)	30-Year Annual Pension Benefit Estimate (Min.)	30-Year Annual Pension Benefit Estimate (Max.)
Information Tech Systems Spec	67,043	99,893	68,585	102,191	70,162	104,541	71,776	106,945	73,427	109,405	2.30%	11.50%	42,441	63,236	60,821	90,623	85,491	127,380
Internal Auditor I-IV	45,015	105,042	46,050	107,458	47,109	109,929	48,193	112,458	49,301	115,044	2.30%	11.50%	28,496	66,495	40,837	95,294	57,401	133,945
Inventory Control Specialist	36,882	54,855	37,730	56,117	38,598	57,408	39,485	58,728	40,394	60,079	2.30%	11.50%	23,347	34,725	33,459	49,765	47,030	69,950
Inventory Management Coord	63,718	95,155	65,183	97,344	66,683	99,583	68,216	101,873	69,785	104,216	2.30%	11.50%	40,336	60,237	57,805	86,324	81,251	121,338
Investment Manager	70,438	105,042	72,058	107,458	73,716	109,929	75,411	112,458	77,145	115,044	2.30%	11.50%	44,590	66,495	63,901	95,294	89,820	133,945
Labor Compliance Specialist	48,158	69,709	49,266	71,312	50,399	72,952	51,558	74,630	52,744	76,347	2.30%	11.50%	30,486	44,128	43,689	63,240	61,409	88,890
Landscape Architect I-II	52,236	90,416	53,437	92,496	54,666	94,623	55,923	96,799	57,210	99,026	2.30%	11.50%	33,067	57,237	47,388	82,025	66,609	115,295
Legal Assistant	43,055	63,125	44,046	64,577	45,059	66,063	46,095	67,582	47,155	69,136	2.30%	11.50%	27,256	39,961	39,060	57,267	54,903	80,495
Legal	45,197	66,360	46,236	67,886	47,300	69,447	48,387	71,044	49,500	72,679	2.30%	11.50%	28,611	42,008	41,002	60,201	57,633	84,619
Legal Secretary	39,251	57,384	40,153	58,704	41,077	60,054	42,022	61,435	42,988	62,848	2.30%	11.50%	24,847	36,326	35,608	52,059	50,051	73,174
Librarian I-IV	45,015	95,155	46,050	97,344	47,109	99,583	48,193	101,873	49,301	104,216	2.30%	11.50%	28,496	60,237	40,837	86,324	57,401	121,338
Library Circulation Attnd I-III	25,947	47,316	26,544	48,404	27,154	49,517	27,779	50,656	28,418	51,821	2.30%	11.50%	16,425	29,953	23,539	42,925	33,087	60,335
Mail Service Worker	31,505	41,233	32,230	42,181	32,971	43,151	33,729	44,144	34,505	45,159		11.50%	19,944	26,102	28,581	37,406	40,174	52,579
Management Asst I-III	47,316	121,056	48,404	123,840	49,517	126,689	50,656	129,603	51,821	132,583	2.30%	11.50%	29,953	76,633	42,925	109,822	60,335	154,366
Management Services Adm	76,794	121,056	78,560	123,840	80,367	126,689	82,215	129,603	84,106	132,583	2.30%	11.50%	48,613	76,633	69,667	109,822	97,925	154,366
Materials Technician	35,173	45,493	35,982	46,540	36,810	47,610	37,656	48,705	38,522	49,825	2.30%	11.50%	22,266	28,799	31,909	41,271	44,851	58,012
Mechanical Plans Examiner I-II	52,145	84,151	53,344	86,087	54,571	88,067	55,826	90,092	57,110	92,165	2.30%	11.50%	33,009	53,271	47,305	76,342	66,493	107,307
Museum Curator	54,855	81,873	56,117	83,756	57,408	85,683	58,728	87,654	60,079	89,670	2.30%	11.50%	34,725	51,829	49,765	74,275	69,950	104,402
Neighborhood Maint Tech I-III	33,989	63,718	34,771	65,183	35,571	66,683	36,389	68,216	37,226	69,785	2.30%	11.50%	21,516	40,336	30,835	57,805	43,342	81,251
Neighborhood Preserv Insp I-II	47,452	81,873	48,543	83,756	49,660	85,683	50,802	87,654	51,970	89,670	2.30%	11.50%	30,039	51,829	43,048	74,275	60,509	104,402
Operations & Maint Supervisor	49,502	74,083	50,640	75,787	51,805	77,530	52,997	79,313	54,216	81,137	2.30%	11.50%	31,337	46,897	44,908	67,208	63,123	94,468
Operations & Maint Tech Trnee	35,173	36,449	35,982	37,287	36,810	38,145	37,656	39,022	38,522	39,920	2.30%	11.50%	22,266	23,074	31,909	33,066	44,851	46,478
Operations & Maintenance Tech	45,493	57,316	46,540	58,635	47,610	59,983	48,705	61,363	49,825	62,774	2.30%	11.50%	28,799	36,283	41,271	51,997	58,012	73,088
Operations Analyst	49,502	74,083	50,640	75,787	51,805	77,530	52,997	79,313	54,216	81,137	2.30%	11.50%	31,337	46,897	44,908	67,208	63,123	94,468
Park Ranger I-III	34,490	60,642	35,283	62,037	36,094	63,464	36,925	64,924	37,774	66,417	2.30%	11.50%	21,833	38,389	31,289	55,015	43,980	77,329
Parks Foreman I-II	38,681	63,718	39,571	65,183	40,481	66,683	41,412	68,216	42,364	69,785	2.30%	11.50%	24,487	40,336	35,091	57,805	49,325	81,251
Parks Special Maintenance Supv	54,855	81,873	56,117	83,756	57,408	85,683	58,728	87,654	60,079	89,670	2.30%	11.50%	34,725	51,829	49,765	74,275	69,950	104,402
Parks Special Operations Supv	63,718	95,155	65,183	97,344	66,683	99,583	68,216	101,873	69,785	104,216	2.30%	11.50%	40,336	60,237	57,805	86,324	81,251	121,338
Parks Supervisor	57,612	86,043	58,937	88,022	60,293	90,046	61,679	92,117	63,098	94,236	2.30%	11.50%	36,471	54,468	52,265	78,058	73,465	109,719
Payroll Supervisor	63,718	95,155	65,183	97,344	66,683	99,583	68,216	101,873	69,785	104,216	2.30%	11.50%	40,336	60,237	57,805	86,324	81,251	121,338
Personnel Aide	37,634	56,017	38,500	57,306	39,385	58,624	40,291	59,972	41,218	61,352	2.30%	11.50%	23,824	35,461	34,141	50,819	47,990	71,431
Personnel Analyst I-II	45,015	77,978	46,050	79,771	47,109	81,606	48,193	83,483	49,301	85,403	2.30%	11.50%	28,496	49,363	40,837	70,741	57,401	99,434
Personnel Clerk I-II	29,797	48,158	30,482	49,266	31,183	50,399	31,900	51,558	32,634	52,744	2.30%	11.50%	18,862	30,486	27,031	43,689	37,996	61,409
Personnel Officer	57,612	86,043	58,937	88,022	60,293	90,046	61,679	92,117	63,098	94,236	2.30%	11.50%	36,471	54,468	52,265	78,058	73,465	109,719
Planner I-III	52,236	99,893	53,437	102,191	54,666	104,541	55,923	106,945	57,210	109,405	2.30%	11.50%	33,067	63,236	47,388	90,623	66,609	127,380
Plumbing/Mech Insp I-II	47,452	84,151	48,543	86,087	49,660	88,067	50,802	90,092	51,970	92,165	2.30%	11.50%	30,039	53,271	43,048	76,342	60,509	107,307
Police Aide	25,947	37,634	26,544	38,500	27,154	39,385	27,779	40,291	28,418	41,218	2.30%	11.50%	16,425	23,824	23,539	34,141	33,087	47,990
Police Lieutenant	68,388	100,758	69,961	103,076	71,570	105,447	73,216	107,872	74,900	110,353	2.30%	11.50%	43,292	63,784	62,041	91,408	87,206	128,483
Police Officer	44,354	69,481	45,374	71,079	46,418	72,714	47,486	74,386	48,578	76,097	2.30%	11.50%	28,078	43,984	40,238	63,033	56,559	88,600

Chart III - U.S. States & Cities - Job Titles - Salaries - Pension Estimates

Arizona-Phoenix	2010 (Min)	2010 (Max)	2011 (Min)	2011 (Max)	2012 (Min)	2012 (Max)	2013 (Min)	2013 (Max)	2014 (Min)	2014 (Max)	5-Year Average % Raise	5-Year Cumulative Raise Estimate**	20-Year Annual Pension Benefit Estimate (Min.)***	20-Year Annual Pension Benefit Estimate (Max.)	25-Year Annual Pension Benefit Estimate (Min.)	25-Year Annual Pension Benefit Estimate (Max.)	30-Year Annual Pension Benefit Estimate (Min.)	30-Year Annual Pension Benefit Estimate (Max.)
rocurement anager	67,043	99,893	68,585	102,191	70,162	104,541	71,776	106,945	73,427	109,405	2.30%	11.50%	42,441	63,236	60,821	90,623	85,491	127,380
rocurement upervisor	54,855	81,873	56,117	83,756	57,408	85,683	58,728	87,654	60,079	89,670	2.30%	11.50%	34,725	51,829	49,765	74,275	69,950	104,402
roject Management ssistant	47,316	70,438	48,404	72,058	49,517	73,716	50,656	75,411	51,821	77,145	2.30%	11.50%	29,953	44,590	42,925	63,901	60,335	89,820
roject Manager	60,642	90,416	62,037	92,496	63,464	94,623	64,924	96,799	66,417	99,026	2.30%	11.50%	38,389	57,237	55,015	82,025	77,329	115,295
ecords Clerk I-III	28,316	54,855	28,967	56,117	29,633	57,408	30,315	58,728	31,012	60,079	2.30%	11.50%	17,925	34,725	25,688	49,765	36,107	69,950
ecreation oordinator I-III	40,640	77,978	41,575	79,771	42,531	81,606	43,510	83,483	44,510	85,403	2.30%	11.50%	25,727	49,363	36,869	70,741	51,823	99,434
afety Analyst I-II	45,015	77,978	46,050	79,771	47,109	81,606	48,193	83,483	49,301	85,403	2.30%	11.50%	28,496	49,363	40,837	70,741	57,401	99,434
ecretary I-III	27,041	57,612	27,663	58,937	28,299	60,293	28,950	61,679	29,616	63,098	2.30%	11.50%	17,118	36,471	24,532	52,265	34,482	73,465
enior Buyer	49,502	74,083	50,640	75,787	51,805	77,530	52,997	79,313	54,216	81,137	2.30%	11.50%	31,337	46,897	44,908	67,208	63,123	94,468
enior Planning echnician	39,251	57,384	40,153	58,704	41,077	60,054	42,022	61,435	42,988	62,848	2.30%	11.50%	24,847	36,326	35,608	52,059	50,051	73,174
enior Programs upervisor I-II	45,015	74,083	46,050	75,787	47,109	77,530	48,193	79,313	49,301	81,137	2.30%	11.50%	28,496	46,897	40,837	67,208	57,401	94,468
enior Workforce ev Spec	57,612	86,043	58,937	88,022	60,293	90,046	61,679	92,117	63,098	94,236	2.30%	11.50%	36,471	54,468	52,265	78,058	73,465	109,719
ign Specialist I-II	31,505	48,569	32,230	49,686	32,971	50,829	33,729	51,998	34,505	53,194	2.30%	11.50%	19,944	30,746	28,581	44,061	40,174	61,933
olid Waste Admin nalyst	52,236	77,978	53,437	79,771	54,666	81,606	55,923	83,483	57,210	85,403	2.30%	11.50%	33,067	49,363	47,388	70,741	66,609	99,434
olid Waste dministrator	66,429	104,563	67,956	106,968	69,519	109,428	71,118	111,945	72,754	114,520	2.30%	11.50%	42,052	66,192	60,264	94,859	84,707	133,335
treet Maint Foreman III	34,922	63,718	35,725	65,183	36,547	66,683	37,388	68,216	38,248	69,785	2.30%	11.50%	22,107	40,336	31,681	57,805	44,532	81,251
treet Maint uperintendent	67,043	99,893	68,585	102,191	70,162	104,541	71,776	106,945	73,427	109,405	2.30%	11.50%	42,441	63,236	60,821	90,623	85,491	127,380
treet Maint upervisor	52,236	77,978	53,437	79,771	54,666	81,606	55,923	83,483	57,210	85,403	2.30%	11.50%	33,067	49,363	47,388	70,741	66,609	99,434
treet Maint Worker II	31,505	46,586	32,230	47,658	32,971	48,754	33,729	49,875	34,505	51,022	2.30%	11.50%	19,944	29,491	28,581	42,263	40,174	59,405
tructural Inspector II	47,452	84,151	48,543	86,087	49,660	88,067	50,802	90,092	51,970	92,165	2.30%	11.50%	30,039	53,271	43,048	76,342	60,509	107,307
tructural Plans xaminer I-II	52,145	84,151	53,344	86,087	54,571	88,067	55,826	90,092	57,110	92,165	2.30%	11.50%	33,009	53,271	47,305	76,342	66,493	107,307
upplies Clerk I-III	32,508	57,612	33,256	58,937	34,021	60,293	34,803	61,679	35,604	63,098	2.30%	11.50%	20,579	36,471	29,492	52,265	41,454	73,465
ax Auditor	45,015	67,043	46,050	68,585	47,109	70,162	48,193	71,776	49,301	73,427	2.30%	11.50%	28,496	42,441	40,837	60,821	57,401	85,491
elecommunications dm	73,194	115,293	74,877	117,945	76,599	120,657	78,361	123,433	80,163	126,272	2.30%	11.50%	46,334	72,985	66,401	104,593	93,334	147,018
elecommunications ide	37,634	54,628	38,500	55,884	39,385	57,169	40,291	58,484	41,218	59,829	2.30%	11.50%	23,824	34,581	34,141	49,558	47,990	69,659
elecommunications enter Supv	38,681	57,612	39,571	58,937	40,481	60,293	41,412	61,679	42,364	63,098	2.30%	11.50%	24,487	36,471	35,091	52,265	49,325	73,465
elecommunications perator	29,661	43,055	30,343	44,046	31,041	45,059	31,755	46,095	32,485	47,155	2.30%	11.50%	18,776	27,256	26,908	39,060	37,822	54,903
elecommunications pecialist	53,808	65,585	55,046	67,094	56,312	68,637	57,607	70,215	58,932	71,830	2.30%	11.50%	34,063	41,518	48,815	59,499	68,614	83,632
elecommunications vcs Asst	49,502	74,083	50,640	75,787	51,805	77,530	52,997	79,313	54,216	81,137	2.30%	11.50%	31,337	46,897	44,908	67,208	63,123	94,468
raffic Engineer I-III	47,316	110,554	48,404	113,097	49,517	115,698	50,656	118,359	51,821	121,081	2.30%	11.50%	29,953	69,985	42,925	100,294	60,335	140,974
raffic Maintenance rmn I-III	34,922	63,718	35,725	65,183	36,547	66,683	37,388	68,216	38,248	69,785	2.30%	11.50%	22,107	40,336	31,681	57,805	44,532	81,251
ree Trimmer I-II	33,397	48,569	34,165	49,686	34,951	50,829	35,754	51,998	36,577	53,194	2.30%	11.50%	21,141	30,746	30,297	44,061	42,586	61,933
ypist I-II	24,717	39,251	25,285	40,153	25,867	41,077	26,462	42,022	27,071	42,988	2.30%	11.50%	15,647	24,847	22,423	35,608	31,518	50,051
ser Support pecialist	45,197	66,360	46,236	67,886	47,300	69,447	48,387	71,044	49,500	72,679	2.30%	11.50%	28,611	42,008	41,002	60,201	57,633	84,619
ser Technology pecialist	57,612	86,043	58,937	88,022	60,293	90,046	61,679	92,117	63,098	94,236	2.30%	11.50%	36,471	54,468	52,265	78,058	73,465	109,719
ater Customer ervices Spv I-II	45,015	77,978	46,050	79,771	47,109	81,606	48,193	83,483	49,301	85,403	2.30%	11.50%	28,496	49,363	40,837	70,741	57,401	99,434

145

Chart III - U.S. States & Cities - Job Titles - Salaries - Pension Estimates

Arizona-Phoenix	2010 (Min)	2010 (Max)	2011 (Min)	2011 (Max)	2012 (Min)	2012 (Max)	2013 (Min)	2013 (Max)	2014 (Min)	2014 (Max)	5-Year Average % Raise	5-Year Cumulative Raise Estimate**	20-Year Annual Pension Benefit Estimate (Min.)***	20-Year Annual Pension Benefit Estimate (Max.)	25-Year Annual Pension Benefit Estimate (Min.)	25-Year Annual Pension Benefit Estimate (Max.)	30-Year Annual Pension Benefit Estimate (Min.)	30-Year Annual Pension Benefit Estimate (Max.)
Water Distribution Supv I-II	47,316	77,978	48,404	79,771	49,517	81,606	50,656	83,483	51,821	85,403	2.30%	11.50%	29,953	49,363	42,925	70,741	60,335	99,434
Water Meter Technician I-II	34,194	47,475	34,980	48,567	35,785	49,684	36,608	50,826	37,450	51,995	2.30%	11.50%	21,646	30,053	31,021	43,069	43,603	60,538
Water Production Supt	80,711	127,139	82,568	130,063	84,467	133,055	86,410	136,115	88,397	139,246	2.30%	11.50%	51,093	80,484	73,221	115,340	102,920	162,123
Water Quality Inspector	41,756	56,177	42,717	57,469	43,699	58,791	44,704	60,143	45,733	61,527	2.30%	11.50%	26,433	35,562	37,881	50,964	53,246	71,635
Water Quality Supervisor	63,718	95,155	65,183	97,344	66,683	99,583	68,216	101,873	69,785	104,216	2.30%	11.50%	40,336	60,237	57,805	86,324	81,251	121,338
Water Resource Specialist	52,236	77,978	53,437	79,771	54,666	81,606	55,923	83,483	57,210	85,403	2.30%	11.50%	33,067	49,363	47,388	70,741	66,609	99,434
Workforce Development Spec	47,316	70,438	48,404	72,058	49,517	73,716	50,656	75,411	51,821	77,145	2.30%	11.50%	29,953	44,590	42,925	63,901	60,335	89,820
Youth Counselor	32,622	47,452	33,373	48,543	34,140	49,660	34,925	50,802	35,729	51,970	2.30%	11.50%	20,651	30,039	29,595	43,048	41,599	60,509

http://www.ci.phoenix.az.us/JOBSPECS/jobsidx.html

Chart III - U.S. States & Cities - Job Titles - Salaries - Pension Estimates

California	2010 (Min)	2010 (Max)	2011 (Min)	2011 (Max)	2012 (Min)	2012 (Max)	2013 (Min)	2013 (Max)	2014 (Min)	2014 (Max)	5-Year Average % Raise	5-Year Cumulative Raise Estimate **	20-Year Pension %	25-Year Pension %	30-Year Pension %	20-Year Annual Pension Benefit Estimate (Min.) ***	20-Year Annual Pension Benefit Estimate (Max.)	25-Year Annual Pension Benefit Estimate (Min.)	25-Year Annual Pension Benefit Estimate (Max.)	30-Year Annual Pension Benefit Estimate (Min.)	30-Year Annual Pension Benefit Estimate (Max.)
Adoptions Specialist	49,370	61,539	51,839	64,616	54,431	67,847	57,152	71,239	60,010	74,801	5.00%	25.00%	2.00%	2.00%	2.00%	45,299	56,464	72,268	90,081	110,681	137,962
Adoptions Supervisor I-II	70,555	93,448	74,083	98,121	77,787	103,027	81,676	108,178	85,760	113,587	5.00%	25.00%	2.00%	2.00%	2.00%	64,737	85,742	103,278	136,789	158,174	209,497
Aging Programs Analyst I-II	38,035	74,236	39,937	77,948	41,934	81,845	44,030	85,938	46,232	90,235	5.00%	25.00%	2.00%	2.00%	2.00%	34,898	68,114	55,675	108,666	85,269	166,426
Agricultural Biologist	39,132	44,356	41,089	46,573	43,143	48,902	45,301	51,347	47,566	53,914	5.00%	25.00%	2.00%	2.00%	2.00%	35,905	40,698	57,282	64,927	87,729	99,439
Agricultural Education Administrator I	88,364	107,437	92,782	112,809	97,421	118,449	102,292	124,372	107,407	130,590	5.00%	25.00%	2.00%	2.00%	2.00%	81,077	98,577	129,346	157,265	198,099	240,858
Agricultural Laboratory Microscopist	46,328	56,261	48,645	59,074	51,077	62,027	53,631	65,129	56,312	68,385	5.00%	25.00%	2.00%	2.00%	2.00%	42,508	51,621	67,815	82,354	103,861	126,128
Agricultural Pest Control Specialist	39,869	48,454	41,862	50,876	43,955	53,420	46,153	56,091	48,461	58,896	5.00%	25.00%	2.00%	2.00%	2.00%	36,581	44,458	58,359	70,926	89,379	108,626
Air Operations Officer I-III	66,721	98,060	70,057	102,963	73,560	108,111	77,238	113,517	81,100	119,193	5.00%	25.00%	2.00%	2.00%	2.00%	61,219	89,974	97,665	143,540	149,578	219,836
Air Pollution Research Specialist	94,282	114,591	98,996	120,321	103,945	126,337	109,143	132,653	114,600	139,286	5.00%	25.00%	2.00%	2.00%	2.00%	86,507	105,141	138,009	167,737	211,365	256,896
Air Pollution Specialist	54,219	62,776	56,929	65,914	59,776	69,210	62,765	72,671	65,903	76,304	5.00%	25.00%	2.00%	2.00%	2.00%	49,747	57,599	79,365	91,890	121,550	140,734
Air Resources Engineer	59,442	68,805	62,414	72,245	65,535	75,857	68,811	79,650	72,252	83,632	5.00%	25.00%	2.00%	2.00%	2.00%	54,540	63,131	87,010	100,716	133,260	154,250
Air Resources Field Relpresentative I-III	51,926	75,598	54,523	79,377	57,249	83,346	60,111	87,514	63,117	91,889	5.00%	25.00%	2.00%	2.00%	2.00%	47,644	69,363	76,009	110,659	116,411	169,478
Air Resources Supervisor I-II	102,478	136,720	107,601	143,556	112,982	150,734	118,631	158,271	124,562	166,184	5.00%	25.00%	2.00%	2.00%	2.00%	94,027	125,446	150,006	200,130	229,740	306,506
Apprenticeship Consultant	64,165	78,015	67,373	81,915	70,742	86,011	74,279	90,312	77,993	94,827	5.00%	25.00%	2.00%	2.00%	2.00%	58,873	71,581	93,924	114,197	143,848	174,897
Architectural Assistant	48,662	56,316	51,095	59,132	53,650	62,089	56,332	65,193	59,149	68,453	5.00%	25.00%	2.00%	2.00%	2.00%	44,649	51,672	71,231	82,435	109,093	126,252
Architectural Associate	68,902	83,724	72,347	87,910	75,964	92,306	79,762	96,921	83,751	101,767	5.00%	25.00%	2.00%	2.00%	2.00%	63,220	76,820	100,858	122,555	154,468	187,697
Architectural Designer	59,442	68,805	62,414	72,245	65,535	75,857	68,811	79,650	72,252	83,632	5.00%	25.00%	2.00%	2.00%	2.00%	54,540	63,131	87,010	100,716	133,260	154,250
Architectural Senior	94,337	114,688	99,054	120,423	104,007	126,444	109,207	132,766	114,667	139,404	5.00%	25.00%	2.00%	2.00%	2.00%	86,558	105,230	138,090	167,880	211,490	257,114
Archivist I-II	53,677	74,834	56,361	78,575	59,179	82,504	62,138	86,629	65,244	90,961	5.00%	25.00%	2.00%	2.00%	2.00%	49,250	68,662	78,572	109,541	120,335	167,766
Arson And Bomb Investigator	69,458	83,766	72,930	87,954	76,577	92,352	80,406	96,969	84,426	101,818	5.00%	25.00%	2.00%	2.00%	2.00%	63,730	76,858	101,671	122,616	155,713	187,790
Assistive Technology Specialist I-II	46,328	59,122	48,645	62,078	51,077	65,182	53,631	68,441	56,312	71,863	5.00%	25.00%	2.00%	2.00%	2.00%	42,508	54,247	67,815	86,543	103,861	132,543
Assistive Technology Supervisor	53,524	65,068	56,200	68,321	59,010	71,737	61,961	75,324	65,059	79,090	5.00%	25.00%	2.00%	2.00%	2.00%	49,110	59,702	78,348	95,246	119,993	145,872
Associate Accounting Analyst	64,165	78,015	67,373	81,915	70,742	86,011	74,279	90,312	77,993	94,827	5.00%	25.00%	2.00%	2.00%	2.00%	58,873	71,581	93,924	114,197	143,848	174,897
Associate Agricultural Biologist	64,359	77,570	67,577	81,449	70,956	85,521	74,504	89,797	78,229	94,287	5.00%	25.00%	2.00%	2.00%	2.00%	59,052	71,173	94,209	113,546	144,284	173,901
Associate Agricultural Economist	61,123	74,292	64,179	78,006	67,388	81,907	70,757	86,002	74,295	90,302	5.00%	25.00%	2.00%	2.00%	2.00%	56,082	68,165	89,471	108,748	137,028	166,551
Associate Architect	87,100	105,812	91,455	111,102	96,027	116,657	100,829	122,490	105,870	128,615	5.00%	25.00%	2.00%	2.00%	2.00%	79,917	97,086	127,496	154,886	195,265	237,214
Associate Arts Grants Administrator	61,123	74,292	64,179	78,006	67,388	81,907	70,757	86,002	74,295	90,302	5.00%	25.00%	2.00%	2.00%	2.00%	56,082	68,165	89,471	108,748	137,028	166,551
Associate Bridge Engineer	87,405	106,201	91,776	111,511	96,364	117,086	101,183	122,940	106,242	129,087	5.00%	25.00%	2.00%	2.00%	2.00%	80,197	97,443	127,943	155,455	195,950	238,086
Associate Budget Analyst	61,123	74,292	64,179	78,006	67,388	81,907	70,757	86,002	74,295	90,302	5.00%	25.00%	2.00%	2.00%	2.00%	56,082	68,165	89,471	108,748	137,028	166,551
Associate Casualty Actuary	97,754	118,842	102,642	124,784	107,774	131,023	113,163	137,574	118,821	144,453	5.00%	25.00%	2.00%	2.00%	2.00%	89,693	109,041	143,092	173,960	219,151	266,426
Associate Civil Engineer	87,405	106,201	91,776	111,511	96,364	117,086	101,183	122,940	106,242	129,087	5.00%	25.00%	2.00%	2.00%	2.00%	80,197	97,443	127,943	155,455	195,950	238,086
Associate Construction Analyst	82,335	100,019	86,452	105,020	90,774	110,271	95,313	115,784	100,079	121,573	5.00%	25.00%	2.00%	2.00%	2.00%	75,545	91,771	120,521	146,407	184,583	224,227
Associate Control Engineer	94,573	114,855	99,302	120,598	104,267	126,628	109,480	132,959	114,954	139,607	5.00%	25.00%	2.00%	2.00%	2.00%	86,774	105,383	138,436	168,124	212,019	257,488
Associate Corrosion Engineer	87,114	105,798	91,469	111,088	96,043	116,642	100,845	122,474	105,887	128,598	5.00%	25.00%	2.00%	2.00%	2.00%	79,930	97,073	127,516	154,866	195,296	237,183

Chart III - U.S. States & Cities - Job Titles - Salaries - Pension Estimates

California	2010 (Min)	2010 (Max)	2011 (Min)	2011 (Max)	2012 (Min)	2012 (Max)	2013 (Min)	2013 (Max)	2014 (Min)	2014 (Max)	5-Year Average % Raise	5-Year Cumulative Raise Estimate **	20-Year Pension %	25-Year Pension %	30-Year Pension %	20-Year Annual Pension Benefit Estimate (Min.) ***	20-Year Annual Pension Benefit Estimate (Max.)	25-Year Annual Pension Benefit Estimate (Min.)	25-Year Annual Pension Benefit Estimate (Max.)	30-Year Annual Pension Benefit Estimate (Min.)	30-Year Annual Pension Benefit Estimate (Max.)
Associate Editor Of Publications	61,123	74,292	64,179	78,006	67,388	81,907	70,757	86,002	74,295	90,302	5.00%	25.00%	2.00%	2.00%	2.00%	56,082	68,165	89,471	108,748	137,028	166,551
Associate Electrical Engineer	87,114	105,798	91,469	111,088	96,043	116,642	100,845	122,474	105,887	128,598	5.00%	25.00%	2.00%	2.00%	2.00%	79,930	97,073	127,516	154,866	195,296	237,183
Associate Electronics Engineer	87,114	105,798	91,469	111,088	96,043	116,642	100,845	122,474	105,887	128,598	5.00%	25.00%	2.00%	2.00%	2.00%	79,930	97,073	127,516	154,866	195,296	237,183
Associate Environmental Planner	64,165	78,015	67,373	81,915	70,742	86,011	74,279	90,312	77,993	94,827	5.00%	25.00%	2.00%	2.00%	2.00%	58,873	71,581	93,924	114,197	143,848	174,897
Associate Equipment Engineer	87,405	106,256	91,776	111,569	96,364	117,147	101,183	123,005	106,242	129,155	5.00%	25.00%	2.00%	2.00%	2.00%	80,197	97,494	127,943	155,537	195,950	238,210
Associate Geochemist	68,902	83,071	72,347	87,225	75,964	91,586	79,762	96,165	83,751	100,974	5.00%	25.00%	2.00%	2.00%	2.00%	63,220	76,221	100,858	121,599	154,468	186,233
Associate Geologist	68,902	83,071	72,347	87,225	75,964	91,586	79,762	96,165	83,751	100,974	5.00%	25.00%	2.00%	2.00%	2.00%	63,220	76,221	100,858	121,599	154,468	186,233
Associate Geophysicist	68,902	83,071	72,347	87,225	75,964	91,586	79,762	96,165	83,751	100,974	5.00%	25.00%	2.00%	2.00%	2.00%	63,220	76,221	100,858	121,599	154,468	186,233
Associate Health Physicist	68,902	87,211	72,347	91,571	75,964	96,150	79,762	100,957	83,751	106,005	5.00%	25.00%	2.00%	2.00%	2.00%	63,220	80,019	100,858	127,658	154,468	195,514
Associate Health Planning Analyst	61,123	74,292	64,179	78,006	67,388	81,907	70,757	86,002	74,295	90,302	5.00%	25.00%	2.00%	2.00%	2.00%	56,082	68,165	89,471	108,748	137,028	166,551
Associate Health Program Adviser	61,123	74,292	64,179	78,006	67,388	81,907	70,757	86,002	74,295	90,302	5.00%	25.00%	2.00%	2.00%	2.00%	56,082	68,165	89,471	108,748	137,028	166,551
Associate Hydraulic Engineer	87,100	105,812	91,455	111,102	96,027	116,657	100,829	122,490	105,870	128,615	5.00%	25.00%	2.00%	2.00%	2.00%	79,917	97,086	127,496	154,886	195,265	237,214
Associate Industrial Hygienist	68,902	91,364	72,347	95,933	75,964	100,729	79,762	105,766	83,751	111,054	5.00%	25.00%	2.00%	2.00%	2.00%	63,220	83,830	100,858	133,738	154,468	204,825
Associate Insurance Examiner	64,165	81,918	67,373	86,014	70,742	90,315	74,279	94,831	77,993	99,572	5.00%	25.00%	2.00%	2.00%	2.00%	58,873	75,163	93,924	119,911	143,848	183,648
Associate Pension Actuary	97,407	118,397	102,278	124,317	107,391	130,533	112,761	137,060	118,399	143,913	5.00%	25.00%	2.00%	2.00%	2.00%	89,375	108,634	142,584	173,309	218,372	265,429
Associate Pension Program Analyst	61,123	74,292	64,179	78,006	67,388	81,907	70,757	86,002	74,295	90,302	5.00%	25.00%	2.00%	2.00%	2.00%	56,082	68,165	89,471	108,748	137,028	166,551
Associate Personnel Analyst	61,123	74,292	64,179	78,006	67,388	81,907	70,757	86,002	74,295	90,302	5.00%	25.00%	2.00%	2.00%	2.00%	56,082	68,165	89,471	108,748	137,028	166,551
Associate Planner	61,123	74,292	64,179	78,006	67,388	81,907	70,757	86,002	74,295	90,302	5.00%	25.00%	2.00%	2.00%	2.00%	56,082	68,165	89,471	108,748	137,028	166,551
Associate Process Safety Engineer	108,381	131,622	113,801	138,203	119,491	145,113	125,465	152,369	131,738	159,987	5.00%	25.00%	2.00%	2.00%	2.00%	99,444	120,768	158,648	192,667	242,975	295,077
Associate Procurement Engineer	87,114	105,798	91,469	111,088	96,043	116,642	100,845	122,474	105,887	128,598	5.00%	25.00%	2.00%	2.00%	2.00%	79,930	97,073	127,516	154,866	195,296	237,183
Associate Program Systems Analyst	64,165	81,918	67,373	86,014	70,742	90,315	74,279	94,831	77,993	99,572	5.00%	25.00%	2.00%	2.00%	2.00%	58,873	75,163	93,924	119,911	143,848	183,648
Associate Programmer Analyst (Specialist)	64,165	81,918	67,373	86,014	70,742	90,315	74,279	94,831	77,993	99,572	5.00%	25.00%	2.00%	2.00%	2.00%	58,873	75,163	93,924	119,911	143,848	183,648
Associate Programmer Analyst (Supervisor)	67,374	86,016	70,742	90,317	74,280	94,833	77,994	99,574	81,893	104,553	5.00%	25.00%	2.00%	2.00%	2.00%	61,818	78,923	98,621	125,910	151,042	192,835
Audiologist I-II	56,677	78,070	59,511	81,974	62,487	86,072	65,611	90,376	68,892	94,895	5.00%	25.00%	2.00%	2.00%	2.00%	52,003	71,632	82,964	114,279	127,062	175,022
Audio-Visual Assistant	50,815	61,762	53,356	64,850	56,024	68,092	58,825	71,497	61,766	75,072	5.00%	25.00%	2.00%	2.00%	2.00%	46,625	56,668	74,383	90,406	113,920	138,460
Automotive Pool Manager I-II	46,370	73,792	48,688	77,481	51,123	81,355	53,679	85,423	56,363	89,694	5.00%	25.00%	2.00%	2.00%	2.00%	42,546	67,706	67,876	108,016	103,954	165,430
Behavior Specialist I-II	50,190	69,249	52,699	72,712	55,334	76,347	58,101	80,165	61,006	84,173	5.00%	25.00%	2.00%	2.00%	2.00%	46,051	63,538	73,468	101,366	112,519	155,246
Biologist (General)	39,132	44,356	41,089	46,573	43,143	48,902	45,301	51,347	47,566	53,914	5.00%	25.00%	2.00%	2.00%	2.00%	35,905	40,698	57,282	64,927	87,729	99,439
Biostatistician II-IV	53,149	89,614	55,806	94,095	58,597	98,800	61,526	103,739	64,603	108,926	5.00%	25.00%	2.00%	2.00%	2.00%	48,766	82,224	77,799	131,176	119,152	200,901
Building Maintenance Worker	44,258	48,579	46,471	51,008	48,795	53,558	51,235	56,236	53,796	59,048	5.00%	25.00%	2.00%	2.00%	2.00%	40,609	44,573	64,785	71,109	99,221	108,906
Business Education Administrator I	88,364	107,437	92,782	112,809	97,421	118,449	102,292	124,372	107,407	130,590	5.00%	25.00%	2.00%	2.00%	2.00%	81,077	98,577	129,346	157,265	198,099	240,858
Business Enterprise Consultant I-II	53,149	96,601	55,806	101,432	58,597	106,503	61,526	111,828	64,603	117,420	5.00%	25.00%	2.00%	2.00%	2.00%	48,766	88,635	77,799	141,404	119,152	216,566
Business Manager I-II	70,555	95,282	74,083	100,046	77,787	105,048	81,676	110,301	85,760	115,816	5.00%	25.00%	2.00%	2.00%	2.00%	64,737	87,424	103,278	139,473	158,174	213,608

Chart III - U.S. States & Cities - Job Titles - Salaries - Pension Estimates

California	2010 (Min)	2010 (Max)	2011 (Min)	2011 (Max)	2012 (Min)	2012 (Max)	2013 (Min)	2013 (Max)	2014 (Min)	2014 (Max)	5-Year Average % Raise	5-Year Cumu-lative Raise Estimate **	20-Year Pension %	25-Year Pension %	30-Year Pension %	20-Year Annual Pension Benefit Estimate (Min.) ***	20-Year Annual Pension Benefit Estimate (Max.)	25-Year Annual Pension Benefit Estimate (Min.)	25-Year Annual Pension Benefit Estimate (Max.)	30-Year Annual Pension Benefit Estimate (Min.)	30-Year Annual Pension Benefit Estimate (Max.)
Business Service Officer I-III	50,815	77,459	53,356	81,332	56,024	85,399	58,825	89,668	61,766	94,152	5.00%	25.00%	2.00%	2.00%	2.00%	46,625	71,071	74,383	113,384	113,920	173,652
Business Taxes Compliance Specialist	64,165	78,015	67,373	81,915	70,742	86,011	74,279	90,312	77,993	94,827	5.00%	25.00%	2.00%	2.00%	2.00%	58,873	71,581	93,924	114,197	143,848	174,897
Business Taxes Compliance Supervisor I-III	64,207	94,157	67,417	98,864	70,788	103,808	74,327	108,998	78,043	114,448	5.00%	25.00%	2.00%	2.00%	2.00%	58,912	86,392	93,985	137,826	143,941	211,085
Career-Vocational Education Administrator I-II	88,364	112,952	92,782	118,599	97,421	124,529	102,292	130,756	107,407	137,294	5.00%	25.00%	2.00%	2.00%	2.00%	81,077	103,637	129,346	165,338	198,099	253,221
Carpenter I-II	50,843	58,358	53,385	61,276	56,054	64,340	58,857	67,557	61,800	70,935	5.00%	25.00%	2.00%	2.00%	2.00%	46,650	53,546	74,423	85,424	113,982	130,830
Chief Engineer I-II	65,665	79,265	68,948	83,228	72,396	87,390	76,016	91,759	79,816	96,347	5.00%	25.00%	2.00%	2.00%	2.00%	60,250	72,728	96,120	116,027	147,211	177,700
Child Development Administrator I-II	88,364	112,952	92,782	118,599	97,421	124,529	102,292	130,756	107,407	137,294	5.00%	25.00%	2.00%	2.00%	2.00%	81,077	103,637	129,346	165,338	198,099	253,221
Child Nutrition Supervisor I-II	67,193	89,850	70,553	94,343	74,080	99,060	77,785	104,013	81,674	109,214	5.00%	25.00%	2.00%	2.00%	2.00%	61,652	82,441	98,357	131,522	150,637	201,431
Civil Engineering Technician II	51,926	63,123	54,523	66,279	57,249	69,593	60,111	73,073	63,117	76,726	5.00%	25.00%	2.00%	2.00%	2.00%	47,644	57,918	76,009	92,399	116,411	141,512
Claim Auditor	38,952	47,342	40,899	49,709	42,944	52,195	45,092	54,805	47,346	57,545	5.00%	25.00%	2.00%	2.00%	2.00%	35,740	43,438	57,017	69,299	87,324	106,134
Clinical Administrator	92,823	102,325	97,464	107,441	102,337	112,813	107,454	118,454	112,827	124,376	5.00%	25.00%	2.00%	2.00%	2.00%	85,168	93,887	135,873	149,782	208,095	229,397
Clinical Dietitian	46,120	57,400	48,426	60,270	50,847	63,283	53,389	66,447	56,059	69,770	5.00%	25.00%	2.00%	2.00%	2.00%	42,317	52,666	67,510	84,021	103,394	128,682
Clinical Laboratory Technologist	55,788	67,818	58,578	71,209	61,507	74,770	64,582	78,508	67,811	82,434	5.00%	25.00%	2.00%	2.00%	2.00%	51,188	62,226	81,662	99,272	125,069	152,039
Coastal Program Analyst I-III	43,147	85,113	45,304	89,369	47,570	93,837	49,948	98,529	52,445	103,456	5.00%	25.00%	2.00%	2.00%	2.00%	39,589	78,094	63,158	124,588	96,729	190,811
Coastal Program Manager	77,459	93,448	81,332	98,121	85,399	103,027	89,668	108,178	94,152	113,587	5.00%	25.00%	2.00%	2.00%	2.00%	71,071	85,742	113,384	136,789	173,652	209,497
Collection Agent	44,244	53,760	46,457	56,448	48,779	59,271	51,218	62,234	53,779	65,346	5.00%	25.00%	2.00%	2.00%	2.00%	40,596	49,327	64,765	78,694	99,189	120,522
Communicable Disease Manager I-III	64,207	93,448	67,417	98,121	70,788	103,027	74,327	108,178	78,043	113,587	5.00%	25.00%	2.00%	2.00%	2.00%	58,912	85,742	93,985	136,789	143,941	209,497
Communicable Disease Specialist I-II	61,123	81,599	64,179	85,679	67,388	89,963	70,757	94,461	74,295	99,184	5.00%	25.00%	2.00%	2.00%	2.00%	56,082	74,870	89,471	119,443	137,028	182,932
Communications Operator	41,897	50,926	43,992	53,473	46,191	56,146	48,501	58,953	50,926	61,901	5.00%	25.00%	2.00%	2.00%	2.00%	38,442	46,727	61,328	74,545	93,926	114,169
Communications Supervisor	53,774	65,346	56,463	68,613	59,286	72,044	62,250	75,646	65,363	79,428	5.00%	25.00%	2.00%	2.00%	2.00%	49,340	59,957	78,714	95,652	120,553	146,495
Community College Program Assistant I-II	59,928	87,919	62,924	92,315	66,071	96,931	69,374	101,778	72,843	106,866	5.00%	25.00%	2.00%	2.00%	2.00%	54,986	80,669	87,722	128,696	134,350	197,102
Community Program Administrator II	98,769	108,882	103,707	114,326	108,892	120,042	114,337	126,044	120,054	132,346	5.00%	25.00%	2.00%	2.00%	2.00%	90,624	99,903	144,577	159,380	221,424	244,096
Community Program Specialist I-IV	50,815	93,448	53,356	98,121	56,024	103,027	58,825	108,178	61,766	113,587	5.00%	25.00%	2.00%	2.00%	2.00%	46,625	85,742	74,383	136,789	113,920	209,497
Computer Operations Specialist I-II	48,551	74,458	50,978	78,181	53,527	82,090	56,204	86,195	59,014	90,505	5.00%	25.00%	2.00%	2.00%	2.00%	44,547	68,318	71,068	108,992	108,844	166,925
Computer Operations Supervisor I-II	51,551	78,459	54,129	82,382	56,835	86,501	59,677	90,826	62,661	95,368	5.00%	25.00%	2.00%	2.00%	2.00%	47,300	71,989	75,460	114,848	115,570	175,894
Conservancy Project Development Analyst III	53,357	93,448	56,025	98,121	58,826	103,027	61,768	108,178	64,856	113,587	5.00%	25.00%	2.00%	2.00%	2.00%	48,957	85,742	78,104	136,789	119,619	209,497
Construction Inspector I-II	56,858	78,904	59,701	82,849	62,686	86,991	65,820	91,341	69,111	95,908	5.00%	25.00%	2.00%	2.00%	2.00%	52,169	72,397	83,228	115,499	127,467	176,890
Construction Supervisor I-III	82,516	136,720	86,641	143,556	90,973	150,734	95,522	158,271	100,298	166,184	5.00%	25.00%	2.00%	2.00%	2.00%	75,711	125,446	120,785	200,130	184,988	306,506
Construction Supervisor I-III Water Resources	68,902	136,720	72,347	143,556	75,964	150,734	79,762	158,271	83,751	166,184	5.00%	25.00%	2.00%	2.00%	2.00%	63,220	125,446	100,858	200,130	154,468	306,506
Corporation Examiner	55,691	67,721	58,476	71,107	61,399	74,662	64,469	78,396	67,693	82,315	5.00%	25.00%	2.00%	2.00%	2.00%	51,098	62,136	81,520	99,129	124,851	151,821
Corporations Counsel	64,929	64,929	68,175	68,175	71,584	71,584	75,163	75,163	78,921	78,921	5.00%	25.00%	2.00%	2.00%	2.00%	59,575	59,575	95,042	95,042	145,561	145,561
Corporations Investigator	50,440	57,900	52,962	60,795	55,610	63,834	58,391	67,026	61,310	70,378	5.00%	25.00%	2.00%	2.00%	2.00%	46,280	53,125	73,834	84,753	113,079	129,803
Correctional Case Records Administrator	77,459	93,448	81,332	98,121	85,399	103,027	89,668	108,178	94,152	113,587	5.00%	25.00%	2.00%	2.00%	2.00%	71,071	85,742	113,384	136,789	173,652	209,497

Chart III - U.S. States & Cities - Job Titles - Salaries - Pension Estimates

California	2010 (Min)	2010 (Max)	2011 (Min)	2011 (Max)	2012 (Min)	2012 (Max)	2013 (Min)	2013 (Max)	2014 (Min)	2014 (Max)	5-Year Average % Raise	5-Year Cumulative Raise Estimate **	20-Year Pension %	25-Year Pension %	30-Year Pension %	20-Year Annual Pension Benefit Estimate (Min.) ***	20-Year Annual Pension Benefit Estimate (Max.)	25-Year Annual Pension Benefit Estimate (Min.)	25-Year Annual Pension Benefit Estimate (Max.)	30-Year Annual Pension Benefit Estimate (Min.)	30-Year Annual Pension Benefit Estimate (Max.)
Correctional Case Records Analyst	39,132	47,592	41,089	49,972	43,143	52,470	45,301	55,094	47,566	57,849	5.00%	25.00%	2.00%	2.00%	2.00%	35,905	43,668	57,282	69,665	87,729	106,69
Correctional Case Records Manager	67,596	81,488	70,976	85,562	74,525	89,840	78,251	94,332	82,163	99,049	5.00%	25.00%	2.00%	2.00%	2.00%	62,022	74,768	98,946	119,281	151,540	182,68
Correctional Case Records Supervisor	58,858	70,791	61,801	74,331	64,891	78,047	68,136	81,950	71,543	86,047	5.00%	25.00%	2.00%	2.00%	2.00%	54,005	64,953	86,156	103,623	131,952	158,70
Correctional Counselor I-III	69,916	123,343	73,412	129,510	77,082	135,985	80,936	142,785	84,983	149,924	5.00%	25.00%	2.00%	2.00%	2.00%	64,150	113,171	102,342	180,548	156,741	276,51
Crime Studies Technician I-II	38,146	55,108	40,053	57,863	42,056	60,756	44,159	63,794	46,367	66,984	5.00%	25.00%	2.00%	2.00%	2.00%	35,000	50,563	55,838	80,666	85,518	123,54
Criminal Identification Specialist I-III	39,966	62,817	41,964	65,958	44,062	69,256	46,265	72,719	48,579	76,355	5.00%	25.00%	2.00%	2.00%	2.00%	36,670	57,637	58,502	91,952	89,597	140,82
Criminal Intelligence Specialist I-III	39,966	62,776	41,964	65,914	44,062	69,210	46,265	72,671	48,579	76,304	5.00%	25.00%	2.00%	2.00%	2.00%	36,670	57,599	58,502	91,890	89,597	140,73
Criminal Justice Specialist I-II	61,123	81,599	64,179	85,679	67,388	89,963	70,757	94,461	74,295	99,184	5.00%	25.00%	2.00%	2.00%	2.00%	56,082	74,870	89,471	119,443	137,028	182,93
Criminalist	43,828	53,913	46,019	56,609	48,320	59,439	50,736	62,411	53,273	65,531	5.00%	25.00%	2.00%	2.00%	2.00%	40,213	49,467	64,155	78,917	98,255	120,86
Criminalist Manager	103,950	120,370	109,148	126,388	114,605	132,708	120,335	139,343	126,352	146,310	5.00%	25.00%	2.00%	2.00%	2.00%	95,378	110,444	152,161	176,196	233,041	269,85
Criminalist Supervisor	85,613	108,645	89,894	114,078	94,389	119,782	99,108	125,771	104,064	132,059	5.00%	25.00%	2.00%	2.00%	2.00%	78,553	99,686	125,320	159,034	191,932	243,56
Data Communications Specialist	112,396	136,595	118,016	143,425	123,917	150,596	130,113	158,126	136,618	166,032	5.00%	25.00%	2.00%	2.00%	2.00%	103,127	125,331	164,524	199,947	251,975	306,22
Data Entry Manager	64,276	78,140	67,490	82,047	70,864	86,149	74,407	90,456	78,128	94,979	5.00%	25.00%	2.00%	2.00%	2.00%	58,975	71,696	94,087	114,380	144,097	175,17
Data Processing Manager I-IV	73,875	125,843	77,569	132,135	81,447	138,742	85,520	145,679	89,796	152,963	5.00%	25.00%	2.00%	2.00%	2.00%	67,783	115,465	108,138	184,208	165,617	282,12
Dental Hygienist	47,453	57,678	49,826	60,561	52,317	63,589	54,933	66,769	57,680	70,107	5.00%	25.00%	2.00%	2.00%	2.00%	43,540	52,921	69,462	84,428	106,383	129,30
Digital Composition Specialist I-III	38,299	68,818	40,214	72,259	42,224	75,872	44,336	79,666	46,553	83,649	5.00%	25.00%	2.00%	2.00%	2.00%	35,141	63,143	56,062	100,736	85,860	154,28
Digital Print Operator I-II	36,215	48,412	38,026	50,832	39,927	53,374	41,924	56,043	44,020	58,845	5.00%	25.00%	2.00%	2.00%	2.00%	33,229	44,420	53,011	70,865	81,189	108,53
Direct Construction Supervisor I-III	77,987	136,720	81,886	143,556	85,981	150,734	90,280	158,271	94,794	166,184	5.00%	25.00%	2.00%	2.00%	2.00%	71,556	125,446	114,157	200,130	174,835	306,50
Disability Evaluation Analyst I-III	39,132	74,292	41,089	78,006	43,143	81,907	45,301	86,002	47,566	90,302	5.00%	25.00%	2.00%	2.00%	2.00%	35,905	68,165	57,282	108,748	87,729	166,55
Disability Evaluation Services Administrator I-III	70,555	103,825	74,083	109,016	77,787	114,467	81,676	120,190	85,760	126,200	5.00%	25.00%	2.00%	2.00%	2.00%	64,737	95,263	103,278	151,978	158,174	232,76
Disability Insurance Program Manager I-III	61,150	89,697	64,208	94,182	67,418	98,891	70,789	103,836	74,329	109,028	5.00%	25.00%	2.00%	2.00%	2.00%	56,108	82,301	89,511	131,298	137,090	201,08
Disability Insurance Specialist I-III	46,328	81,599	48,645	85,679	51,077	89,963	53,631	94,461	56,312	99,184	5.00%	25.00%	2.00%	2.00%	2.00%	42,508	74,870	67,815	119,443	103,861	182,93
Disaster Assistance Programs Specialist I-II	48,273	75,750	50,687	79,538	53,221	83,515	55,882	87,690	58,676	92,075	5.00%	25.00%	2.00%	2.00%	2.00%	44,292	69,504	70,662	110,883	108,221	169,82
Driver Safety Manager I-III	61,150	90,045	64,208	94,547	67,418	99,274	70,789	104,238	74,329	109,450	5.00%	25.00%	2.00%	2.00%	2.00%	56,108	82,619	89,511	131,807	137,090	201,84
Education And Outreach Specialist	61,123	74,292	64,179	78,006	67,388	81,907	70,757	86,002	74,295	90,302	5.00%	25.00%	2.00%	2.00%	2.00%	56,082	68,165	89,471	108,748	137,028	166,55
Education And Outreach Supervisor	74,083	85,113	77,788	89,369	81,677	93,837	85,761	98,529	90,049	103,456	5.00%	25.00%	2.00%	2.00%	2.00%	67,974	78,094	108,443	124,588	166,084	190,8
Education Programs Assistant	59,928	72,778	62,924	76,416	66,071	80,237	69,374	84,249	72,843	88,462	5.00%	25.00%	2.00%	2.00%	2.00%	54,986	66,776	87,722	106,531	134,350	163,15
Elections Specialist	67,138	81,599	70,495	85,679	74,019	89,963	77,720	94,461	81,606	99,184	5.00%	25.00%	2.00%	2.00%	2.00%	61,601	74,870	98,275	119,443	150,513	182,93
Electrical Construction Inspector	53,149	64,595	55,806	67,825	58,597	71,217	61,526	74,777	64,603	78,516	5.00%	25.00%	2.00%	2.00%	2.00%	48,766	59,269	77,799	94,554	119,152	144,8
Electrical Construction Supervisor I-II	68,902	114,688	72,347	120,423	75,964	126,444	79,762	132,766	83,751	139,404	5.00%	25.00%	2.00%	2.00%	2.00%	63,220	105,230	100,858	167,880	154,468	257,11
Electrical Engineer	59,442	68,805	62,414	72,245	65,535	75,857	68,811	79,650	72,252	83,632	5.00%	25.00%	2.00%	2.00%	2.00%	54,540	63,131	87,010	100,716	133,260	154,28
Electrical Engineering Technician I-III	45,314	72,666	47,580	76,300	49,959	80,115	52,457	84,120	55,080	88,327	5.00%	25.00%	2.00%	2.00%	2.00%	41,577	66,674	66,330	106,368	101,587	162,90

150

Chart III - U.S. States & Cities - Job Titles - Salaries - Pension Estimates

California	2010 (Min)	2010 (Max)	2011 (Min)	2011 (Max)	2012 (Min)	2012 (Max)	2013 (Min)	2013 (Max)	2014 (Min)	2014 (Max)	5-Year Average % Raise	5-Year Cumulative Raise Estimate **	20-Year Pension %	25-Year Pension %	30-Year Pension %	20-Year Annual Pension Benefit Estimate (Min.) ***	20-Year Annual Pension Benefit Estimate (Max.)	25-Year Annual Pension Benefit Estimate (Min.)	25-Year Annual Pension Benefit Estimate (Max.)	30-Year Annual Pension Benefit Estimate (Min.)	30-Year Annual Pension Benefit Estimate (Max.)
Electrical Estimator I-III	56,997	96,240	59,847	101,052	62,839	106,105	65,981	111,410	69,280	116,981	5.00%	25.00%	2.00%	2.00%	2.00%	52,297	88,304	83,431	140,876	127,778	215,757
Electrical Inspector I-II	51,926	76,028	54,523	79,830	57,249	83,821	60,111	88,012	63,117	92,413	5.00%	25.00%	2.00%	2.00%	2.00%	47,644	69,759	76,009	111,289	116,411	170,444
Electrician I-III	53,177	70,388	55,835	73,908	58,627	77,603	61,559	81,483	64,637	85,557	5.00%	25.00%	2.00%	2.00%	2.00%	48,791	64,584	77,840	103,034	119,214	157,800
Employment Development Planner III	73,750	89,614	77,437	94,095	81,309	98,800	85,375	103,739	89,644	108,926	5.00%	25.00%	2.00%	2.00%	2.00%	67,668	82,224	107,955	131,176	165,336	200,901
Employment Development Specialist I-III	46,328	81,599	48,645	85,679	51,077	89,963	53,631	94,461	56,312	99,184	5.00%	25.00%	2.00%	2.00%	2.00%	42,508	74,870	67,815	119,443	103,861	182,932
Employment Program Manager I-III	61,150	89,697	64,208	94,182	67,418	98,891	70,789	103,836	74,329	109,028	5.00%	25.00%	2.00%	2.00%	2.00%	56,108	82,301	89,511	131,298	137,090	201,088
Employment Program Supervisor I-II	50,843	67,763	53,385	71,151	56,054	74,708	58,857	78,444	61,800	82,366	5.00%	25.00%	2.00%	2.00%	2.00%	46,650	62,175	74,423	99,190	113,982	151,914
Energy Resources Specialist I-III	61,123	90,045	64,179	94,547	67,388	99,274	70,757	104,238	74,295	109,450	5.00%	25.00%	2.00%	2.00%	2.00%	56,082	82,619	89,471	131,807	137,028	201,867
Environmental Planner	43,147	47,578	45,304	49,957	47,570	52,455	49,948	55,078	52,445	57,832	5.00%	25.00%	2.00%	2.00%	2.00%	39,589	43,655	63,158	69,645	96,729	106,664
Epidemiologic Interviewer I-II	40,674	53,760	42,708	56,448	44,843	59,271	47,086	62,234	49,440	65,346	5.00%	25.00%	2.00%	2.00%	2.00%	37,320	49,327	59,539	78,694	91,186	120,522
Executive Secretary I-II	41,952	55,510	44,050	58,286	46,252	61,200	48,565	64,260	50,993	67,473	5.00%	25.00%	2.00%	2.00%	2.00%	38,493	50,933	61,409	81,256	94,051	124,446
Financial Aid Analyst	42,369	51,510	44,488	54,085	46,712	56,789	49,048	59,629	51,500	62,610	5.00%	25.00%	2.00%	2.00%	2.00%	38,875	47,262	62,019	75,399	94,985	115,477
Financial Aid Manager I-II	67,193	89,031	70,553	93,482	74,080	98,156	77,785	103,064	81,674	108,217	5.00%	25.00%	2.00%	2.00%	2.00%	61,652	81,689	98,357	130,322	150,637	199,593
Financial Institutions Examiner	43,147	55,733	45,304	58,519	47,570	61,445	49,948	64,518	52,445	67,743	5.00%	25.00%	2.00%	2.00%	2.00%	39,589	51,137	63,158	81,581	96,729	124,944
Financial Institutions Manager	94,643	109,562	99,375	115,040	104,344	120,792	109,561	126,832	115,039	133,174	5.00%	25.00%	2.00%	2.00%	2.00%	86,838	100,527	138,537	160,376	212,175	245,622
Fire Apparatus Engineer	46,189	53,468	48,499	56,142	50,924	58,949	53,470	61,896	56,143	64,991	5.00%	25.00%	2.00%	2.00%	2.00%	42,380	49,059	67,611	78,267	103,549	119,868
Fire Captain	50,676	61,567	53,210	64,645	55,871	67,878	58,664	71,272	61,597	74,835	5.00%	25.00%	2.00%	2.00%	2.00%	46,497	56,490	74,179	90,121	113,609	138,024
Fire Chief	59,108	71,222	62,064	74,783	65,167	78,522	68,425	82,448	71,847	86,570	5.00%	25.00%	2.00%	2.00%	2.00%	54,234	65,348	86,522	104,254	132,512	159,669
Fire Prevention Officer I-II	66,721	89,100	70,057	93,555	73,560	98,233	77,238	103,144	81,100	108,302	5.00%	25.00%	2.00%	2.00%	2.00%	61,219	81,752	97,665	130,424	149,578	199,749
Fire Prevention Specialist I-II	39,924	55,497	41,920	58,271	44,016	61,185	46,217	64,244	48,528	67,456	5.00%	25.00%	2.00%	2.00%	2.00%	36,632	50,920	58,441	81,235	89,504	124,415
Fire Service Training Specialist I-III	60,345	92,059	63,362	96,662	66,530	101,495	69,857	106,570	73,349	111,898	5.00%	25.00%	2.00%	2.00%	2.00%	55,368	84,467	88,332	134,755	135,284	206,383
Fire Service Training Supervisor	81,363	98,352	85,431	103,269	89,702	108,433	94,187	113,855	98,897	119,547	5.00%	25.00%	2.00%	2.00%	2.00%	74,653	90,241	119,098	143,967	182,403	220,490
Firefighter/Security Officer	49,162	59,067	51,620	62,020	54,201	65,121	56,911	68,377	59,757	71,796	5.00%	25.00%	2.00%	2.00%	2.00%	45,108	54,196	71,963	86,461	110,214	132,419
Fiscal Officer I	70,555	85,113	74,083	89,369	77,787	93,837	81,676	98,529	85,760	103,456	5.00%	25.00%	2.00%	2.00%	2.00%	64,737	78,094	103,278	124,588	158,174	190,811
Forester I-III	66,721	102,561	70,057	107,689	73,560	113,073	77,238	118,727	81,100	124,663	5.00%	25.00%	2.00%	2.00%	2.00%	61,219	94,103	97,665	150,128	149,578	229,926
Forestry Equipment Manager I-II	65,471	84,516	68,744	88,742	72,181	93,179	75,790	97,838	79,580	102,730	5.00%	25.00%	2.00%	2.00%	2.00%	60,072	77,546	95,835	123,714	146,775	189,472
Forestry Logistics Officer I-II	42,564	56,177	44,692	58,986	46,926	61,935	49,273	65,032	51,736	68,284	5.00%	25.00%	2.00%	2.00%	2.00%	39,054	51,545	62,304	82,232	95,421	125,941
Grain And Commodity Inspector	39,869	47,453	41,862	49,826	43,955	52,317	46,153	54,933	48,461	57,680	5.00%	25.00%	2.00%	2.00%	2.00%	36,581	43,540	58,359	69,462	89,379	106,383
Grain And Commodity Supervisor I-II	49,732	62,595	52,218	65,725	54,829	69,011	57,571	72,462	60,449	76,085	5.00%	25.00%	2.00%	2.00%	2.00%	45,630	57,433	72,797	91,626	111,491	140,329
Graphic Designer I-III	44,828	73,750	47,069	77,437	49,423	81,309	51,894	85,375	54,489	89,644	5.00%	25.00%	2.00%	2.00%	2.00%	41,131	67,668	65,619	107,955	100,497	165,336
Health Analyst	39,132	47,592	41,089	49,972	43,143	52,470	45,301	55,094	47,566	57,849	5.00%	25.00%	2.00%	2.00%	2.00%	35,905	43,668	57,282	69,665	87,729	106,695
Health And Safety Officer	64,207	77,459	67,417	81,332	70,788	85,399	74,327	89,668	78,043	94,152	5.00%	25.00%	2.00%	2.00%	2.00%	58,912	71,071	93,985	113,384	143,941	173,652
Health And Safety Program Specialist I-III	67,138	97,824	70,495	102,715	74,019	107,851	77,720	113,243	81,606	118,906	5.00%	25.00%	2.00%	2.00%	2.00%	61,601	89,757	98,275	143,194	150,513	219,307

151

Chart III - U.S. States & Cities - Job Titles - Salaries - Pension Estimates

California	2010 (Min)	2010 (Max)	2011 (Min)	2011 (Max)	2012 (Min)	2012 (Max)	2013 (Min)	2013 (Max)	2014 (Min)	2014 (Max)	5-Year Average % Raise	5-Year Cumulative Raise Estimate **	20-Year Pension %	25-Year Pension %	30-Year Pension %	20-Year Annual Pension Benefit Estimate (Min.) ***	20-Year Annual Pension Benefit Estimate (Max.)	25-Year Annual Pension Benefit Estimate (Min.)	25-Year Annual Pension Benefit Estimate (Max.)	30-Year Annual Pension Benefit Estimate (Min.)	30-Year Annual Pension Benefit Estimate (Max.)
Health Careers Education Administrator I	88,364	107,437	92,782	112,809	97,421	118,449	102,292	124,372	107,407	130,590	5.00%	25.00%	2.00%	2.00%	2.00%	81,077	98,577	129,346	157,265	198,099	240,858
Health Education Consultant I-III	46,231	85,752	48,542	90,040	50,970	94,542	53,518	99,269	56,194	104,232	5.00%	25.00%	2.00%	2.00%	2.00%	42,418	78,681	67,672	125,523	103,643	192,244
Health Facilities Evaluator I-II	53,468	81,363	56,142	85,431	58,949	89,702	61,896	94,187	64,991	98,897	5.00%	25.00%	2.00%	2.00%	2.00%	49,059	74,653	78,267	119,098	119,868	182,403
Health Facilities Evaluator Manager I-II	70,555	93,448	74,083	98,121	77,787	103,027	81,676	108,178	85,760	113,587	5.00%	25.00%	2.00%	2.00%	2.00%	64,737	85,742	103,278	136,789	158,174	209,497
Hospital Administrative Resident I-II	64,207	85,113	67,417	89,369	70,788	93,837	74,327	98,529	78,043	103,456	5.00%	25.00%	2.00%	2.00%	2.00%	58,912	78,094	93,985	124,588	143,941	190,811
Hospital Administrator	108,562	119,689	113,990	125,674	119,690	131,957	125,674	138,555	131,958	145,483	5.00%	25.00%	2.00%	2.00%	2.00%	99,609	109,819	158,912	175,200	243,380	268,325
Hospital General Services Administrator I-II	53,413	77,459	56,083	81,332	58,888	85,399	61,832	89,668	64,924	94,152	5.00%	25.00%	2.00%	2.00%	2.00%	49,008	71,071	78,185	113,384	119,744	173,652
Housing And Community Development Representative I-II	43,147	78,015	45,304	81,915	47,570	86,011	49,948	90,312	52,445	94,827	5.00%	25.00%	2.00%	2.00%	2.00%	39,589	71,581	63,158	114,197	96,729	174,897
Housing And Community Development Specialist I-II	67,138	89,614	70,495	94,095	74,019	98,800	77,720	103,739	81,606	108,926	5.00%	25.00%	2.00%	2.00%	2.00%	61,601	82,224	98,275	131,176	150,513	200,901
Housing And Comunity Development Manager I	70,555	85,113	74,083	89,369	77,787	93,837	81,676	98,529	85,760	103,456	5.00%	25.00%	2.00%	2.00%	2.00%	64,737	78,094	103,278	124,588	158,174	190,811
Information Officer I-III	61,123	108,882	64,179	114,326	67,388	120,042	70,757	126,044	74,295	132,346	5.00%	25.00%	2.00%	2.00%	2.00%	56,082	99,903	89,471	159,380	137,028	244,096
Information Systems Manager	98,880	114,452	103,824	120,175	109,015	126,183	114,466	132,493	120,189	139,117	5.00%	25.00%	2.00%	2.00%	2.00%	90,726	105,014	144,739	167,534	221,674	256,585
Information Systems Supervisor I-IV	51,593	103,561	54,173	108,739	56,881	114,176	59,725	119,885	62,712	125,879	5.00%	25.00%	2.00%	2.00%	2.00%	47,338	95,021	75,521	151,592	115,664	232,169
Information Systems Technician Specialist I-II	48,551	74,458	50,978	78,181	53,527	82,090	56,204	86,195	59,014	90,505	5.00%	25.00%	2.00%	2.00%	2.00%	44,547	68,318	71,068	108,992	108,844	166,925
Information Systems Technician Supervisor I-II	51,551	78,459	54,129	82,382	56,835	86,501	59,677	90,826	62,661	95,368	5.00%	25.00%	2.00%	2.00%	2.00%	47,300	71,989	75,460	114,848	115,570	175,894
Information Technology Specialist I-III	43,175	108,409	45,334	113,830	47,600	119,521	49,980	125,497	52,479	131,772	5.00%	25.00%	2.00%	2.00%	2.00%	39,614	99,469	63,199	158,689	96,791	243,037
Inheritance And Gift Tax Examiner III	64,165	81,918	67,373	86,014	70,742	90,315	74,279	94,831	77,993	99,572	5.00%	25.00%	2.00%	2.00%	2.00%	58,873	75,163	93,924	119,911	143,848	183,648
Insurance Claims Specialist	81,001	98,449	85,051	103,372	89,304	108,540	93,769	113,967	98,458	119,665	5.00%	25.00%	2.00%	2.00%	2.00%	74,322	90,330	118,569	144,109	181,593	220,708
Insurance Examiner	43,147	49,954	45,304	52,452	47,570	55,074	49,948	57,828	52,445	60,719	5.00%	25.00%	2.00%	2.00%	2.00%	39,589	45,834	63,158	73,122	96,729	111,989
Insurance Investigator	41,244	46,925	43,306	49,272	45,471	51,735	47,745	54,322	50,132	57,038	5.00%	25.00%	2.00%	2.00%	2.00%	37,843	43,056	60,372	68,689	92,463	105,200
Insurance Rate Analyst	43,147	47,578	45,304	49,957	47,570	52,455	49,948	55,078	52,445	57,832	5.00%	25.00%	2.00%	2.00%	2.00%	39,589	43,655	63,158	69,645	96,729	106,664
Labor Relations Analyst	61,150	74,320	64,208	78,036	67,418	81,937	70,789	86,034	74,329	90,336	5.00%	25.00%	2.00%	2.00%	2.00%	56,108	68,191	89,511	108,788	137,090	166,613
Labor Relations Counsel I-IV	78,404	145,638	82,324	152,920	86,440	160,566	90,762	168,595	95,300	177,024	5.00%	25.00%	2.00%	2.00%	2.00%	71,938	133,628	114,767	213,184	175,769	326,500
Labor Relations Manager I-II	85,752	103,825	90,040	109,016	94,542	114,467	99,269	120,190	104,232	126,200	5.00%	25.00%	2.00%	2.00%	2.00%	78,681	95,263	125,523	151,978	192,244	232,760
Labor Relations Specialist	70,555	85,113	74,083	89,369	77,787	93,837	81,676	98,529	85,760	103,456	5.00%	25.00%	2.00%	2.00%	2.00%	64,737	78,094	103,278	124,588	158,174	190,811
Laborer	37,326	40,688	39,193	42,723	41,152	44,859	43,210	47,102	45,371	49,457	5.00%	25.00%	2.00%	2.00%	2.00%	34,248	37,333	54,638	59,559	83,680	91,217
Land And Water Use Program Manager I	83,946	101,338	88,144	106,405	92,551	111,726	97,178	117,312	102,037	123,178	5.00%	25.00%	2.00%	2.00%	2.00%	77,024	92,982	122,880	148,338	188,195	227,186
Land And Water Use Scientist	44,356	51,023	46,573	53,575	48,902	56,253	51,347	59,066	53,914	62,019	5.00%	25.00%	2.00%	2.00%	2.00%	40,698	46,816	64,927	74,688	99,439	114,387
Land Surveyor Supervisor	83,932	102,033	88,129	107,135	92,536	112,491	97,162	118,116	102,020	124,022	5.00%	25.00%	2.00%	2.00%	2.00%	77,011	93,619	122,860	149,355	188,164	228,743

152

Chart III - U.S. States & Cities - Job Titles - Salaries - Pension Estimates

California	2010 (Min)	2010 (Max)	2011 (Min)	2011 (Max)	2012 (Min)	2012 (Max)	2013 (Min)	2013 (Max)	2014 (Min)	2014 (Max)	5-Year Average % Raise	5-Year Cumulative Raise Estimate **	20-Year Pension %	25-Year Pension %	30-Year Pension %	20-Year Annual Pension Benefit Estimate (Min.) ***	20-Year Annual Pension Benefit Estimate (Max.)	25-Year Annual Pension Benefit Estimate (Min.)	25-Year Annual Pension Benefit Estimate (Max.)	30-Year Annual Pension Benefit Estimate (Min.)	30-Year Annual Pension Benefit Estimate (Max.)
Landscape Architect	59,442	68,805	62,414	72,245	65,535	75,857	68,811	79,650	72,252	83,632	5.00%	25.00%	2.00%	2.00%	2.00%	54,540	63,131	87,010	100,716	133,260	154,250
Landscape Technician	45,314	55,052	47,580	57,805	49,959	60,695	52,457	63,730	55,080	66,916	5.00%	25.00%	2.00%	2.00%	2.00%	41,577	50,512	66,330	80,585	101,587	123,418
Legal Analyst	53,357	64,873	56,025	68,117	58,826	71,523	61,768	75,099	64,856	78,854	5.00%	25.00%	2.00%	2.00%	2.00%	48,957	59,524	78,104	94,961	119,619	145,436
Legal Counsel	64,929	64,929	68,175	68,175	71,584	71,584	75,163	75,163	78,921	78,921	5.00%	25.00%	2.00%	2.00%	2.00%	59,575	59,575	95,042	95,042	145,561	145,561
Librarian	58,275	70,805	61,189	74,345	64,248	78,062	67,460	81,966	70,833	86,064	5.00%	25.00%	2.00%	2.00%	2.00%	53,469	64,966	85,302	103,644	130,644	158,734
Library Technical Assistant I-II	38,493	51,621	40,418	54,202	42,439	56,912	44,561	59,758	46,789	62,745	5.00%	25.00%	2.00%	2.00%	2.00%	35,319	47,364	56,346	75,562	86,296	115,726
Licensed Vocational Nurse	36,285	46,328	38,099	48,645	40,004	51,077	42,004	53,631	44,104	56,312	5.00%	25.00%	2.00%	2.00%	2.00%	33,292	42,508	53,113	67,815	81,345	103,861
Licensing Program Analyst	38,035	46,828	39,937	49,170	41,934	51,628	44,030	54,210	46,232	56,920	5.00%	25.00%	2.00%	2.00%	2.00%	34,898	42,967	55,675	68,547	85,269	104,982
Licensing Program Manager I-III	70,555	103,825	74,083	109,016	77,787	114,467	81,676	120,190	85,760	126,200	5.00%	25.00%	2.00%	2.00%	2.00%	64,737	95,263	103,278	151,978	158,174	232,760
Lifeguard Supervisor IV	63,762	101,491	66,950	106,566	70,298	111,894	73,812	117,489	77,503	123,363	5.00%	25.00%	2.00%	2.00%	2.00%	58,504	93,122	93,334	148,562	142,945	227,528
Loan Officer	61,123	74,292	64,179	78,006	67,388	81,907	70,757	86,002	74,295	90,302	5.00%	25.00%	2.00%	2.00%	2.00%	56,082	68,165	89,471	108,748	137,028	166,551
Lottery Agent	64,971	78,237	68,219	82,149	71,630	86,256	75,212	90,569	78,972	95,097	5.00%	25.00%	2.00%	2.00%	2.00%	59,613	71,785	95,103	114,523	145,654	175,396
Marine Safety Inspector	57,164	68,916	60,022	72,362	63,023	75,980	66,174	79,779	69,483	83,768	5.00%	25.00%	2.00%	2.00%	2.00%	52,450	63,233	83,675	100,878	128,152	154,499
Marine Safety Operations Supervisor	79,807	96,185	83,797	100,994	87,987	106,044	92,386	111,346	97,006	116,913	5.00%	25.00%	2.00%	2.00%	2.00%	73,225	88,253	116,820	140,794	178,915	215,632
Marine Safety Specialist I-II	65,804	83,280	69,094	87,444	72,549	91,816	76,176	96,406	79,985	101,227	5.00%	25.00%	2.00%	2.00%	2.00%	60,378	76,412	96,323	121,904	147,523	186,700
Marine Safety Supervisor	72,541	87,447	76,168	91,819	79,977	96,410	83,976	101,231	88,175	106,292	5.00%	25.00%	2.00%	2.00%	2.00%	66,559	80,236	106,185	128,004	162,627	196,043
Mason I-II	50,843	58,358	53,385	61,276	56,054	64,340	58,857	67,557	61,800	70,935	5.00%	25.00%	2.00%	2.00%	2.00%	46,650	53,546	74,423	85,424	113,982	130,830
Materials And Stores Specialist	39,966	47,509	41,964	49,884	44,062	52,379	46,265	54,998	48,579	57,747	5.00%	25.00%	2.00%	2.00%	2.00%	36,670	43,591	58,502	69,543	89,597	106,508
Materials And Stores Supervisor	44,258	53,177	46,471	55,835	48,795	58,627	51,235	61,559	53,796	64,637	5.00%	25.00%	2.00%	2.00%	2.00%	40,609	48,791	64,785	77,840	99,221	119,214
Mechanical Construction Inspector	53,149	64,595	55,806	67,825	58,597	71,217	61,526	74,777	64,603	78,516	5.00%	25.00%	2.00%	2.00%	2.00%	48,766	59,269	77,799	94,554	119,152	144,813
Mechanical Construction Supervisor I-II	68,902	114,688	72,347	120,423	75,964	126,444	79,762	132,766	83,751	139,404	5.00%	25.00%	2.00%	2.00%	2.00%	63,220	105,230	100,858	167,880	154,468	257,114
Mechanical Engineer	59,442	68,805	62,414	72,245	65,535	75,857	68,811	79,650	72,252	83,632	5.00%	25.00%	2.00%	2.00%	2.00%	54,540	63,131	87,010	100,716	133,260	154,250
Mechanical Engineering Technician I-III	45,314	72,666	47,580	76,300	49,959	80,115	52,457	84,120	55,080	88,327	5.00%	25.00%	2.00%	2.00%	2.00%	41,577	66,674	66,330	106,368	101,587	162,907
Mechanical Estimator I-III	68,902	96,240	72,347	101,052	75,964	106,105	79,762	111,410	83,751	116,981	5.00%	25.00%	2.00%	2.00%	2.00%	63,220	88,304	100,858	140,876	154,468	215,757
Mechanical Inspector II	51,926	76,028	54,523	79,830	57,249	83,821	60,111	88,012	63,117	92,413	5.00%	25.00%	2.00%	2.00%	2.00%	47,644	69,759	76,009	111,289	116,411	170,444
Mental Health Nurse I	43,730	64,679	45,917	67,913	48,213	71,308	50,623	74,874	53,155	78,618	5.00%	25.00%	2.00%	2.00%	2.00%	40,124	59,345	64,012	94,676	98,037	145,000
Mortgage Insurance Representative I-II	42,369	74,292	44,488	78,006	46,712	81,907	49,048	86,002	51,500	90,302	5.00%	25.00%	2.00%	2.00%	2.00%	38,875	68,165	62,019	108,748	94,985	166,551
Mortgage Insurance Specialist	67,138	81,599	70,495	85,679	74,019	89,963	77,720	94,461	81,606	99,184	5.00%	25.00%	2.00%	2.00%	2.00%	61,601	74,870	98,275	119,443	150,513	182,932
Mortgage Insurance Supervisor	67,193	81,057	70,553	85,110	74,080	89,365	77,785	93,833	81,674	98,525	5.00%	25.00%	2.00%	2.00%	2.00%	61,652	74,373	98,357	118,650	150,637	181,718
Mortgage Loan Accountant	39,869	48,454	41,862	50,876	43,955	53,420	46,153	56,091	48,461	58,896	5.00%	25.00%	2.00%	2.00%	2.00%	36,581	44,458	58,359	70,926	89,379	108,626
Mortgage Loan Accounting Administrator	77,459	93,448	81,332	98,121	85,399	103,027	89,668	108,178	94,152	113,587	5.00%	25.00%	2.00%	2.00%	2.00%	71,071	85,742	113,384	136,789	173,652	209,497
Mortgage Loan Accounting Officer	53,357	64,873	56,025	68,117	58,826	71,523	61,768	75,099	64,856	78,854	5.00%	25.00%	2.00%	2.00%	2.00%	48,957	59,524	78,104	94,961	119,619	145,436
Mortgage Loan Accounting Supervisor	64,207	77,459	67,417	81,332	70,788	85,399	74,327	89,668	78,043	94,152	5.00%	25.00%	2.00%	2.00%	2.00%	58,912	71,071	93,985	113,384	143,941	173,652

Chart III - U.S. States & Cities - Job Titles - Salaries - Pension Estimates

California	2010 (Min)	2010 (Max)	2011 (Min)	2011 (Max)	2012 (Min)	2012 (Max)	2013 (Min)	2013 (Max)	2014 (Min)	2014 (Max)	5-Year Average % Raise	5-Year Cumulative Raise Estimate **	20-Year Pension %	25-Year Pension %	30-Year Pension %	20-Year Annual Pension Benefit Estimate (Min.) ***	20-Year Annual Pension Benefit Estimate (Max.)	25-Year Annual Pension Benefit Estimate (Min.)	25-Year Annual Pension Benefit Estimate (Max.)	30-Year Annual Pension Benefit Estimate (Min.)	30-Year Annual Pension Benefit Estimate (Max.)
Motor Vehicle Program Supervisor I-II	38,132	49,870	40,039	52,364	42,041	54,982	44,143	57,731	46,350	60,618	5.00%	25.00%	2.00%	2.00%	2.00%	34,988	45,758	55,818	73,000	85,487	111,80
Museum Curator I-III	48,579	81,057	51,008	85,110	53,558	89,365	56,236	93,833	59,048	98,525	5.00%	25.00%	2.00%	2.00%	2.00%	44,573	74,373	71,109	118,650	108,906	181,7
Nursing Coordinator	73,667	95,560	77,350	100,338	81,217	105,354	85,278	110,622	89,542	116,153	5.00%	25.00%	2.00%	2.00%	2.00%	67,592	87,679	107,833	139,879	165,150	214,23
Nursing Treatment Specialist	58,956	76,362	61,903	80,180	64,998	84,189	68,248	88,398	71,661	92,818	5.00%	25.00%	2.00%	2.00%	2.00%	54,094	70,064	86,299	111,777	132,170	171,19
Nutrition Education Administrator	88,364	107,437	92,782	112,809	97,421	118,449	102,292	124,372	107,407	130,590	5.00%	25.00%	2.00%	2.00%	2.00%	81,077	98,577	129,346	157,265	198,099	240,85
Nutrition Education Assistant	59,928	72,778	62,924	76,416	66,071	80,237	69,374	84,249	72,843	88,462	5.00%	25.00%	2.00%	2.00%	2.00%	54,986	66,776	87,722	106,531	134,350	163,18
Occupational Therapist	45,022	61,817	47,273	64,908	49,637	68,153	52,119	71,561	54,725	75,139	5.00%	25.00%	2.00%	2.00%	2.00%	41,310	56,719	65,903	90,487	100,933	138,58
Office Services Manager I-II	55,219	77,112	57,980	80,967	60,879	85,016	63,923	89,266	67,119	93,730	5.00%	25.00%	2.00%	2.00%	2.00%	50,665	70,753	80,829	112,875	123,792	172,87
Office Services Supervisor I-III	36,646	56,747	38,478	59,584	40,402	62,563	42,422	65,691	44,543	68,976	5.00%	25.00%	2.00%	2.00%	2.00%	33,624	52,067	53,642	83,065	82,154	127,2
Oil Spill Prevention Supervisor I-II	70,319	94,282	73,835	98,996	77,526	103,945	81,403	109,143	85,473	114,600	5.00%	25.00%	2.00%	2.00%	2.00%	64,520	86,507	102,932	138,009	157,644	211,36
Operations Research Specialist II-III	65,610	91,823	68,890	96,414	72,335	101,235	75,951	106,296	79,749	111,611	5.00%	25.00%	2.00%	2.00%	2.00%	60,199	84,251	96,039	134,409	147,087	205,88
Painter I-III	50,843	67,193	53,385	70,553	56,054	74,080	58,857	77,785	61,800	81,674	5.00%	25.00%	2.00%	2.00%	2.00%	46,650	61,652	74,423	98,357	113,982	150,6
Park Maintenance Chief I-III	57,038	83,168	59,890	87,327	62,885	91,693	66,029	96,278	69,331	101,092	5.00%	25.00%	2.00%	2.00%	2.00%	52,335	76,310	83,492	121,741	127,872	186,48
Parole Agent I-III Adult Parole	69,916	127,246	73,412	133,608	77,082	140,289	80,936	147,303	84,983	154,668	5.00%	25.00%	2.00%	2.00%	2.00%	64,150	116,753	102,342	186,262	156,741	285,26
Parole Agent I-III Youth Authority	69,916	127,246	73,412	133,608	77,082	140,289	80,936	147,303	84,983	154,668	5.00%	25.00%	2.00%	2.00%	2.00%	64,150	116,753	102,342	186,262	156,741	285,26
Pathologist	124,426	173,644	130,647	182,326	137,180	191,442	144,039	201,014	151,241	211,065	5.00%	25.00%	2.00%	2.00%	2.00%	114,165	159,324	182,134	254,178	278,945	389,28
Payroll Operations Supervisor	50,815	61,762	53,356	64,850	56,024	68,092	58,825	71,497	61,766	75,072	5.00%	25.00%	2.00%	2.00%	2.00%	46,625	56,668	74,383	90,406	113,920	138,44
Payroll Specialist	36,146	43,925	37,953	46,121	39,851	48,427	41,843	50,849	43,935	53,391	5.00%	25.00%	2.00%	2.00%	2.00%	33,165	40,303	52,910	64,297	81,033	98,47
Pension Program Analyst	39,132	47,592	41,089	49,972	43,143	52,470	45,301	55,094	47,566	57,849	5.00%	25.00%	2.00%	2.00%	2.00%	35,905	43,668	57,282	69,665	87,729	106,6
Pension Program Manager I-III	71,041	104,547	74,593	109,775	78,323	115,264	82,239	121,027	86,351	127,078	5.00%	25.00%	2.00%	2.00%	2.00%	65,183	95,926	103,989	153,036	159,264	234,3
Pension Program Supervisor	64,651	78,015	67,884	81,915	71,278	86,011	74,842	90,312	78,584	94,827	5.00%	25.00%	2.00%	2.00%	2.00%	59,320	71,581	94,636	114,197	144,938	174,8
Personnel Program Advisor	85,752	94,573	90,040	99,302	94,542	104,267	99,269	109,480	104,232	114,954	5.00%	25.00%	2.00%	2.00%	2.00%	78,681	86,774	125,523	138,436	192,244	212,0
Personnel Program Analyst	61,150	74,292	64,208	78,006	67,418	81,907	70,789	86,002	74,329	90,302	5.00%	25.00%	2.00%	2.00%	2.00%	56,108	68,165	89,511	108,748	137,090	166,58
Personnel Program Manager I-II	89,822	103,825	94,314	109,016	99,029	114,467	103,981	120,190	109,180	126,200	5.00%	25.00%	2.00%	2.00%	2.00%	82,415	95,263	131,481	151,978	201,369	232,7
Personnel Services Supervisor I	46,523	56,566	48,849	59,394	51,291	62,364	53,856	65,482	56,549	68,757	5.00%	25.00%	2.00%	2.00%	2.00%	42,686	51,901	68,099	82,801	104,297	126,8
Personnel Specialist	36,146	43,925	37,953	46,121	39,851	48,427	41,843	50,849	43,935	53,391	5.00%	25.00%	2.00%	2.00%	2.00%	33,165	40,303	52,910	64,297	81,033	98,47
Personnel Supervisor I-II	50,815	67,957	53,356	71,355	56,024	74,923	58,825	78,669	61,766	82,602	5.00%	25.00%	2.00%	2.00%	2.00%	46,625	62,353	74,383	99,475	113,920	152,3
Pharmacist I-II	75,209	103,214	78,969	108,375	82,917	113,793	87,063	119,483	91,417	125,457	5.00%	25.00%	2.00%	2.00%	2.00%	69,007	94,702	110,090	151,084	168,606	231,3
Plumber I-III	53,177	70,388	55,835	73,908	58,627	77,603	61,559	81,483	64,637	85,557	5.00%	25.00%	2.00%	2.00%	2.00%	48,791	64,584	77,840	103,034	119,214	157,8
Polygraph Examiner	70,513	85,099	74,039	89,354	77,741	93,822	81,628	98,513	85,709	103,439	5.00%	25.00%	2.00%	2.00%	2.00%	64,698	78,082	103,217	124,568	158,080	190,7
Polygraph Examiner Supervisor	77,473	93,670	81,347	98,354	85,414	103,272	89,685	108,435	94,169	113,857	5.00%	25.00%	2.00%	2.00%	2.00%	71,084	85,946	113,404	137,114	173,683	209,9
Principal Architect	136,720	150,764	143,556	158,303	150,734	166,218	158,271	174,529	166,184	183,255	5.00%	25.00%	2.00%	2.00%	2.00%	125,446	138,332	200,130	220,688	306,506	337,9
Principal Buyer	64,207	77,459	67,417	81,332	70,788	85,399	74,327	89,668	78,043	94,152	5.00%	25.00%	2.00%	2.00%	2.00%	58,912	71,071	93,985	113,384	143,941	173,6
Principal Claim Auditor	51,579	62,053	54,158	65,156	56,866	68,414	59,709	71,834	62,695	75,426	5.00%	25.00%	2.00%	2.00%	2.00%	47,326	56,936	75,501	90,833	115,633	139,1
Principal Geologist	105,923	116,828	111,219	122,669	116,780	128,802	122,619	135,242	128,750	142,005	5.00%	25.00%	2.00%	2.00%	2.00%	97,188	107,193	155,049	171,011	237,463	261,9
Principal Hydraulic Engineer	136,720	150,764	143,556	158,303	150,734	166,218	158,271	174,529	166,184	183,255	5.00%	25.00%	2.00%	2.00%	2.00%	125,446	138,332	200,130	220,688	306,506	337,9

Chart III - U.S. States & Cities - Job Titles - Salaries - Pension Estimates

California	2010 (Min)	2010 (Max)	2011 (Min)	2011 (Max)	2012 (Min)	2012 (Max)	2013 (Min)	2013 (Max)	2014 (Min)	2014 (Max)	5-Year Average % Raise	5-Year Cumulative Raise Estimate **	20-Year Pension %	25-Year Pension %	30-Year Pension %	20-Year Annual Pension Benefit Estimate (Min.) ***	20-Year Annual Pension Benefit Estimate (Max.)	25-Year Annual Pension Benefit Estimate (Min.)	25-Year Annual Pension Benefit Estimate (Max.)	30-Year Annual Pension Benefit Estimate (Min.)	30-Year Annual Pension Benefit Estimate (Max.)
Principal Librarian	80,404	97,727	84,424	102,613	88,645	107,744	93,078	113,131	97,732	118,787	5.00%	25.00%	2.00%	2.00%	2.00%	73,773	89,668	117,695	143,051	180,254	219,089
Principal Program Budget Analyst I-III	94,198	114,327	98,908	120,043	103,854	126,046	109,046	132,348	114,499	138,965	5.00%	25.00%	2.00%	2.00%	2.00%	86,430	104,899	137,887	167,351	211,179	256,304
Principal Safety Engineer -Construction-	124,398	137,220	130,618	144,081	137,149	151,285	144,007	158,850	151,207	166,792	5.00%	25.00%	2.00%	2.00%	2.00%	114,140	125,904	182,093	200,862	278,883	307,627
Principal State Metrologist	87,697	87,697	92,082	92,082	96,686	96,686	101,520	101,520	106,596	106,596	5.00%	25.00%	2.00%	2.00%	2.00%	80,465	80,465	128,370	128,370	196,604	196,604
Principal Structural Engineer	136,720	150,764	143,556	158,303	150,734	166,218	158,271	174,529	166,184	183,255	5.00%	25.00%	2.00%	2.00%	2.00%	125,446	138,332	200,130	220,688	306,506	337,992
Principal Water Resource Control Engineer	136,720	150,764	143,556	158,303	150,734	166,218	158,271	174,529	166,184	183,255	5.00%	25.00%	2.00%	2.00%	2.00%	125,446	138,332	200,130	220,688	306,506	337,992
Prison Industries Administrator	98,769	108,882	103,707	114,326	108,892	120,042	114,337	126,044	120,054	132,346	5.00%	25.00%	2.00%	2.00%	2.00%	90,624	99,903	144,577	159,380	221,424	244,096
Prison Industries Engineer	115,786	127,607	121,575	133,988	127,654	140,687	134,036	147,721	140,738	155,107	5.00%	25.00%	2.00%	2.00%	2.00%	106,237	117,084	169,486	186,790	259,574	286,077
Prison Industries Superintendent I-II	59,845	79,154	62,837	83,111	65,979	87,267	69,278	91,630	72,741	96,212	5.00%	25.00%	2.00%	2.00%	2.00%	54,909	72,626	87,600	115,865	134,163	177,451
Procurement And Services Officer I-II	58,567	77,459	61,495	81,332	64,570	85,399	67,798	89,668	71,188	94,152	5.00%	25.00%	2.00%	2.00%	2.00%	53,737	71,071	85,729	113,384	131,298	173,652
Programmer I-II	45,314	71,500	47,580	75,075	49,959	78,828	52,457	82,770	55,080	86,908	5.00%	25.00%	2.00%	2.00%	2.00%	41,577	65,603	66,330	104,660	101,587	160,291
Project Director I-III	87,114	136,720	91,469	143,556	96,043	150,734	100,845	158,271	105,887	166,184	5.00%	25.00%	2.00%	2.00%	2.00%	79,930	125,446	127,516	200,130	195,296	306,506
Property Controller I-II	40,313	61,067	42,329	64,120	44,445	67,326	46,667	70,693	49,001	74,227	5.00%	25.00%	2.00%	2.00%	2.00%	36,989	56,031	59,010	89,389	90,376	136,903
Psychologist (Clinical)	66,860	92,170	70,203	96,779	73,713	101,618	77,399	106,698	81,268	112,033	5.00%	25.00%	2.00%	2.00%	2.00%	61,346	84,569	97,869	134,918	149,890	206,632
Psychologist (Educational)	66,860	92,170	70,203	96,779	73,713	101,618	77,399	106,698	81,268	112,033	5.00%	25.00%	2.00%	2.00%	2.00%	61,346	84,569	97,869	134,918	149,890	206,632
Public Health Medical Officer II-III	121,009	170,588	127,059	179,117	133,412	188,073	140,083	197,476	147,087	207,350	5.00%	25.00%	2.00%	2.00%	2.00%	111,030	156,520	177,132	249,705	271,284	382,432
Public Health Microbiologist I-II	53,524	81,112	56,200	85,168	59,010	89,426	61,961	93,898	65,059	98,593	5.00%	25.00%	2.00%	2.00%	2.00%	49,110	74,424	78,348	118,732	119,993	181,842
Public Land Management Specialist I-IV	45,314	91,837	47,580	96,429	49,959	101,250	52,457	106,312	55,080	111,628	5.00%	25.00%	2.00%	2.00%	2.00%	41,577	84,263	66,330	134,430	101,587	205,884
Public Land Manager I-II	77,459	103,825	81,332	109,016	85,399	114,467	89,668	120,190	94,152	126,200	5.00%	25.00%	2.00%	2.00%	2.00%	71,071	95,263	113,384	151,978	173,652	232,760
Public Utilities Regulatory Analyst I-V	40,827	103,144	42,868	108,302	45,012	113,717	47,262	119,403	49,626	125,373	5.00%	25.00%	2.00%	2.00%	2.00%	37,460	94,639	59,762	150,982	91,528	231,234
Public Utility Financial Examiner II-IV	53,149	98,588	55,806	103,517	58,597	108,693	61,526	114,128	64,603	119,834	5.00%	25.00%	2.00%	2.00%	2.00%	48,766	90,458	77,799	144,312	119,152	221,020
Real Estate License Examiner I-II	50,815	74,292	53,356	78,006	56,024	81,907	58,825	86,002	61,766	90,302	5.00%	25.00%	2.00%	2.00%	2.00%	46,625	68,165	74,383	108,748	113,920	166,551
Records Management Analyst I-II	50,815	74,292	53,356	78,006	56,024	81,907	58,825	86,002	61,766	90,302	5.00%	25.00%	2.00%	2.00%	2.00%	46,625	68,165	74,383	108,748	113,920	166,551
Records Manager I-II	67,193	90,045	70,553	94,547	74,080	99,274	77,785	104,238	81,674	109,450	5.00%	25.00%	2.00%	2.00%	2.00%	61,652	82,619	98,357	131,807	150,637	201,867
Recycling Program Manager I-II	81,432	103,728	85,504	108,914	89,779	114,360	94,268	120,078	98,981	126,082	5.00%	25.00%	2.00%	2.00%	2.00%	74,717	95,174	119,199	151,836	182,558	232,542
Research Analyst I-II	43,147	78,015	45,304	81,915	47,570	86,011	49,948	90,312	52,445	94,827	5.00%	25.00%	2.00%	2.00%	2.00%	39,589	71,581	63,158	114,197	96,729	174,897
Research Assistant I-V	38,952	77,792	40,899	81,682	42,944	85,766	45,092	90,054	47,346	94,557	5.00%	25.00%	2.00%	2.00%	2.00%	35,740	71,377	57,017	113,872	87,324	174,399
Research Scientist I-V	67,138	123,787	70,495	129,977	74,019	136,475	77,720	143,299	81,606	150,464	5.00%	25.00%	2.00%	2.00%	2.00%	61,601	113,579	98,275	181,199	150,513	277,512
Research Scientist Supervisor I-II	89,031	127,191	93,482	133,550	98,156	140,228	103,064	147,239	108,217	154,601	5.00%	25.00%	2.00%	2.00%	2.00%	81,689	116,702	130,322	186,180	199,593	285,142
Research Specialist I-V	70,347	137,234	73,864	144,096	77,557	151,301	81,435	158,866	85,507	166,809	5.00%	25.00%	2.00%	2.00%	2.00%	64,545	125,917	102,973	200,882	157,707	307,659
Restoration Architect	87,100	105,812	91,455	111,102	96,027	116,657	100,829	122,490	105,870	128,615	5.00%	25.00%	2.00%	2.00%	2.00%	79,917	97,086	127,496	154,886	195,265	237,214
Restoration Supervisor I-II	59,845	79,154	62,837	83,111	65,979	87,267	69,278	91,630	72,741	96,212	5.00%	25.00%	2.00%	2.00%	2.00%	54,909	72,626	87,600	115,865	134,163	177,451
Restoration Work Specialist	54,510	59,831	57,236	62,822	60,098	65,963	63,102	69,262	66,258	72,725	5.00%	25.00%	2.00%	2.00%	2.00%	50,015	54,897	79,792	87,580	122,204	134,132

Chart III - U.S. States & Cities - Job Titles - Salaries - Pension Estimates

California	2010 (Min)	2010 (Max)	2011 (Min)	2011 (Max)	2012 (Min)	2012 (Max)	2013 (Min)	2013 (Max)	2014 (Min)	2014 (Max)	5-Year Average % Raise	5-Year Cumulative Raise Estimate **	20-Year Pension %	25-Year Pension %	30-Year Pension %	20-Year Annual Pension Benefit Estimate (Min.) ***	20-Year Annual Pension Benefit Estimate (Max.)	25-Year Annual Pension Benefit Estimate (Min.)	25-Year Annual Pension Benefit Estimate (Max.)	30-Year Annual Pension Benefit Estimate (Min.)	30-Year Annual Pension Benefit Estimate (Max.)
Retirement Program Specialist I-II	39,132	74,292	41,089	78,006	43,143	81,907	45,301	86,002	47,566	90,302	5.00%	25.00%	2.00%	2.00%	2.00%	35,905	68,165	57,282	108,748	87,729	166,551
School Facilities Program Administrator I-III	67,193	98,880	70,553	103,824	74,080	109,015	77,785	114,466	81,674	120,189	5.00%	25.00%	2.00%	2.00%	2.00%	61,652	90,726	98,357	144,739	150,637	221,674
School Facilities Program Analyst I-II	39,132	74,292	41,089	78,006	43,143	81,907	45,301	86,002	47,566	90,302	5.00%	25.00%	2.00%	2.00%	2.00%	35,905	68,165	57,282	108,748	87,729	166,551
Social Service Administrator II	75,598	91,892	79,377	96,487	83,346	101,311	87,514	106,377	91,889	111,696	5.00%	25.00%	2.00%	2.00%	2.00%	69,363	84,314	110,659	134,511	169,478	206,009
Social Service Consultant I-III	49,370	74,320	51,839	78,036	54,431	81,937	57,152	86,034	60,010	90,336	5.00%	25.00%	2.00%	2.00%	2.00%	45,299	68,191	72,268	108,788	110,681	166,613
Special Education Administrator I-II	88,364	112,952	92,782	118,599	97,421	124,529	102,292	130,756	107,407	137,294	5.00%	25.00%	2.00%	2.00%	2.00%	81,077	103,637	129,346	165,338	198,099	253,221
Special Investigator I	54,205	62,234	56,915	65,346	59,761	68,613	62,749	72,044	65,886	75,646	5.00%	25.00%	2.00%	2.00%	2.00%	49,735	57,102	79,344	91,097	121,519	139,519
Specification Writer I-II	54,482	76,028	57,207	79,830	60,067	83,821	63,070	88,012	66,224	92,413	5.00%	25.00%	2.00%	2.00%	2.00%	49,990	69,759	79,751	111,289	122,142	170,444
Speech Pathologist I-II	56,677	77,765	59,511	81,653	62,487	85,735	65,611	90,022	68,892	94,523	5.00%	25.00%	2.00%	2.00%	2.00%	52,003	71,352	82,964	113,831	127,062	174,337
Staff Psychiatrist	126,774	165,670	133,113	173,954	139,768	182,651	146,757	191,784	154,094	201,373	5.00%	25.00%	2.00%	2.00%	2.00%	116,319	152,008	185,570	242,506	284,208	371,408
Staff Risk Manager	70,555	85,113	74,083	89,369	77,787	93,837	81,676	98,529	85,760	103,456	5.00%	25.00%	2.00%	2.00%	2.00%	64,737	78,094	103,278	124,588	158,174	190,811
State Facilities Manager I-II	77,459	103,825	81,332	109,016	85,399	114,467	89,668	120,190	94,152	126,200	5.00%	25.00%	2.00%	2.00%	2.00%	71,071	95,263	113,384	151,978	173,652	232,760
State Park Ranger	46,453	55,302	48,776	58,067	51,215	60,971	53,775	64,019	56,464	67,220	5.00%	25.00%	2.00%	2.00%	2.00%	42,622	50,742	67,998	80,951	104,141	123,979
State Park Superintendent I-V	69,888	123,593	73,383	129,772	77,052	136,261	80,904	143,074	84,949	150,228	5.00%	25.00%	2.00%	2.00%	2.00%	64,125	113,401	102,302	180,914	156,679	277,076
Stationary Engineer	68,402	68,402	71,822	71,822	75,413	75,413	79,184	79,184	83,143	83,143	5.00%	25.00%	2.00%	2.00%	2.00%	62,761	62,761	100,126	100,126	153,347	153,347
Surgical Nurse I-II	68,888	94,518	72,332	99,244	75,949	104,206	79,746	109,416	83,734	114,887	5.00%	25.00%	2.00%	2.00%	2.00%	63,207	86,723	100,838	138,354	154,437	211,895
Tax Research Specialist I-III	67,138	98,449	70,495	103,372	74,019	108,540	77,720	113,967	81,606	119,665	5.00%	25.00%	2.00%	2.00%	2.00%	61,601	90,330	98,275	144,109	150,513	220,708
Teacher -Business Education- I-VI	48,707	78,275	51,142	82,189	53,700	86,298	56,385	90,613	59,204	95,144	5.00%	25.00%	2.00%	2.00%	2.00%	44,690	71,820	71,297	114,578	109,194	175,481
Teacher -Emotionally Handicapped- I-VI	48,707	78,275	51,142	82,189	53,700	86,298	56,385	90,613	59,204	95,144	5.00%	25.00%	2.00%	2.00%	2.00%	44,690	71,820	71,297	114,578	109,194	175,481
Teacher -High School Education- I-VI	48,707	78,275	51,142	82,189	53,700	86,298	56,385	90,613	59,204	95,144	5.00%	25.00%	2.00%	2.00%	2.00%	44,690	71,820	71,297	114,578	109,194	175,481
Telecommunications Maintenance Supervisor I-III	68,777	100,561	72,216	105,589	75,826	110,868	79,618	116,411	83,599	122,232	5.00%	25.00%	2.00%	2.00%	2.00%	63,105	92,268	100,675	147,200	154,187	225,442
Telecommunications Systems Analyst I-II	39,132	78,015	41,089	81,915	43,143	86,011	45,301	90,312	47,566	94,827	5.00%	25.00%	2.00%	2.00%	2.00%	35,905	71,581	57,282	114,197	87,729	174,897
Telecommunications Systems Manager I-II	67,138	77,473	70,495	81,347	74,019	85,414	77,720	89,685	81,606	94,169	5.00%	25.00%	2.00%	2.00%	2.00%	61,601	71,084	98,275	113,404	150,513	173,683
Telecommunications Technician	62,609	72,194	65,739	75,804	69,026	79,594	72,478	83,574	76,102	87,752	5.00%	25.00%	2.00%	2.00%	2.00%	57,446	66,241	91,646	105,677	140,360	161,849
Television Assistant	50,815	61,762	53,356	64,850	56,024	68,092	58,825	71,497	61,766	75,072	5.00%	25.00%	2.00%	2.00%	2.00%	46,625	56,668	74,383	90,406	113,920	138,460
Television Specialist	61,123	74,292	64,179	78,006	67,388	81,907	70,757	86,002	74,295	90,302	5.00%	25.00%	2.00%	2.00%	2.00%	56,082	68,165	89,471	108,748	137,028	166,551
Training Officer I-III	61,123	93,448	64,179	98,121	67,388	103,027	70,757	108,178	74,295	113,587	5.00%	25.00%	2.00%	2.00%	2.00%	56,082	85,742	89,471	136,789	137,028	209,497
Transportation Analyst	43,147	47,578	45,304	49,957	47,570	52,455	49,948	55,078	52,445	57,832	5.00%	25.00%	2.00%	2.00%	2.00%	39,589	43,655	63,158	69,645	96,729	106,664
Treasury Program Manager I-III	70,555	109,020	74,083	114,472	77,787	120,195	81,676	126,205	85,760	132,515	5.00%	25.00%	2.00%	2.00%	2.00%	64,737	100,030	103,278	159,583	158,174	244,408
Treatment Team Supervisor	94,546	114,910	99,273	120,656	104,236	126,689	109,448	133,023	114,921	139,674	5.00%	25.00%	2.00%	2.00%	2.00%	86,749	105,434	138,395	168,205	211,957	257,612
Tree Maintenance Supervisor	49,732	59,845	52,218	62,837	54,829	65,979	57,571	69,278	60,449	72,741	5.00%	25.00%	2.00%	2.00%	2.00%	45,630	54,909	72,797	87,600	111,491	134,163
Tree Maintenance Worker	43,341	49,732	45,509	52,218	47,784	54,829	50,173	57,571	52,682	60,449	5.00%	25.00%	2.00%	2.00%	2.00%	39,767	45,630	63,443	72,797	97,165	111,491
Truck Driver	42,383	46,370	44,502	48,688	46,727	51,123	49,064	53,679	51,517	56,363	5.00%	25.00%	2.00%	2.00%	2.00%	38,888	42,546	62,040	67,876	95,016	103,954
Veterinary Medical Officer I-IV	62,553	105,228	65,681	110,490	68,965	116,014	72,413	121,815	76,034	127,905	5.00%	25.00%	2.00%	2.00%	2.00%	57,395	96,550	91,565	154,032	140,235	235,906
Victim Compensation Specialist	39,591	48,106	41,570	50,512	43,649	53,037	45,831	55,689	48,123	58,473	5.00%	25.00%	2.00%	2.00%	2.00%	36,326	44,139	57,953	70,418	88,757	107,847

Chart III - U.S. States & Cities - Job Titles - Salaries - Pension Estimates

California	2010 (Min)	2010 (Max)	2011 (Min)	2011 (Max)	2012 (Min)	2012 (Max)	2013 (Min)	2013 (Max)	2014 (Min)	2014 (Max)	5-Year Average % Raise	5-Year Cumulative Raise Estimate **	20-Year Pension %	25-Year Pension %	30-Year Pension %	20-Year Annual Pension Benefit Estimate (Min.) ***	20-Year Annual Pension Benefit Estimate (Max.)	25-Year Annual Pension Benefit Estimate (Min.)	25-Year Annual Pension Benefit Estimate (Max.)	30-Year Annual Pension Benefit Estimate (Min.)	30-Year Annual Pension Benefit Estimate (Max.)
Victim Compensation Supervisor	53,427	64,207	56,098	67,417	58,903	70,788	61,848	74,327	64,940	78,043	5.00%	25.00%	2.00%	2.00%	2.00%	49,021	58,912	78,206	93,985	119,775	143,941
Vocational Psychologist	66,860	92,170	70,203	96,779	73,713	101,618	77,399	106,698	81,268	112,033	5.00%	25.00%	2.00%	2.00%	2.00%	61,346	84,569	97,869	134,918	149,890	206,632
Vocational Resource Specialist	50,815	61,762	53,356	64,850	56,024	68,092	58,825	71,497	61,766	75,072	5.00%	25.00%	2.00%	2.00%	2.00%	46,625	56,668	74,383	90,406	113,920	138,460
Warehouse Manager I-II	48,579	70,388	51,008	73,908	53,558	77,603	56,236	81,483	59,048	85,557	5.00%	25.00%	2.00%	2.00%	2.00%	44,573	64,584	71,109	103,034	108,906	157,800
Waste Management Engineer	59,442	68,805	62,414	72,245	65,535	75,857	68,811	79,650	72,252	83,632	5.00%	25.00%	2.00%	2.00%	2.00%	54,540	63,131	87,010	100,716	133,260	154,250
Water And Power Dispatcher	75,598	91,225	79,377	95,787	83,346	100,576	87,514	105,605	91,889	110,885	5.00%	25.00%	2.00%	2.00%	2.00%	69,363	83,703	110,659	133,535	169,478	204,514
Water And Sewage Plant Supervisor	68,402	68,402	71,822	71,822	75,413	75,413	79,184	79,184	83,143	83,143	5.00%	25.00%	2.00%	2.00%	2.00%	62,761	62,761	100,126	100,126	153,347	153,347
Water Quality Biologist	39,132	44,356	41,089	46,573	43,143	48,902	45,301	51,347	47,566	53,914	5.00%	25.00%	2.00%	2.00%	2.00%	35,905	40,698	57,282	64,927	87,729	99,439
Water Resources Technician I-II	45,314	66,207	47,580	69,517	49,959	72,993	52,457	76,643	55,080	80,475	5.00%	25.00%	2.00%	2.00%	2.00%	41,577	60,747	66,330	96,913	101,587	148,426
Water Services Supervisor	75,709	92,017	79,494	96,618	83,469	101,449	87,642	106,522	92,024	111,848	5.00%	25.00%	2.00%	2.00%	2.00%	69,465	84,429	110,822	134,694	169,728	206,289
Wildlife Forensic Specialist	39,132	44,356	41,089	46,573	43,143	48,902	45,301	51,347	47,566	53,914	5.00%	25.00%	2.00%	2.00%	2.00%	35,905	40,698	57,282	64,927	87,729	99,439
Wildlife Habitat Supervisor I-II	49,829	72,778	52,320	76,416	54,936	80,237	57,683	84,249	60,567	88,462	5.00%	25.00%	2.00%	2.00%	2.00%	45,720	66,776	72,939	106,531	111,709	163,157
Wildlife Veterinarian	62,553	75,556	65,681	79,334	68,965	83,300	72,413	87,465	76,034	91,839	5.00%	25.00%	2.00%	2.00%	2.00%	57,395	69,325	91,565	110,598	140,235	169,385
Workers' Compensation Claims Adjuster	43,147	47,578	45,304	49,957	47,570	52,455	49,948	55,078	52,445	57,832	5.00%	25.00%	2.00%	2.00%	2.00%	39,589	43,655	63,158	69,645	96,729	106,664
Workers' Compensation Compliance Officer	64,165	78,015	67,373	81,915	70,742	86,011	74,279	90,312	77,993	94,827	5.00%	25.00%	2.00%	2.00%	2.00%	58,873	71,581	93,924	114,197	143,848	174,897
Workers' Compensation Insurance Supervisor II	56,080	81,918	58,884	86,014	61,828	90,315	64,920	94,831	68,166	99,572	5.00%	25.00%	2.00%	2.00%	2.00%	51,455	75,163	82,089	119,911	125,723	183,648
Workers' Compensation Insurance Technician	35,673	43,369	37,457	45,538	39,330	47,815	41,296	50,205	43,361	52,716	5.00%	25.00%	2.00%	2.00%	2.00%	32,732	39,793	52,218	63,484	79,974	97,227
Workers' Compensation Judge	104,103	125,899	109,308	132,194	114,773	138,803	120,512	145,743	126,538	153,031	5.00%	25.00%	2.00%	2.00%	2.00%	95,518	115,516	152,385	184,289	233,383	282,246
Workers' Compensation Manager	85,752	94,573	90,040	99,302	94,542	104,267	99,269	109,480	104,232	114,954	5.00%	25.00%	2.00%	2.00%	2.00%	78,681	86,774	125,523	138,436	192,244	212,019
Workers' Compensation Payroll Auditor	43,147	49,954	45,304	52,452	47,570	55,074	49,948	57,828	52,445	60,719	5.00%	25.00%	2.00%	2.00%	2.00%	39,589	45,834	63,158	73,122	96,729	111,989
Youth Correctional Counselor	42,369	42,369	44,488	44,488	46,712	46,712	49,048	49,048	51,500	51,500	5.00%	25.00%	2.00%	2.00%	2.00%	38,875	38,875	62,019	62,019	94,985	94,985
Youth Correctional Officer	42,369	42,369	44,488	44,488	46,712	46,712	49,048	49,048	51,500	51,500	5.00%	25.00%	2.00%	2.00%	2.00%	38,875	38,875	62,019	62,019	94,985	94,985
Youthful Offender Parole Board Representative	104,936	115,744	110,183	121,531	115,692	127,608	121,477	133,988	127,551	140,688	5.00%	25.00%	2.00%	2.00%	2.00%	96,283	106,199	153,605	169,425	235,252	259,481

http://www.dpa.ca.gov/publications/pay-scales/index.htm
http://www.my.ca.gov/

Chart III - U.S. States & Cities - Job Titles - Salaries - Pension Estimates

Colorado	2010 (Min)	2010 (Max)	2011 (Min)	2011 (Max)	2012 (Min)	2012 (Max)	2013 (Min)	2013 (Max)	2014 (Min)	2014 (Max)	5-Year Average % Raise	5-Year Cumulative Raise Estimate**	20-Year Annual Pension Benefit Estimate (Min.)***	20-Year Annual Pension Benefit Estimate (Max.)	25-Year Annual Pension Benefit Estimate (Min.)	25-Year Annual Pension Benefit Estimate (Max.)	30-Year Annual Pension Benefit Estimate (Min.)	30-Year Annual Pension Benefit Estimate (Max.)
Admin Assistant Int	24,266	34,012	24,812	34,778	25,371	35,560	25,942	36,360	26,525	37,178	2.25%	11.25%	18,110	25,383	25,301	35,463	33,934	47,563
Accountant I-IV	44,244	111,849	45,239	114,365	46,257	116,938	47,298	119,570	48,362	122,260	2.25%	11.25%	33,019	83,472	46,130	116,618	61,871	156,410
Accounting Technician I-IV	29,985	67,212	30,660	68,724	31,350	70,270	32,055	71,851	32,777	73,468	2.25%	11.25%	22,378	50,160	31,264	70,078	41,932	93,989
Actuary I-IV	64,680	119,522	66,135	122,211	67,623	124,961	69,145	127,773	70,701	130,648	2.25%	11.25%	48,270	89,199	67,438	124,619	90,449	167,141
Admin Assistant I-III	26,746	51,366	27,347	52,522	27,963	53,704	28,592	54,912	29,235	56,148	2.25%	11.25%	19,960	38,334	27,886	53,557	37,401	71,831
Admin Law Judge I-III	79,660	119,522	81,452	122,211	83,285	124,961	85,158	127,773	87,075	130,648	2.25%	11.25%	59,449	89,199	83,057	124,619	111,397	167,141
Air Environ Sys Tech I-II	55,878	92,842	57,136	94,931	58,421	97,067	59,736	99,251	61,080	101,484	2.25%	11.25%	41,702	69,287	58,261	96,801	78,141	129,831
Air Traffic Contrl I-III	61,033	114,839	62,407	117,423	63,811	120,065	65,247	122,767	66,715	125,529	2.25%	11.25%	45,549	85,704	63,636	119,737	85,350	160,592
Ang Patrol Officer I-III	32,622	59,184	33,356	60,516	34,106	61,877	34,874	63,269	35,659	64,693	2.25%	11.25%	24,346	44,169	34,013	61,708	45,619	82,763
Animal Care I-III	29,198	59,459	29,855	60,797	30,527	62,165	31,214	63,564	31,916	64,994	2.25%	11.25%	21,791	44,374	30,444	61,995	40,831	83,148
App Programmer I-III	44,558	78,125	45,561	79,883	46,586	81,680	47,634	83,518	48,706	85,397	2.25%	11.25%	33,254	58,304	46,459	81,456	62,311	109,250
Architect I-III	64,680	118,486	66,135	121,152	67,623	123,878	69,145	126,665	70,701	129,515	2.25%	11.25%	48,270	88,425	67,438	123,539	90,449	165,692
Archivist I-II	37,475	60,902	38,318	62,273	39,181	63,674	40,062	65,106	40,964	66,571	2.25%	11.25%	27,968	45,451	39,073	63,499	52,406	85,166
Arts Professional I-IV	36,505	77,744	37,326	79,494	38,166	81,282	39,025	83,111	39,903	84,981	2.25%	11.25%	27,243	58,020	38,061	81,060	51,048	108,719
Arts Technician I-II	25,959	43,299	26,543	44,273	27,140	45,270	27,750	46,288	28,375	47,330	2.25%	11.25%	19,373	32,314	27,066	45,146	36,301	60,550
Budget & Policy Anlst III-V	66,779	119,522	68,281	122,211	69,817	124,961	71,388	127,773	72,995	130,648	2.25%	11.25%	49,836	89,199	69,626	124,619	93,384	167,141
Budget Analyst I-II	47,497	79,502	48,565	81,291	49,658	83,120	50,775	84,990	51,918	86,902	2.25%	11.25%	35,446	59,332	49,522	82,892	66,420	111,176
Chaplain I-II	53,911	81,666	55,124	83,504	56,364	85,383	57,632	87,304	58,929	89,268	2.25%	11.25%	40,233	60,947	56,210	85,149	75,389	114,203
Civil Eng Proj Manager I-II	61,611	97,499	62,997	99,692	64,414	101,935	65,864	104,229	67,345	106,574	2.25%	11.25%	45,980	72,763	64,238	101,656	86,157	136,343
Client Care Aide I-II	22,915	38,341	23,431	39,204	23,958	40,086	24,497	40,988	25,048	41,910	2.25%	11.25%	17,102	28,614	23,893	39,976	32,045	53,616
Clin Behav Spec II-III	49,976	79,686	51,100	81,479	52,250	83,312	53,426	85,186	54,628	87,103	2.25%	11.25%	37,297	59,469	52,107	83,084	69,887	111,433
Clinical Therapist I-V	36,518	87,818	37,339	89,794	38,180	91,815	39,039	93,880	39,917	95,993	2.25%	11.25%	27,253	65,538	38,075	91,563	51,067	122,806
Collections Rep I-III	24,804	61,086	25,362	62,460	25,933	63,866	26,516	65,303	27,113	66,772	2.25%	11.25%	18,511	45,588	25,862	63,691	34,686	85,423
Community Worker I-II	24,699	41,358	25,255	42,288	25,823	43,240	26,404	44,213	26,998	45,208	2.25%	11.25%	18,433	30,865	25,753	43,122	34,540	57,835
Comp Insurance Spec I-VI	42,263	114,839	43,214	117,423	44,186	120,065	45,180	122,767	46,197	125,529	2.25%	11.25%	31,541	85,704	44,065	119,737	59,101	160,592
Compl Investigator I-III	48,900	99,217	50,000	101,449	51,125	103,732	52,276	106,066	53,452	108,452	2.25%	11.25%	36,494	74,045	50,986	103,448	68,382	138,746
Compl Investigator Int	42,263	60,902	43,214	62,273	44,186	63,674	45,180	65,106	46,197	66,571	2.25%	11.25%	31,541	45,451	44,065	63,499	59,101	85,166
Computer Oper Supv I-II	52,953	90,219	54,145	92,249	55,363	94,324	56,609	96,447	57,882	98,617	2.25%	11.25%	39,519	67,330	55,212	94,066	74,050	126,163
Computer Operator I-II	32,517	55,380	33,249	56,626	33,997	57,900	34,762	59,203	35,544	60,535	2.25%	11.25%	24,267	41,330	33,904	57,742	45,472	77,444
Computer Prod Coord I	28,083	39,377	28,715	40,263	29,361	41,169	30,022	42,095	30,698	43,043	2.25%	11.25%	20,959	29,387	29,281	41,056	39,272	55,065
Computer Prod Coord Int	25,473	35,718	26,046	36,521	26,632	37,343	27,232	38,183	27,844	39,042	2.25%	11.25%	19,010	26,656	26,560	37,241	35,622	49,948
Controller I-III	70,163	119,522	71,741	122,211	73,356	124,961	75,006	127,773	76,694	130,648	2.25%	11.25%	52,362	89,199	73,155	124,619	98,116	167,141
Corr Or Yth Sec Off IV-V	58,594	91,806	59,912	93,872	61,260	95,984	62,638	98,143	64,048	100,351	2.25%	11.25%	43,728	68,514	61,092	95,721	81,938	128,382
Corr Supp Lic Trades Supv I-III	47,169	83,280	48,230	85,154	49,315	87,070	50,425	89,029	51,559	91,032	2.25%	11.25%	35,202	62,151	49,180	86,831	65,961	116,459
Corr Supp Trades Supv I-IV	45,896	91,806	46,929	93,872	47,985	95,984	49,065	98,143	50,169	100,351	2.25%	11.25%	34,252	68,514	47,854	95,721	64,182	128,382
Corr/Yth/Clin Sec Off I-II	41,646	65,257	42,584	66,725	43,542	68,227	44,521	69,762	45,523	71,331	2.25%	11.25%	31,080	48,701	43,422	68,040	58,239	91,256
Corr/Yth/Cln Sec Spec III	50,605	71,934	51,744	73,552	52,908	75,207	54,099	76,899	55,316	78,629	2.25%	11.25%	37,766	53,684	52,763	75,001	70,767	100,593
Corrections Case Mgr I-III	50,605	83,280	51,744	85,154	52,908	87,070	54,099	89,029	55,316	91,032	2.25%	11.25%	37,766	62,151	52,763	86,831	70,767	116,459
Correctl Indus Supv I-III	43,562	90,547	44,542	92,584	45,544	94,667	46,569	96,797	47,616	98,975	2.25%	11.25%	32,510	67,574	45,419	94,408	60,917	126,62?

158

Chart III - U.S. States & Cities - Job Titles - Salaries - Pension Estimates

Colorado	2010 (Min)	2010 (Max)	2011 (Min)	2011 (Max)	2012 (Min)	2012 (Max)	2013 (Min)	2013 (Max)	2014 (Min)	2014 (Max)	5-Year Average % Raise	5-Year Cumulative Raise Estimate**	20-Year Annual Pension Benefit Estimate (Min.)***	20-Year Annual Pension Benefit Estimate (Max.)	25-Year Annual Pension Benefit Estimate (Min.)	25-Year Annual Pension Benefit Estimate (Max.)	30-Year Annual Pension Benefit Estimate (Min.)	30-Year Annual Pension Benefit Estimate (Max.)
Criminal Investigator I-IV	58,594	119,522	59,912	122,211	61,260	124,961	62,638	127,773	64,048	130,648	2.25%	11.25%	43,728	89,199	61,092	124,619	81,938	167,141
Cust Support Coord I-III	42,407	81,837	43,361	83,678	44,337	85,561	45,335	87,486	46,355	89,455	2.25%	11.25%	31,648	61,074	44,216	85,327	59,303	114,442
Custodian I-IV	21,997	57,151	22,492	58,437	22,998	59,751	23,516	61,096	24,045	62,471	2.25%	11.25%	16,416	42,651	22,935	59,588	30,761	79,920
Data Entry Operator I-II	27,336	43,444	27,951	44,421	28,580	45,420	29,223	46,442	29,880	47,487	2.25%	11.25%	20,401	32,422	28,502	45,296	38,227	60,752
Data Specialist	35,836	50,251	36,642	51,382	37,466	52,538	38,309	53,720	39,171	54,929	2.25%	11.25%	26,744	37,502	37,364	52,394	50,113	70,272
Data Supervisor	40,400	56,626	41,309	57,900	42,239	59,203	43,189	60,535	44,161	61,897	2.25%	11.25%	30,151	42,260	42,123	59,041	56,496	79,186
Dental Care I-V	26,549	72,288	27,146	73,914	27,757	75,577	28,381	77,278	29,020	79,017	2.25%	11.25%	19,813	53,948	27,681	75,370	37,126	101,088
Dentist I-III	110,091	161,182	112,568	164,808	115,101	168,516	117,691	172,308	120,339	176,185	2.25%	11.25%	82,160	120,289	114,786	168,055	153,952	225,398
Diag Proced Technol I-IV	34,760	90,232	35,542	92,262	36,342	94,338	37,160	96,461	37,996	98,631	2.25%	11.25%	25,941	67,339	36,242	94,080	48,609	126,181
Dietitian I-III	43,168	75,882	44,139	77,589	45,132	79,335	46,148	81,120	47,186	82,945	2.25%	11.25%	32,216	56,630	45,009	79,118	60,367	106,114
Dining Services I-V	19,518	46,998	19,957	48,056	20,406	49,137	20,865	50,243	21,335	51,373	2.25%	11.25%	14,566	35,074	20,350	49,002	27,294	65,723
Driver's Lic Exam I-IV	31,625	72,235	32,337	73,861	33,064	75,522	33,808	77,222	34,569	78,959	2.25%	11.25%	23,602	53,909	32,974	75,316	44,225	101,015
Early Childhood Educ I-II	24,503	39,535	25,054	40,424	25,618	41,334	26,194	42,264	26,783	43,215	2.25%	11.25%	18,286	29,504	25,547	41,221	34,265	55,286
Electrical Trades I-III	40,571	78,243	41,484	80,003	42,417	81,803	43,371	83,644	44,347	85,526	2.25%	11.25%	30,278	58,392	42,301	81,580	56,735	109,416
Electronic Engineer I-IV	71,304	119,522	72,908	122,211	74,549	124,961	76,226	127,773	77,941	130,648	2.25%	11.25%	53,214	89,199	74,345	124,619	99,712	167,141
Electronics Spec I-IV	41,699	92,842	42,637	94,931	43,597	97,067	44,577	99,251	45,580	101,484	2.25%	11.25%	31,120	69,287	43,477	96,801	58,312	129,831
Engineer-In-Training I-III	52,088	92,842	53,260	94,931	54,458	97,067	55,683	99,251	56,936	101,484	2.25%	11.25%	38,873	69,287	54,309	96,801	72,840	129,831
Engr/Phys Sci Asst I-III	26,168	49,372	26,757	50,483	27,359	51,619	27,975	52,781	28,604	53,968	2.25%	11.25%	19,529	36,846	27,284	51,478	36,594	69,043
Engr/Phys Sci Tech I-III	44,978	76,393	45,990	78,112	47,025	79,870	48,083	81,667	49,165	83,504	2.25%	11.25%	33,567	57,012	46,896	79,651	62,898	106,829
Environ Protect Spec I-V	54,685	119,522	55,915	122,211	57,173	124,961	58,460	127,773	59,775	130,648	2.25%	11.25%	40,811	89,199	57,017	124,619	76,472	167,141
Equipment Mechanic I-IV	35,849	70,963	36,655	72,560	37,480	74,192	38,323	75,862	39,186	77,568	2.25%	11.25%	26,754	52,959	37,378	73,989	50,131	99,235
Equipment Operator I-IV	26,772	52,980	27,374	54,172	27,990	55,390	28,620	56,637	29,264	57,911	2.25%	11.25%	19,980	39,538	27,913	55,239	37,438	74,087
Fin/Credit Examiner I-V	54,960	117,463	56,197	120,106	57,461	122,808	58,754	125,571	60,076	128,397	2.25%	11.25%	41,016	87,662	57,304	122,472	76,857	164,261
Fingerprint Examiner I-III	43,378	83,857	44,354	85,744	45,352	87,673	46,372	89,646	47,416	91,663	2.25%	11.25%	32,373	62,582	45,228	87,433	60,660	117,266
Food Serv Mgr I-IV	42,263	99,217	43,214	101,449	44,186	103,732	45,180	106,066	46,197	108,452	2.25%	11.25%	31,541	74,045	44,065	103,448	59,101	138,746
General Labor I-III	28,083	49,372	28,715	50,483	29,361	51,619	30,022	52,781	30,698	53,968	2.25%	11.25%	20,959	36,846	29,281	51,478	39,272	69,043
General Professional I-VII	37,475	114,839	38,318	117,423	39,181	120,065	40,062	122,767	40,964	125,529	2.25%	11.25%	27,968	85,704	39,073	119,737	52,406	160,592
Grounds & Nursery I-III	32,517	57,151	33,249	58,437	33,997	59,751	34,762	61,096	35,544	62,471	2.25%	11.25%	24,267	42,651	33,904	59,588	45,472	79,920
Health Care Tech I-IV	32,215	59,459	32,940	60,797	33,681	62,165	34,439	63,564	35,214	64,994	2.25%	11.25%	24,042	44,374	33,589	61,995	45,050	83,148
Health Professional I-VII	42,237	117,686	43,187	120,334	44,159	123,041	45,152	125,810	46,168	128,640	2.25%	11.25%	31,521	87,828	44,038	122,704	59,064	164,573
Hearings Officer I-III	44,362	99,217	45,360	101,449	46,380	103,732	47,424	106,066	48,491	108,452	2.25%	11.25%	33,107	74,045	46,253	103,448	62,036	138,746
Inspector I-III	43,562	78,243	44,542	80,003	45,544	81,803	46,569	83,644	47,616	85,526	2.25%	11.25%	32,510	58,392	45,419	81,580	60,917	109,416
Investment Officer I-III	60,561	119,522	61,924	122,211	63,317	124,961	64,742	127,773	66,198	130,648	2.25%	11.25%	45,196	89,199	63,144	124,619	84,689	167,141
IT Professional I-VII	51,602	119,522	52,763	122,211	53,951	124,961	55,164	127,773	56,406	130,648	2.25%	11.25%	38,510	89,199	53,803	124,619	72,161	167,141
IT Technician I-II	42,420	67,526	43,375	69,046	44,351	70,599	45,349	72,188	46,369	73,812	2.25%	11.25%	31,658	50,394	44,229	70,406	59,321	94,429
Labor/Employment Spec I-V	42,263	109,383	43,214	111,844	44,186	114,360	45,180	116,933	46,197	119,564	2.25%	11.25%	31,541	81,632	44,065	114,047	59,101	152,962
Laboratory Coord I-III	43,798	86,520	44,783	88,466	45,791	90,457	46,821	92,492	47,874	94,573	2.25%	11.25%	32,686	64,569	45,665	90,209	61,247	120,990
Laboratory Support I-III	24,699	48,940	25,255	50,041	25,823	51,167	26,404	52,318	26,998	53,495	2.25%	11.25%	18,433	36,523	25,753	51,027	34,540	68,437

Chart III - U.S. States & Cities - Job Titles - Salaries - Pension Estimates

Colorado	2010 (Min)	2010 (Max)	2011 (Min)	2011 (Max)	2012 (Min)	2012 (Max)	2013 (Min)	2013 (Max)	2014 (Min)	2014 (Max)	5-Year Average % Raise	5-Year Cumulative Raise Estimate**	20-Year Annual Pension Benefit Estimate (Min.)***	20-Year Annual Pension Benefit Estimate (Max.)	25-Year Annual Pension Benefit Estimate (Min.)	25-Year Annual Pension Benefit Estimate (Max.)	30-Year Annual Pension Benefit Estimate (Min.)	30-Year Annual Pension Benefit Estimate (Max.)
Laboratory Technology I-IV	40,243	81,876	41,148	83,719	42,074	85,602	43,021	87,528	43,989	89,498	2.25%	11.25%	30,033	61,104	41,959	85,368	56,276	114,497
Landscape Architect I-III	57,413	107,507	58,705	109,926	60,026	112,399	61,376	114,928	62,757	117,514	2.25%	11.25%	42,847	80,232	59,861	112,092	80,287	150,339
Legal Assistant I-II	44,362	74,045	45,360	75,711	46,380	77,415	47,424	79,157	48,491	80,938	2.25%	11.25%	33,107	55,260	46,253	77,203	62,036	103,546
Lottery Sales Rep I-III	37,475	70,517	38,318	72,104	39,181	73,726	40,062	75,385	40,964	77,081	2.25%	11.25%	27,968	52,626	39,073	73,524	52,406	98,612
Ltc Operations I-II	54,370	84,355	55,593	86,253	56,844	88,194	58,123	90,178	59,431	92,208	2.25%	11.25%	40,576	62,954	56,689	87,953	76,031	117,963
Machining Trades I-IV	38,656	80,368	39,526	82,176	40,415	84,025	41,324	85,916	42,254	87,849	2.25%	11.25%	28,849	59,978	40,304	83,795	54,057	112,387
Materials Handler I-III	27,480	57,151	28,098	58,437	28,731	59,751	29,377	61,096	30,038	62,471	2.25%	11.25%	20,508	42,651	28,652	59,588	38,428	79,920
Media Specialist I-V	29,395	76,065	30,057	77,777	30,733	79,527	31,424	81,316	32,131	83,146	2.25%	11.25%	21,937	56,767	30,649	79,309	41,106	106,371
Medical Records Tech I-III	34,878	65,559	35,663	67,034	36,465	68,542	37,286	70,084	38,125	71,661	2.25%	11.25%	26,029	48,926	36,365	68,354	48,774	91,678
Mental Hlth Clinician I-III	34,760	61,112	35,542	62,487	36,342	63,893	37,160	65,331	37,996	66,801	2.25%	11.25%	25,941	45,608	36,242	63,718	48,609	85,460
Nurse I-III	52,455	90,232	53,635	92,262	54,842	94,338	56,076	96,461	57,338	98,631	2.25%	11.25%	39,147	67,339	54,692	94,080	73,353	126,181
Nurse V-VI	77,482	119,522	79,225	122,211	81,008	124,961	82,831	127,773	84,694	130,648	2.25%	11.25%	57,824	89,199	80,786	124,619	108,352	167,141
Office Manager I-II	43,562	67,330	44,542	68,844	45,544	70,393	46,569	71,977	47,616	73,597	2.25%	11.25%	32,510	50,248	45,419	70,201	60,917	94,154
Park Manager I-VI	37,475	109,383	38,318	111,844	39,181	114,360	40,062	116,933	40,964	119,564	2.25%	11.25%	27,968	81,632	39,073	114,047	52,406	152,962
Pharmacy I-III	81,378	119,522	83,209	122,211	85,081	124,961	86,995	127,773	88,953	130,648	2.25%	11.25%	60,732	89,199	84,848	124,619	113,800	167,141
Pharmacy Technician I-II	29,198	46,592	29,855	47,640	30,527	48,712	31,214	49,808	31,916	50,928	2.25%	11.25%	21,791	34,771	30,444	48,578	40,831	65,154
Phy Sci Res/Scientist I-V	54,685	119,522	55,915	122,211	57,173	124,961	58,460	127,773	59,775	130,648	2.25%	11.25%	40,811	89,199	57,017	124,619	76,472	167,141
Physician I-II	143,513	161,182	146,742	164,808	150,044	168,516	153,420	172,308	156,872	176,185	2.25%	11.25%	107,103	120,289	149,633	168,055	200,690	225,398
Pipe/Mech Trades I-III	39,522	74,518	40,411	76,194	41,320	77,909	42,250	79,662	43,200	81,454	2.25%	11.25%	29,495	55,612	41,207	77,695	55,267	104,206
Police Administrator I-II	73,127	114,656	74,773	117,235	76,455	119,873	78,175	122,570	79,934	125,328	2.25%	11.25%	54,574	85,567	76,246	119,545	102,262	160,336
Police Officer I-III	47,169	89,838	48,230	91,860	49,315	93,927	50,425	96,040	51,559	98,201	2.25%	11.25%	35,202	67,046	49,180	93,669	65,961	125,631
Port Of Entry I-III	39,390	72,458	40,277	74,089	41,183	75,756	42,109	77,460	43,057	79,203	2.25%	11.25%	29,397	54,075	41,070	75,548	55,084	101,326
Production I-V	23,112	59,984	23,632	61,334	24,164	62,714	24,708	64,125	25,264	65,568	2.25%	11.25%	17,248	44,766	24,098	62,542	32,320	83,882
Prof Land Surveyor I-II	61,611	97,499	62,997	99,692	64,414	101,935	65,864	104,229	67,345	106,574	2.25%	11.25%	45,980	72,763	64,238	101,656	86,157	136,343
Professional Engineer I-IV	69,756	119,522	71,326	122,211	72,931	124,961	74,571	127,773	76,249	130,648	2.25%	11.25%	52,059	89,199	72,731	124,619	97,548	167,141
Program Assistant I-II	37,475	60,902	38,318	62,273	39,181	63,674	40,062	65,106	40,964	66,571	2.25%	11.25%	27,968	45,451	39,073	63,499	52,406	85,166
Project Planner I-II	52,927	86,257	54,118	88,198	55,336	90,183	56,581	92,212	57,854	94,287	2.25%	11.25%	39,499	64,373	55,184	89,936	74,014	120,623
Property Tax Spec I-IV	47,497	111,849	48,565	114,365	49,658	116,938	50,775	119,570	51,918	122,260	2.25%	11.25%	35,446	83,472	49,522	116,618	66,420	156,410
Psychologist I-II	68,786	106,772	70,333	109,175	71,916	111,631	73,534	114,143	75,188	116,711	2.25%	11.25%	51,334	79,684	71,719	111,326	96,190	149,311
Pub Hlth Med Admin I-II	143,513	161,182	146,742	164,808	150,044	168,516	153,420	172,308	156,872	176,185	2.25%	11.25%	107,103	120,289	149,633	168,055	200,690	225,398
Rate/Financial Anlyst I-V	48,769	119,522	49,866	122,211	50,988	124,961	52,136	127,773	53,309	130,648	2.25%	11.25%	36,396	89,199	50,849	124,619	68,199	167,141
Records Administrator I-II	52,757	88,028	53,944	90,009	55,157	92,034	56,398	94,105	57,667	96,222	2.25%	11.25%	39,372	65,695	55,006	91,782	73,775	123,099
Rehabilitation Couns I-II	48,900	77,744	50,000	79,494	51,125	81,282	52,276	83,111	53,452	84,981	2.25%	11.25%	36,494	58,020	50,986	81,060	68,382	108,719
Rehabilitation Supv I-II	65,546	104,162	67,020	106,506	68,528	108,902	70,070	111,352	71,647	113,858	2.25%	11.25%	48,916	77,736	68,341	108,604	91,660	145,661
Revenue Agent I-IV	48,769	111,849	49,866	114,365	50,988	116,938	52,136	119,570	53,309	122,260	2.25%	11.25%	36,396	83,472	50,849	116,618	68,199	156,410
Safety Security Off I-III	47,169	83,280	48,230	85,154	49,315	87,070	50,425	89,029	51,559	91,032	2.25%	11.25%	35,202	62,151	49,180	86,831	65,961	116,459
Sales Assistant I-III	22,483	42,237	22,988	43,187	23,506	44,159	24,035	45,152	24,575	46,168	2.25%	11.25%	16,779	31,521	23,441	44,038	31,440	59,064
Sales Manager I-III	37,475	70,517	38,318	72,104	39,181	73,726	40,062	75,385	40,964	77,081	2.25%	11.25%	27,968	52,626	39,073	73,524	52,406	98,612
Security I-III	28,871	52,980	29,520	54,172	30,184	55,390	30,863	56,637	31,558	57,911	2.25%	11.25%	21,546	39,538	30,102	55,239	40,373	74,087

160

Chart III - U.S. States & Cities - Job Titles - Salaries - Pension Estimates

Colorado	2010 (Min)	2010 (Max)	2011 (Min)	2011 (Max)	2012 (Min)	2012 (Max)	2013 (Min)	2013 (Max)	2014 (Min)	2014 (Max)	5-Year Average % Raise	5-Year Cumulative Raise Estimate**	20-Year Annual Pension Benefit Estimate (Min.)***	20-Year Annual Pension Benefit Estimate (Max.)	25-Year Annual Pension Benefit Estimate (Min.)	25-Year Annual Pension Benefit Estimate (Max.)	30-Year Annual Pension Benefit Estimate (Min.)	30-Year Annual Pension Benefit Estimate (Max.)
Social Work/ Counselor I-IV	42,237	79,686	43,187	81,479	44,159	83,312	45,152	85,186	46,168	87,103	2.25%	11.25%	31,521	59,469	44,038	83,084	59,064	111,433
State Patrol Admin I-II	71,186	113,344	72,788	115,894	74,425	118,502	76,100	121,168	77,812	123,894	2.25%	11.25%	53,126	84,588	74,222	118,178	99,547	158,501
State Patrol Trooper I-III	53,137	79,384	54,333	81,170	55,555	82,997	56,805	84,864	58,083	86,773	2.25%	11.25%	39,656	59,244	55,403	82,769	74,307	111,011
State Serv Prof Train I-II	33,999	55,288	34,764	56,532	35,546	57,804	36,346	59,105	37,164	60,435	2.25%	11.25%	25,373	41,261	35,449	57,646	47,545	77,315
State Service Trainee I-V	18,088	43,444	18,495	44,421	18,911	45,420	19,337	46,442	19,772	47,487	2.25%	11.25%	13,499	32,422	18,860	45,296	25,295	60,752
Statistical Analyst I-IV	49,595	115,928	50,711	118,536	51,852	121,203	53,019	123,931	54,212	126,719	2.25%	11.25%	37,013	86,516	51,710	120,872	69,355	162,115
Structural Trades I-III	31,809	64,378	32,524	65,827	33,256	67,308	34,004	68,822	34,770	70,371	2.25%	11.25%	23,739	48,045	33,165	67,124	44,482	90,027
Student Trainee I-IV	30,851	60,902	31,545	62,273	32,255	63,674	32,981	65,106	33,723	66,571	2.25%	11.25%	23,024	45,451	32,167	63,499	43,143	85,166
Tax Compliance Agent I-III	49,831	92,042	50,953	94,113	52,099	96,230	53,271	98,396	54,470	100,610	2.25%	11.25%	37,189	68,690	51,957	95,967	69,685	128,712
Tax Conferee I-II	77,325	117,463	79,065	120,106	80,843	122,808	82,662	125,571	84,522	128,397	2.25%	11.25%	57,707	87,662	80,622	122,472	108,132	164,261
Tax Examiner I-V	40,151	101,473	41,055	103,756	41,978	106,091	42,923	108,478	43,889	110,919	2.25%	11.25%	29,965	75,729	41,863	105,800	56,148	141,901
Teacher I-II	46,316	113,646	47,358	116,203	48,424	118,817	49,513	121,491	50,627	124,224	2.25%	11.25%	34,565	84,813	48,291	118,492	64,769	158,923
Technician I-V	29,395	77,744	30,057	79,494	30,733	81,282	31,424	83,111	32,131	84,981	2.25%	11.25%	21,937	58,020	30,649	81,060	41,106	108,719
Telephone Operator II	23,112	37,502	23,632	38,345	24,164	39,208	24,708	40,090	25,264	40,992	2.25%	11.25%	17,248	27,987	24,098	39,101	32,320	52,442
Therapist I-IV	45,306	99,466	46,326	101,704	47,368	103,993	48,434	106,332	49,523	108,725	2.25%	11.25%	33,812	74,231	47,238	103,708	63,356	139,094
Therapy Assistant I-IV	32,215	59,459	32,940	60,797	33,681	62,165	34,439	63,564	35,214	64,994	2.25%	11.25%	24,042	44,374	33,589	61,995	45,050	83,148
Transportation Mtc III	34,117	66,123	34,885	67,611	35,670	69,132	36,472	70,687	37,293	72,278	2.25%	11.25%	25,462	49,347	35,572	68,943	47,710	92,467
Utility Plant Oper I-II	43,562	74,518	44,542	76,194	45,544	77,909	46,569	79,662	47,616	81,454	2.25%	11.25%	32,510	55,612	45,419	77,695	60,917	104,206
Veterinarian I-III	79,660	119,522	81,452	122,211	83,285	124,961	85,158	127,773	87,075	130,648	2.25%	11.25%	59,449	89,199	83,057	124,619	111,397	167,141
Veterinary Technology I-IV	31,546	64,129	32,256	65,572	32,982	67,047	33,724	68,556	34,483	70,098	2.25%	11.25%	23,543	47,859	32,892	66,864	44,115	89,679
Wildlife Manager I-VI	39,390	114,839	40,277	117,423	41,183	120,065	42,109	122,767	43,057	125,529	2.25%	11.25%	29,397	85,704	41,070	119,737	55,084	160,592
Youth Serv Counselor I-III	48,900	89,996	50,000	92,021	51,125	94,091	52,276	96,208	53,452	98,373	2.25%	11.25%	36,494	67,163	50,986	93,834	68,382	125,851

http://www.colorado.gov/dpa/dhr/comp/compplan.htm

Chart III - U.S. States & Cities - Job Titles - Salaries - Pension Estimates

CO-Denver	2010 (Min)	2010 (Max)	2011 (Min)	2011 (Max)	2012 (Min)	2012 (Max)	2013 (Min)	2013 (Max)	2014 (Min)	2014 (Max)	5-Year Average % Raise	5-Year Cumulative Raise Estimate**	20-Year Annual Pension Benefit Estimate (Min.)***	20-Year Annual Pension Benefit Estimate (Max.)	25-Year Annual Pension Benefit Estimate (Min.)	25-Year Annual Pension Benefit Estimate (Max.)	30-Year Annual Pension Benefit Estimate (Min.)	30-Year Annual Pension Benefit Estimate (Max.)
3-1-1 Customer Service Agent	31,114	45,424	31,814	46,446	32,529	47,491	33,261	48,560	34,010	49,652	2.25%	11.25%	23,220	33,900	32,440	47,361	43,509	63,522
3-1-1 Customer Service Operations Supervisor	36,360	58,003	37,178	59,308	38,015	60,643	38,870	62,007	39,745	63,403	2.25%	11.25%	27,135	43,288	37,911	60,477	50,847	81,112
911 Lead Operator	35,560	51,904	36,360	53,072	37,178	54,266	38,015	55,487	38,870	56,735	2.25%	11.25%	26,538	38,736	37,077	54,117	49,728	72,583
911 Operator	34,012	49,648	34,778	50,765	35,560	51,907	36,360	53,075	37,178	54,269	2.25%	11.25%	25,383	37,052	35,463	51,765	47,563	69,428
Accounting Manager	66,280	105,775	67,772	108,155	69,296	110,589	70,856	113,077	72,450	115,621	2.25%	11.25%	49,464	78,940	69,107	110,286	92,687	147,917
Accounting Supervisor	62,004	98,942	63,399	101,168	64,826	103,444	66,284	105,771	67,776	108,151	2.25%	11.25%	46,273	73,839	64,648	103,161	86,707	138,361
Accounting Technician	37,174	54,265	38,010	55,486	38,865	56,734	39,740	58,011	40,634	59,316	2.25%	11.25%	27,742	40,498	38,759	56,579	51,984	75,885
Administrative Analyst	46,447	74,085	47,492	75,752	48,561	77,456	49,654	79,199	50,771	80,981	2.25%	11.25%	34,663	55,289	48,428	77,244	64,952	103,601
Administrative Officer	79,200	126,382	80,982	129,226	82,805	132,133	84,668	135,106	86,573	138,146	2.25%	11.25%	59,107	94,318	82,578	131,772	110,755	176,734
Administrative Support Assistant I-V	24,476	51,038	25,027	52,187	25,590	53,361	26,166	54,561	26,755	55,789	2.25%	11.25%	18,267	38,090	25,520	53,215	34,228	71,372
Agency Trainer	49,648	79,200	50,765	80,982	51,907	82,805	53,075	84,668	54,269	86,573	2.25%	11.25%	37,052	59,107	51,765	82,578	69,428	110,755
Agent	62,004	98,942	63,399	101,168	64,826	103,444	66,284	105,771	67,776	108,151	2.25%	11.25%	46,273	73,839	64,648	103,161	86,707	138,361
Analyst Specialist	60,640	96,764	62,004	98,941	63,399	101,167	64,826	103,444	66,284	105,771	2.25%	11.25%	45,255	72,214	63,226	100,891	84,799	135,316
Analyst Technician	40,636	59,302	41,551	60,636	42,486	62,001	43,442	63,396	44,419	64,822	2.25%	11.25%	30,327	44,257	42,369	61,831	56,826	82,928
Architect	67,290	107,350	68,804	109,765	70,352	112,235	71,935	114,760	73,554	117,342	2.25%	11.25%	50,218	80,114	70,160	111,927	94,099	150,119
Associate Agency Budget Analyst	44,427	70,858	45,427	72,452	46,449	74,083	47,494	75,749	48,563	77,454	2.25%	11.25%	33,156	52,881	46,322	73,880	62,127	99,088
Associate Analyst	46,447	74,085	47,492	75,752	48,561	77,456	49,654	79,199	50,771	80,981	2.25%	11.25%	34,663	55,289	48,428	77,244	64,952	103,601
Associate Buyer	46,447	74,085	47,492	75,752	48,561	77,456	49,654	79,199	50,771	80,981	2.25%	11.25%	34,663	55,289	48,428	77,244	64,952	103,601
Associate City Inspector	43,444	63,394	44,421	64,821	45,420	66,279	46,442	67,771	47,487	69,295	2.25%	11.25%	32,422	47,311	45,296	66,098	60,752	88,651
Associate City Planner	48,205	76,892	49,290	78,622	50,399	80,391	51,533	82,200	52,692	84,049	2.25%	11.25%	35,975	57,384	50,261	80,171	67,410	107,526
Associate Human Resources Professional	49,648	79,200	50,765	80,982	51,907	82,805	53,075	84,668	54,269	86,573	2.25%	11.25%	37,052	59,107	51,765	82,578	69,428	110,755
Associate Information Technology Developer	59,026	94,180	60,355	96,299	61,713	98,466	63,101	100,681	64,521	102,947	2.25%	11.25%	44,051	70,286	61,544	98,196	82,543	131,702
Associate Information Technology System Administrator	55,209	88,094	56,452	90,076	57,722	92,103	59,021	94,175	60,349	96,294	2.25%	11.25%	41,202	65,744	57,564	91,850	77,205	123,191
Associate Information Technology Systems Analyst	59,026	94,180	60,355	96,299	61,713	98,466	63,101	100,681	64,521	102,947	2.25%	11.25%	44,051	70,286	61,544	98,196	82,543	131,702
Associate Information Technology Technician	45,175	65,979	46,191	67,463	47,231	68,981	48,293	70,533	49,380	72,120	2.25%	11.25%	33,714	49,239	47,101	68,792	63,173	92,265
Board Of Adjustment Code Investigator	41,555	60,640	42,490	62,004	43,446	63,399	44,423	64,826	45,423	66,284	2.25%	11.25%	31,012	45,255	43,327	63,226	58,110	84,799
Boating Ranger	26,024	38,013	26,610	38,868	27,208	39,743	27,821	40,637	28,447	41,551	2.25%	11.25%	19,422	28,369	27,134	39,634	36,392	53,158
Body Repair Worker	44,545	65,008	45,548	66,471	46,572	67,966	47,620	69,495	48,692	71,059	2.25%	11.25%	33,244	48,515	46,445	67,780	62,293	90,908
Business Analyst	53,071	84,670	54,265	86,575	55,486	88,523	56,735	90,515	58,011	92,552	2.25%	11.25%	39,607	63,189	55,335	88,281	74,215	118,404
Business Development Associate	46,447	74,085	47,492	75,752	48,561	77,456	49,654	79,199	50,771	80,981	2.25%	11.25%	34,663	55,289	48,428	77,244	64,952	103,601
Business Development Representative I-II	53,071	96,764	54,265	98,941	55,486	101,167	56,735	103,444	58,011	105,771	2.25%	11.25%	39,607	72,214	55,335	100,891	74,215	135,316
Carpenter	38,984	56,875	39,861	58,155	40,758	59,463	41,675	60,801	42,612	62,169	2.25%	11.25%	29,093	42,446	40,646	59,301	54,515	79,535
Case Management Coordinator	37,410	54,632	38,251	55,862	39,112	57,118	39,992	58,404	40,892	59,718	2.25%	11.25%	27,919	40,772	39,005	56,962	52,314	76,398
Certified Public Accountant I-IV	42,486	113,082	43,442	115,626	44,419	118,228	45,419	120,888	46,441	123,608	2.25%	11.25%	31,707	84,392	44,298	117,904	59,413	158,134
Chemist	55,078	87,871	56,318	89,848	57,585	91,869	58,880	93,937	60,205	96,050	2.25%	11.25%	41,105	65,577	57,427	91,618	77,022	122,879

162

Chart III - U.S. States & Cities - Job Titles - Salaries - Pension Estimates

CO-Denver	2010 (Min)	2010 (Max)	2011 (Min)	2011 (Max)	2012 (Min)	2012 (Max)	2013 (Min)	2013 (Max)	2014 (Min)	2014 (Max)	5-Year Average % Raise	5-Year Cumulative Raise Estimate**	20-Year Annual Pension Benefit Estimate (Min.)***	20-Year Annual Pension Benefit Estimate (Max.)	25-Year Annual Pension Benefit Estimate (Min.)	25-Year Annual Pension Benefit Estimate (Max.)	30-Year Annual Pension Benefit Estimate (Min.)	30-Year Annual Pension Benefit Estimate (Max.)
City Council Aide I-III	38,013	96,764	38,868	98,941	39,743	101,167	40,637	103,444	41,551	105,771	2.25%	11.25%	28,369	72,214	39,634	100,891	53,158	135,316
City Forester	69,297	110,589	70,856	113,078	72,451	115,622	74,081	118,223	75,748	120,883	2.25%	11.25%	51,716	82,532	72,252	115,305	96,906	154,649
City Inspector	39,745	58,003	40,639	59,308	41,553	60,643	42,488	62,007	43,444	63,403	2.25%	11.25%	29,661	43,288	41,439	60,477	55,579	81,112
Claims Adjuster I-II	40,636	74,085	41,551	75,752	42,486	77,456	43,442	79,199	44,419	80,981	2.25%	11.25%	30,327	55,289	42,369	77,244	56,826	103,601
Community Development Representative I-II	53,071	96,764	54,265	98,941	55,486	101,167	56,735	103,444	58,011	105,771	2.25%	11.25%	39,607	72,214	55,335	100,891	74,215	135,316
Computer Operator	37,816	55,209	38,667	56,452	39,537	57,722	40,427	59,021	41,336	60,349	2.25%	11.25%	28,222	41,202	39,429	57,564	52,883	77,205
Construction Inspector	48,690	71,068	49,786	72,667	50,906	74,302	52,051	75,974	53,223	77,683	2.25%	11.25%	36,337	53,038	50,767	74,099	68,089	99,382
Contract Compliance Coordinator	46,447	74,085	47,492	75,752	48,561	77,456	49,654	79,199	50,771	80,981	2.25%	11.25%	34,663	55,289	48,428	77,244	64,952	103,601
Contract Compliance Technician	40,636	59,302	41,551	60,636	42,486	62,001	43,442	63,396	44,419	64,822	2.25%	11.25%	30,327	44,257	42,369	61,831	56,826	82,928
Court Interpreter	48,559	70,858	49,652	72,452	50,769	74,083	51,911	75,749	53,079	77,454	2.25%	11.25%	36,239	52,881	50,630	73,880	67,906	99,088
Court Technical Clerk	39,941	58,358	40,840	59,671	41,759	61,013	42,698	62,386	43,659	63,790	2.25%	11.25%	29,808	43,552	41,645	60,846	55,854	81,608
Criminal/Civil Investigator	46,408	67,736	47,452	69,260	48,520	70,819	49,611	72,412	50,728	74,041	2.25%	11.25%	34,634	50,551	48,387	70,625	64,897	94,723
Criminal/Civil Investigator Specialist	64,785	103,375	66,243	105,701	67,733	108,079	69,257	110,511	70,815	112,998	2.25%	11.25%	48,349	77,148	67,548	107,783	90,596	144,561
Data Network Inventory Analyst	51,629	75,397	52,790	77,093	53,978	78,828	55,192	80,601	56,434	82,415	2.25%	11.25%	38,530	56,268	53,830	78,612	72,198	105,435
Data Team Administrator	55,209	88,094	56,452	90,076	57,722	92,103	59,021	94,175	60,349	96,294	2.25%	11.25%	41,202	65,744	57,564	91,850	77,205	123,191
Data Training Coordinator	48,284	77,089	49,370	78,823	50,481	80,597	51,617	82,410	52,778	84,264	2.25%	11.25%	36,034	57,531	50,343	80,376	67,520	107,801
Database Administrator	67,461	107,651	68,979	110,073	70,531	112,550	72,118	115,082	73,740	117,672	2.25%	11.25%	50,346	80,339	70,338	112,242	94,338	150,540
Dental Assistant	27,401	39,994	28,018	40,894	28,648	41,814	29,293	42,755	29,952	43,716	2.25%	11.25%	20,449	29,847	28,570	41,699	38,318	55,928
Drafter	38,590	56,311	39,458	57,578	40,346	58,874	41,254	60,198	42,182	61,553	2.25%	11.25%	28,800	42,025	40,236	58,713	53,965	78,746
Economic Crime Specialist	34,773	50,763	35,556	51,905	36,356	53,073	37,174	54,267	38,010	55,488	2.25%	11.25%	25,951	37,884	36,256	52,928	48,627	70,987
Economic Development Specialist - Business Development	50,763	80,984	51,905	82,807	53,073	84,670	54,267	86,575	55,488	88,523	2.25%	11.25%	37,884	60,438	52,928	84,438	70,987	113,249
Education Program Assistant	42,486	62,004	43,442	63,399	44,419	64,826	45,419	66,284	46,441	67,776	2.25%	11.25%	31,707	46,273	44,298	64,648	59,413	86,707
Education Program Coordinator	46,447	74,085	47,492	75,752	48,561	77,456	49,654	79,199	50,771	80,981	2.25%	11.25%	34,663	55,289	48,428	77,244	64,952	103,601
Election Service Worker	24,476	35,731	25,027	36,535	25,590	37,357	26,166	38,197	26,755	39,057	2.25%	11.25%	18,267	26,666	25,520	37,254	34,228	49,966
Electrical Inspector	48,690	71,068	49,786	72,667	50,906	74,302	52,051	75,974	53,223	77,683	2.25%	11.25%	36,337	53,038	50,767	74,099	68,089	99,382
Electrician	46,565	67,972	47,613	69,502	48,684	71,065	49,780	72,664	50,900	74,299	2.25%	11.25%	34,751	50,727	48,551	70,871	65,117	95,053
Electrocardiograph Technician	32,740	47,785	33,477	48,860	34,230	49,960	35,000	51,084	35,788	52,233	2.25%	11.25%	24,434	35,662	34,136	49,823	45,784	66,823
	34,222	49,963	34,992	51,087	35,780	52,236	36,585	53,412	37,408	54,613	2.25%	11.25%	25,540	37,287	35,682	52,093	47,857	69,868
Electronic Equipment Installer	35,665	52,048	36,468	53,219	37,288	54,417	38,127	55,641	38,985	56,893	2.25%	11.25%	26,617	38,843	37,186	54,268	49,874	72,785
Electronic Monitoring Probation Officer	45,424	66,280	46,446	67,772	47,491	69,296	48,560	70,856	49,652	72,450	2.25%	11.25%	33,900	49,464	47,361	69,107	63,522	92,687
Electronic Systems Technician	46,565	67,972	47,613	69,502	48,684	71,065	49,780	72,664	50,900	74,299	2.25%	11.25%	34,751	50,727	48,551	70,871	65,117	95,053
Elevator Inspector	48,690	71,068	49,786	72,667	50,906	74,302	52,051	75,974	53,223	77,683	2.25%	11.25%	36,337	53,038	50,767	74,099	68,089	99,382
Eligibility Supervisor I-II	41,817	76,288	42,758	78,005	43,720	79,760	44,704	81,555	45,709	83,390	2.25%	11.25%	31,208	56,934	43,600	79,542	58,477	106,682
Eligibility Technician	35,783	52,245	36,588	53,421	37,412	54,622	38,253	55,851	39,114	57,108	2.25%	11.25%	26,705	38,990	37,309	54,473	50,040	73,060
Emergency Exercise And Training Officer	49,648	79,200	50,765	80,982	51,907	82,805	53,075	84,668	54,269	86,573	2.25%	11.25%	37,052	59,107	51,765	82,578	69,428	110,755

Chart III - U.S. States & Cities - Job Titles - Salaries - Pension Estimates

CO-Denver	2010 (Min)	2010 (Max)	2011 (Min)	2011 (Max)	2012 (Min)	2012 (Max)	2013 (Min)	2013 (Max)	2014 (Min)	2014 (Max)	5-Year Average % Raise	5-Year Cumulative Raise Estimate**	20-Year Annual Pension Benefit Estimate (Min.)***	20-Year Annual Pension Benefit Estimate (Max.)	25-Year Annual Pension Benefit Estimate (Min.)	25-Year Annual Pension Benefit Estimate (Max.)	30-Year Annual Pension Benefit Estimate (Min.)	30-Year Annual Pension Benefit Estimate (Max.)
Emergency Management Coordinator	49,648	79,200	50,765	80,982	51,907	82,805	53,075	84,668	54,269	86,573	2.25%	11.25%	37,052	59,107	51,765	82,578	69,428	110,755
EMT - Basic	29,946	43,719	30,620	44,703	31,309	45,708	32,013	46,737	32,734	47,788	2.25%	11.25%	22,349	32,627	31,223	45,583	41,877	61,137
Engineer	67,290	107,350	68,804	109,765	70,352	112,235	71,935	114,760	73,554	117,342	2.25%	11.25%	50,218	80,114	70,160	111,927	94,099	150,119
Engineering Aide	30,891	45,096	31,586	46,111	32,296	47,148	33,023	48,209	33,766	49,294	2.25%	11.25%	23,053	33,655	32,208	47,019	43,198	63,063
Engineering Associate	42,184	61,558	43,133	62,943	44,104	64,359	45,096	65,807	46,111	67,288	2.25%	11.25%	31,482	45,940	43,983	64,183	58,991	86,083
Engineering Drawings Technician	30,576	44,650	31,264	45,655	31,967	46,682	32,686	47,732	33,422	48,806	2.25%	11.25%	22,818	33,322	31,880	46,554	42,757	62,439
Engineering Manager	76,892	122,683	78,622	125,444	80,391	128,266	82,200	131,152	84,049	134,103	2.25%	11.25%	57,384	91,558	80,171	127,915	107,526	171,561
Entry Paralegal	38,839	56,692	39,713	57,967	40,607	59,271	41,521	60,605	42,455	61,969	2.25%	11.25%	28,986	42,309	40,496	59,109	54,313	79,278
Environmental Associate	44,427	64,824	45,427	66,283	46,449	67,774	47,494	69,299	48,563	70,858	2.25%	11.25%	33,156	48,378	46,322	67,589	62,127	90,651
Environmental Health Analyst	56,731	90,520	58,007	92,557	59,313	94,640	60,647	96,769	62,012	98,946	2.25%	11.25%	42,338	67,555	59,150	94,381	79,333	126,585
Environmental Inspector	39,745	58,003	40,639	59,308	41,553	60,643	42,488	62,007	43,444	63,403	2.25%	11.25%	29,661	43,288	41,439	60,477	55,579	81,112
Environmental Scientist I-II	51,537	100,424	52,696	102,683	53,882	104,994	55,094	107,356	56,334	109,772	2.25%	11.25%	38,462	74,946	53,734	104,706	72,069	140,433
Environmental Specialist I-II	49,648	87,871	50,765	89,848	51,907	91,869	53,075	93,937	54,269	96,050	2.25%	11.25%	37,052	65,577	51,765	91,618	69,428	122,879
Equipment Operator	33,357	48,690	34,107	49,786	34,874	50,906	35,659	52,051	36,461	53,223	2.25%	11.25%	24,894	36,337	34,779	50,767	46,646	68,089
Equipment Operator Specialist	36,465	53,216	37,286	54,413	38,125	55,637	38,982	56,889	39,860	58,169	2.25%	11.25%	27,214	39,715	38,020	55,485	50,993	74,417
Executive	110,589	176,476	113,078	180,447	115,622	184,507	118,223	188,658	120,883	192,903	2.25%	11.25%	82,532	131,703	115,305	184,002	154,649	246,786
Executive Assistant I-III	38,866	62,004	39,740	63,399	40,634	64,826	41,549	66,284	42,483	67,776	2.25%	11.25%	29,005	46,273	40,523	64,648	54,350	86,707
Facility Maintenance Technician	38,984	58,882	39,861	60,207	40,758	61,562	41,675	62,947	42,612	64,363	2.25%	11.25%	29,093	43,943	40,646	61,393	54,515	82,341
Financial Management Specialist	62,004	98,942	63,399	101,168	64,826	103,444	66,284	105,771	67,776	108,151	2.25%	11.25%	46,273	73,839	64,648	103,161	86,707	138,361
Fleet Maintenance Engineer	76,892	122,683	78,622	125,444	80,391	128,266	82,200	131,152	84,049	134,103	2.25%	11.25%	57,384	91,558	80,171	127,915	107,526	171,561
Forensic Pathologist	130,449	208,154	133,384	212,837	136,385	217,626	139,453	222,523	142,591	227,529	2.25%	11.25%	97,353	155,344	136,011	217,030	182,420	291,084
Forensic Quality Assurance Specialist	60,640	96,764	62,004	98,941	63,399	101,167	64,826	103,444	66,284	105,771	2.25%	11.25%	45,255	72,214	63,226	100,891	84,799	135,316
Forensic Scientist I-II	51,537	100,424	52,696	102,683	53,882	104,994	55,094	107,356	56,334	109,772	2.25%	11.25%	38,462	74,946	53,734	104,706	72,069	140,433
Geographic Information System Analyst	49,372	72,117	50,483	73,740	51,619	75,399	52,781	77,096	53,968	78,830	2.25%	11.25%	36,846	53,821	51,478	75,193	69,043	100,849
Geographic Information System Data Administrator	63,106	100,686	64,526	102,952	65,978	105,268	67,462	107,636	68,980	110,058	2.25%	11.25%	47,096	75,141	65,797	104,980	88,248	140,800
Graphic Designer	41,555	66,280	42,490	67,772	43,446	69,296	44,423	70,856	45,423	72,450	2.25%	11.25%	31,012	49,464	43,327	69,107	58,110	92,687
Graphics Technician	38,866	56,731	39,740	58,007	40,634	59,313	41,549	60,647	42,483	62,012	2.25%	11.25%	29,005	42,338	40,523	59,150	54,350	79,333
Health Care Technician	28,648	41,817	29,292	42,758	29,951	43,720	30,625	44,704	31,314	45,709	2.25%	11.25%	21,379	31,208	29,869	43,600	40,061	58,477
Hearings Officer	90,455	144,353	92,490	147,601	94,571	150,922	96,699	154,317	98,875	157,789	2.25%	11.25%	67,506	107,729	94,312	150,508	126,493	201,864
Heavy Equipment Operator	39,863	58,161	40,759	59,469	41,677	60,807	42,614	62,176	43,573	63,575	2.25%	11.25%	29,749	43,405	41,562	60,641	55,744	81,333
Hotline Operator	29,762	43,444	30,432	44,421	31,117	45,420	31,817	46,442	32,533	47,487	2.25%	11.25%	22,212	32,422	31,032	45,296	41,620	60,752
Human Resources Specialist	64,824	103,454	66,283	105,781	67,774	108,162	69,299	110,595	70,858	113,084	2.25%	11.25%	48,378	77,207	67,589	107,866	90,651	144,671
Human Services Outreach Representative	34,222	49,963	34,992	51,087	35,780	52,236	36,585	53,412	37,408	54,613	2.25%	11.25%	25,540	37,287	35,682	52,093	47,857	69,868
Information Security Manager	72,117	115,089	73,740	117,678	75,399	120,326	77,096	123,033	78,830	125,801	2.25%	11.25%	53,821	85,890	75,193	119,996	100,849	160,941

Chart III - U.S. States & Cities - Job Titles - Salaries - Pension Estimates

CO-Denver	2010 (Min)	2010 (Max)	2011 (Min)	2011 (Max)	2012 (Min)	2012 (Max)	2013 (Min)	2013 (Max)	2014 (Min)	2014 (Max)	5-Year Average % Raise	5-Year Cumulative Raise Estimate**	20-Year Annual Pension Benefit Estimate (Min.)***	20-Year Annual Pension Benefit Estimate (Max.)	25-Year Annual Pension Benefit Estimate (Min.)	25-Year Annual Pension Benefit Estimate (Max.)	30-Year Annual Pension Benefit Estimate (Min.)	30-Year Annual Pension Benefit Estimate (Max.)
Information Technology Communications Technician	49,372	72,117	50,483	73,740	51,619	75,399	52,781	77,096	53,968	78,830	2.25%	11.25%	36,846	53,821	51,478	75,193	69,043	100,849
Information Technology Division Director	94,180	140,614	96,299	143,778	98,466	147,013	100,681	150,321	102,947	153,703	2.25%	11.25%	70,286	104,940	98,196	146,611	131,702	196,636
Information Technology Project Manager	72,117	115,089	73,740	117,678	75,399	120,326	77,096	123,033	78,830	125,801	2.25%	11.25%	53,821	85,890	75,193	119,996	100,849	160,941
Information Technology Supervisor	77,089	123,024	78,823	125,792	80,597	128,623	82,410	131,517	84,264	134,476	2.25%	11.25%	57,531	91,812	80,376	128,271	107,801	172,038
Information Technology System Architect	72,117	115,089	73,740	117,678	75,399	120,326	77,096	123,033	78,830	125,801	2.25%	11.25%	53,821	85,890	75,193	119,996	100,849	160,941
Information Technology Technical Writer	48,284	77,089	49,370	78,823	50,481	80,597	51,617	82,410	52,778	84,264	2.25%	11.25%	36,034	57,531	50,343	80,376	67,520	107,801
Information Technology Technician Supervisor	55,209	88,094	56,452	90,076	57,722	92,103	59,021	94,175	60,349	96,294	2.25%	11.25%	41,202	65,744	57,564	91,850	77,205	123,191
Institution Food Steward	34,012	49,648	34,778	50,765	35,560	51,907	36,360	53,075	37,178	54,269	2.25%	11.25%	25,383	37,052	35,463	51,765	47,563	69,428
Land Surveyor	62,948	100,424	64,365	102,683	65,813	104,994	67,294	107,356	68,808	109,772	2.25%	11.25%	46,978	74,946	65,633	104,706	88,028	140,433
Laundry Worker	21,774	31,809	22,264	32,524	22,765	33,256	23,277	34,004	23,801	34,770	2.25%	11.25%	16,250	23,739	22,703	33,165	30,449	44,482
Legal Research Assistant	48,520	70,819	49,611	72,412	50,728	74,041	51,869	75,707	53,036	77,411	2.25%	11.25%	36,210	52,852	50,589	73,839	67,850	99,033
Legal Secretary	39,941	58,358	40,840	59,671	41,759	61,013	42,698	62,386	43,659	63,790	2.25%	11.25%	29,808	43,552	41,645	60,846	55,854	81,608
Licensed Practical Nurse	35,783	52,245	36,588	53,421	37,412	54,622	38,253	55,851	39,114	57,108	2.25%	11.25%	26,705	38,990	37,309	54,473	50,040	73,060
Maintenance Control Technician	37,174	54,265	38,010	55,486	38,865	56,734	39,740	58,011	40,634	59,316	2.25%	11.25%	27,742	40,498	38,759	56,579	51,984	75,885
Maintenance Liaison	37,174	54,265	38,010	55,486	38,865	56,734	39,740	58,011	40,634	59,316	2.25%	11.25%	27,742	40,498	38,759	56,579	51,984	75,885
Maintenance Machinist	40,755	59,472	41,671	60,811	42,609	62,179	43,568	63,578	44,548	65,008	2.25%	11.25%	30,415	44,384	42,492	62,009	56,991	83,167
Maintenance Technician	34,104	49,792	34,872	50,912	35,656	52,058	36,458	53,229	37,279	54,427	2.25%	11.25%	25,452	37,160	35,559	51,915	47,692	69,630
Management Analyst	54,265	86,572	55,486	88,520	56,734	90,512	58,011	92,548	59,316	94,631	2.25%	11.25%	40,498	64,608	56,579	90,264	75,885	121,063
Manager 1-2	74,085	160,211	75,752	163,816	77,456	167,502	79,199	171,270	80,981	175,124	2.25%	11.25%	55,289	119,564	77,244	167,043	103,601	224,041
Marketing/Public Relations Specialist	60,640	96,764	62,004	98,941	63,399	101,167	64,826	103,444	66,284	105,771	2.25%	11.25%	45,255	72,214	63,226	100,891	84,799	135,316
Medical Interpreter	29,762	43,444	30,432	44,421	31,117	45,420	31,817	46,442	32,533	47,487	2.25%	11.25%	22,212	32,422	31,032	45,296	41,620	60,752
Medical Office Assistant	29,946	43,719	30,620	44,703	31,309	45,708	32,013	46,737	32,734	47,788	2.25%	11.25%	22,349	32,627	31,223	45,583	41,877	61,137
Medical Services Representative	31,310	45,713	32,015	46,741	32,735	47,793	33,472	48,868	34,225	49,968	2.25%	11.25%	23,367	34,115	32,645	47,662	43,785	63,925
Medical Technologist	52,140	83,175	53,313	85,046	54,513	86,960	55,739	88,916	56,993	90,917	2.25%	11.25%	38,912	62,073	54,364	86,722	72,913	116,313
Medical Transcriptionist	33,422	48,808	34,174	49,907	34,943	51,029	35,729	52,178	36,533	53,352	2.25%	11.25%	24,943	36,425	34,847	50,890	46,738	68,254
Nurse Practitioner	72,773	116,125	74,411	118,738	76,085	121,409	77,797	124,141	79,547	126,934	2.25%	11.25%	54,310	86,663	75,876	121,077	101,767	162,390
Nursing Administrator	68,077	108,622	69,609	111,066	71,175	113,565	72,777	116,120	74,414	118,733	2.25%	11.25%	50,806	81,064	70,980	113,254	95,200	151,898
Nursing Clinical Coordinator	63,683	101,617	65,116	103,904	66,581	106,242	68,079	108,632	69,611	111,076	2.25%	11.25%	47,526	75,836	66,399	105,951	89,055	142,103
Occupational Therapy Assistant	33,409	48,769	34,161	49,866	34,929	50,988	35,715	52,136	36,519	53,309	2.25%	11.25%	24,933	36,396	34,834	50,849	46,719	68,199
Painter	38,984	56,875	39,861	58,155	40,758	59,463	41,675	60,801	42,612	62,169	2.25%	11.25%	29,093	42,446	40,646	59,301	54,515	79,535
Paralegal	44,388	64,785	45,387	66,243	46,408	67,733	47,452	69,257	48,520	70,815	2.25%	11.25%	33,126	48,349	46,281	67,548	62,072	90,596
Paramedic	44,703	65,283	45,709	66,752	46,737	68,254	47,789	69,790	48,864	71,360	2.25%	11.25%	33,361	48,721	46,609	68,067	62,513	91,293
Paramedic Dispatcher	42,486	62,004	43,442	63,399	44,419	64,826	45,419	66,284	46,441	67,776	2.25%	11.25%	31,707	46,273	44,298	64,648	59,413	86,707
Parking Operations Analyst	46,447	67,776	47,492	69,300	48,561	70,860	49,654	72,454	50,771	74,084	2.25%	11.25%	34,663	50,580	48,428	70,666	64,952	94,778

Chart III - U.S. States & Cities - Job Titles - Salaries - Pension Estimates

CO-Denver	2010 (Min)	2010 (Max)	2011 (Min)	2011 (Max)	2012 (Min)	2012 (Max)	2013 (Min)	2013 (Max)	2014 (Min)	2014 (Max)	5-Year Average % Raise	5-Year Cumulative Raise Estimate**	20-Year Annual Pension Benefit Estimate (Min.)***	20-Year Annual Pension Benefit Estimate (Max.)	25-Year Annual Pension Benefit Estimate (Min.)	25-Year Annual Pension Benefit Estimate (Max.)	30-Year Annual Pension Benefit Estimate (Min.)	30-Year Annual Pension Benefit Estimate (Max.)
Patient Representative	34,012	49,648	34,778	50,765	35,560	51,907	36,360	53,075	37,178	54,269	2.25%	11.25%	25,383	37,052	35,463	51,765	47,563	69,428
Permit Supervisor	48,205	76,892	49,290	78,622	50,399	80,391	51,533	82,200	52,692	84,049	2.25%	11.25%	35,975	57,384	50,261	80,171	67,410	107,526
Personnel Technician	42,486	62,004	43,442	63,399	44,419	64,826	45,419	66,284	46,441	67,776	2.25%	11.25%	31,707	46,273	44,298	64,648	59,413	86,707
Physical Therapist	52,140	83,175	53,313	85,046	54,513	86,960	55,739	88,916	56,993	90,917	2.25%	11.25%	38,912	62,073	54,364	86,722	72,913	116,313
Plumber	46,565	67,972	47,613	69,502	48,684	71,065	49,780	72,664	50,900	74,299	2.25%	11.25%	34,751	50,727	48,551	70,871	65,117	95,053
Plumbing Inspector	48,690	71,068	49,786	72,667	50,906	74,302	52,051	75,974	53,223	77,683	2.25%	11.25%	36,337	53,038	50,767	74,099	68,089	99,382
Police Dispatcher	42,486	62,004	43,442	63,399	44,419	64,826	45,419	66,284	46,441	67,776	2.25%	11.25%	31,707	46,273	44,298	64,648	59,413	86,707
Police Fleet Technician	42,604	62,175	43,563	63,574	44,543	65,004	45,545	66,466	46,570	67,962	2.25%	11.25%	31,795	46,400	44,421	64,826	59,578	86,945
Police Lead Dispatcher	44,427	64,824	45,427	66,283	46,449	67,774	47,494	69,299	48,563	70,858	2.25%	11.25%	33,156	48,378	46,322	67,589	62,127	90,651
Pool Maintenance Technician	38,984	56,875	39,861	58,155	40,758	59,463	41,675	60,801	42,612	62,169	2.25%	11.25%	29,093	42,446	40,646	59,301	54,515	79,535
Principal City Planner	62,948	100,424	64,365	102,683	65,813	104,994	67,294	107,356	68,808	109,772	2.25%	11.25%	46,978	74,946	65,633	104,706	88,028	140,433
Program Coordinator	46,447	74,085	47,492	75,752	48,561	77,456	49,654	79,199	50,771	80,981	2.25%	11.25%	34,663	55,289	48,428	77,244	64,952	103,601
Program Evaluator	60,640	96,764	62,004	98,941	63,399	101,167	64,826	103,444	66,284	105,771	2.25%	11.25%	45,255	72,214	63,226	100,891	84,799	135,316
Program Manager	64,824	103,454	66,283	105,781	67,774	108,162	69,299	110,595	70,858	113,084	2.25%	11.25%	48,378	77,207	67,589	107,866	90,651	144,671
Program Quality Assurance Technician	39,745	58,003	40,639	59,308	41,553	60,643	42,488	62,007	43,444	63,403	2.25%	11.25%	29,661	43,288	41,439	60,477	55,579	81,112
Project Inspector	51,537	82,204	52,696	84,054	53,882	85,945	55,094	87,879	56,334	89,856	2.25%	11.25%	38,462	61,348	53,734	85,710	72,069	114,955
Property and Evidence Technician	38,013	55,485	38,868	56,733	39,743	58,010	40,637	59,315	41,551	60,650	2.25%	11.25%	28,369	41,408	39,634	57,851	53,158	77,591
Psychiatric Technician	27,401	39,994	28,018	40,894	28,648	41,814	29,293	42,755	29,952	43,716	2.25%	11.25%	20,449	29,847	28,570	41,699	38,318	55,928
Psychologist	63,683	101,617	65,116	103,904	66,581	106,242	68,079	108,632	69,611	111,076	2.25%	11.25%	47,526	75,836	66,399	105,951	89,055	142,103
Public Art Coordinator	41,555	66,280	42,490	67,772	43,446	69,296	44,423	70,856	45,423	72,450	2.25%	11.25%	31,012	49,464	43,327	69,107	58,110	92,687
Publication Assistant	38,866	56,731	39,740	58,007	40,634	59,313	41,549	60,647	42,483	62,012	2.25%	11.25%	29,005	42,338	40,523	59,150	54,350	79,333
Real Property Appraiser Specialist	58,003	92,554	59,308	94,636	60,643	96,765	62,007	98,943	63,403	101,169	2.25%	11.25%	43,288	69,072	60,477	96,500	81,112	129,428
Recreational Therapist	42,670	68,077	43,630	69,609	44,611	71,175	45,615	72,777	46,641	74,414	2.25%	11.25%	31,844	50,806	44,489	70,980	59,670	95,200
Registered Nurse	55,721	88,920	56,975	90,921	58,257	92,967	59,567	95,058	60,908	97,197	2.25%	11.25%	41,584	66,361	58,097	92,712	77,921	124,347
Research Supervisor	64,824	103,454	66,283	105,781	67,774	108,162	69,299	110,595	70,858	113,084	2.25%	11.25%	48,378	77,207	67,589	107,866	90,651	144,671
Respiratory Therapist	40,899	59,722	41,819	61,065	42,760	62,439	43,722	63,844	44,706	65,281	2.25%	11.25%	30,523	44,570	42,643	62,269	57,193	83,515
Risk Analyst	53,071	84,670	54,265	86,575	55,486	88,523	56,735	90,515	58,011	92,552	2.25%	11.25%	39,607	63,189	55,335	88,281	74,215	118,404
Safety and Industrial Hygiene Professional I-II	46,447	84,670	47,492	86,575	48,561	88,523	49,654	90,515	50,771	92,552	2.25%	11.25%	34,663	63,189	48,428	88,281	64,952	118,404
Security Guard	30,431	44,427	31,116	45,427	31,816	46,449	32,532	47,494	33,264	48,563	2.25%	11.25%	22,711	33,156	31,729	46,322	42,556	62,127
Social Case Worker	39,915	63,683	40,813	65,116	41,731	66,581	42,670	68,079	43,630	69,611	2.25%	11.25%	29,788	47,526	41,617	66,399	55,818	89,055
Special Education Teacher	52,140	83,175	53,313	85,046	54,513	86,960	55,739	88,916	56,993	90,917	2.25%	11.25%	38,912	62,073	54,364	86,722	72,913	116,313
Staff Analyst	40,636	59,302	41,551	60,636	42,486	62,001	43,442	63,396	44,419	64,822	2.25%	11.25%	30,327	44,257	42,369	61,831	56,826	82,928
Staff Buyer	40,636	59,302	41,551	60,636	42,486	62,001	43,442	63,396	44,419	64,822	2.25%	11.25%	30,327	44,257	42,369	61,831	56,826	82,928
Supervisor of Administrative Support I-II	39,062	71,291	39,941	72,895	40,840	74,535	41,759	76,212	42,698	77,927	2.25%	11.25%	29,152	53,204	40,728	74,331	54,625	99,694
Tax Analyst	42,486	62,004	43,442	63,399	44,419	64,826	45,419	66,284	46,441	67,776	2.25%	11.25%	31,707	46,273	44,298	64,648	59,413	86,707
Tax Revenue Agent I-II	40,636	64,824	41,551	66,283	42,486	67,774	43,442	69,299	44,419	70,858	2.25%	11.25%	30,327	48,378	42,369	67,589	56,826	90,651
Transportation Worker	24,411	35,665	24,960	36,468	25,522	37,288	26,096	38,127	26,683	38,985	2.25%	11.25%	18,218	26,617	25,452	37,186	34,136	49,874
Utility Worker	29,185	42,604	29,842	43,563	30,513	44,543	31,200	45,545	31,902	46,570	2.25%	11.25%	21,781	31,795	30,430	44,421	40,813	59,578

Chart III - U.S. States & Cities - Job Titles - Salaries - Pension Estimates

CO-Denver	2010 (Min)	2010 (Max)	2011 (Min)	2011 (Max)	2012 (Min)	2012 (Max)	2013 (Min)	2013 (Max)	2014 (Min)	2014 (Max)	5-Year Average % Raise	5-Year Cumulative Raise Estimate**	20-Year Annual Pension Benefit Estimate (Min.)***	20-Year Annual Pension Benefit Estimate (Max.)	25-Year Annual Pension Benefit Estimate (Min.)	25-Year Annual Pension Benefit Estimate (Max.)	30-Year Annual Pension Benefit Estimate (Min.)	30-Year Annual Pension Benefit Estimate (Max.)
Wastewater Systems Data Investigator	43,444	63,394	44,421	64,821	45,420	66,279	46,442	67,771	47,487	69,295	2.25%	11.25%	32,422	47,311	45,296	66,098	60,752	88,651
Water Conservation Analyst	46,447	67,776	47,492	69,300	48,561	70,860	49,654	72,454	50,771	74,084	2.25%	11.25%	34,663	50,580	48,428	70,666	64,952	94,778
Water Quality Investigator	47,497	69,297	48,565	70,856	49,658	72,451	50,775	74,081	51,918	75,748	2.25%	11.25%	35,446	51,716	49,522	72,252	66,420	96,906
Zoo Veterinarian	71,553	114,144	73,163	116,712	74,809	119,338	76,493	122,024	78,214	124,769	2.25%	11.25%	53,400	85,185	74,605	119,012	100,061	159,620
Zoo Veterinary Technician	39,115	57,125	39,995	58,410	40,895	59,724	41,815	61,068	42,756	62,442	2.25%	11.25%	29,191	42,632	40,783	59,561	54,699	79,883
Zookeeper	38,866	56,731	39,740	58,007	40,634	59,313	41,549	60,647	42,483	62,012	2.25%	11.25%	29,005	42,338	40,523	59,150	54,350	79,333

http://www.denvergov.org/redirect_404/tabid/367615/tabid/382603/Default.aspx?

Chart III - U.S. States & Cities - Job Titles - Salaries - Pension Estimates

District of Columbia	2010 (Min)	2010 (Max)	2011 (Min)	2011 (Max)	2012 (Min)	2012 (Max)	2013 (Min)	2013 (Max)	2014 (Min)	2014 (Max)	5-Year Average % Raise	5-Year Cumulative Raise Estimate**	20-Year Annual Pension Benefit Estimate (Min.)***	20-Year Annual Pension Benefit Estimate (Max.)	25-Year Annual Pension Benefit Estimate (Min.)	25-Year Annual Pension Benefit Estimate (Max.)	30-Year Annual Pension Benefit Estimate (Min.)	30-Year Annual Pension Benefit Estimate (Max.)
Accountant	45,915	65,994	46,971	67,512	48,051	69,065	49,157	70,653	50,287	72,278	2.30%	11.50%	29,066	41,777	41,654	59,870	58,549	84,153
Accounting Technician	30,961	65,994	31,673	67,512	32,401	69,065	33,147	70,653	33,909	72,278	2.30%	11.50%	19,599	41,777	28,088	59,870	39,480	84,153
Actuary	45,915	65,994	46,971	67,512	48,051	69,065	49,157	70,653	50,287	72,278	2.30%	11.50%	29,066	41,777	41,654	59,870	58,549	84,153
Administration & Program Specialist	30,961	65,994	31,673	67,512	32,401	69,065	33,147	70,653	33,909	72,278	2.30%	11.50%	19,599	41,777	28,088	59,870	39,480	84,153
Administrative Assistant	25,043	65,994	25,619	67,512	26,209	69,065	26,811	70,653	27,428	72,278	2.30%	11.50%	15,853	41,777	22,719	59,870	31,934	84,153
Architect	45,915	65,994	46,971	67,512	48,051	69,065	49,157	70,653	50,287	72,278	2.30%	11.50%	29,066	41,777	41,654	59,870	58,549	84,153
Archivist	45,915	65,994	46,971	67,512	48,051	69,065	49,157	70,653	50,287	72,278	2.30%	11.50%	29,066	41,777	41,654	59,870	58,549	84,153
Assessor	45,915	65,994	46,971	67,512	48,051	69,065	49,157	70,653	50,287	72,278	2.30%	11.50%	29,066	41,777	41,654	59,870	58,549	84,153
Auditor	45,915	65,994	46,971	67,512	48,051	69,065	49,157	70,653	50,287	72,278	2.30%	11.50%	29,066	41,777	41,654	59,870	58,549	84,153
Biological Science Technician	30,961	65,994	31,673	67,512	32,401	69,065	33,147	70,653	33,909	72,278	2.30%	11.50%	19,599	41,777	28,088	59,870	39,480	84,153
Biologist	45,915	65,994	46,971	67,512	48,051	69,065	49,157	70,653	50,287	72,278	2.30%	11.50%	29,066	41,777	41,654	59,870	58,549	84,153
Budget Analyst	45,915	65,994	46,971	67,512	48,051	69,065	49,157	70,653	50,287	72,278	2.30%	11.50%	29,066	41,777	41,654	59,870	58,549	84,153
Chemist	45,915	65,994	46,971	67,512	48,051	69,065	49,157	70,653	50,287	72,278	2.30%	11.50%	29,066	41,777	41,654	59,870	58,549	84,153
Civil Engineer	45,915	65,994	46,971	67,512	48,051	69,065	49,157	70,653	50,287	72,278	2.30%	11.50%	29,066	41,777	41,654	59,870	58,549	84,153
Clerk Typist	25,043	65,994	25,619	67,512	26,209	69,065	26,811	70,653	27,428	72,278	2.30%	11.50%	15,853	41,777	22,719	59,870	31,934	84,153
Community Planner	45,915	65,994	46,971	67,512	48,051	69,065	49,157	70,653	50,287	72,278	2.30%	11.50%	29,066	41,777	41,654	59,870	58,549	84,153
Computer Assistant	25,043	65,994	25,619	67,512	26,209	69,065	26,811	70,653	27,428	72,278	2.30%	11.50%	15,853	41,777	22,719	59,870	31,934	84,153
Computer Operator	30,961	65,994	31,673	67,512	32,401	69,065	33,147	70,653	33,909	72,278	2.30%	11.50%	19,599	41,777	28,088	59,870	39,480	84,153
Computer Specialist	30,961	65,994	31,673	67,512	32,401	69,065	33,147	70,653	33,909	72,278	2.30%	11.50%	19,599	41,777	28,088	59,870	39,480	84,153
Construction Analyst	45,915	65,994	46,971	67,512	48,051	69,065	49,157	70,653	50,287	72,278	2.30%	11.50%	29,066	41,777	41,654	59,870	58,549	84,153
Consumer Safety Inspector	30,961	65,994	31,673	67,512	32,401	69,065	33,147	70,653	33,909	72,278	2.30%	11.50%	19,599	41,777	28,088	59,870	39,480	84,153
Contract Specialist	45,915	65,994	46,971	67,512	48,051	69,065	49,157	70,653	50,287	72,278	2.30%	11.50%	29,066	41,777	41,654	59,870	58,549	84,153
Correctional Officer	37,744	65,994	38,612	67,512	39,500	69,065	40,408	70,653	41,338	72,278	2.30%	11.50%	23,893	41,777	34,241	59,870	48,129	84,153
Correctional Program Specialist	33,213	65,994	33,977	67,512	34,758	69,065	35,557	70,653	36,375	72,278	2.30%	11.50%	21,025	41,777	30,130	59,870	42,352	84,153
Criminal Investigator	33,213	65,994	33,977	67,512	34,758	69,065	35,557	70,653	36,375	72,278	2.30%	11.50%	21,025	41,777	30,130	59,870	42,352	84,153
Early Childhood Education Specialist	45,915	65,994	46,971	67,512	48,051	69,065	49,157	70,653	50,287	72,278	2.30%	11.50%	29,066	41,777	41,654	59,870	58,549	84,153
Editorial Assistant	25,043	65,994	25,619	67,512	26,209	69,065	26,811	70,653	27,428	72,278	2.30%	11.50%	15,853	41,777	22,719	59,870	31,934	84,153
Educational Specialist	45,915	65,994	46,971	67,512	48,051	69,065	49,157	70,653	50,287	72,278	2.30%	11.50%	29,066	41,777	41,654	59,870	58,549	84,153
Electrical Engineer	45,915	65,994	46,971	67,512	48,051	69,065	49,157	70,653	50,287	72,278	2.30%	11.50%	29,066	41,777	41,654	59,870	58,549	84,153
Elevator Inspector	45,915	65,994	46,971	67,512	48,051	69,065	49,157	70,653	50,287	72,278	2.30%	11.50%	29,066	41,777	41,654	59,870	58,549	84,153
EMT/Paramedic	37,744	65,994	38,612	67,512	39,500	69,065	40,408	70,653	41,338	72,278	2.30%	11.50%	23,893	41,777	34,241	59,870	48,129	84,153
Engineer	45,915	65,994	46,971	67,512	48,051	69,065	49,157	70,653	50,287	72,278	2.30%	11.50%	29,066	41,777	41,654	59,870	58,549	84,153
Enviromental Protection Specialist	45,915	65,994	46,971	67,512	48,051	69,065	49,157	70,653	50,287	72,278	2.30%	11.50%	29,066	41,777	41,654	59,870	58,549	84,153
Equal Opportunity Specialist	45,915	65,994	46,971	67,512	48,051	69,065	49,157	70,653	50,287	72,278	2.30%	11.50%	29,066	41,777	41,654	59,870	58,549	84,153
Equipment Specialist	30,961	65,994	31,673	67,512	32,401	69,065	33,147	70,653	33,909	72,278	2.30%	11.50%	19,599	41,777	28,088	59,870	39,480	84,153
Financial Economist	45,915	65,994	46,971	67,512	48,051	69,065	49,157	70,653	50,287	72,278	2.30%	11.50%	29,066	41,777	41,654	59,870	58,549	84,153
Financial/Accounting/ Budget Specialist	45,915	65,994	46,971	67,512	48,051	69,065	49,157	70,653	50,287	72,278	2.30%	11.50%	29,066	41,777	41,654	59,870	58,549	84,153
Fingerprint Examiner	30,961	65,994	31,673	67,512	32,401	69,065	33,147	70,653	33,909	72,278	2.30%	11.50%	19,599	41,777	28,088	59,870	39,480	84,153
Fire Protection Specialist	33,213	65,994	33,977	67,512	34,758	69,065	35,557	70,653	36,375	72,278	2.30%	11.50%	21,025	41,777	30,130	59,870	42,352	84,153
Health Physicist	45,915	65,994	46,971	67,512	48,051	69,065	49,157	70,653	50,287	72,278	2.30%	11.50%	29,066	41,777	41,654	59,870	58,549	84,153
Health/Medical Specialist	45,915	65,994	46,971	67,512	48,051	69,065	49,157	70,653	50,287	72,278	2.30%	11.50%	29,066	41,777	41,654	59,870	58,549	84,153

Chart III - U.S. States & Cities - Job Titles - Salaries - Pension Estimates

District of Columbia	2010 (Min)	2010 (Max)	2011 (Min)	2011 (Max)	2012 (Min)	2012 (Max)	2013 (Min)	2013 (Max)	2014 (Min)	2014 (Max)	5-Year Average % Raise	5-Year Cumulative Raise Estimate**	20-Year Annual Pension Benefit Estimate (Min.)***	20-Year Annual Pension Benefit Estimate (Max.)	25-Year Annual Pension Benefit Estimate (Min.)	25-Year Annual Pension Benefit Estimate (Max.)	30-Year Annual Pension Benefit Estimate (Min.)	30-Year Annual Pension Benefit Estimate (Max.)
Highway Safety Specialist	45,915	65,994	46,971	67,512	48,051	69,065	49,157	70,653	50,287	72,278	2.30%	11.50%	29,066	41,777	41,654	59,870	58,549	84,153
Information Technology Specialist	30,961	65,994	31,673	67,512	32,401	69,065	33,147	70,653	33,909	72,278	2.30%	11.50%	19,599	41,777	28,088	59,870	39,480	84,153
Insurance Examiner	30,961	65,994	31,673	67,512	32,401	69,065	33,147	70,653	33,909	72,278	2.30%	11.50%	19,599	41,777	28,088	59,870	39,480	84,153
Investigator Specialist	30,961	65,994	31,673	67,512	32,401	69,065	33,147	70,653	33,909	72,278	2.30%	11.50%	19,599	41,777	28,088	59,870	39,480	84,153
Law Clerk	45,915	65,994	46,971	67,512	48,051	69,065	49,157	70,653	50,287	72,278	2.30%	11.50%	29,066	41,777	41,654	59,870	58,549	84,153
Legal Administrative Specialist	45,915	65,994	46,971	67,512	48,051	69,065	49,157	70,653	50,287	72,278	2.30%	11.50%	29,066	41,777	41,654	59,870	58,549	84,153
Legal Assistant	25,043	65,994	25,619	67,512	26,209	69,065	26,811	70,653	27,428	72,278	2.30%	11.50%	15,853	41,777	22,719	59,870	31,934	84,153
Legal Instruments Examiner	30,961	65,994	31,673	67,512	32,401	69,065	33,147	70,653	33,909	72,278	2.30%	11.50%	19,599	41,777	28,088	59,870	39,480	84,153
Librarian	45,915	65,994	46,971	67,512	48,051	69,065	49,157	70,653	50,287	72,278	2.30%	11.50%	29,066	41,777	41,654	59,870	58,549	84,153
Licensed Practical Nurse	35,794	65,994	36,617	67,512	37,460	69,065	38,321	70,653	39,202	72,278	2.30%	11.50%	22,659	41,777	32,472	59,870	45,643	84,153
Loan Specialist	45,915	65,994	46,971	67,512	48,051	69,065	49,157	70,653	50,287	72,278	2.30%	11.50%	29,066	41,777	41,654	59,870	58,549	84,153
Logistics Management Specialist	45,915	65,994	46,971	67,512	48,051	69,065	49,157	70,653	50,287	72,278	2.30%	11.50%	29,066	41,777	41,654	59,870	58,549	84,153
Mail/File Clerk	25,043	65,994	25,619	67,512	26,209	69,065	26,811	70,653	27,428	72,278	2.30%	11.50%	15,853	41,777	22,719	59,870	31,934	84,153
Management/Program Analyst	45,915	65,994	46,971	67,512	48,051	69,065	49,157	70,653	50,287	72,278	2.30%	11.50%	29,066	41,777	41,654	59,870	58,549	84,153
Manpower Development Specialist	30,961	65,994	31,673	67,512	32,401	69,065	33,147	70,653	33,909	72,278	2.30%	11.50%	19,599	41,777	28,088	59,870	39,480	84,153
Mechanical Engineer	45,915	65,994	46,971	67,512	48,051	69,065	49,157	70,653	50,287	72,278	2.30%	11.50%	29,066	41,777	41,654	59,870	58,549	84,153
Medical Instrument Technician	35,794	65,994	36,617	67,512	37,460	69,065	38,321	70,653	39,202	72,278	2.30%	11.50%	22,659	41,777	32,472	59,870	45,643	84,153
Medical Records Technician	30,961	65,994	31,673	67,512	32,401	69,065	33,147	70,653	33,909	72,278	2.30%	11.50%	19,599	41,777	28,088	59,870	39,480	84,153
Medical Technologist	35,794	65,994	36,617	67,512	37,460	69,065	38,321	70,653	39,202	72,278	2.30%	11.50%	22,659	41,777	32,472	59,870	45,643	84,153
Nursing Assistant	25,043	65,994	25,619	67,512	26,209	69,065	26,811	70,653	27,428	72,278	2.30%	11.50%	15,853	41,777	22,719	59,870	31,934	84,153
Operations Research Analyst	45,915	65,994	46,971	67,512	48,051	69,065	49,157	70,653	50,287	72,278	2.30%	11.50%	29,066	41,777	41,654	59,870	58,549	84,153
Paralegal Specialist	30,961	65,994	31,673	67,512	32,401	69,065	33,147	70,653	33,909	72,278	2.30%	11.50%	19,599	41,777	28,088	59,870	39,480	84,153
Pharmacist	45,915	65,994	46,971	67,512	48,051	69,065	49,157	70,653	50,287	72,278	2.30%	11.50%	29,066	41,777	41,654	59,870	58,549	84,153
Photographer	30,961	65,994	31,673	67,512	32,401	69,065	33,147	70,653	33,909	72,278	2.30%	11.50%	19,599	41,777	28,088	59,870	39,480	84,153
Program Compliance Technician	30,961	65,994	31,673	67,512	32,401	69,065	33,147	70,653	33,909	72,278	2.30%	11.50%	19,599	41,777	28,088	59,870	39,480	84,153
Property Disposal Specialist	45,915	65,994	46,971	67,512	48,051	69,065	49,157	70,653	50,287	72,278	2.30%	11.50%	29,066	41,777	41,654	59,870	58,549	84,153
Public Affairs Specialist	45,915	65,994	46,971	67,512	48,051	69,065	49,157	70,653	50,287	72,278	2.30%	11.50%	29,066	41,777	41,654	59,870	58,549	84,153
Purchasing Agent	30,961	65,994	31,673	67,512	32,401	69,065	33,147	70,653	33,909	72,278	2.30%	11.50%	19,599	41,777	28,088	59,870	39,480	84,153
Receptionist	25,043	65,994	25,619	67,512	26,209	69,065	26,811	70,653	27,428	72,278	2.30%	11.50%	15,853	41,777	22,719	59,870	31,934	84,153
Recreation Specialist	30,961	65,994	31,673	67,512	32,401	69,065	33,147	70,653	33,909	72,278	2.30%	11.50%	19,599	41,777	28,088	59,870	39,480	84,153
Revenue Officer	45,915	65,994	46,971	67,512	48,051	69,065	49,157	70,653	50,287	72,278	2.30%	11.50%	29,066	41,777	41,654	59,870	58,549	84,153
Safety and Occupational Health Specialist	45,915	65,994	46,971	67,512	48,051	69,065	49,157	70,653	50,287	72,278	2.30%	11.50%	29,066	41,777	41,654	59,870	58,549	84,153
Sanitarian	35,794	65,994	36,617	67,512	37,460	69,065	38,321	70,653	39,202	72,278	2.30%	11.50%	22,659	41,777	32,472	59,870	45,643	84,153
Secretary	25,043	65,994	25,619	67,512	26,209	69,065	26,811	70,653	27,428	72,278	2.30%	11.50%	15,853	41,777	22,719	59,870	31,934	84,153
Social Insurance Specialist	45,915	65,994	46,971	67,512	48,051	69,065	49,157	70,653	50,287	72,278	2.30%	11.50%	29,066	41,777	41,654	59,870	58,549	84,153
Social Work Associate	45,915	65,994	46,971	67,512	48,051	69,065	49,157	70,653	50,287	72,278	2.30%	11.50%	29,066	41,777	41,654	59,870	58,549	84,153
Special Police Officer	37,744	65,994	38,612	67,512	39,500	69,065	40,408	70,653	41,338	72,278	2.30%	11.50%	23,893	41,777	34,241	59,870	48,129	84,153

Chart III - U.S. States & Cities - Job Titles - Salaries - Pension Estimates

District of Columbia	2010 (Min)	2010 (Max)	2011 (Min)	2011 (Max)	2012 (Min)	2012 (Max)	2013 (Min)	2013 (Max)	2014 (Min)	2014 (Max)	5-Year Average % Raise	5-Year Cumulative Raise Estimate**	20-Year Annual Pension Benefit Estimate (Min.)***	20-Year Annual Pension Benefit Estimate (Max.)	25-Year Annual Pension Benefit Estimate (Min.)	25-Year Annual Pension Benefit Estimate (Max.)	30-Year Annual Pension Benefit Estimate (Min.)	30-Year Annual Pension Benefit Estimate (Max.)
Speech and Language Specialist	45,915	65,994	46,971	67,512	48,051	69,065	49,157	70,653	50,287	72,278	2.30%	11.50%	29,066	41,777	41,654	59,870	58,549	84,153
Statistician	45,915	65,994	46,971	67,512	48,051	69,065	49,157	70,653	50,287	72,278	2.30%	11.50%	29,066	41,777	41,654	59,870	58,549	84,153
Supply Management Specialist	30,961	65,994	31,673	67,512	32,401	69,065	33,147	70,653	33,909	72,278	2.30%	11.50%	19,599	41,777	28,088	59,870	39,480	84,153
Tax Auditor	45,915	65,994	46,971	67,512	48,051	69,065	49,157	70,653	50,287	72,278	2.30%	11.50%	29,066	41,777	41,654	59,870	58,549	84,153
Technical Writer	30,961	65,994	31,673	67,512	32,401	69,065	33,147	70,653	33,909	72,278	2.30%	11.50%	19,599	41,777	28,088	59,870	39,480	84,153
Telecommunications Equipment Operator	33,213	65,994	33,977	67,512	34,758	69,065	35,557	70,653	36,375	72,278	2.30%	11.50%	21,025	41,777	30,130	59,870	42,352	84,153
Telecommunications Specialist	30,961	65,994	31,673	67,512	32,401	69,065	33,147	70,653	33,909	72,278	2.30%	11.50%	19,599	41,777	28,088	59,870	39,480	84,153
Training Instructor	45,915	65,994	46,971	67,512	48,051	69,065	49,157	70,653	50,287	72,278	2.30%	11.50%	29,066	41,777	41,654	59,870	58,549	84,153
Transportation Specialist	45,915	65,994	46,971	67,512	48,051	69,065	49,157	70,653	50,287	72,278	2.30%	11.50%	29,066	41,777	41,654	59,870	58,549	84,153
Unemploy Comp Claims Examiner	45,915	65,994	46,971	67,512	48,051	69,065	49,157	70,653	50,287	72,278	2.30%	11.50%	29,066	41,777	41,654	59,870	58,549	84,153
Video Production Specialist	68,450	65,994	70,025	67,512	71,635	69,065	73,283	70,653	74,968	72,278	2.30%	11.50%	43,332	41,777	62,098	59,870	87,285	84,153
Vocational Rehabilitation Specialist	45,915	65,994	46,971	67,512	48,051	69,065	49,157	70,653	50,287	72,278	2.30%	11.50%	29,066	41,777	41,654	59,870	58,549	84,153
Workers Comp Claims Examiner	30,961	65,994	31,673	67,512	32,401	69,065	33,147	70,653	33,909	72,278	2.30%	11.50%	19,599	41,777	28,088	59,870	39,480	84,153

http://www.dcop.dc.gov/dcop/cwp/view,a,1219,q,529980,dcopNav,|31656|.asp

Chart III - U.S. States & Cities - Job Titles - Salaries - Pension Estimates

Florida	2010 (Min)	2010 (Max)	2011 (Min)	2011 (Max)	2012 (Min)	2012 (Max)	2013 (Min)	2013 (Max)	2014 (Min)	2014 (Max)	5-Year Average % Raise	5-Year Cumulative Raise Estimate**	20-Year Annual Pension Benefit Estimate (Min.)***	20-Year Annual Pension Benefit Estimate (Max.)	25-Year Annual Pension Benefit Estimate (Min.)	25-Year Annual Pension Benefit Estimate (Max.)	30-Year Annual Pension Benefit Estimate (Min.)	30-Year Annual Pension Benefit Estimate (Max.)
Accountants And Auditors Level 1-4	23,712	94,813	24,245	96,947	24,791	99,128	25,349	101,358	25,919	103,639	2.25%	11.25%	10,838	43,336	15,142	60,544	20,308	81,203
Actuaries Level 3-5	33,472	205,929	34,226	210,563	34,996	215,300	35,783	220,145	36,588	225,098	2.25%	11.25%	15,299	94,123	21,374	131,499	28,667	176,368
Administrat Law Judge/Adjud/Hear Officer Level 1-5	25,846	173,325	26,428	177,224	27,022	181,212	27,630	185,289	28,252	189,458	2.25%	11.25%	11,813	79,221	16,504	110,679	22,136	148,444
Administrative Services Managers Level 1-4	51,721	215,057	52,884	219,896	54,074	224,843	55,291	229,902	56,535	235,075	2.25%	11.25%	23,640	98,295	33,027	137,328	44,296	184,186
Agricultural Inspectors Level 2-4	25,846	86,987	26,428	88,944	27,022	90,945	27,630	92,991	28,252	95,084	2.25%	11.25%	11,813	39,759	16,504	55,547	22,136	74,500
Archivists Level 1-3	19,959	86,987	20,408	88,944	20,867	90,945	21,336	92,991	21,816	95,084	2.25%	11.25%	9,122	39,759	12,745	55,547	17,094	74,500
Art Directors Level 3-4	30,708	86,987	31,399	88,944	32,105	90,945	32,828	92,991	33,566	95,084	2.25%	11.25%	14,036	39,759	19,609	55,547	26,300	74,500
Automotive Service Technician & Mechanic Level 1-2	18,311	61,622	18,723	63,008	19,144	64,426	19,575	65,875	20,015	67,358	2.25%	11.25%	8,369	28,165	11,692	39,349	15,682	52,776
Biological Scientists, All Other Level 1-3	25,846	94,813	26,428	96,947	27,022	99,128	27,630	101,358	28,252	103,639	2.25%	11.25%	11,813	43,336	16,504	60,544	22,136	81,203
Biological Technicians Level 1-2	19,959	67,169	20,408	68,680	20,867	70,225	21,336	71,805	21,816	73,421	2.25%	11.25%	9,122	30,700	12,745	42,891	17,094	57,527
Business Operation Specialist, All Other Level 1-4	21,755	103,348	22,245	105,673	22,745	108,051	23,257	110,482	23,780	112,968	2.25%	11.25%	9,943	47,237	13,892	65,994	18,632	88,512
Cashiers Level 1-2	19,959	56,536	20,408	57,808	20,867	59,109	21,336	60,439	21,816	61,799	2.25%	11.25%	9,122	25,841	12,745	36,102	17,094	48,420
Chemists Level 1-2	25,846	86,987	26,428	88,944	27,022	90,945	27,630	92,991	28,252	95,084	2.25%	11.25%	11,813	39,759	16,504	55,547	22,136	74,500
Chief Executives Level 1-3	51,721	309,682	52,884	316,650	54,074	323,775	55,291	331,059	56,535	338,508	2.25%	11.25%	23,640	141,545	33,027	197,752	44,296	265,227
Claims Adjuster, Examiner & Investigator Level 1-4	21,755	103,348	22,245	105,673	22,745	108,051	23,257	110,482	23,780	112,968	2.25%	11.25%	9,943	47,237	13,892	65,994	18,632	88,512
Community And Social Service Managers Level 1-4	23,126	187,806	23,646	192,032	24,178	196,353	24,722	200,771	25,279	205,288	2.25%	11.25%	10,570	85,840	14,767	119,926	19,806	160,847
Community/Social Service Spec/All Other Level 1-4	19,959	94,813	20,408	96,947	20,867	99,128	21,336	101,358	21,816	103,639	2.25%	11.25%	9,122	43,336	12,745	60,544	17,094	81,203
Comp, Benefit & Job Analysis Spec Level 1-4	21,755	103,348	22,245	105,673	22,745	108,051	23,257	110,482	23,780	112,968	2.25%	11.25%	9,943	47,237	13,892	65,994	18,632	88,512
Compensation And Benefits Managers Level 1-3	51,721	187,806	52,884	192,032	54,074	196,353	55,291	200,771	56,535	205,288	2.25%	11.25%	23,640	85,840	33,027	119,926	44,296	160,847
Compliance Officers Level 1-4	21,755	103,348	22,245	105,673	22,745	108,051	23,257	110,482	23,780	112,968	2.25%	11.25%	9,943	47,237	13,892	65,994	18,632	88,512
Computer & Information Systems Managers Level 1-3	51,721	187,806	52,884	192,032	54,074	196,353	55,291	200,771	56,535	205,288	2.25%	11.25%	23,640	85,840	33,027	119,926	44,296	160,847
Computer Programmers Level 1-4	23,712	94,813	24,245	96,947	24,791	99,128	25,349	101,358	25,919	103,639	2.25%	11.25%	10,838	43,336	15,142	60,544	20,308	81,203
Computer Specialists, All Other Level 1-4	23,712	94,813	24,245	96,947	24,791	99,128	25,349	101,358	25,919	103,639	2.25%	11.25%	10,838	43,336	15,142	60,544	20,308	81,203
Computer Support Specialists Level 1-4	23,712	94,813	24,245	96,947	24,791	99,128	25,349	101,358	25,919	103,639	2.25%	11.25%	10,838	43,336	15,142	60,544	20,308	81,203
Computer Systems Analysts Level 3-4	33,472	94,813	34,226	96,947	34,996	99,128	35,783	101,358	36,588	103,639	2.25%	11.25%	15,299	43,336	21,374	60,544	28,667	81,203
Construction Managers Level 1-3	51,721	150,248	52,884	153,629	54,074	157,085	55,291	160,620	56,535	164,234	2.25%	11.25%	23,640	68,673	33,027	95,943	44,296	128,680
Correctional Enforcement Level 1-6	30,708	122,789	31,399	125,552	32,105	128,377	32,828	131,265	33,566	134,219	2.25%	11.25%	14,036	56,123	19,609	78,409	26,300	105,163
Counselors, All Other Level 1-3	19,959	79,803	20,408	81,599	20,867	83,435	21,336	85,312	21,816	87,231	2.25%	11.25%	9,122	36,475	12,745	50,959	17,094	68,347
Database Administrators Level 2-4	28,173	94,813	28,807	96,947	29,455	99,128	30,118	101,358	30,796	103,639	2.25%	11.25%	12,877	43,336	17,990	60,544	24,129	81,203

Chart III - U.S. States & Cities - Job Titles - Salaries - Pension Estimates

Florida	2010 (Min)	2010 (Max)	2011 (Min)	2011 (Max)	2012 (Min)	2012 (Max)	2013 (Min)	2013 (Max)	2014 (Min)	2014 (Max)	5-Year Average % Raise	5-Year Cumulative Raise Estimate**	20-Year Annual Pension Benefit Estimate (Min.)***	20-Year Annual Pension Benefit Estimate (Max.)	25-Year Annual Pension Benefit Estimate (Min.)	25-Year Annual Pension Benefit Estimate (Max.)	30-Year Annual Pension Benefit Estimate (Min.)	30-Year Annual Pension Benefit Estimate (Max.)
Dental Assistants Level 2-3	21,755	61,622	22,245	63,008	22,745	64,426	23,257	65,875	23,780	67,358	2.25%	11.25%	9,943	28,165	13,892	39,349	18,632	52,776
Detectives And Criminal Investigators Level 1-5	25,846	122,789	26,428	125,552	27,022	128,377	27,630	131,265	28,252	134,219	2.25%	11.25%	11,813	56,123	16,504	78,409	22,136	105,163
Dietitians And Nutritionists Level 1-4	28,173	103,348	28,807	105,673	29,455	108,051	30,118	110,482	30,796	112,968	2.25%	11.25%	12,877	47,237	17,990	65,994	24,129	88,512
Education Administrators, All Other Level 1-3	51,721	150,248	52,884	153,629	54,074	157,085	55,291	160,620	56,535	164,234	2.25%	11.25%	23,640	68,673	33,027	95,943	44,296	128,680
Education/Train/ Library Worker/All Other Level 2-4	25,846	94,813	26,428	96,947	27,022	99,128	27,630	101,358	28,252	103,639	2.25%	11.25%	11,813	43,336	16,504	60,544	22,136	81,203
Electric/Electron Repr/Comr Indust Equip Level 1-3	18,311	73,215	18,723	74,862	19,144	76,547	19,575	78,269	20,015	80,030	2.25%	11.25%	8,369	33,464	11,692	46,752	15,682	62,705
Engineering Managers Level 1-4	51,721	187,806	52,884	192,032	54,074	196,353	55,291	200,771	56,535	205,288	2.25%	11.25%	23,640	85,840	33,027	119,926	44,296	160,847
Engineering Technicians, All Other Level 1-2	21,755	73,215	22,245	74,862	22,745	76,547	23,257	78,269	23,780	80,030	2.25%	11.25%	9,943	33,464	13,892	46,752	18,632	62,705
Engineering, All Other Level 2-5	28,173	122,789	28,807	125,552	29,455	128,377	30,118	131,265	30,796	134,219	2.25%	11.25%	12,877	56,123	17,990	78,409	24,129	105,163
Environ Science/ Protect Tech, Incl Hlth Level 1-4	19,959	94,813	20,408	96,947	20,867	99,128	21,336	101,358	21,816	103,639	2.25%	11.25%	9,122	43,336	12,745	60,544	17,094	81,203
Environmen Scientist & Spec, Incl Hlth Level 1-4	25,846	122,789	26,428	125,552	27,022	128,377	27,630	131,265	28,252	134,219	2.25%	11.25%	11,813	56,123	16,504	78,409	22,136	105,163
Executive Secretaries & Admin Assistants Level 1-5	18,311	103,348	18,723	105,673	19,144	108,051	19,575	110,482	20,015	112,968	2.25%	11.25%	8,369	47,237	11,692	65,994	15,682	88,512
Farm, Ranch & Other Agricultural Manager Level 2-4	28,908	187,806	29,558	192,032	30,223	196,353	30,903	200,771	31,598	205,288	2.25%	11.25%	13,213	85,840	18,459	119,926	24,758	160,847
Farm, Ranch & Other Agricultural Managerlevel 1	51,721	215,057	52,884	219,896	54,074	224,843	55,291	229,902	56,535	235,075	2.25%	11.25%	23,640	98,295	33,027	137,328	44,296	184,186
File Clerks Level 2-3	21,755	67,169	22,245	68,680	22,745	70,225	23,257	71,805	23,780	73,421	2.25%	11.25%	9,943	30,700	13,892	42,891	18,632	57,527
Financial Analysts Level 1-4	23,712	94,813	24,245	96,947	24,791	99,128	25,349	101,358	25,919	103,639	2.25%	11.25%	10,838	43,336	15,142	60,544	20,308	81,203
Financial Managers Level 1-4	51,721	187,806	52,884	192,032	54,074	196,353	55,291	200,771	56,535	205,288	2.25%	11.25%	23,640	85,840	33,027	119,926	44,296	160,847
Financial Specialists, All Other Level 1-4	23,712	94,813	24,245	96,947	24,791	99,128	25,349	101,358	25,919	103,639	2.25%	11.25%	10,838	43,336	15,142	60,544	20,308	81,203
Food Service Manager Level 1-3	23,126	150,248	23,646	153,629	24,178	157,085	24,722	160,620	25,279	164,234	2.25%	11.25%	10,570	68,673	14,767	95,943	19,806	128,680
Forensic Science Technicians Level 1-4	19,959	94,813	20,408	96,947	20,867	99,128	21,336	101,358	21,816	103,639	2.25%	11.25%	9,122	43,336	12,745	60,544	17,094	81,203
Forest And Conservation Workers Level 1-2	30,708	86,987	31,399	88,944	32,105	90,945	32,828	92,991	33,566	95,084	2.25%	11.25%	14,036	39,759	19,609	55,547	26,300	74,500
General And Operations Managers Level 1-4	51,721	187,806	52,884	192,032	54,074	196,353	55,291	200,771	56,535	205,288	2.25%	11.25%	23,640	85,840	33,027	119,926	44,296	160,847
Geoscientist/ Except Hydrologi & Geograph Level 2-4	33,472	122,789	34,226	125,552	34,996	128,377	35,783	131,265	36,588	134,219	2.25%	11.25%	15,299	56,123	21,374	78,409	28,667	105,163
Health Care Support Workers, All Other Level 1-3	19,959	61,622	20,408	63,008	20,867	64,426	21,336	65,875	21,816	67,358	2.25%	11.25%	9,122	28,165	12,745	39,349	17,094	52,776
Health Educators Level 1-4	19,959	94,813	20,408	96,947	20,867	99,128	21,336	101,358	21,816	103,639	2.25%	11.25%	9,122	43,336	12,745	60,544	17,094	81,203
Heating/Air Cond/ Refrig Mechanc/ Instaler Level 2-3	23,712	73,215	24,245	74,862	24,791	76,547	25,349	78,269	25,919	80,030	2.25%	11.25%	10,838	33,464	15,142	46,752	20,308	62,705
Highway Maintenance Workers Level 1-3	19,959	73,215	20,408	74,862	20,867	76,547	21,336	78,269	21,816	80,030	2.25%	11.25%	9,122	33,464	12,745	46,752	17,094	62,705
Historians Level 1-4	25,846	112,648	26,428	115,183	27,022	117,775	27,630	120,425	28,252	123,134	2.25%	11.25%	11,813	51,488	16,504	71,933	22,136	96,478

Chart III - U.S. States & Cities - Job Titles - Salaries - Pension Estimates

Florida	2010 (Min)	2010 (Max)	2011 (Min)	2011 (Max)	2012 (Min)	2012 (Max)	2013 (Min)	2013 (Max)	2014 (Min)	2014 (Max)	5-Year Average % Raise	5-Year Cumulative Raise Estimate**	20-Year Annual Pension Benefit Estimate (Min.)***	20-Year Annual Pension Benefit Estimate (Max.)	25-Year Annual Pension Benefit Estimate (Min.)	25-Year Annual Pension Benefit Estimate (Max.)	30-Year Annual Pension Benefit Estimate (Min.)	30-Year Annual Pension Benefit Estimate (Max.)
Home Health Aides Level 1-3	19,959	61,622	20,408	63,008	20,867	64,426	21,336	65,875	21,816	67,358	2.25%	11.25%	9,122	28,165	12,745	39,349	17,094	52,776
Human Resour/Train/Labr Relat Spec, Othr Level 1-4	21,755	103,348	22,245	105,673	22,745	108,051	23,257	110,482	23,780	112,968	2.25%	11.25%	9,943	47,237	13,892	65,994	18,632	88,512
Human Resources Managers Level 1-3	51,721	150,248	52,884	153,629	54,074	157,085	55,291	160,620	56,535	164,234	2.25%	11.25%	23,640	68,673	33,027	95,943	44,296	128,680
Human Resources Managers, All Other Level 1-4	51,721	187,806	52,884	192,032	54,074	196,353	55,291	200,771	56,535	205,288	2.25%	11.25%	23,640	85,840	33,027	119,926	44,296	160,847
Information And Record Clerks, All Other Level 2-3	21,755	67,169	22,245	68,680	22,745	70,225	23,257	71,805	23,780	73,421	2.25%	11.25%	9,943	30,700	13,892	42,891	18,632	57,527
Install, Maint/Repair Worker, All Other Level 1-3	18,311	73,215	18,723	74,862	19,144	76,547	19,575	78,269	20,015	80,030	2.25%	11.25%	8,369	33,464	11,692	46,752	15,682	62,705
Insurance Analysts/Advisors Level 1-3	23,712	86,987	24,245	88,944	24,791	90,945	25,349	92,991	25,919	95,084	2.25%	11.25%	10,838	39,759	15,142	55,547	20,308	74,500
Law Clerks Level 1-3	25,846	103,348	26,428	105,673	27,022	108,051	27,630	110,482	28,252	112,968	2.25%	11.25%	11,813	47,237	16,504	65,994	22,136	88,512
Lawyers Level 3-5	39,768	173,325	40,663	177,224	41,578	181,212	42,513	185,289	43,470	189,458	2.25%	11.25%	18,177	79,221	25,394	110,679	34,059	148,444
Management Analysts Level 1-4	21,755	103,348	22,245	105,673	22,745	108,051	23,257	110,482	23,780	112,968	2.25%	11.25%	9,943	47,237	13,892	65,994	18,632	88,512
Managers, All Other Level 1-2	51,721	258,068	52,884	263,875	54,074	269,812	55,291	275,883	56,535	282,090	2.25%	11.25%	23,640	117,954	33,027	164,793	44,296	221,023
Market Research Analysts Level 1-4	25,846	112,648	26,428	115,183	27,022	117,775	27,630	120,425	28,252	123,134	2.25%	11.25%	11,813	51,488	16,504	71,933	22,136	96,478
Marketing Managers Level 1-Level 4	23,126	187,806	23,646	192,032	24,178	196,353	24,722	200,771	25,279	205,288	2.25%	11.25%	10,570	85,840	14,767	119,926	19,806	160,847
Medical & Clinical Lab Technologists Level 3-4	25,846	94,813	26,428	96,947	27,022	99,128	27,630	101,358	28,252	103,639	2.25%	11.25%	11,813	43,336	16,504	60,544	22,136	81,203
Medical & Clinical Laboratory Technician Level 1-3	19,959	67,169	20,408	68,680	20,867	70,225	21,336	71,805	21,816	73,421	2.25%	11.25%	9,122	30,700	12,745	42,891	17,094	57,527
Medical And Health Services Managers Level 1-4	51,721	187,806	52,884	192,032	54,074	196,353	55,291	200,771	56,535	205,288	2.25%	11.25%	23,640	85,840	33,027	119,926	44,296	160,847
Medical Assistants Level 2	21,755	56,536	22,245	57,808	22,745	59,109	23,257	60,439	23,780	61,799	2.25%	11.25%	9,943	25,841	13,892	36,102	18,632	48,420
Motor Vehicle Supertors, All Other Level 1	18,311	47,585	18,723	48,655	19,144	49,750	19,575	50,870	20,015	52,014	2.25%	11.25%	8,369	21,749	11,692	30,386	15,682	40,754
Natural Sciences Managers Level 1-4	51,721	187,806	52,884	192,032	54,074	196,353	55,291	200,771	56,535	205,288	2.25%	11.25%	23,640	85,840	33,027	119,926	44,296	160,847
Network & Computer Systems Administrator Level 1-4	28,173	94,813	28,807	96,947	29,455	99,128	30,118	101,358	30,796	103,639	2.25%	11.25%	12,877	43,336	17,990	60,544	24,129	81,203
Network System & Data Communicat Analyst Level 1-4	23,712	94,813	24,245	96,947	24,791	99,128	25,349	101,358	25,919	103,639	2.25%	11.25%	10,838	43,336	15,142	60,544	20,308	81,203
Office & Admin Support Worker, All Other Level 1-5	18,311	103,348	18,723	105,673	19,144	108,051	19,575	110,482	20,015	112,968	2.25%	11.25%	8,369	47,237	11,692	65,994	15,682	88,512
Paralegals And Legal Assistants Level 1	25,846	67,169	26,428	68,680	27,022	70,225	27,630	71,805	28,252	73,421	2.25%	11.25%	11,813	30,700	16,504	42,891	22,136	57,527
Physical Scientists, All Other Level 1-4	25,846	122,789	26,428	125,552	27,022	128,377	27,630	131,265	28,252	134,219	2.25%	11.25%	11,813	56,123	16,504	78,409	22,136	105,163
Probation Officer & Corr Treatment Spec Level 1-4	23,712	86,987	24,245	88,944	24,791	90,945	25,349	92,991	25,919	95,084	2.25%	11.25%	10,838	39,759	15,142	55,547	20,308	74,500
Property And Real Estate Managers Level 1-4	23,126	187,806	23,646	192,032	24,178	196,353	24,722	200,771	25,279	205,288	2.25%	11.25%	10,570	85,840	14,767	119,926	19,806	160,847
Public Relations Managers Level 1-3	51,721	187,806	52,884	192,032	54,074	196,353	55,291	200,771	56,535	205,288	2.25%	11.25%	23,640	85,840	33,027	119,926	44,296	160,847
Public Relations Specialists Level 1-2	21,755	73,215	22,245	74,862	22,745	76,547	23,257	78,269	23,780	80,030	2.25%	11.25%	9,943	33,464	13,892	46,752	18,632	62,705
Purchasing Managers Level 1-3	51,721	150,248	52,884	153,629	54,074	157,085	55,291	160,620	56,535	164,234	2.25%	11.25%	23,640	68,673	33,027	95,943	44,296	128,680

Chart III - U.S. States & Cities - Job Titles - Salaries - Pension Estimates

Florida	2010 (Min)	2010 (Max)	2011 (Min)	2011 (Max)	2012 (Min)	2012 (Max)	2013 (Min)	2013 (Max)	2014 (Min)	2014 (Max)	5-Year Average % Raise	5-Year Cumulative Raise Estimate**	20-Year Annual Pension Benefit Estimate (Min.)***	20-Year Annual Pension Benefit Estimate (Max.)	25-Year Annual Pension Benefit Estimate (Min.)	25-Year Annual Pension Benefit Estimate (Max.)	30-Year Annual Pension Benefit Estimate (Min.)	30-Year Annual Pension Benefit Estimate (Max.)
Registered Nurses Level 1-4	28,173	103,348	28,807	105,673	29,455	108,051	30,118	110,482	30,796	112,968	2.25%	11.25%	12,877	47,237	17,990	65,994	24,129	88,512
Rehabilitation Counselors Level 2-4	25,846	94,813	26,428	96,947	27,022	99,128	27,630	101,358	28,252	103,639	2.25%	11.25%	11,813	43,336	16,504	60,544	22,136	81,203
Social And Human Service Assistants Level 1	19,959	51,867	20,408	53,034	20,867	54,227	21,336	55,447	21,816	56,695	2.25%	11.25%	9,122	23,707	12,745	33,120	17,094	44,422
Statisticians Level 1-3	21,755	86,987	22,245	88,944	22,745	90,945	23,257	92,991	23,780	95,084	2.25%	11.25%	9,943	39,759	13,892	55,547	18,632	74,500
Surveyors Level 2-5	28,173	122,789	28,807	125,552	29,455	128,377	30,118	131,265	30,796	134,219	2.25%	11.25%	12,877	56,123	17,990	78,409	24,129	105,163
Teachers And Instructors, All Other Level 2-4	25,846	94,813	26,428	96,947	27,022	99,128	27,630	101,358	28,252	103,639	2.25%	11.25%	11,813	43,336	16,504	60,544	22,136	81,203
Telecomm Equp Instal/Repr Ex Line Instal Level 1-3	18,311	73,215	18,723	74,862	19,144	76,547	19,575	78,269	20,015	80,030	2.25%	11.25%	8,369	33,464	11,692	46,752	15,682	62,705
Training And Development Managers Level 1-3	51,721	150,248	52,884	153,629	54,074	157,085	55,291	160,620	56,535	164,234	2.25%	11.25%	23,640	68,673	33,027	95,943	44,296	128,680
Training And Development Specialists Level 1-4	21,755	103,348	22,245	105,673	22,745	108,051	23,257	110,482	23,780	112,968	2.25%	11.25%	9,943	47,237	13,892	65,994	18,632	88,512
Transportation, Storage & Distribut Mgr Level 1	23,126	96,158	23,646	98,321	24,178	100,533	24,722	102,795	25,279	105,108	2.25%	11.25%	10,570	43,950	14,767	61,403	19,806	82,354
Word Processors And Typists Level 1-2	18,311	56,536	18,723	57,808	19,144	59,109	19,575	60,439	20,015	61,799	2.25%	11.25%	8,369	25,841	11,692	36,102	15,682	48,420

http://sun6.dms.state.fl.us/owa_broadband/owa/broadband_www.BROADBAND_MENU.BB_MENU

Chart III - U.S. States & Cities - Job Titles - Salaries - Pension Estimates

FL-Miami	2010 (Min)	2010 (Max)	2011 (Min)	2011 (Max)	2012 (Min)	2012 (Max)	2013 (Min)	2013 (Max)	2014 (Min)	2014 (Max)	5-Year Average % Raise	5-Year Cumula-tive Raise Esti-mate**	20-Year Annual Pension Benefit Estimate (Min.)***	20-Year Annual Pension Benefit Estimate (Max.)	25-Year Annual Pension Benefit Estimate (Min.)	25-Year Annual Pension Benefit Estimate (Max.)	30-Year Annual Pension Benefit Estimate (Min.)	30-Year Annual Pension Benefit Estimate (Max.)
Account Clerk	32,383	88,597	33,128	90,635	33,890	92,719	34,669	94,852	35,467	97,034	2.30%	11.50%	20,500	56,085	29,378	80,375	41,294	112,976
Accountant	41,545	69,636	42,500	71,238	43,478	72,876	44,478	74,553	45,501	76,267	2.30%	11.50%	26,299	44,082	37,689	63,174	52,976	88,798
Accountant Supervisor	55,702	76,497	56,983	78,257	58,293	80,056	59,634	81,898	61,006	83,781	2.30%	11.50%	35,261	48,426	50,532	69,398	71,029	97,546
Administrative Aide	37,732	63,098	38,600	64,550	39,488	66,034	40,396	67,553	41,325	69,107	2.30%	11.50%	23,886	39,944	34,231	57,243	48,115	80,461
Administrative Aide I-II	37,733	69,636	38,601	71,238	39,488	72,876	40,397	74,553	41,326	76,267	2.30%	11.50%	23,886	44,082	34,231	63,174	48,115	88,798
Administrative Assistant I-III	48,143	108,139	49,250	110,626	50,383	113,170	51,542	115,773	52,727	118,436	2.30%	11.50%	30,476	68,456	43,675	98,103	61,390	137,895
Administrative Secretary I-II	35,842	66,350	36,667	67,876	37,510	69,437	38,373	71,034	39,255	72,668	2.30%	11.50%	22,689	42,002	32,516	60,193	45,705	84,607
Application Developer	67,713	113,466	69,270	116,076	70,864	118,745	72,493	121,477	74,161	124,271	2.30%	11.50%	42,865	71,828	61,429	102,936	86,345	144,688
Architect I-III	50,609	88,597	51,773	90,635	52,964	92,719	54,182	94,852	55,428	97,034	2.30%	11.50%	32,038	56,085	45,913	80,375	64,535	112,976
Audit Manager	71,076	119,104	72,711	121,844	74,384	124,646	76,094	127,513	77,845	130,446	2.30%	11.50%	44,994	75,398	64,480	108,051	90,634	151,878
Auditor	43,626	73,130	44,629	74,812	45,656	76,533	46,706	78,293	47,780	80,094	2.30%	11.50%	27,617	46,294	39,577	66,343	55,630	93,253
Auditor Assistant	35,842	60,158	36,667	61,541	37,510	62,957	38,373	64,405	39,255	65,886	2.30%	11.50%	22,689	38,082	32,516	54,575	45,705	76,711
Automotive Parts Specialist I-II	30,910	46,953	31,621	48,033	32,348	49,138	33,092	50,268	33,853	51,424	2.30%	11.50%	19,567	29,723	28,041	42,596	39,415	59,873
Budget & Financial Support Advisor	45,900	76,763	46,956	78,528	48,036	80,334	49,141	82,182	50,271	84,072	2.30%	11.50%	29,057	48,594	41,641	69,639	58,530	97,885
Budget Analyst	53,107	88,905	54,328	90,950	55,578	93,042	56,856	95,181	58,164	97,371	2.30%	11.50%	33,619	56,280	48,178	80,654	67,720	113,368
Budget and Financial Support Advisor, Senior	58,425	98,003	59,768	100,257	61,143	102,562	62,549	104,921	63,988	107,335	2.30%	11.50%	36,985	62,039	53,003	88,908	74,501	124,969
Budget Assistant	41,545	57,157	42,500	58,472	43,478	59,817	44,478	61,192	45,501	62,600	2.30%	11.50%	26,299	36,183	37,689	51,853	52,976	72,885
Budget Coordinator	61,436	103,019	62,849	105,388	64,294	107,812	65,773	110,292	67,286	112,829	2.30%	11.50%	38,891	65,215	55,734	93,459	78,340	131,366
Building Inspector I-III	53,107	84,322	54,329	86,261	55,578	88,245	56,857	90,275	58,164	92,351	2.30%	11.50%	33,619	53,379	48,179	76,497	67,721	107,524
Building Roofing Inspector I	50,609	69,395	51,773	70,991	52,964	72,624	54,182	74,295	55,428	76,003	2.30%	11.50%	32,038	43,930	45,913	62,955	64,535	88,490
Business Developer	50,609	69,395	51,773	70,991	52,964	72,624	54,182	74,295	55,428	76,003	2.30%	11.50%	32,038	43,930	45,913	62,955	64,535	88,490
Business Development Coordinator	74,664	124,985	76,381	127,860	78,138	130,800	79,935	133,809	81,774	136,887	2.30%	11.50%	47,265	79,120	67,735	113,386	95,209	159,376
Business Development Supervisor	64,479	108,139	65,962	110,626	67,479	113,170	69,031	115,773	70,618	118,436	2.30%	11.50%	40,817	68,456	58,495	98,103	82,221	137,895
Business Process Analyst	61,436	103,019	62,849	105,388	64,294	107,812	65,773	110,292	67,286	112,829	2.30%	11.50%	38,891	65,215	55,734	93,459	78,340	131,366
Business System Administrator	67,713	113,466	69,270	116,076	70,864	118,745	72,493	121,477	74,161	124,271	2.30%	11.50%	42,865	71,828	61,429	102,936	86,345	144,688
CADD Operator	45,900	76,763	46,956	78,528	48,036	80,334	49,141	82,182	50,271	84,072	2.30%	11.50%	29,057	48,594	41,641	69,639	58,531	97,885
Capital Improvements Assistant	50,609	93,298	51,773	95,444	52,964	97,639	54,182	99,885	55,428	102,182	2.30%	11.50%	32,037	59,061	45,912	84,640	64,535	118,971
Capital Improvements Procurement Administrator	82,319	137,796	84,213	140,966	86,150	144,208	88,131	147,525	90,158	150,918	2.30%	11.50%	52,111	87,230	74,680	125,008	104,971	175,713
Carpenter	39,590	54,468	40,501	55,721	41,433	57,002	42,386	58,313	43,360	59,655	2.30%	11.50%	25,062	34,480	35,916	49,413	50,484	69,456
Case Management Assistant	41,544	69,636	42,500	71,238	43,477	72,876	44,477	74,553	45,500	76,267	2.30%	11.50%	26,299	44,082	37,689	63,174	52,976	88,798
Case Management Supervisor	55,701	93,298	56,983	95,444	58,293	97,639	59,634	99,885	61,005	102,182	2.30%	11.50%	35,261	59,061	50,532	84,640	71,028	118,971
Case Manager	48,143	80,637	49,250	82,492	50,383	84,389	51,541	86,330	52,727	88,316	2.30%	11.50%	30,476	51,046	43,675	73,154	61,390	102,826
Cashier I-II	29,404	88,597	30,081	90,635	30,772	92,719	31,480	94,852	32,204	97,034	2.30%	11.50%	18,614	56,085	26,676	80,375	37,495	112,976
Claims Account Specialist	41,545	57,157	42,500	58,472	43,478	59,817	44,478	61,192	45,501	62,600	2.30%	11.50%	26,299	36,183	37,689	51,853	52,976	72,885
Claims Adjustor I-III	41,545	84,615	42,500	86,561	43,478	88,552	44,478	90,589	45,501	92,673	2.30%	11.50%	26,299	53,565	37,689	76,763	52,976	107,898
Claims Manager	67,713	113,466	69,270	116,076	70,864	118,745	72,493	121,477	74,161	124,271	2.30%	11.50%	42,865	71,828	61,429	102,936	86,345	144,688
Claims Supervisor	61,436	103,019	62,849	105,388	64,294	107,812	65,773	110,292	67,286	112,829	2.30%	11.50%	38,891	65,215	55,734	93,459	78,340	131,366

Chart III - U.S. States & Cities - Job Titles - Salaries - Pension Estimates

FL-Miami	2010 (Min)	2010 (Max)	2011 (Min)	2011 (Max)	2012 (Min)	2012 (Max)	2013 (Min)	2013 (Max)	2014 (Min)	2014 (Max)	5-Year Average % Raise	5-Year Cumulative Raise Estimate**	20-Year Annual Pension Benefit Estimate (Min.)***	20-Year Annual Pension Benefit Estimate (Max.)	25-Year Annual Pension Benefit Estimate (Min.)	25-Year Annual Pension Benefit Estimate (Max.)	30-Year Annual Pension Benefit Estimate (Min.)	30-Year Annual Pension Benefit Estimate (Max.)
Clerk I--IV	25,336	51,814	25,919	53,006	26,515	54,225	27,125	55,472	27,749	56,748	2.30%	11.50%	16,039	32,800	22,985	47,005	32,308	66,071
Client Services Coordinator	67,713	113,466	69,270	116,076	70,864	118,745	72,493	121,477	74,161	124,271	2.30%	11.50%	42,865	71,828	61,429	102,936	86,345	144,688
Client Services Specialist	48,143	80,637	49,250	82,492	50,383	84,389	51,541	86,330	52,727	88,316	2.30%	11.50%	30,476	51,046	43,675	73,154	61,390	102,826
Code Enforcement Assistant	45,900	76,763	46,956	78,528	48,036	80,334	49,141	82,182	50,271	84,072	2.30%	11.50%	29,057	48,594	41,641	69,639	58,530	97,885
Code Enforcement Coordinator	61,436	103,019	62,849	105,388	64,294	107,812	65,773	110,292	67,286	112,829	2.30%	11.50%	38,891	65,215	55,734	93,459	78,340	131,366
Computer Operator I-II	37,733	57,157	38,601	58,472	39,488	59,817	40,397	61,192	41,326	62,600	2.30%	11.50%	23,886	36,183	34,231	51,853	48,115	72,885
Computer Training Specialist	50,609	84,615	51,773	86,561	52,964	88,552	54,182	90,589	55,428	92,673	2.30%	11.50%	32,037	53,565	45,912	76,763	64,535	107,898
Contracts Manager	74,664	124,985	76,381	127,860	78,138	130,800	79,935	133,809	81,774	136,887	2.30%	11.50%	47,265	79,120	67,735	113,386	95,209	159,376
Crime Analyst I-II	41,545	62,880	42,500	64,326	43,478	65,806	44,478	67,319	45,501	68,867	2.30%	11.50%	26,299	39,805	37,689	57,044	52,976	80,182
Crime Scene Investigator I-II	41,545	69,395	42,500	70,991	43,478	72,624	44,478	74,295	45,501	76,003	2.30%	11.50%	26,299	43,930	37,689	62,955	52,976	88,490
Criminal Intelligence Analyst I-II	50,609	93,298	51,773	95,444	52,964	97,639	54,182	99,885	55,428	102,182	2.30%	11.50%	32,037	59,061	45,912	84,640	64,535	118,971
Custodian I-II	26,380	32,206	26,987	32,947	27,608	33,705	28,243	34,480	28,892	35,273	2.30%	11.50%	16,700	20,388	23,932	29,217	33,639	41,068
Customer Service Representative I-III	64,479	54,468	65,962	55,721	67,479	57,002	69,031	58,313	70,618	59,655	2.30%	11.50%	40,817	34,480	58,495	49,413	82,221	69,456
Data Librarian	37,733	51,814	38,601	53,006	39,488	54,225	40,397	55,472	41,326	56,748	2.30%	11.50%	23,886	32,800	34,231	47,005	48,115	66,071
Database Manager	74,664	124,985	76,381	127,860	78,138	130,800	79,935	133,809	81,774	136,887	2.30%	11.50%	47,265	79,120	67,735	113,386	95,209	159,376
Duplicating Equipment Operator I-II	30,910	49,400	31,621	50,537	32,348	51,699	33,092	52,888	33,853	54,105	2.30%	11.50%	19,567	31,272	28,041	44,816	39,415	62,994
Electrical Inspector I-III	53,107	84,322	54,329	86,261	55,578	88,245	56,857	90,275	58,164	92,351	2.30%	11.50%	33,619	53,379	48,179	76,497	67,721	107,524
Engineer I-II	53,107	80,358	54,329	82,206	55,578	84,097	56,857	86,031	58,164	88,010	2.30%	11.50%	33,619	50,870	48,179	72,901	67,721	102,470
Engineering Technician I-IV	34,178	72,877	34,964	74,553	35,768	76,268	36,590	78,022	37,432	79,816	2.30%	11.50%	21,636	46,134	31,006	66,114	43,582	92,930
Fire Supplies Clerk I-II	27,995	88,597	28,639	90,635	29,298	92,719	29,972	94,852	30,661	97,034	2.30%	11.50%	17,722	56,085	25,397	80,375	35,698	112,976
Information Analyst	50,609	84,615	51,773	86,561	52,964	88,552	54,182	90,589	55,428	92,673	2.30%	11.50%	32,038	53,565	45,913	76,763	64,535	107,898
Information Analyst Coordinator	64,478	108,139	65,961	110,626	67,478	113,170	69,030	115,773	70,618	118,436	2.30%	11.50%	40,817	68,456	58,494	98,103	82,220	137,895
Information Center Specialist	61,436	84,322	62,849	86,261	64,295	88,245	65,773	90,275	67,286	92,351	2.30%	11.50%	38,891	53,379	55,735	76,497	78,341	107,524
Information Services Liaison	37,733	63,098	38,601	64,550	39,488	66,034	40,397	67,553	41,326	69,107	2.30%	11.50%	23,886	39,944	34,231	57,243	48,115	80,461
Information Technology Technician I-III	37,733	66,121	38,601	67,641	39,488	69,197	40,397	70,789	41,326	72,417	2.30%	11.50%	23,886	41,857	34,231	59,984	48,115	84,315
Job Placement Specialist	41,544	69,636	42,500	71,238	43,477	72,876	44,477	74,553	45,500	76,267	2.30%	11.50%	26,299	44,082	37,689	63,174	52,976	88,798
Laborer I-III	27,708	35,556	28,346	36,374	28,998	37,211	29,665	38,066	30,347	38,942	2.30%	11.50%	17,540	22,508	25,137	32,257	35,333	45,340
Law Office Manager	61,436	103,019	62,849	105,388	64,294	107,812	65,773	110,292	67,286	112,829	2.30%	11.50%	38,891	65,215	55,734	93,459	78,340	131,366
Legislative Services Representative I-III	35,842	80,637	36,667	82,492	37,510	84,389	38,373	86,330	39,255	88,316	2.30%	11.50%	22,690	51,046	32,516	73,154	45,705	102,826
Mechanical Inspector I-III	53,107	84,322	54,329	86,261	55,578	88,245	56,857	90,275	58,164	92,351	2.30%	11.50%	33,619	53,379	48,179	76,497	67,721	107,524
Park Tender I-II	64,479	49,400	65,962	50,537	67,479	51,699	69,031	52,888	70,618	54,105	2.30%	11.50%	40,817	31,272	58,495	44,816	82,221	62,994
Parks and Recreation Manager I-II	43,626	69,395	44,630	70,991	45,656	72,624	46,706	74,295	47,781	76,003	2.30%	11.50%	27,617	43,930	39,578	62,955	55,631	88,490
Personnel Specialist I-II	45,900	66,121	46,956	67,641	48,036	69,197	49,141	70,789	50,271	72,417	2.30%	11.50%	29,057	41,857	41,641	59,984	58,531	84,315
Plumbing Inspector I-III	53,107	84,322	54,329	86,261	55,578	88,245	56,857	90,275	58,164	92,351	2.30%	11.50%	33,619	53,379	48,179	76,497	67,721	107,524
Police Captain	64,304	86,325	65,783	88,311	67,296	90,342	68,844	92,420	70,427	94,546	2.30%	11.50%	40,707	54,647	58,336	78,314	81,998	110,079
Police Lieutenant	55,598	74,546	56,877	76,261	58,185	78,015	59,523	79,809	60,892	81,645	2.30%	11.50%	35,196	47,191	50,438	67,628	70,896	95,059

Chart III - U.S. States & Cities - Job Titles - Salaries - Pension Estimates

FL-Miami	2010 (Min)	2010 (Max)	2011 (Min)	2011 (Max)	2012 (Min)	2012 (Max)	2013 (Min)	2013 (Max)	2014 (Min)	2014 (Max)	5-Year Average % Raise	5-Year Cumulative Raise Estimate**	20-Year Annual Pension Benefit Estimate (Min.)***	20-Year Annual Pension Benefit Estimate (Max.)	25-Year Annual Pension Benefit Estimate (Min.)	25-Year Annual Pension Benefit Estimate (Max.)	30-Year Annual Pension Benefit Estimate (Min.)	30-Year Annual Pension Benefit Estimate (Max.)
Police Officer	41,418	55,598	42,371	56,877	43,345	58,185	44,342	59,523	45,362	60,892	2.30%	11.50%	26,219	35,196	37,574	50,438	52,815	70,896
Police Property Specialist I-II	64,479	49,400	65,962	50,537	67,479	51,699	69,031	52,888	70,618	54,105	2.30%	11.50%	40,817	31,272	58,495	44,816	82,221	62,994
Procurement Aide	35,842	49,400	36,667	50,537	37,510	51,699	38,373	52,888	39,255	54,105	2.30%	11.50%	22,690	31,272	32,516	44,816	45,705	62,994
Procurement Contract Officer	58,425	80,358	59,768	82,206	61,143	84,097	62,549	86,031	63,988	88,010	2.30%	11.50%	36,985	50,870	53,003	72,901	74,501	102,470
Procurement Specialist	48,143	66,121	49,250	67,641	50,383	69,197	51,542	70,789	52,727	72,417	2.30%	11.50%	30,476	41,857	43,675	59,984	61,390	84,315
Procurement Supervisor	71,077	119,104	72,712	121,844	74,384	124,646	76,095	127,513	77,845	130,446	2.30%	11.50%	44,994	75,398	64,481	108,051	90,635	151,878
Professional Engineer II-IV	64,479	131,282	65,962	134,301	67,479	137,390	69,031	140,550	70,618	143,783	2.30%	11.50%	40,817	83,106	58,495	119,098	82,221	167,406
Programmer	55,702	76,497	56,983	78,257	58,293	80,056	59,634	81,898	61,006	83,781	2.30%	11.50%	35,261	48,426	50,532	69,398	71,029	97,546
Project Manager-IT	78,347	131,282	80,149	134,301	81,993	137,390	83,879	140,550	85,808	143,783	2.30%	11.50%	49,597	83,106	71,077	119,098	99,906	167,406
Sanitation Inspector II	39,590	66,121	40,501	67,641	41,433	69,197	42,386	70,789	43,360	72,417	2.30%	11.50%	25,062	41,857	35,916	59,984	50,484	84,315
Technical Support Analyst	53,107	72,877	54,329	74,553	55,578	76,268	56,857	78,022	58,164	79,816	2.30%	11.50%	33,619	46,134	48,179	66,114	67,721	92,930
Technical Writer	53,107	88,905	54,328	90,950	55,578	93,042	56,856	95,181	58,164	97,371	2.30%	11.50%	33,619	56,280	48,178	80,654	67,720	113,368
Telecommunications Processing Aide	39,590	54,468	40,501	55,721	41,433	57,002	42,386	58,313	43,360	59,655	2.30%	11.50%	25,062	34,480	35,916	49,413	50,484	69,456
Telecommunications Systems Development Manager	71,077	97,663	72,712	99,909	74,384	102,207	76,095	104,558	77,845	106,963	2.30%	11.50%	44,994	61,824	64,481	88,600	90,635	124,536
Telecommunications Technical Specialist	39,590	54,468	40,501	55,721	41,433	57,002	42,386	58,313	43,360	59,655	2.30%	11.50%	25,062	34,480	35,916	49,413	50,484	69,456
Telecommunications Technician	67,713	113,466	69,270	116,076	70,864	118,745	72,493	121,477	74,161	124,271	2.30%	11.50%	42,865	71,828	61,429	102,936	86,345	144,688
Telecommunications Technician Assistant	55,701	93,298	56,983	95,444	58,293	97,639	59,634	99,885	61,005	102,182	2.30%	11.50%	35,261	59,061	50,532	84,640	71,028	118,971
Training & Development Coordinator	64,478	108,139	65,961	110,626	67,478	113,170	69,030	115,773	70,618	118,436	2.30%	11.50%	40,817	68,456	58,494	98,103	82,220	137,895
Training and Development Specialist	53,107	88,905	54,328	90,950	55,578	93,042	56,856	95,181	58,164	97,371	2.30%	11.50%	33,619	56,280	48,178	80,654	67,720	113,368
Waste Collector Operator I-II	29,141	38,098	29,811	38,975	30,496	39,871	31,198	40,788	31,915	41,726	2.30%	11.50%	18,447	24,118	26,436	34,563	37,159	48,582
Waste Equipment Operator	31,705	39,838	32,434	40,754	33,180	41,691	33,943	42,650	34,724	43,631	2.30%	11.50%	20,070	25,219	28,762	36,141	40,428	50,800
Web Administrator	67,713	113,466	69,270	116,076	70,864	118,745	72,493	121,477	74,161	124,271	2.30%	11.50%	42,865	71,828	61,429	102,936	86,345	144,688
Web Developer I-II	50,609	76,497	51,773	78,257	52,964	80,056	54,182	81,898	55,428	83,781	2.30%	11.50%	32,038	48,426	45,913	69,398	64,535	97,546

http://www.ci.miami.fl.us/Personnel/ClassificationPage.asp

Chart III - U.S. States & Cities - Job Titles - Salaries - Pension Estimates

Iowa	2010 (Min)	2010 (Max)	2011 (Min)	2011 (Max)	2012 (Min)	2012 (Max)	2013 (Min)	2013 (Max)	2014 (Min)	2014 (Max)	5-Year Average % Raise	5-Year Cumulative Raise Estimate**	20-Year Annual Pension Benefit Estimate (Min.)***	20-Year Annual Pension Benefit Estimate (Max.)	25-Year Annual Pension Benefit Estimate (Min.)	25-Year Annual Pension Benefit Estimate (Max.)	30-Year Annual Pension Benefit Estimate (Min.)	30-Year Annual Pension Benefit Estimate (Max.)
Accountant 2-4	34,877	90,940	35,679	93,032	36,500	95,172	37,339	97,361	38,198	99,600	2.30%	11.50%	22,079	57,569	31,640	82,501	44,474	115,964
Accountant/Auditor 1	34,877	51,530	35,679	52,715	36,500	53,927	37,339	55,168	38,198	56,437	2.30%	11.50%	22,079	32,620	31,640	46,748	44,474	65,709
Actuarial Administrator	124,792	177,438	127,663	181,519	130,599	185,694	133,603	189,965	136,675	194,335	2.30%	11.50%	78,998	112,325	113,211	160,972	159,131	226,263
Actuary A.S.A.	83,992	119,576	85,924	122,326	87,900	125,139	89,922	128,018	91,990	130,962	2.30%	11.50%	53,170	75,696	76,197	108,479	107,104	152,478
Admin Law Judge 1-3	62,009	114,063	63,435	116,686	64,894	119,370	66,387	122,115	67,914	124,924	2.30%	11.50%	39,254	72,206	56,254	103,477	79,072	145,449
Administrative Secretary	38,454	56,564	39,338	57,865	40,243	59,196	41,169	60,558	42,115	61,951	2.30%	11.50%	24,343	35,807	34,885	51,315	49,035	72,129
Administrator Of Nursing	72,944	103,811	74,621	106,199	76,338	108,642	78,093	111,140	79,890	113,697	2.30%	11.50%	46,176	65,716	66,174	94,177	93,015	132,377
Agriculture Marketing Spec	43,010	65,175	43,999	66,674	45,011	68,208	46,046	69,777	47,105	71,382	2.30%	11.50%	27,227	41,258	39,018	59,127	54,845	83,109
Agriculture Program Mgr 3	62,009	95,383	63,435	97,576	64,894	99,821	66,387	102,116	67,914	104,465	2.30%	11.50%	39,254	60,381	56,254	86,531	79,072	121,628
Attorney 1-3	47,179	108,778	48,264	111,279	49,374	113,839	50,509	116,457	51,671	119,136	2.30%	11.50%	29,866	68,860	42,800	98,683	60,161	138,709
Attorney Supervisor	92,244	131,216	94,366	134,234	96,537	137,322	98,757	140,480	101,028	143,711	2.30%	11.50%	58,394	83,065	83,684	119,039	117,627	167,323
Bank Examination Analyst	101,351	143,974	103,682	147,285	106,067	150,673	108,506	154,138	111,002	157,683	2.30%	11.50%	64,159	91,141	91,945	130,612	129,239	183,590
Bank Examiner Supervisor	112,536	159,920	115,125	163,598	117,773	167,361	120,481	171,210	123,252	175,148	2.30%	11.50%	71,240	101,235	102,093	145,079	143,502	203,924
Bridge Inspector 1-2	36,449	65,175	37,287	66,674	38,145	68,208	39,022	69,777	39,920	71,382	2.30%	11.50%	23,074	41,258	33,066	59,127	46,478	83,109
Budget Analyst 1-4	36,449	82,830	37,287	84,735	38,145	86,684	39,022	88,678	39,920	90,718	2.30%	11.50%	23,074	52,435	33,066	75,143	46,478	105,622
Captain	62,009	95,383	63,435	97,576	64,894	99,821	66,387	102,116	67,914	104,465	2.30%	11.50%	39,254	60,381	56,254	86,531	79,072	121,628
Carpenter 1-2	34,695	49,138	35,493	50,268	36,309	51,424	37,144	52,607	37,999	53,817	2.30%	11.50%	21,963	31,106	31,475	44,578	44,242	62,659
Chemist	43,010	65,175	43,999	66,674	45,011	68,208	46,046	69,777	47,105	71,382	2.30%	11.50%	27,227	41,258	39,018	59,127	54,845	83,109
Chemist Supervisor	48,568	75,336	49,685	77,068	50,828	78,841	51,997	80,654	53,193	82,509	2.30%	11.50%	30,746	47,690	44,061	68,344	61,933	96,065
Chief Benefits Officer	83,992	119,576	85,924	122,326	87,900	125,139	89,922	128,018	91,990	130,962	2.30%	11.50%	53,170	75,696	76,197	108,479	107,104	152,478
Child Support Recovery Officer	38,454	56,564	39,338	57,865	40,243	59,196	41,169	60,558	42,115	61,951	2.30%	11.50%	24,343	35,807	34,885	51,315	49,035	72,129
Child Support Recovery Supervisor	48,568	75,336	49,685	77,068	50,828	78,841	51,997	80,654	53,193	82,509	2.30%	11.50%	30,746	47,690	44,061	68,344	61,933	96,065
Communications Engineer	48,568	75,336	49,685	77,068	50,828	78,841	51,997	80,654	53,193	82,509	2.30%	11.50%	30,746	47,690	44,061	68,344	61,933	96,065
Compliance Officer 1-2	47,179	82,830	48,264	84,735	49,374	86,684	50,509	88,678	51,671	90,718	2.30%	11.50%	29,866	52,435	42,800	75,143	60,161	105,622
Conservation Officer	41,142	62,487	42,088	63,924	43,056	65,395	44,046	66,899	45,059	68,438	2.30%	11.50%	26,044	39,557	37,324	56,688	52,463	79,682
Consumer Advocate	89,574	137,049	91,634	140,201	93,742	143,425	95,898	146,724	98,103	150,099	2.30%	11.50%	56,704	86,757	81,261	124,330	114,221	174,759
Correctional Bldg Services Coordinator	36,449	54,013	37,287	55,255	38,145	56,526	39,022	57,826	39,920	59,156	2.30%	11.50%	23,074	34,192	33,066	49,000	46,478	68,875
Correctional Counselor	45,060	68,615	46,096	70,193	47,157	71,808	48,241	73,459	49,351	75,149	2.30%	11.50%	28,525	43,436	40,878	62,248	57,459	87,496
Correctional Officer	36,449	54,013	37,287	55,255	38,145	56,526	39,022	57,826	39,920	59,156	2.30%	11.50%	23,074	34,192	33,066	49,000	46,478	68,875
Correctional Services Manager	48,568	75,336	49,685	77,068	50,828	78,841	51,997	80,654	53,193	82,509	2.30%	11.50%	30,746	47,690	44,061	68,344	61,933	96,065
Correctional Supervisor 1-2	43,010	71,782	43,999	73,433	45,011	75,122	46,046	76,850	47,105	78,617	2.30%	11.50%	27,227	45,441	39,018	65,120	54,845	91,534
Criminalist	53,557	82,830	54,789	84,735	56,049	86,684	57,338	88,678	58,657	90,718	2.30%	11.50%	33,904	52,435	48,587	75,143	68,294	105,622
Criminalist Supervisor	59,093	90,940	60,452	93,032	61,843	95,172	63,265	97,361	64,720	99,600	2.30%	11.50%	37,408	57,569	53,609	82,501	75,353	115,964
Data Warehouse Analyst	62,009	95,383	63,435	97,576	64,894	99,821	66,387	102,116	67,914	104,465	2.30%	11.50%	39,254	60,381	56,254	86,531	79,072	121,628
Dentist	83,992	119,576	85,924	122,326	87,900	125,139	89,922	128,018	91,990	130,962	2.30%	11.50%	53,170	75,696	76,197	108,479	107,104	152,478
Disability Examiner	43,010	65,175	43,999	66,674	45,011	68,208	46,046	69,777	47,105	71,382	2.30%	11.50%	27,227	41,258	39,018	59,127	54,845	83,109
Disability Examiner Specialist	47,179	71,782	48,264	73,433	49,374	75,122	50,509	76,850	51,671	78,617	2.30%	11.50%	29,866	45,441	42,800	65,120	60,161	91,534
Drivers License Examiner	36,449	54,013	37,287	55,255	38,145	56,526	39,022	57,826	39,920	59,156	2.30%	11.50%	23,074	34,192	33,066	49,000	46,478	68,875

Chart III - U.S. States & Cities - Job Titles - Salaries - Pension Estimates

Iowa	2010 (Min)	2010 (Max)	2011 (Min)	2011 (Max)	2012 (Min)	2012 (Max)	2013 (Min)	2013 (Max)	2014 (Min)	2014 (Max)	5-Year Average % Raise	5-Year Cumulative Raise Estimate**	20-Year Annual Pension Benefit Estimate (Min.)***	20-Year Annual Pension Benefit Estimate (Max.)	25-Year Annual Pension Benefit Estimate (Min.)	25-Year Annual Pension Benefit Estimate (Max.)	30-Year Annual Pension Benefit Estimate (Min.)	30-Year Annual Pension Benefit Estimate (Max.)
Drug Abuse Prevention Coor	77,887	119,166	79,678	121,907	81,511	124,710	83,386	127,579	85,303	130,513	2.30%	11.50%	49,305	75,436	70,659	108,107	99,318	151,956
Education Supervisor	47,179	71,782	48,264	73,433	49,374	75,122	50,509	76,850	51,671	78,617	2.30%	11.50%	29,866	45,441	42,800	65,120	60,161	91,534
Electrical Maintenance Spe	45,060	68,615	46,096	70,193	47,157	71,808	48,241	73,459	49,351	75,149	2.30%	11.50%	28,525	43,436	40,878	62,248	57,459	87,496
Electrician	41,370	54,013	42,321	55,255	43,295	56,526	44,290	57,826	45,309	59,156	2.30%	11.50%	26,189	34,192	37,530	49,000	52,753	68,875
Emergency Management Spec	36,449	71,782	37,287	73,433	38,145	75,122	39,022	76,850	39,920	78,617	2.30%	11.50%	23,074	45,441	33,066	65,120	46,478	91,534
Engineering Operations Tec	41,142	62,487	42,088	63,924	43,056	65,395	44,046	66,899	45,059	68,438	2.30%	11.50%	26,044	39,557	37,324	56,688	52,463	79,682
Environmental Engineer	48,568	75,336	49,685	77,068	50,828	78,841	51,997	80,654	53,193	82,509	2.30%	11.50%	30,746	47,690	44,061	68,344	61,933	96,065
Environmental Engineer Senior	59,093	90,940	60,452	93,032	61,843	95,172	63,265	97,361	64,720	99,600	2.30%	11.50%	37,408	57,569	53,609	82,501	75,353	115,964
Exec Off 1-5	47,179	125,180	48,264	128,059	49,374	131,004	50,509	134,017	51,671	137,100	2.30%	11.50%	29,866	79,243	42,800	113,563	60,161	159,625
Executive Secretary	43,010	65,175	43,999	66,674	45,011	68,208	46,046	69,777	47,105	71,382	2.30%	11.50%	27,227	41,258	39,018	59,127	54,845	83,109
Facilities Engineer 1-2	51,051	90,940	52,226	93,032	53,427	95,172	54,656	97,361	55,913	99,600	2.30%	11.50%	32,317	57,569	46,314	82,501	65,099	115,964
Field Auditor Supervisor	47,179	71,782	48,264	73,433	49,374	75,122	50,509	76,850	51,671	78,617	2.30%	11.50%	29,866	45,441	42,800	65,120	60,161	91,534
Fire Inspector 1-2	41,142	68,615	42,088	70,193	43,056	71,808	44,046	73,459	45,059	75,149	2.30%	11.50%	26,044	43,436	37,324	62,248	52,463	87,496
Fire Prevention Supervisor	62,009	95,383	63,435	97,576	64,894	99,821	66,387	102,116	67,914	104,465	2.30%	11.50%	39,254	60,381	56,254	86,531	79,072	121,628
Fire Service Coordinator	51,051	79,049	52,226	80,867	53,427	82,727	54,656	84,630	55,913	86,576	2.30%	11.50%	32,317	50,041	46,314	71,713	65,099	100,800
Fiscal & Policy Analyst	43,010	82,830	43,999	84,735	45,011	86,684	46,046	88,678	47,105	90,718	2.30%	11.50%	27,227	52,435	39,018	75,143	54,845	105,622
Fiscal & Policy Analyst Senior	53,557	95,383	54,789	97,576	56,049	99,821	57,338	102,116	58,657	104,465	2.30%	11.50%	33,904	60,381	48,587	86,531	68,294	121,628
Food Production Supervisor	36,449	54,013	37,287	55,255	38,145	56,526	39,022	57,826	39,920	59,156	2.30%	11.50%	23,074	34,192	33,066	49,000	46,478	68,875
Food Services Assistant Di	41,142	62,487	42,088	63,924	43,056	65,395	44,046	66,899	45,059	68,438	2.30%	11.50%	26,044	39,557	37,324	56,688	52,463	79,682
Forester 2-3	45,060	75,336	46,096	77,068	47,157	78,841	48,241	80,654	49,351	82,509	2.30%	11.50%	28,525	47,690	40,878	68,344	57,459	96,065
Geologist 2-4	45,060	90,940	46,096	93,032	47,157	95,172	48,241	97,361	49,351	99,600	2.30%	11.50%	28,525	57,569	40,878	82,501	57,459	115,964
Graphic Artist	34,877	51,530	35,679	52,715	36,500	53,927	37,339	55,168	38,198	56,437	2.30%	11.50%	22,079	32,620	31,640	46,748	44,474	65,709
Health Facilities Officer 1-2	56,268	95,383	57,562	97,576	58,886	99,821	60,241	102,116	61,626	104,465	2.30%	11.50%	35,620	60,381	51,046	86,531	71,751	121,628
Health Facilities Survey Supervisor	56,268	86,726	57,562	88,721	58,886	90,761	60,241	92,849	61,626	94,984	2.30%	11.50%	35,620	54,901	51,046	78,677	71,751	110,590
Health Physicist 1-3	43,010	82,830	43,999	84,735	45,011	86,684	46,046	88,678	47,105	90,718	2.30%	11.50%	27,227	52,435	39,018	75,143	54,845	105,622
Health Professions Investi	47,179	71,782	48,264	73,433	49,374	75,122	50,509	76,850	51,671	78,617	2.30%	11.50%	29,866	45,441	42,800	65,120	60,161	91,534
Highway Division Administr	112,536	159,920	115,125	163,598	117,773	167,361	120,481	171,210	123,252	175,148	2.30%	11.50%	71,240	101,235	102,093	145,079	143,502	203,924
Highway Maintenance Supervisor	51,051	79,049	52,226	80,867	53,427	82,727	54,656	84,630	55,913	86,576	2.30%	11.50%	32,317	50,041	46,314	71,713	65,099	100,800
Human Resources Technical Specialist	34,877	51,530	35,679	52,715	36,500	53,927	37,339	55,168	38,198	56,437	2.30%	11.50%	22,079	32,620	31,640	46,748	44,474	65,709
Human Services Admin Field	80,120	114,063	81,962	116,686	83,847	119,370	85,776	122,115	87,749	124,924	2.30%	11.50%	50,719	72,206	72,684	103,477	102,166	145,449
Human Services Quality Assurance Coordinator	48,568	75,336	49,685	77,068	50,828	78,841	51,997	80,654	53,193	82,509	2.30%	11.50%	30,746	47,690	44,061	68,344	61,933	96,065
Income Maint Worker 2-6	38,454	75,336	39,338	77,068	40,243	78,841	41,169	80,654	42,115	82,509	2.30%	11.50%	24,343	47,690	34,885	68,344	49,035	96,065
Income Maintenance Administrator	51,051	79,049	52,226	80,867	53,427	82,727	54,656	84,630	55,913	86,576	2.30%	11.50%	32,317	50,041	46,314	71,713	65,099	100,800
Income Maintenance Supervisor	47,179	71,782	48,264	73,433	49,374	75,122	50,509	76,850	51,671	78,617	2.30%	11.50%	29,866	45,441	42,800	65,120	60,161	91,534
Info Tech Admin 1-4	59,093	137,481	60,452	140,643	61,843	143,878	63,265	147,187	64,720	150,573	2.30%	11.50%	37,408	87,031	53,609	124,722	75,353	175,311

179

Chart III - U.S. States & Cities - Job Titles - Salaries - Pension Estimates

Iowa	2010 (Min)	2010 (Max)	2011 (Min)	2011 (Max)	2012 (Min)	2012 (Max)	2013 (Min)	2013 (Max)	2014 (Min)	2014 (Max)	5-Year Average % Raise	5-Year Cumulative Raise Estimate**	20-Year Annual Pension Benefit Estimate (Min.)***	20-Year Annual Pension Benefit Estimate (Max.)	25-Year Annual Pension Benefit Estimate (Min.)	25-Year Annual Pension Benefit Estimate (Max.)	30-Year Annual Pension Benefit Estimate (Min.)	30-Year Annual Pension Benefit Estimate (Max.)
Info Tech Enterprise Expert	65,084	150,990	66,581	154,463	68,113	158,015	69,679	161,650	71,282	165,368	2.30%	11.50%	41,201	95,582	59,044	136,978	82,993	192,537
Info Tech Specialist 1-5	36,449	95,383	37,287	97,576	38,145	99,821	39,022	102,116	39,920	104,465	2.30%	11.50%	23,074	60,381	33,066	86,531	46,478	121,628
Info Tech Supervisor 1-2	38,454	65,175	39,338	66,674	40,243	68,208	41,169	69,777	42,115	71,382	2.30%	11.50%	24,343	41,258	34,885	59,127	49,035	83,109
Internal Auditor	47,179	71,782	48,264	73,433	49,374	75,122	50,509	76,850	51,671	78,617	2.30%	11.50%	29,866	45,441	42,800	65,120	60,161	91,534
Investigator 1-4	36,449	71,782	37,287	73,433	38,145	75,122	39,022	76,850	39,920	78,617	2.30%	11.50%	23,074	45,441	33,066	65,120	46,478	91,534
Investigator Supervisor	47,179	71,782	48,264	73,433	49,374	75,122	50,509	76,850	51,671	78,617	2.30%	11.50%	29,866	45,441	42,800	65,120	60,161	91,534
Labor Safety Officer	62,009	95,383	63,435	97,576	64,894	99,821	66,387	102,116	67,914	104,465	2.30%	11.50%	39,254	60,381	56,254	86,531	79,072	121,628
Land Surveyor	47,179	71,782	48,264	73,433	49,374	75,122	50,509	76,850	51,671	78,617	2.30%	11.50%	29,866	45,441	42,800	65,120	60,161	91,534
Land Surveyor Senior	53,557	82,830	54,789	84,735	56,049	86,684	57,338	88,678	58,657	90,718	2.30%	11.50%	33,904	52,435	48,587	75,143	68,294	105,622
Law Enforcement Instructor	48,568	75,336	49,685	77,068	50,828	78,841	51,997	80,654	53,193	82,509	2.30%	11.50%	30,746	47,690	44,061	68,344	61,933	96,065
Legal Instructor	56,268	86,726	57,562	88,721	58,886	90,761	60,241	92,849	61,626	94,984	2.30%	11.50%	35,620	54,901	51,046	78,677	71,751	110,590
Librarian 1-3	39,707	75,336	40,620	77,068	41,554	78,841	42,510	80,654	43,488	82,509	2.30%	11.50%	25,136	47,690	36,022	68,344	50,632	96,065
Librarian Supervisor	48,568	75,336	49,685	77,068	50,828	78,841	51,997	80,654	53,193	82,509	2.30%	11.50%	30,746	47,690	44,061	68,344	61,933	96,065
Library Consultant	47,179	71,782	48,264	73,433	49,374	75,122	50,509	76,850	51,671	78,617	2.30%	11.50%	29,866	45,441	42,800	65,120	60,161	91,534
Library Program Director	62,009	95,383	63,435	97,576	64,894	99,821	66,387	102,116	67,914	104,465	2.30%	11.50%	39,254	60,381	56,254	86,531	79,072	121,628
Licensed Practical Nurse	36,449	54,013	37,287	55,255	38,145	56,526	39,022	57,826	39,920	59,156	2.30%	11.50%	23,074	34,192	33,066	49,000	46,478	68,875
Lieutenant	56,268	86,726	57,562	88,721	58,886	90,761	60,241	92,849	61,626	94,984	2.30%	11.50%	35,620	54,901	51,046	78,677	71,751	110,590
Machinist	43,648	56,564	44,652	57,865	45,679	59,196	46,729	60,558	47,804	61,951	2.30%	11.50%	27,631	35,807	39,597	51,315	55,658	72,129
Maintenance Engineer	41,142	62,487	42,088	63,924	43,056	65,395	44,046	66,899	45,059	68,438	2.30%	11.50%	26,044	39,557	37,324	56,688	52,463	79,682
Maintenance Repairer	34,695	44,673	35,493	45,700	36,309	46,751	37,144	47,827	37,999	48,927	2.30%	11.50%	21,963	28,280	31,475	40,527	44,242	56,965
Maintenance Repairs Supv	39,707	59,389	40,620	60,755	41,554	62,152	42,510	63,582	43,488	65,044	2.30%	11.50%	25,136	37,596	36,022	53,878	50,632	75,731
Management Analyst 1-4	34,877	86,726	35,679	88,721	36,500	90,761	37,339	92,849	38,198	94,984	2.30%	11.50%	22,079	54,901	31,640	78,677	44,474	110,590
Mechanic	39,593	51,530	40,503	52,715	41,435	53,927	42,388	55,168	43,363	56,437	2.30%	11.50%	25,064	32,620	35,918	46,748	50,487	65,709
Mechanical Maintenance Sup	43,010	65,175	43,999	66,674	45,011	68,208	46,046	69,777	47,105	71,382	2.30%	11.50%	27,227	41,258	39,018	59,127	54,845	83,109
Medicaid Administrator	92,244	131,216	94,366	134,234	96,537	137,322	98,757	140,480	101,028	143,711	2.30%	11.50%	58,394	83,065	83,684	119,039	117,627	167,323
Medical Technologist	39,707	59,389	40,620	60,755	41,554	62,152	42,510	63,582	43,488	65,044	2.30%	11.50%	25,136	37,596	36,022	53,878	50,632	75,731
Microbiologist	43,010	65,175	43,999	66,674	45,011	68,208	46,046	69,777	47,105	71,382	2.30%	11.50%	27,227	41,258	39,018	59,127	54,845	83,109
Microbiologist Supervisor	48,568	75,336	49,685	77,068	50,828	78,841	51,997	80,654	53,193	82,509	2.30%	11.50%	30,746	47,690	44,061	68,344	61,933	96,065
Motor Vehicle Captain	51,051	79,049	52,226	80,867	53,427	82,727	54,656	84,630	55,913	86,576	2.30%	11.50%	32,317	50,041	46,314	71,713	65,099	100,800
Motor Vehicle Commander, Uniform	62,009	95,383	63,435	97,576	64,894	99,821	66,387	102,116	67,914	104,465	2.30%	11.50%	39,254	60,381	56,254	86,531	79,072	121,628
Motor Vehicle Investigator	43,010	65,175	43,999	66,674	45,011	68,208	46,046	69,777	47,105	71,382	2.30%	11.50%	27,227	41,258	39,018	59,127	54,845	83,109
Motor Vehicle Officer	39,707	59,389	40,620	60,755	41,554	62,152	42,510	63,582	43,488	65,044	2.30%	11.50%	25,136	37,596	36,022	53,878	50,632	75,731
Motor Vehicle Sergeant	43,010	65,175	43,999	66,674	45,011	68,208	46,046	69,777	47,105	71,382	2.30%	11.50%	27,227	41,258	39,018	59,127	54,845	83,109
Natural Resources Biologist	45,060	68,615	46,096	70,193	47,157	71,808	48,241	73,459	49,351	75,149	2.30%	11.50%	28,525	43,436	40,878	62,248	57,459	87,496
Natural Resources Biometrician	48,568	75,336	49,685	77,068	50,828	78,841	51,997	80,654	53,193	82,509	2.30%	11.50%	30,746	47,690	44,061	68,344	61,933	96,065
Natural Resources Engr Sup	59,093	90,940	60,452	93,032	61,843	95,172	63,265	97,361	64,720	99,600	2.30%	11.50%	37,408	57,569	53,609	82,501	75,353	115,964
Nurse Clinician	48,568	75,336	49,685	77,068	50,828	78,841	51,997	80,654	53,193	82,509	2.30%	11.50%	30,746	47,690	44,061	68,344	61,933	96,065
Nurse Practitioner	65,084	99,779	66,581	102,074	68,113	104,422	69,679	106,824	71,282	109,280	2.30%	11.50%	41,201	63,164	59,044	90,519	82,993	127,235

180

Chart III - U.S. States & Cities - Job Titles - Salaries - Pension Estimates

Iowa	2010 (Min)	2010 (Max)	2011 (Min)	2011 (Max)	2012 (Min)	2012 (Max)	2013 (Min)	2013 (Max)	2014 (Min)	2014 (Max)	5-Year Average % Raise	5-Year Cumula-tive Raise Esti-mate**	20-Year Annual Pension Benefit Estimate (Min.)***	20-Year Annual Pension Benefit Estimate (Max.)	25-Year Annual Pension Benefit Estimate (Min.)	25-Year Annual Pension Benefit Estimate (Max.)	30-Year Annual Pension Benefit Estimate (Min.)	30-Year Annual Pension Benefit Estimate (Max.)
urse Specialist	53,557	82,830	54,789	84,735	56,049	86,684	57,338	88,678	58,657	90,718	2.30%	11.50%	33,904	52,435	48,587	75,143	68,294	105,622
urse Supervisor 1-2	51,051	86,726	52,226	88,721	53,427	90,761	54,656	92,849	55,913	94,984	2.30%	11.50%	32,317	54,901	46,314	78,677	65,099	110,590
ursing Services rector	62,009	95,383	63,435	97,576	64,894	99,821	66,387	102,116	67,914	104,465	2.30%	11.50%	39,254	60,381	56,254	86,531	79,072	121,628
ccupational herapist 1-2	45,060	75,336	46,096	77,068	47,157	78,841	48,241	80,654	49,351	82,509	2.30%	11.50%	28,525	47,690	40,878	68,344	57,459	96,065
ainter 1-2	34,695	49,138	35,493	50,268	36,309	51,424	37,144	52,607	37,999	53,817	2.30%	11.50%	21,963	31,106	31,475	44,578	44,242	62,659
aralegal	36,449	54,013	37,287	55,255	38,145	56,526	39,022	57,826	39,920	59,156	2.30%	11.50%	23,074	34,192	33,066	49,000	46,478	68,875
ark Manager	41,142	62,487	42,088	63,924	43,056	65,395	44,046	66,899	45,059	68,438	2.30%	11.50%	26,044	39,557	37,324	56,688	52,463	79,682
ark Ranger	41,142	62,487	42,088	63,924	43,056	65,395	44,046	66,899	45,059	68,438	2.30%	11.50%	26,044	39,557	37,324	56,688	52,463	79,682
arole Board Chair	67,726	103,629	69,284	106,012	70,878	108,451	72,508	110,945	74,176	113,497	2.30%	11.50%	42,873	65,601	61,441	94,012	86,362	132,144
arole Board Liaison fficer	43,010	65,175	43,999	66,674	45,011	68,208	46,046	69,777	47,105	71,382	2.30%	11.50%	27,227	41,258	39,018	59,127	54,845	83,109
arole Board ember	67,726	103,629	69,284	106,012	70,878	108,451	72,508	110,945	74,176	113,497	2.30%	11.50%	42,873	65,601	61,441	94,012	86,362	132,144
ension System ttorney	83,992	119,576	85,924	122,326	87,900	125,139	89,922	128,018	91,990	130,962	2.30%	11.50%	53,170	75,696	76,197	108,479	107,104	152,478
ersonnel Mgmt Prog oord	62,009	95,383	63,435	97,576	64,894	99,821	66,387	102,116	67,914	104,465	2.30%	11.50%	39,254	60,381	56,254	86,531	79,072	121,628
ersonnel Mgmt pecialist	34,877	65,175	35,679	66,674	36,500	68,208	37,339	69,777	38,198	71,382	2.30%	11.50%	22,079	41,258	31,640	59,127	44,474	83,109
esticide Investigator	43,010	65,175	43,999	66,674	45,011	68,208	46,046	69,777	47,105	71,382	2.30%	11.50%	27,227	41,258	39,018	59,127	54,845	83,109
harmacist	59,093	90,940	60,452	93,032	61,843	95,172	63,265	97,361	64,720	99,600	2.30%	11.50%	37,408	57,569	53,609	82,501	75,353	115,964
harmacy Consultant	72,944	103,811	74,621	106,199	76,338	108,642	78,093	111,140	79,890	113,697	2.30%	11.50%	46,176	65,716	66,174	94,177	93,015	132,377
harmacy Supervisor	72,944	103,811	74,621	106,199	76,338	108,642	78,093	111,140	79,890	113,697	2.30%	11.50%	46,176	65,716	66,174	94,177	93,015	132,377
hysical Therapist 2	53,557	90,940	54,789	93,032	56,049	95,172	57,338	97,361	58,657	99,600	2.30%	11.50%	33,904	57,569	48,587	82,501	68,294	115,964
hysician	92,244	246,281	94,366	251,946	96,537	257,741	98,757	263,669	101,028	269,733	2.30%	11.50%	58,394	155,905	83,684	223,426	117,627	314,049
hysician Assistant	65,084	99,779	66,581	102,074	68,113	104,422	69,679	106,824	71,282	109,280	2.30%	11.50%	41,201	63,164	59,044	90,519	82,993	127,235
hysician Supervisor	92,244	246,281	94,366	251,946	96,537	257,741	98,757	263,669	101,028	269,733	2.30%	11.50%	58,394	155,905	83,684	223,426	117,627	314,049
ant Operations anager 1-3	41,142	79,049	42,088	80,867	43,056	82,727	44,046	84,630	45,059	86,576	2.30%	11.50%	26,044	50,041	37,324	71,713	52,463	100,800
ant Pathologist	45,060	68,615	46,096	70,193	47,157	71,808	48,241	73,459	49,351	75,149	2.30%	11.50%	28,525	43,436	40,878	62,248	57,459	87,496
umber 1-2	34,695	49,138	35,493	50,268	36,309	51,424	37,144	52,607	37,999	53,817	2.30%	11.50%	21,963	31,106	31,475	44,578	44,242	62,659
rogram & Planning dmin 1-2	51,051	82,830	52,226	84,735	53,427	86,684	54,656	88,678	55,913	90,718	2.30%	11.50%	32,317	52,435	46,314	75,143	65,099	105,622
rogram dministrator	56,268	86,726	57,562	88,721	58,886	90,761	60,241	92,849	61,626	94,984	2.30%	11.50%	35,620	54,901	51,046	78,677	71,751	110,590
rogram Planner 1-3	36,449	71,782	37,287	73,433	38,145	75,122	39,022	76,850	39,920	78,617	2.30%	11.50%	23,074	45,441	33,066	65,120	46,478	91,534
sychologist 1-4	45,060	90,940	46,096	93,032	47,157	95,172	48,241	97,361	49,351	99,600	2.30%	11.50%	28,525	57,569	40,878	82,501	57,459	115,964
sychologist upervisor	53,557	82,830	54,789	84,735	56,049	86,684	57,338	88,678	58,657	90,718	2.30%	11.50%	33,904	52,435	48,587	75,143	68,294	105,622
sychology dministrator	62,009	95,383	63,435	97,576	64,894	99,821	66,387	102,116	67,914	104,465	2.30%	11.50%	39,254	60,381	56,254	86,531	79,072	121,628
ublic Defender 1-3	47,179	108,778	48,264	111,279	49,374	113,839	50,509	116,457	51,671	119,136	2.30%	11.50%	29,866	68,860	42,800	98,683	60,161	138,709
ublic Health Dental ygie	43,010	65,175	43,999	66,674	45,011	68,208	46,046	69,777	47,105	71,382	2.30%	11.50%	27,227	41,258	39,018	59,127	54,845	83,109
ublic Health Service hie	92,244	131,216	94,366	134,234	96,537	137,322	98,757	140,480	101,028	143,711	2.30%	11.50%	58,394	83,065	83,684	119,039	117,627	167,323
ublic Information ssista	41,142	62,487	42,088	63,924	43,056	65,395	44,046	66,899	45,059	68,438	2.30%	11.50%	26,044	39,557	37,324	56,688	52,463	79,682
ublic Safety Chief	92,244	131,216	94,366	134,234	96,537	137,322	98,757	140,480	101,028	143,711	2.30%	11.50%	58,394	83,065	83,684	119,039	117,627	167,323
ublic Safety eserve Peac	43,010	65,175	43,999	66,674	45,011	68,208	46,046	69,777	47,105	71,382	2.30%	11.50%	27,227	41,258	39,018	59,127	54,845	83,109
ublic Service xecutive 1-6	47,179	137,481	48,264	140,643	49,374	143,878	50,509	147,187	51,671	150,573	2.30%	11.50%	29,866	87,031	42,800	124,722	60,161	175,311
urchasing Agent 1-4	34,877	82,830	35,679	84,735	36,500	86,684	37,339	88,678	38,198	90,718	2.30%	11.50%	22,079	52,435	31,640	75,143	44,474	105,622

Chart III - U.S. States & Cities - Job Titles - Salaries - Pension Estimates

Iowa	2010 (Min)	2010 (Max)	2011 (Min)	2011 (Max)	2012 (Min)	2012 (Max)	2013 (Min)	2013 (Max)	2014 (Min)	2014 (Max)	5-Year Average % Raise	5-Year Cumulative Raise Estimate**	20-Year Annual Pension Benefit Estimate (Min.)***	20-Year Annual Pension Benefit Estimate (Max.)	25-Year Annual Pension Benefit Estimate (Min.)	25-Year Annual Pension Benefit Estimate (Max.)	30-Year Annual Pension Benefit Estimate (Min.)	30-Year Annual Pension Benefit Estimate (Max.)
Racing Steward, Equine	76,406	108,778	78,164	111,279	79,961	113,839	81,800	116,457	83,682	119,136	2.30%	11.50%	48,368	68,860	69,316	98,683	97,431	138,70
Racing Veterinarian Canine	80,120	114,063	81,962	116,686	83,847	119,370	85,776	122,115	87,749	124,924	2.30%	11.50%	50,719	72,206	72,684	103,477	102,166	145,44
Racing Veterinarian, Equin	106,226	150,990	108,669	154,463	111,169	158,015	113,726	161,650	116,341	165,368	2.30%	11.50%	67,245	95,582	96,368	136,978	135,456	192,53
Radiological Electronics Technician	34,877	51,530	35,679	52,715	36,500	53,927	37,339	55,168	38,198	56,437	2.30%	11.50%	22,079	32,620	31,640	46,748	44,474	65,709
Refugee Specialist 1-2	34,877	56,564	35,679	57,865	36,500	59,196	37,339	60,558	38,198	61,951	2.30%	11.50%	22,079	35,807	31,640	51,315	44,474	72,129
Registered Nurse	45,060	68,615	46,096	70,193	47,157	71,808	48,241	73,459	49,351	75,149	2.30%	11.50%	28,525	43,436	40,878	62,248	57,459	87,496
Rehabilitation Consultant	53,557	82,830	54,789	84,735	56,049	86,684	57,338	88,678	58,657	90,718	2.30%	11.50%	33,904	52,435	48,587	75,143	68,294	105,62
Rehabilitation Counselor	45,060	68,615	46,096	70,193	47,157	71,808	48,241	73,459	49,351	75,149	2.30%	11.50%	28,525	43,436	40,878	62,248	57,459	87,496
Rehabilitation Counselor Specialist	48,568	75,336	49,685	77,068	50,828	78,841	51,997	80,654	53,193	82,509	2.30%	11.50%	30,746	47,690	44,061	68,344	61,933	96,065
Research Associate	36,449	54,013	37,287	55,255	38,145	56,526	39,022	57,826	39,920	59,156	2.30%	11.50%	23,074	34,192	33,066	49,000	46,478	68,875
Resident Treatment Technician	34,877	51,530	35,679	52,715	36,500	53,927	37,339	55,168	38,198	56,437	2.30%	11.50%	22,079	32,620	31,640	46,748	44,474	65,709
Respiratory Therapy Technician	36,449	54,013	37,287	55,255	38,145	56,526	39,022	57,826	39,920	59,156	2.30%	11.50%	23,074	34,192	33,066	49,000	46,478	68,875
Revenue Auditor 2-3	43,010	71,782	43,999	73,433	45,011	75,122	46,046	76,850	47,105	78,617	2.30%	11.50%	27,227	45,441	39,018	65,120	54,845	91,534
Right Of Way Agent 1-4	36,449	75,336	37,287	77,068	38,145	78,841	39,022	80,654	39,920	82,509	2.30%	11.50%	23,074	47,690	33,066	68,344	46,478	96,065
Safety Inspection Coordinator	48,568	75,336	49,685	77,068	50,828	78,841	51,997	80,654	53,193	82,509	2.30%	11.50%	30,746	47,690	44,061	68,344	61,933	96,065
Safety/Health Consultant	41,142	62,487	42,088	63,924	43,056	65,395	44,046	66,899	45,059	68,438	2.30%	11.50%	26,044	39,557	37,324	56,688	52,463	79,682
Sergeant	51,051	79,049	52,226	80,867	53,427	82,727	54,656	84,630	55,913	86,576	2.30%	11.50%	32,317	50,041	46,314	71,713	65,099	100,80
Social Work Administrator	56,268	86,726	57,562	88,721	58,886	90,761	60,241	92,849	61,626	94,984	2.30%	11.50%	35,620	54,901	51,046	78,677	71,751	110,59
Social Work Supervisor	48,568	75,336	49,685	77,068	50,828	78,841	51,997	80,654	53,193	82,509	2.30%	11.50%	30,746	47,690	44,061	68,344	61,933	96,065
Social Worker 2-6	39,707	75,336	40,620	77,068	41,554	78,841	42,510	80,654	43,488	82,509	2.30%	11.50%	25,136	47,690	36,022	68,344	50,632	96,065
Soils Party Chief	38,454	56,564	39,338	57,865	40,243	59,196	41,169	60,558	42,115	61,951	2.30%	11.50%	24,343	35,807	34,885	51,315	49,035	72,129
Soils Party Supervisor	41,142	62,487	42,088	63,924	43,056	65,395	44,046	66,899	45,059	68,438	2.30%	11.50%	26,044	39,557	37,324	56,688	52,463	79,682
Special Agent	51,051	79,049	52,226	80,867	53,427	82,727	54,656	84,630	55,913	86,576	2.30%	11.50%	32,317	50,041	46,314	71,713	65,099	100,80
Special Agent In Charge	62,009	95,383	63,435	97,576	64,894	99,821	66,387	102,116	67,914	104,465	2.30%	11.50%	39,254	60,381	56,254	86,531	79,072	121,62
Special Agent Supervisor	56,268	86,726	57,562	88,721	58,886	90,761	60,241	92,849	61,626	94,984	2.30%	11.50%	35,620	54,901	51,046	78,677	71,751	110,59
Special Investigator	47,179	71,782	48,264	73,433	49,374	75,122	50,509	76,850	51,671	78,617	2.30%	11.50%	29,866	45,441	42,800	65,120	60,161	91,534
Speech/Language Pathologis	43,010	71,782	43,999	73,433	45,011	75,122	46,046	76,850	47,105	78,617	2.30%	11.50%	27,227	45,441	39,018	65,120	54,845	91,534
Statistical Research Analyst 1-3	34,877	71,782	35,679	73,433	36,500	75,122	37,339	76,850	38,198	78,617	2.30%	11.50%	22,079	45,441	31,640	65,120	44,474	91,534
Superintendent Banking Div	89,574	137,049	91,634	140,201	93,742	143,425	95,898	146,724	98,103	150,099	2.30%	11.50%	56,704	86,757	81,261	124,330	114,221	174,75
Superintendent Credit Unio	89,574	137,049	91,634	140,201	93,742	143,425	95,898	146,724	98,103	150,099	2.30%	11.50%	56,704	86,757	81,261	124,330	114,221	174,75
Surveys Supervisor	56,268	86,726	57,562	88,721	58,886	90,761	60,241	92,849	61,626	94,984	2.30%	11.50%	35,620	54,901	51,046	78,677	71,751	110,59
Tax Performance System Analyst	47,179	71,782	48,264	73,433	49,374	75,122	50,509	76,850	51,671	78,617	2.30%	11.50%	29,866	45,441	42,800	65,120	60,161	91,534
Taxpayer Service Specialis	47,179	71,782	48,264	73,433	49,374	75,122	50,509	76,850	51,671	78,617	2.30%	11.50%	29,866	45,441	42,800	65,120	60,161	91,534
Technical Service Spec Sen	38,454	56,564	39,338	57,865	40,243	59,196	41,169	60,558	42,115	61,951	2.30%	11.50%	24,343	35,807	34,885	51,315	49,035	72,129
Technical Tax Specialist 1-4	47,179	99,779	48,264	102,074	49,374	104,422	50,509	106,824	51,671	109,280	2.30%	11.50%	29,866	63,164	42,800	90,519	60,161	127,23
Telecommunications Account Consultant	53,557	82,830	54,789	84,735	56,049	86,684	57,338	88,678	58,657	90,718	2.30%	11.50%	33,904	52,435	48,587	75,143	68,294	105,62

Chart III - U.S. States & Cities - Job Titles - Salaries - Pension Estimates

Iowa	2010 (Min)	2010 (Max)	2011 (Min)	2011 (Max)	2012 (Min)	2012 (Max)	2013 (Min)	2013 (Max)	2014 (Min)	2014 (Max)	5-Year Average % Raise	5-Year Cumulative Raise Estimate**	20-Year Annual Pension Benefit Estimate (Min.)***	20-Year Annual Pension Benefit Estimate (Max.)	25-Year Annual Pension Benefit Estimate (Min.)	25-Year Annual Pension Benefit Estimate (Max.)	30-Year Annual Pension Benefit Estimate (Min.)	30-Year Annual Pension Benefit Estimate (Max.)
Telecommunications Admin	83,992	119,576	85,924	122,326	87,900	125,139	89,922	128,018	91,990	130,962	2.30%	11.50%	53,170	75,696	76,197	108,479	107,104	152,478
Telecommunications Design	51,051	79,049	52,226	80,867	53,427	82,727	54,656	84,630	55,913	86,576	2.30%	11.50%	32,317	50,041	46,314	71,713	65,099	100,800
Telecommunications Eng Sen	45,060	90,940	46,096	93,032	47,157	95,172	48,241	97,361	49,351	99,600	2.30%	11.50%	28,525	57,569	40,878	82,501	57,459	115,964
Telecommunications Enginee	41,142	82,830	42,088	84,735	43,056	86,684	44,046	88,678	45,059	90,718	2.30%	11.50%	26,044	52,435	37,324	75,143	52,463	105,622
Telecommunications Manager	45,060	90,940	46,096	93,032	47,157	95,172	48,241	97,361	49,351	99,600	2.30%	11.50%	28,525	57,569	40,878	82,501	57,459	115,964
Telecommunications Marketing Analyst	48,568	75,336	49,685	77,068	50,828	78,841	51,997	80,654	53,193	82,509	2.30%	11.50%	30,746	47,690	44,061	68,344	61,933	96,065
Telecommunications Marketing Analyst, Senior	53,557	82,830	54,789	84,735	56,049	86,684	57,338	88,678	58,657	90,718	2.30%	11.50%	33,904	52,435	48,587	75,143	68,294	105,622
Telecommunications Sales Engineer	62,009	95,383	63,435	97,576	64,894	99,821	66,387	102,116	67,914	104,465	2.30%	11.50%	39,254	60,381	56,254	86,531	79,072	121,628
Telecommunications Tech En	59,093	119,576	60,452	122,326	61,843	125,139	63,265	128,018	64,720	130,962	2.30%	11.50%	37,408	75,696	53,609	108,479	75,353	152,478
Transportation Engineer	53,557	82,830	54,789	84,735	56,049	86,684	57,338	88,678	58,657	90,718	2.30%	11.50%	33,904	52,435	48,587	75,143	68,294	105,622
Transportation Engineer Manager	62,009	95,383	63,435	97,576	64,894	99,821	66,387	102,116	67,914	104,465	2.30%	11.50%	39,254	60,381	56,254	86,531	79,072	121,628
Transportation Engineer Specialist	62,009	95,383	63,435	97,576	64,894	99,821	66,387	102,116	67,914	104,465	2.30%	11.50%	39,254	60,381	56,254	86,531	79,072	121,628
Transportation Planner 1-4	38,454	95,383	39,338	97,576	40,243	99,821	41,169	102,116	42,115	104,465	2.30%	11.50%	24,343	60,381	34,885	86,531	49,035	121,628
Treatment Program Admin	59,093	90,940	60,452	93,032	61,843	95,172	63,265	97,361	64,720	99,600	2.30%	11.50%	37,408	57,569	53,609	82,501	75,353	115,964
Treatment Program Manager	45,060	68,615	46,096	70,193	47,157	71,808	48,241	73,459	49,351	75,149	2.30%	11.50%	28,525	43,436	40,878	62,248	57,459	87,496
Treatment Program Supervisor	43,010	65,175	43,999	66,674	45,011	68,208	46,046	69,777	47,105	71,382	2.30%	11.50%	27,227	41,258	39,018	59,127	54,845	83,109
Treatment Services Director	51,051	79,049	52,226	80,867	53,427	82,727	54,656	84,630	55,913	86,576	2.30%	11.50%	32,317	50,041	46,314	71,713	65,099	100,800
Trooper	43,010	65,175	43,999	66,674	45,011	68,208	46,046	69,777	47,105	71,382	2.30%	11.50%	27,227	41,258	39,018	59,127	54,845	83,109
Trooper Pilot	45,060	68,615	46,096	70,193	47,157	71,808	48,241	73,459	49,351	75,149	2.30%	11.50%	28,525	43,436	40,878	62,248	57,459	87,496
Trooper Pilot Senior	46,290	68,205	47,355	69,774	48,444	71,379	49,558	73,020	50,698	74,700	2.30%	11.50%	29,303	43,176	41,994	61,876	59,028	86,973
Trooper, Senior	44,331	65,267	45,351	66,768	46,394	68,303	47,461	69,874	48,552	71,481	2.30%	11.50%	28,063	41,316	40,217	59,210	56,529	83,226
Utilities Regulation Engineer 1-3	47,179	103,811	48,264	106,199	49,374	108,642	50,509	111,140	51,671	113,697	2.30%	11.50%	29,866	65,716	42,800	94,177	60,161	132,377
Utilities Regulation Inspe	45,060	68,615	46,096	70,193	47,157	71,808	48,241	73,459	49,351	75,149	2.30%	11.50%	28,525	43,436	40,878	62,248	57,459	87,496
Utility Administrator 1-2	80,120	137,481	81,962	140,643	83,847	143,878	85,776	147,187	87,749	150,573	2.30%	11.50%	50,719	87,031	72,684	124,722	102,166	175,311
Utility Analyst 1-2	39,707	71,782	40,620	73,433	41,554	75,122	42,510	76,850	43,488	78,617	2.30%	11.50%	25,136	45,441	36,022	65,120	50,632	91,534
Utility Attorney 1-2	65,084	131,216	66,581	134,234	68,113	137,322	69,679	140,480	71,282	143,711	2.30%	11.50%	41,201	83,065	59,044	119,039	82,993	167,323
Veterans Benefits Specialist	36,449	54,013	37,287	55,255	38,145	56,526	39,022	57,826	39,920	59,156	2.30%	11.50%	23,074	34,192	33,066	49,000	46,478	68,875
Veterinarian	56,268	86,726	57,562	88,721	58,886	90,761	60,241	92,849	61,626	94,984	2.30%	11.50%	35,620	54,901	51,046	78,677	71,751	110,590
Veterinarian Supervisor	59,093	90,940	60,452	93,032	61,843	95,172	63,265	97,361	64,720	99,600	2.30%	11.50%	37,408	57,569	53,609	82,501	75,353	115,964
Vocational Instructor	36,449	54,013	37,287	55,255	38,145	56,526	39,022	57,826	39,920	59,156	2.30%	11.50%	23,074	34,192	33,066	49,000	46,478	68,875
Vocational Instructor Supv	41,142	62,487	42,088	63,924	43,056	65,395	44,046	66,899	45,059	68,438	2.30%	11.50%	26,044	39,557	37,324	56,688	52,463	79,682
Vocational Rehabilitation Specialist	41,142	62,487	42,088	63,924	43,056	65,395	44,046	66,899	45,059	68,438	2.30%	11.50%	26,044	39,557	37,324	56,688	52,463	79,682
Welder	39,593	51,530	40,503	52,715	41,435	53,927	42,388	55,168	43,363	56,437	2.30%	11.50%	25,064	32,620	35,918	46,748	50,487	65,709
Workers Compensation Comm	77,887	119,166	79,678	121,907	81,511	124,710	83,386	127,579	85,303	130,513	2.30%	11.50%	49,305	75,436	70,659	108,107	99,318	151,956
Workforce Development Supr	41,142	62,487	42,088	63,924	43,056	65,395	44,046	66,899	45,059	68,438	2.30%	11.50%	26,044	39,557	37,324	56,688	52,463	79,682

Chart III - U.S. States & Cities - Job Titles - Salaries - Pension Estimates

Iowa	2010 (Min)	2010 (Max)	2011 (Min)	2011 (Max)	2012 (Min)	2012 (Max)	2013 (Min)	2013 (Max)	2014 (Min)	2014 (Max)	5-Year Average % Raise	5-Year Cumulative Raise Estimate**	20-Year Annual Pension Benefit Estimate (Min.)***	20-Year Annual Pension Benefit Estimate (Max.)	25-Year Annual Pension Benefit Estimate (Min.)	25-Year Annual Pension Benefit Estimate (Max.)	30-Year Annual Pension Benefit Estimate (Min.)	30-Year Annual Pension Benefit Estimate (Max.)
Workforce Program Coordina	48,568	75,336	49,685	77,068	50,828	78,841	51,997	80,654	53,193	82,509	2.30%	11.50%	30,746	47,690	44,061	68,344	61,933	96,065
Youth Counselor	39,707	59,389	40,620	60,755	41,554	62,152	42,510	63,582	43,488	65,044	2.30%	11.50%	25,136	37,596	36,022	53,878	50,632	75,731
Youth Counselor Supervisor	45,060	68,615	46,096	70,193	47,157	71,808	48,241	73,459	49,351	75,149	2.30%	11.50%	28,525	43,436	40,878	62,248	57,459	87,496

https://www.iowaonline.state.ia.us/idopapptrack/ICPJobClassPrompt.asp?partialCls=all

Chart III - U.S. States & Cities - Job Titles - Salaries - Pension Estimates

IL-Chicago	2010 (Min)	2010 (Max)	2011 (Min)	2011 (Max)	2012 (Min)	2012 (Max)	2013 (Min)	2013 (Max)	2014 (Min)	2014 (Max)	5-Year Average % Raise	5-Year Cumulative Raise Estimate**	20-Year Annual Pension Benefit Estimate (Min.)***	20-Year Annual Pension Benefit Estimate (Max.)	25-Year Annual Pension Benefit Estimate (Min.)	25-Year Annual Pension Benefit Estimate (Max.)	30-Year Annual Pension Benefit Estimate (Min.)	30-Year Annual Pension Benefit Estimate (Max.)
Accountant I-V	44,717	83,577	45,745	85,499	46,797	87,465	47,874	89,477	48,975	91,535	2.30%	11.50%	28,307	52,907	40,567	75,820	57,021	106,574
Accounting Technician I-III	34,535	84,272	35,329	86,210	36,142	88,193	36,973	90,221	37,824	92,296	2.30%	11.50%	21,862	53,347	31,330	76,451	44,038	107,460
Administrative Asst I-III	31,497	84,272	32,222	86,210	32,963	88,193	33,721	90,221	34,497	92,296	2.30%	11.50%	19,939	53,347	28,574	76,451	40,164	107,460
Administrative Legal Clerk	34,535	58,129	35,329	59,466	36,142	60,834	36,973	62,233	37,824	63,664	2.30%	11.50%	21,862	36,798	31,330	52,735	44,038	74,124
Administrative Services Officer I-II	45,618	93,140	46,667	95,283	47,740	97,474	48,838	99,716	49,962	102,010	2.30%	11.50%	28,878	58,961	41,384	84,497	58,170	118,769
Airport Operations Supvsr I-II	50,084	92,484	51,236	94,611	52,415	96,787	53,620	99,013	54,853	101,291	2.30%	11.50%	31,705	58,546	45,436	83,901	63,866	117,932
Animal Care Aide I-II	31,497	58,129	32,222	59,466	32,963	60,834	33,721	62,233	34,497	63,664	2.30%	11.50%	19,939	36,798	28,574	52,735	40,164	74,124
Animal Control Officer	37,985	63,316	38,858	64,773	39,752	66,263	40,666	67,787	41,602	69,346	2.30%	11.50%	24,046	40,082	34,460	57,440	48,437	80,739
Animal Shelter Manager	60,304	106,283	61,691	108,727	63,110	111,228	64,562	113,786	66,047	116,403	2.30%	11.50%	38,175	67,281	54,708	96,419	76,898	135,528
Architect I-IV	49,299	91,287	50,433	93,387	51,593	95,534	52,780	97,732	53,993	99,980	2.30%	11.50%	31,208	57,788	44,724	82,815	62,864	116,406
Asst Specialist In Aging	37,895	63,793	38,766	65,260	39,658	66,761	40,570	68,296	41,503	69,867	2.30%	11.50%	23,989	40,383	34,378	57,873	48,322	81,346
Asst Specialist In Disability	37,895	63,793	38,766	65,260	39,658	66,761	40,570	68,296	41,503	69,867	2.30%	11.50%	23,989	40,383	34,378	57,873	48,322	81,346
Asst Supt Of Forestry	54,950	92,484	56,214	94,611	57,507	96,787	58,829	99,013	60,182	101,291	2.30%	11.50%	34,785	58,546	49,850	83,901	70,070	117,932
Asst Supt Of Laborers	60,304	106,283	61,691	108,727	63,110	111,228	64,562	113,786	66,047	116,403	2.30%	11.50%	38,175	67,281	54,708	96,419	76,898	135,528
Auditor I-IV	49,299	121,484	50,433	124,278	51,593	127,137	52,780	130,061	53,993	133,052	2.30%	11.50%	31,208	76,904	44,724	110,210	62,864	154,912
Battalion Chief	86,016	125,288	87,994	128,169	90,018	131,117	92,089	134,133	94,207	137,218	2.30%	11.50%	54,451	79,312	78,033	113,661	109,684	159,762
Battalion Chief-Paramedic	131,402	127,598	134,424	130,533	137,516	133,535	140,679	136,607	143,914	139,749	2.30%	11.50%	83,182	80,774	119,207	115,757	167,559	162,709
Business Consultant	50,084	92,484	51,236	94,611	52,415	96,787	53,620	99,013	54,853	101,291	2.30%	11.50%	31,705	58,546	45,436	83,901	63,866	117,932
Buyer	54,950	93,140	56,214	95,283	57,507	97,474	58,829	99,716	60,182	102,010	2.30%	11.50%	34,785	58,961	49,850	84,497	70,070	118,769
Captain	78,113	123,962	79,909	126,813	81,747	129,730	83,627	132,714	85,551	135,766	2.30%	11.50%	49,448	78,473	70,863	112,458	99,606	158,072
Captain-Paramedic	83,583	123,248	85,506	126,082	87,472	128,982	89,484	131,949	91,542	134,984	2.30%	11.50%	52,911	78,020	75,826	111,810	106,582	157,161
Cartographer III	41,576	84,272	42,532	86,210	43,510	88,193	44,511	90,221	45,535	92,296	2.30%	11.50%	26,319	53,347	37,718	76,451	53,016	107,460
Case Manager Asst	37,895	63,793	38,766	65,260	39,658	66,761	40,570	68,296	41,503	69,867	2.30%	11.50%	23,989	40,383	34,378	57,873	48,322	81,346
City Planner III-V	49,299	88,288	50,433	90,318	51,593	92,396	52,780	94,521	53,993	96,695	2.30%	11.50%	31,208	55,889	44,724	80,094	62,864	112,581
Civil Engineer II-V	54,293	121,484	55,542	124,278	56,820	127,137	58,126	130,061	59,463	133,052	2.30%	11.50%	34,370	76,904	49,255	110,210	69,233	154,912
Clerk II-IV	26,156	58,129	26,757	59,466	27,373	60,834	28,002	62,233	28,646	63,664	2.30%	11.50%	16,557	36,798	23,728	52,735	33,353	74,124
Clinical Therapist I-III	44,717	88,288	45,745	90,318	46,797	92,396	47,874	94,521	48,975	96,695	2.30%	11.50%	28,307	55,889	40,567	80,094	57,021	112,581
Communicable Disease Control Investigator I-II	37,895	84,272	38,766	86,210	39,658	88,193	40,570	90,221	41,503	92,296	2.30%	11.50%	23,989	53,347	34,378	76,451	48,322	107,460
Communications Operator I-II	34,535	63,793	35,329	65,260	36,142	66,761	36,973	68,296	37,824	69,867	2.30%	11.50%	21,862	40,383	31,330	57,873	44,038	81,346
Community Outreach Coord	50,084	84,272	51,236	86,210	52,415	88,193	53,620	90,221	54,853	92,296	2.30%	11.50%	31,705	53,347	45,436	76,451	63,866	107,460
Community Services Representative	45,618	76,806	46,667	78,573	47,740	80,380	48,838	82,229	49,962	84,120	2.30%	11.50%	28,878	48,621	41,384	69,678	58,170	97,940
Computer Applications Analyst	54,950	93,140	56,214	95,283	57,507	97,474	58,829	99,716	60,182	102,010	2.30%	11.50%	34,785	58,961	49,850	84,497	70,070	118,769
Computer Graphics Technician III	37,895	63,793	38,766	65,260	39,658	66,761	40,570	68,296	41,503	69,867	2.30%	11.50%	23,989	40,383	34,378	57,873	48,322	81,346
Construction Equipment Inspector	101,627	101,627	103,965	103,965	106,356	106,356	108,802	108,802	111,304	111,304	2.30%	11.50%	64,334	64,334	92,196	92,196	129,591	129,591
Consumer Investigator I-II	41,576	76,806	42,532	78,573	43,510	80,380	44,511	82,229	45,535	84,120	2.30%	11.50%	26,319	48,621	37,718	69,678	53,016	97,940
Contracts Compliance Coord	54,950	93,140	56,214	95,283	57,507	97,474	58,829	99,716	60,182	102,010	2.30%	11.50%	34,785	58,961	49,850	84,497	70,070	118,769
Contracts Compliance Officer	41,576	84,272	42,532	86,210	43,510	88,193	44,511	90,221	45,535	92,296	2.30%	11.50%	26,319	53,347	37,718	76,451	53,016	107,460

Chart III - U.S. States & Cities - Job Titles - Salaries - Pension Estimates

IL-Chicago	2010 (Min)	2010 (Max)	2011 (Min)	2011 (Max)	2012 (Min)	2012 (Max)	2013 (Min)	2013 (Max)	2014 (Min)	2014 (Max)	5-Year Average % Raise	5-Year Cumulative Raise Estimate**	20-Year Annual Pension Benefit Estimate (Min.)***	20-Year Annual Pension Benefit Estimate (Max.)	25-Year Annual Pension Benefit Estimate (Min.)	25-Year Annual Pension Benefit Estimate (Max.)	30-Year Annual Pension Benefit Estimate (Min.)	30-Year Annual Pension Benefit Estimate (Max.)
Contracts Coord	66,148	116,632	67,670	119,314	69,226	122,058	70,818	124,866	72,447	127,738	2.30%	11.50%	41,874	73,832	60,009	105,808	84,350	148,724
Contracts Development Specialist	41,576	84,272	42,532	86,210	43,510	88,193	44,511	90,221	45,535	92,296	2.30%	11.50%	26,319	53,347	37,718	76,451	53,016	107,460
Contracts Manager	45,618	76,806	46,667	78,573	47,740	80,380	48,838	82,229	49,962	84,120	2.30%	11.50%	28,878	48,621	41,384	69,678	58,170	97,940
Contracts Negotiator	66,148	116,632	67,670	119,314	69,226	122,058	70,818	124,866	72,447	127,738	2.30%	11.50%	41,874	73,832	60,009	105,808	84,350	148,724
Contracts Review Specialist I-II	37,895	76,806	38,766	78,573	39,658	80,380	40,570	82,229	41,503	84,120	2.30%	11.50%	23,989	48,621	34,378	69,678	48,322	97,940
Criminalist III	59,931	83,577	61,310	85,499	62,720	87,465	64,162	89,477	65,638	91,535	2.30%	11.50%	37,939	52,907	54,369	75,820	76,422	106,574
Customer Services Supvsr	45,618	84,272	46,667	86,210	47,740	88,193	48,838	90,221	49,962	92,296	2.30%	11.50%	28,878	53,347	41,384	76,451	58,170	107,460
Data Base Analyst	54,293	76,626	55,542	78,388	56,820	80,191	58,126	82,036	59,463	83,922	2.30%	11.50%	34,370	48,507	49,255	69,515	69,233	97,711
Data Entry Operator	28,691	48,334	29,351	49,445	30,026	50,583	30,717	51,746	31,423	52,936	2.30%	11.50%	18,163	30,597	26,029	43,848	36,586	61,633
Data Services Administrator	66,148	116,632	67,670	119,314	69,226	122,058	70,818	124,866	72,447	127,738	2.30%	11.50%	41,874	73,832	60,009	105,808	84,350	148,724
Dir Of Administration I-II	54,950	106,283	56,214	108,727	57,507	111,228	58,829	113,786	60,182	116,403	2.30%	11.50%	34,785	67,281	49,850	96,419	70,070	135,528
Disability Specialist I-III	40,585	88,288	41,518	90,318	42,473	92,396	43,450	94,521	44,449	96,695	2.30%	11.50%	25,692	55,889	36,818	80,094	51,752	112,581
Elder Protective Investigator I-III	44,717	88,288	45,745	90,318	46,797	92,396	47,874	94,521	48,975	96,695	2.30%	11.50%	28,307	55,889	40,567	80,094	57,021	112,581
Elderly Aide II	27,404	46,068	28,034	47,128	28,679	48,212	29,339	49,321	30,014	50,455	2.30%	11.50%	17,348	29,163	24,861	41,793	34,945	58,745
Electrical Engineer II-IV	54,293	91,287	55,542	93,387	56,820	95,534	58,126	97,732	59,463	99,980	2.30%	11.50%	34,370	57,788	49,255	82,815	69,233	116,406
Electrical Inspector	85,121	85,121	87,079	87,079	89,082	89,082	91,131	91,131	93,227	93,227	2.30%	11.50%	53,885	53,885	77,222	77,222	108,544	108,544
Electrical Mechanic	80,989	80,989	82,852	82,852	84,758	84,758	86,707	86,707	88,702	88,702	2.30%	11.50%	51,269	51,269	73,473	73,473	103,275	103,275
Engineering Technician II-VI	31,497	92,484	32,222	94,611	32,963	96,787	33,721	99,013	34,497	101,291	2.30%	11.50%	19,939	58,546	28,574	83,901	40,164	117,932
Environmental Engineer I-III	54,293	91,287	55,542	93,387	56,820	95,534	58,126	97,732	59,463	99,980	2.30%	11.50%	34,370	57,788	49,255	82,815	69,233	116,406
Epidemiologist II-IV	59,931	117,198	61,310	119,893	62,720	122,651	64,162	125,472	65,638	128,358	2.30%	11.50%	37,939	74,191	54,369	106,322	76,422	149,447
Equipment Services Coord	66,148	111,315	67,670	113,876	69,226	116,495	70,818	119,174	72,447	121,915	2.30%	11.50%	41,874	70,467	60,009	100,985	84,350	141,94
Executive Asst	78,113	115,183	79,909	117,833	81,747	120,543	83,627	123,315	85,551	126,152	2.30%	11.50%	49,448	72,915	70,863	104,494	99,606	146,87
Executive Legal Secretary	41,576	70,010	42,532	71,620	43,510	73,267	44,511	74,952	45,535	76,676	2.30%	11.50%	26,319	44,319	37,718	63,513	53,016	89,274
Executive Secretary I-II	34,535	70,010	35,329	71,620	36,142	73,267	36,973	74,952	37,824	76,676	2.30%	11.50%	21,862	44,319	31,330	63,513	44,038	89,274
Explosives Technician I-III	69,044	123,962	70,632	126,813	72,257	129,730	73,919	132,714	75,619	135,766	2.30%	11.50%	43,708	78,473	62,637	112,458	88,043	158,072
Field Service Specialist II-III	45,618	84,272	46,667	86,210	47,740	88,193	48,838	90,221	49,962	92,296	2.30%	11.50%	28,878	53,347	41,384	76,451	58,170	107,46
Field Services Dir	72,571	116,632	74,240	119,314	75,948	122,058	77,695	124,866	79,482	127,738	2.30%	11.50%	45,940	73,832	65,836	105,808	92,540	148,724
Field Supvsr	60,304	106,283	61,691	108,727	63,110	111,228	64,562	113,786	66,047	116,403	2.30%	11.50%	38,175	67,281	54,708	96,419	76,898	135,528
Filtration Engineer II-V	54,293	121,484	55,542	124,278	56,820	127,137	58,126	130,061	59,463	133,052	2.30%	11.50%	34,370	76,904	49,255	110,210	69,233	154,912
Financial Analyst	54,950	93,140	56,214	95,283	57,507	97,474	58,829	99,716	60,182	102,010	2.30%	11.50%	34,785	58,961	49,850	84,497	70,070	118,769
Financial Planning Analyst	72,571	121,484	74,240	124,278	75,948	127,137	77,695	130,061	79,482	133,052	2.30%	11.50%	45,940	76,904	65,836	110,210	92,540	154,912
Fingerprint Technician I-IV	31,497	93,140	32,222	95,283	32,963	97,474	33,721	99,716	34,497	102,010	2.30%	11.50%	19,939	58,961	28,574	84,497	40,164	118,769
Fire Communications Operator I-II	42,541	79,432	43,520	81,259	44,521	83,128	45,545	85,040	46,592	86,996	2.30%	11.50%	26,930	50,283	38,593	72,060	54,247	101,289
Fire Engineer	61,830	93,700	63,252	95,855	64,707	98,060	66,195	100,316	67,717	102,623	2.30%	11.50%	39,141	59,316	56,092	85,005	78,843	119,483
Fire Engineer-Paramedic	66,155	100,259	67,676	102,565	69,233	104,923	70,825	107,337	72,454	109,805	2.30%	11.50%	41,878	63,467	60,015	90,954	84,358	127,84
Fire Marshal	49,054	87,812	50,183	89,831	51,337	91,897	52,518	94,011	53,726	96,173	2.30%	11.50%	31,053	55,588	44,502	79,662	62,553	111,974
Fire Prevention Engineer III	66,110	91,287	67,630	93,387	69,186	95,534	70,777	97,732	72,405	99,980	2.30%	11.50%	41,850	57,788	59,974	82,815	84,301	116,40

Chart III - U.S. States & Cities - Job Titles - Salaries - Pension Estimates

IL-Chicago	2010 (Min)	2010 (Max)	2011 (Min)	2011 (Max)	2012 (Min)	2012 (Max)	2013 (Min)	2013 (Max)	2014 (Min)	2014 (Max)	5-Year Average % Raise	5-Year Cumulative Raise Estimate**	20-Year Annual Pension Benefit Estimate (Min.)***	20-Year Annual Pension Benefit Estimate (Max.)	25-Year Annual Pension Benefit Estimate (Min.)	25-Year Annual Pension Benefit Estimate (Max.)	30-Year Annual Pension Benefit Estimate (Min.)	30-Year Annual Pension Benefit Estimate (Max.)
Firearms Identification Technician I	69,044	103,052	70,632	105,422	72,257	107,847	73,919	110,327	75,619	112,865	2.30%	11.50%	43,708	65,236	62,637	93,488	88,043	131,408
Firefighter	49,054	87,812	50,183	89,831	51,337	91,897	52,518	94,011	53,726	96,173	2.30%	11.50%	31,053	55,588	44,502	79,662	62,553	111,974
Firefighter/Paramedic	59,777	93,958	61,152	96,119	62,558	98,330	63,997	100,591	65,469	102,905	2.30%	11.50%	37,841	59,479	54,229	85,238	76,225	119,812
Fiscal Administrator	72,571	116,632	74,240	119,314	75,948	122,058	77,695	124,866	79,482	127,738	2.30%	11.50%	45,940	73,832	65,836	105,808	92,540	148,724
Fiscal Policy Analyst	59,931	88,288	61,310	90,318	62,720	92,396	64,162	94,521	65,638	96,695	2.30%	11.50%	37,939	55,889	54,369	80,094	76,422	112,581
Gis Data Base Analyst	72,571	121,484	74,240	124,278	75,948	127,137	77,695	130,061	79,482	133,052	2.30%	11.50%	45,940	76,904	65,836	110,210	92,540	154,912
Grants Research Specialist	59,931	83,577	61,310	85,499	62,720	87,465	64,162	89,477	65,638	91,535	2.30%	11.50%	37,939	52,907	54,369	75,820	76,422	106,574
Grants Specialist	41,576	84,272	42,532	86,210	43,510	88,193	44,511	90,221	45,535	92,296	2.30%	11.50%	26,319	53,347	37,718	76,451	53,016	107,460
Graphic Artist II-III	34,535	84,272	35,329	86,210	36,142	88,193	36,973	90,221	37,824	92,296	2.30%	11.50%	21,862	53,347	31,330	76,451	44,038	107,460
Health Educator	41,576	84,272	42,532	86,210	43,510	88,193	44,511	90,221	45,535	92,296	2.30%	11.50%	26,319	53,347	37,718	76,451	53,016	107,460
Help Desk Manager	72,571	116,632	74,240	119,314	75,948	122,058	77,695	124,866	79,482	127,738	2.30%	11.50%	45,940	73,832	65,836	105,808	92,540	148,724
Help Desk Supervisor	60,304	106,283	61,691	108,727	63,110	111,228	64,562	113,786	66,047	116,403	2.30%	11.50%	38,175	67,281	54,708	96,419	76,898	135,528
Help Desk Technician	41,576	84,272	42,532	86,210	43,510	88,193	44,511	90,221	45,535	92,296	2.30%	11.50%	26,319	53,347	37,718	76,451	53,016	107,460
Human Relations Investigator II-III	54,293	83,577	55,542	85,499	56,820	87,465	58,126	89,477	59,463	91,535	2.30%	11.50%	34,370	52,907	49,255	75,820	69,233	106,574
Human Relations Specialist I-II	41,576	84,272	42,532	86,210	43,510	88,193	44,511	90,221	45,535	92,296	2.30%	11.50%	26,319	53,347	37,718	76,451	53,016	107,460
Human Service Specialist II	45,618	76,806	46,667	78,573	47,740	80,380	48,838	82,229	49,962	84,120	2.30%	11.50%	28,878	48,621	41,384	69,678	58,170	97,940
Inquiry Aide I-III	27,404	55,503	28,034	56,780	28,679	58,086	29,339	59,422	30,014	60,788	2.30%	11.50%	17,348	35,136	24,861	50,352	34,945	70,776
Inventory Analyst	37,895	63,793	38,766	65,260	39,658	66,761	40,570	68,296	41,503	69,867	2.30%	11.50%	23,989	40,383	34,378	57,873	48,322	81,346
Investigator	50,084	92,484	51,236	94,611	52,415	96,787	53,620	99,013	54,853	101,291	2.30%	11.50%	31,705	58,546	45,436	83,901	63,866	117,932
Investigator - Ops I-III	50,084	101,456	51,236	103,789	52,415	106,176	53,620	108,618	54,853	111,117	2.30%	11.50%	31,705	64,225	45,436	92,040	63,866	129,373
Investigator Specialist	54,950	93,140	56,214	95,283	57,507	97,474	58,829	99,716	60,182	102,010	2.30%	11.50%	34,785	58,961	49,850	84,497	70,070	118,769
Labor Relations Specialist II-III	49,299	88,288	50,433	90,318	51,593	92,396	52,780	94,521	53,993	96,695	2.30%	11.50%	31,208	55,889	44,724	80,094	62,864	112,581
Laboratory Technician III	34,535	58,129	35,329	59,466	36,142	60,834	36,973	62,233	37,824	63,664	2.30%	11.50%	21,862	36,798	31,330	52,735	44,038	74,124
Landscape Architect	44,717	63,497	45,745	64,957	46,797	66,451	47,874	67,979	48,975	69,543	2.30%	11.50%	28,307	40,196	40,567	57,604	57,021	80,969
Leasing Agent II	45,618	76,806	46,667	78,573	47,740	80,380	48,838	82,229	49,962	84,120	2.30%	11.50%	28,878	48,621	41,384	69,678	58,170	97,940
Legislative Asst II	34,535	58,129	35,329	59,466	36,142	60,834	36,973	62,233	37,824	63,664	2.30%	11.50%	21,862	36,798	31,330	52,735	44,038	74,124
Librarian I-IV	44,717	83,577	45,745	85,499	46,797	87,465	47,874	89,477	48,975	91,535	2.30%	11.50%	28,307	52,907	40,567	75,820	57,021	106,574
Lieutenant	69,044	115,183	70,632	117,833	72,257	120,543	73,919	123,315	75,619	126,152	2.30%	11.50%	43,708	72,915	62,637	104,494	88,043	146,878
Mason Inspector	85,541	85,541	87,508	87,508	89,521	89,521	91,580	91,580	93,686	93,686	2.30%	11.50%	54,151	54,151	77,602	77,602	109,079	109,079
Mechanical Engineer II-V	54,293	121,484	55,542	124,278	56,820	127,137	58,126	130,061	59,463	133,052	2.30%	11.50%	34,370	76,904	49,255	110,210	69,233	154,912
Medical Records Coord	41,576	84,272	42,532	86,210	43,510	88,193	44,511	90,221	45,535	92,296	2.30%	11.50%	26,319	53,347	37,718	76,451	53,016	107,460
Mgr Data Entry And Operations	60,304	106,283	61,691	108,727	63,110	111,228	64,562	113,786	66,047	116,403	2.30%	11.50%	38,175	67,281	54,708	96,419	76,898	135,528
Microbiologist II-IV	49,299	83,577	50,433	85,499	51,593	87,465	52,780	89,477	53,993	91,535	2.30%	11.50%	31,208	52,907	44,724	75,820	62,864	106,574
Nurse Practitioner	72,507	113,838	74,175	116,457	75,881	119,135	77,626	121,875	79,411	124,678	2.30%	11.50%	45,900	72,064	65,778	103,274	92,458	145,163
Nutrition Technician	31,497	52,968	32,222	54,186	32,963	55,432	33,721	56,707	34,497	58,011	2.30%	11.50%	19,939	33,530	28,574	48,052	40,164	67,542
Occupational Health Nurse	51,539	80,861	52,724	82,721	53,937	84,623	55,177	86,569	56,446	88,561	2.30%	11.50%	32,626	51,188	46,756	73,357	65,720	103,111
Paralegal I-II	37,895	76,806	38,766	78,573	39,658	80,380	40,570	82,229	41,503	84,120	2.30%	11.50%	23,989	48,621	34,378	69,678	48,322	97,940
Paramedic	49,054	87,812	50,183	89,831	51,337	91,897	52,518	94,011	53,726	96,173	2.30%	11.50%	31,053	55,588	44,502	79,662	62,553	111,974
Paramedic Field Officer	86,016	125,288	87,994	128,169	90,018	131,117	92,089	134,133	94,207	137,218	2.30%	11.50%	54,451	79,312	78,033	113,661	109,684	159,762
Parking Analyst	45,618	76,806	46,667	78,573	47,740	80,380	48,838	82,229	49,962	84,120	2.30%	11.50%	28,878	48,621	41,384	69,678	58,170	97,940

Chart III - U.S. States & Cities - Job Titles - Salaries - Pension Estimates

IL-Chicago	2010 (Min)	2010 (Max)	2011 (Min)	2011 (Max)	2012 (Min)	2012 (Max)	2013 (Min)	2013 (Max)	2014 (Min)	2014 (Max)	5-Year Average % Raise	5-Year Cumulative Raise Estimate**	20-Year Annual Pension Benefit Estimate (Min.)***	20-Year Annual Pension Benefit Estimate (Max.)	25-Year Annual Pension Benefit Estimate (Min.)	25-Year Annual Pension Benefit Estimate (Max.)	30-Year Annual Pension Benefit Estimate (Min.)	30-Year Annual Pension Benefit Estimate (Max.)
Parking Enforcement Aide	34,625	57,691	35,422	59,018	36,236	60,376	37,070	61,764	37,922	63,185	2.30%	11.50%	21,919	36,521	31,412	52,338	44,153	73,566
Parking Meter Mechanic	37,895	68,105	38,766	69,671	39,658	71,274	40,570	72,913	41,503	74,590	2.30%	11.50%	23,989	43,113	34,378	61,784	48,322	86,845
Parking Revenue Security Specialist	45,618	84,272	46,667	86,210	47,740	88,193	48,838	90,221	49,962	92,296	2.30%	11.50%	28,878	53,347	41,384	76,451	58,170	107,460
Parking Revenue Security Supvsr	60,304	106,283	61,691	108,727	63,110	111,228	64,562	113,786	66,047	116,403	2.30%	11.50%	38,175	67,281	54,708	96,419	76,898	135,528
Payment Services Representative	34,535	58,129	35,329	59,466	36,142	60,834	36,973	62,233	37,824	63,664	2.30%	11.50%	21,862	36,798	31,330	52,735	44,038	74,124
Payroll Administrator	66,148	116,632	67,670	119,314	69,226	122,058	70,818	124,866	72,447	127,738	2.30%	11.50%	41,874	73,832	60,009	105,808	84,350	148,724
Personal Computer Operator I-III	28,691	58,129	29,351	59,466	30,026	60,834	30,717	62,233	31,423	63,664	2.30%	11.50%	18,163	36,798	26,029	52,735	36,586	74,124
Personnel Analyst I-III	44,717	88,288	45,745	90,318	46,797	92,396	47,874	94,521	48,975	96,695	2.30%	11.50%	28,307	55,889	40,567	80,094	57,021	112,581
Personnel Assistant	31,497	52,968	32,222	54,186	32,963	55,432	33,721	56,707	34,497	58,011	2.30%	11.50%	19,939	33,530	28,574	48,052	40,164	67,542
Police Agent	59,777	103,052	61,152	105,422	62,558	107,847	63,997	110,327	65,469	112,865	2.30%	11.50%	37,841	65,236	54,229	93,488	76,225	131,408
Police Communications Operator I-II	45,734	83,641	46,785	85,565	47,861	87,533	48,962	89,546	50,088	91,606	2.30%	11.50%	28,951	52,948	41,489	75,879	58,318	106,656
Police Forensic Investigator I-III	69,044	123,962	70,632	126,813	72,257	129,730	73,919	132,714	75,619	135,766	2.30%	11.50%	43,708	78,473	62,637	112,458	88,043	158,072
Police Legal Officer I	69,044	103,052	70,632	105,422	72,257	107,847	73,919	110,327	75,619	112,865	2.30%	11.50%	43,708	65,236	62,637	93,488	88,043	131,408
Police Officer	46,236	86,602	47,299	88,593	48,387	90,631	49,500	92,716	50,638	94,848	2.30%	11.50%	29,269	54,822	41,945	78,565	58,958	110,431
Police Technician	59,777	103,052	61,152	105,422	62,558	107,847	63,997	110,327	65,469	112,865	2.30%	11.50%	37,841	65,236	54,229	93,488	76,225	131,408
Principal Computer Console Operator	45,618	84,272	46,667	86,210	47,740	88,193	48,838	90,221	49,962	92,296	2.30%	11.50%	28,878	53,347	41,384	76,451	58,170	107,460
Principal Data Base Analyst	79,265	117,198	81,088	119,893	82,953	122,651	84,861	125,472	86,812	128,358	2.30%	11.50%	50,177	74,191	71,909	106,322	101,075	149,447
Principal Operations Analyst	66,110	98,354	67,630	100,616	69,186	102,930	70,777	105,297	72,405	107,719	2.30%	11.50%	41,850	62,261	59,974	89,226	84,301	125,417
Principal Programmer/Analyst	79,265	117,198	81,088	119,893	82,953	122,651	84,861	125,472	86,812	128,358	2.30%	11.50%	50,177	74,191	71,909	106,322	101,075	149,447
Principal Revenue Analyst	54,293	76,626	55,542	78,388	56,820	80,191	58,126	82,036	59,463	83,922	2.30%	11.50%	34,370	48,507	49,255	69,515	69,233	97,711
Principal Systems Programmer	79,265	117,198	81,088	119,893	82,953	122,651	84,861	125,472	86,812	128,358	2.30%	11.50%	50,177	74,191	71,909	106,322	101,075	149,447
Principal Telecommunications Specialist	66,148	116,632	67,670	119,314	69,226	122,058	70,818	124,866	72,447	127,738	2.30%	11.50%	41,874	73,832	60,009	105,808	84,350	148,724
Program Auditor I-III	41,576	84,272	42,532	86,210	43,510	88,193	44,511	90,221	45,535	92,296	2.30%	11.50%	26,319	53,347	37,718	76,451	53,016	107,460
Program Specialist II	45,618	84,272	46,667	86,210	47,740	88,193	48,838	90,221	49,962	92,296	2.30%	11.50%	28,878	53,347	41,384	76,451	58,170	107,460
Programmer/Analyst	54,293	84,272	55,542	86,210	56,820	88,193	58,126	90,221	59,463	92,296	2.30%	11.50%	34,370	53,347	49,255	76,451	69,233	107,460
Psychologist	59,931	83,577	61,310	85,499	62,720	87,465	64,162	89,477	65,638	91,535	2.30%	11.50%	37,939	52,907	54,369	75,820	76,422	106,574
Public Health Administrator I-III	41,576	106,283	42,532	108,727	43,510	111,228	44,511	113,786	45,535	116,403	2.30%	11.50%	26,319	67,281	37,718	96,419	53,016	135,528
Public Health Aide	28,691	48,334	29,351	49,445	30,026	50,583	30,717	51,746	31,423	52,936	2.30%	11.50%	18,163	30,597	26,029	43,848	36,586	61,633
Public Health Nurse I-IV	51,539	108,419	52,724	110,913	53,937	113,464	55,177	116,074	56,446	118,743	2.30%	11.50%	32,626	68,633	46,756	98,358	65,720	138,252
Public Health Nutritionist I-III	36,710	70,100	37,555	71,712	38,419	73,362	39,302	75,049	40,206	76,775	2.30%	11.50%	23,239	44,376	33,304	63,594	46,812	89,389
Public Information Officer	45,618	76,806	46,667	78,573	47,740	80,380	48,838	82,229	49,962	84,120	2.30%	11.50%	28,878	48,621	41,384	69,678	58,170	97,940
Public Relations Representative I-III	41,576	92,484	42,532	94,611	43,510	96,787	44,511	99,013	45,535	101,291	2.30%	11.50%	26,319	58,546	37,718	83,901	53,016	117,932
Reprographics Technician II-IV	28,691	70,010	29,351	71,620	30,026	73,267	30,717	74,952	31,423	76,676	2.30%	11.50%	18,163	44,319	26,029	63,513	36,586	89,274
Resident Services Coord I-II	40,585	70,100	41,518	71,712	42,473	73,362	43,450	75,049	44,449	76,775	2.30%	11.50%	25,692	44,376	36,818	63,594	51,752	89,389
Revenue Account Specialist II	37,895	63,793	38,766	65,260	39,658	66,761	40,570	68,296	41,503	69,867	2.30%	11.50%	23,989	40,383	34,378	57,873	48,322	81,346
Revenue Investigator I-II	41,576	76,806	42,532	78,573	43,510	80,380	44,511	82,229	45,535	84,120	2.30%	11.50%	26,319	48,621	37,718	69,678	53,016	97,940

Chart III - U.S. States & Cities - Job Titles - Salaries - Pension Estimates

IL-Chicago	2010 (Min)	2010 (Max)	2011 (Min)	2011 (Max)	2012 (Min)	2012 (Max)	2013 (Min)	2013 (Max)	2014 (Min)	2014 (Max)	5-Year Average % Raise	5-Year Cumulative Raise Estimate**	20-Year Annual Pension Benefit Estimate (Min.)***	20-Year Annual Pension Benefit Estimate (Max.)	25-Year Annual Pension Benefit Estimate (Min.)	25-Year Annual Pension Benefit Estimate (Max.)	30-Year Annual Pension Benefit Estimate (Min.)	30-Year Annual Pension Benefit Estimate (Max.)
Safety Specialist	45,618	76,806	46,667	78,573	47,740	80,380	48,838	82,229	49,962	84,120	2.30%	11.50%	28,878	48,621	41,384	69,678	58,170	97,940
Sanitarian I-II	41,576	76,806	42,532	78,573	43,510	80,380	44,511	82,229	45,535	84,120	2.30%	11.50%	26,319	48,621	37,718	69,678	53,016	97,940
Sanitary Engineer I-IV	54,293	91,287	55,542	93,387	56,820	95,534	58,126	97,732	59,463	99,980	2.30%	11.50%	34,370	57,788	49,255	82,815	69,233	116,406
Senior Computer Console Operator	34,535	58,129	35,329	59,466	36,142	60,834	36,973	62,233	37,824	63,664	2.30%	11.50%	21,862	36,798	31,330	52,735	44,038	74,124
Senior Data Base Analyst	66,110	98,354	67,630	100,616	69,186	102,930	70,777	105,297	72,405	107,719	2.30%	11.50%	41,850	62,261	59,974	89,226	84,301	125,417
Senior Data Controller	37,895	63,793	38,766	65,260	39,658	66,761	40,570	68,296	41,503	69,867	2.30%	11.50%	23,989	40,383	34,378	57,873	48,322	81,346
Senior Emergency Management Coord	60,304	106,283	61,691	108,727	63,110	111,228	64,562	113,786	66,047	116,403	2.30%	11.50%	38,175	67,281	54,708	96,419	76,898	135,528
Senior Help Desk Technician	50,084	92,484	51,236	94,611	52,415	96,787	53,620	99,013	54,853	101,291	2.30%	11.50%	31,705	58,546	45,436	83,901	63,866	117,932
Senior Legal Investigator	45,618	76,806	46,667	78,573	47,740	80,380	48,838	82,229	49,962	84,120	2.30%	11.50%	28,878	48,621	41,384	69,678	58,170	97,940
Senior Operations Analyst	54,293	84,272	55,542	86,210	56,820	88,193	58,126	90,221	59,463	92,296	2.30%	11.50%	34,370	53,347	49,255	76,451	69,233	107,460
Senior Personnel Assistant	37,895	63,793	38,766	65,260	39,658	66,761	40,570	68,296	41,503	69,867	2.30%	11.50%	23,989	40,383	34,378	57,873	48,322	81,346
Senior Public Information Officer	54,950	93,140	56,214	95,283	57,507	97,474	58,829	99,716	60,182	102,010	2.30%	11.50%	34,785	58,961	49,850	84,497	70,070	118,769
Senior Research Analyst	49,299	70,100	50,433	71,712	51,593	73,362	52,780	75,049	53,993	76,775	2.30%	11.50%	31,208	44,376	44,724	63,594	62,864	89,389
Senior Research Asst	41,576	84,272	42,532	86,210	43,510	88,193	44,511	90,221	45,535	92,296	2.30%	11.50%	26,319	53,347	37,718	76,451	53,016	107,460
Senior Systems Programmer	66,110	98,354	67,630	100,616	69,186	102,930	70,777	105,297	72,405	107,719	2.30%	11.50%	41,850	62,261	59,974	89,226	84,301	125,417
Senior Telecommunications Specialist	54,950	93,140	56,214	95,283	57,507	97,474	58,829	99,716	60,182	102,010	2.30%	11.50%	34,785	58,961	49,850	84,497	70,070	118,769
Social Work Supvsr	66,110	98,354	67,630	100,616	69,186	102,930	70,777	105,297	72,405	107,719	2.30%	11.50%	41,850	62,261	59,974	89,226	84,301	125,417
Social Worker III	54,293	84,272	55,542	86,210	56,820	88,193	58,126	90,221	59,463	92,296	2.30%	11.50%	34,370	53,347	49,255	76,451	69,233	107,460
Specialist In Aging III	40,585	88,288	41,518	90,318	42,473	92,396	43,450	94,521	44,449	96,695	2.30%	11.50%	25,692	55,889	36,818	80,094	51,752	112,581
Training Agent I-II	45,618	84,272	46,667	86,210	47,740	88,193	48,838	90,221	49,962	92,296	2.30%	11.50%	28,878	53,347	41,384	76,451	58,170	107,460
Training Technician I-III	41,576	76,806	42,532	78,573	43,510	80,380	44,511	82,229	45,535	84,120	2.30%	11.50%	26,319	48,621	37,718	69,678	53,016	97,940
Water Chemist II-IV	49,299	83,577	50,433	85,499	51,593	87,465	52,780	89,477	53,993	91,535	2.30%	11.50%	31,208	52,907	44,724	75,820	62,864	106,574

http://egov.cityofchicago.org/city/webportal/portalContentItemAction.do?

189

Chart III - U.S. States & Cities - Job Titles - Salaries - Pension Estimates

Maryland	2010 (Min)	2010 (Max)	2011 (Min)	2011 (Max)	2012 (Min)	2012 (Max)	2013 (Min)	2013 (Max)	2014 (Min)	2014 (Max)	5-Year Average % Raise	5-Year Cumulative Raise Estimate**	20-Year Annual Pension Benefit Estimate (Min.)***	20-Year Annual Pension Benefit Estimate (Max.)	25-Year Annual Pension Benefit Estimate (Min.)	25-Year Annual Pension Benefit Estimate (Max.)	30-Year Annual Pension Benefit Estimate (Min.)	30-Year Annual Pension Benefit Estimate (Max.)
Accountant I-II	38,190	64,663	39,069	66,150	39,967	67,672	40,887	69,228	41,827	70,820	2.30%	11.50%	24,176	40,934	34,646	58,662	48,699	82,456
Accountant Supervisor I-II	46,028	78,661	47,086	80,470	48,169	82,321	49,277	84,215	50,411	86,151	2.30%	11.50%	29,137	49,795	41,756	71,361	58,693	100,30
Accountant, Advanced	43,237	69,022	44,232	70,610	45,249	72,234	46,290	73,895	47,354	75,595	2.30%	11.50%	27,371	43,694	39,225	62,617	55,135	88,014
Acquisition Agent I-II	31,790	56,786	32,521	58,092	33,269	59,428	34,034	60,795	34,817	62,194	2.30%	11.50%	20,124	35,948	28,840	51,516	40,537	72,412
Acquisition Agent Supervisor	38,190	60,600	39,069	61,994	39,967	63,419	40,887	64,878	41,827	66,370	2.30%	11.50%	24,176	38,362	34,646	54,976	48,699	77,275
Acquisition Specialist	43,237	69,022	44,232	70,610	45,249	72,234	46,290	73,895	47,354	75,595	2.30%	11.50%	27,371	43,694	39,225	62,617	55,135	88,014
Activity Therapy Manager	40,627	64,663	41,562	66,150	42,518	67,672	43,496	69,228	44,496	70,820	2.30%	11.50%	25,719	40,934	36,857	58,662	51,806	82,456
Admin Aide	31,790	49,918	32,521	51,066	33,269	52,241	34,034	53,442	34,817	54,671	2.30%	11.50%	20,124	31,600	28,840	45,286	40,537	63,654
Admin Officer I-III	35,910	64,663	36,736	66,150	37,581	67,672	38,445	69,228	39,330	70,820	2.30%	11.50%	22,732	40,934	32,578	58,662	45,791	82,456
Admin Spec II-III	31,790	53,227	32,521	54,451	33,269	55,703	34,034	56,985	34,817	58,295	2.30%	11.50%	20,124	33,694	28,840	48,287	40,537	67,873
Agency Budget Specialist I-II	35,910	64,663	36,736	66,150	37,581	67,672	38,445	69,228	39,330	70,820	2.30%	11.50%	22,732	40,934	32,578	58,662	45,791	82,456
Agency Procurement Specialist I-II	35,910	64,663	36,736	66,150	37,581	67,672	38,445	69,228	39,330	70,820	2.30%	11.50%	22,732	40,934	32,578	58,662	45,791	82,456
Alcoh & Other Drug Abuse Prevent Crd	35,910	56,786	36,736	58,092	37,581	59,428	38,445	60,795	39,330	62,194	2.30%	11.50%	22,732	35,948	32,578	51,516	45,791	72,412
Alcoh & Other Drug Abuse Prevent Supv	40,627	64,663	41,562	66,150	42,518	67,672	43,496	69,228	44,496	70,820	2.30%	11.50%	25,719	40,934	36,857	58,662	51,806	82,456
Architect I-II	43,237	73,687	44,232	75,381	45,249	77,115	46,290	78,889	47,354	80,703	2.30%	11.50%	27,371	46,646	39,225	66,848	55,135	93,963
Architectural Tech I-II	35,910	64,663	36,736	66,150	37,581	67,672	38,445	69,228	39,330	70,820	2.30%	11.50%	22,732	40,934	32,578	58,662	45,791	82,456
Archivist I-II	38,190	69,022	39,069	70,610	39,967	72,234	40,887	73,895	41,827	75,595	2.30%	11.50%	24,176	43,694	34,646	62,617	48,699	88,014
Art Therapist I-II	33,781	56,786	34,558	58,092	35,353	59,428	36,166	60,795	36,998	62,194	2.30%	11.50%	21,385	35,948	30,646	51,516	43,076	72,412
Assoc Librarian I-II	33,781	60,600	34,558	61,994	35,353	63,419	36,166	64,878	36,998	66,370	2.30%	11.50%	21,385	38,362	30,646	54,976	43,076	77,275
Automotive Services Supv I-II	31,790	53,227	32,521	54,451	33,269	55,703	34,034	56,985	34,817	58,295	2.30%	11.50%	20,124	33,694	28,840	48,287	40,537	67,873
Chemist I-III	35,910	64,663	36,736	66,150	37,581	67,672	38,445	69,228	39,330	70,820	2.30%	11.50%	22,732	40,934	32,578	58,662	45,791	82,456
Child Support Specialist I-II	31,790	53,227	32,521	54,451	33,269	55,703	34,034	56,985	34,817	58,295	2.30%	11.50%	20,124	33,694	28,840	48,287	40,537	67,873
Computer Network Spec I-II	43,237	73,687	44,232	75,381	45,249	77,115	46,290	78,889	47,354	80,703	2.30%	11.50%	27,371	46,646	39,225	66,848	55,135	93,963
Computer Operator Mgr I	49,016	78,661	50,143	80,470	51,296	82,321	52,476	84,215	53,683	86,151	2.30%	11.50%	31,029	49,795	44,467	71,361	62,503	100,30
Contributions Specialist I-II	31,790	53,227	32,521	54,451	33,269	55,703	34,034	56,985	34,817	58,295	2.30%	11.50%	20,124	33,694	28,840	48,287	40,537	67,873
Corr Officer I-II	33,781	56,786	34,558	58,092	35,353	59,428	36,166	60,795	36,998	62,194	2.30%	11.50%	21,385	35,948	30,646	51,516	43,076	72,412
Corr Rec Officer I-III	33,781	60,600	34,558	61,994	35,353	63,419	36,166	64,878	36,998	66,370	2.30%	11.50%	21,385	38,362	30,646	54,976	43,076	77,275
Correctional Hearing Officer I-II	46,028	78,661	47,086	80,470	48,169	82,321	49,277	84,215	50,411	86,151	2.30%	11.50%	29,137	49,795	41,756	71,361	58,693	100,30
Data Base Spec I-II	43,237	78,661	44,232	80,470	45,249	82,321	46,290	84,215	47,354	86,151	2.30%	11.50%	27,371	49,795	39,225	71,361	55,135	100,30
Data Base Spec Supervisor	52,252	83,892	53,454	85,821	54,683	87,795	55,941	89,815	57,228	91,880	2.30%	11.50%	33,077	53,107	47,403	76,106	66,630	106,97
Data Communications Tech I-II	33,781	60,600	34,558	61,994	35,353	63,419	36,166	64,878	36,998	66,370	2.30%	11.50%	21,385	38,362	30,646	54,976	43,076	77,275
Dentist I-III	63,466	116,108	64,926	118,778	66,419	121,510	67,947	124,305	69,509	127,164	2.30%	11.50%	40,176	73,501	57,576	105,333	80,930	148,05
Dp Functional Analyst I-II	40,627	69,022	41,562	70,610	42,518	72,234	43,496	73,895	44,496	75,595	2.30%	11.50%	25,719	43,694	36,857	62,617	51,806	88,014
Dp Functional Analyst Lead	46,028	73,687	47,086	75,381	48,169	77,115	49,277	78,889	50,411	80,703	2.30%	11.50%	29,137	46,646	41,756	66,848	58,693	93,963
Dp Functional Analyst Supervisor	49,016	78,661	50,143	80,470	51,296	82,321	52,476	84,215	53,683	86,151	2.30%	11.50%	31,029	49,795	44,467	71,361	62,503	100,30
Dp Production Control Spec Lead	33,781	53,227	34,558	54,451	35,353	55,703	36,166	56,985	36,998	58,295	2.30%	11.50%	21,385	33,694	30,646	48,287	43,076	67,873
Dp Production Control Spec Supr	35,910	56,786	36,736	58,092	37,581	59,428	38,445	60,795	39,330	62,194	2.30%	11.50%	22,732	35,948	32,578	51,516	45,791	72,41

Chart III - U.S. States & Cities - Job Titles - Salaries - Pension Estimates

Maryland	2010 (Min)	2010 (Max)	2011 (Min)	2011 (Max)	2012 (Min)	2012 (Max)	2013 (Min)	2013 (Max)	2014 (Min)	2014 (Max)	5-Year Average % Raise	5-Year Cumulative Raise Estimate**	20-Year Annual Pension Benefit Estimate (Min.)***	20-Year Annual Pension Benefit Estimate (Max.)	25-Year Annual Pension Benefit Estimate (Min.)	25-Year Annual Pension Benefit Estimate (Max.)	30-Year Annual Pension Benefit Estimate (Min.)	30-Year Annual Pension Benefit Estimate (Max.)
Dp Programmer	35,910	56,786	36,736	58,092	37,581	59,428	38,445	60,795	39,330	62,194	2.30%	11.50%	22,732	35,948	32,578	51,516	45,791	72,412
Dp Programmer Analyst I-II	43,237	73,687	44,232	75,381	45,249	77,115	46,290	78,889	47,354	80,703	2.30%	11.50%	27,371	46,646	39,225	66,848	55,135	93,963
Dp Programmer Analyst Lead/ Advanced	49,016	78,661	50,143	80,470	51,296	82,321	52,476	84,215	53,683	86,151	2.30%	11.50%	31,029	49,795	44,467	71,361	62,503	100,306
Dp Programmer Analyst Supervisor	52,252	83,892	53,454	85,821	54,683	87,795	55,941	89,815	57,228	91,880	2.30%	11.50%	33,077	53,107	47,403	76,106	66,630	106,976
Dp Programmer Analyst Trainee	40,627	64,663	41,562	66,150	42,518	67,672	43,496	69,228	44,496	70,820	2.30%	11.50%	25,719	40,934	36,857	58,662	51,806	82,456
Dp Programmer Trainee	29,931	46,866	30,620	47,944	31,324	49,046	32,044	50,174	32,781	51,328	2.30%	11.50%	18,948	29,668	27,154	42,516	38,167	59,761
Dp Quality Assurance Spec	49,016	78,661	50,143	80,470	51,296	82,321	52,476	84,215	53,683	86,151	2.30%	11.50%	31,029	49,795	44,467	71,361	62,503	100,306
Dp Quality Assurance Spec Supervisor	52,252	83,892	53,454	85,821	54,683	87,795	55,941	89,815	57,228	91,880	2.30%	11.50%	33,077	53,107	47,403	76,106	66,630	106,976
Dp Staff Spec	46,028	73,687	47,086	75,381	48,169	77,115	49,277	78,889	50,411	80,703	2.30%	11.50%	29,137	46,646	41,756	66,848	58,693	93,963
Dp Staff Spec Supervisor	52,252	83,892	53,454	85,821	54,683	87,795	55,941	89,815	57,228	91,880	2.30%	11.50%	33,077	53,107	47,403	76,106	66,630	106,976
Dp Technical Support Spec I-II	43,237	78,661	44,232	80,470	45,249	82,321	46,290	84,215	47,354	86,151	2.30%	11.50%	27,371	49,795	39,225	71,361	55,135	100,306
Dp Technical Support Spec Supervisor	52,252	83,892	53,454	85,821	54,683	87,795	55,941	89,815	57,228	91,880	2.30%	11.50%	33,077	53,107	47,403	76,106	66,630	106,976
Dp Technical Support Spec Trainee	40,627	64,663	41,562	66,150	42,518	67,672	43,496	69,228	44,496	70,820	2.30%	11.50%	25,719	40,934	36,857	58,662	51,806	82,456
Election Director I-III	43,237	91,935	44,232	94,050	45,249	96,213	46,290	98,426	47,354	100,690	2.30%	11.50%	27,371	58,198	39,225	83,403	55,135	117,232
Elevator Inspector I-II	35,910	60,600	36,736	61,994	37,581	63,419	38,445	64,878	39,330	66,370	2.30%	11.50%	22,732	38,362	32,578	54,976	45,791	77,275
Emp Selection Spec I-II	38,190	73,687	39,069	75,381	39,967	77,115	40,887	78,889	41,827	80,703	2.30%	11.50%	24,176	46,646	34,646	66,848	48,699	93,963
Emp Training Spec I-II	35,910	60,600	36,736	61,994	37,581	63,419	38,445	64,878	39,330	66,370	2.30%	11.50%	22,732	38,362	32,578	54,976	45,791	77,275
Ems Comm Oper I-II	29,931	49,918	30,620	51,066	31,324	52,241	32,044	53,442	32,781	54,671	2.30%	11.50%	18,948	31,600	27,154	45,286	38,167	63,654
Engr I-III	35,910	69,022	36,736	70,610	37,581	72,234	38,445	73,895	39,330	75,595	2.30%	11.50%	22,732	43,694	32,578	62,617	45,791	88,014
Engr Sr Civil General	46,028	73,687	47,086	75,381	48,169	77,115	49,277	78,889	50,411	80,703	2.30%	11.50%	29,137	46,646	41,756	66,848	58,693	93,963
Engr Sr Civil Geotechcl	46,028	73,687	47,086	75,381	48,169	77,115	49,277	78,889	50,411	80,703	2.30%	11.50%	29,137	46,646	41,756	66,848	58,693	93,963
Engr Sr Civil Hydrology	46,028	73,687	47,086	75,381	48,169	77,115	49,277	78,889	50,411	80,703	2.30%	11.50%	29,137	46,646	41,756	66,848	58,693	93,963
Engr Sr Electrical	46,028	73,687	47,086	75,381	48,169	77,115	49,277	78,889	50,411	80,703	2.30%	11.50%	29,137	46,646	41,756	66,848	58,693	93,963
Engr Sr Mechanical	46,028	73,687	47,086	75,381	48,169	77,115	49,277	78,889	50,411	80,703	2.30%	11.50%	29,137	46,646	41,756	66,848	58,693	93,963
Engr Sr Registered Civil	49,016	78,661	50,143	80,470	51,296	82,321	52,476	84,215	53,683	86,151	2.30%	11.50%	31,029	49,795	44,467	71,361	62,503	100,306
Engr Sr Registered Electrical	49,016	78,661	50,143	80,470	51,296	82,321	52,476	84,215	53,683	86,151	2.30%	11.50%	31,029	49,795	44,467	71,361	62,503	100,306
Engr Sr Registered Mechanical	49,016	78,661	50,143	80,470	51,296	82,321	52,476	84,215	53,683	86,151	2.30%	11.50%	31,029	49,795	44,467	71,361	62,503	100,306
Engr Sr Structural	46,028	73,687	47,086	75,381	48,169	77,115	49,277	78,889	50,411	80,703	2.30%	11.50%	29,137	46,646	41,756	66,848	58,693	93,963
Entmolgst I-II	33,781	60,600	34,558	61,994	35,353	63,419	36,166	64,878	36,998	66,370	2.30%	11.50%	21,385	38,362	30,646	54,976	43,076	77,275
Envrmntl Enforcement Inspector I-II	29,931	53,227	30,620	54,451	31,324	55,703	32,044	56,985	32,781	58,295	2.30%	11.50%	18,948	33,694	27,154	48,287	38,167	67,873
Envrmntl Health Asst Dir I-III	40,627	78,661	41,562	80,470	42,518	82,321	43,496	84,215	44,496	86,151	2.30%	11.50%	25,719	49,795	36,857	71,361	51,806	100,306
Envrmntl Prgm Mgr I Air Mgt	52,252	83,892	53,454	85,821	54,683	87,795	55,941	89,815	57,228	91,880	2.30%	11.50%	33,077	53,107	47,403	76,106	66,630	106,976
Envrmntl Prgm Mgr I General	52,252	83,892	53,454	85,821	54,683	87,795	55,941	89,815	57,228	91,880	2.30%	11.50%	33,077	53,107	47,403	76,106	66,630	106,976
Financial Agent Supervisor I-II	33,781	56,786	34,558	58,092	35,353	59,428	36,166	60,795	36,998	62,194	2.30%	11.50%	21,385	35,948	30,646	51,516	43,076	72,412
Financial Compliance Auditor I-II	38,190	64,663	39,069	66,150	39,967	67,672	40,887	69,228	41,827	70,820	2.30%	11.50%	24,176	40,934	34,646	58,662	48,699	82,456
Fire Protection Eng II	49,016	78,661	50,143	80,470	51,296	82,321	52,476	84,215	53,683	86,151	2.30%	11.50%	31,029	49,795	44,467	71,361	62,503	100,306

191

Chart III - U.S. States & Cities - Job Titles - Salaries - Pension Estimates

Maryland	2010 (Min)	2010 (Max)	2011 (Min)	2011 (Max)	2012 (Min)	2012 (Max)	2013 (Min)	2013 (Max)	2014 (Min)	2014 (Max)	5-Year Average % Raise	5-Year Cumulative Raise Estimate**	20-Year Annual Pension Benefit Estimate (Min.)***	20-Year Annual Pension Benefit Estimate (Max.)	25-Year Annual Pension Benefit Estimate (Min.)	25-Year Annual Pension Benefit Estimate (Max.)	30-Year Annual Pension Benefit Estimate (Min.)	30-Year Annual Pension Benefit Estimate (Max.)
Fiscal Accounts Clerk Manager	38,190	60,600	39,069	61,994	39,967	63,419	40,887	64,878	41,827	66,370	2.30%	11.50%	24,176	38,362	34,646	54,976	48,699	77,275
Fiscal Accounts Clerk Supervisor	33,781	53,227	34,558	54,451	35,353	55,703	36,166	56,985	36,998	58,295	2.30%	11.50%	21,385	33,694	30,646	48,287	43,076	67,873
Fiscal Accounts Clerk, Lead	29,931	46,866	30,620	47,944	31,324	49,046	32,044	50,174	32,781	51,328	2.30%	11.50%	18,948	29,668	27,154	42,516	38,167	59,761
Fiscal Accounts Technician I-II	29,931	49,918	30,620	51,066	31,324	52,241	32,044	53,442	32,781	54,671	2.30%	11.50%	18,948	31,600	27,154	45,286	38,167	63,654
Fiscal Accounts Technician Supv	35,910	56,786	36,736	58,092	37,581	59,428	38,445	60,795	39,330	62,194	2.30%	11.50%	22,732	35,948	32,578	51,516	45,791	72,412
Fiscal Services Chief I-II	49,016	83,892	50,143	85,821	51,296	87,795	52,476	89,815	53,683	91,880	2.30%	11.50%	31,029	53,107	44,467	76,106	62,503	106,976
Fiscal Services Officer I-II	43,237	73,687	44,232	75,381	45,249	77,115	46,290	78,889	47,354	80,703	2.30%	11.50%	27,371	46,646	39,225	66,848	55,135	93,963
Food Administrator I-Iv	35,910	69,022	36,736	70,610	37,581	72,234	38,445	73,895	39,330	75,595	2.30%	11.50%	22,732	43,694	32,578	62,617	45,791	88,014
Food Service Mgr I-II	31,790	53,227	32,521	54,451	33,269	55,703	34,034	56,985	34,817	58,295	2.30%	11.50%	20,124	33,694	28,840	48,287	40,537	67,873
Forensic Photographer I-II	29,931	49,918	30,620	51,066	31,324	52,241	32,044	53,442	32,781	54,671	2.30%	11.50%	18,948	31,600	27,154	45,286	38,167	63,654
Forester I	33,781	53,227	34,558	54,451	35,353	55,703	36,166	56,985	36,998	58,295	2.30%	11.50%	21,385	33,694	30,646	48,287	43,076	67,873
Forestry Manager I-III	40,627	73,687	41,562	75,381	42,518	77,115	43,496	78,889	44,496	80,703	2.30%	11.50%	25,719	46,646	36,857	66,848	51,806	93,963
Forestry Supervisor I-III	31,790	56,786	32,521	58,092	33,269	59,428	34,034	60,795	34,817	62,194	2.30%	11.50%	20,124	35,948	28,840	51,516	40,537	72,412
Hearing Exam I-III	52,252	101,908	53,454	104,252	54,683	106,650	55,941	109,103	57,228	111,612	2.30%	11.50%	33,077	64,512	47,403	92,451	66,630	129,950
Hearing Officer I-II	46,028	78,661	47,086	80,470	48,169	82,321	49,277	84,215	50,411	86,151	2.30%	11.50%	29,137	49,795	41,756	71,361	58,693	100,306
Hearing Reporter I-II	33,781	64,663	34,558	66,150	35,353	67,672	36,166	69,228	36,998	70,820	2.30%	11.50%	21,385	40,934	30,646	58,662	43,076	82,456
Hlth Fac Survey Coordinator I-II	43,237	73,687	44,232	75,381	45,249	77,115	46,290	78,889	47,354	80,703	2.30%	11.50%	27,371	46,646	39,225	66,848	55,135	93,963
Hlth Fac Surveyor I-III	35,910	64,663	36,736	66,150	37,581	67,672	38,445	69,228	39,330	70,820	2.30%	11.50%	22,732	40,934	32,578	58,662	45,791	82,456
Hlth Fac Surveyor Nurse I	46,028	73,687	47,086	75,381	48,169	77,115	49,277	78,889	50,411	80,703	2.30%	11.50%	29,137	46,646	41,756	66,848	58,693	93,963
Hlth Fac Surveyor Nurse II	49,016	78,661	50,143	80,470	51,296	82,321	52,476	84,215	53,683	86,151	2.30%	11.50%	31,029	49,795	44,467	71,361	62,503	100,306
Hlth Occupations Invest I-Iv	31,790	60,600	32,521	61,994	33,269	63,419	34,034	64,878	34,817	66,370	2.30%	11.50%	20,124	38,362	28,840	54,976	40,537	77,275
Hlth Physicist I-III	38,190	69,022	39,069	70,610	39,967	72,234	40,887	73,895	41,827	75,595	2.30%	11.50%	24,176	43,694	34,646	62,617	48,699	88,014
Hlth Planner I-Iv	33,781	73,687	34,558	75,381	35,353	77,115	36,166	78,889	36,998	80,703	2.30%	11.50%	21,385	46,646	30,646	66,848	43,076	93,963
Hlth Planning & Dev Admin I-II	49,016	89,496	50,143	91,555	51,296	93,660	52,476	95,814	53,683	98,018	2.30%	11.50%	31,029	56,654	44,467	81,191	62,503	114,122
Hlth Policy Analyst I-II	43,237	73,687	44,232	75,381	45,249	77,115	46,290	78,889	47,354	80,703	2.30%	11.50%	27,371	46,646	39,225	66,848	55,135	93,963
Hlth Svs Rate Analyst I-II	43,237	73,687	44,232	75,381	45,249	77,115	46,290	78,889	47,354	80,703	2.30%	11.50%	27,371	46,646	39,225	66,848	55,135	93,963
Housing Rehab Spec I-II	33,781	56,786	34,558	58,092	35,353	59,428	36,166	60,795	36,998	62,194	2.30%	11.50%	21,385	35,948	30,646	51,516	43,076	72,412
Hum Ser Admin I-II	46,028	78,661	47,086	80,470	48,169	82,321	49,277	84,215	50,411	86,151	2.30%	11.50%	29,137	49,795	41,756	71,361	58,693	100,306
Hum Ser Spec I-V	33,781	69,022	34,558	70,610	35,353	72,234	36,166	73,895	36,998	75,595	2.30%	11.50%	21,385	43,694	30,646	62,617	43,076	88,014
Human Relations Representative I-III	33,781	64,663	34,558	66,150	35,353	67,672	36,166	69,228	36,998	70,820	2.30%	11.50%	21,385	40,934	30,646	58,662	43,076	82,456
Income Maint Spec I-Iv	29,931	56,786	30,620	58,092	31,324	59,428	32,044	60,795	32,781	62,194	2.30%	11.50%	18,948	35,948	27,154	51,516	38,167	72,412
Income Maint Supv I-II	40,627	69,022	41,562	70,610	42,518	72,234	43,496	73,895	44,496	75,595	2.30%	11.50%	25,719	43,694	36,857	62,617	51,806	88,014
Industrial Hygienist I-III	35,910	69,022	36,736	70,610	37,581	72,234	38,445	73,895	39,330	75,595	2.30%	11.50%	22,732	43,694	32,578	62,617	45,791	88,014
Industrial Hygienist Lead	46,028	73,687	47,086	75,381	48,169	77,115	49,277	78,889	50,411	80,703	2.30%	11.50%	29,137	46,646	41,756	66,848	58,693	93,963
Industrial Hygienist Supervisor	49,016	78,661	50,143	80,470	51,296	82,321	52,476	84,215	53,683	86,151	2.30%	11.50%	31,029	49,795	44,467	71,361	62,503	100,306
Internal Auditor I-II	38,190	69,022	39,069	70,610	39,967	72,234	40,887	73,895	41,827	75,595	2.30%	11.50%	24,176	43,694	34,646	62,617	48,699	88,014
Internal Auditor Lead	46,028	73,687	47,086	75,381	48,169	77,115	49,277	78,889	50,411	80,703	2.30%	11.50%	29,137	46,646	41,756	66,848	58,693	93,963

Chart III - U.S. States & Cities - Job Titles - Salaries - Pension Estimates

Maryland	2010 (Min)	2010 (Max)	2011 (Min)	2011 (Max)	2012 (Min)	2012 (Max)	2013 (Min)	2013 (Max)	2014 (Min)	2014 (Max)	5-Year Average % Raise	5-Year Cumulative Raise Estimate**	20-Year Annual Pension Benefit Estimate (Min.)***	20-Year Annual Pension Benefit Estimate (Max.)	25-Year Annual Pension Benefit Estimate (Min.)	25-Year Annual Pension Benefit Estimate (Max.)	30-Year Annual Pension Benefit Estimate (Min.)	30-Year Annual Pension Benefit Estimate (Max.)
Internal Auditor Officer	46,028	73,687	47,086	75,381	48,169	77,115	49,277	78,889	50,411	80,703	2.30%	11.50%	29,137	46,646	41,756	66,848	58,693	93,963
Internal Auditor Prog Super	52,252	83,892	53,454	85,821	54,683	87,795	55,941	89,815	57,228	91,880	2.30%	11.50%	33,077	53,107	47,403	76,106	66,630	106,976
Internal Auditor Super	49,016	78,661	50,143	80,470	51,296	82,321	52,476	84,215	53,683	86,151	2.30%	11.50%	31,029	49,795	44,467	71,361	62,503	100,306
Internal Auditor Trainee	35,910	56,786	36,736	58,092	37,581	59,428	38,445	60,795	39,330	62,194	2.30%	11.50%	22,732	35,948	32,578	51,516	45,791	72,412
Job Service Spec I-Iv	29,931	56,786	30,620	58,092	31,324	59,428	32,044	60,795	32,781	62,194	2.30%	11.50%	18,948	35,948	27,154	51,516	38,167	72,412
Job Service Spec Supv I-II	38,190	64,663	39,069	66,150	39,967	67,672	40,887	69,228	41,827	70,820	2.30%	11.50%	24,176	40,934	34,646	58,662	48,699	82,456
Lab Scientist Surveyor I-II	40,627	69,022	41,562	70,610	42,518	72,234	43,496	73,895	44,496	75,595	2.30%	11.50%	25,719	43,694	36,857	62,617	51,806	88,014
Landscape Architect I-V	35,910	78,661	36,736	80,470	37,581	82,321	38,445	84,215	39,330	86,151	2.30%	11.50%	22,732	49,795	32,578	71,361	45,791	100,306
Laundry Manager I-Iv	31,790	69,022	32,521	70,610	33,269	72,234	34,034	73,895	34,817	75,595	2.30%	11.50%	20,124	43,694	28,840	62,617	40,537	88,014
Legal Officer I-Iv Unemp Insurance	38,190	78,661	39,069	80,470	39,967	82,321	40,887	84,215	41,827	86,151	2.30%	11.50%	24,176	49,795	34,646	71,361	48,699	100,306
Licensed Practical Nurse I-III	31,790	56,786	32,521	58,092	33,269	59,428	34,034	60,795	34,817	62,194	2.30%	11.50%	20,124	35,948	28,840	51,516	40,537	72,412
Loan/Insur Underwriter Asst	29,931	46,866	30,620	47,944	31,324	49,046	32,044	50,174	32,781	51,328	2.30%	11.50%	18,948	29,668	27,154	42,516	38,167	59,761
Maint Chief I-Iv	29,931	56,786	30,620	58,092	31,324	59,428	32,044	60,795	32,781	62,194	2.30%	11.50%	18,948	35,948	27,154	51,516	38,167	72,412
Maint Engineer I-II	40,627	73,687	41,562	75,381	42,518	77,115	43,496	78,889	44,496	80,703	2.30%	11.50%	25,719	46,646	36,857	66,848	51,806	93,963
Maint Engineering Asst Mgr	49,016	78,661	50,143	80,470	51,296	82,321	52,476	84,215	53,683	86,151	2.30%	11.50%	31,029	49,795	44,467	71,361	62,503	100,306
Management Associate	35,910	56,786	36,736	58,092	37,581	59,428	38,445	60,795	39,330	62,194	2.30%	11.50%	22,732	35,948	32,578	51,516	45,791	72,412
Management Development Spec	43,237	69,022	44,232	70,610	45,249	72,234	46,290	73,895	47,354	75,595	2.30%	11.50%	27,371	43,694	39,225	62,617	55,135	88,014
Management Specialist I-V	33,781	78,661	34,558	80,470	35,353	82,321	36,166	84,215	36,998	86,151	2.30%	11.50%	21,385	49,795	30,646	71,361	43,076	100,306
Med Care Prgm Assoc I-II	29,931	49,918	30,620	51,066	31,324	52,241	32,044	53,442	32,781	54,671	2.30%	11.50%	18,948	31,600	27,154	45,286	38,167	63,654
Medical Serv Reviewing Nurse I-II	43,237	73,687	44,232	75,381	45,249	77,115	46,290	78,889	47,354	80,703	2.30%	11.50%	27,371	46,646	39,225	66,848	55,135	93,963
Meteorologist I-III	35,910	69,022	36,736	70,610	37,581	72,234	38,445	73,895	39,330	75,595	2.30%	11.50%	22,732	43,694	32,578	62,617	45,791	88,014
Nat Res Planner I-V	33,781	78,661	34,558	80,470	35,353	82,321	36,166	84,215	36,998	86,151	2.30%	11.50%	21,385	49,795	30,646	71,361	43,076	100,306
Nutritionist I-V	38,190	78,661	39,069	80,470	39,967	82,321	40,887	84,215	41,827	86,151	2.30%	11.50%	24,176	49,795	34,646	71,361	48,699	100,306
Occupational Therapist I-III	38,190	73,687	39,069	75,381	39,967	77,115	40,887	78,889	41,827	80,703	2.30%	11.50%	24,176	46,646	34,646	66,848	48,699	93,963
Occupational Therapist Institutional	40,627	64,663	41,562	66,150	42,518	67,672	43,496	69,228	44,496	70,820	2.30%	11.50%	25,719	40,934	36,857	58,662	51,806	82,456
Occupational Therapist Supervisor	49,016	78,661	50,143	80,470	51,296	82,321	52,476	84,215	53,683	86,151	2.30%	11.50%	31,029	49,795	44,467	71,361	62,503	100,306
Occupational Therapy Consultant	49,016	78,661	50,143	80,470	51,296	82,321	52,476	84,215	53,683	86,151	2.30%	11.50%	31,029	49,795	44,467	71,361	62,503	100,306
Office Manager	35,910	56,786	36,736	58,092	37,581	59,428	38,445	60,795	39,330	62,194	2.30%	11.50%	22,732	35,948	32,578	51,516	45,791	72,412
Office Processing Clerk Supr	29,931	46,866	30,620	47,944	31,324	49,046	32,044	50,174	32,781	51,328	2.30%	11.50%	18,948	29,668	27,154	42,516	38,167	59,761
Office Supervisor	31,790	49,918	32,521	51,066	33,269	52,241	34,034	53,442	34,817	54,671	2.30%	11.50%	20,124	31,600	28,840	45,286	40,537	63,654
Paralegal I-II	29,931	53,227	30,620	54,451	31,324	55,703	32,044	56,985	32,781	58,295	2.30%	11.50%	18,948	33,694	27,154	48,287	38,167	67,873
Park Services Associate I-II	33,781	56,786	34,558	58,092	35,353	59,428	36,166	60,795	36,998	62,194	2.30%	11.50%	21,385	35,948	30,646	51,516	43,076	72,412
Park Services Associate Lead	40,627	64,663	41,562	66,150	42,518	67,672	43,496	69,228	44,496	70,820	2.30%	11.50%	25,719	40,934	36,857	58,662	51,806	82,456
Park Services Associate Supervisor	43,237	69,022	44,232	70,610	45,249	72,234	46,290	73,895	47,354	75,595	2.30%	11.50%	27,371	43,694	39,225	62,617	55,135	88,014
Park Services Associate Trainee	31,790	49,918	32,521	51,066	33,269	52,241	34,034	53,442	34,817	54,671	2.30%	11.50%	20,124	31,600	28,840	45,286	40,537	63,654
Park Services Asst Manager	46,028	73,687	47,086	75,381	48,169	77,115	49,277	78,889	50,411	80,703	2.30%	11.50%	29,137	46,646	41,756	66,848	58,693	93,963

Chart III - U.S. States & Cities - Job Titles - Salaries - Pension Estimates

Maryland	2010 (Min)	2010 (Max)	2011 (Min)	2011 (Max)	2012 (Min)	2012 (Max)	2013 (Min)	2013 (Max)	2014 (Min)	2014 (Max)	5-Year Average % Raise	5-Year Cumula-tive Raise Esti-mate**	20-Year Annual Pension Benefit Estimate (Min.)***	20-Year Annual Pension Benefit Estimate (Max.)	25-Year Annual Pension Benefit Estimate (Min.)	25-Year Annual Pension Benefit Estimate (Max.)	30-Year Annual Pension Benefit Estimate (Min.)	30-Year Annual Pension Benefit Estimate (Max.)
Park Services Manager I-II	49,016	83,892	50,143	85,821	51,296	87,795	52,476	89,815	53,683	91,880	2.30%	11.50%	31,029	53,107	44,467	76,106	62,503	106,976
Park Services Specialist	48,296	79,504	49,407	81,333	50,543	83,204	51,706	85,117	52,895	87,075	2.30%	11.50%	30,573	50,329	43,814	72,126	61,585	101,381
Personnel Administrator I-II	46,028	78,661	47,086	80,470	48,169	82,321	49,277	84,215	50,411	86,151	2.30%	11.50%	29,137	49,795	41,756	71,361	58,693	100,306
Personnel Analyst Adv/Lead Budget & Mgmt	46,028	73,687	47,086	75,381	48,169	77,115	49,277	78,889	50,411	80,703	2.30%	11.50%	29,137	46,646	41,756	66,848	58,693	93,963
Personnel Analyst Budget & Mgmt	43,237	69,022	44,232	70,610	45,249	72,234	46,290	73,895	47,354	75,595	2.30%	11.50%	27,371	43,694	39,225	62,617	55,135	88,014
Personnel Analyst Supv Budget & Mgmt	49,016	78,661	50,143	80,470	51,296	82,321	52,476	84,215	53,683	86,151	2.30%	11.50%	31,029	49,795	44,467	71,361	62,503	100,306
Personnel Associate I-Iv	29,931	56,786	30,620	58,092	31,324	59,428	32,044	60,795	32,781	62,194	2.30%	11.50%	18,948	35,948	27,154	51,516	38,167	72,412
Personnel Officer I-III	38,190	69,022	39,069	70,610	39,967	72,234	40,887	73,895	41,827	75,595	2.30%	11.50%	24,176	43,694	34,646	62,617	48,699	88,014
Personnel Specialist	35,910	56,786	36,736	58,092	37,581	59,428	38,445	60,795	39,330	62,194	2.30%	11.50%	22,732	35,948	32,578	51,516	45,791	72,412
Personnel Specialist Trainee	33,781	53,227	34,558	54,451	35,353	55,703	36,166	56,985	36,998	58,295	2.30%	11.50%	21,385	33,694	30,646	48,287	43,076	67,873
Personnel Technician I-Iv	29,931	56,786	30,620	58,092	31,324	59,428	32,044	60,795	32,781	62,194	2.30%	11.50%	18,948	35,948	27,154	51,516	38,167	72,412
Ph Engineer I-Iv	35,910	78,661	36,736	80,470	37,581	82,321	38,445	84,215	39,330	86,151	2.30%	11.50%	22,732	49,795	32,578	71,361	45,791	100,306
Physical Therapist I-III	38,190	73,687	39,069	75,381	39,967	77,115	40,887	78,889	41,827	80,703	2.30%	11.50%	24,176	46,646	34,646	66,848	48,699	93,963
Physician Assistant I-II	33,781	60,600	34,558	61,994	35,353	63,419	36,166	64,878	36,998	66,370	2.30%	11.50%	21,385	38,362	30,646	54,976	43,076	77,275
Physician Clinical Specialist	120,630	199,010	123,405	203,587	126,243	208,269	129,146	213,060	132,117	217,960	2.30%	11.50%	76,363	125,980	109,435	180,541	153,823	253,770
Physician Clinical Staff	96,249	158,471	98,463	162,116	100,728	165,845	103,044	169,659	105,414	173,561	2.30%	11.50%	60,929	100,318	87,317	143,764	122,734	202,077
Physician Program Specialist	111,868	184,442	114,441	188,684	117,073	193,024	119,766	197,464	122,521	202,005	2.30%	11.50%	70,817	116,759	101,487	167,325	142,650	235,194
Physician Program Staff	89,295	146,909	91,348	150,288	93,449	153,744	95,599	157,280	97,798	160,898	2.30%	11.50%	56,527	92,999	81,008	133,275	113,865	187,33
Physician Supervisor	103,758	170,959	106,145	174,891	108,586	178,913	111,083	183,028	113,638	187,238	2.30%	11.50%	65,683	108,223	94,129	155,093	132,309	218,00
Planner I-V	33,781	78,661	34,558	80,470	35,353	82,321	36,166	84,215	36,998	86,151	2.30%	11.50%	21,385	49,795	30,646	71,361	43,076	100,306
Plumber Supervisor	29,931	46,866	30,620	47,944	31,324	49,046	32,044	50,174	32,781	51,328	2.30%	11.50%	18,948	29,668	27,154	42,516	38,167	59,761
Police Chief I-II	44,251	82,548	45,269	84,447	46,310	86,389	47,375	88,376	48,465	90,409	2.30%	11.50%	28,013	52,256	40,145	74,887	56,428	105,262
Police Comm Systems Technician I-II	33,781	56,786	34,558	58,092	35,353	59,428	36,166	60,795	36,998	62,194	2.30%	11.50%	21,385	35,948	30,646	51,516	43,076	72,412
Police Officer I-III	34,606	59,675	35,402	61,048	36,216	62,452	37,049	63,888	37,901	65,358	2.30%	11.50%	21,907	37,777	31,394	54,137	44,128	76,096
Police Officer Manager	47,100	72,516	48,183	74,184	49,292	75,890	50,425	77,635	51,585	79,421	2.30%	11.50%	29,816	45,905	42,729	65,786	60,060	92,470
Police Officer Military	33,781	53,227	34,558	54,451	35,353	55,703	36,166	56,985	36,998	58,295	2.30%	11.50%	21,385	33,694	30,646	48,287	43,076	67,873
Police Officer Supervisor	41,591	63,674	42,548	65,139	43,526	66,637	44,527	68,169	45,552	69,737	2.30%	11.50%	26,329	40,308	37,731	57,765	53,035	81,195
Police Officer Trainee	32,577	49,219	33,327	50,351	34,093	51,509	34,877	52,694	35,680	53,906	2.30%	11.50%	20,623	31,158	29,554	44,652	41,542	62,763
Pretrial Release Invstgtns Supv	31,790	49,918	32,521	51,066	33,269	52,241	34,034	53,442	34,817	54,671	2.30%	11.50%	20,124	31,600	28,840	45,286	40,537	63,654
Prgm Admin I-III	43,237	78,661	44,232	80,470	45,249	82,321	46,290	84,215	47,354	86,151	2.30%	11.50%	27,371	49,795	39,225	71,361	55,135	100,306
Prgm Analyst Bdgt & Mgmt I-III	38,190	78,661	39,069	80,470	39,967	82,321	40,887	84,215	41,827	86,151	2.30%	11.50%	24,176	49,795	34,646	71,361	48,699	100,306
Prgm Analyst Sr Bdgt & Mgmt	55,739	89,496	57,021	91,555	58,333	93,660	59,674	95,814	61,047	98,018	2.30%	11.50%	35,285	56,654	50,566	81,191	71,077	114,12
Procurement Analyst Bdgt & Mgmt I-III	43,237	89,496	44,232	91,555	45,249	93,660	46,290	95,814	47,354	98,018	2.30%	11.50%	27,371	56,654	39,225	81,191	55,135	114,122
Procurement Analyst Supv Bdgt & Mgmt	59,472	95,485	60,840	97,681	62,239	99,928	63,670	102,226	65,135	104,577	2.30%	11.50%	37,648	60,445	53,953	86,624	75,836	121,75
Psc Regulatory Economist I-III	43,237	78,661	44,232	80,470	45,249	82,321	46,290	84,215	47,354	86,151	2.30%	11.50%	27,371	49,795	39,225	71,361	55,135	100,30
Psychologist I-II	49,016	83,892	50,143	85,821	51,296	87,795	52,476	89,815	53,683	91,880	2.30%	11.50%	31,029	53,107	44,467	76,106	62,503	106,97

Chart III - U.S. States & Cities - Job Titles - Salaries - Pension Estimates

Maryland	2010 (Min)	2010 (Max)	2011 (Min)	2011 (Max)	2012 (Min)	2012 (Max)	2013 (Min)	2013 (Max)	2014 (Min)	2014 (Max)	5-Year Average % Raise	5-Year Cumulative Raise Estimate**	20-Year Annual Pension Benefit Estimate (Min.)***	20-Year Annual Pension Benefit Estimate (Max.)	25-Year Annual Pension Benefit Estimate (Min.)	25-Year Annual Pension Benefit Estimate (Max.)	30-Year Annual Pension Benefit Estimate (Min.)	30-Year Annual Pension Benefit Estimate (Max.)
Pub Affairs Officer I-II	35,910	64,663	36,736	66,150	37,581	67,672	38,445	69,228	39,330	70,820	2.30%	11.50%	22,732	40,934	32,578	58,662	45,791	82,456
Pub Serv Engr I-III	38,190	78,661	39,069	80,470	39,967	82,321	40,887	84,215	41,827	86,151	2.30%	11.50%	24,176	49,795	34,646	71,361	48,699	100,306
Pub Utility Auditor	43,237	69,022	44,232	70,610	45,249	72,234	46,290	73,895	47,354	75,595	2.30%	11.50%	27,371	43,694	39,225	62,617	55,135	88,014
Pub Utility Auditor Senior	46,028	73,687	47,086	75,381	48,169	77,115	49,277	78,889	50,411	80,703	2.30%	11.50%	29,137	46,646	41,756	66,848	58,693	93,963
Qual Develop Disabil Prof	35,910	56,786	36,736	58,092	37,581	59,428	38,445	60,795	39,330	62,194	2.30%	11.50%	22,732	35,948	32,578	51,516	45,791	72,412
Qual Develop Disabil Prof Sup	38,190	60,600	39,069	61,994	39,967	63,419	40,887	64,878	41,827	66,370	2.30%	11.50%	24,176	38,362	34,646	54,976	48,699	77,275
Radio Tech I-Iv	29,931	60,600	30,620	61,994	31,324	63,419	32,044	64,878	32,781	66,370	2.30%	11.50%	18,948	38,362	27,154	54,976	38,167	77,275
Radiologic Technologist Supv	31,790	49,918	32,521	51,066	33,269	52,241	34,034	53,442	34,817	54,671	2.30%	11.50%	20,124	31,600	28,840	45,286	40,537	63,654
Ranger I-II	42,440	74,279	43,416	75,988	44,415	77,735	45,436	79,523	46,481	81,352	2.30%	11.50%	26,866	47,021	38,501	67,386	54,118	94,718
Real Estate Reviewing Appraiser I Dgs	43,237	69,022	44,232	70,610	45,249	72,234	46,290	73,895	47,354	75,595	2.30%	11.50%	27,371	43,694	39,225	62,617	55,135	88,014
Recreation Specialist I-II	33,781	56,786	34,558	58,092	35,353	59,428	36,166	60,795	36,998	62,194	2.30%	11.50%	21,385	35,948	30,646	51,516	43,076	72,412
Registered Dietitian I-V	35,910	78,661	36,736	80,470	37,581	82,321	38,445	84,215	39,330	86,151	2.30%	11.50%	22,732	49,795	32,578	71,361	45,791	100,306
Registered Nurse	43,237	69,022	44,232	70,610	45,249	72,234	46,290	73,895	47,354	75,595	2.30%	11.50%	27,371	43,694	39,225	62,617	55,135	88,014
Regulatory Economist I-III	43,237	78,661	44,232	80,470	45,249	82,321	46,290	84,215	47,354	86,151	2.30%	11.50%	27,371	49,795	39,225	71,361	55,135	100,306
Research Analyst	35,910	56,786	36,736	58,092	37,581	59,428	38,445	60,795	39,330	62,194	2.30%	11.50%	22,732	35,948	32,578	51,516	45,791	72,412
Research Statistician I-Iv	35,910	73,687	36,736	75,381	37,581	77,115	38,445	78,889	39,330	80,703	2.30%	11.50%	22,732	46,646	32,578	66,848	45,791	93,963
Resident Physician Specialist	55,739	89,496	57,021	91,555	58,333	93,660	59,674	95,814	61,047	98,018	2.30%	11.50%	35,285	56,654	50,566	81,191	71,077	114,122
Respiratory Care Nurse	46,028	73,687	47,086	75,381	48,169	77,115	49,277	78,889	50,411	80,703	2.30%	11.50%	29,137	46,646	41,756	66,848	58,693	93,963
Respiratory Care Practitioner I-II	33,781	60,600	34,558	61,994	35,353	63,419	36,166	64,878	36,998	66,370	2.30%	11.50%	21,385	38,362	30,646	54,976	43,076	77,275
Respiratory Therapist I-II	33,781	60,600	34,558	61,994	35,353	63,419	36,166	64,878	36,998	66,370	2.30%	11.50%	21,385	38,362	30,646	54,976	43,076	77,275
Security Attend I-III	31,790	56,786	32,521	58,092	33,269	59,428	34,034	60,795	34,817	62,194	2.30%	11.50%	20,124	35,948	28,840	51,516	40,537	72,412
Security Attend Manager I-II	43,237	73,687	44,232	75,381	45,249	77,115	46,290	78,889	47,354	80,703	2.30%	11.50%	27,371	46,646	39,225	66,848	55,135	93,963
Services Supervisor I-III	29,931	53,227	30,620	54,451	31,324	55,703	32,044	56,985	32,781	58,295	2.30%	11.50%	18,948	33,694	27,154	48,287	38,167	67,873
Social Service Admin I-III	43,237	78,661	44,232	80,470	45,249	82,321	46,290	84,215	47,354	86,151	2.30%	11.50%	27,371	49,795	39,225	71,361	55,135	100,306
Staff Atty Pub Ser Comm I-III	52,252	95,485	53,454	97,681	54,683	99,928	55,941	102,226	57,228	104,577	2.30%	11.50%	33,077	60,445	47,403	86,624	66,630	121,759
Tax Consultant I-II	40,627	73,687	41,562	75,381	42,518	77,115	43,496	78,889	44,496	80,703	2.30%	11.50%	25,719	46,646	36,857	66,848	51,806	93,963
Tax Revenue Analyst	52,252	83,892	53,454	85,821	54,683	87,795	55,941	89,815	57,228	91,880	2.30%	11.50%	33,077	53,107	47,403	76,106	66,630	106,976
Therapeutic Recreator I-II	33,781	56,786	34,558	58,092	35,353	59,428	36,166	60,795	36,998	62,194	2.30%	11.50%	21,385	35,948	30,646	51,516	43,076	72,412
Therapeutic Recreator Supervisor	38,190	60,600	39,069	61,994	39,967	63,419	40,887	64,878	41,827	66,370	2.30%	11.50%	24,176	38,362	34,646	54,976	48,699	77,275
Treasury Spec I-V	33,781	69,022	34,558	70,610	35,353	72,234	36,166	73,895	36,998	75,595	2.30%	11.50%	21,385	43,694	30,646	62,617	43,076	88,014
Trns Supervisor I-II	31,790	56,786	32,521	58,092	33,269	59,428	34,034	60,795	34,817	62,194	2.30%	11.50%	20,124	35,948	28,840	51,516	40,537	72,412
Unemp Insurance Assoc Supr I-II	33,781	56,786	34,558	58,092	35,353	59,428	36,166	60,795	36,998	62,194	2.30%	11.50%	21,385	35,948	30,646	51,516	43,076	72,412
Unemp Insurance Legal Case Manager I-II	33,781	56,786	34,558	58,092	35,353	59,428	36,166	60,795	36,998	62,194	2.30%	11.50%	21,385	35,948	30,646	51,516	43,076	72,412
Unemp Insurance Spec Supv I-II	38,190	64,663	39,069	66,150	39,967	67,672	40,887	69,228	41,827	70,820	2.30%	11.50%	24,176	40,934	34,646	58,662	48,699	82,456
Unemp Insurance Staff Spec I-II	33,781	56,786	34,558	58,092	35,353	59,428	36,166	60,795	36,998	62,194	2.30%	11.50%	21,385	35,948	30,646	51,516	43,076	72,412
Veterans Serv Prog Appeals Supv	35,910	56,786	36,736	58,092	37,581	59,428	38,445	60,795	39,330	62,194	2.30%	11.50%	22,732	35,948	32,578	51,516	45,791	72,412

Chart III - U.S. States & Cities - Job Titles - Salaries - Pension Estimates

Maryland	2010 (Min)	2010 (Max)	2011 (Min)	2011 (Max)	2012 (Min)	2012 (Max)	2013 (Min)	2013 (Max)	2014 (Min)	2014 (Max)	5-Year Average % Raise	5-Year Cumulative Raise Estimate**	20-Year Annual Pension Benefit Estimate (Min.)***	20-Year Annual Pension Benefit Estimate (Max.)	25-Year Annual Pension Benefit Estimate (Min.)	25-Year Annual Pension Benefit Estimate (Max.)	30-Year Annual Pension Benefit Estimate (Min.)	30-Year Annual Pension Benefit Estimate (Max.)
Veterans Serv Prog Area Supv	35,910	56,786	36,736	58,092	37,581	59,428	38,445	60,795	39,330	62,194	2.30%	11.50%	22,732	35,948	32,578	51,516	45,791	72,412
Veterans Serv Prog Manager	40,627	64,663	41,562	66,150	42,518	67,672	43,496	69,228	44,496	70,820	2.30%	11.50%	25,719	40,934	36,857	58,662	51,806	82,456
Veterinarian I-Iv	46,028	89,496	47,086	91,555	48,169	93,660	49,277	95,814	50,411	98,018	2.30%	11.50%	29,137	56,654	41,756	81,191	58,693	114,122
Veterinary Epidemiologist I-III	49,016	89,496	50,143	91,555	51,296	93,660	52,476	95,814	53,683	98,018	2.30%	11.50%	31,029	56,654	44,467	81,191	62,503	114,122
Water Res Engr I-V	35,910	83,892	36,736	85,821	37,581	87,795	38,445	89,815	39,330	91,880	2.30%	11.50%	22,732	53,107	32,578	76,106	45,791	106,976
Waterways Improvement Tech I	31,790	49,918	32,521	51,066	33,269	52,241	34,034	53,442	34,817	54,671	2.30%	11.50%	20,124	31,600	28,840	45,286	40,537	63,654
Waterways Improvement Tech II	33,781	53,227	34,558	54,451	35,353	55,703	36,166	56,985	36,998	58,295	2.30%	11.50%	21,385	33,694	30,646	48,287	43,076	67,873
Waterways Improvement Tech III	35,910	56,786	36,736	58,092	37,581	59,428	38,445	60,795	39,330	62,194	2.30%	11.50%	22,732	35,948	32,578	51,516	45,791	72,412
Webmaster I-II	43,237	73,687	44,232	75,381	45,249	77,115	46,290	78,889	47,354	80,703	2.30%	11.50%	27,371	46,646	39,225	66,848	55,135	93,963
Webmaster Supr	52,252	83,892	53,454	85,821	54,683	87,795	55,941	89,815	57,228	91,880	2.30%	11.50%	33,077	53,107	47,403	76,106	66,630	106,976
Workers Comp Rehab Spec	35,910	56,786	36,736	58,092	37,581	59,428	38,445	60,795	39,330	62,194	2.30%	11.50%	22,732	35,948	32,578	51,516	45,791	72,412
Workers Comp Rehab Supv	40,627	64,663	41,562	66,150	42,518	67,672	43,496	69,228	44,496	70,820	2.30%	11.50%	25,719	40,934	36,857	58,662	51,806	82,456

http://www.dbm.maryland.gov/portal/server.pt?open=514&objID=2903&parentname=CommunityPage&parentid=5&mode=2&in_hi_userid=1332&cached=true

Chart III - U.S. States & Cities - Job Titles - Salaries - Pension Estimates

New Jersey	2010 (Min)	2010 (Max)	2011 (Min)	2011 (Max)	2012 (Min)	2012 (Max)	2013 (Min)	2013 (Max)	2014 (Min)	2014 (Max)	5-Year Average % Raise	5-Year Cumulative Raise Estimate**	20-Year Annual Pension Benefit Estimate (Min.)***	20-Year Annual Pension Benefit Estimate (Max.)	25-Year Annual Pension Benefit Estimate (Min.)	25-Year Annual Pension Benefit Estimate (Max.)	30-Year Annual Pension Benefit Estimate (Min.)	30-Year Annual Pension Benefit Estimate (Max.)
Accountant 1	56,768	88,700	58,045	90,696	59,351	92,736	60,687	94,823	62,052	96,956	2.25%	11.25%	35,638	55,685	50,948	79,607	71,439	111,623
Accountant/Auditor Data Processing 1-4	68,184	97,403	69,718	99,594	71,287	101,835	72,891	104,126	74,531	106,469	2.25%	11.25%	42,805	61,149	61,194	87,418	85,805	122,575
Administrative Analyst 1--4	47,374	102,080	48,440	104,377	49,530	106,725	50,644	109,126	51,784	111,582	2.25%	11.25%	29,741	64,085	42,518	91,615	59,617	128,461
Administrative Assistant State Parole Board	56,768	80,787	58,045	82,605	59,351	84,463	60,687	86,364	62,052	88,307	2.25%	11.25%	35,638	50,718	50,948	72,505	71,439	101,665
Administrative Director Health & Senior Services	82,297	115,490	84,149	118,088	86,042	120,745	87,978	123,462	89,958	126,240	2.25%	11.25%	51,666	72,504	73,861	103,650	103,566	145,336
Administrator Employee Relations	82,061	117,572	83,907	120,217	85,795	122,922	87,726	125,688	89,699	128,516	2.25%	11.25%	51,517	73,811	73,649	105,519	103,268	147,957
Administrator Fiscal Operations Youth and Family Services	82,297	115,490	84,149	118,088	86,042	120,745	87,978	123,462	89,958	126,240	2.25%	11.25%	51,666	72,504	73,861	103,650	103,566	145,336
Administrator Law Enforcement Standards	82,297	115,490	84,149	118,088	86,042	120,745	87,978	123,462	89,958	126,240	2.25%	11.25%	51,666	72,504	73,861	103,650	103,566	145,336
Administrator Natural Lands Management	74,644	104,768	76,323	107,125	78,041	109,535	79,796	112,000	81,592	114,520	2.25%	11.25%	46,861	65,773	66,992	94,028	93,934	131,843
Administrator Of Insurance	71,089	99,768	72,689	102,013	74,324	104,308	75,997	106,655	77,707	109,055	2.25%	11.25%	44,629	62,634	63,802	89,540	89,461	125,551
Administrator Psychiatric Social Services	71,089	99,768	72,689	102,013	74,324	104,308	75,997	106,655	77,707	109,055	2.25%	11.25%	44,629	62,634	63,802	89,540	89,461	125,551
Admitting Officer	45,300	64,120	46,320	65,563	47,362	67,038	48,428	68,546	49,517	70,089	2.25%	11.25%	28,439	40,254	40,656	57,547	57,008	80,691
Advocate Representative 1-3	45,300	84,659	46,320	86,564	47,362	88,512	48,428	90,503	49,517	92,540	2.25%	11.25%	28,439	53,148	40,656	75,980	57,008	106,538
Affirmative Action Assistant Public Contracts	51,843	73,643	53,009	75,300	54,202	76,995	55,422	78,727	56,669	80,498	2.25%	11.25%	32,547	46,233	46,528	66,094	65,241	92,675
Affirmative Action Investigator Public Contracts	78,333	112,155	80,096	114,679	81,898	117,259	83,741	119,897	85,625	122,595	2.25%	11.25%	49,177	70,410	70,303	100,658	98,578	141,140
Affirmative Action Officer 1-3	62,197	97,403	63,596	99,594	65,027	101,835	66,490	104,126	67,986	106,469	2.25%	11.25%	39,047	61,149	55,821	87,418	78,270	122,575
Affirmative Action Specialist 1-3	45,300	84,659	46,320	86,564	47,362	88,512	48,428	90,503	49,517	92,540	2.25%	11.25%	28,439	53,148	40,656	75,980	57,008	106,538
Agricultural Marketing Specialist 1-4	43,325	92,945	44,300	95,036	45,297	97,175	46,316	99,361	47,358	101,597	2.25%	11.25%	27,199	58,350	38,884	83,417	54,522	116,965
Agricultural Resource Specialist 1-3	43,325	80,787	44,300	82,605	45,297	84,463	46,316	86,364	47,358	88,307	2.25%	11.25%	27,199	50,718	38,884	72,505	54,522	101,665
Agricultural Statistician 1-3	45,300	84,659	46,320	86,564	47,362	88,512	48,428	90,503	49,517	92,540	2.25%	11.25%	28,439	53,148	40,656	75,980	57,008	106,538
Appeals Examiner 1-2	49,554	84,659	50,669	86,564	51,809	88,512	52,974	90,503	54,166	92,540	2.25%	11.25%	31,109	53,148	44,474	75,980	62,360	106,538
Archivist 1-2	49,554	84,659	50,669	86,564	51,809	88,512	52,974	90,503	54,166	92,540	2.25%	11.25%	31,109	53,148	44,474	75,980	62,360	106,538
Area Coordinator Community Involvement	45,300	64,120	46,320	65,563	47,362	67,038	48,428	68,546	49,517	70,089	2.25%	11.25%	28,439	40,254	40,656	57,547	57,008	80,691
Area Supervisor Bridge Operations	47,374	67,155	48,440	68,666	49,530	70,211	50,644	71,790	51,784	73,406	2.25%	11.25%	29,741	42,159	42,518	60,270	59,617	84,510
Area Supervisor Highway Maintenance	49,554	70,327	50,669	71,910	51,809	73,528	52,974	75,182	54,166	76,874	2.25%	11.25%	31,109	44,151	44,474	63,118	62,360	88,502
Area Supervisor Institutional Assistance	59,415	84,659	60,752	86,564	62,118	88,512	63,516	90,503	64,945	92,540	2.25%	11.25%	37,300	53,148	53,324	75,980	74,769	106,538
Assistant Attorney General	115,796	162,501	118,401	166,158	121,065	169,896	123,789	173,719	126,575	177,628	2.25%	11.25%	72,696	102,017	103,925	145,843	145,722	204,497
Assistant Biologist	45,300	67,155	46,320	68,666	47,362	70,211	48,428	71,790	49,517	73,406	2.25%	11.25%	28,439	42,159	40,656	60,270	57,008	84,510
Assistant Business Manager 1	71,404	102,080	73,011	104,377	74,653	106,725	76,333	109,126	78,051	111,582	2.25%	11.25%	44,827	64,085	64,084	91,615	89,857	128,461
Assistant Buyer	43,325	61,251	44,300	62,629	45,297	64,038	46,316	65,479	47,358	66,952	2.25%	11.25%	27,199	38,453	38,884	54,972	54,522	77,080
Attorney Assistant	47,374	67,155	48,440	68,666	49,530	70,211	50,644	71,790	51,784	73,406	2.25%	11.25%	29,741	42,159	42,518	60,270	59,617	84,510

197

Chart III - U.S. States & Cities - Job Titles - Salaries - Pension Estimates

New Jersey	2010 (Min)	2010 (Max)	2011 (Min)	2011 (Max)	2012 (Min)	2012 (Max)	2013 (Min)	2013 (Max)	2014 (Min)	2014 (Max)	5-Year Average % Raise	5-Year Cumulative Raise Estimate**	20-Year Annual Pension Benefit Estimate (Min.)***	20-Year Annual Pension Benefit Estimate (Max.)	25-Year Annual Pension Benefit Estimate (Min.)	25-Year Annual Pension Benefit Estimate (Max.)	30-Year Annual Pension Benefit Estimate (Min.)	30-Year Annual Pension Benefit Estimate (Max.)
Auditor 1	65,117	97,403	66,582	99,594	68,081	101,835	69,612	104,126	71,179	106,469	2.25%	11.25%	40,880	61,149	58,442	87,418	81,946	122,575
Budget Analyst 1-3	47,374	88,700	48,440	90,696	49,530	92,736	50,644	94,823	51,784	96,956	2.25%	11.25%	29,741	55,685	42,518	79,607	59,617	111,623
Building Management Services Specialist 1-4	43,325	92,945	44,300	95,036	45,297	97,175	46,316	99,361	47,358	101,597	2.25%	11.25%	27,199	58,350	38,884	83,417	54,522	116,965
Business Manager 1-3	61,407	115,490	62,788	118,088	64,201	120,745	65,646	123,462	67,123	126,240	2.25%	11.25%	38,551	72,504	55,112	103,650	77,276	145,336
Business Representative 1-3	45,300	80,787	46,320	82,605	47,362	84,463	48,428	86,364	49,517	88,307	2.25%	11.25%	28,439	50,718	40,656	72,505	57,008	101,665
Buyer	49,554	77,138	50,669	78,874	51,809	80,649	52,974	82,463	54,166	84,319	2.25%	11.25%	31,109	48,427	44,474	69,231	62,360	97,074
Chemist	45,300	70,327	46,320	71,910	47,362	73,528	48,428	75,182	49,517	76,874	2.25%	11.25%	28,439	44,151	40,656	63,118	57,008	88,502
Claims Examiner Unemployment & Disability Insurance	41,441	58,540	42,374	59,857	43,327	61,204	44,302	62,581	45,299	63,989	2.25%	11.25%	26,017	36,751	37,193	52,539	52,151	73,668
Classification Officer 1-3	45,300	88,700	46,320	90,696	47,362	92,736	48,428	94,823	49,517	96,956	2.25%	11.25%	28,439	55,685	40,656	79,607	57,008	111,623
Clinical Director 1-2	90,733	110,006	92,775	112,481	94,862	115,012	96,997	117,600	99,179	120,246	2.25%	11.25%	56,962	69,061	81,432	98,729	114,182	138,435
Clinical Laboratory Evaluator 1-4	51,843	102,080	53,009	104,377	54,202	106,725	55,422	109,126	56,669	111,582	2.25%	11.25%	32,547	64,085	46,528	91,615	65,241	128,461
Clinical Psychologist 1-2	65,117	106,984	66,582	109,392	68,081	111,853	69,612	114,370	71,179	116,943	2.25%	11.25%	40,880	67,164	58,442	96,017	81,946	134,633
Community Program Analyst 1	54,245	77,138	55,466	78,874	56,714	80,649	57,990	82,463	59,294	84,319	2.25%	11.25%	34,055	48,427	48,684	69,231	68,264	97,074
Community Program Specialist	45,300	64,120	46,320	65,563	47,362	67,038	48,428	68,546	49,517	70,089	2.25%	11.25%	28,439	40,254	40,656	57,547	57,008	80,691
Community Service Officer 1-3	62,197	61,251	63,596	62,629	65,027	64,038	66,490	65,479	67,986	66,952	2.25%	11.25%	39,047	38,453	55,821	54,972	78,270	77,080
Compliance Officer 1-2 Code Enforcement	59,415	72,828	60,752	74,467	62,118	76,142	63,516	77,855	64,945	79,607	2.25%	11.25%	37,300	45,721	53,324	65,362	74,769	91,649
Computer Operator 1-3	45,300	48,822	46,320	49,920	47,362	51,043	48,428	52,192	49,517	53,366	2.25%	11.25%	28,439	30,650	40,656	43,817	57,008	61,439
Conservation Officer 1-3	67,175	80,339	68,687	82,147	70,232	83,995	71,812	85,885	73,428	87,817	2.25%	11.25%	42,172	50,436	60,289	72,103	84,536	101,101
Construction And Maintenance Technician 1-5	51,843	44,133	53,009	45,126	54,202	46,141	55,422	47,179	56,669	48,241	2.25%	11.25%	32,547	27,706	46,528	39,609	65,241	55,538
Construction Management Specialist 1-4	82,297	73,643	84,149	75,300	86,042	76,995	87,978	78,727	89,958	80,498	2.25%	11.25%	51,666	46,233	73,861	66,094	103,566	92,675
Consultant Curriculum And Instruction 1-2	68,184	88,700	69,718	90,696	71,287	92,736	72,891	94,823	74,531	96,956	2.25%	11.25%	42,805	55,685	61,194	79,607	85,805	111,623
Contract Administrator 1-2	62,197	77,138	63,596	78,874	65,027	80,649	66,490	82,463	67,986	84,319	2.25%	11.25%	39,047	48,427	55,821	69,231	78,270	97,074
Crew Supervisor	45,300	64,120	46,320	65,563	47,362	67,038	48,428	68,546	49,517	70,089	2.25%	11.25%	28,439	40,254	40,656	57,547	57,008	80,691
Curator	74,785	106,984	76,467	109,392	78,188	111,853	79,947	114,370	81,746	116,943	2.25%	11.25%	46,949	67,164	67,118	96,017	94,112	134,633
Customer Representative 1-3 Public Utilities	56,768	61,251	58,045	62,629	59,351	64,038	60,687	65,479	62,052	66,952	2.25%	11.25%	35,638	38,453	50,948	54,972	71,439	77,080
Customer Service Representative 1-4	43,325	42,692	44,300	43,653	45,297	44,635	46,316	45,639	47,358	46,666	2.25%	11.25%	27,199	26,802	38,884	38,316	54,522	53,726
Customized Training Representative 1-3	59,415	64,120	60,752	65,563	62,118	67,038	63,516	68,546	64,945	70,089	2.25%	11.25%	37,300	40,254	53,324	57,547	74,769	80,691
Data Base Analyst 1-2	71,404	92,945	73,011	95,036	74,653	97,175	76,333	99,361	78,051	101,597	2.25%	11.25%	44,827	58,350	64,084	83,417	89,857	116,965
Data Processing Analyst 1-2	71,404	88,700	73,011	90,696	74,653	92,736	76,333	94,823	78,051	96,956	2.25%	11.25%	44,827	55,685	64,084	79,607	89,857	111,623
Data Processing Input/Output Control Specialist 1-3	47,374	48,822	48,440	49,920	49,530	51,043	50,644	52,192	51,784	53,366	2.25%	11.25%	29,741	30,650	42,518	43,817	59,617	61,439
Data Processing Scheduler 1-2	56,768	67,155	58,045	68,666	59,351	70,211	60,687	71,790	62,052	73,406	2.25%	11.25%	35,638	42,159	50,948	60,270	71,439	84,510
Data Processing Systems Programmer 1-2	71,404	88,700	73,011	90,696	74,653	92,736	76,333	94,823	78,051	96,956	2.25%	11.25%	44,827	55,685	64,084	79,607	89,857	111,623

Chart III - U.S. States & Cities - Job Titles - Salaries - Pension Estimates

New Jersey	2010 (Min)	2010 (Max)	2011 (Min)	2011 (Max)	2012 (Min)	2012 (Max)	2013 (Min)	2013 (Max)	2014 (Min)	2014 (Max)	5-Year Average % Raise	5-Year Cumulative Raise Estimate**	20-Year Annual Pension Benefit Estimate (Min.)***	20-Year Annual Pension Benefit Estimate (Max.)	25-Year Annual Pension Benefit Estimate (Min.)	25-Year Annual Pension Benefit Estimate (Max.)	30-Year Annual Pension Benefit Estimate (Min.)	30-Year Annual Pension Benefit Estimate (Max.)
Dental Assistant 1-2	103,678	50,503	106,011	51,640	108,396	52,801	110,835	53,989	113,328	55,204	2.25%	11.25%	65,088	31,706	93,049	45,326	130,472	63,555
Deputy Attorney General 1-5	100,029	74,454	102,280	76,129	104,581	77,842	106,934	79,594	109,340	81,385	2.25%	11.25%	62,798	46,742	89,775	66,822	125,880	93,696
Deputy Public Advocate 1-2	105,031	127,319	107,394	130,183	109,810	133,112	112,281	136,107	114,807	139,170	2.25%	11.25%	65,938	79,930	94,264	114,267	132,174	160,222
Deputy Public Defender 1-2	105,031	127,319	107,394	130,183	109,810	133,112	112,281	136,107	114,807	139,170	2.25%	11.25%	65,938	79,930	94,264	114,267	132,174	160,222
Director Of Custody Operations 1-2	83,749	117,099	85,633	119,734	87,560	122,428	89,530	125,182	91,544	127,999	2.25%	11.25%	52,577	73,514	75,163	105,095	105,392	147,361
Director Of Medical Security	58,481	82,085	59,797	83,932	61,142	85,820	62,518	87,751	63,925	89,726	2.25%	11.25%	36,714	51,532	52,486	73,670	73,595	103,298
Director Of Programming P B A	95,267	133,682	97,411	136,690	99,603	139,766	101,844	142,911	104,135	146,126	2.25%	11.25%	59,808	83,925	85,501	119,978	119,888	168,230
Dispute Resolution Specialist 1-3	65,117	112,155	66,582	114,679	68,081	117,259	69,612	119,897	71,179	122,595	2.25%	11.25%	40,880	70,410	58,442	100,658	81,946	141,140
Driver Improvement Analyst 1-3	56,768	67,155	58,045	68,666	59,351	70,211	60,687	71,790	62,052	73,406	2.25%	11.25%	35,638	42,159	50,948	60,270	71,439	84,510
Driver License Examiner 1-2	40,985	50,502	41,907	51,638	42,850	52,800	43,814	53,988	44,800	55,203	2.25%	11.25%	25,730	31,705	36,784	45,325	51,577	63,553
Economic Development Representative 1-4	74,785	67,155	76,467	68,666	78,188	70,211	79,947	71,790	81,746	73,406	2.25%	11.25%	46,949	42,159	67,118	60,270	94,112	84,510
Education Planner	51,843	73,643	53,009	75,300	54,202	76,995	55,422	78,727	56,669	80,498	2.25%	11.25%	32,547	46,233	46,528	66,094	65,241	92,675
Education Program Development Specialist 1-3	74,785	88,700	76,467	90,696	78,188	92,736	79,947	94,823	81,746	96,956	2.25%	11.25%	46,949	55,685	67,118	79,607	94,112	111,623
Education Program Specialist 1-3	74,785	88,700	76,467	90,696	78,188	92,736	79,947	94,823	81,746	96,956	2.25%	11.25%	46,949	55,685	67,118	79,607	94,112	111,623
Election Specialist 1	50,518	70,890	51,655	72,485	52,817	74,116	54,005	75,783	55,220	77,489	2.25%	11.25%	31,715	44,504	45,339	63,623	63,573	89,210
Emergency Response Specialist 1-4	74,785	70,327	76,467	71,910	78,188	73,528	79,947	75,182	81,746	76,874	2.25%	11.25%	46,949	44,151	67,118	63,118	94,112	88,502
Employee Relations Coordinator	71,404	102,080	73,011	104,377	74,653	106,725	76,333	109,126	78,051	111,582	2.25%	11.25%	44,827	64,085	64,084	91,615	89,857	128,461
Employment And Training Specialist 1-2	56,768	70,327	58,045	71,910	59,351	73,528	60,687	75,182	62,052	76,874	2.25%	11.25%	35,638	44,151	50,948	63,118	71,439	88,502
Employment Services Specialist 1-3	56,768	61,251	58,045	62,629	59,351	64,038	60,687	65,479	62,052	66,952	2.25%	11.25%	35,638	38,453	50,948	54,972	71,439	77,080
Employment Supervisor 1-2	65,117	84,659	66,582	86,564	68,081	88,512	69,612	90,503	71,179	92,540	2.25%	11.25%	40,880	53,148	58,442	75,980	81,946	106,538
Engineer In Charge Maintenance 1-4	67,703	77,138	69,227	78,874	70,784	80,649	72,377	82,463	74,005	84,319	2.25%	11.25%	42,504	48,427	60,763	69,231	85,200	97,074
Engineering Technician 1-5	47,374	44,625	48,440	45,629	49,530	46,655	50,644	47,705	51,784	48,778	2.25%	11.25%	29,741	28,015	42,518	40,050	59,617	56,157
Entomologist 1-2	51,843	64,120	53,009	65,563	54,202	67,038	55,422	68,546	56,669	70,089	2.25%	11.25%	32,547	40,254	46,528	57,547	65,241	80,691
Environmental Compliance Inspector 1-3	51,843	55,301	53,009	56,545	54,202	57,818	55,422	59,119	56,669	60,449	2.25%	11.25%	32,547	34,718	46,528	49,632	65,241	69,593
Environmental Scientist 1-4	74,785	73,643	76,467	75,300	78,188	76,995	79,947	78,727	81,746	80,498	2.25%	11.25%	46,949	46,233	67,118	66,094	94,112	92,675
Environmental Specialist	68,184	102,080	69,718	104,377	71,287	106,725	72,891	109,126	74,531	111,582	2.25%	11.25%	42,805	64,085	61,194	91,615	85,805	128,461
Erosion Control Engineer	68,184	97,403	69,718	99,594	71,287	101,835	72,891	104,126	74,531	106,469	2.25%	11.25%	42,805	61,149	61,194	87,418	85,805	122,575
Executive Assistant 1-4	82,061	77,138	83,907	78,874	85,795	80,649	87,726	82,463	89,699	84,319	2.25%	11.25%	51,517	48,427	73,649	69,231	103,268	97,074
Family Service Specialist 1-2	56,768	73,643	58,045	75,300	59,351	76,995	60,687	78,727	62,052	80,498	2.25%	11.25%	35,638	46,233	50,948	66,094	71,439	92,675
Farm Supervisor 1-2	54,245	70,327	55,466	71,910	56,714	73,528	57,990	75,182	59,294	76,874	2.25%	11.25%	34,055	44,151	48,684	63,118	68,264	88,502
Field Service Supervisor 1-3	65,117	77,138	66,582	78,874	68,081	80,649	69,612	82,463	71,179	84,319	2.25%	11.25%	40,880	48,427	58,442	69,231	81,946	97,074
Financial Examiner 1-4	74,785	67,155	76,467	68,666	78,188	70,211	79,947	71,790	81,746	73,406	2.25%	11.25%	46,949	42,159	67,118	60,270	94,112	84,510
Fire Code Assistance Representative 1-2	58,758	72,828	60,080	74,467	61,432	76,142	62,814	77,855	64,227	79,607	2.25%	11.25%	36,888	45,721	52,734	65,362	73,943	91,649

199

Chart III - U.S. States & Cities - Job Titles - Salaries - Pension Estimates

New Jersey	2010 (Min)	2010 (Max)	2011 (Min)	2011 (Max)	2012 (Min)	2012 (Max)	2013 (Min)	2013 (Max)	2014 (Min)	2014 (Max)	5-Year Average % Raise	5-Year Cumulative Raise Estimate**	20-Year Annual Pension Benefit Estimate (Min.)***	20-Year Annual Pension Benefit Estimate (Max.)	25-Year Annual Pension Benefit Estimate (Min.)	25-Year Annual Pension Benefit Estimate (Max.)	30-Year Annual Pension Benefit Estimate (Min.)	30-Year Annual Pension Benefit Estimate (Max.)
Fire Code Specialist	65,117	92,945	66,582	95,036	68,081	97,175	69,612	99,361	71,179	101,597	2.25%	11.25%	40,880	58,350	58,442	83,417	81,946	116,965
Fire Investigator	59,415	84,659	60,752	86,564	62,118	88,512	63,516	90,503	64,945	92,540	2.25%	11.25%	37,300	53,148	53,324	75,980	74,769	106,538
Fiscal Analyst	43,325	61,251	44,300	62,629	45,297	64,038	46,316	65,479	47,358	66,952	2.25%	11.25%	27,199	38,453	38,884	54,972	54,522	77,080
Forest Fire Equipment Maintenance Specialist 1-2	40,985	52,829	41,907	54,018	42,850	55,233	43,814	56,476	44,800	57,747	2.25%	11.25%	25,730	33,166	36,784	47,414	51,577	66,482
Forest Fire Pilot	49,554	70,327	50,669	71,910	51,809	73,528	52,974	75,182	54,166	76,874	2.25%	11.25%	31,109	44,151	44,474	63,118	62,360	88,502
Forester	45,300	64,120	46,320	65,563	47,362	67,038	48,428	68,546	49,517	70,089	2.25%	11.25%	28,439	40,254	40,656	57,547	57,008	80,691
Forms Analyst 1-3	43,325	80,787	44,300	82,605	45,297	84,463	46,316	86,364	47,358	88,307	2.25%	11.25%	27,199	50,718	38,884	72,505	54,522	101,665
Garage Supervisor 1-2	59,415	73,643	60,752	75,300	62,118	76,995	63,516	78,727	64,945	80,498	2.25%	11.25%	37,300	46,233	53,324	66,094	74,769	92,675
Geographic Information Systems Specialist 1-3	68,184	73,643	69,718	75,300	71,287	76,995	72,891	78,727	74,531	80,498	2.25%	11.25%	42,805	46,233	61,194	66,094	85,805	92,675
Governmental Relations Specialist 1-3	62,197	61,251	63,596	62,629	65,027	64,038	66,490	65,479	67,986	66,952	2.25%	11.25%	39,047	38,453	55,821	54,972	78,270	77,080
Guardianship Services Specialist 1-3	62,197	64,120	63,596	65,563	65,027	67,038	66,490	68,546	67,986	70,089	2.25%	11.25%	39,047	40,254	55,821	57,547	78,270	80,691
Hazardous Site Mitigation Specialist 1-4	68,184	64,120	69,718	65,563	71,287	67,038	72,891	68,546	74,531	70,089	2.25%	11.25%	42,805	40,254	61,194	57,547	85,805	80,691
Health Economics Research Specialist 1-3	71,404	73,643	73,011	75,300	74,653	76,995	76,333	78,727	78,051	80,498	2.25%	11.25%	44,827	46,233	64,084	66,094	89,857	92,675
Health Systems Specialist 1-3	71,404	84,659	73,011	86,564	74,653	88,512	76,333	90,503	78,051	92,540	2.25%	11.25%	44,827	53,148	64,084	75,980	89,857	106,538
Hearing Officer 1-4	59,415	129,236	60,752	132,144	62,118	135,117	63,516	138,157	64,945	141,266	2.25%	11.25%	37,300	81,133	53,324	115,987	74,769	162,635
Highway Safety Specialist	45,300	64,120	46,320	65,563	47,362	67,038	48,428	68,546	49,517	70,089	2.25%	11.25%	28,439	40,254	40,656	57,547	57,008	80,691
Human Resource Consultant 1-5	45,300	102,080	46,320	104,377	47,362	106,725	48,428	109,126	49,517	111,582	2.25%	11.25%	28,439	64,085	40,656	91,615	57,008	128,461
Institution Fire Chief	45,300	64,120	46,320	65,563	47,362	67,038	48,428	68,546	49,517	70,089	2.25%	11.25%	28,439	40,254	40,656	57,547	57,008	80,691
Institutional Trade Instructor 1-2	44,802	55,303	45,810	56,547	46,841	57,819	47,895	59,120	48,972	60,450	2.25%	11.25%	28,126	34,719	40,209	49,633	56,380	69,595
Insurance Analyst 1-4	71,404	64,120	73,011	65,563	74,653	67,038	76,333	68,546	78,051	70,089	2.25%	11.25%	44,827	40,254	64,084	57,547	89,857	80,691
Insurance Examiner 1-3	62,197	67,155	63,596	68,666	65,027	70,211	66,490	71,790	67,986	73,406	2.25%	11.25%	39,047	42,159	55,821	60,270	78,270	84,510
Investigator Insurance Fraud Prevention	45,300	64,120	46,320	65,563	47,362	67,038	48,428	68,546	49,517	70,089	2.25%	11.25%	28,439	40,254	40,656	57,547	57,008	80,691
Labor Market Analyst 1-4	45,300	84,659	46,320	86,564	47,362	88,512	48,428	90,503	49,517	92,540	2.25%	11.25%	28,439	53,148	40,656	75,980	57,008	106,538
Landscape Designer 1-3	62,197	67,155	63,596	68,666	65,027	70,211	66,490	71,790	67,986	73,406	2.25%	11.25%	39,047	42,159	55,821	60,270	78,270	84,510
Legal Services Assistant 1-2	43,325	53,419	44,300	54,621	45,297	55,850	46,316	57,107	47,358	58,391	2.25%	11.25%	27,199	33,536	38,884	47,943	54,522	67,224
Legal Services Coordinator	56,768	80,787	58,045	82,605	59,351	84,463	60,687	86,364	62,052	88,307	2.25%	11.25%	35,638	50,718	50,948	72,505	71,439	101,665
Librarian 1-3	43,325	70,327	44,300	71,910	45,297	73,528	46,316	75,182	47,358	76,874	2.25%	11.25%	27,199	44,151	38,884	63,118	54,522	88,502
License Examiner 1-3	59,415	64,120	60,752	65,563	62,118	67,038	63,516	68,546	64,945	70,089	2.25%	11.25%	37,300	40,254	53,324	57,547	74,769	80,691
Management Assistant	43,325	61,251	44,300	62,629	45,297	64,038	46,316	65,479	47,358	66,952	2.25%	11.25%	27,199	38,453	38,884	54,972	54,522	77,080
Management Information Systems Specialist 2-3	71,404	112,155	73,011	114,679	74,653	117,259	76,333	119,897	78,051	122,595	2.25%	11.25%	44,827	70,410	64,084	100,658	89,857	141,140
Manager 1-4	68,184	133,682	69,718	136,690	71,287	139,766	72,891	142,911	74,531	146,126	2.25%	11.25%	42,805	83,925	61,194	119,978	85,805	168,230
Manager Word Processing System 1-2	53,044	73,643	54,237	75,300	55,458	76,995	56,705	78,727	57,981	80,498	2.25%	11.25%	33,301	46,233	47,606	66,094	66,752	92,675
Market Conduct Examiner 1-4	68,184	64,120	69,718	65,563	71,287	67,038	72,891	68,546	74,531	70,089	2.25%	11.25%	42,805	40,254	61,194	57,547	85,805	80,691

Chart III - U.S. States & Cities - Job Titles - Salaries - Pension Estimates

New Jersey	2010 (Min)	2010 (Max)	2011 (Min)	2011 (Max)	2012 (Min)	2012 (Max)	2013 (Min)	2013 (Max)	2014 (Min)	2014 (Max)	5-Year Average % Raise	5-Year Cumulative Raise Estimate**	20-Year Annual Pension Benefit Estimate (Min.)***	20-Year Annual Pension Benefit Estimate (Max.)	25-Year Annual Pension Benefit Estimate (Min.)	25-Year Annual Pension Benefit Estimate (Max.)	30-Year Annual Pension Benefit Estimate (Min.)	30-Year Annual Pension Benefit Estimate (Max.)
Media Technician 1-3	49,554	53,419	50,669	54,621	51,809	55,850	52,974	57,107	54,166	58,391	2.25%	11.25%	31,109	33,536	44,474	47,943	62,360	67,224
Medical Records Administrator	62,197	88,700	63,596	90,696	65,027	92,736	66,490	94,823	67,986	96,956	2.25%	11.25%	39,047	55,685	55,821	79,607	78,270	111,623
Medical Review Analyst	62,197	88,700	63,596	90,696	65,027	92,736	66,490	94,823	67,986	96,956	2.25%	11.25%	39,047	55,685	55,821	79,607	78,270	111,623
Medical Social Work Consultant 1-2	68,184	84,659	69,718	86,564	71,287	88,512	72,891	90,503	74,531	92,540	2.25%	11.25%	42,805	53,148	61,194	75,980	85,805	106,538
Microbiologist 1-5	71,089	64,120	72,689	65,563	74,324	67,038	75,997	68,546	77,707	70,089	2.25%	11.25%	44,629	40,254	63,802	57,547	89,461	80,691
Municipal Finance Auditor 1-3	59,415	64,120	60,752	65,563	62,118	67,038	63,516	68,546	64,945	70,089	2.25%	11.25%	37,300	40,254	53,324	57,547	74,769	80,691
Network Administrator 1-2	62,197	106,984	63,596	109,392	65,027	111,853	66,490	114,370	67,986	116,943	2.25%	11.25%	39,047	67,164	55,821	96,017	78,270	134,633
Occupational Analyst	45,300	64,120	46,320	65,563	47,362	67,038	48,428	68,546	49,517	70,089	2.25%	11.25%	28,439	40,254	40,656	57,547	57,008	80,691
Occupational Health Consultant 1-4	65,117	61,251	66,582	62,629	68,081	64,038	69,612	65,479	71,179	66,952	2.25%	11.25%	40,880	38,453	58,442	54,972	81,946	77,080
Occupational Safety Consultant 1-2	59,415	73,643	60,752	75,300	62,118	76,995	63,516	78,727	64,945	80,498	2.25%	11.25%	37,300	46,233	53,324	66,094	74,769	92,675
Occupational Therapist	47,374	67,155	48,440	68,666	49,530	70,211	50,644	71,790	51,784	73,406	2.25%	11.25%	29,741	42,159	42,518	60,270	59,617	84,510
Office Automation Specialist 1-3	59,415	64,120	60,752	65,563	62,118	67,038	63,516	68,546	64,945	70,089	2.25%	11.25%	37,300	40,254	53,324	57,547	74,769	80,691
Operations Analyst	43,325	61,251	44,300	62,629	45,297	64,038	46,316	65,479	47,358	66,952	2.25%	11.25%	27,199	38,453	38,884	54,972	54,522	77,080
Paralegal Technician 1-2	47,374	58,540	48,440	59,857	49,530	61,204	50,644	62,581	51,784	63,989	2.25%	11.25%	29,741	36,751	42,518	52,539	59,617	73,668
Parks Maintenance Supervisor 1-2	49,554	64,120	50,669	65,563	51,809	67,038	52,974	68,546	54,166	70,089	2.25%	11.25%	31,109	40,254	44,474	57,547	62,360	80,691
Payroll Analyst 1-3	59,415	61,251	60,752	62,629	62,118	64,038	63,516	65,479	64,945	66,952	2.25%	11.25%	37,300	38,453	53,324	54,972	74,769	77,080
Pensions Benefits Specialist 1-3	56,768	61,251	58,045	62,629	59,351	64,038	60,687	65,479	62,052	66,952	2.25%	11.25%	35,638	38,453	50,948	54,972	71,439	77,080
Permit Coordination Officer 1-2	62,197	77,138	63,596	78,874	65,027	80,649	66,490	82,463	67,986	84,319	2.25%	11.25%	39,047	48,427	55,821	69,231	78,270	97,074
Personnel And Labor Analyst 1-4	49,554	102,080	50,669	104,377	51,809	106,725	52,974	109,126	54,166	111,582	2.25%	11.25%	31,109	64,085	44,474	91,615	62,360	128,461
Personnel Assistant 1-4	68,184	64,120	69,718	65,563	71,287	67,038	72,891	68,546	74,531	70,089	2.25%	11.25%	42,805	40,254	61,194	57,547	85,805	80,691
Physical Therapist	49,554	70,327	50,669	71,910	51,809	73,528	52,974	75,182	54,166	76,874	2.25%	11.25%	31,109	44,151	44,474	63,118	62,360	88,502
Physician 1-3	82,061	135,472	83,907	138,520	85,795	141,637	87,726	144,824	89,699	148,082	2.25%	11.25%	51,517	85,048	73,649	121,584	103,268	170,482
Physician Specialist 1-2	125,200	148,992	128,017	152,344	130,897	155,772	133,842	159,277	136,854	162,860	2.25%	11.25%	78,599	93,536	112,365	133,718	157,555	187,496
Planned Real Estate Development Analyst 1-2	65,117	73,643	66,582	75,300	68,081	76,995	69,612	78,727	71,179	80,498	2.25%	11.25%	40,880	46,233	58,442	66,094	81,946	92,675
Planning Associate 1-3	74,785	88,700	76,467	90,696	78,188	92,736	79,947	94,823	81,746	96,956	2.25%	11.25%	46,949	55,685	67,118	79,607	94,112	111,623
Police Lieutenant Pip	67,175	97,654	68,687	99,852	70,232	102,098	71,812	104,396	73,428	106,744	2.25%	11.25%	42,172	61,307	60,289	87,643	84,536	122,892
Police Officer P I P	50,137	72,902	51,265	74,543	52,418	76,220	53,598	77,935	54,804	79,688	2.25%	11.25%	31,476	45,768	44,997	65,429	63,094	91,743
Police Sergeant Pip	58,024	84,357	59,330	86,255	60,665	88,196	62,030	90,180	63,425	92,209	2.25%	11.25%	36,427	52,959	52,076	75,709	73,019	106,158
Principal Engineer Civil	56,768	88,700	58,045	90,696	59,351	92,736	60,687	94,823	62,052	96,956	2.25%	11.25%	35,638	55,685	50,948	79,607	71,439	111,623
Principal Engineer Industrial	62,197	88,700	63,596	90,696	65,027	92,736	66,490	94,823	67,986	96,956	2.25%	11.25%	39,047	55,685	55,821	79,607	78,270	111,623
Principal Engineer Mechanical	62,197	88,700	63,596	90,696	65,027	92,736	66,490	94,823	67,986	96,956	2.25%	11.25%	39,047	55,685	55,821	79,607	78,270	111,623
Principal Engineer Traffic	62,197	88,700	63,596	90,696	65,027	92,736	66,490	94,823	67,986	96,956	2.25%	11.25%	39,047	55,685	55,821	79,607	78,270	111,623
Principal Fiscal Analyst	56,768	80,787	58,045	82,605	59,351	84,463	60,687	86,364	62,052	88,307	2.25%	11.25%	35,638	50,718	50,948	72,505	71,439	101,665
Principal Investigator Public Defender	59,415	84,659	60,752	86,564	62,118	88,512	63,516	90,503	64,945	92,540	2.25%	11.25%	37,300	53,148	53,324	75,980	74,769	106,538
Principal Laboratory Technician	43,325	61,251	44,300	62,629	45,297	64,038	46,316	65,479	47,358	66,952	2.25%	11.25%	27,199	38,453	38,884	54,972	54,522	77,080
Principal Medical Technologist	56,768	80,787	58,045	82,605	59,351	84,463	60,687	86,364	62,052	88,307	2.25%	11.25%	35,638	50,718	50,948	72,505	71,439	101,665

Chart III - U.S. States & Cities - Job Titles - Salaries - Pension Estimates

New Jersey	2010 (Min)	2010 (Max)	2011 (Min)	2011 (Max)	2012 (Min)	2012 (Max)	2013 (Min)	2013 (Max)	2014 (Min)	2014 (Max)	5-Year Average % Raise	5-Year Cumulative Raise Estimate**	20-Year Annual Pension Benefit Estimate (Min.)***	20-Year Annual Pension Benefit Estimate (Max.)	25-Year Annual Pension Benefit Estimate (Min.)	25-Year Annual Pension Benefit Estimate (Max.)	30-Year Annual Pension Benefit Estimate (Min.)	30-Year Annual Pension Benefit Estimate (Max.)
Principal Occupational Analyst	59,415	84,659	60,752	86,564	62,118	88,512	63,516	90,503	64,945	92,540	2.25%	11.25%	37,300	53,148	53,324	75,980	74,769	106,538
Principal Planner	59,415	84,659	60,752	86,564	62,118	88,512	63,516	90,503	64,945	92,540	2.25%	11.25%	37,300	53,148	53,324	75,980	74,769	106,538
Principal Procedures Analyst	56,768	80,787	58,045	82,605	59,351	84,463	60,687	86,364	62,052	88,307	2.25%	11.25%	35,638	50,718	50,948	72,505	71,439	101,665
Principal Statistician	56,768	80,787	58,045	82,605	59,351	84,463	60,687	86,364	62,052	88,307	2.25%	11.25%	35,638	50,718	50,948	72,505	71,439	101,665
Principal Traffic Control Analyst	62,197	88,700	63,596	90,696	65,027	92,736	66,490	94,823	67,986	96,956	2.25%	11.25%	39,047	55,685	55,821	79,607	78,270	111,623
Principal Transportation Analyst	62,197	88,700	63,596	90,696	65,027	92,736	66,490	94,823	67,986	96,956	2.25%	11.25%	39,047	55,685	55,821	79,607	78,270	111,623
Procedures Analyst	43,325	61,251	44,300	62,629	45,297	64,038	46,316	65,479	47,358	66,952	2.25%	11.25%	27,199	38,453	38,884	54,972	54,522	77,080
Procurement Controller	41,441	58,540	42,374	59,857	43,327	61,204	44,302	62,581	45,299	63,989	2.25%	11.25%	26,017	36,751	37,193	52,539	52,151	73,668
Procurement Specialist 1-3	59,415	64,120	60,752	65,563	62,118	67,038	63,516	68,546	64,945	70,089	2.25%	11.25%	37,300	40,254	53,324	57,547	74,769	80,691
Program Analyst 1-4 Budget And Accounting	47,374	88,700	48,440	90,696	49,530	92,736	50,644	94,823	51,784	96,956	2.25%	11.25%	29,741	55,685	42,518	79,607	59,617	111,623
Program Development Specialist 1-3	43,325	88,700	44,300	90,696	45,297	92,736	46,316	94,823	47,358	96,956	2.25%	11.25%	27,199	55,685	38,884	79,607	54,522	111,623
Program Support Specialist 1-3	65,117	73,643	66,582	75,300	68,081	76,995	69,612	78,727	71,179	80,498	2.25%	11.25%	40,880	46,233	58,442	66,094	81,946	92,675
Project Engineer Industrial	71,404	102,080	73,011	104,377	74,653	106,725	76,333	109,126	78,051	111,582	2.25%	11.25%	44,827	64,085	64,084	91,615	89,857	128,461
Project Engineer Planning	71,404	102,080	73,011	104,377	74,653	106,725	76,333	109,126	78,051	111,582	2.25%	11.25%	44,827	64,085	64,084	91,615	89,857	128,461
Project Engineer Research	71,404	102,080	73,011	104,377	74,653	106,725	76,333	109,126	78,051	111,582	2.25%	11.25%	44,827	64,085	64,084	91,615	89,857	128,461
Project Engineer Traffic	71,404	102,080	73,011	104,377	74,653	106,725	76,333	109,126	78,051	111,582	2.25%	11.25%	44,827	64,085	64,084	91,615	89,857	128,461
Project Engineer Utilities	71,404	102,080	73,011	104,377	74,653	106,725	76,333	109,126	78,051	111,582	2.25%	11.25%	44,827	64,085	64,084	91,615	89,857	128,461
Project Manager Data Processing	74,785	106,984	76,467	109,392	78,188	111,853	79,947	114,370	81,746	116,943	2.25%	11.25%	46,949	67,164	67,118	96,017	94,112	134,633
Property Management Services Specialist 1-4	43,325	92,945	44,300	95,036	45,297	97,175	46,316	99,361	47,358	101,597	2.25%	11.25%	27,199	58,350	38,884	83,417	54,522	116,965
Public Employment Relations Specialist 1-4	90,082	84,659	92,109	86,564	94,181	88,512	96,300	90,503	98,467	92,540	2.25%	11.25%	56,553	53,148	80,847	75,980	113,362	106,538
Public Health Consultant 1-2	56,768	97,403	58,045	99,594	59,351	101,835	60,687	104,126	62,052	106,469	2.25%	11.25%	35,638	61,149	50,948	87,418	71,439	122,575
Public Health Physician	82,061	117,572	83,907	120,217	85,795	122,922	87,726	125,688	89,699	128,516	2.25%	11.25%	51,517	73,811	73,649	105,519	103,268	147,957
Public Health Project Nurse	49,554	70,327	50,669	71,910	51,809	73,528	52,974	75,182	54,166	76,874	2.25%	11.25%	31,109	44,151	44,474	63,118	62,360	88,502
Public Health Representative 1-3	56,768	61,251	58,045	62,629	59,351	64,038	60,687	65,479	62,052	66,952	2.25%	11.25%	35,638	38,453	50,948	54,972	71,439	77,080
Public Information Officer	67,704	95,017	69,228	97,155	70,785	99,341	72,378	101,576	74,006	103,861	2.25%	11.25%	42,504	59,651	60,764	85,276	85,201	119,573
Real Estate Appraiser 1-3	51,843	102,080	53,009	104,377	54,202	106,725	55,422	109,126	56,669	111,582	2.25%	11.25%	32,547	64,085	46,528	91,615	65,241	128,461
Records Analyst 1-3	43,325	70,327	44,300	71,910	45,297	73,528	46,316	75,182	47,358	76,874	2.25%	11.25%	27,199	44,151	38,884	63,118	54,522	88,502
Registered Environmental Health Inspector 1-3	45,300	88,700	46,320	90,696	47,362	92,736	48,428	94,823	49,517	96,956	2.25%	11.25%	28,439	55,685	40,656	79,607	57,008	111,623
Regulatory Officer 1-4	51,843	112,155	53,009	114,679	54,202	117,259	55,422	119,897	56,669	122,595	2.25%	11.25%	32,547	70,410	46,528	100,658	65,241	141,140
Research Analyst	43,325	61,251	44,300	62,629	45,297	64,038	46,316	65,479	47,358	66,952	2.25%	11.25%	27,199	38,453	38,884	54,972	54,522	77,080
Research Economist 1-4	74,785	73,643	76,467	75,300	78,188	76,995	79,947	78,727	81,746	80,498	2.25%	11.25%	46,949	46,233	67,118	66,094	94,112	92,675
Research Scientist 1-3	59,415	156,238	60,752	159,753	62,118	163,347	63,516	167,023	64,945	170,781	2.25%	11.25%	37,300	98,085	53,324	140,221	74,769	196,615

Chart III - U.S. States & Cities - Job Titles - Salaries - Pension Estimates

New Jersey	2010 (Min)	2010 (Max)	2011 (Min)	2011 (Max)	2012 (Min)	2012 (Max)	2013 (Min)	2013 (Max)	2014 (Min)	2014 (Max)	5-Year Average % Raise	5-Year Cumulative Raise Estimate**	20-Year Annual Pension Benefit Estimate (Min.)***	20-Year Annual Pension Benefit Estimate (Max.)	25-Year Annual Pension Benefit Estimate (Min.)	25-Year Annual Pension Benefit Estimate (Max.)	30-Year Annual Pension Benefit Estimate (Min.)	30-Year Annual Pension Benefit Estimate (Max.)
Resource Interpretive Specialist 1-4	47,374	97,403	48,440	99,594	49,530	101,835	50,644	104,126	51,784	106,469	2.25%	11.25%	29,741	61,149	42,518	87,418	59,617	122,575
Securities Market Trader 1-3	71,404	73,643	73,011	75,300	74,653	76,995	76,333	78,727	78,051	80,498	2.25%	11.25%	44,827	46,233	64,084	66,094	89,857	92,675
Site Manager	74,785	106,984	76,467	109,392	78,188	111,853	79,947	114,370	81,746	116,943	2.25%	11.25%	46,949	67,164	67,118	96,017	94,112	134,633
Social Work Supervisor 1-3	65,117	77,138	66,582	78,874	68,081	80,649	69,612	82,463	71,179	84,319	2.25%	11.25%	40,880	48,427	58,442	69,231	81,946	97,074
Social Worker 1-2	47,374	61,251	48,440	62,629	49,530	64,038	50,644	65,479	51,784	66,952	2.25%	11.25%	29,741	38,453	42,518	54,972	59,617	77,080
Software Development Specialist 1-4	49,554	112,155	50,669	114,679	51,809	117,259	52,974	119,897	54,166	122,595	2.25%	11.25%	31,109	70,410	44,474	100,658	62,360	141,140
Special Agent 1-3	70,535	76,515	72,122	78,237	73,745	79,997	75,404	81,797	77,101	83,638	2.25%	11.25%	44,282	48,036	63,304	68,671	88,764	96,290
Special Staff Officer 1-3	51,843	64,120	53,009	65,563	54,202	67,038	55,422	68,546	56,669	70,089	2.25%	11.25%	32,547	40,254	46,528	57,547	65,241	80,691
Specification Writer 1-2	54,245	77,138	55,466	78,874	56,714	80,649	57,990	82,463	59,294	84,319	2.25%	11.25%	34,055	48,427	48,684	69,231	68,264	97,074
Staff Clinical Psychologist 1-3	43,325	80,787	44,300	82,605	45,297	84,463	46,316	86,364	47,358	88,307	2.25%	11.25%	27,199	50,718	38,884	72,505	54,522	101,665
Statistical Engineer 1-2	74,785	92,945	76,467	95,036	78,188	97,175	79,947	99,361	81,746	101,597	2.25%	11.25%	46,949	58,350	67,118	83,417	94,112	116,965
Storekeeper 1-2	43,325	55,919	44,300	57,177	45,297	58,463	46,316	59,779	47,358	61,124	2.25%	11.25%	27,199	35,105	38,884	50,186	54,522	70,370
Student Financial Aid Administrator 1-2	47,374	61,251	48,440	62,629	49,530	64,038	50,644	65,479	51,784	66,952	2.25%	11.25%	29,741	38,453	42,518	54,972	59,617	77,080
Substance Abuse Counselor 1-2	51,843	61,251	53,009	62,629	54,202	64,038	55,422	65,479	56,669	66,952	2.25%	11.25%	32,547	38,453	46,528	54,972	65,241	77,080
Superintendent Parks And Forestry 1-4	74,785	80,787	76,467	82,605	78,188	84,463	79,947	86,364	81,746	88,307	2.25%	11.25%	46,949	50,718	67,118	72,505	94,112	101,665
Tax Services Specialist 1-3	71,404	77,138	73,011	78,874	74,653	80,649	76,333	82,463	78,051	84,319	2.25%	11.25%	44,827	48,427	64,084	69,231	89,857	97,074
Taxpayer Service Representative 1-3	56,768	61,251	58,045	62,629	59,351	64,038	60,687	65,479	62,052	66,952	2.25%	11.25%	35,638	38,453	50,948	54,972	71,439	77,080
Telecommunications Systems Analyst 1-3	78,333	84,659	80,096	86,564	81,898	88,512	83,741	90,503	85,625	92,540	2.25%	11.25%	49,177	53,148	70,303	75,980	98,578	106,538
Test Development Specialist 1-4	45,300	84,659	46,320	86,564	47,362	88,512	48,428	90,503	49,517	92,540	2.25%	11.25%	28,439	53,148	40,656	75,980	57,008	106,538
Title Officer 2	65,117	92,945	66,582	95,036	68,081	97,175	69,612	99,361	71,179	101,597	2.25%	11.25%	40,880	58,350	58,442	83,417	81,946	116,965
Tourism Representative 1-3	62,197	64,120	63,596	65,563	65,027	67,038	66,490	68,546	67,986	70,089	2.25%	11.25%	39,047	40,254	55,821	57,547	78,270	80,691
Transportation Analyst	47,374	67,155	48,440	68,666	49,530	70,211	50,644	71,790	51,784	73,406	2.25%	11.25%	29,741	42,159	42,518	60,270	59,617	84,510
Transportation Services Specialist 1-4	65,117	61,251	66,582	62,629	68,081	64,038	69,612	65,479	71,179	66,952	2.25%	11.25%	40,880	38,453	58,442	54,972	81,946	77,080
Trooper 1-2	58,581	92,318	59,899	94,395	61,246	96,519	62,624	98,690	64,033	100,911	2.25%	11.25%	36,777	57,956	52,575	82,854	73,720	116,175
Unemployment Insurance Technician 1-3	59,415	64,120	60,752	65,563	62,118	67,038	63,516	68,546	64,945	70,089	2.25%	11.25%	37,300	40,254	53,324	57,547	74,769	80,691
Veterans Service Officer 1-3	45,300	73,643	46,320	75,300	47,362	76,995	48,428	78,727	49,517	80,498	2.25%	11.25%	28,439	46,233	40,656	66,094	57,008	92,675
Vocational Rehabilitation Counselor 1-2	47,374	77,138	48,440	78,874	49,530	80,649	50,644	82,463	51,784	84,319	2.25%	11.25%	29,741	48,427	42,518	69,231	59,617	97,074
Work Program Specialist 1-2	54,245	64,120	55,466	65,563	56,714	67,038	57,990	68,546	59,294	70,089	2.25%	11.25%	34,055	40,254	48,684	57,547	68,264	80,691

http://webapps.dop.state.nj.us/TitleList/StateList.aspx
http://webapps.dop.state.nj.us/Comp/EmpGroup.aspx

Chart III - U.S. States & Cities - Job Titles - Salaries - Pension Estimates

NV-Las Vegas	2010 (Min)	2010 (Max)	2011 (Min)	2011 (Max)	2012 (Min)	2012 (Max)	2013 (Min)	2013 (Max)	2014 (Min)	2014 (Max)	5-Year Average % Raise	5-Year Cumulative Raise Estimate**	20-Year Annual Pension Benefit Estimate (Min.)***	20-Year Annual Pension Benefit Estimate (Max.)	25-Year Annual Pension Benefit Estimate (Min.)	25-Year Annual Pension Benefit Estimate (Max.)	30-Year Annual Pension Benefit Estimate (Min.)	30-Year Annual Pension Benefit Estimate (Max.)
Agenda Technician I-II	42,540	65,994	43,518	67,512	44,519	69,065	45,543	70,653	46,590	72,278	2.30%	11.50%	26,929	41,777	38,592	59,870	54,245	84,153
Animal Control Officer I-II	44,666	69,293	45,694	70,887	46,745	72,517	47,820	74,185	48,920	75,891	2.30%	11.50%	28,276	43,865	40,521	62,862	56,957	88,360
Architectural Technician I-II	46,901	75,758	47,979	77,500	49,083	79,283	50,212	81,106	51,367	82,972	2.30%	11.50%	29,690	47,958	42,548	68,727	59,806	96,604
Business Specialist I-II	59,858	92,860	61,235	94,996	62,643	97,181	64,084	99,416	65,558	101,702	2.30%	11.50%	37,893	58,784	54,303	84,242	76,329	118,412
Account Clerk	41,514	58,416	42,469	59,759	43,446	61,134	44,445	62,540	45,468	63,978	2.30%	11.50%	26,280	36,979	37,662	52,995	52,938	74,490
Accounting Manager	92,278	138,416	94,400	141,600	96,572	144,857	98,793	148,189	101,065	151,597	2.30%	11.50%	58,415	87,623	83,714	125,571	117,670	176,504
Accounting Supervisor	64,403	90,622	65,885	92,706	67,400	94,839	68,950	97,020	70,536	99,251	2.30%	11.50%	40,770	57,367	58,427	82,212	82,125	115,558
Administrative Assistant	50,461	71,004	51,622	72,638	52,809	74,308	54,024	76,017	55,266	77,766	2.30%	11.50%	31,944	44,948	45,778	64,415	64,346	90,542
Administrative Officer	64,891	115,361	66,383	118,014	67,910	120,729	69,472	123,505	71,070	126,346	2.30%	11.50%	41,078	73,028	58,869	104,655	82,746	147,104
Administrative Projects Specialist	58,460	103,928	59,804	106,318	61,180	108,764	62,587	111,265	64,026	113,824	2.30%	11.50%	37,007	65,790	53,034	94,283	74,546	132,525
Administrative Secretary	45,714	73,024	46,765	74,704	47,841	76,422	48,941	78,179	50,066	79,978	2.30%	11.50%	28,938	46,227	41,471	66,247	58,292	93,118
Administrative Services Manager	92,278	138,416	94,400	141,600	96,572	144,857	98,793	148,189	101,065	151,597	2.30%	11.50%	58,415	87,623	83,714	125,571	117,670	176,504
Alternative Sentencing & Education Manager	92,278	138,416	94,400	141,600	96,572	144,857	98,793	148,189	101,065	151,597	2.30%	11.50%	58,415	87,623	83,714	125,571	117,670	176,504
Animal Control Supervisor	62,850	88,437	64,296	90,471	65,775	92,552	67,288	94,681	68,835	96,858	2.30%	11.50%	39,787	55,984	57,018	80,230	80,145	112,772
Aquatic Biologist	61,336	86,306	62,746	88,291	64,190	90,321	65,666	92,399	67,176	94,524	2.30%	11.50%	38,828	54,635	55,644	78,296	78,213	110,054
Architectural Project Manager	84,226	118,515	86,163	121,241	88,145	124,030	90,172	126,882	92,246	129,801	2.30%	11.50%	53,318	75,024	76,409	107,517	107,402	151,126
Architectural Superintendent	92,278	138,416	94,400	141,600	96,572	144,857	98,793	148,189	101,065	151,597	2.30%	11.50%	58,415	87,623	83,714	125,571	117,670	176,504
Associate Court Clerk	39,538	55,634	40,447	56,914	41,377	58,223	42,329	59,562	43,302	60,932	2.30%	11.50%	25,029	35,218	35,868	50,471	50,417	70,943
Audio-Visual Production Specialist	50,461	71,004	51,622	72,638	52,809	74,308	54,024	76,017	55,266	77,766	2.30%	11.50%	31,944	44,948	45,778	64,415	64,346	90,542
Auditor	61,336	86,306	62,746	88,291	64,190	90,321	65,666	92,399	67,176	94,524	2.30%	11.50%	38,828	54,635	55,644	78,296	78,213	110,054
Bail Bond Technician	44,666	62,850	45,694	64,296	46,745	65,775	47,820	67,288	48,920	68,835	2.30%	11.50%	28,276	39,787	40,521	57,018	56,957	80,145
Budget Analyst	58,460	103,928	59,804	106,318	61,180	108,764	62,587	111,265	64,026	113,824	2.30%	11.50%	37,007	65,790	53,034	94,283	74,546	132,525
Building Inspector I-II	54,293	84,226	55,542	86,163	56,820	88,145	58,127	90,172	59,463	92,246	2.30%	11.50%	34,370	53,318	49,255	76,410	69,233	107,402
Bus Driver	43,591	61,336	44,594	62,746	45,619	64,190	46,668	65,666	47,742	67,176	2.30%	11.50%	27,595	38,828	39,546	55,644	55,586	78,213
Buyer I-II	50,461	78,282	51,622	80,082	52,809	81,924	54,024	83,809	55,266	85,736	2.30%	11.50%	31,944	49,555	45,778	71,017	64,346	99,822
Caseworker	54,293	76,396	55,542	78,153	56,820	79,951	58,127	81,790	59,463	83,671	2.30%	11.50%	34,370	48,362	49,255	69,306	69,233	97,418
Chemist	61,336	86,306	62,746	88,291	64,190	90,321	65,666	92,399	67,176	94,524	2.30%	11.50%	38,828	54,635	55,644	78,296	78,213	110,054
Civil Engineer	72,758	102,378	74,431	104,733	76,143	107,142	77,894	109,606	79,686	112,127	2.30%	11.50%	46,058	64,809	66,006	92,877	92,778	130,549
Classification & Compensation Administrator	64,891	115,361	66,383	118,014	67,910	120,729	69,472	123,505	71,070	126,346	2.30%	11.50%	41,078	73,028	58,869	104,655	82,746	147,104
Clean Water Coalition Engineering Manager	99,199	148,798	101,480	152,220	103,814	155,722	106,202	159,303	108,645	162,967	2.30%	11.50%	62,796	94,195	89,993	134,989	126,495	189,742
Collections Officer	45,770	64,403	46,823	65,885	47,900	67,400	49,002	68,950	50,129	70,536	2.30%	11.50%	28,974	40,770	41,523	58,427	58,365	82,125
Collections Supervisor	52,985	74,554	54,203	76,269	55,450	78,023	56,725	79,817	58,030	81,653	2.30%	11.50%	33,541	47,195	48,068	67,635	67,564	95,069
Communications Specialist	50,823	78,886	51,992	80,700	53,187	82,556	54,411	84,455	55,662	86,397	2.30%	11.50%	32,173	49,938	46,106	71,565	64,807	100,592
Computer Infrastructure Supervisor	80,215	112,871	82,060	115,468	83,948	118,123	85,878	120,840	87,854	123,619	2.30%	11.50%	50,779	71,452	72,771	102,397	102,288	143,930
Computer Systems Technician I-II	45,770	71,004	46,823	72,637	47,900	74,308	49,002	76,017	50,129	77,765	2.30%	11.50%	28,974	44,948	41,523	64,415	58,365	90,542
Construction Control Specialist	67,623	95,153	69,179	97,341	70,770	99,580	72,398	101,871	74,063	104,214	2.30%	11.50%	42,808	60,235	61,348	86,322	86,231	121,336

Chart III - U.S. States & Cities - Job Titles - Salaries - Pension Estimates

NV-Las Vegas	2010 (Min)	2010 (Max)	2011 (Min)	2011 (Max)	2012 (Min)	2012 (Max)	2013 (Min)	2013 (Max)	2014 (Min)	2014 (Max)	5-Year Average % Raise	5-Year Cumulative Raise Estimate**	20-Year Annual Pension Benefit Estimate (Min.)***	20-Year Annual Pension Benefit Estimate (Max.)	25-Year Annual Pension Benefit Estimate (Min.)	25-Year Annual Pension Benefit Estimate (Max.)	30-Year Annual Pension Benefit Estimate (Min.)	30-Year Annual Pension Benefit Estimate (Max.)
Construction Inspection Supervisor	76,396	107,496	78,153	109,969	79,951	112,498	81,790	115,085	83,671	117,732	2.30%	11.50%	48,362	68,049	69,306	97,520	97,418	137,075
Construction Inspector I-II	54,293	84,226	55,542	86,163	56,820	88,145	58,127	90,172	59,463	92,246	2.30%	11.50%	34,370	53,318	49,255	76,410	69,233	107,402
Contracts Officer	64,891	115,361	66,383	118,014	67,910	120,729	69,472	123,505	71,070	126,346	2.30%	11.50%	41,078	73,028	58,869	104,655	82,746	147,104
Contracts Specialist	67,623	95,153	69,179	97,341	70,770	99,580	72,398	101,871	74,063	104,214	2.30%	11.50%	42,808	60,235	61,348	86,322	86,231	121,336
Corrections Officer	52,919	81,216	54,136	83,084	55,381	84,995	56,655	86,950	57,958	88,950	2.30%	11.50%	33,500	51,413	48,008	73,679	67,480	103,564
Court Administrator	123,234	184,852	126,069	189,103	128,968	193,453	131,935	197,902	134,969	202,454	2.30%	11.50%	78,012	117,018	111,798	167,697	157,144	235,716
Court Clerk	44,666	62,850	45,694	64,296	46,745	65,775	47,820	67,288	48,920	68,835	2.30%	11.50%	28,276	39,787	40,521	57,018	56,957	80,145
Court Specialist	49,246	69,293	50,378	70,886	51,537	72,517	52,722	74,185	53,935	75,891	2.30%	11.50%	31,174	43,865	44,675	62,862	62,796	88,359
Deputy Human Resources Director	106,639	159,958	109,091	163,637	111,600	167,401	114,167	171,251	116,793	175,190	2.30%	11.50%	67,506	101,260	96,742	145,114	135,982	203,973
Deputy Information Technologies Director	106,639	159,958	109,091	163,637	111,600	167,401	114,167	171,251	116,793	175,190	2.30%	11.50%	67,506	101,260	96,742	145,114	135,982	203,973
Deputy Planning & Development Director	106,639	159,958	109,091	163,637	111,600	167,401	114,167	171,251	116,793	175,190	2.30%	11.50%	67,506	101,260	96,742	145,114	135,982	203,973
Director, Human Resources	123,234	184,852	126,069	189,103	128,968	193,453	131,935	197,902	134,969	202,454	2.30%	11.50%	78,012	117,018	111,798	167,697	157,144	235,716
Director, Information Technologies	123,234	184,852	126,069	189,103	128,968	193,453	131,935	197,902	134,969	202,454	2.30%	11.50%	78,012	117,018	111,798	167,697	157,144	235,716
Director, Leisure Services	123,234	184,852	126,069	189,103	128,968	193,453	131,935	197,902	134,969	202,454	2.30%	11.50%	78,012	117,018	111,798	167,697	157,144	235,716
Director, Neighborhood Services	123,234	184,852	126,069	189,103	128,968	193,453	131,935	197,902	134,969	202,454	2.30%	11.50%	78,012	117,018	111,798	167,697	157,144	235,716
Director, Planning & Development	123,234	184,852	126,069	189,103	128,968	193,453	131,935	197,902	134,969	202,454	2.30%	11.50%	78,012	117,018	111,798	167,697	157,144	235,716
Director, Public Works	123,234	184,852	126,069	189,103	128,968	193,453	131,935	197,902	134,969	202,454	2.30%	11.50%	78,012	117,018	111,798	167,697	157,144	235,716
Crisis Intervention Administrator	52,667	93,631	53,878	95,784	55,118	97,987	56,385	100,241	57,682	102,546	2.30%	11.50%	33,340	59,272	47,779	84,941	67,159	119,394
Cultural Activities Specialist	46,901	65,994	47,979	67,512	49,083	69,064	50,212	70,653	51,367	72,278	2.30%	11.50%	29,690	41,776	42,548	59,869	59,806	84,153
Cultural Affairs Manager	92,278	138,416	94,400	141,600	96,572	144,857	98,793	148,189	101,065	151,597	2.30%	11.50%	58,415	87,623	83,714	125,571	117,670	176,504
Custodian I-II	34,155	53,985	34,940	55,227	35,744	56,497	36,566	57,796	37,407	59,126	2.30%	11.50%	21,621	34,175	30,985	48,975	43,553	68,840
Database Administrator	64,891	115,361	66,383	118,014	67,910	120,729	69,472	123,505	71,070	126,346	2.30%	11.50%	41,078	73,028	58,869	104,655	82,746	147,104
Database Architect	77,730	144,357	79,518	147,677	81,347	151,074	83,218	154,548	85,132	158,103	2.30%	11.50%	49,206	91,383	70,517	130,960	99,119	184,079
Deputy Building & Safety Director	106,639	159,958	109,091	163,637	111,600	167,401	114,167	171,251	116,793	175,190	2.30%	11.50%	67,506	101,260	96,742	145,114	135,982	203,973
Deputy Business Development Director	106,639	159,958	109,091	163,637	111,600	167,401	114,167	171,251	116,793	175,190	2.30%	11.50%	67,506	101,260	96,742	145,114	135,982	203,973
Deputy City Attorney IV	62,661	159,153	64,102	162,814	65,577	166,558	67,085	170,389	68,628	174,308	2.30%	11.50%	39,667	100,750	56,846	144,383	79,903	202,946
Deputy City Manager	141,720	212,579	144,979	217,469	148,314	222,471	151,725	227,587	155,215	232,822	2.30%	11.50%	89,714	134,571	128,568	192,851	180,716	271,074
Deputy City Marshal	53,437	82,012	54,666	83,899	55,923	85,828	57,210	87,802	58,525	89,822	2.30%	11.50%	33,828	51,917	48,478	74,401	68,141	104,579
Deputy Finance and Business Services Director	106,639	159,958	109,091	163,637	111,600	167,401	114,167	171,251	116,793	175,190	2.30%	11.50%	67,506	101,260	96,742	145,114	135,982	203,973
Deputy Fire Chief	106,639	159,958	109,091	163,637	111,600	167,401	114,167	171,251	116,793	175,190	2.30%	11.50%	67,506	101,260	96,742	145,114	135,982	203,973
Deputy Fire Marshal	76,646	119,999	78,409	122,759	80,212	125,583	82,057	128,471	83,944	131,426	2.30%	11.50%	48,520	75,964	69,533	108,863	97,736	153,019
Director, Administrative Services	114,637	171,954	117,274	175,909	119,971	179,955	122,730	184,094	125,553	188,328	2.30%	11.50%	72,569	108,853	103,998	155,996	146,181	219,270
Director, Building and Safety	123,234	184,852	126,069	189,103	128,968	193,453	131,935	197,902	134,969	202,454	2.30%	11.50%	78,012	117,018	111,798	167,697	157,144	235,716
Director, Business Operations	123,234	184,852	126,069	189,103	128,968	193,453	131,935	197,902	134,969	202,454	2.30%	11.50%	78,012	117,018	111,798	167,697	157,144	235,716
Director, Communications	114,637	171,954	117,274	175,909	119,971	179,955	122,730	184,094	125,553	188,328	2.30%	11.50%	72,569	108,853	103,998	155,996	146,181	219,270
Director, Detention & Enforcement	123,234	184,852	126,069	189,103	128,968	193,453	131,935	197,902	134,969	202,454	2.30%	11.50%	78,012	117,018	111,798	167,697	157,144	235,716

Chart III - U.S. States & Cities - Job Titles - Salaries - Pension Estimates

NV-Las Vegas	2010 (Min)	2010 (Max)	2011 (Min)	2011 (Max)	2012 (Min)	2012 (Max)	2013 (Min)	2013 (Max)	2014 (Min)	2014 (Max)	5-Year Average % Raise	5-Year Cumulative Raise Estimate**	20-Year Annual Pension Benefit Estimate (Min.)***	20-Year Annual Pension Benefit Estimate (Max.)	25-Year Annual Pension Benefit Estimate (Min.)	25-Year Annual Pension Benefit Estimate (Max.)	30-Year Annual Pension Benefit Estimate (Min.)	30-Year Annual Pension Benefit Estimate (Max.)
Director, Field Operations	123,234	184,852	126,069	189,103	128,968	193,453	131,935	197,902	134,969	202,454	2.30%	11.50%	78,012	117,018	111,798	167,697	157,144	235,716
Director, Finance & Business Services	123,234	184,852	126,069	189,103	128,968	193,453	131,935	197,902	134,969	202,454	2.30%	11.50%	78,012	117,018	111,798	167,697	157,144	235,716
Director, Fire & Rescue	123,234	184,852	126,069	189,103	128,968	193,453	131,935	197,902	134,969	202,454	2.30%	11.50%	78,012	117,018	111,798	167,697	157,144	235,716
Director, Government & Community Affairs	114,637	171,954	117,274	175,909	119,971	179,955	122,730	184,094	125,553	188,328	2.30%	11.50%	72,569	108,853	103,998	155,996	146,181	219,270
Economic Development Manager	92,278	138,416	94,400	141,600	96,572	144,857	98,793	148,189	101,065	151,597	2.30%	11.50%	58,415	87,623	83,714	125,571	117,670	176,504
Economic Development Officer	59,858	84,226	61,235	86,163	62,643	88,145	64,084	90,172	65,558	92,246	2.30%	11.50%	37,893	53,318	54,303	76,409	76,329	107,402
Emergency Management Officer	64,891	115,361	66,383	118,014	67,910	120,729	69,472	123,505	71,070	126,346	2.30%	11.50%	41,078	73,028	58,869	104,655	82,746	147,104
Employee Benefits Administrator	64,891	115,361	66,383	118,014	67,910	120,729	69,472	123,505	71,070	126,346	2.30%	11.50%	41,078	73,028	58,869	104,655	82,746	147,104
Employee Benefits Specialist	51,708	72,758	52,897	74,431	54,114	76,143	55,358	77,894	56,631	79,686	2.30%	11.50%	32,733	46,058	46,909	66,006	65,936	92,778
EMS Field Coordinator	65,510	102,177	67,016	104,527	68,558	106,931	70,135	109,390	71,748	111,906	2.30%	11.50%	41,470	64,682	59,430	92,694	83,536	130,292
Engineering Project Manager	84,226	118,515	86,163	121,241	88,145	124,030	90,172	126,882	92,246	129,801	2.30%	11.50%	53,318	75,024	76,409	107,517	107,402	151,126
Environmental Manager	106,639	159,958	109,091	163,637	111,600	167,401	114,167	171,251	116,793	175,190	2.30%	11.50%	67,506	101,260	96,742	145,114	135,982	203,973
Environmental Officer	80,215	112,871	82,060	115,468	83,948	118,123	85,878	120,840	87,854	123,619	2.30%	11.50%	50,779	71,452	72,771	102,397	102,288	143,930
Environmental Systems Technician I-III	50,461	92,860	51,622	94,996	52,809	97,181	54,024	99,416	55,266	101,702	2.30%	11.50%	31,944	58,784	45,778	84,242	64,346	118,412
Equipment Operator II	48,058	67,623	49,164	69,179	50,294	70,770	51,451	72,398	52,635	74,063	2.30%	11.50%	30,423	42,808	43,598	61,348	61,282	86,231
Executive Assistant	49,424	82,375	50,561	84,270	51,724	86,208	52,913	88,191	54,130	90,219	2.30%	11.50%	31,287	52,146	44,837	74,730	63,024	105,042
Facilities Engineer	76,396	107,496	78,153	109,969	79,951	112,498	81,790	115,085	83,671	117,732	2.30%	11.50%	48,362	68,049	69,306	97,520	97,418	137,075
Facilities Field Supervisor	65,994	92,860	67,512	94,995	69,064	97,180	70,653	99,415	72,278	101,702	2.30%	11.50%	41,776	58,784	59,869	84,242	84,153	118,411
Facilities Maintenance Supervisor	69,293	97,502	70,886	99,745	72,517	102,039	74,185	104,386	75,891	106,787	2.30%	11.50%	43,865	61,723	62,862	88,454	88,359	124,331
Field Electrician II	54,293	76,396	55,542	78,153	56,820	79,951	58,127	81,790	59,463	83,671	2.30%	11.50%	34,370	48,362	49,255	69,306	69,233	97,418
Field Lighting Supervisor	69,293	97,502	70,886	99,745	72,517	102,039	74,185	104,386	75,891	106,787	2.30%	11.50%	43,865	61,723	62,862	88,454	88,359	124,331
Financial Analyst I	49,424	82,375	50,561	84,270	51,724	86,208	52,913	88,191	54,130	90,219	2.30%	11.50%	31,287	52,146	44,837	74,730	63,024	105,042
Financial Analyst II	52,667	93,631	53,878	95,784	55,118	97,987	56,385	100,241	57,682	102,546	2.30%	11.50%	33,340	59,272	47,779	84,941	67,159	119,394
Financial Services Manager	99,199	148,798	101,480	152,220	103,814	155,722	106,202	159,303	108,645	162,967	2.30%	11.50%	62,796	94,195	89,993	134,989	126,495	189,742
Financial Specialist	65,994	92,860	67,512	94,995	69,064	97,180	70,653	99,415	72,278	101,702	2.30%	11.50%	41,776	58,784	59,869	84,242	84,153	118,411
Fire Battalion Chief	76,646	119,547	78,409	122,296	80,212	125,109	82,057	127,987	83,944	130,930	2.30%	11.50%	48,520	75,678	69,533	108,453	97,736	152,442
Fire Captain	65,510	102,177	67,016	104,527	68,558	106,931	70,135	109,390	71,748	111,906	2.30%	11.50%	41,470	64,682	59,430	92,694	83,536	130,292
Fire Communications Supervisor	76,936	119,999	78,706	122,759	80,516	125,583	82,368	128,471	84,262	131,426	2.30%	11.50%	48,703	75,964	69,796	108,863	98,106	153,019
Fire Communications Technician I	53,310	82,827	54,536	84,732	55,790	86,681	57,074	88,675	58,386	90,714	2.30%	11.50%	33,747	52,433	48,363	75,141	67,979	105,614
Fire Communications Technician II	60,776	94,669	62,174	96,846	63,604	99,074	65,067	101,352	66,563	103,684	2.30%	11.50%	38,474	59,929	55,136	85,883	77,500	120,718
Fire Communications Training Specialist	63,268	98,617	64,723	100,885	66,212	103,206	67,734	105,579	69,292	108,008	2.30%	11.50%	40,051	62,428	57,396	89,465	80,677	125,752
Fire Engineer	58,070	90,381	59,405	92,460	60,772	94,586	62,169	96,762	63,599	98,987	2.30%	11.50%	36,760	57,215	52,681	81,993	74,049	115,251
Fire Equipment Mechanic Foreman	65,756	102,563	67,268	104,922	68,816	107,335	70,398	109,804	72,018	112,330	2.30%	11.50%	41,626	64,926	59,654	93,045	83,850	130,785
Fire Equipment Mechanic I	50,823	78,886	51,992	80,700	53,187	82,556	54,411	84,455	55,662	86,397	2.30%	11.50%	32,173	49,938	46,106	71,565	64,807	100,594
Fire Equipment Mechanic II	55,802	86,776	57,085	88,771	58,398	90,813	59,741	92,902	61,115	95,039	2.30%	11.50%	35,324	54,932	50,623	78,723	71,156	110,653

Chart III - U.S. States & Cities - Job Titles - Salaries - Pension Estimates

NV-Las Vegas	2010 (Min)	2010 (Max)	2011 (Min)	2011 (Max)	2012 (Min)	2012 (Max)	2013 (Min)	2013 (Max)	2014 (Min)	2014 (Max)	5-Year Average % Raise	5-Year Cumulative Raise Estimate**	20-Year Annual Pension Benefit Estimate (Min.)***	20-Year Annual Pension Benefit Estimate (Max.)	25-Year Annual Pension Benefit Estimate (Min.)	25-Year Annual Pension Benefit Estimate (Max.)	30-Year Annual Pension Benefit Estimate (Min.)	30-Year Annual Pension Benefit Estimate (Max.)
Fire Equipment Mechanic III	60,776	94,669	62,174	96,846	63,604	99,074	65,067	101,352	66,563	103,684	2.30%	11.50%	38,474	59,929	55,136	85,883	77,500	120,718
Fire Equipment Service Technician	48,333	74,935	49,445	76,659	50,582	78,422	51,746	80,226	52,936	82,071	2.30%	11.50%	30,597	47,437	43,848	67,981	61,633	95,555
Fire Health & Safety Training Officer	68,244	106,508	69,814	108,958	71,420	111,464	73,062	114,028	74,743	116,650	2.30%	11.50%	43,201	67,424	61,911	96,624	87,023	135,815
Fire Investigator I	60,548	94,313	61,941	96,482	63,366	98,701	64,823	100,971	66,314	103,294	2.30%	11.50%	38,329	59,704	54,929	85,560	77,209	120,264
Fire Investigator II	65,510	102,177	67,016	104,527	68,558	106,931	70,135	109,390	71,748	111,906	2.30%	11.50%	41,470	64,682	59,430	92,694	83,536	130,292
Fire Prevention Inspection Supervisor	65,756	102,563	67,268	104,922	68,816	107,335	70,398	109,804	72,018	112,330	2.30%	11.50%	41,626	64,926	59,654	93,045	83,850	130,785
Fire Prevention Inspector I-II	50,823	90,723	51,992	92,810	53,187	94,944	54,411	97,128	55,662	99,362	2.30%	11.50%	32,173	57,431	46,106	82,304	64,807	115,687
Firefighter	53,110	82,516	54,331	84,414	55,581	86,356	56,859	88,342	58,167	90,374	2.30%	11.50%	33,620	52,236	48,181	74,859	67,723	105,222
Fleet & Transportation Services Manager	92,278	138,416	94,400	141,600	96,572	144,857	98,793	148,189	101,065	151,597	2.30%	11.50%	58,415	87,623	83,714	125,571	117,670	176,504
Fleet Coordinator	51,708	72,758	52,897	74,431	54,114	76,143	55,358	77,894	56,631	79,686	2.30%	11.50%	32,733	46,058	46,909	66,006	65,936	92,778
Landscape Architect	84,226	118,515	86,163	121,241	88,145	124,030	90,172	126,882	92,246	129,801	2.30%	11.50%	53,318	75,024	76,409	107,517	107,402	151,126
Law Enforcement Support Supervisor	55,634	78,282	56,914	80,083	58,223	81,925	59,562	83,809	60,932	85,736	2.30%	11.50%	35,218	49,555	50,471	71,017	70,943	99,823
Firefighter Trainee	45,845	70,988	46,899	72,621	47,978	74,291	49,082	76,000	50,210	77,748	2.30%	11.50%	29,022	44,938	41,590	64,400	58,460	90,521
Firefighter/Paramedic	60,548	94,313	61,941	96,482	63,366	98,701	64,823	100,971	66,314	103,294	2.30%	11.50%	38,329	59,704	54,929	85,560	77,209	120,264
GIS Programmer/ Analyst	62,850	88,437	64,296	90,471	65,775	92,552	67,288	94,681	68,835	96,858	2.30%	11.50%	39,787	55,984	57,018	80,230	80,145	112,772
GIS Technician	51,708	72,758	52,897	74,431	54,114	76,143	55,358	77,894	56,631	79,686	2.30%	11.50%	32,733	46,058	46,909	66,006	65,936	92,778
Grant Coordinator	62,850	88,437	64,296	90,471	65,775	92,552	67,288	94,681	68,835	96,858	2.30%	11.50%	39,787	55,984	57,018	80,230	80,145	112,772
Graphic Artist I-II	44,666	69,293	45,694	70,887	46,745	72,517	47,820	74,185	48,920	75,891	2.30%	11.50%	28,276	43,865	40,521	62,862	56,957	88,360
Graphic Illustrator	57,007	80,215	58,319	82,060	59,660	83,948	61,032	85,878	62,436	87,854	2.30%	11.50%	36,088	50,779	51,717	72,771	72,694	102,288
Housing Rehabilitation Specialist	55,634	78,282	56,914	80,083	58,223	81,925	59,562	83,809	60,932	85,736	2.30%	11.50%	35,218	49,555	50,471	71,017	70,943	99,823
Housing Rehabilitation Technician	50,461	71,004	51,622	72,638	52,809	74,308	54,024	76,017	55,266	77,766	2.30%	11.50%	31,944	44,948	45,778	64,415	64,346	90,542
Human Resources Manager	92,278	138,416	94,400	141,600	96,572	144,857	98,793	148,189	101,065	151,597	2.30%	11.50%	58,415	87,623	83,714	125,571	117,670	176,504
Human Resources Specialist	58,416	82,196	59,759	84,087	61,134	86,021	62,540	87,999	63,978	90,023	2.30%	11.50%	36,979	52,033	52,995	74,568	74,490	104,814
Information Security & Contingency Administrator	64,891	115,361	66,383	118,014	67,910	120,729	69,472	123,505	71,070	126,346	2.30%	11.50%	41,078	73,028	58,869	104,655	82,746	147,104
Information Systems Coordinator	69,293	97,502	70,886	99,745	72,517	102,039	74,185	104,386	75,891	106,787	2.30%	11.50%	43,865	61,723	62,862	88,454	88,359	124,331
Information Technologies Development Supervisor	80,215	112,871	82,060	115,468	83,948	118,123	85,878	120,840	87,854	123,619	2.30%	11.50%	50,779	71,452	72,771	102,397	102,288	143,930
Information Technologies Manager	92,278	138,416	94,400	141,600	96,572	144,857	98,793	148,189	101,065	151,597	2.30%	11.50%	58,415	87,623	83,714	125,571	117,670	176,504
Information Technologies Project Coordinator	69,293	97,502	70,886	99,745	72,517	102,039	74,185	104,386	75,891	106,787	2.30%	11.50%	43,865	61,723	62,862	88,454	88,359	124,331
Information Technologies Training Specialist	58,416	82,196	59,759	84,087	61,134	86,021	62,540	87,999	63,978	90,023	2.30%	11.50%	36,979	52,033	52,995	74,568	74,490	104,814
Internal Auditor I-II	49,424	93,631	50,561	95,785	51,724	97,988	52,913	100,241	54,130	102,547	2.30%	11.50%	31,287	59,272	44,837	84,942	63,024	119,395
Internet Developer/ Analyst	65,994	92,860	67,512	94,995	69,064	97,180	70,653	99,415	72,278	101,702	2.30%	11.50%	41,776	58,784	59,869	84,242	84,153	118,411
Janitor	22,016	30,978	22,523	31,691	23,041	32,420	23,570	33,165	24,113	33,928	2.30%	11.50%	13,937	19,610	19,973	28,103	28,074	39,503
Land Development Superintendent	92,278	138,416	94,400	141,600	96,572	144,857	98,793	148,189	101,065	151,597	2.30%	11.50%	58,415	87,623	83,714	125,571	117,670	176,504
Land Surveyor	69,293	97,502	70,886	99,745	72,517	102,039	74,185	104,386	75,891	106,787	2.30%	11.50%	43,865	61,723	62,862	88,454	88,359	124,331

Chart III - U.S. States & Cities - Job Titles - Salaries - Pension Estimates

NV-Las Vegas	2010 (Min)	2010 (Max)	2011 (Min)	2011 (Max)	2012 (Min)	2012 (Max)	2013 (Min)	2013 (Max)	2014 (Min)	2014 (Max)	5-Year Average % Raise	5-Year Cumulative Raise Estimate**	20-Year Annual Pension Benefit Estimate (Min.)***	20-Year Annual Pension Benefit Estimate (Max.)	25-Year Annual Pension Benefit Estimate (Min.)	25-Year Annual Pension Benefit Estimate (Max.)	30-Year Annual Pension Benefit Estimate (Min.)	30-Year Annual Pension Benefit Estimate (Max.)
Legal Assistant I-II	41,184	73,024	42,131	74,704	43,100	76,422	44,091	78,179	45,105	79,978	2.30%	11.50%	26,071	46,227	37,362	66,247	52,516	93,118
Legal Secretary	46,901	65,994	47,979	67,512	49,083	69,064	50,212	70,653	51,367	72,278	2.30%	11.50%	29,690	41,776	42,548	59,869	59,806	84,153
Legal Technician I-II	39,538	61,336	40,447	62,747	41,377	64,190	42,329	65,666	43,302	67,177	2.30%	11.50%	25,029	38,828	35,868	55,644	50,417	78,213
Legislative Officer	64,891	115,361	66,383	118,014	67,910	120,729	69,472	123,505	71,070	126,346	2.30%	11.50%	41,078	73,028	58,869	104,655	82,746	147,104
Management Analyst I-II	49,424	93,631	50,561	95,785	51,724	97,988	52,913	100,241	54,130	102,547	2.30%	11.50%	31,287	59,272	44,837	84,942	63,024	119,395
Marketing Supervisor	64,403	90,622	65,885	92,706	67,400	94,839	68,950	97,020	70,536	99,251	2.30%	11.50%	40,770	57,367	58,427	82,212	82,125	115,558
Paralegal	51,708	72,758	52,897	74,431	54,114	76,143	55,358	77,894	56,631	79,686	2.30%	11.50%	32,733	46,058	46,909	66,006	65,936	92,778
Personnel Services Administrator	58,460	103,928	59,804	106,318	61,180	108,764	62,587	111,265	64,026	113,824	2.30%	11.50%	37,007	65,790	53,034	94,283	74,546	132,525
Medical Services Physician	86,282	160,237	88,266	163,922	90,296	167,692	92,373	171,549	94,498	175,495	2.30%	11.50%	54,619	101,436	78,274	145,366	110,023	204,328
Microbiologist	61,336	86,306	62,746	88,291	64,190	90,321	65,666	92,399	67,176	94,524	2.30%	11.50%	38,828	54,635	55,644	78,296	78,213	110,054
Municipal Court Marshal	53,437	82,012	54,666	83,899	55,923	85,828	57,210	87,802	58,525	89,822	2.30%	11.50%	33,828	51,917	48,478	74,401	68,141	104,579
Municipal Court Marshal Lieutenant	72,028	128,050	73,685	130,995	75,380	134,008	77,114	137,090	78,887	140,243	2.30%	11.50%	45,597	81,061	65,344	116,167	91,848	163,285
Municipal Court Marshal Sergeant	66,737	102,423	68,272	104,779	69,843	107,189	71,449	109,654	73,092	112,176	2.30%	11.50%	42,247	64,838	60,544	92,918	85,101	130,606
Municipal Court Office Supervisor	57,007	80,215	58,319	82,060	59,660	83,948	61,032	85,878	62,436	87,854	2.30%	11.50%	36,088	50,779	51,717	72,771	72,694	102,288
Office Specialist I-II	35,862	55,634	36,687	56,914	37,531	58,223	38,394	59,562	39,277	60,932	2.30%	11.50%	22,702	35,218	32,534	50,471	45,730	70,942
Office Supervisor	50,461	71,004	51,622	72,638	52,809	74,308	54,024	76,017	55,266	77,766	2.30%	11.50%	31,944	44,948	45,778	64,415	64,346	90,542
Personnel Analyst I-II	49,424	93,631	50,561	95,785	51,724	97,988	52,913	100,241	54,130	102,547	2.30%	11.50%	31,287	59,272	44,837	84,942	63,024	119,395
Programmer I-II	51,708	80,215	52,897	82,060	54,114	83,947	55,358	85,878	56,631	87,853	2.30%	11.50%	32,733	50,779	46,909	72,771	65,936	102,287
Project Engineer	76,396	107,496	78,153	109,969	79,951	112,498	81,790	115,085	83,671	117,732	2.30%	11.50%	48,362	68,049	69,306	97,520	97,418	137,075
Public Information Officer	52,667	93,631	53,878	95,784	55,118	97,987	56,385	100,241	57,682	102,546	2.30%	11.50%	33,340	59,272	47,779	84,941	67,159	119,394
Public Information Specialist	57,007	80,215	58,319	82,060	59,660	83,948	61,032	85,878	62,436	87,854	2.30%	11.50%	36,088	50,779	51,717	72,771	72,694	102,288
Public Safety Technician	48,058	67,623	49,164	69,179	50,294	70,770	51,451	72,398	52,635	74,063	2.30%	11.50%	30,423	42,808	43,598	61,348	61,282	86,231
Purchasing & Contracts Manager	92,278	138,416	94,400	141,600	96,572	144,857	98,793	148,189	101,065	151,597	2.30%	11.50%	58,415	87,623	83,714	125,571	117,670	176,504
Purchasing Technician	48,058	67,623	49,164	69,179	50,294	70,770	51,451	72,398	52,635	74,063	2.30%	11.50%	30,423	42,808	43,598	61,348	61,282	86,231
Quality Assurance Administrator	64,891	115,361	66,383	118,014	67,910	120,729	69,472	123,505	71,070	126,346	2.30%	11.50%	41,078	73,028	58,869	104,655	82,746	147,104
Quality Assurance Officer	64,403	90,622	65,885	92,706	67,400	94,839	68,950	97,020	70,536	99,251	2.30%	11.50%	40,770	57,367	58,427	82,212	82,125	115,558
Quality Assurance Specialist	62,850	88,437	64,296	90,471	65,775	92,552	67,288	94,681	68,835	96,858	2.30%	11.50%	39,787	55,984	57,018	80,230	80,145	112,772
Safety & Health Officer	58,460	103,928	59,804	106,318	61,180	108,764	62,587	111,265	64,026	113,824	2.30%	11.50%	37,007	65,790	53,034	94,283	74,546	132,525
Secretary	44,666	62,850	45,694	64,296	46,745	65,775	47,820	67,288	48,920	68,835	2.30%	11.50%	28,276	39,787	40,521	57,018	56,957	80,145
Software Architect	64,891	115,361	66,383	118,014	67,910	120,729	69,472	123,505	71,070	126,346	2.30%	11.50%	41,078	73,028	58,869	104,655	82,746	147,104
Sr Auditor	67,623	95,153	69,179	97,341	70,770	99,580	72,398	101,871	74,063	104,214	2.30%	11.50%	42,808	60,235	61,348	86,322	86,231	121,336
Sr Business Specialist	72,758	102,378	74,431	104,733	76,143	107,142	77,894	109,606	79,686	112,127	2.30%	11.50%	46,058	64,809	66,006	92,877	92,778	130,549
Sr Buyer	61,336	86,306	62,746	88,291	64,190	90,321	65,666	92,399	67,176	94,524	2.30%	11.50%	38,828	54,635	55,644	78,296	78,213	110,054
Sr Carpenter	59,858	84,226	61,235	86,163	62,643	88,145	64,084	90,172	65,558	92,246	2.30%	11.50%	37,893	53,318	54,303	76,409	76,329	107,402
Sr Construction Inspector	65,994	92,860	67,512	94,995	69,064	97,180	70,653	99,415	72,278	101,702	2.30%	11.50%	41,776	58,784	59,869	84,242	84,153	118,411
Sr Contracts Technician	48,058	67,623	49,164	69,179	50,294	70,770	51,451	72,398	52,635	74,063	2.30%	11.50%	30,423	42,808	43,598	61,348	61,282	86,231
Sr Corrections Officer	58,415	89,647	59,758	91,709	61,133	93,818	62,539	95,976	63,977	98,184	2.30%	11.50%	36,979	56,750	52,994	81,328	74,488	114,315
Sr Economic Development Officer	65,994	92,860	67,512	94,995	69,064	97,180	70,653	99,415	72,278	101,702	2.30%	11.50%	41,776	58,784	59,869	84,242	84,153	118,411

Chart III - U.S. States & Cities - Job Titles - Salaries - Pension Estimates

NV-Las Vegas	2010 (Min)	2010 (Max)	2011 (Min)	2011 (Max)	2012 (Min)	2012 (Max)	2013 (Min)	2013 (Max)	2014 (Min)	2014 (Max)	5-Year Average % Raise	5-Year Cumulative Raise Estimate**	20-Year Annual Pension Benefit Estimate (Min.)***	20-Year Annual Pension Benefit Estimate (Max.)	25-Year Annual Pension Benefit Estimate (Min.)	25-Year Annual Pension Benefit Estimate (Max.)	30-Year Annual Pension Benefit Estimate (Min.)	30-Year Annual Pension Benefit Estimate (Max.)
r Electrical Construction Inspector	65,994	92,860	67,512	94,995	69,064	97,180	70,653	99,415	72,278	101,702	2.30%	11.50%	41,776	58,784	59,869	84,242	84,153	118,411
r Engineering Associate	69,293	97,502	70,886	99,745	72,517	102,039	74,185	104,386	75,891	106,787	2.30%	11.50%	43,865	61,723	62,862	88,454	88,359	124,331
r Executive Assistant	52,667	93,631	53,878	95,784	55,118	97,987	56,385	100,241	57,682	102,546	2.30%	11.50%	33,340	59,272	47,779	84,941	67,159	119,394
r Field Electrician	59,858	84,226	61,235	86,163	62,643	88,145	64,084	90,172	65,558	92,246	2.30%	11.50%	37,893	53,318	54,303	76,409	76,329	107,402
r Financial Analyst	58,460	103,928	59,804	106,318	61,180	108,764	62,587	111,265	64,026	113,824	2.30%	11.50%	37,007	65,790	53,034	94,283	74,546	132,525
r Fire Investigator	70,779	110,534	72,407	113,077	74,072	115,677	75,776	118,338	77,519	121,060	2.30%	11.50%	44,806	69,972	64,210	100,276	90,255	140,949
r GIS Analyst - System Adminstration	69,293	97,502	70,886	99,745	72,517	102,039	74,185	104,386	75,891	106,787	2.30%	11.50%	43,865	61,723	62,862	88,454	88,359	124,331
r Graphic Artist	54,293	76,396	55,542	78,153	56,820	79,951	58,127	81,790	59,463	83,671	2.30%	11.50%	34,370	48,362	49,255	69,306	69,233	97,418
r Information Technology Auditor	64,891	115,361	66,383	118,014	67,910	120,729	69,472	123,505	71,070	126,346	2.30%	11.50%	41,078	73,028	58,869	104,655	82,746	147,104
r Internal Auditor	58,460	103,928	59,804	106,318	61,180	108,764	62,587	111,265	64,026	113,824	2.30%	11.50%	37,007	65,790	53,034	94,283	74,546	132,525
r Management Analyst	58,460	103,928	59,804	106,318	61,180	108,764	62,587	111,265	64,026	113,824	2.30%	11.50%	37,007	65,790	53,034	94,283	74,546	132,525
r Mechanic	59,858	84,226	61,235	86,163	62,643	88,145	64,084	90,172	65,558	92,246	2.30%	11.50%	37,893	53,318	54,303	76,409	76,329	107,402
r Office Specialist	43,591	61,336	44,594	62,746	45,619	64,190	46,668	65,666	47,742	67,176	2.30%	11.50%	27,595	38,828	39,546	55,644	55,586	78,213
r Personnel Analyst	58,460	103,928	59,804	106,318	61,180	108,764	62,587	111,265	64,026	113,824	2.30%	11.50%	37,007	65,790	53,034	94,283	74,546	132,525
r Statistical Analyst	76,396	107,496	78,153	109,969	79,951	112,498	81,790	115,085	83,671	117,732	2.30%	11.50%	48,362	68,049	69,306	97,520	97,418	137,075
r Systems Analyst	69,293	97,502	70,886	99,745	72,517	102,039	74,185	104,386	75,891	106,787	2.30%	11.50%	43,865	61,723	62,862	88,454	88,359	124,331
tatistical Analyst I-II	61,336	95,153	62,746	97,342	64,190	99,580	65,666	101,871	67,176	104,214	2.30%	11.50%	38,828	60,235	55,644	86,322	78,213	121,336
ystems Adminstration Specialist	69,293	97,502	70,886	99,745	72,517	102,039	74,185	104,386	75,891	106,787	2.30%	11.50%	43,865	61,723	62,862	88,454	88,359	124,331
ystems Analyst I-II	57,007	88,437	58,319	90,471	59,660	92,552	61,032	94,681	62,436	96,858	2.30%	11.50%	36,088	55,984	51,717	80,230	72,694	112,772
echnical Writer	46,901	65,994	47,979	67,512	49,083	69,064	50,212	70,653	51,367	72,278	2.30%	11.50%	29,690	41,776	42,548	59,869	59,806	84,153
raffic Electrician I-II	49,246	76,396	50,378	78,153	51,537	79,951	52,722	81,789	53,935	83,671	2.30%	11.50%	31,174	48,361	44,675	69,306	62,796	97,417
raffic Signal Field Supervisor	69,293	97,502	70,886	99,745	72,517	102,039	74,185	104,386	75,891	106,787	2.30%	11.50%	43,865	61,723	62,862	88,454	88,359	124,331
ransportation Services Supervisor	50,461	71,004	51,622	72,638	52,809	74,308	54,024	76,017	55,266	77,766	2.30%	11.50%	31,944	44,948	45,778	64,415	64,346	90,542
ideographer	44,666	62,850	45,694	64,296	46,745	65,775	47,820	67,288	48,920	68,835	2.30%	11.50%	28,276	39,787	40,521	57,018	56,957	80,145
olunteer Program Coordinator	46,901	65,994	47,979	67,512	49,083	69,064	50,212	70,653	51,367	72,278	2.30%	11.50%	29,690	41,776	42,548	59,869	59,806	84,153
ater Systems Technician	52,985	74,554	54,203	76,269	55,450	78,023	56,725	79,817	58,030	81,653	2.30%	11.50%	33,541	47,195	48,068	67,635	67,564	95,069
elder	54,293	76,396	55,542	78,153	56,820	79,951	58,127	81,790	59,463	83,671	2.30%	11.50%	34,370	48,362	49,255	69,306	69,233	97,418
orkers' Compensation Specialist	51,708	72,758	52,897	74,431	54,114	76,143	55,358	77,894	56,631	79,686	2.30%	11.50%	32,733	46,058	46,909	66,006	65,936	92,778

ttp://www3.lasvegasnevada.gov/HRJobDescriptions/Default.aspx?ID=#

Chart III - U.S. States & Cities - Job Titles - Salaries - Pension Estimates

NY-New York City	2010 (Min)	2010 (Max)	2011 (Min)	2011 (Max)	2012 (Min)	2012 (Max)	2013 (Min)	2013 (Max)	2014 (Min)	2014 (Max)	5-Year Average % Raise	5-Year Cumulative Raise Estimate**	20-Year Annual Pension Benefit Estimate (Min.)***	20-Year Annual Pension Benefit Estimate (Max.)	25-Year Annual Pension Benefit Estimate (Min.)	25-Year Annual Pension Benefit Estimate (Max.)	30-Year Annual Pension Benefit Estimate (Min.)	30-Year Annual Pension Benefit Estimate (Max.)
Accountant	43,056	56,236	44,089	57,585	45,147	58,967	46,231	60,383	47,340	61,832	2.40%	12.00%	27,713	36,196	39,909	52,126	56,372	73,628
Administrative Accountant	51,974	168,391	53,221	172,433	54,499	176,571	55,807	180,809	57,146	185,148	2.40%	12.00%	33,453	108,385	48,176	156,086	68,048	220,470
Administrative Actuary	51,974	168,391	53,221	172,433	54,499	176,571	55,807	180,809	57,146	185,148	2.40%	12.00%	33,453	108,385	48,176	156,086	68,048	220,470
Administrative Architect	51,974	168,391	53,221	172,433	54,499	176,571	55,807	180,809	57,146	185,148	2.40%	12.00%	33,453	108,385	48,176	156,086	68,048	220,470
Administrative Assessor	51,974	168,391	53,221	172,433	54,499	176,571	55,807	180,809	57,146	185,148	2.40%	12.00%	33,453	108,385	48,176	156,086	68,048	220,470
Administrative Budget Analyst	50,955	165,089	52,178	169,052	53,430	173,109	54,712	177,263	56,025	181,518	2.40%	12.00%	32,797	106,260	47,231	153,025	66,713	216,147
Administrative Claim Examiner	51,974	168,391	53,221	172,433	54,499	176,571	55,807	180,809	57,146	185,148	2.40%	12.00%	33,453	108,385	48,176	156,086	68,048	220,470
Administrative Construction Project Manager	51,974	168,391	53,221	172,433	54,499	176,571	55,807	180,809	57,146	185,148	2.40%	12.00%	33,453	108,385	48,176	156,086	68,048	220,470
Administrative Crime Laboratory Manager	51,974	168,391	53,221	172,433	54,499	176,571	55,807	180,809	57,146	185,148	2.40%	12.00%	33,453	108,385	48,176	156,086	68,048	220,470
Administrative Deputy Register	51,974	168,391	53,221	172,433	54,499	176,571	55,807	180,809	57,146	185,148	2.40%	12.00%	33,453	108,385	48,176	156,086	68,048	220,470
Administrative Education Officer	36,284	124,795	37,155	127,790	38,046	130,857	38,960	133,997	39,895	137,213	2.40%	12.00%	23,354	80,324	33,632	115,675	47,505	163,394
Administrative Housing Development Specialist	51,974	168,391	53,221	172,433	54,499	176,571	55,807	180,809	57,146	185,148	2.40%	12.00%	33,453	108,385	48,176	156,086	68,048	220,470
Administrative Juvenile Counselor	51,974	168,391	53,221	172,433	54,499	176,571	55,807	180,809	57,146	185,148	2.40%	12.00%	33,453	108,385	48,176	156,086	68,048	220,470
Administrative Labor Relations Analyst	51,974	168,391	53,221	172,433	54,499	176,571	55,807	180,809	57,146	185,148	2.40%	12.00%	33,453	108,385	48,176	156,086	68,048	220,470
Administrative Manager	51,974	168,391	53,221	172,433	54,499	176,571	55,807	180,809	57,146	185,148	2.40%	12.00%	33,453	108,385	48,176	156,086	68,048	220,470
Administrative Organizational Research Analyst	50,955	165,089	52,178	169,052	53,430	173,109	54,712	177,263	56,025	181,518	2.40%	12.00%	32,797	106,260	47,231	153,025	66,713	216,147
Administrative Personnel Analyst	50,955	165,089	52,178	169,052	53,430	173,109	54,712	177,263	56,025	181,518	2.40%	12.00%	32,797	106,260	47,231	153,025	66,713	216,147
Administrative Personnel Investigator	50,955	165,089	52,178	169,052	53,430	173,109	54,712	177,263	56,025	181,518	2.40%	12.00%	32,797	106,260	47,231	153,025	66,713	216,147
Administrative Plant Manager	50,955	165,089	52,178	169,052	53,430	173,109	54,712	177,263	56,025	181,518	2.40%	12.00%	32,797	106,260	47,231	153,025	66,713	216,147
Administrative Procurement Analyst	51,974	168,391	53,221	172,433	54,499	176,571	55,807	180,809	57,146	185,148	2.40%	12.00%	33,453	108,385	48,176	156,086	68,048	220,470
Administrative Project Manager	51,974	168,391	53,221	172,433	54,499	176,571	55,807	180,809	57,146	185,148	2.40%	12.00%	33,453	108,385	48,176	156,086	68,048	220,470
Administrative Psychologist	51,974	168,391	53,221	172,433	54,499	176,571	55,807	180,809	57,146	185,148	2.40%	12.00%	33,453	108,385	48,176	156,086	68,048	220,470
Administrative Public Health Sanitarian	51,974	168,391	53,221	172,433	54,499	176,571	55,807	180,809	57,146	185,148	2.40%	12.00%	33,453	108,385	48,176	156,086	68,048	220,470
Administrative Retirement Benefits Specialist	51,974	168,391	53,221	172,433	54,499	176,571	55,807	180,809	57,146	185,148	2.40%	12.00%	33,453	108,385	48,176	156,086	68,048	220,470
Administrative School Security Manager	43,050	171,524	44,083	175,640	45,141	179,856	46,225	184,172	47,334	188,592	2.40%	12.00%	27,709	110,401	39,904	158,989	56,364	224,574
Administrative Superintendent Of Bridge Operations	51,974	168,391	53,221	172,433	54,499	176,571	55,807	180,809	57,146	185,148	2.40%	12.00%	33,453	108,385	48,176	156,086	68,048	220,470
Administrative Transportation Coordinator	51,974	168,391	53,221	172,433	54,499	176,571	55,807	180,809	57,146	185,148	2.40%	12.00%	33,453	108,385	48,176	156,086	68,048	220,470
Adult Education Teacher	20,350	104,202	20,838	106,703	21,338	109,264	21,850	111,886	22,375	114,571	2.40%	12.00%	13,098	67,069	18,863	96,587	26,643	136,424
Adult Educator Assistant Coord	73,014	78,502	74,767	80,386	76,561	82,315	78,398	84,291	80,280	86,314	2.40%	12.00%	46,996	50,528	67,678	72,765	95,595	102,784
Air Pollution Control Engineer I-III	52,705	82,634	53,970	84,617	55,265	86,648	56,592	88,727	57,950	90,857	2.40%	12.00%	33,924	53,187	48,854	76,595	69,005	108,194
Air Pollution Inspector I-II	28,804	54,083	29,495	55,381	30,203	56,710	30,928	58,071	31,670	59,465	2.40%	12.00%	18,540	34,810	26,699	50,131	37,712	70,809

Chart III - U.S. States & Cities - Job Titles - Salaries - Pension Estimates

NY-New York City	2010 (Min)	2010 (Max)	2011 (Min)	2011 (Max)	2012 (Min)	2012 (Max)	2013 (Min)	2013 (Max)	2014 (Min)	2014 (Max)	5-Year Average % Raise	5-Year Cumulative Raise Estimate**	20-Year Annual Pension Benefit Estimate (Min.)***	20-Year Annual Pension Benefit Estimate (Max.)	25-Year Annual Pension Benefit Estimate (Min.)	25-Year Annual Pension Benefit Estimate (Max.)	30-Year Annual Pension Benefit Estimate (Min.)	30-Year Annual Pension Benefit Estimate (Max.)
Architect I-III	64,217	100,686	65,758	103,102	67,336	105,576	68,952	108,110	70,607	110,705	2.40%	12.00%	41,333	64,806	59,524	93,328	84,077	131,825
Aspiring Principal	98,956	131,941	101,331	135,108	103,763	138,351	106,253	141,671	108,803	145,071	2.40%	12.00%	63,693	84,924	91,725	122,299	129,560	172,747
Assistant Accountant	38,122	47,756	39,037	48,902	39,974	50,076	40,933	51,278	41,916	52,508	2.40%	12.00%	24,537	30,738	35,336	44,266	49,912	62,526
Assistant Building Custodian	26,050	34,032	26,675	34,849	27,315	35,685	27,971	36,542	28,642	37,419	2.40%	12.00%	16,767	21,905	24,146	31,545	34,106	44,557
Assistant City Assessor I-II	39,039	49,275	39,976	50,457	40,936	51,668	41,918	52,908	42,924	54,178	2.40%	12.00%	25,128	31,716	36,186	45,674	51,113	64,514
Assistant Civil Engineer	54,097	70,584	55,395	72,278	56,725	74,013	58,086	75,789	59,480	77,608	2.40%	12.00%	34,820	45,431	50,144	65,426	70,828	92,414
Assistant Highway Transportation Specialist	46,752	59,809	47,874	61,244	49,023	62,714	50,200	64,219	51,405	65,761	2.40%	12.00%	30,092	38,496	43,336	55,438	61,211	78,306
Assistant Principal	97,195	115,031	99,527	117,792	101,916	120,619	104,362	123,513	106,867	126,478	2.40%	12.00%	62,559	74,040	90,092	106,625	127,254	150,607
Assistant Space Analyst	54,097	70,584	55,395	72,278	56,725	74,013	58,086	75,789	59,480	77,608	2.40%	12.00%	34,820	45,431	50,144	65,426	70,828	92,414
Assistant Superintendent	127,066	188,058	130,116	192,572	133,239	197,193	136,436	201,926	139,711	206,772	2.40%	12.00%	81,786	121,044	117,780	174,315	166,364	246,219
Assistant Superintendent Schls	176,160	181,473	180,388	185,829	184,718	190,289	189,151	194,855	193,690	199,532	2.40%	12.00%	113,386	116,805	163,287	168,212	230,642	237,598
Associate Attorney	59,633	77,180	61,064	79,033	62,530	80,929	64,031	82,872	65,567	84,861	2.40%	12.00%	38,383	49,677	55,275	71,540	78,076	101,050
Associate Call Center Representative (Local 1180)	56,322	80,860	57,674	82,801	59,058	84,788	60,476	86,823	61,927	88,907	2.40%	12.00%	36,252	52,046	52,207	74,951	73,741	105,868
Associate Claim Examiner I-II	41,907	52,008	42,913	53,256	43,942	54,534	44,997	55,843	46,077	57,183	2.40%	12.00%	26,973	33,475	38,844	48,207	54,867	68,093
Associate Fingerprint Technician I-IV	32,880	60,791	33,669	62,250	34,477	63,744	35,304	65,274	36,152	66,840	2.40%	12.00%	21,163	39,128	30,477	56,348	43,049	79,592
Associate Human Rights Specialist I-II	55,397	86,305	56,726	88,376	58,088	90,497	59,482	92,669	60,909	94,893	2.40%	12.00%	35,656	55,550	51,348	79,998	72,529	112,997
Associate Job Opportunity Specialist I-III	42,007	70,981	43,015	72,685	44,047	74,429	45,105	76,215	46,187	78,045	2.40%	12.00%	27,038	45,687	38,937	65,794	54,998	92,934
Associate Job Opportunity Specialist I-III	42,007	70,981	43,015	72,685	44,047	74,429	45,105	76,215	46,187	78,045	2.40%	12.00%	27,038	45,687	38,937	65,794	54,998	92,934
Associate Market Agent I-II	48,411	75,190	49,573	76,995	50,763	78,843	51,981	80,735	53,229	82,672	2.40%	12.00%	31,160	48,396	44,874	69,695	63,384	98,444
Associate Park Service Worker	42,922	53,242	43,952	54,519	45,007	55,828	46,087	57,168	47,193	58,540	2.40%	12.00%	27,626	34,269	39,785	49,351	56,196	69,708
Associate Park Service Worker - Crew Chief	40,723	53,242	41,700	54,519	42,701	55,828	43,726	57,168	44,775	58,540	2.40%	12.00%	26,211	34,269	37,747	49,351	53,317	69,708
Associate Project Manager I-III	64,217	100,686	65,758	103,102	67,336	105,576	68,952	108,110	70,607	110,705	2.40%	12.00%	41,333	64,806	59,524	93,328	84,077	131,825
Associate Retirement Benefits Examiner I-III	44,940	72,075	46,019	73,805	47,123	75,576	48,254	77,390	49,412	79,248	2.40%	12.00%	28,926	46,391	41,656	66,808	58,839	94,366
Associate Sanitation Enforcement Agent I-II	48,015	66,734	49,167	68,335	50,347	69,975	51,555	71,655	52,793	73,375	2.40%	12.00%	30,905	42,953	44,506	61,857	62,864	87,373
Associate Space Analyst	64,217	80,872	65,758	82,813	67,336	84,801	68,952	86,836	70,607	88,920	2.40%	12.00%	41,333	52,053	59,524	74,962	84,077	105,884
Associate Staff Analyst	64,987	84,142	66,546	86,162	68,143	88,230	69,779	90,347	71,454	92,515	2.40%	12.00%	41,829	54,158	60,238	77,993	85,085	110,165
Associate Staff Analyst (Osa)	44,495	57,610	45,563	58,993	46,656	60,408	47,776	61,858	48,923	63,343	2.40%	12.00%	28,639	37,081	41,243	53,400	58,256	75,427
Associate Taxi & Limousine Inspector I-II	43,775	59,375	44,825	60,800	45,901	62,259	47,003	63,753	48,131	65,283	2.40%	12.00%	28,176	38,216	40,576	55,036	57,313	77,738
Associate Traffic Enforcement Agent	56,624	66,734	57,983	68,335	59,374	69,975	60,799	71,655	62,258	73,375	2.40%	12.00%	36,446	42,953	52,486	61,857	74,136	87,373
Associate Urban Park Ranger	49,390	49,390	50,575	50,575	51,789	51,789	53,032	53,032	54,305	54,305	2.40%	12.00%	31,790	31,790	45,781	45,781	64,665	64,665
Associate Water Use Inpector I-III	48,242	70,064	49,400	71,746	50,586	73,468	51,800	75,231	53,043	77,036	2.40%	12.00%	31,051	45,097	44,717	64,944	63,162	91,733
Attorney	46,899	62,984	48,024	64,496	49,177	66,044	50,357	67,629	51,566	69,252	2.40%	12.00%	30,186	40,540	43,471	58,382	61,403	82,464

211

Chart III - U.S. States & Cities - Job Titles - Salaries - Pension Estimates

NY-New York City	2010 (Min)	2010 (Max)	2011 (Min)	2011 (Max)	2012 (Min)	2012 (Max)	2013 (Min)	2013 (Max)	2014 (Min)	2014 (Max)	5-Year Average % Raise	5-Year Cumulative Raise Estimate**	20-Year Annual Pension Benefit Estimate (Min.)***	20-Year Annual Pension Benefit Estimate (Max.)	25-Year Annual Pension Benefit Estimate (Min.)	25-Year Annual Pension Benefit Estimate (Max.)	30-Year Annual Pension Benefit Estimate (Min.)	30-Year Annual Pension Benefit Estimate (Max.)
Audiologist (Health)	51,309	57,061	52,540	58,431	53,801	59,833	55,092	61,269	56,415	62,740	2.40%	12.00%	33,025	36,727	47,559	52,891	67,177	74,709
Auditor Of Accounts	45,020	57,918	46,100	59,308	47,206	60,731	48,339	62,189	49,499	63,681	2.40%	12.00%	28,977	37,279	41,730	53,685	58,943	75,830
Auto Mechanic	60,769	60,769	62,227	62,227	63,721	63,721	65,250	65,250	66,816	66,816	2.40%	12.00%	39,114	39,114	56,328	56,328	79,563	79,563
Battalion Chief	106,360	133,398	108,913	136,600	111,527	139,878	114,203	143,235	116,944	146,673	2.40%	12.00%	68,459	85,862	98,588	123,650	139,254	174,654
Bookkeeper I-II	36,358	47,422	37,230	48,560	38,124	49,726	39,039	50,919	39,976	52,141	2.40%	12.00%	23,402	30,523	33,701	43,956	47,602	62,088
Bricklayer	76,817	76,817	78,660	78,660	80,548	80,548	82,481	82,481	84,461	84,461	2.40%	12.00%	49,443	49,443	71,203	71,203	100,574	100,574
Bridge Operator	37,939	46,673	38,849	47,793	39,782	48,940	40,736	50,115	41,714	51,318	2.40%	12.00%	24,419	30,041	35,166	43,262	49,672	61,108
Budget Analyst I-II	35,085	45,371	35,927	46,460	36,790	47,575	37,673	48,717	38,577	49,886	2.40%	12.00%	22,583	29,203	32,521	42,056	45,936	59,403
Building Custodian	28,600	36,884	29,287	37,769	29,990	38,676	30,710	39,604	31,447	40,555	2.40%	12.00%	18,409	23,740	26,510	34,189	37,446	48,291
Captain (Fire)	93,048	102,448	95,282	104,907	97,568	107,425	99,910	110,003	102,308	112,643	2.40%	12.00%	59,890	65,941	86,249	94,961	121,825	134,132
Captain D/A Deputy Inspector (Rec N/S)	99,777	119,880	102,172	122,757	104,624	125,703	107,135	128,720	109,706	131,809	2.40%	12.00%	64,222	77,160	92,486	111,119	130,636	156,955
Carpenter	51,546	51,546	52,783	52,783	54,050	54,050	55,347	55,347	56,676	56,676	2.40%	12.00%	33,178	33,178	47,779	47,779	67,488	67,488
Cashier	37,927	51,773	38,837	53,015	39,769	54,288	40,723	55,591	41,701	56,925	2.40%	12.00%	24,411	33,323	35,155	47,989	49,656	67,784
Certified It Administrator (Database) I-IV	73,822	116,931	75,594	119,737	77,408	122,611	79,266	125,554	81,168	128,567	2.40%	12.00%	47,516	75,262	68,428	108,386	96,653	153,094
Certified It Administrator (LAN-WAN) I-IV	73,822	116,931	75,594	119,737	77,408	122,611	79,266	125,554	81,168	128,567	2.40%	12.00%	47,516	75,262	68,428	108,386	96,653	153,094
Certified It Developer (Applications) I-IV	76,904	116,931	78,750	119,737	80,640	122,611	82,575	125,554	84,557	128,567	2.40%	12.00%	49,499	75,262	71,284	108,386	100,688	153,094
Chemical Engineer I-III	64,217	100,686	65,758	103,102	67,336	105,576	68,952	108,110	70,607	110,705	2.40%	12.00%	41,333	64,806	59,524	93,328	84,077	131,825
Chief Inspector	51,974	168,391	53,221	172,433	54,499	176,571	55,807	180,809	57,146	185,148	2.40%	12.00%	33,453	108,385	48,176	156,086	68,048	220,470
Chief Marine Engineer	65,291	65,291	66,858	66,858	68,463	68,463	70,106	70,106	71,788	71,788	2.40%	12.00%	42,025	42,025	60,520	60,520	85,484	85,484
Chief Surgeon	105,772	118,037	108,310	120,870	110,910	123,771	113,572	126,741	116,297	129,783	2.40%	12.00%	68,080	75,974	98,042	109,411	138,484	154,542
Child Protective Specialist I-II	41,832	68,685	42,836	70,334	43,864	72,022	44,917	73,750	45,995	75,520	2.40%	12.00%	26,925	44,209	38,775	63,666	54,769	89,928
Child Protective Specialist Supervisor	45,431	68,685	46,521	70,334	47,638	72,022	48,781	73,750	49,952	75,520	2.40%	12.00%	29,241	44,209	42,111	63,666	59,481	89,928
Child Welfare Specialist I-II	39,325	65,641	40,269	67,216	41,235	68,829	42,225	70,481	43,238	72,173	2.40%	12.00%	25,312	42,250	36,451	60,844	51,487	85,942
Child Welfare Specialist Supervisor I-II	55,541	83,110	56,874	85,105	58,239	87,147	59,636	89,239	61,068	91,380	2.40%	12.00%	35,749	53,494	51,482	77,036	72,718	108,813
City Planner I-II	52,325	79,113	53,580	81,012	54,866	82,956	56,183	84,947	57,532	86,986	2.40%	12.00%	33,679	50,921	48,501	73,332	68,507	103,581
City Tax Auditor I-II	43,056	73,852	44,089	75,624	45,147	77,439	46,231	79,298	47,340	81,201	2.40%	12.00%	27,713	47,535	39,909	68,455	56,372	96,692
Civil Engineer I-III	64,217	100,686	65,758	103,102	67,336	105,576	68,952	108,110	70,607	110,705	2.40%	12.00%	41,333	64,806	59,524	93,328	84,077	131,825
Civil Engineering Drafter	34,528	44,171	35,357	45,231	36,205	46,316	37,074	47,428	37,964	48,566	2.40%	12.00%	22,224	28,430	32,005	40,943	45,206	57,831
Claim Specialist I-III	56,993	70,733	58,361	72,430	59,762	74,169	61,196	75,949	62,665	77,771	2.40%	12.00%	36,684	45,527	52,828	65,564	74,619	92,608
Classification Specialist	44,495	57,610	45,563	58,993	46,656	60,408	47,776	61,858	48,923	63,343	2.40%	12.00%	28,639	37,081	41,243	53,400	58,256	75,427
Clerical Aide	27,943	33,844	28,614	34,656	29,300	35,488	30,004	36,340	30,724	37,212	2.40%	12.00%	17,985	21,784	25,901	31,371	36,585	44,311
Clerical Associate	37,927	51,773	38,837	53,015	39,769	54,288	40,723	55,591	41,701	56,925	2.40%	12.00%	24,411	33,323	35,155	47,989	49,656	67,784
College Security Director	79,441	107,411	81,347	109,989	83,300	112,629	85,299	115,332	87,346	118,100	2.40%	12.00%	51,132	69,135	73,635	99,562	104,010	140,630
College Security Specialist	52,893	72,397	54,163	74,135	55,462	75,914	56,794	77,736	58,157	79,602	2.40%	12.00%	34,045	46,598	49,028	67,107	69,251	94,788
Computer Aide	42,085	54,302	43,095	55,605	44,129	56,939	45,188	58,306	46,273	59,705	2.40%	12.00%	27,088	34,951	39,009	50,333	55,101	71,095
Computer Associate (Operations) I-III	48,557	92,397	49,722	94,615	50,915	96,886	52,137	99,211	53,389	101,592	2.40%	12.00%	31,253	59,472	45,008	85,645	63,574	120,973
Computer Associate (Software) I-III	63,119	92,397	64,633	94,615	66,185	96,886	67,773	99,211	69,400	101,592	2.40%	12.00%	40,626	59,472	58,506	85,645	82,639	120,973
Computer Associate (Technical Support) I-III	47,032	89,924	48,160	92,082	49,316	94,292	50,500	96,555	51,712	98,872	2.40%	12.00%	30,272	57,879	43,595	83,352	61,577	117,734

212

Chart III - U.S. States & Cities - Job Titles - Salaries - Pension Estimates

NY-New York City	2010 (Min)	2010 (Max)	2011 (Min)	2011 (Max)	2012 (Min)	2012 (Max)	2013 (Min)	2013 (Max)	2014 (Min)	2014 (Max)	5-Year Average % Raise	5-Year Cumulative Raise Estimate**	20-Year Annual Pension Benefit Estimate (Min.)***	20-Year Annual Pension Benefit Estimate (Max.)	25-Year Annual Pension Benefit Estimate (Min.)	25-Year Annual Pension Benefit Estimate (Max.)	30-Year Annual Pension Benefit Estimate (Min.)	30-Year Annual Pension Benefit Estimate (Max.)
Computer Operations Manager	51,974	168,391	53,221	172,433	54,499	176,571	55,807	180,809	57,146	185,148	2.40%	12.00%	33,453	108,385	48,176	156,086	68,048	220,470
Computer Operator Manager	79,441	107,411	81,347	109,989	83,300	112,629	85,299	115,332	87,346	118,100	2.40%	12.00%	51,132	69,135	73,635	99,562	104,010	140,630
Computer Programmer	33,719	44,314	34,528	45,377	35,357	46,466	36,205	47,581	37,074	48,723	2.40%	12.00%	21,703	28,522	31,255	41,075	44,147	58,019
Computer Programmer Analyst II	48,557	69,015	49,722	70,672	50,915	72,368	52,137	74,105	53,389	75,883	2.40%	12.00%	31,253	44,422	45,008	63,972	63,574	90,360
Computer Service Technician	42,085	54,961	43,095	56,280	44,129	57,631	45,188	59,014	46,273	60,431	2.40%	12.00%	27,088	35,376	39,009	50,945	55,101	71,959
Computer Specialist (Software) I-IV	77,671	112,868	79,535	115,577	81,444	118,351	83,398	121,191	85,400	124,100	2.40%	12.00%	49,993	72,647	71,995	104,620	101,692	147,775
Computer Systems Manager	79,441	107,411	81,347	109,989	83,300	112,629	85,299	115,332	87,346	118,100	2.40%	12.00%	51,132	69,135	73,635	99,562	104,010	140,630
Computer Systems Manager	51,974	168,391	53,221	172,433	54,499	176,571	55,807	180,809	57,146	185,148	2.40%	12.00%	33,453	108,385	48,176	156,086	68,048	220,470
Congregate Care Specialist I-II	35,215	62,625	36,060	64,128	36,926	65,667	37,812	67,243	38,719	68,857	2.40%	12.00%	22,666	40,308	32,642	58,048	46,106	81,993
Construction Manager	53,452	70,990	54,734	72,694	56,048	74,438	57,393	76,225	58,771	78,054	2.40%	12.00%	34,404	45,693	49,546	65,802	69,983	92,945
Consumer Affairs Inspector	27,643	33,885	28,306	34,698	28,986	35,531	29,681	36,383	30,394	37,257	2.40%	12.00%	17,792	21,810	25,623	31,409	36,192	44,364
Contract Specialist II	39,355	65,080	40,299	66,642	41,267	68,241	42,257	69,879	43,271	71,556	2.40%	12.00%	25,331	41,889	36,479	60,324	51,526	85,207
Correction Officer	29,321	69,609	30,024	71,280	30,745	72,990	31,483	74,742	32,238	76,536	2.40%	12.00%	18,872	44,804	27,178	64,522	38,389	91,137
Correctional Counselor	39,317	52,575	40,261	53,837	41,227	55,129	42,217	56,452	43,230	57,807	2.40%	12.00%	25,307	33,840	36,444	48,733	51,477	68,835
County Detective	35,586	50,343	36,440	51,552	37,314	52,789	38,210	54,056	39,127	55,353	2.40%	12.00%	22,905	32,403	32,985	46,664	46,591	65,913
Custodial Supervisor	32,923	42,845	33,713	43,873	34,522	44,926	35,350	46,004	36,199	47,108	2.40%	12.00%	21,191	27,577	30,517	39,714	43,105	56,095
Custodian I-IV	31,011	66,544	31,755	68,141	32,517	69,776	33,297	71,451	34,097	73,165	2.40%	12.00%	19,960	42,831	28,744	61,681	40,601	87,123
Dental Hygienist I-III	30,266	61,931	30,993	63,417	31,736	64,939	32,498	66,498	33,278	68,094	2.40%	12.00%	19,481	39,862	28,054	57,405	39,627	81,085
Dietitian I-III	42,002	57,656	43,011	59,040	44,043	60,457	45,100	61,908	46,182	63,394	2.40%	12.00%	27,035	37,110	38,933	53,443	54,993	75,488
Director Of Television II	38,289	58,582	39,208	59,988	40,149	61,428	41,113	62,902	42,100	64,412	2.40%	12.00%	24,645	37,706	35,491	54,301	50,131	76,700
Economist	43,056	56,653	44,089	58,013	45,147	59,405	46,231	60,831	47,340	62,291	2.40%	12.00%	27,713	36,465	39,909	52,513	56,372	74,175
Electrical Engineer I-III	64,217	100,686	65,758	103,102	67,336	105,576	68,952	108,110	70,607	110,705	2.40%	12.00%	41,333	64,806	59,524	93,328	84,077	131,825
Electrician	88,388	88,388	90,509	90,509	92,681	92,681	94,905	94,905	97,183	97,183	2.40%	12.00%	56,891	56,891	81,928	81,928	115,723	115,723
Eligibility Specialist	37,971	48,946	38,882	50,121	39,815	51,323	40,771	52,555	41,749	53,817	2.40%	12.00%	24,440	31,504	35,196	45,369	49,714	64,083
Environmental Engineer I-III	64,217	100,686	65,758	103,102	67,336	105,576	68,952	108,110	70,607	110,705	2.40%	12.00%	41,333	64,806	59,524	93,328	84,077	131,825
Environmental Police Officer I-III	30,848	56,714	31,588	58,075	32,346	59,469	33,123	60,896	33,918	62,358	2.40%	12.00%	19,855	36,504	28,594	52,569	40,388	74,254
Estimator (Electrical)	54,097	70,584	55,395	72,278	56,725	74,013	58,086	75,789	59,480	77,608	2.40%	12.00%	34,820	45,431	50,144	65,426	70,828	92,414
Estimator (General Construction)	54,097	70,584	55,395	72,278	56,725	74,013	58,086	75,789	59,480	77,608	2.40%	12.00%	34,820	45,431	50,144	65,426	70,828	92,414
Film Editor	38,504	45,444	39,428	46,535	40,374	47,651	41,343	48,795	42,335	49,966	2.40%	12.00%	24,783	29,250	35,690	42,123	50,412	59,498
Film Manager I-II	52,302	66,345	53,557	67,937	54,842	69,567	56,158	71,237	57,506	72,947	2.40%	12.00%	33,664	42,703	48,479	61,496	68,477	86,863
Fingerprint Technician	32,880	38,488	33,669	39,412	34,477	40,358	35,304	41,327	36,152	42,318	2.40%	12.00%	21,163	24,773	30,477	35,676	43,049	50,392
Fire Protection Inspector	42,095	51,403	43,105	52,637	44,140	53,900	45,199	55,194	46,284	56,518	2.40%	12.00%	27,094	33,086	39,019	47,647	55,113	67,301
Firefighter	47,496	69,609	48,635	71,280	49,803	72,990	50,998	74,742	52,222	76,536	2.40%	12.00%	30,571	44,804	44,025	64,522	62,185	91,137
Graphic Artist I-II	43,213	82,538	44,250	84,519	45,312	86,548	46,400	88,625	47,513	90,752	2.40%	12.00%	27,814	53,126	40,055	76,506	56,578	108,065
Guidance Counselor	40,864	92,476	41,845	94,695	42,849	96,968	43,878	99,295	44,931	101,678	2.40%	12.00%	26,302	59,522	37,878	85,718	53,503	121,075
Health Resources Coordinator	34,005	42,278	34,821	43,293	35,656	44,332	36,512	45,396	37,388	46,486	2.40%	12.00%	21,887	27,212	31,520	39,189	44,521	55,354
Highway Repairer	50,324	50,324	51,531	51,531	52,768	52,768	54,034	54,034	55,331	55,331	2.40%	12.00%	32,391	32,391	46,646	46,646	65,887	65,887

213

Chart III - U.S. States & Cities - Job Titles - Salaries - Pension Estimates

NY-New York City	2010 (Min)	2010 (Max)	2011 (Min)	2011 (Max)	2012 (Min)	2012 (Max)	2013 (Min)	2013 (Max)	2014 (Min)	2014 (Max)	5-Year Average % Raise	5-Year Cumulative Raise Estimate**	20-Year Annual Pension Benefit Estimate (Min.)***	20-Year Annual Pension Benefit Estimate (Max.)	25-Year Annual Pension Benefit Estimate (Min.)	25-Year Annual Pension Benefit Estimate (Max.)	30-Year Annual Pension Benefit Estimate (Min.)	30-Year Annual Pension Benefit Estimate (Max.)
Highway Transportation Specialist I-III	54,097	90,170	55,395	92,334	56,725	94,550	58,086	96,819	59,480	99,143	2.40%	12.00%	34,820	58,038	50,144	83,580	70,828	118,057
Housekeeper	34,765	40,278	35,600	41,245	36,454	42,235	37,329	43,249	38,225	44,287	2.40%	12.00%	22,377	25,925	32,225	37,335	45,517	52,735
Housing Development Specialist I-II	42,061	45,834	43,070	46,934	44,104	48,061	45,162	49,214	46,246	50,395	2.40%	12.00%	27,072	29,501	38,987	42,485	55,069	60,009
Industrial Hygienist I-II	44,916	62,074	45,994	63,564	47,098	65,089	48,228	66,651	49,386	68,251	2.40%	12.00%	28,910	39,954	41,634	57,538	58,807	81,272
Information Systems Associate	59,374	72,568	60,799	74,309	62,258	76,093	63,752	77,919	65,282	79,789	2.40%	12.00%	38,216	46,708	55,035	67,265	77,736	95,011
Information Systems Specialist	72,568	92,359	74,309	94,576	76,093	96,845	77,919	99,170	79,789	101,550	2.40%	12.00%	46,708	59,447	67,265	85,610	95,011	120,923
Insurance Advisor	50,455	66,248	51,666	67,838	52,906	69,466	54,176	71,133	55,476	72,840	2.40%	12.00%	32,476	42,640	46,768	61,407	66,060	86,736
Investment Analyst	43,056	55,683	44,089	57,019	45,147	58,387	46,231	59,789	47,340	61,224	2.40%	12.00%	27,713	35,840	39,909	51,613	56,372	72,904
Junior Building Custodian	24,558	30,620	25,147	31,355	25,751	32,108	26,369	32,878	27,001	33,667	2.40%	12.00%	15,806	19,709	22,763	28,383	32,153	40,090
Juvenile Counselor I-II	39,317	54,590	40,261	55,900	41,227	57,241	42,217	58,615	43,230	60,022	2.40%	12.00%	25,307	35,137	36,444	50,600	51,477	71,473
Labor Relations Analyst	58,589	66,248	59,995	67,838	61,435	69,466	62,909	71,133	64,419	72,840	2.40%	12.00%	37,710	42,640	54,307	61,407	76,708	86,736
Laboratory Microbiologist I-II	42,704	62,730	43,729	64,236	44,778	65,778	45,853	67,356	46,953	68,973	2.40%	12.00%	27,486	40,376	39,583	58,146	55,911	82,131
Landscape Architect I-III	64,217	100,686	65,758	103,102	67,336	105,576	68,952	108,110	70,607	110,705	2.40%	12.00%	41,333	64,806	59,524	93,328	84,077	131,825
Lieutenant (Fire)	72,427	89,252	74,165	91,394	75,945	93,587	77,768	95,833	79,634	98,133	2.40%	12.00%	46,618	57,447	67,134	82,729	94,827	116,855
Lieutenant (Police) (Recur Ns)	92,531	102,448	94,751	104,907	97,025	107,425	99,354	110,003	101,738	112,643	2.40%	12.00%	59,557	65,941	85,769	94,961	121,147	134,132
Lieutenant D/A Special Assignmet (Recur Ns)	104,282	112,697	106,785	115,401	109,348	118,171	111,972	121,007	114,659	123,911	2.40%	12.00%	67,121	72,537	96,661	104,461	136,533	147,550
Local Instructional Supervisor	155,945	155,945	159,688	159,688	163,520	163,520	167,444	167,444	171,463	171,463	2.40%	12.00%	100,374	100,374	144,549	144,549	204,174	204,174
Management Auditor	53,088	73,852	54,362	75,624	55,667	77,439	57,003	79,298	58,371	81,201	2.40%	12.00%	34,170	47,535	49,208	68,455	69,506	96,692
Mechanical Engineer I-III	64,217	100,686	65,758	103,102	67,336	105,576	68,952	108,110	70,607	110,705	2.40%	12.00%	41,333	64,806	59,524	93,328	84,077	131,825
Medical Record Librarian	41,866	47,420	42,871	48,558	43,900	49,723	44,953	50,917	46,032	52,139	2.40%	12.00%	26,947	30,522	38,807	43,954	54,814	62,085
Motor Vehicle Operator	37,876	41,146	38,785	42,133	39,716	43,145	40,669	44,180	41,645	45,240	2.40%	12.00%	24,379	26,484	35,108	38,139	49,590	53,871
Nutritionist	55,891	61,477	57,233	62,952	58,606	64,463	60,013	66,010	61,453	67,595	2.40%	12.00%	35,974	39,570	51,807	56,984	73,177	80,490
Office Aide (Typing)	21,528	29,342	22,045	30,046	22,574	30,767	23,116	31,505	23,671	32,261	2.40%	12.00%	13,857	18,886	19,955	27,197	28,187	38,416
Oiler	88,824	88,824	90,956	90,956	93,139	93,139	95,374	95,374	97,663	97,663	2.40%	12.00%	57,172	57,172	82,333	82,333	116,295	116,295
Operations Communications Specialist I-II	37,997	51,043	38,909	52,268	39,843	53,522	40,799	54,807	41,778	56,122	2.40%	12.00%	24,457	32,854	35,220	47,313	49,748	66,829
Organizational Research Analyst	40,740	45,371	41,718	46,460	42,719	47,575	43,744	48,717	44,794	49,886	2.40%	12.00%	26,222	29,203	37,763	42,056	53,340	59,403
Painter	54,740	54,740	56,054	56,054	57,399	57,399	58,777	58,777	60,188	60,188	2.40%	12.00%	35,234	35,234	50,740	50,740	71,670	71,670
Park Services Worker	32,798	44,298	33,586	45,361	34,392	46,450	35,217	47,565	36,062	48,706	2.40%	12.00%	21,111	28,513	30,402	41,061	42,942	57,998
Parking Control Specialist	37,646	44,856	38,550	45,932	39,475	47,035	40,422	48,163	41,392	49,319	2.40%	12.00%	24,231	28,871	34,895	41,578	49,289	58,728
Personnel Analyst	40,740	45,371	41,718	46,460	42,719	47,575	43,744	48,717	44,794	49,886	2.40%	12.00%	26,222	29,203	37,763	42,056	53,340	59,403
Pharmacist	61,057	62,695	62,522	64,200	64,023	65,741	65,559	67,319	67,133	68,934	2.40%	12.00%	39,299	40,354	56,595	58,114	79,940	82,085
Photographer	40,240	49,276	41,206	50,458	42,195	51,669	43,207	52,909	44,244	54,179	2.40%	12.00%	25,900	31,716	37,299	45,675	52,685	64,515
Physical Therapist	49,931	55,641	51,129	56,976	52,356	58,344	53,613	59,744	54,900	61,178	2.40%	12.00%	32,138	35,813	46,282	51,575	65,373	72,849
Physician's Assistant I-II	67,473	84,344	69,092	86,368	70,750	88,441	72,448	90,563	74,187	92,737	2.40%	12.00%	43,429	54,288	62,542	78,180	88,340	110,424
Physicist	64,217	80,872	65,758	82,813	67,336	84,801	68,952	86,836	70,607	88,920	2.40%	12.00%	41,333	52,053	59,524	74,962	84,077	105,884
Plasterer	66,773	66,773	68,375	68,375	70,016	70,016	71,697	71,697	73,417	73,417	2.40%	12.00%	42,978	42,978	61,893	61,893	87,424	87,424
Plumber	54,057	54,057	55,355	55,355	56,683	56,683	58,044	58,044	59,437	59,437	2.40%	12.00%	34,794	34,794	50,107	50,107	70,776	70,776

Chart III - U.S. States & Cities - Job Titles - Salaries - Pension Estimates

NY-New York City	2010 (Min)	2010 (Max)	2011 (Min)	2011 (Max)	2012 (Min)	2012 (Max)	2013 (Min)	2013 (Max)	2014 (Min)	2014 (Max)	5-Year Average % Raise	5-Year Cumulative Raise Estimate**	20-Year Annual Pension Benefit Estimate (Min.)***	20-Year Annual Pension Benefit Estimate (Max.)	25-Year Annual Pension Benefit Estimate (Min.)	25-Year Annual Pension Benefit Estimate (Max.)	30-Year Annual Pension Benefit Estimate (Min.)	30-Year Annual Pension Benefit Estimate (Max.)
Pol Off D/A Detective 2nd Gr (Intelligence) (Recur Ns)	82,924	86,526	84,914	88,603	86,952	90,729	89,039	92,907	91,176	95,136	2.40%	12.00%	53,374	55,692	76,864	80,203	108,570	113,286
Pol Off D/A Detective 3rd Gr Intelligence (Recur Ns)	68,460	77,001	70,103	78,849	71,786	80,741	73,508	82,679	75,273	84,663	2.40%	12.00%	44,064	49,562	63,457	71,374	89,633	100,815
Police Officer D/A Detective 1st Gr (Recur Ns)	94,297	99,320	96,561	101,704	98,878	104,145	101,251	106,644	103,681	109,203	2.40%	12.00%	60,694	63,927	87,406	92,062	123,461	130,037
Police Officer D/A Detective 2nd Gr (Recur Ns)	82,924	86,526	84,914	88,603	86,952	90,729	89,039	92,907	91,176	95,136	2.40%	12.00%	53,374	55,692	76,864	80,203	108,570	113,286
Police Officer D/A Detective 3rd Grade (Recur Ns)	68,460	77,001	70,103	78,849	71,786	80,741	73,508	82,679	75,273	84,663	2.40%	12.00%	44,064	49,562	63,457	71,374	89,633	100,815
Police Officer, Det. Specialist (Recur Ns)	68,460	77,001	70,103	78,849	71,786	80,741	73,508	82,679	75,273	84,663	2.40%	12.00%	44,064	49,562	63,457	71,374	89,633	100,815
Principal Administrative Associate I-III	43,435	71,445	44,478	73,160	45,545	74,916	46,638	76,714	47,757	78,555	2.40%	12.00%	27,957	45,986	40,261	66,224	56,868	93,541
Principal Air Pollution Inspector	61,385	73,464	62,858	75,227	64,366	77,032	65,911	78,881	67,493	80,774	2.40%	12.00%	39,510	47,285	56,899	68,095	80,369	96,184
Principal Custodial Supervisor	55,558	66,878	56,892	68,483	58,257	70,126	59,655	71,809	61,087	73,533	2.40%	12.00%	35,760	43,046	51,498	61,990	72,741	87,561
Principal Investigator	39,852	48,589	40,808	49,755	41,788	50,949	42,791	52,172	43,818	53,424	2.40%	12.00%	25,651	31,274	36,940	45,038	52,177	63,616
Principal Pharmacist	75,532	83,088	77,345	85,082	79,201	87,124	81,102	89,215	83,048	91,356	2.40%	12.00%	48,616	53,479	70,012	77,016	98,892	108,785
Principal Planner	54,685	72,220	55,998	73,954	57,342	75,728	58,718	77,546	60,127	79,407	2.40%	12.00%	35,198	46,485	50,689	66,943	71,598	94,556
Principal Title Examiner	51,531	67,237	52,768	68,851	54,034	70,503	55,331	72,196	56,659	73,928	2.40%	12.00%	33,168	43,277	47,765	62,324	67,468	88,032
Probation Officer	45,278	65,554	46,365	67,127	47,477	68,738	48,617	70,388	49,784	72,077	2.40%	12.00%	29,143	42,194	41,969	60,763	59,281	85,828
Procurement Analyst	55,230	80,731	56,555	82,668	57,912	84,652	59,302	86,684	60,726	88,764	2.40%	12.00%	35,548	51,962	51,193	74,831	72,310	105,698
Program Producer I-III	39,565	77,119	40,514	78,969	41,487	80,865	42,482	82,806	43,502	84,793	2.40%	12.00%	25,466	49,637	36,674	71,483	51,801	100,969
Project Coordinator	47,425	59,725	48,563	61,159	49,729	62,627	50,922	64,130	52,145	65,669	2.40%	12.00%	30,525	38,442	43,959	55,361	62,092	78,197
Psychologist I-III	60,596	88,668	62,051	90,796	63,540	92,975	65,065	95,206	66,626	97,491	2.40%	12.00%	39,003	57,071	56,168	82,188	79,337	116,090
Public Health Adviser	36,823	49,214	37,706	50,395	38,611	51,605	39,538	52,843	40,487	54,112	2.40%	12.00%	23,701	31,677	34,132	45,618	48,211	64,435
Public Health Educator I-III	48,476	67,897	49,640	69,527	50,831	71,195	52,051	72,904	53,300	74,654	2.40%	12.00%	31,202	43,702	44,934	62,935	63,469	88,896
Public Health Epidemiologist	52,250	60,929	53,504	62,392	54,788	63,889	56,103	65,422	57,449	66,993	2.40%	12.00%	33,631	39,217	48,432	56,477	68,409	79,773
Public Health Nurse I-III	62,835	69,008	64,343	70,664	65,887	72,360	67,468	74,096	69,088	75,875	2.40%	12.00%	40,444	44,417	58,243	63,965	82,268	90,350
Public Health Sanitarian I-II	43,067	66,527	44,100	68,124	45,159	69,759	46,243	71,433	47,352	73,147	2.40%	12.00%	27,720	42,820	39,920	61,665	56,386	87,102
Purchasing Agent	57,817	76,047	59,204	77,872	60,625	79,741	62,080	81,654	63,570	83,614	2.40%	12.00%	37,214	48,947	53,592	70,489	75,698	99,566
Quality Assurance Specialist I-II	41,542	56,990	42,539	58,358	43,560	59,758	44,605	61,192	45,676	62,661	2.40%	12.00%	26,738	36,681	38,506	52,825	54,389	74,615
Radio And Tevevision Operator	33,323	42,573	34,123	43,595	34,942	44,641	35,780	45,713	36,639	46,810	2.40%	12.00%	21,448	27,402	30,888	39,462	43,629	55,740
Real Property Manager I-III	41,678	59,986	42,678	61,426	43,703	62,900	44,752	64,410	45,826	65,955	2.40%	12.00%	26,826	38,610	38,632	55,602	54,568	78,538
Rehabilitation Counselor	49,275	54,983	50,457	56,303	51,668	57,654	52,908	59,038	54,178	60,455	2.40%	12.00%	31,716	35,390	45,674	50,965	64,514	71,988
Rent Examiner	23,394	31,170	23,956	31,918	24,531	32,684	25,119	33,469	25,722	34,272	2.40%	12.00%	15,058	20,063	21,685	28,892	30,629	40,810
Research Assistant	43,056	56,653	44,089	58,013	45,147	59,405	46,231	60,831	47,340	62,291	2.40%	12.00%	27,713	36,465	39,909	52,513	56,372	74,175
Sanitation Worker	39,534	63,103	40,483	64,618	41,454	66,168	42,449	67,757	43,468	69,383	2.40%	12.00%	25,446	40,616	36,645	58,492	51,761	82,619
School Custodian	37,754	77,331	38,660	79,187	39,588	81,087	40,538	83,033	41,511	85,026	2.40%	12.00%	24,300	49,774	34,995	71,680	49,430	101,247
School Medical Inspector	102,285	132,722	104,740	135,907	107,254	139,169	109,828	142,509	112,464	145,929	2.40%	12.00%	65,836	85,426	94,811	123,023	133,919	173,769
School Medical Inspector	64,170	69,339	65,710	71,003	67,287	72,707	68,902	74,452	70,555	76,238	2.40%	12.00%	41,303	44,630	59,480	64,271	84,015	90,783
School Psycholgist	48,208	93,781	49,365	96,031	50,550	98,336	51,763	100,696	53,005	103,113	2.40%	12.00%	31,029	60,362	44,685	86,927	63,117	122,784

Chart III - U.S. States & Cities - Job Titles - Salaries - Pension Estimates

NY-New York City	2010 (Min)	2010 (Max)	2011 (Min)	2011 (Max)	2012 (Min)	2012 (Max)	2013 (Min)	2013 (Max)	2014 (Min)	2014 (Max)	5-Year Average % Raise	5-Year Cumulative Raise Estimate**	20-Year Annual Pension Benefit Estimate (Min.)***	20-Year Annual Pension Benefit Estimate (Max.)	25-Year Annual Pension Benefit Estimate (Min.)	25-Year Annual Pension Benefit Estimate (Max.)	30-Year Annual Pension Benefit Estimate (Min.)	30-Year Annual Pension Benefit Estimate (Max.)
School Secretary	31,068	58,479	31,813	59,882	32,577	61,319	33,359	62,791	34,159	64,298	2.40%	12.00%	19,997	37,640	28,797	54,205	40,676	76,564
School Social Worker	48,208	93,781	49,365	96,031	50,550	98,336	51,763	100,696	53,005	103,113	2.40%	12.00%	31,029	60,362	44,685	86,927	63,117	122,784
Scientist (Water Ecology) I-III	43,066	77,457	44,099	79,316	45,158	81,220	46,241	83,169	47,351	85,165	2.40%	12.00%	27,719	49,855	39,919	71,797	56,385	101,413
Senior Air Pollution Inspector	49,474	60,576	50,661	62,030	51,877	63,519	53,122	65,044	54,397	66,605	2.40%	12.00%	31,844	38,990	45,858	56,150	64,774	79,311
Senior Custodial Supervisor	35,501	46,961	36,353	48,088	37,226	49,242	38,119	50,424	39,034	51,634	2.40%	12.00%	22,850	30,227	32,907	43,529	46,480	61,485
Senior Detective Investigator	51,188	68,277	52,416	69,916	53,674	71,594	54,962	73,312	56,282	75,072	2.40%	12.00%	32,947	43,947	47,447	63,288	67,019	89,394
Senior Economist	53,088	69,938	54,362	71,616	55,667	73,335	57,003	75,095	58,371	76,897	2.40%	12.00%	34,170	45,015	49,208	64,827	69,506	91,567
Senior Estimator (Mechanical)	64,217	80,872	65,758	82,813	67,336	84,801	68,952	86,836	70,607	88,920	2.40%	12.00%	41,333	52,053	59,524	74,962	84,077	105,884
Senior Fingerprint Technician	35,525	44,105	36,378	45,163	37,251	46,247	38,145	47,357	39,060	48,494	2.40%	12.00%	22,866	28,388	32,929	40,882	46,512	57,745
Senior Public Health Educator	55,376	64,410	56,705	65,956	58,066	67,539	59,459	69,160	60,886	70,820	2.40%	12.00%	35,643	41,458	51,329	59,703	72,502	84,331
Senior Rent Examiner	28,824	36,586	29,515	37,464	30,224	38,363	30,949	39,284	31,692	40,227	2.40%	12.00%	18,552	23,549	26,717	33,913	37,738	47,901
Senior Transportation Inspector	40,634	50,144	41,609	51,348	42,607	52,580	43,630	53,842	44,677	55,134	2.40%	12.00%	26,154	32,275	37,664	46,480	53,200	65,652
Sergeant D/A Spec Assign (Harbor) (Recur Ns)	88,511	96,427	90,635	98,741	92,810	101,111	95,038	103,538	97,319	106,023	2.40%	12.00%	56,970	62,065	82,042	89,380	115,884	126,249
Sergeant D/A Special Assignment (Recur Ns)	88,511	96,427	90,635	98,741	92,810	101,111	95,038	103,538	97,319	106,023	2.40%	12.00%	56,970	62,065	82,042	89,380	115,884	126,249
Sergeant D/A Supervisor Detective Squad (Recur Ns)	88,511	96,427	90,635	98,741	92,810	101,111	95,038	103,538	97,319	106,023	2.40%	12.00%	56,970	62,065	82,042	89,380	115,884	126,249
Sheet Metal Worker	59,300	59,300	60,723	60,723	62,181	62,181	63,673	63,673	65,201	65,201	2.40%	12.00%	38,168	38,168	54,966	54,966	77,640	77,640
Special Officer	32,456	40,179	33,235	41,144	34,033	42,131	34,850	43,142	35,686	44,178	2.40%	12.00%	20,891	25,861	30,085	37,243	42,494	52,606
Staff Analyst	57,491	64,029	58,871	65,566	60,284	67,139	61,731	68,751	63,212	70,401	2.40%	12.00%	37,004	41,212	53,290	59,350	75,272	83,831
Statistician	43,056	56,236	44,089	57,585	45,147	58,967	46,231	60,383	47,340	61,832	2.40%	12.00%	27,713	36,196	39,909	52,126	56,372	73,628
Superintendent Of Construction	47,425	59,725	48,563	61,159	49,729	62,627	50,922	64,130	52,145	65,669	2.40%	12.00%	30,525	38,442	43,959	55,361	62,092	78,197
Supervising Audiologist	60,819	69,845	62,279	71,522	63,774	73,238	65,304	74,996	66,872	76,796	2.40%	12.00%	39,146	44,956	56,375	64,741	79,629	91,446
Supervising Claim Examiner	41,907	52,008	42,913	53,256	43,942	54,534	44,997	55,843	46,077	57,183	2.40%	12.00%	26,973	33,475	38,844	48,207	54,867	68,093
Supervising Economist	56,319	76,446	57,671	78,280	59,055	80,159	60,472	82,083	61,924	84,053	2.40%	12.00%	36,250	49,204	52,203	70,859	73,737	100,088
Supervising Pharmacist	69,797	76,471	71,472	78,306	73,187	80,186	74,944	82,110	76,743	84,081	2.40%	12.00%	44,925	49,221	64,696	70,883	91,383	100,121
Supervising Public Health Adviser	51,115	62,759	52,342	64,265	53,598	65,808	54,885	67,387	56,202	69,004	2.40%	12.00%	32,900	40,395	47,380	58,173	66,924	82,169
Supervisor (Sanitation)	70,158	84,758	71,841	86,792	73,566	88,875	75,331	91,008	77,139	93,192	2.40%	12.00%	45,157	54,554	65,031	78,564	91,855	110,971
Supervisor Machinist	51,448	51,448	52,683	52,683	53,948	53,948	55,242	55,242	56,568	56,568	2.40%	12.00%	33,115	33,115	47,689	47,689	67,360	67,360
Surveyor I-IV	59,157	90,170	60,577	92,334	62,031	94,550	63,519	96,819	65,044	99,143	2.40%	12.00%	38,076	58,038	54,834	83,580	77,453	118,057
Tax Auditor	33,056	43,172	33,849	44,208	34,661	45,269	35,493	46,356	36,345	47,468	2.40%	12.00%	21,276	27,788	30,640	40,017	43,279	56,524
Taxi And Limousine Inspector	37,212	46,441	38,105	47,556	39,019	48,697	39,956	49,866	40,915	51,063	2.40%	12.00%	23,951	29,892	34,492	43,047	48,720	60,804
Teacher Aide	20,014	30,507	20,495	31,239	20,987	31,989	21,490	32,757	22,006	33,543	2.40%	12.00%	12,882	19,636	18,552	28,278	26,204	39,942
Teacher Special Education	40,700	98,247	41,676	100,605	42,677	103,019	43,701	105,492	44,750	108,024	2.40%	12.00%	26,196	63,237	37,725	91,067	53,287	128,632
Technical Support Aide	26,907	36,730	27,553	37,612	28,214	38,514	28,891	39,439	29,585	40,385	2.40%	12.00%	17,319	23,641	24,941	34,046	35,229	48,090
Telecommunication Manager	51,974	168,391	53,221	172,433	54,499	176,571	55,807	180,809	57,146	185,148	2.40%	12.00%	33,453	108,385	48,176	156,086	68,048	220,470
Telecommunications Associate I-III	41,127	74,605	42,114	76,396	43,125	78,229	44,160	80,107	45,220	82,029	2.40%	12.00%	26,472	48,020	38,122	69,153	53,847	97,678

Chart III - U.S. States & Cities - Job Titles - Salaries - Pension Estimates

NY-New York City	2010 (Min)	2010 (Max)	2011 (Min)	2011 (Max)	2012 (Min)	2012 (Max)	2013 (Min)	2013 (Max)	2014 (Min)	2014 (Max)	5-Year Average % Raise	5-Year Cumulative Raise Estimate**	20-Year Annual Pension Benefit Estimate (Min.)***	20-Year Annual Pension Benefit Estimate (Max.)	25-Year Annual Pension Benefit Estimate (Min.)	25-Year Annual Pension Benefit Estimate (Max.)	30-Year Annual Pension Benefit Estimate (Min.)	30-Year Annual Pension Benefit Estimate (Max.)
Telecommunications Specialist	68,868	93,474	70,521	95,717	72,213	98,014	73,946	100,367	75,721	102,776	2.40%	12.00%	44,327	60,164	63,835	86,643	90,167	122,383
Telephone Service Technician I-II	49,593	69,875	50,784	71,552	52,003	73,269	53,251	75,028	54,529	76,828	2.40%	12.00%	31,921	44,975	45,969	64,769	64,931	91,485
Television Lighting Technician	38,504	45,444	39,428	46,535	40,374	47,651	41,343	48,795	42,335	49,966	2.40%	12.00%	24,783	29,250	35,690	42,123	50,412	59,498
Title Examiner	37,756	49,275	38,662	50,457	39,590	51,668	40,540	52,908	41,513	54,178	2.40%	12.00%	24,302	31,716	34,997	45,674	49,433	64,514
Traffic Control Inspector I-II	47,322	64,141	48,458	65,680	49,621	67,257	50,811	68,871	52,031	70,524	2.40%	12.00%	30,459	41,284	43,864	59,454	61,957	83,978
Traffic Enforcement Agent I-II	32,842	37,299	33,631	38,194	34,438	39,111	35,264	40,049	36,111	41,010	2.40%	12.00%	21,139	24,007	30,442	34,573	43,000	48,834
Training Development Specialist I-II	49,510	84,142	50,698	86,162	51,915	88,230	53,161	90,347	54,437	92,515	2.40%	12.00%	31,867	54,158	45,892	77,993	64,822	110,165
Transportation Inspector	35,955	44,523	36,818	45,591	37,702	46,685	38,607	47,806	39,533	48,953	2.40%	12.00%	23,142	28,657	33,328	41,269	47,075	58,292
Unemployment Insurance Specialist II	30,602	52,006	31,336	53,254	32,088	54,532	32,858	55,841	33,647	57,181	2.40%	12.00%	19,697	33,473	28,365	48,205	40,066	68,090
University Architect	63,667	75,059	65,195	76,861	66,760	78,705	68,362	80,594	70,003	82,529	2.40%	12.00%	40,979	48,312	59,015	69,574	83,358	98,273
University Engineer	63,667	75,059	65,195	76,861	66,760	78,705	68,362	80,594	70,003	82,529	2.40%	12.00%	40,979	48,312	59,015	69,574	83,358	98,273
Urban Park Ranger	36,934	36,934	37,820	37,820	38,728	38,728	39,657	39,657	40,609	40,609	2.40%	12.00%	23,772	23,772	34,235	34,235	48,356	48,356
Water Plant Operator	38,767	46,205	39,697	47,314	40,650	48,449	41,625	49,612	42,624	50,803	2.40%	12.00%	24,952	29,740	35,934	42,828	50,756	60,495
Watershed Maintainer	38,767	49,306	39,697	50,490	40,650	51,702	41,625	52,942	42,624	54,213	2.40%	12.00%	24,952	31,736	35,934	45,703	50,756	64,556
Welder	54,432	54,432	55,739	55,739	57,077	57,077	58,446	58,446	59,849	59,849	2.40%	12.00%	35,035	35,035	50,455	50,455	71,267	71,267
Worker's Compensation Benefits Examiner I-V	39,228	62,624	40,170	64,127	41,134	65,666	42,121	67,242	43,132	68,856	2.40%	12.00%	25,249	40,308	36,362	58,047	51,361	81,991
X-Ray Technician I-III	45,662	56,723	46,757	58,084	47,880	59,478	49,029	60,906	50,205	62,367	2.40%	12.00%	29,390	36,510	42,325	52,578	59,783	74,265

http://www.nyc.gov/html/dcas/home.html

Chart III - U.S. States & Cities - Job Titles - Salaries - Pension Estimates

TX-Dallas	2010 (Min)	2010 (Max)	2011 (Min)	2011 (Max)	2012 (Min)	2012 (Max)	2013 (Min)	2013 (Max)	2014 (Min)	2014 (Max)	5-Year Average % Raise	5-Year Cumulative Raise Estimate**	20-Year Annual Pension Benefit Estimate (Min.)***	20-Year Annual Pension Benefit Estimate (Max.)	25-Year Annual Pension Benefit Estimate (Min.)	25-Year Annual Pension Benefit Estimate (Max.)	30-Year Annual Pension Benefit Estimate (Min.)	30-Year Annual Pension Benefit Estimate (Max.)
911/311 Call Taker	30,942	51,055	31,654	52,229	32,382	53,430	33,127	54,659	33,889	55,917	2.30%	11.50%	19,588	32,320	28,071	46,317	39,456	65,103
911/311 Call Taker Trainee	28,130	46,413	28,777	47,481	29,439	48,573	30,116	49,690	30,808	50,833	2.30%	11.50%	17,807	29,381	25,519	42,106	35,870	59,185
Accountant I-III	34,036	69,992	34,819	71,602	35,620	73,249	36,439	74,934	37,277	76,657	2.30%	11.50%	21,546	44,308	30,878	63,497	43,402	89,252
Administrative Audit Assistant	49,833	84,691	50,979	86,639	52,151	88,632	53,351	90,671	54,578	92,756	2.30%	11.50%	31,546	53,613	45,208	76,832	63,545	107,995
Administrative Hearing Officer I-II	34,036	69,992	34,819	71,602	35,620	73,249	36,439	74,934	37,277	76,657	2.30%	11.50%	21,546	44,308	30,878	63,497	43,402	89,252
Animal Research Technician	30,942	51,055	31,654	52,229	32,382	53,430	33,127	54,659	33,889	55,917	2.30%	11.50%	19,588	32,320	28,071	46,317	39,456	65,103
Animal Services Officer	28,130	46,413	28,777	47,481	29,439	48,573	30,116	49,690	30,808	50,833	2.30%	11.50%	17,807	29,381	25,519	42,106	35,870	59,185
Arborist	37,440	63,629	38,301	65,093	39,182	66,590	40,083	68,121	41,005	69,688	2.30%	11.50%	23,701	40,280	33,966	57,724	47,742	81,138
Architect	54,816	93,160	56,077	95,302	57,366	97,494	58,686	99,737	60,036	102,031	2.30%	11.50%	34,700	58,974	49,729	84,514	69,899	118,794
Architect Assistant	45,303	76,992	46,345	78,763	47,411	80,574	48,501	82,428	49,617	84,323	2.30%	11.50%	28,678	48,739	41,099	69,847	57,769	98,177
Audiovisual Technician	28,130	46,413	28,777	47,481	29,439	48,573	30,116	49,690	30,808	50,833	2.30%	11.50%	17,807	29,381	25,519	42,106	35,870	59,185
Audit Accountant	66,328	112,724	67,853	115,316	69,414	117,969	71,010	120,682	72,644	123,458	2.30%	11.50%	41,988	71,358	60,172	102,263	84,579	143,74
Auditor	49,833	84,691	50,979	86,639	52,151	88,632	53,351	90,671	54,578	92,756	2.30%	11.50%	31,546	53,613	45,208	76,832	63,545	107,99
Automotive Body Repairer II	30,942	51,055	31,654	52,229	32,382	53,430	33,127	54,659	33,889	55,917	2.30%	11.50%	19,588	32,320	28,071	46,317	39,456	65,103
Bailiff	34,036	57,845	34,819	59,176	35,620	60,537	36,439	61,929	37,277	63,353	2.30%	11.50%	21,546	36,618	30,878	52,477	43,402	73,762
Benefits Specialist	41,185	69,992	42,132	71,602	43,101	73,249	44,092	74,934	45,106	76,657	2.30%	11.50%	26,071	44,308	37,363	63,497	52,517	89,252
Branch Delivery Assistant	28,130	46,413	28,777	47,481	29,439	48,573	30,116	49,690	30,808	50,833	2.30%	11.50%	17,807	29,381	25,519	42,106	35,870	59,185
Budget Analyst I-II	37,440	69,992	38,301	71,602	39,182	73,249	40,083	74,934	41,005	76,657	2.30%	11.50%	23,701	44,308	33,966	63,497	47,742	89,252
Buyer I-III	34,036	69,992	34,819	71,602	35,620	73,249	36,439	74,934	37,277	76,657	2.30%	11.50%	21,546	44,308	30,878	63,497	43,402	89,252
Carpenter	25,572	42,195	26,161	43,165	26,762	44,158	27,378	45,173	28,007	46,212	2.30%	11.50%	16,188	26,711	23,199	38,279	32,609	53,805
Caseworker I-II	37,440	69,992	38,301	71,602	39,182	73,249	40,083	74,934	41,005	76,657	2.30%	11.50%	23,701	44,308	33,966	63,497	47,742	89,252
Cash Management Analyst	45,303	76,992	46,345	78,763	47,411	80,574	48,501	82,428	49,617	84,323	2.30%	11.50%	28,678	48,739	41,099	69,847	57,769	98,177
Chemist	41,185	69,992	42,132	71,602	43,101	73,249	44,092	74,934	45,106	76,657	2.30%	11.50%	26,071	44,308	37,363	63,497	52,517	89,252
City Archivist	45,303	76,992	46,345	78,763	47,411	80,574	48,501	82,428	49,617	84,323	2.30%	11.50%	28,678	48,739	41,099	69,847	57,769	98,177
City Controller	80,257	136,396	82,103	139,533	83,991	142,742	85,923	146,025	87,899	149,384	2.30%	11.50%	50,806	86,344	72,809	123,738	102,341	173,92
City Marshal	66,328	112,724	67,853	115,316	69,414	117,969	71,010	120,682	72,644	123,458	2.30%	11.50%	41,988	71,358	60,172	102,263	84,579	143,74
Collector	30,942	51,055	31,654	52,229	32,382	53,430	33,127	54,659	33,889	55,917	2.30%	11.50%	19,588	32,320	28,071	46,317	39,456	65,103
Community Outreach Representative	34,036	57,845	34,819	59,176	35,620	60,537	36,439	61,929	37,277	63,353	2.30%	11.50%	21,546	36,618	30,878	52,477	43,402	73,762
Computer Aided Drafting Technician	30,942	51,055	31,654	52,229	32,382	53,430	33,127	54,659	33,889	55,917	2.30%	11.50%	19,588	32,320	28,071	46,317	39,456	65,103
Computer Forms Analyst	34,036	57,845	34,819	59,176	35,620	60,537	36,439	61,929	37,277	63,353	2.30%	11.50%	21,546	36,618	30,878	52,477	43,402	73,762
Computer Operator I-II	25,572	57,845	26,161	59,176	26,762	60,537	27,378	61,929	28,007	63,353	2.30%	11.50%	16,188	36,618	23,199	52,477	32,609	73,762
Construction Contract Administrator	41,185	69,992	42,132	71,602	43,101	73,249	44,092	74,934	45,106	76,657	2.30%	11.50%	26,071	44,308	37,363	63,497	52,517	89,252
Contract Compliance Administrator	34,036	57,845	34,819	59,176	35,620	60,537	36,439	61,929	37,277	63,353	2.30%	11.50%	21,546	36,618	30,878	52,477	43,402	73,762
Coordinator I-V	37,440	84,691	38,301	86,639	39,182	88,632	40,083	90,671	41,005	92,756	2.30%	11.50%	23,701	53,613	33,966	76,832	47,742	107,99
Court Specialist I-II	25,572	46,413	26,161	47,481	26,762	48,573	27,378	49,690	28,007	50,833	2.30%	11.50%	16,188	29,381	23,199	42,106	32,609	59,185
Court Specialist Supervisor	37,440	63,629	38,301	65,093	39,182	66,590	40,083	68,121	41,005	69,688	2.30%	11.50%	23,701	40,280	33,966	57,724	47,742	81,138
Crime Scene Analyst	41,185	69,992	42,132	71,602	43,101	73,249	44,092	74,934	45,106	76,657	2.30%	11.50%	26,071	44,308	37,363	63,497	52,517	89,252
Crime Scene Technician	34,036	57,845	34,819	59,176	35,620	60,537	36,439	61,929	37,277	63,353	2.30%	11.50%	21,546	36,618	30,878	52,477	43,402	73,762
Crime Technician	30,942	51,055	31,654	52,229	32,382	53,430	33,127	54,659	33,889	55,917	2.30%	11.50%	19,588	32,320	28,071	46,317	39,456	65,103

Chart III - U.S. States & Cities - Job Titles - Salaries - Pension Estimates

TX-Dallas	2010 (Min)	2010 (Max)	2011 (Min)	2011 (Max)	2012 (Min)	2012 (Max)	2013 (Min)	2013 (Max)	2014 (Min)	2014 (Max)	5-Year Average % Raise	5-Year Cumulative Raise Estimate**	20-Year Annual Pension Benefit Estimate (Min.)***	20-Year Annual Pension Benefit Estimate (Max.)	25-Year Annual Pension Benefit Estimate (Min.)	25-Year Annual Pension Benefit Estimate (Max.)	30-Year Annual Pension Benefit Estimate (Min.)	30-Year Annual Pension Benefit Estimate (Max.)
Customer Service Representative I-II	25,572	46,413	26,161	47,481	26,762	48,573	27,378	49,690	28,007	50,833	2.30%	11.50%	16,188	29,381	23,199	42,106	32,609	59,185
Database Analyst	54,816	93,160	56,077	95,302	57,366	97,494	58,686	99,737	60,036	102,031	2.30%	11.50%	34,700	58,974	49,729	84,514	69,899	118,794
Departmental Technology Analyst	45,303	76,992	46,345	78,763	47,411	80,574	48,501	82,428	49,617	84,323	2.30%	11.50%	28,678	48,739	41,099	69,847	57,769	98,177
Deputy City Marshal	34,036	57,845	34,819	59,176	35,620	60,537	36,439	61,929	37,277	63,353	2.30%	11.50%	21,546	36,618	30,878	52,477	43,402	73,762
Design Technician I-II	25,572	57,845	26,161	59,176	26,762	60,537	27,378	61,929	28,007	63,353	2.30%	11.50%	16,188	36,618	23,199	52,477	32,609	73,762
Detention Officer	28,130	46,413	28,777	47,481	29,439	48,573	30,116	49,690	30,808	50,833	2.30%	11.50%	17,807	29,381	25,519	42,106	35,870	59,185
Director I-II	97,110	181,543	99,344	185,719	101,629	189,990	103,966	194,360	106,357	198,830	2.30%	11.50%	61,474	114,923	88,098	164,695	123,831	231,497
Drafter	30,942	51,055	31,654	52,229	32,382	53,430	33,127	54,659	33,889	55,917	2.30%	11.50%	19,588	32,320	28,071	46,317	39,456	65,103
Economic Development Analyst	45,303	76,992	46,345	78,763	47,411	80,574	48,501	82,428	49,617	84,323	2.30%	11.50%	28,678	48,739	41,099	69,847	57,769	98,177
Election Manager	54,816	93,160	56,077	95,302	57,366	97,494	58,686	99,737	60,036	102,031	2.30%	11.50%	34,700	58,974	49,729	84,514	69,899	118,794
Electrician	34,036	57,845	34,819	59,176	35,620	60,537	36,439	61,929	37,277	63,353	2.30%	11.50%	21,546	36,618	30,878	52,477	43,402	73,762
Electrician Assistant	28,130	46,413	28,777	47,481	29,439	48,573	30,116	49,690	30,808	50,833	2.30%	11.50%	17,807	29,381	25,519	42,106	35,870	59,185
Engineer	54,816	93,160	56,077	95,302	57,366	97,494	58,686	99,737	60,036	102,031	2.30%	11.50%	34,700	58,974	49,729	84,514	69,899	118,794
Engineer Assistant	45,303	76,992	46,345	78,763	47,411	80,574	48,501	82,428	49,617	84,323	2.30%	11.50%	28,678	48,739	41,099	69,847	57,769	98,177
Environmental Coordinator I-III	41,185	93,160	42,132	95,302	43,101	97,494	44,092	99,737	45,106	102,031	2.30%	11.50%	26,071	58,974	37,363	84,514	52,517	118,794
Environmental Specialist I-III	28,130	63,629	28,777	65,093	29,439	66,590	30,116	68,121	30,808	69,688	2.30%	11.50%	17,807	40,280	25,519	57,724	35,870	81,138
Environmental Specialist Trainee	25,572	42,195	26,161	43,165	26,762	44,158	27,378	45,173	28,007	46,212	2.30%	11.50%	16,188	26,711	23,199	38,279	32,609	53,805
Epidemiologist	49,833	84,691	50,979	86,639	52,151	88,632	53,351	90,671	54,578	92,756	2.30%	11.50%	31,546	53,613	45,208	76,832	63,545	107,995
Equipment Operator	25,572	42,195	26,161	43,165	26,762	44,158	27,378	45,173	28,007	46,212	2.30%	11.50%	16,188	26,711	23,199	38,279	32,609	53,805
Executive Assistant	45,303	76,992	46,345	78,763	47,411	80,574	48,501	82,428	49,617	84,323	2.30%	11.50%	28,678	48,739	41,099	69,847	57,769	98,177
Executive Assistant City Attorney	88,165	169,760	90,193	173,664	92,268	177,658	94,390	181,744	96,561	185,925	2.30%	11.50%	55,812	107,464	79,983	154,005	112,425	216,471
Executive Secretary	30,942	51,055	31,654	52,229	32,382	53,430	33,127	54,659	33,889	55,917	2.30%	11.50%	19,588	32,320	28,071	46,317	39,456	65,103
Fair Housing Administrator	66,328	112,724	67,853	115,316	69,414	117,969	71,010	120,682	72,644	123,458	2.30%	11.50%	41,988	71,358	60,172	102,263	84,579	143,741
Fair Housing Conciliator	37,440	63,629	38,301	65,093	39,182	66,590	40,083	68,121	41,005	69,688	2.30%	11.50%	23,701	40,280	33,966	57,724	47,742	81,138
Fair Housing Investigator	34,036	57,845	34,819	59,176	35,620	60,537	36,439	61,929	37,277	63,353	2.30%	11.50%	21,546	36,618	30,878	52,477	43,402	73,762
Financial Specialist	30,942	51,055	31,654	52,229	32,382	53,430	33,127	54,659	33,889	55,917	2.30%	11.50%	19,588	32,320	28,071	46,317	39,456	65,103
Fire and Rescue Officer	45,660	67,435	46,710	68,986	47,784	70,573	48,883	72,196	50,008	73,856	2.30%	11.50%	28,904	42,689	41,422	61,177	58,224	85,991
Fire and Rescue Officer Trainee I-III	45,660	45,660	46,710	46,710	47,784	47,784	48,883	48,883	50,008	50,008	2.30%	11.50%	28,904	28,904	41,422	41,422	58,224	58,224
Fire Assistant Chief	71,954	129,452	73,609	132,429	75,302	135,475	77,034	138,591	78,806	141,779	2.30%	11.50%	45,550	81,948	65,276	117,438	91,753	165,073
Fire Battalion Section Chief	64,924	97,876	66,417	100,127	67,945	102,430	69,507	104,786	71,106	107,196	2.30%	11.50%	41,099	61,959	58,899	88,793	82,788	124,808
Fire Captain	59,173	89,185	60,534	91,236	61,926	93,335	63,350	95,481	64,807	97,678	2.30%	11.50%	37,459	56,457	53,681	80,908	75,455	113,726
Fire Chief	94,692	159,415	96,870	163,082	99,098	166,833	101,377	170,670	103,709	174,595	2.30%	11.50%	59,943	100,916	85,904	144,621	120,748	203,280
Fire Deputy Chief	70,993	103,149	72,626	105,522	74,297	107,949	76,006	110,431	77,754	112,971	2.30%	11.50%	44,941	65,297	64,405	93,577	90,528	131,532
Fire Driver - Engineer	46,941	74,343	48,021	76,053	49,125	77,802	50,255	79,591	51,411	81,422	2.30%	11.50%	29,716	47,062	42,585	67,443	59,858	94,799
Fire Lieutenant	53,923	81,424	55,164	83,297	56,432	85,213	57,730	87,173	59,058	89,178	2.30%	11.50%	34,135	51,545	48,919	73,868	68,761	103,829
Fire Prevention Captain	59,173	89,185	60,534	91,236	61,926	93,335	63,350	95,481	64,807	97,678	2.30%	11.50%	37,459	56,457	53,681	80,908	75,455	113,726
Fire Prevention Lieutenant	53,923	81,424	55,164	83,297	56,432	85,213	57,730	87,173	59,058	89,178	2.30%	11.50%	34,135	51,545	48,919	73,868	68,761	103,829
Fire Prevention Officer	46,941	67,435	48,021	68,986	49,125	70,573	50,255	72,196	51,411	73,856	2.30%	11.50%	29,716	42,689	42,585	61,177	59,858	85,991
Fire Prevention Officer Trainee I-III	45,660	45,660	46,710	46,710	47,784	47,784	48,883	48,883	50,008	50,008	2.30%	11.50%	28,904	28,904	41,422	41,422	58,224	58,224

Chart III - U.S. States & Cities - Job Titles - Salaries - Pension Estimates

TX-Dallas	2010 (Min)	2010 (Max)	2011 (Min)	2011 (Max)	2012 (Min)	2012 (Max)	2013 (Min)	2013 (Max)	2014 (Min)	2014 (Max)	5-Year Average % Raise	5-Year Cumulative Raise Estimate**	20-Year Annual Pension Benefit Estimate (Min.)***	20-Year Annual Pension Benefit Estimate (Max.)	25-Year Annual Pension Benefit Estimate (Min.)	25-Year Annual Pension Benefit Estimate (Max.)	30-Year Annual Pension Benefit Estimate (Min.)	30-Year Annual Pension Benefit Estimate (Max.)
Fire Prevention Section Chief	64,924	97,766	66,417	100,015	67,945	102,315	69,507	104,668	71,106	107,076	2.30%	11.50%	41,099	61,890	58,899	88,693	82,788	124,668
Fire Second Driver	46,062	67,435	47,121	68,986	48,205	70,573	49,314	72,196	50,448	73,856	2.30%	11.50%	29,159	42,689	41,787	61,177	58,736	85,991
Fire Senior Prevention Officer	46,941	74,343	48,021	76,053	49,125	77,802	50,255	79,591	51,411	81,422	2.30%	11.50%	29,716	47,062	42,585	67,443	59,858	94,799
Fire Technician Specialist	49,833	84,691	50,979	86,639	52,151	88,632	53,351	90,671	54,578	92,756	2.30%	11.50%	31,546	53,613	45,208	76,832	63,545	107,995
First Assistant City Manager	129,254	219,667	132,227	224,719	135,268	229,888	138,379	235,175	141,562	240,584	2.30%	11.50%	81,822	139,057	117,259	199,281	164,820	280,111
Forensic Video Specialist	37,440	63,629	38,301	65,093	39,182	66,590	40,083	68,121	41,005	69,688	2.30%	11.50%	23,701	40,280	33,966	57,724	47,742	81,138
Fuel Transport Operator	30,942	51,055	31,654	52,229	32,382	53,430	33,127	54,659	33,889	55,917	2.30%	11.50%	19,588	32,320	28,071	46,317	39,456	65,103
Fund Analyst	45,303	76,992	46,345	78,763	47,411	80,574	48,501	82,428	49,617	84,323	2.30%	11.50%	28,678	48,739	41,099	69,847	57,769	98,177
Fund Development Representative	41,185	69,992	42,132	71,602	43,101	73,249	44,092	74,934	45,106	76,657	2.30%	11.50%	26,071	44,308	37,363	63,497	52,517	89,252
Geographic Information Systems Analyst I-III	41,185	84,691	42,132	86,639	43,101	88,632	44,092	90,671	45,106	92,756	2.30%	11.50%	26,071	53,613	37,363	76,832	52,517	107,995
Geographic Information Systems Data Administrator	41,185	69,992	42,132	71,602	43,101	73,249	44,092	74,934	45,106	76,657	2.30%	11.50%	26,071	44,308	37,363	63,497	52,517	89,252
Geographic Information Systems Manager	66,328	112,724	67,853	115,316	69,414	117,969	71,010	120,682	72,644	123,458	2.30%	11.50%	41,988	71,358	60,172	102,263	84,579	143,741
Geographic Information Systems Support Technician	30,942	51,055	31,654	52,229	32,382	53,430	33,127	54,659	33,889	55,917	2.30%	11.50%	19,588	32,320	28,071	46,317	39,456	65,103
Geographic Information Systems Technician Manager	60,297	102,476	61,684	104,833	63,103	107,244	64,554	109,710	66,039	112,234	2.30%	11.50%	38,171	64,871	54,702	92,966	76,889	130,673
Graphics Designer	41,185	69,992	42,132	71,602	43,101	73,249	44,092	74,934	45,106	76,657	2.30%	11.50%	26,071	44,308	37,363	63,497	52,517	89,252
Greens Superintendent	41,185	69,992	42,132	71,602	43,101	73,249	44,092	74,934	45,106	76,657	2.30%	11.50%	26,071	44,308	37,363	63,497	52,517	89,252
Hazardous Waste Inspector	34,036	57,845	34,819	59,176	35,620	60,537	36,439	61,929	37,277	63,353	2.30%	11.50%	21,546	36,618	30,878	52,477	43,402	73,762
Heating, Ventilation, Air Conditioning Mechanic	25,572	42,195	26,161	43,165	26,762	44,158	27,378	45,173	28,007	46,212	2.30%	11.50%	16,188	26,711	23,199	38,279	32,609	53,805
Heavy Equipment Operator	28,130	46,413	28,777	47,481	29,439	48,573	30,116	49,690	30,808	50,833	2.30%	11.50%	17,807	29,381	25,519	42,106	35,870	59,185
Housing Compliance Administrator	72,960	123,996	74,639	126,848	76,355	129,765	78,111	132,750	79,908	135,803	2.30%	11.50%	46,187	78,494	66,189	112,488	93,037	158,115
Human Resources Analyst I-II	37,440	69,992	38,301	71,602	39,182	73,249	40,083	74,934	41,005	76,657	2.30%	11.50%	23,701	44,308	33,966	63,497	47,742	89,252
Human Resources Assistant	37,440	63,629	38,301	65,093	39,182	66,590	40,083	68,121	41,005	69,688	2.30%	11.50%	23,701	40,280	33,966	57,724	47,742	81,138
Human Services Program Specialist	41,185	69,992	42,132	71,602	43,101	73,249	44,092	74,934	45,106	76,657	2.30%	11.50%	26,071	44,308	37,363	63,497	52,517	89,252
Information Technology Analyst I-II	41,185	76,992	42,132	78,763	43,101	80,574	44,092	82,428	45,106	84,323	2.30%	11.50%	26,071	48,739	37,363	69,847	52,517	98,177
Information Technology Architect	72,960	123,996	74,639	126,848	76,355	129,765	78,111	132,750	79,908	135,803	2.30%	11.50%	46,187	78,494	66,189	112,488	93,037	158,115
Information Technology Consultant	60,297	102,476	61,684	104,833	63,103	107,244	64,554	109,710	66,039	112,234	2.30%	11.50%	38,171	64,871	54,702	92,966	76,889	130,673
Information Technology Engineer	54,816	93,160	56,077	95,302	57,366	97,494	58,686	99,737	60,036	102,031	2.30%	11.50%	34,700	58,974	49,729	84,514	69,899	118,794
Information Technology Manager	66,328	112,724	67,853	115,316	69,414	117,969	71,010	120,682	72,644	123,458	2.30%	11.50%	41,988	71,358	60,172	102,263	84,579	143,741
Inspector I-III	28,130	63,629	28,777	65,093	29,439	66,590	30,116	68,121	30,808	69,688	2.30%	11.50%	17,807	40,280	25,519	57,724	35,870	81,138
Instructor	37,440	63,629	38,301	65,093	39,182	66,590	40,083	68,121	41,005	69,688	2.30%	11.50%	23,701	40,280	33,966	57,724	47,742	81,138
Intern I-II	25,572	46,413	26,161	47,481	26,762	48,573	27,378	49,690	28,007	50,833	2.30%	11.50%	16,188	29,381	23,199	42,106	32,609	59,185
Internal Control Specialist	41,185	69,992	42,132	71,602	43,101	73,249	44,092	74,934	45,106	76,657	2.30%	11.50%	26,071	44,308	37,363	63,497	52,517	89,252

Chart III - U.S. States & Cities - Job Titles - Salaries - Pension Estimates

TX-Dallas	2010 (Min)	2010 (Max)	2011 (Min)	2011 (Max)	2012 (Min)	2012 (Max)	2013 (Min)	2013 (Max)	2014 (Min)	2014 (Max)	5-Year Average % Raise	5-Year Cumulative Raise Estimate**	20-Year Annual Pension Benefit Estimate (Min.)***	20-Year Annual Pension Benefit Estimate (Max.)	25-Year Annual Pension Benefit Estimate (Min.)	25-Year Annual Pension Benefit Estimate (Max.)	30-Year Annual Pension Benefit Estimate (Min.)	30-Year Annual Pension Benefit Estimate (Max.)
Judicial Hearing Officer	66,328	112,724	67,853	115,316	69,414	117,969	71,010	120,682	72,644	123,458	2.30%	11.50%	41,988	71,358	60,172	102,263	84,579	143,741
Laborer I-II	23,247	42,195	23,782	43,165	24,329	44,158	24,888	45,173	25,461	46,212	2.30%	11.50%	14,716	26,711	21,090	38,279	29,644	53,805
Landscape Architect	49,833	84,691	50,979	86,639	52,151	88,632	53,351	90,671	54,578	92,756	2.30%	11.50%	31,546	53,613	45,208	76,832	63,545	107,995
Lead Custodian	25,572	42,195	26,161	43,165	26,762	44,158	27,378	45,173	28,007	46,212	2.30%	11.50%	16,188	26,711	23,199	38,279	32,609	53,805
Legal Assistant	41,185	67,954	42,132	69,517	43,101	71,116	44,092	72,752	45,106	74,425	2.30%	11.50%	26,071	43,018	37,363	61,648	52,517	86,653
Legal Secretary	25,572	42,195	26,161	43,165	26,762	44,158	27,378	45,173	28,007	46,212	2.30%	11.50%	16,188	26,711	23,199	38,279	32,609	53,805
Librarian I-II	41,185	76,992	42,132	78,763	43,101	80,574	44,092	82,428	45,106	84,323	2.30%	11.50%	26,071	48,739	37,363	69,847	52,517	98,177
Library Associate	30,942	51,055	31,654	52,229	32,382	53,430	33,127	54,659	33,889	55,917	2.30%	11.50%	19,588	32,320	28,071	46,317	39,456	65,103
Litigation Manager	60,297	102,476	61,684	104,833	63,103	107,244	64,554	109,710	66,039	112,234	2.30%	11.50%	38,171	64,871	54,702	92,966	76,889	130,673
Loan Services Representative	37,440	63,629	38,301	65,093	39,182	66,590	40,083	68,121	41,005	69,688	2.30%	11.50%	23,701	40,280	33,966	57,724	47,742	81,138
Machinist	25,572	42,195	26,161	43,165	26,762	44,158	27,378	45,173	28,007	46,212	2.30%	11.50%	16,188	26,711	23,199	38,279	32,609	53,805
Management Development Associate	41,185	69,992	42,132	71,602	43,101	73,249	44,092	74,934	45,106	76,657	2.30%	11.50%	26,071	44,308	37,363	63,497	52,517	89,252
Manager I-III	45,303	112,724	46,345	115,316	47,411	117,969	48,501	120,682	49,617	123,458	2.30%	11.50%	28,678	71,358	41,099	102,263	57,769	143,741
Master Electrician	45,303	76,992	46,345	78,763	47,411	80,574	48,501	82,428	49,617	84,323	2.30%	11.50%	28,678	48,739	41,099	69,847	57,769	98,177
Mechanic I-II	25,572	51,055	26,161	52,229	26,762	53,430	27,378	54,659	28,007	55,917	2.30%	11.50%	16,188	32,320	23,199	46,317	32,609	65,103
Network Analyst I-II	45,303	84,691	46,345	86,639	47,411	88,632	48,501	90,671	49,617	92,756	2.30%	11.50%	28,678	53,613	41,099	76,832	57,769	107,995
Network Technician	37,440	63,629	38,301	65,093	39,182	66,590	40,083	68,121	41,005	69,688	2.30%	11.50%	23,701	40,280	33,966	57,724	47,742	81,138
Nutritionist	37,440	63,629	38,301	65,093	39,182	66,590	40,083	68,121	41,005	69,688	2.30%	11.50%	23,701	40,280	33,966	57,724	47,742	81,138
Office Assistant I-II	23,247	46,413	23,782	47,481	24,329	48,573	24,888	49,690	25,461	50,833	2.30%	11.50%	14,716	29,381	21,090	42,106	29,644	59,185
Painter	28,130	46,413	28,777	47,481	29,439	48,573	30,116	49,690	30,808	50,833	2.30%	11.50%	17,807	29,381	25,519	42,106	35,870	59,185
Park Planner	54,816	93,160	56,077	95,302	57,366	97,494	58,686	99,737	60,036	102,031	2.30%	11.50%	34,700	58,974	49,729	84,514	69,899	118,794
Park Ranger	45,660	67,435	46,710	68,986	47,784	70,573	48,883	72,196	50,008	73,856	2.30%	11.50%	28,904	42,689	41,422	61,177	58,224	85,991
Park Ranger Supervisor	53,923	81,424	55,164	83,297	56,432	85,213	57,730	87,173	59,058	89,178	2.30%	11.50%	34,135	51,545	48,919	73,868	68,761	103,829
Parking Attendant	23,247	38,358	23,782	39,240	24,329	40,143	24,888	41,066	25,461	42,011	2.30%	11.50%	14,716	24,282	21,090	34,798	29,644	48,913
Parking Enforcement Officer	28,130	46,413	28,777	47,481	29,439	48,573	30,116	49,690	30,808	50,833	2.30%	11.50%	17,807	29,381	25,519	42,106	35,870	59,185
Payroll Specialist	28,130	46,413	28,777	47,481	29,439	48,573	30,116	49,690	30,808	50,833	2.30%	11.50%	17,807	29,381	25,519	42,106	35,870	59,185
Pension Benefits Specialist	41,185	69,992	42,132	71,602	43,101	73,249	44,092	74,934	45,106	76,657	2.30%	11.50%	26,071	44,308	37,363	63,497	52,517	89,252
Photographic Technician	25,572	42,195	26,161	43,165	26,762	44,158	27,378	45,173	28,007	46,212	2.30%	11.50%	16,188	26,711	23,199	38,279	32,609	53,805
Physician	80,257	136,396	82,103	139,533	83,991	142,742	85,923	146,025	87,899	149,384	2.30%	11.50%	50,806	86,344	72,809	123,738	102,341	173,927
Physician Manager	88,282	150,036	90,312	153,487	92,389	157,017	94,514	160,628	96,688	164,323	2.30%	11.50%	55,885	94,978	80,089	136,112	112,573	191,320
Planner I-II	37,440	69,992	38,301	71,602	39,182	73,249	40,083	74,934	41,005	76,657	2.30%	11.50%	23,701	44,308	33,966	63,497	47,742	89,252
Planning Technician	28,130	46,413	28,777	47,481	29,439	48,573	30,116	49,690	30,808	50,833	2.30%	11.50%	17,807	29,381	25,519	42,106	35,870	59,185
Plans Examiner	37,440	63,629	38,301	65,093	39,182	66,590	40,083	68,121	41,005	69,688	2.30%	11.50%	23,701	40,280	33,966	57,724	47,742	81,138
Plumber	25,572	42,195	26,161	43,165	26,762	44,158	27,378	45,173	28,007	46,212	2.30%	11.50%	16,188	26,711	23,199	38,279	32,609	53,805
Police Assistant Chief	71,954	129,452	73,609	132,429	75,302	135,475	77,034	138,591	78,806	141,779	2.30%	11.50%	45,550	81,948	65,276	117,438	91,753	165,073
Police Auto Pound Attendant	25,572	42,195	26,161	43,165	26,762	44,158	27,378	45,173	28,007	46,212	2.30%	11.50%	16,188	26,711	23,199	38,279	32,609	53,805
Police Cadet	28,130	46,413	28,777	47,481	29,439	48,573	30,116	49,690	30,808	50,833	2.30%	11.50%	17,807	29,381	25,519	42,106	35,870	59,185
Police Captain	64,924	97,876	66,417	100,127	67,945	102,430	69,507	104,786	71,106	107,196	2.30%	11.50%	41,099	61,959	58,899	88,793	82,788	124,808
Police Chief	94,692	193,770	96,870	198,227	99,098	202,786	101,377	207,450	103,709	212,221	2.30%	11.50%	59,943	122,664	85,904	175,788	120,748	247,089
Police Corporal	45,660	67,435	46,710	68,986	47,784	70,573	48,883	72,196	50,008	73,856	2.30%	11.50%	28,904	42,689	41,422	61,177	58,224	85,991
Police Deputy Chief	70,993	103,149	72,626	105,522	74,297	107,949	76,006	110,431	77,754	112,971	2.30%	11.50%	44,941	65,297	64,405	93,577	90,528	131,532
Police Dispatcher	34,036	57,845	34,819	59,176	35,620	60,537	36,439	61,929	37,277	63,353	2.30%	11.50%	21,546	36,618	30,878	52,477	43,402	73,762

Chart III - U.S. States & Cities - Job Titles - Salaries - Pension Estimates

TX-Dallas	2010 (Min)	2010 (Max)	2011 (Min)	2011 (Max)	2012 (Min)	2012 (Max)	2013 (Min)	2013 (Max)	2014 (Min)	2014 (Max)	5-Year Average % Raise	5-Year Cumulative Raise Estimate**	20-Year Annual Pension Benefit Estimate (Min.)***	20-Year Annual Pension Benefit Estimate (Max.)	25-Year Annual Pension Benefit Estimate (Min.)	25-Year Annual Pension Benefit Estimate (Max.)	30-Year Annual Pension Benefit Estimate (Min.)	30-Year Annual Pension Benefit Estimate (Max.)
Police Lieutenant	59,173	89,185	60,534	91,236	61,926	93,335	63,350	95,481	64,807	97,678	2.30%	11.50%	37,459	56,457	53,681	80,908	75,455	113,726
Police Officer	45,660	67,435	46,710	68,986	47,784	70,573	48,883	72,196	50,008	73,856	2.30%	11.50%	28,904	42,689	41,422	61,177	58,224	85,991
Police Officer Trainee I-III	45,660	45,660	46,710	46,710	47,784	47,784	48,883	48,883	50,008	50,008	2.30%	11.50%	28,904	28,904	41,422	41,422	58,224	58,224
Police Report Representative	30,942	51,055	31,654	52,229	32,382	53,430	33,127	54,659	33,889	55,917	2.30%	11.50%	19,588	32,320	28,071	46,317	39,456	65,103
Police Research Specialist	37,440	63,629	38,301	65,093	39,182	66,590	40,083	68,121	41,005	69,688	2.30%	11.50%	23,701	40,280	33,966	57,724	47,742	81,138
Police Senior Corporal	46,941	74,343	48,021	76,053	49,125	77,802	50,255	79,591	51,411	81,422	2.30%	11.50%	29,716	47,062	42,585	67,443	59,858	94,799
Police Sergeant	53,923	81,424	55,164	83,297	56,432	85,213	57,730	87,173	59,058	89,178	2.30%	11.50%	34,135	51,545	48,919	73,868	68,761	103,829
Pool Mechanic	30,942	51,055	31,654	52,229	32,382	53,430	33,127	54,659	33,889	55,917	2.30%	11.50%	19,588	32,320	28,071	46,317	39,456	65,103
Press Operator	25,572	42,195	26,161	43,165	26,762	44,158	27,378	45,173	28,007	46,212	2.30%	11.50%	16,188	26,711	23,199	38,279	32,609	53,805
Programmer/Analyst I-II	41,185	76,992	42,132	78,763	43,101	80,574	44,092	82,428	45,106	84,323	2.30%	11.50%	26,071	48,739	37,363	69,847	52,517	98,177
Programming Analyst Division Manager	72,960	123,996	74,639	126,848	76,355	129,765	78,111	132,750	79,908	135,803	2.30%	11.50%	46,187	78,494	66,189	112,488	93,037	158,115
Programming Analyst Project Manager	66,328	112,724	67,853	115,316	69,414	117,969	71,010	120,682	72,644	123,458	2.30%	11.50%	41,988	71,358	60,172	102,263	84,579	143,741
Project Assistant	34,036	57,845	34,819	59,176	35,620	60,537	36,439	61,929	37,277	63,353	2.30%	11.50%	21,546	36,618	30,878	52,477	43,402	73,762
Project Coordinator I-III	41,185	84,691	42,132	86,639	43,101	88,632	44,092	90,671	45,106	92,756	2.30%	11.50%	26,071	53,613	37,363	76,832	52,517	107,995
Psychologist	72,960	123,996	74,639	126,848	76,355	129,765	78,111	132,750	79,908	135,803	2.30%	11.50%	46,187	78,494	66,189	112,488	93,037	158,115
Public Health Nurse	41,185	69,992	42,132	71,602	43,101	73,249	44,092	74,934	45,106	76,657	2.30%	11.50%	26,071	44,308	37,363	63,497	52,517	89,252
Public Health Nurse Practitioner	54,816	93,160	56,077	95,302	57,366	97,494	58,686	99,737	60,036	102,031	2.30%	11.50%	34,700	58,974	49,729	84,514	69,899	118,794
Public Health Nutritionist	41,185	69,992	42,132	71,602	43,101	73,249	44,092	74,934	45,106	76,657	2.30%	11.50%	26,071	44,308	37,363	63,497	52,517	89,252
Public Information Officer	45,303	76,992	46,345	78,763	47,411	80,574	48,501	82,428	49,617	84,323	2.30%	11.50%	28,678	48,739	41,099	69,847	57,769	98,177
Public Information Representative I-II	30,942	63,629	31,654	65,093	32,382	66,590	33,127	68,121	33,889	69,688	2.30%	11.50%	19,588	40,280	28,071	57,724	39,456	81,138
Public Service Officer	25,572	42,195	26,161	43,165	26,762	44,158	27,378	45,173	28,007	46,212	2.30%	11.50%	16,188	26,711	23,199	38,279	32,609	53,805
Radio Announcer - WRR	30,942	51,055	31,654	52,229	32,382	53,430	33,127	54,659	33,889	55,917	2.30%	11.50%	19,588	32,320	28,071	46,317	39,456	65,103
Records Management Officer	54,816	93,160	56,077	95,302	57,366	97,494	58,686	99,737	60,036	102,031	2.30%	11.50%	34,700	58,974	49,729	84,514	69,899	118,794
Recreation Center Assistant	23,247	38,358	23,782	39,240	24,329	40,143	24,888	41,066	25,461	42,011	2.30%	11.50%	14,716	24,282	21,090	34,798	29,644	48,913
Recreation Program Specialist	25,572	42,195	26,161	43,165	26,762	44,158	27,378	45,173	28,007	46,212	2.30%	11.50%	16,188	26,711	23,199	38,279	32,609	53,805
Risk Analyst	41,185	69,992	42,132	71,602	43,101	73,249	44,092	74,934	45,106	76,657	2.30%	11.50%	26,071	44,308	37,363	63,497	52,517	89,252
Safety Officer I-II	37,440	69,992	38,301	71,602	39,182	73,249	40,083	74,934	41,005	76,657	2.30%	11.50%	23,701	44,308	33,966	63,497	47,742	89,252
Sanitarian	37,440	63,629	38,301	65,093	39,182	66,590	40,083	68,121	41,005	69,688	2.30%	11.50%	23,701	40,280	33,966	57,724	47,742	81,138
Sanitarian Trainee	30,942	51,055	31,654	52,229	32,382	53,430	33,127	54,659	33,889	55,917	2.30%	11.50%	19,588	32,320	28,071	46,317	39,456	65,103
Security Analyst	41,185	69,992	42,132	71,602	43,101	73,249	44,092	74,934	45,106	76,657	2.30%	11.50%	26,071	44,308	37,363	63,497	52,517	89,252
Security Officer	30,942	51,055	31,654	52,229	32,382	53,430	33,127	54,659	33,889	55,917	2.30%	11.50%	19,588	32,320	28,071	46,317	39,456	65,103
Senior 911/311 Call Taker	34,036	57,845	34,819	59,176	35,620	60,537	36,439	61,929	37,277	63,353	2.30%	11.50%	21,546	36,618	30,878	52,477	43,402	73,762
Senior Accountant	45,303	76,992	46,345	78,763	47,411	80,574	48,501	82,428	49,617	84,323	2.30%	11.50%	28,678	48,739	41,099	69,847	57,769	98,177
Senior Administrative Hearing Officer	45,303	76,992	46,345	78,763	47,411	80,574	48,501	82,428	49,617	84,323	2.30%	11.50%	28,678	48,739	41,099	69,847	57,769	98,177
Senior Architect	66,328	112,724	67,853	115,316	69,414	117,969	71,010	120,682	72,644	123,458	2.30%	11.50%	41,988	71,358	60,172	102,263	84,579	143,741
Senior Assistant City Attorney I-II	65,713	142,379	67,225	145,654	68,771	149,004	70,353	152,431	71,971	155,937	2.30%	11.50%	41,599	90,131	59,615	129,166	83,795	181,555
Senior Auditor	60,297	102,476	61,684	104,833	63,103	107,244	64,554	109,710	66,039	112,234	2.30%	11.50%	38,171	64,871	54,702	92,966	76,889	130,677
Senior Benefits Specialist	45,303	76,992	46,345	78,763	47,411	80,574	48,501	82,428	49,617	84,323	2.30%	11.50%	28,678	48,739	41,099	69,847	57,769	98,177

222

Chart III - U.S. States & Cities - Job Titles - Salaries - Pension Estimates

TX-Dallas	2010 (Min)	2010 (Max)	2011 (Min)	2011 (Max)	2012 (Min)	2012 (Max)	2013 (Min)	2013 (Max)	2014 (Min)	2014 (Max)	5-Year Average % Raise	5-Year Cumulative Raise Estimate**	20-Year Annual Pension Benefit Estimate (Min.)***	20-Year Annual Pension Benefit Estimate (Max.)	25-Year Annual Pension Benefit Estimate (Min.)	25-Year Annual Pension Benefit Estimate (Max.)	30-Year Annual Pension Benefit Estimate (Min.)	30-Year Annual Pension Benefit Estimate (Max.)
Senior Budget Analyst	45,303	76,992	46,345	78,763	47,411	80,574	48,501	82,428	49,617	84,323	2.30%	11.50%	28,678	48,739	41,099	69,847	57,769	98,177
Senior Buyer	45,303	76,992	46,345	78,763	47,411	80,574	48,501	82,428	49,617	84,323	2.30%	11.50%	28,678	48,739	41,099	69,847	57,769	98,177
Senior Carpenter	28,130	46,413	28,777	47,481	29,439	48,573	30,116	49,690	30,808	50,833	2.30%	11.50%	17,807	29,381	25,519	42,106	35,870	59,185
Senior Caseworker	45,303	76,992	46,345	78,763	47,411	80,574	48,501	82,428	49,617	84,323	2.30%	11.50%	28,678	48,739	41,099	69,847	57,769	98,177
Senior Chemist	45,303	76,992	46,345	78,763	47,411	80,574	48,501	82,428	49,617	84,323	2.30%	11.50%	28,678	48,739	41,099	69,847	57,769	98,177
Senior Contract Compliance Administrator	41,185	69,992	42,132	71,602	43,101	73,249	44,092	74,934	45,106	76,657	2.30%	11.50%	26,071	44,308	37,363	63,497	52,517	89,252
Senior Coordinator	60,297	102,476	61,684	104,833	63,103	107,244	64,554	109,710	66,039	112,234	2.30%	11.50%	38,171	64,871	54,702	92,966	76,889	130,673
Senior Court Specialist	30,942	51,055	31,654	52,229	32,382	53,430	33,127	54,659	33,889	55,917	2.30%	11.50%	19,588	32,320	28,071	46,317	39,456	65,103
Senior Customer Service Representative	30,942	51,055	31,654	52,229	32,382	53,430	33,127	54,659	33,889	55,917	2.30%	11.50%	19,588	32,320	28,071	46,317	39,456	65,103
Senior Electronic Technician	37,440	63,629	38,301	65,093	39,182	66,590	40,083	68,121	41,005	69,688	2.30%	11.50%	23,701	40,280	33,966	57,724	47,742	81,138
Senior Engineer	66,328	112,724	67,853	115,316	69,414	117,969	71,010	120,682	72,644	123,458	2.30%	11.50%	41,988	71,358	60,172	102,263	84,579	143,741
Senior Environmental Coordinator	60,297	102,476	61,684	104,833	63,103	107,244	64,554	109,710	66,039	112,234	2.30%	11.50%	38,171	64,871	54,702	92,966	76,889	130,673
Senior Executive Assistant	49,833	84,691	50,979	86,639	52,151	88,632	53,351	90,671	54,578	92,756	2.30%	11.50%	31,546	53,613	45,208	76,832	63,545	107,995
Senior Executive Assistant City Attorney	131,427	262,854	134,450	268,899	137,542	275,084	140,705	281,411	143,942	287,883	2.30%	11.50%	83,198	166,396	119,230	238,460	167,591	335,181
Senior Executive Secretary	37,440	63,629	38,301	65,093	39,182	66,590	40,083	68,121	41,005	69,688	2.30%	11.50%	23,701	40,280	33,966	57,724	47,742	81,138
Senior Geographic Information Systems Analyst	54,816	93,160	56,077	95,302	57,366	97,494	58,686	99,737	60,036	102,031	2.30%	11.50%	34,700	58,974	49,729	84,514	69,899	118,794
Senior Human Resources Analyst	45,303	76,992	46,345	78,763	47,411	80,574	48,501	82,428	49,617	84,323	2.30%	11.50%	28,678	48,739	41,099	69,847	57,769	98,177
Senior Information Technology Analyst	49,833	84,691	50,979	86,639	52,151	88,632	53,351	90,671	54,578	92,756	2.30%	11.50%	31,546	53,613	45,208	76,832	63,545	107,995
Senior Information Technology Consultant	66,328	112,724	67,853	115,316	69,414	117,969	71,010	120,682	72,644	123,458	2.30%	11.50%	41,988	71,358	60,172	102,263	84,579	143,741
Senior Information Technology Engineer	66,328	112,724	67,853	115,316	69,414	117,969	71,010	120,682	72,644	123,458	2.30%	11.50%	41,988	71,358	60,172	102,263	84,579	143,741
Senior Information Technology Manager	72,960	123,996	74,639	126,848	76,355	129,765	78,111	132,750	79,908	135,803	2.30%	11.50%	46,187	78,494	66,189	112,488	93,037	158,115
Senior Inspector	41,185	69,992	42,132	71,602	43,101	73,249	44,092	74,934	45,106	76,657	2.30%	11.50%	26,071	44,308	37,363	63,497	52,517	89,252
Senior Intern	37,440	63,629	38,301	65,093	39,182	66,590	40,083	68,121	41,005	69,688	2.30%	11.50%	23,701	40,280	33,966	57,724	47,742	81,138
Senior Legal Secretary	30,942	51,055	31,654	52,229	32,382	53,430	33,127	54,659	33,889	55,917	2.30%	11.50%	19,588	32,320	28,071	46,317	39,456	65,103
Senior Librarian	49,833	84,691	50,979	86,639	52,151	88,632	53,351	90,671	54,578	92,756	2.30%	11.50%	31,546	53,613	45,208	76,832	63,545	107,995
Senior Machinist	34,036	57,845	34,819	59,176	35,620	60,537	36,439	61,929	37,277	63,353	2.30%	11.50%	21,546	36,618	30,878	52,477	43,402	73,762
Senior Maintenance Worker	28,130	46,413	28,777	47,481	29,439	48,573	30,116	49,690	30,808	50,833	2.30%	11.50%	17,807	29,381	25,519	42,106	35,870	59,185
Senior Mechanic	34,036	57,845	34,819	59,176	35,620	60,537	36,439	61,929	37,277	63,353	2.30%	11.50%	21,546	36,618	30,878	52,477	43,402	73,762
Senior Office Assistant	34,036	57,845	34,819	59,176	35,620	60,537	36,439	61,929	37,277	63,353	2.30%	11.50%	21,546	36,618	30,878	52,477	43,402	73,762
Senior Parking Enforcement Officer	30,942	51,055	31,654	52,229	32,382	53,430	33,127	54,659	33,889	55,917	2.30%	11.50%	19,588	32,320	28,071	46,317	39,456	65,103
Senior Parks and Recreation Manager	72,960	123,996	74,639	126,848	76,355	129,765	78,111	132,750	79,908	135,803	2.30%	11.50%	46,187	78,494	66,189	112,488	93,037	158,115
Senior Payroll Specialist	30,942	51,055	31,654	52,229	32,382	53,430	33,127	54,659	33,889	55,917	2.30%	11.50%	19,588	32,320	28,071	46,317	39,456	65,103
Senior Pension Specialist	54,816	93,160	56,077	95,302	57,366	97,494	58,686	99,737	60,036	102,031	2.30%	11.50%	34,700	58,974	49,729	84,514	69,899	118,794
Senior Planner	49,833	84,691	50,979	86,639	52,151	88,632	53,351	90,671	54,578	92,756	2.30%	11.50%	31,546	53,613	45,208	76,832	63,545	107,995
Senior Plans Examiner	41,185	69,992	42,132	71,602	43,101	73,249	44,092	74,934	45,106	76,657	2.30%	11.50%	26,071	44,308	37,363	63,497	52,517	89,252

Chart III - U.S. States & Cities - Job Titles - Salaries - Pension Estimates

TX-Dallas	2010 (Min)	2010 (Max)	2011 (Min)	2011 (Max)	2012 (Min)	2012 (Max)	2013 (Min)	2013 (Max)	2014 (Min)	2014 (Max)	5-Year Average % Raise	5-Year Cumulative Raise Estimate**	20-Year Annual Pension Benefit Estimate (Min.)***	20-Year Annual Pension Benefit Estimate (Max.)	25-Year Annual Pension Benefit Estimate (Min.)	25-Year Annual Pension Benefit Estimate (Max.)	30-Year Annual Pension Benefit Estimate (Min.)	30-Year Annual Pension Benefit Estimate (Max.)
Senior Plumber	34,036	57,845	34,819	59,176	35,620	60,537	36,439	61,929	37,277	63,353	2.30%	11.50%	21,546	36,618	30,878	52,477	43,402	73,762
Senior Police Dispatcher	41,185	69,992	42,132	71,602	43,101	73,249	44,092	74,934	45,106	76,657	2.30%	11.50%	26,071	44,308	37,363	63,497	52,517	89,252
Senior Program Manager	72,960	123,996	74,639	126,848	76,355	129,765	78,111	132,750	79,908	135,803	2.30%	11.50%	46,187	78,494	66,189	112,488	93,037	158,115
Senior Programmer/ Analyst	49,833	84,691	50,979	86,639	52,151	88,632	53,351	90,671	54,578	92,756	2.30%	11.50%	31,546	53,613	45,208	76,832	63,545	107,995
Senior Project Coordinator	60,297	102,476	61,684	104,833	63,103	107,244	64,554	109,710	66,039	112,234	2.30%	11.50%	38,171	64,871	54,702	92,966	76,889	130,673
Senior Public Health Nurse	45,303	76,992	46,345	78,763	47,411	80,574	48,501	82,428	49,617	84,323	2.30%	11.50%	28,678	48,739	41,099	69,847	57,769	98,177
Senior Public Information Officer	49,833	84,691	50,979	86,639	52,151	88,632	53,351	90,671	54,578	92,756	2.30%	11.50%	31,546	53,613	45,208	76,832	63,545	107,995
Senior Public Information Representative	41,185	69,992	42,132	71,602	43,101	73,249	44,092	74,934	45,106	76,657	2.30%	11.50%	26,071	44,308	37,363	63,497	52,517	89,252
Senior Real Estate Specialist	45,303	76,992	46,345	78,763	47,411	80,574	48,501	82,428	49,617	84,323	2.30%	11.50%	28,678	48,739	41,099	69,847	57,769	98,177
Senior Risk Analyst	45,303	76,992	46,345	78,763	47,411	80,574	48,501	82,428	49,617	84,323	2.30%	11.50%	28,678	48,739	41,099	69,847	57,769	98,177
Senior Security Analyst	54,816	93,160	56,077	95,302	57,366	97,494	58,686	99,737	60,036	102,031	2.30%	11.50%	34,700	58,974	49,729	84,514	69,899	118,794
Senior Security Officer	34,036	57,845	34,819	59,176	35,620	60,537	36,439	61,929	37,277	63,353	2.30%	11.50%	21,546	36,618	30,878	52,477	43,402	73,762
Senior Systems Programmer	60,297	102,476	61,684	104,833	63,103	107,244	64,554	109,710	66,039	112,234	2.30%	11.50%	38,171	64,871	54,702	92,966	76,889	130,673
Senior Telecommunications Analyst	49,833	84,691	50,979	86,639	52,151	88,632	53,351	90,671	54,578	92,756	2.30%	11.50%	31,546	53,613	45,208	76,832	63,545	107,995
Senior Therapeutic Recreation Specialist	41,185	69,992	42,132	71,602	43,101	73,249	44,092	74,934	45,106	76,657	2.30%	11.50%	26,071	44,308	37,363	63,497	52,517	89,252
Senior Truck Driver	28,130	46,413	28,777	47,481	29,439	48,573	30,116	49,690	30,808	50,833	2.30%	11.50%	17,807	29,381	25,519	42,106	35,870	59,185
Senior Water Field Representative	34,036	57,845	34,819	59,176	35,620	60,537	36,439	61,929	37,277	63,353	2.30%	11.50%	21,546	36,618	30,878	52,477	43,402	73,762
Service Agent	34,036	57,845	34,819	59,176	35,620	60,537	36,439	61,929	37,277	63,353	2.30%	11.50%	21,546	36,618	30,878	52,477	43,402	73,762
Supervisor I-IV	37,440	84,691	38,301	86,639	39,182	88,632	40,083	90,671	41,005	92,756	2.30%	11.50%	23,701	53,613	33,966	76,832	47,742	107,995
Survey Crew Chief	34,036	57,845	34,819	59,176	35,620	60,537	36,439	61,929	37,277	63,353	2.30%	11.50%	21,546	36,618	30,878	52,477	43,402	73,762
Surveyor	54,816	93,160	56,077	95,302	57,366	97,494	58,686	99,737	60,036	102,031	2.30%	11.50%	34,700	58,974	49,729	84,514	69,899	118,794
Surveyor Assistant	28,130	46,413	28,777	47,481	29,439	48,573	30,116	49,690	30,808	50,833	2.30%	11.50%	17,807	29,381	25,519	42,106	35,870	59,185
Surveyor Trainee	45,303	76,992	46,345	78,763	47,411	80,574	48,501	82,428	49,617	84,323	2.30%	11.50%	28,678	48,739	41,099	69,847	57,769	98,177
Systems Programmer	54,816	93,160	56,077	95,302	57,366	97,494	58,686	99,737	60,036	102,031	2.30%	11.50%	34,700	58,974	49,729	84,514	69,899	118,794
Telecommunications Analyst	45,303	76,992	46,345	78,763	47,411	80,574	48,501	82,428	49,617	84,323	2.30%	11.50%	28,678	48,739	41,099	69,847	57,769	98,177
Telecommunications Manager	60,297	102,476	61,684	104,833	63,103	107,244	64,554	109,710	66,039	112,234	2.30%	11.50%	38,171	64,871	54,702	92,966	76,889	130,673
Telecommunications Service Representative	34,036	57,845	34,819	59,176	35,620	60,537	36,439	61,929	37,277	63,353	2.30%	11.50%	21,546	36,618	30,878	52,477	43,402	73,762
Therapeutic Recreation Specialist	37,440	63,629	38,301	65,093	39,182	66,590	40,083	68,121	41,005	69,688	2.30%	11.50%	23,701	40,280	33,966	57,724	47,742	81,138
Title Examiner	37,440	63,629	38,301	65,093	39,182	66,590	40,083	68,121	41,005	69,688	2.30%	11.50%	23,701	40,280	33,966	57,724	47,742	81,138
Traffic Control System Operator	30,942	51,055	31,654	52,229	32,382	53,430	33,127	54,659	33,889	55,917	2.30%	11.50%	19,588	32,320	28,071	46,317	39,456	65,103
Traffic Management Specialist	37,440	63,629	38,301	65,093	39,182	66,590	40,083	68,121	41,005	69,688	2.30%	11.50%	23,701	40,280	33,966	57,724	47,742	81,138
Translator	34,036	57,845	34,819	59,176	35,620	60,537	36,439	61,929	37,277	63,353	2.30%	11.50%	21,546	36,618	30,878	52,477	43,402	73,762
Truck Driver	23,247	38,358	23,782	39,240	24,329	40,143	24,888	41,066	25,461	42,011	2.30%	11.50%	14,716	24,282	21,090	34,798	29,644	48,913
Truck Driver II	25,572	42,195	26,161	43,165	26,762	44,158	27,378	45,173	28,007	46,212	2.30%	11.50%	16,188	26,711	23,199	38,279	32,609	53,805
Urban Policy Analyst	54,816	93,160	56,077	95,302	57,366	97,494	58,686	99,737	60,036	102,031	2.30%	11.50%	34,700	58,974	49,729	84,514	69,899	118,794
Veterinarian	60,297	102,476	61,684	104,833	63,103	107,244	64,554	109,710	66,039	112,234	2.30%	11.50%	38,171	64,871	54,702	92,966	76,889	130,673
Veterinary Technologist	30,942	51,055	31,654	52,229	32,382	53,430	33,127	54,659	33,889	55,917	2.30%	11.50%	19,588	32,320	28,071	46,317	39,456	65,103

Chart III - U.S. States & Cities - Job Titles - Salaries - Pension Estimates

TX-Dallas	2010 (Min)	2010 (Max)	2011 (Min)	2011 (Max)	2012 (Min)	2012 (Max)	2013 (Min)	2013 (Max)	2014 (Min)	2014 (Max)	5-Year Average % Raise	5-Year Cumulative Raise Estimate**	20-Year Annual Pension Benefit Estimate (Min.)***	20-Year Annual Pension Benefit Estimate (Max.)	25-Year Annual Pension Benefit Estimate (Min.)	25-Year Annual Pension Benefit Estimate (Max.)	30-Year Annual Pension Benefit Estimate (Min.)	30-Year Annual Pension Benefit Estimate (Max.)
Video Specialist	34,036	57,845	34,819	59,176	35,620	60,537	36,439	61,929	37,277	63,353	2.30%	11.50%	21,546	36,618	30,878	52,477	43,402	73,762
Water Field Representative I-II	25,572	51,055	26,161	52,229	26,762	53,430	27,378	54,659	28,007	55,917	2.30%	11.50%	16,188	32,320	23,199	46,317	32,609	65,103
Water Instrument Technician	34,036	57,845	34,819	59,176	35,620	60,537	36,439	61,929	37,277	63,353	2.30%	11.50%	21,546	36,618	30,878	52,477	43,402	73,762
Water Meter Reader	23,247	38,358	23,782	39,240	24,329	40,143	24,888	41,066	25,461	42,011	2.30%	11.50%	14,716	24,282	21,090	34,798	29,644	48,913
Water Meter Reading Representative	30,942	51,055	31,654	52,229	32,382	53,430	33,127	54,659	33,889	55,917	2.30%	11.50%	19,588	32,320	28,071	46,317	39,456	65,103
Water Plant Operator	34,036	57,845	34,819	59,176	35,620	60,537	36,439	61,929	37,277	63,353	2.30%	11.50%	21,546	36,618	30,878	52,477	43,402	73,762
Web Designer	49,833	84,691	50,979	86,639	52,151	88,632	53,351	90,671	54,578	92,756	2.30%	11.50%	31,546	53,613	45,208	76,832	63,545	107,995
Welder	25,572	42,195	26,161	43,165	26,762	44,158	27,378	45,173	28,007	46,212	2.30%	11.50%	16,188	26,711	23,199	38,279	32,609	53,805
Wholesale Service Representative	45,303	76,992	46,345	78,763	47,411	80,574	48,501	82,428	49,617	84,323	2.30%	11.50%	28,678	48,739	41,099	69,847	57,769	98,177
Zoo Curator	54,816	93,160	56,077	95,302	57,366	97,494	58,686	99,737	60,036	102,031	2.30%	11.50%	34,700	58,974	49,729	84,514	69,899	118,794
Zoologist	37,440	63,629	38,301	65,093	39,182	66,590	40,083	68,121	41,005	69,688	2.30%	11.50%	23,701	40,280	33,966	57,724	47,742	81,13

http://www.dallascityhall.com/

Chart III - U.S. States & Cities - Job Titles - Salaries - Pension Estimates

Virginia	2010 (Min)	2010 (Max)	2011 (Min)	2011 (Max)	2012 (Min)	2012 (Max)	2013 (Min)	2013 (Max)	2014 (Min)	2014 (Max)	5-Year Average % Raise	5-Year Cumulative Raise Estimate**	20-Year Annual Pension Benefit Estimate (Min.)***	20-Year Annual Pension Benefit Estimate (Max.)	25-Year Annual Pension Benefit Estimate (Min.)	25-Year Annual Pension Benefit Estimate (Max.)	30-Year Annual Pension Benefit Estimate (Min.)	30-Year Annual Pension Benefit Estimate (Max.)
Administrative & Office Specialist I-III	16,187	51,871	16,560	53,064	16,941	54,284	17,330	55,533	17,729	56,810	2.30%	11.50%	10,247	32,836	14,685	47,057	20,642	66,144
Agricultural Manager I-IV	33,017	151,088	33,776	154,563	34,553	158,118	35,348	161,755	36,161	165,475	2.30%	11.50%	20,901	95,644	29,953	137,067	42,102	192,662
Agricultural Specialist III-V	25,273	88,526	25,855	90,562	26,449	92,645	27,058	94,776	27,680	96,955	2.30%	11.50%	15,999	56,040	22,928	80,310	32,228	112,885
Archeologist I-III	25,273	88,526	25,855	90,562	26,449	92,645	27,058	94,776	27,680	96,955	2.30%	11.50%	15,999	56,040	22,928	80,310	32,228	112,885
Architect I-II	43,134	115,649	44,126	118,309	45,141	121,030	46,180	123,814	47,242	126,661	2.30%	11.50%	27,306	73,210	39,131	104,916	55,003	147,471
Architect/ Engineer I	43,134	88,526	44,126	90,562	45,141	92,645	46,180	94,776	47,242	96,955	2.30%	11.50%	27,306	56,040	39,131	80,310	55,003	112,885
Architecture/ Engineering Manager I	43,134	88,526	44,126	90,562	45,141	92,645	46,180	94,776	47,242	96,955	2.30%	11.50%	27,306	56,040	39,131	80,310	55,003	112,885
Audit Manager I-IV	43,134	197,382	44,126	201,922	45,141	206,566	46,180	211,317	47,242	216,177	2.30%	11.50%	27,306	124,950	39,131	179,064	55,003	251,695
Auditor I-III	33,017	115,649	33,776	118,309	34,553	121,030	35,348	123,814	36,161	126,661	2.30%	11.50%	20,901	73,210	29,953	104,916	42,102	147,471
Civil Engineer I-II	43,134	115,649	44,126	118,309	45,141	121,030	46,180	123,814	47,242	126,661	2.30%	11.50%	27,306	73,210	39,131	104,916	55,003	147,471
Civil Engineering Technician I-IV	21,149	88,526	21,635	90,562	22,133	92,645	22,642	94,776	23,163	96,955	2.30%	11.50%	13,388	56,040	19,186	80,310	26,968	112,885
Compliance/Safety Manager I-III	43,134	151,088	44,126	154,563	45,141	158,118	46,180	161,755	47,242	165,475	2.30%	11.50%	27,306	95,644	39,131	137,067	55,003	192,662
Compliance/Safety Officer I-IV	21,149	88,526	21,635	90,562	22,133	92,645	22,642	94,776	23,163	96,955	2.30%	11.50%	13,388	56,040	19,186	80,310	26,968	112,885
Compliance/Safety Specialist III-IV	33,017	88,526	33,776	90,562	34,553	92,645	35,348	94,776	36,161	96,955	2.30%	11.50%	20,901	56,040	29,953	80,310	42,102	112,885
Computer Operations Tech I-II	25,273	67,764	25,855	69,322	26,449	70,917	27,058	72,548	27,680	74,216	2.30%	11.50%	15,999	42,897	22,928	61,475	32,228	86,410
Counselor I-II	25,273	67,764	25,855	69,322	26,449	70,917	27,058	72,548	27,680	74,216	2.30%	11.50%	15,999	42,897	22,928	61,475	32,228	86,410
Counselor Manager	43,134	88,526	44,126	90,562	45,141	92,645	46,180	94,776	47,242	96,955	2.30%	11.50%	27,306	56,040	39,131	80,310	55,003	112,885
Dental Manager	73,619	151,088	75,312	154,563	77,044	158,118	78,816	161,755	80,629	165,475	2.30%	11.50%	46,603	95,644	66,787	137,067	93,876	192,662
Dentist I-II	56,351	151,088	57,647	154,563	58,973	158,118	60,330	161,755	61,717	165,475	2.30%	11.50%	35,673	95,644	51,122	137,067	71,857	192,662
Direct Service Associate I-IV	16,187	67,764	16,560	69,322	16,941	70,917	17,330	72,548	17,729	74,216	2.30%	11.50%	10,247	42,897	14,685	61,475	20,642	86,410
Education Administration Coordinator I-II	43,134	115,649	44,126	118,309	45,141	121,030	46,180	123,814	47,242	126,661	2.30%	11.50%	27,306	73,210	39,131	104,916	55,003	147,471
Education Administrator I-IV	33,017	151,088	33,776	154,563	34,553	158,118	35,348	161,755	36,161	165,475	2.30%	11.50%	20,901	95,644	29,953	137,067	42,102	192,662
Education Support Specialist I-III	21,149	67,764	21,635	69,322	22,133	70,917	22,642	72,548	23,163	74,216	2.30%	11.50%	13,388	42,897	19,186	61,475	26,968	86,410
ELECTRICAL ENGINEERS I-II	43,134	115,649	44,126	118,309	45,141	121,030	46,180	123,814	47,242	126,661	2.30%	11.50%	27,306	73,210	39,131	104,916	55,003	147,471
Electronics Technician I-III	25,273	88,526	25,855	90,562	26,449	92,645	27,058	94,776	27,680	96,955	2.30%	11.50%	15,999	56,040	22,928	80,310	32,228	112,885
Emergency Coordinator I-III	25,273	88,526	25,855	90,562	26,449	92,645	27,058	94,776	27,680	96,955	2.30%	11.50%	15,999	56,040	22,928	80,310	32,228	112,885
Emergency Coordinator Manager I-III	43,134	151,088	44,126	154,563	45,141	158,118	46,180	161,755	47,242	165,475	2.30%	11.50%	27,306	95,644	39,131	137,067	55,003	192,662
Engineer I-II	43,134	115,649	44,126	118,309	45,141	121,030	46,180	123,814	47,242	126,661	2.30%	11.50%	27,306	73,210	39,131	104,916	55,003	147,471
Engineering Manager I-IV	43,134	197,382	44,126	201,922	45,141	206,566	46,180	211,317	47,242	216,177	2.30%	11.50%	27,306	124,950	39,131	179,064	55,003	251,695
Engineering Technician I-IV	21,149	88,526	21,635	90,562	22,133	92,645	22,642	94,776	23,163	96,955	2.30%	11.50%	13,388	56,040	19,186	80,310	26,968	112,885
ENVIRONMENTAL ENGINEER I-II	43,134	115,649	44,126	118,309	45,141	121,030	46,180	123,814	47,242	126,661	2.30%	11.50%	27,306	73,210	39,131	104,916	55,003	147,471
Environmental Manager I-III	43,134	151,088	44,126	154,563	45,141	158,118	46,180	161,755	47,242	165,475	2.30%	11.50%	27,306	95,644	39,131	137,067	55,003	192,662
Environmental Specialist I-II	33,017	88,526	33,776	90,562	34,553	92,645	35,348	94,776	36,161	96,955	2.30%	11.50%	20,901	56,040	29,953	80,310	42,102	112,885
Equipment Service and Repair Technician I-II	25,273	67,764	25,855	69,322	26,449	70,917	27,058	72,548	27,680	74,216	2.30%	11.50%	15,999	42,897	22,928	61,475	32,228	86,410
Financial Services Manager I-IV	43,134	197,382	44,126	201,922	45,141	206,566	46,180	211,317	47,242	216,177	2.30%	11.50%	27,306	124,950	39,131	179,064	55,003	251,695

Chart III - U.S. States & Cities - Job Titles - Salaries - Pension Estimates

Virginia	2010 (Min)	2010 (Max)	2011 (Min)	2011 (Max)	2012 (Min)	2012 (Max)	2013 (Min)	2013 (Max)	2014 (Min)	2014 (Max)	5-Year Average % Raise	5-Year Cumulative Raise Estimate**	20-Year Annual Pension Benefit Estimate (Min.)***	20-Year Annual Pension Benefit Estimate (Max.)	25-Year Annual Pension Benefit Estimate (Min.)	25-Year Annual Pension Benefit Estimate (Max.)	30-Year Annual Pension Benefit Estimate (Min.)	30-Year Annual Pension Benefit Estimate (Max.)
Financial Services Specialist I-III	33,017	115,649	33,776	118,309	34,553	121,030	35,348	123,814	36,161	126,661	2.30%	11.50%	20,901	73,210	29,953	104,916	42,102	147,471
Food Services Technician I-III	16,187	51,871	16,560	53,064	16,941	54,284	17,330	55,533	17,729	56,810	2.30%	11.50%	10,247	32,836	14,685	47,057	20,642	66,144
Forensic Science Manager I-II	73,619	197,382	75,312	201,922	77,044	206,566	78,816	211,317	80,629	216,177	2.30%	11.50%	46,603	124,950	66,787	179,064	93,876	251,695
Forensic Scientist I-III	33,017	115,649	33,776	118,309	34,553	121,030	35,348	123,814	36,161	126,661	2.30%	11.50%	20,901	73,210	29,953	104,916	42,102	147,471
General Admin Supv I/Coord I-II	33,017	88,526	33,776	90,562	34,553	92,645	35,348	94,776	36,161	96,955	2.30%	11.50%	20,901	56,040	29,953	80,310	42,102	112,885
General Administration Coordinator I-II	33,017	88,526	33,776	90,562	34,553	92,645	35,348	94,776	36,161	96,955	2.30%	11.50%	20,901	56,040	29,953	80,310	42,102	112,885
General Administration Manager I-IV	43,134	197,382	44,126	201,922	45,141	206,566	46,180	211,317	47,242	216,177	2.30%	11.50%	27,306	124,950	39,131	179,064	55,003	251,695
General Administration Supervisor I-II	33,017	88,526	33,776	90,562	34,553	92,645	35,348	94,776	36,161	96,955	2.30%	11.50%	20,901	56,040	29,953	80,310	42,102	112,885
Health Care Compliance Manager	56,351	115,649	57,647	118,309	58,973	121,030	60,330	123,814	61,717	126,661	2.30%	11.50%	35,673	73,210	51,122	104,916	71,857	147,471
Health Care Compliance Specialist I-II	33,017	88,526	33,776	90,562	34,553	92,645	35,348	94,776	36,161	96,955	2.30%	11.50%	20,901	56,040	29,953	80,310	42,102	112,885
Health Care Manager	43,134	88,526	44,126	90,562	45,141	92,645	46,180	94,776	47,242	96,955	2.30%	11.50%	27,306	56,040	39,131	80,310	55,003	112,885
Health Care Technologist I-III	25,273	88,526	25,855	90,562	26,449	92,645	27,058	94,776	27,680	96,955	2.30%	11.50%	15,999	56,040	22,928	80,310	32,228	112,885
Hearing and Legal Services Manager I-III	43,134	151,088	44,126	154,563	45,141	158,118	46,180	161,755	47,242	165,475	2.30%	11.50%	27,306	95,644	39,131	137,067	55,003	192,662
Hearing and Legal Services Officer I-III	33,017	115,649	33,776	118,309	34,553	121,030	35,348	123,814	36,161	126,661	2.30%	11.50%	20,901	73,210	29,953	104,916	42,102	147,471
Historian I-III	25,273	88,526	25,855	90,562	26,449	92,645	27,058	94,776	27,680	96,955	2.30%	11.50%	15,999	56,040	22,928	80,310	32,228	112,885
Historian/ Archeologist and Preservationist Manager	43,134	88,526	44,126	90,562	45,141	92,645	46,180	94,776	47,242	96,955	2.30%	11.50%	27,306	56,040	39,131	80,310	55,003	112,885
Housekeeping and/or Apparel Manager I-II	25,273	67,764	25,855	69,322	26,449	70,917	27,058	72,548	27,680	74,216	2.30%	11.50%	15,999	42,897	22,928	61,475	32,228	86,410
Housekeeping and/or Apparel Worker I-II	16,187	43,403	16,560	44,401	16,941	45,422	17,330	46,467	17,729	47,536	2.30%	11.50%	10,247	27,475	14,685	39,375	20,642	55,345
Housekeeping Manager I-II	25,273	67,764	25,855	69,322	26,449	70,917	27,058	72,548	27,680	74,216	2.30%	11.50%	15,999	42,897	22,928	61,475	32,228	86,410
Housekeeping Worker II	21,149	43,403	21,635	44,401	22,133	45,422	22,642	46,467	23,163	47,536	2.30%	11.50%	13,388	27,475	19,186	39,375	26,968	55,345
Human Resource Analyst I-III	33,017	115,649	33,776	118,309	34,553	121,030	35,348	123,814	36,161	126,661	2.30%	11.50%	20,901	73,210	29,953	104,916	42,102	147,471
Human Resource Manager I-III	43,134	151,088	44,126	154,563	45,141	158,118	46,180	161,755	47,242	165,475	2.30%	11.50%	27,306	95,644	39,131	137,067	55,003	192,662
Information Technology Manager I-III	56,351	197,382	57,647	201,922	58,973	206,566	60,330	211,317	61,717	216,177	2.30%	11.50%	35,673	124,950	51,122	179,064	71,857	251,695
Information Technology Specialist I-IV	33,017	151,088	33,776	154,563	34,553	158,118	35,348	161,755	36,161	165,475	2.30%	11.50%	20,901	95,644	29,953	137,067	42,102	192,662
Lab & Research Specialist I-II	25,273	67,764	25,855	69,322	26,449	70,917	27,058	72,548	27,680	74,216	2.30%	11.50%	15,999	42,897	22,928	61,475	32,228	86,410
Laboratory and Research Aide	16,187	33,224	16,560	33,988	16,941	34,769	17,330	35,569	17,729	36,387	2.30%	11.50%	10,247	21,032	14,685	30,140	20,642	42,366
Laboratory and Research Manager	43,134	88,526	44,126	90,562	45,141	92,645	46,180	94,776	47,242	96,955	2.30%	11.50%	27,306	56,040	39,131	80,310	55,003	112,885
Laboratory and Research Specialist I	25,273	51,871	25,855	53,064	26,449	54,284	27,058	55,533	27,680	56,810	2.30%	11.50%	15,999	32,836	22,928	47,057	32,228	66,144
Laboratory and Research Technician	21,149	43,403	21,635	44,401	22,133	45,422	22,642	46,467	23,163	47,536	2.30%	11.50%	13,388	27,475	19,186	39,375	26,968	55,345
Land Acquisition and Property Management Agent I-III	25,273	88,526	25,855	90,562	26,449	92,645	27,058	94,776	27,680	96,955	2.30%	11.50%	15,999	56,040	22,928	80,310	32,228	112,885

Chart III - U.S. States & Cities - Job Titles - Salaries - Pension Estimates

Virginia	2010 (Min)	2010 (Max)	2011 (Min)	2011 (Max)	2012 (Min)	2012 (Max)	2013 (Min)	2013 (Max)	2014 (Min)	2014 (Max)	5-Year Average % Raise	5-Year Cumulative Raise Estimate**	20-Year Annual Pension Benefit Estimate (Min.)***	20-Year Annual Pension Benefit Estimate (Max.)	25-Year Annual Pension Benefit Estimate (Min.)	25-Year Annual Pension Benefit Estimate (Max.)	30-Year Annual Pension Benefit Estimate (Min.)	30-Year Annual Pension Benefit Estimate (Max.)
Land Acquisition and Property Management Manager I-II	43,134	115,649	44,126	118,309	45,141	121,030	46,180	123,814	47,242	126,661	2.30%	11.50%	27,306	73,210	39,131	104,916	55,003	147,471
Law Enforcement Manager I-III	43,134	151,088	44,126	154,563	45,141	158,118	46,180	161,755	47,242	165,475	2.30%	11.50%	27,306	95,644	39,131	137,067	55,003	192,662
Law Enforcement Officer I-III	25,273	88,526	25,855	90,562	26,449	92,645	27,058	94,776	27,680	96,955	2.30%	11.50%	15,999	56,040	22,928	80,310	32,228	112,885
Library Manager	56,351	115,649	57,647	118,309	58,973	121,030	60,330	123,814	61,717	126,661	2.30%	11.50%	35,673	73,210	51,122	104,916	71,857	147,471
Library Specialist I-III	25,273	88,526	25,855	90,562	26,449	92,645	27,058	94,776	27,680	96,955	2.30%	11.50%	15,999	56,040	22,928	80,310	32,228	112,885
Licensed Practical Nurse	25,273	51,871	25,855	53,064	26,449	54,284	27,058	55,533	27,680	56,810	2.30%	11.50%	15,999	32,836	22,928	47,057	32,228	66,144
Life and Physical Science I	33,017	67,764	33,776	69,322	34,553	70,917	35,348	72,548	36,161	74,216	2.30%	11.50%	20,901	42,897	29,953	61,475	42,102	86,410
Media Manager I	33,017	67,764	33,776	69,322	34,553	70,917	35,348	72,548	36,161	74,216	2.30%	11.50%	20,901	42,897	29,953	61,475	42,102	86,410
Media Specialist II-IV	25,273	88,526	25,855	90,562	26,449	92,645	27,058	94,776	27,680	96,955	2.30%	11.50%	15,999	56,040	22,928	80,310	32,228	112,885
Mineral Manager I-II	56,351	151,088	57,647	154,563	58,973	158,118	60,330	161,755	61,717	165,475	2.30%	11.50%	35,673	95,644	51,122	137,067	71,857	192,662
Natural Resource Specialist I-IV	21,149	88,526	21,635	90,562	22,133	92,645	22,642	94,776	23,163	96,955	2.30%	11.50%	13,388	56,040	19,186	80,310	26,968	112,885
Pharmacist I-II	43,134	115,649	44,126	118,309	45,141	121,030	46,180	123,814	47,242	126,661	2.30%	11.50%	27,306	73,210	39,131	104,916	55,003	147,471
Pharmacy Manager	56,351	115,649	57,647	118,309	58,973	121,030	60,330	123,814	61,717	126,661	2.30%	11.50%	35,673	73,210	51,122	104,916	71,857	147,471
Physician Assistant	43,134	88,526	44,126	90,562	45,141	92,645	46,180	94,776	47,242	96,955	2.30%	11.50%	27,306	56,040	39,131	80,310	55,003	112,885
Physician I-II	73,619	197,382	75,312	201,922	77,044	206,566	78,816	211,317	80,629	216,177	2.30%	11.50%	46,603	124,950	66,787	179,064	93,876	251,695
Physician Manager I-II	96,174	0	98,386	0	100,649	0	102,964	0	105,332	0	2.30%	11.50%	60,882	0	87,248	0	122,637	-
Pilot I-II	33,017	88,526	33,776	90,562	34,553	92,645	35,348	94,776	36,161	96,955	2.30%	11.50%	20,901	56,040	29,953	80,310	42,102	112,885
Policy and Planning Manager I-IV	43,134	197,382	44,126	201,922	45,141	206,566	46,180	211,317	47,242	216,177	2.30%	11.50%	27,306	124,950	39,131	179,064	55,003	251,695
Policy and Planning Specialist I-IV	33,017	151,088	33,776	154,563	34,553	158,118	35,348	161,755	36,161	165,475	2.30%	11.50%	20,901	95,644	29,953	137,067	42,102	192,662
Printing Manager I-II	33,017	88,526	33,776	90,562	34,553	92,645	35,348	94,776	36,161	96,955	2.30%	11.50%	20,901	56,040	29,953	80,310	42,102	112,885
Printing Technician I-IV	16,187	67,764	16,560	69,322	16,941	70,917	17,330	72,548	17,729	74,216	2.30%	11.50%	10,247	42,897	14,685	61,475	20,642	86,410
Probation Officer I-II	33,017	88,526	33,776	90,562	34,553	92,645	35,348	94,776	36,161	96,955	2.30%	11.50%	20,901	56,040	29,953	80,310	42,102	112,885
Procurement Manager I-IV	33,017	151,088	33,776	154,563	34,553	158,118	35,348	161,755	36,161	165,475	2.30%	11.50%	20,901	95,644	29,953	137,067	42,102	192,662
Procurement Officer I-III	33,017	115,649	33,776	118,309	34,553	121,030	35,348	123,814	36,161	126,661	2.30%	11.50%	20,901	73,210	29,953	104,916	42,102	147,471
Program Administration Manager I-III	33,017	115,649	33,776	118,309	34,553	121,030	35,348	123,814	36,161	126,661	2.30%	11.50%	20,901	73,210	29,953	104,916	42,102	147,471
Program Administration Specialist I-III	33,017	115,649	33,776	118,309	34,553	121,030	35,348	123,814	36,161	126,661	2.30%	11.50%	20,901	73,210	29,953	104,916	42,102	147,471
Psychologist I-III	33,017	115,649	33,776	118,309	34,553	121,030	35,348	123,814	36,161	126,661	2.30%	11.50%	20,901	73,210	29,953	104,916	42,102	147,471
Psychology Manager	56,351	115,649	57,647	118,309	58,973	121,030	60,330	123,814	61,717	126,661	2.30%	11.50%	35,673	73,210	51,122	104,916	71,857	147,471
Public Relations and Marketing Manager I-IV	33,017	151,088	33,776	154,563	34,553	158,118	35,348	161,755	36,161	165,475	2.30%	11.50%	20,901	95,644	29,953	137,067	42,102	192,662
Public Relations and Marketing Specialist I-V	21,149	115,649	21,635	118,309	22,133	121,030	22,642	123,814	23,163	126,661	2.30%	11.50%	13,388	73,210	19,186	104,916	26,968	147,471
Registered Nurse I-III	33,017	115,649	33,776	118,309	34,553	121,030	35,348	123,814	36,161	126,661	2.30%	11.50%	20,901	73,210	29,953	104,916	42,102	147,471
Registered Nurse Manager I-II	43,134	115,649	44,126	118,309	45,141	121,030	46,180	123,814	47,242	126,661	2.30%	11.50%	27,306	73,210	39,131	104,916	55,003	147,471
Retail Manager I-III	25,273	88,526	25,855	90,562	26,449	92,645	27,058	94,776	27,680	96,955	2.30%	11.50%	15,999	56,040	22,928	80,310	32,228	112,885
Retail Specialist I-II	21,149	51,871	21,635	53,064	22,133	54,284	22,642	55,533	23,163	56,810	2.30%	11.50%	13,388	32,836	19,186	47,057	26,968	66,144
Scientist I-III	33,017	115,649	33,776	118,309	34,553	121,030	35,348	123,814	36,161	126,661	2.30%	11.50%	20,901	73,210	29,953	104,916	42,102	147,471
Scientist Manager I-III	43,134	151,088	44,126	154,563	45,141	158,118	46,180	161,755	47,242	165,475	2.30%	11.50%	27,306	95,644	39,131	137,067	55,003	192,662

Chart III - U.S. States & Cities - Job Titles - Salaries - Pension Estimates

Virginia	2010 (Min)	2010 (Max)	2011 (Min)	2011 (Max)	2012 (Min)	2012 (Max)	2013 (Min)	2013 (Max)	2014 (Min)	2014 (Max)	5-Year Average % Raise	5-Year Cumulative Raise Estimate**	20-Year Annual Pension Benefit Estimate (Min.)***	20-Year Annual Pension Benefit Estimate (Max.)	25-Year Annual Pension Benefit Estimate (Min.)	25-Year Annual Pension Benefit Estimate (Max.)	30-Year Annual Pension Benefit Estimate (Min.)	30-Year Annual Pension Benefit Estimate (Max.)
Security Manager I-V	33,017	197,382	33,776	201,922	34,553	206,566	35,348	211,317	36,161	216,177	2.30%	11.50%	20,901	124,950	29,953	179,064	42,102	251,695
Security Officer III-IV	25,273	67,764	25,855	69,322	26,449	70,917	27,058	72,548	27,680	74,216	2.30%	11.50%	15,999	42,897	22,928	61,475	32,228	86,410
Stores and Warehouse Specialist III	16,187	51,871	16,560	53,064	16,941	54,284	17,330	55,533	17,729	56,810	2.30%	11.50%	10,247	32,836	14,685	47,057	20,642	66,144
Therapist Assistant/ Therapist I	25,273	51,871	25,855	53,064	26,449	54,284	27,058	55,533	27,680	56,810	2.30%	11.50%	15,999	32,836	22,928	47,057	32,228	66,144
Therapist I-III	25,273	88,526	25,855	90,562	26,449	92,645	27,058	94,776	27,680	96,955	2.30%	11.50%	15,999	56,040	22,928	80,310	32,228	112,885
Therapy Manager I-II	43,134	115,649	44,126	118,309	45,141	121,030	46,180	123,814	47,242	126,661	2.30%	11.50%	27,306	73,210	39,131	104,916	55,003	147,471
Trades Manager I-II	43,134	115,649	44,126	118,309	45,141	121,030	46,180	123,814	47,242	126,661	2.30%	11.50%	27,306	73,210	39,131	104,916	55,003	147,471
Trades Technician I-IV	21,149	67,764	21,635	69,322	22,133	70,917	22,642	72,548	23,163	74,216	2.30%	11.50%	13,388	42,897	19,186	61,475	26,968	86,410
Trainer and Instructor III	25,273	88,526	25,855	90,562	26,449	92,645	27,058	94,776	27,680	96,955	2.30%	11.50%	15,999	56,040	22,928	80,310	32,228	112,885
Training and Instruction Manager I-II	43,134	115,649	44,126	118,309	45,141	121,030	46,180	123,814	47,242	126,661	2.30%	11.50%	27,306	73,210	39,131	104,916	55,003	147,471
Transportation Operations Manager I-III	25,273	88,526	25,855	90,562	26,449	92,645	27,058	94,776	27,680	96,955	2.30%	11.50%	15,999	56,040	22,928	80,310	32,228	112,885
Transportation Operator I-III	16,187	51,871	16,560	53,064	16,941	54,284	17,330	55,533	17,729	56,810	2.30%	11.50%	10,247	32,836	14,685	47,057	20,642	66,144
Utility Plant Manager II	33,017	88,526	33,776	90,562	34,553	92,645	35,348	94,776	36,161	96,955	2.30%	11.50%	20,901	56,040	29,953	80,310	42,102	112,885
Utility Plant Specialist	25,273	51,871	25,855	53,064	26,449	54,284	27,058	55,533	27,680	56,810	2.30%	11.50%	15,999	32,836	22,928	47,057	32,228	66,144
Veterinarian I-III	43,134	151,088	44,126	154,563	45,141	158,118	46,180	161,755	47,242	165,475	2.30%	11.50%	27,306	95,644	39,131	137,067	55,003	192,662
Veterinary Manager	73,619	151,088	75,312	154,563	77,044	158,118	78,816	161,755	80,629	165,475	2.30%	11.50%	46,603	95,644	66,787	137,067	93,876	192,662
Warehouse Manager II	33,017	88,526	33,776	90,562	34,553	92,645	35,348	94,776	36,161	96,955	2.30%	11.50%	20,901	56,040	29,953	80,310	42,102	112,885
Watercraft Operations Manager I	33,017	67,764	33,776	69,322	34,553	70,917	35,348	72,548	36,161	74,216	2.30%	11.50%	20,901	42,897	29,953	61,475	42,102	86,410
Watercraft Operator II	25,273	51,871	25,855	53,064	26,449	54,284	27,058	55,533	27,680	56,810	2.30%	11.50%	15,999	32,836	22,928	47,057	32,228	66,144

http://www.state.va.us/cmsportal2/

229

Chart III - U.S. States & Cities - Job Titles - Salaries - Pension Estimates

WA-Seattle	2010 (Min)	2010 (Max)	2011 (Min)	2011 (Max)	2012 (Min)	2012 (Max)	2013 (Min)	2013 (Max)	2014 (Min)	2014 (Max)	5-Year Average % Raise	5-Year Cumulative Raise Estimate**	20-Year Annual Pension Benefit Estimate (Min.)***	20-Year Annual Pension Benefit Estimate (Max.)	25-Year Annual Pension Benefit Estimate (Min.)	25-Year Annual Pension Benefit Estimate (Max.)	30-Year Annual Pension Benefit Estimate (Min.)	30-Year Annual Pension Benefit Estimate (Max.)
Accountant	51,865	60,418	53,058	61,808	54,278	63,229	55,527	64,683	56,804	66,171	2.30%	11.50%	32,833	38,247	47,052	54,811	66,137	77,043
Accountant,Prin	67,050	78,072	68,592	79,868	70,169	81,705	71,783	83,584	73,434	85,506	2.30%	11.50%	42,445	49,423	60,827	70,827	85,499	99,555
Actg Tech I - III	39,562	52,323	40,472	53,526	41,403	54,758	42,355	56,017	43,329	57,305	2.30%	11.50%	25,044	33,122	35,891	47,467	50,448	66,720
Admin Spec I - III	39,562	51,293	40,472	52,473	41,403	53,680	42,355	54,914	43,329	56,177	2.30%	11.50%	25,044	32,470	35,891	46,533	50,448	65,407
Admin Staff Anlyst	60,875	70,914	62,275	72,545	63,708	74,214	65,173	75,921	66,672	77,667	2.30%	11.50%	38,536	44,891	55,226	64,333	77,626	90,428
Admin Staff Asst	53,237	62,064	54,462	63,492	55,714	64,952	56,996	66,446	58,307	67,974	2.30%	11.50%	33,701	39,289	48,297	56,305	67,886	79,142
Administrator-Law	87,402	101,444	89,413	103,777	91,469	106,164	93,573	108,605	95,725	111,103	2.30%	11.50%	55,329	64,218	79,291	92,029	111,452	129,35
Adms Personnel Supv	56,370	65,838	57,667	67,352	58,993	68,901	60,350	70,486	61,738	72,107	2.30%	11.50%	35,684	41,678	51,139	59,728	71,881	83,954
Animal Contrl Ofcr I - II	44,044	51,842	45,057	53,034	46,094	54,254	47,154	55,502	48,238	56,779	2.30%	11.50%	27,882	32,818	39,957	47,031	56,164	66,107
Appraiser	67,599	78,850	69,153	80,663	70,744	82,519	72,371	84,416	74,035	86,358	2.30%	11.50%	42,792	49,915	61,325	71,532	86,199	100,54
Appraiser,Sr	73,682	85,802	75,376	87,775	77,110	89,794	78,883	91,859	80,698	93,972	2.30%	11.50%	46,643	54,316	66,844	77,839	93,956	109,41
Aquarium Biologist 1 - 3	40,271	60,875	41,197	62,275	42,145	63,707	43,114	65,173	44,106	66,672	2.30%	11.50%	25,493	38,536	36,534	55,226	51,352	77,626
Architect,Assoc	67,050	78,072	68,592	79,868	70,169	81,705	71,783	83,584	73,434	85,506	2.30%	11.50%	42,445	49,423	60,827	70,827	85,499	99,555
Architect,Sr	75,168	87,402	76,897	89,413	78,665	91,469	80,475	93,573	82,326	95,725	2.30%	11.50%	47,584	55,329	68,192	79,291	95,851	111,452
Arts Prgm Spec	55,364	64,649	56,637	66,135	57,940	67,657	59,273	69,213	60,636	70,805	2.30%	11.50%	35,047	40,925	50,226	58,649	70,598	82,438
Auto Engr	65,838	76,609	67,352	78,371	68,901	80,173	70,486	82,017	72,107	83,904	2.30%	11.50%	41,678	48,496	59,728	69,499	83,954	97,689
Auto Engr,Sr	68,262	79,582	69,832	81,412	71,438	83,284	73,081	85,200	74,762	87,160	2.30%	11.50%	43,212	50,378	61,927	72,196	87,045	101,48
Auto Mechanic	58,154	62,865	59,492	64,311	60,860	65,790	62,260	67,303	63,692	68,851	2.30%	11.50%	36,814	39,796	52,757	57,031	74,156	80,163
Bldg Enrgy Res Spec	67,050	78,072	68,592	79,868	70,169	81,705	71,783	83,584	73,434	85,506	2.30%	11.50%	42,445	49,423	60,827	70,827	85,499	99,555
Bldg Inspector Supv	73,682	85,802	75,376	87,775	77,110	89,794	78,883	91,859	80,698	93,972	2.30%	11.50%	46,643	54,316	66,844	77,839	93,956	109,41
Bldg Inspector,Strucl	70,914	82,554	72,545	84,453	74,214	86,396	75,921	88,383	77,667	90,415	2.30%	11.50%	44,891	52,260	64,333	74,893	90,428	105,27
Bldg Operating Engr	56,393	60,875	57,690	62,275	59,017	63,708	60,374	65,173	61,763	66,672	2.30%	11.50%	35,699	38,536	51,160	55,226	71,910	77,626
Bldg Plans Examiner	65,838	76,609	67,352	78,371	68,901	80,173	70,486	82,017	72,107	83,904	2.30%	11.50%	41,678	48,496	59,728	69,499	83,954	97,689
Bldg Plans Examiner Supv	75,168	87,402	76,897	89,413	78,665	91,469	80,475	93,573	82,326	95,725	2.30%	11.50%	47,584	55,329	68,192	79,291	95,851	111,452
Bldg Plans Examiner,Sr	70,914	82,554	72,545	84,453	74,214	86,396	75,921	88,383	77,667	90,415	2.30%	11.50%	44,891	52,260	64,333	74,893	90,428	105,27
Bldg Prjt Coord	67,050	78,072	68,592	79,868	70,169	81,705	71,783	83,584	73,434	85,506	2.30%	11.50%	42,445	49,423	60,827	70,827	85,499	99,555
Bldg Prjt Coord,Sr	70,914	82,554	72,545	84,453	74,214	86,396	75,921	88,383	77,667	90,415	2.30%	11.50%	44,891	52,260	64,333	74,893	90,428	105,27
Bldg/Facilities Opns Supv	52,323	60,875	53,526	62,275	54,757	63,708	56,016	65,173	57,305	66,672	2.30%	11.50%	33,122	38,536	47,467	55,226	66,720	77,626
Bridge Elecl CC	59,755	64,557	61,129	66,042	62,535	67,561	63,973	69,115	65,445	70,704	2.30%	11.50%	37,827	40,867	54,209	58,566	76,197	82,32
Buyer	60,875	70,914	62,275	72,545	63,708	74,214	65,173	75,921	66,672	77,667	2.30%	11.50%	38,536	44,891	55,226	64,333	77,626	90,428
Buyer,Asst	53,237	62,064	54,462	63,492	55,714	64,952	56,996	66,446	58,307	67,974	2.30%	11.50%	33,701	39,289	48,297	56,305	67,886	79,142
Buyer,Sr	67,050	78,072	68,592	79,868	70,169	81,705	71,783	83,584	73,434	85,506	2.30%	11.50%	42,445	49,423	60,827	70,827	85,499	99,555
Capital Prjts Coord	69,497	81,182	71,095	83,049	72,730	84,960	74,403	86,914	76,114	88,913	2.30%	11.50%	43,994	51,391	63,047	73,648	88,620	103,52
Capital Prjts Coord Supv	76,609	88,912	78,371	90,957	80,173	93,049	82,017	95,189	83,904	97,378	2.30%	11.50%	48,496	56,284	69,499	80,660	97,689	113,37
Capital Prjts Coord,Asst	64,580	75,214	66,065	76,944	67,585	78,713	69,139	80,524	70,729	82,376	2.30%	11.50%	40,881	47,613	58,587	68,234	82,350	95,910
Capital Prjts Coord,Chief	76,609	88,912	78,371	90,957	80,173	93,049	82,017	95,189	83,904	97,378	2.30%	11.50%	48,496	56,284	69,499	80,660	97,689	113,37
Capital Prjts Coord,Sr	73,499	85,733	75,189	87,705	76,918	89,722	78,688	91,786	80,497	93,897	2.30%	11.50%	46,527	54,272	66,678	77,777	93,723	109,32
Carpenter,Sr	59,160	61,676	60,521	63,094	61,913	64,545	63,337	66,030	64,794	67,549	2.30%	11.50%	37,451	39,043	53,670	55,952	75,439	78,647
City Attorney	143,132	0	146,424	0	149,792	0	153,237	0	156,762	0	2.30%	11.50%	90,608	0	129,849	0	182,517	-
City Attorney,Asst	58,954	141,029	60,310	144,272	61,697	147,590	63,116	150,985	64,568	154,458	2.30%	11.50%	37,320	89,276	53,483	127,941	75,176	179,83
Civil Engr Supv	81,480	94,514	83,354	96,688	85,271	98,912	87,232	101,187	89,238	103,514	2.30%	11.50%	51,580	59,831	73,918	85,743	103,900	120,52
Civil Engr,Asst I - III	55,753	73,064	57,035	74,744	58,347	76,464	59,689	78,222	61,062	80,021	2.30%	11.50%	35,294	46,252	50,579	66,283	71,094	93,169

Chart III - U.S. States & Cities - Job Titles - Salaries - Pension Estimates

WA-Seattle	2010 (Min)	2010 (Max)	2011 (Min)	2011 (Max)	2012 (Min)	2012 (Max)	2013 (Min)	2013 (Max)	2014 (Min)	2014 (Max)	5-Year Average % Raise	5-Year Cumulative Raise Estimate**	20-Year Annual Pension Benefit Estimate (Min.)***	20-Year Annual Pension Benefit Estimate (Max.)	25-Year Annual Pension Benefit Estimate (Min.)	25-Year Annual Pension Benefit Estimate (Max.)	30-Year Annual Pension Benefit Estimate (Min.)	30-Year Annual Pension Benefit Estimate (Max.)
Civil Engr,Sr	77,318	90,009	79,096	92,080	80,915	94,198	82,776	96,364	84,680	98,580	2.30%	11.50%	48,945	56,979	70,142	81,656	98,593	114,777
Civil Engrng Spec Supv	79,444	88,912	81,272	90,957	83,141	93,049	85,053	95,189	87,009	97,378	2.30%	11.50%	50,291	56,284	72,072	80,660	101,305	113,377
Cmputr Op	37,275	43,358	38,133	44,355	39,010	45,376	39,907	46,419	40,825	47,487	2.30%	11.50%	23,597	27,447	33,816	39,334	47,532	55,289
Cmputr Op,Lead	45,691	53,237	46,742	54,462	47,817	55,714	48,917	56,996	50,042	58,307	2.30%	11.50%	28,924	33,701	41,451	48,297	58,263	67,886
Cmputr Op,Sr	43,358	48,412	44,355	49,526	45,376	50,665	46,419	51,830	47,487	53,022	2.30%	11.50%	27,447	30,647	39,334	43,919	55,289	61,733
Cmputr Opns Supv	56,370	65,838	57,667	67,352	58,993	68,901	60,350	70,486	61,738	72,107	2.30%	11.50%	35,684	41,678	51,139	59,728	71,881	83,954
Com Dev Spec	60,875	70,914	62,275	72,545	63,708	74,214	65,173	75,921	66,672	77,667	2.30%	11.50%	38,536	44,891	55,226	64,333	77,626	90,428
Com Dev Spec,Sr	72,264	84,201	73,926	86,138	75,626	88,119	77,365	90,145	79,145	92,219	2.30%	11.50%	45,746	53,302	65,557	76,387	92,148	107,370
Comms Elctn I - II	75,008	80,999	76,733	82,862	78,498	84,768	80,303	86,717	82,150	88,712	2.30%	11.50%	47,483	51,275	68,047	73,482	95,647	103,287
Comms Engr,Assoc	67,599	78,850	69,153	80,663	70,744	82,519	72,371	84,416	74,035	86,358	2.30%	11.50%	42,792	49,915	61,325	71,532	86,199	100,546
Complaint Investigator	53,237	62,064	54,462	63,492	55,714	64,952	56,996	66,446	58,307	67,974	2.30%	11.50%	33,701	39,289	48,297	56,305	67,886	79,142
Constr Mgmt Spec	65,838	70,914	67,352	72,545	68,901	74,214	70,486	75,921	72,107	77,667	2.30%	11.50%	41,678	44,891	59,728	64,333	83,954	90,428
Constr Mgmt Supv	72,264	84,201	73,926	86,138	75,626	88,119	77,365	90,145	79,145	92,219	2.30%	11.50%	45,746	53,302	65,557	76,387	92,148	107,370
Court Cashier Supv	45,348	52,849	46,391	54,064	47,458	55,308	48,549	56,580	49,666	57,881	2.30%	11.50%	28,707	33,455	41,139	47,944	57,826	67,391
Court Clerk	42,535	49,487	43,513	50,625	44,514	51,789	45,538	52,981	46,585	54,199	2.30%	11.50%	26,926	31,327	38,588	44,894	54,239	63,104
Court Clerk Supv	48,412	56,370	49,526	57,667	50,665	58,993	51,830	60,350	53,022	61,738	2.30%	11.50%	30,647	35,684	43,919	51,139	61,733	71,881
Court Clerk,Sr	45,073	52,597	46,110	53,807	47,171	55,044	48,255	56,310	49,365	57,605	2.30%	11.50%	28,533	33,296	40,890	47,716	57,476	67,070
Court Commissioner	117,680	0	120,387	0	123,156	0	125,988	0	128,886	0	2.30%	11.50%	74,496	0	106,759	0	150,061	-
Court Interpreter	54,266	63,322	55,514	64,779	56,791	66,269	58,098	67,793	59,434	69,352	2.30%	11.50%	34,353	40,085	49,230	57,446	69,199	80,746
Court Interpreter Coord	65,838	76,609	67,352	78,371	68,901	80,173	70,486	82,017	72,107	83,904	2.30%	11.50%	41,678	48,496	59,728	69,499	83,954	97,689
Cust Svc Rep	42,992	48,161	43,981	49,268	44,993	50,401	46,028	51,561	47,086	52,747	2.30%	11.50%	27,216	30,487	39,002	43,691	54,822	61,413
Cust Svc Rep Supv	50,928	59,297	52,099	60,661	53,297	62,056	54,523	63,484	55,777	64,944	2.30%	11.50%	32,239	37,537	46,201	53,794	64,941	75,614
Cust Svc Rep,Sr	46,308	51,911	47,373	53,105	48,463	54,326	49,578	55,576	50,718	56,854	2.30%	11.50%	29,315	32,862	42,011	47,093	59,051	66,195
Dev Fin Spec	60,875	70,914	62,275	72,545	63,708	74,214	65,173	75,921	66,672	77,667	2.30%	11.50%	38,536	44,891	55,226	64,333	77,626	90,428
Dev Fin Spec I	55,364	64,649	56,637	66,135	57,940	67,657	59,273	69,213	60,636	70,805	2.30%	11.50%	35,047	40,925	50,226	58,649	70,598	82,438
Dev Fin Spec,Sr	69,497	81,159	71,095	83,026	72,730	84,936	74,403	86,889	76,114	88,888	2.30%	11.50%	43,994	51,377	63,047	73,628	88,620	103,492
Drainage&Wstwtr Coll Lead Wkr	50,859	54,907	52,029	56,170	53,225	57,461	54,450	58,783	55,702	60,135	2.30%	11.50%	32,196	34,758	46,139	49,811	64,854	70,015
Economist	67,050	78,072	68,592	79,868	70,169	81,705	71,783	83,584	73,434	85,506	2.30%	11.50%	42,445	49,423	60,827	70,827	85,499	99,555
Economist,Prin	79,582	92,319	81,412	94,442	83,284	96,615	85,200	98,837	87,160	101,110	2.30%	11.50%	50,378	58,441	72,196	83,752	101,480	117,722
Economist,Sr	75,168	87,402	76,897	89,413	78,665	91,469	80,475	93,573	82,326	95,725	2.30%	11.50%	47,584	55,329	68,192	79,291	95,851	111,452
Ed Prgm Supv	59,686	69,497	61,059	71,095	62,463	72,730	63,900	74,403	65,370	76,114	2.30%	11.50%	37,784	43,994	54,147	63,047	76,110	88,620
Ed Prgms Spec	45,691	53,237	46,742	54,462	47,817	55,714	48,917	56,996	50,042	58,307	2.30%	11.50%	28,924	33,701	41,451	48,297	58,263	67,886
EDP Equip Op,Lead-MC	45,691	53,237	46,742	54,462	47,817	55,714	48,917	56,996	50,042	58,307	2.30%	11.50%	28,924	33,701	41,451	48,297	58,263	67,886
EDP Equip Op,Sr-MC	43,358	48,412	44,355	49,526	45,376	50,665	46,419	51,830	47,487	53,022	2.30%	11.50%	27,447	30,647	39,334	43,919	55,289	61,733
EDP Equip Op-MC	37,275	43,358	38,133	44,355	39,010	45,376	39,907	46,419	40,825	47,487	2.30%	11.50%	23,597	27,447	33,816	39,334	47,532	55,289
EEO Anlyst	65,838	76,609	67,352	78,371	68,901	80,173	70,486	82,017	72,107	83,904	2.30%	11.50%	41,678	48,496	59,728	69,499	83,954	97,689
Elctn	56,782	61,424	58,088	62,837	59,424	64,282	60,791	65,761	62,189	67,273	2.30%	11.50%	35,945	38,884	51,512	55,724	72,406	78,326
Elctn,Sr	60,281	62,545	61,667	63,983	63,086	65,455	64,536	66,960	66,021	68,500	2.30%	11.50%	38,160	39,593	54,686	56,740	76,868	79,755
Elecl Engr,Asst I-III	55,753	73,064	57,035	74,745	58,347	76,464	59,689	78,222	61,062	80,021	2.30%	11.50%	35,294	46,252	50,579	66,283	71,094	93,169
Elecl Engr,Sr	77,318	90,009	79,096	92,080	80,915	94,198	82,776	96,364	84,680	98,580	2.30%	11.50%	48,945	56,979	70,142	81,656	98,593	114,777
Elecl Engrng Spec Supv	79,444	88,912	81,272	90,957	83,141	93,049	85,053	95,189	87,009	97,378	2.30%	11.50%	50,291	56,284	72,072	80,660	101,305	113,377
Elecl Engrng Spec,Asst I-III	49,007	68,971	50,134	70,557	51,287	72,180	52,467	73,840	53,673	75,538	2.30%	11.50%	31,023	43,661	44,459	62,570	62,492	87,949
Elecl Engrng Spec,Sr	75,808	84,933	77,552	86,886	79,336	88,885	81,160	90,929	83,027	93,020	2.30%	11.50%	47,989	53,766	68,773	77,051	96,668	108,303

231

Chart III - U.S. States & Cities - Job Titles - Salaries - Pension Estimates

WA-Seattle	2010 (Min)	2010 (Max)	2011 (Min)	2011 (Max)	2012 (Min)	2012 (Max)	2013 (Min)	2013 (Max)	2014 (Min)	2014 (Max)	5-Year Average % Raise	5-Year Cumulative Raise Estimate**	20-Year Annual Pension Benefit Estimate (Min.)***	20-Year Annual Pension Benefit Estimate (Max.)	25-Year Annual Pension Benefit Estimate (Min.)	25-Year Annual Pension Benefit Estimate (Max.)	30-Year Annual Pension Benefit Estimate (Min.)	30-Year Annual Pension Benefit Estimate (Max.)
Elecl Svc Engr	75,968	88,386	77,716	90,419	79,503	92,498	81,332	94,626	83,202	96,802	2.30%	11.50%	48,091	55,951	68,918	80,183	96,872	112,706
Elecl Svc Rep	51,293	59,686	52,473	61,059	53,680	62,463	54,915	63,900	56,178	65,370	2.30%	11.50%	32,471	37,784	46,533	54,147	65,408	76,110
Elecl Svc Rep,Sr	55,364	64,649	56,637	66,135	57,940	67,657	59,273	69,213	60,636	70,805	2.30%	11.50%	35,047	40,925	50,226	58,649	70,598	82,438
Enrgy Res&Eval Anlyst	67,050	78,072	68,592	79,868	70,169	81,705	71,783	83,584	73,434	85,506	2.30%	11.50%	42,445	49,423	60,827	70,827	85,499	99,555
Envrnmtl Anlyst,Assoc	63,322	73,682	64,779	75,376	66,269	77,110	67,793	78,883	69,352	80,698	2.30%	11.50%	40,085	46,643	57,446	66,844	80,746	93,956
Envrnmtl Anlyst,Sr	72,264	84,201	73,926	86,138	75,626	88,119	77,365	90,145	79,145	92,219	2.30%	11.50%	45,746	53,302	65,557	76,387	92,148	107,370
Envrnmtl Fld Spec	48,412	56,370	49,526	57,667	50,665	58,993	51,830	60,350	53,022	61,738	2.30%	11.50%	30,647	35,684	43,919	51,139	61,733	71,881
Envrnmtl Fld Spec,Sr	52,323	60,875	53,526	62,275	54,757	63,708	56,016	65,173	57,305	66,672	2.30%	11.50%	33,122	38,536	47,467	55,226	66,720	77,626
Events Booking Rep	54,266	63,322	55,514	64,779	56,791	66,269	58,098	67,793	59,434	69,352	2.30%	11.50%	34,353	40,085	49,230	57,446	69,199	80,746
Events Svc Rep	54,266	63,322	55,514	64,779	56,791	66,269	58,098	67,793	59,434	69,352	2.30%	11.50%	34,353	40,085	49,230	57,446	69,199	80,746
Evidence Warehouser	45,302	48,915	46,344	50,040	47,410	51,191	48,500	52,369	49,616	53,573	2.30%	11.50%	28,678	30,965	41,098	44,376	57,767	62,375
Exec Asst	72,264	84,201	73,926	86,138	75,626	88,119	77,365	90,145	79,145	92,219	2.30%	11.50%	45,746	53,302	65,557	76,387	92,148	107,370
Exec Asst,Sr	75,168	87,402	76,897	89,413	78,665	91,469	80,475	93,573	82,326	95,725	2.30%	11.50%	47,584	55,329	68,192	79,291	95,851	111,452
Exec Asst/Secretary	55,364	64,649	56,637	66,135	57,940	67,657	59,273	69,213	60,636	70,805	2.30%	11.50%	35,047	40,925	50,226	58,649	70,598	82,438
Exec Manager-City Auditor	77,546	191,522	79,330	195,927	81,154	200,433	83,021	205,043	84,930	209,759	2.30%	11.50%	49,090	121,240	70,350	173,748	98,884	244,222
Executive1-4	73,156	198,702	74,838	203,272	76,559	207,948	78,320	212,730	80,122	217,623	2.30%	11.50%	46,310	125,786	66,366	180,262	93,285	253,378
Facilities Maint Wkr	48,023	51,774	49,128	52,965	50,258	54,183	51,414	55,429	52,596	56,704	2.30%	11.50%	30,401	32,775	43,567	46,969	61,238	66,020
Facilities Support Coord	65,838	76,609	67,352	78,371	68,901	80,173	70,486	82,017	72,107	83,904	2.30%	11.50%	41,678	48,496	59,728	69,499	83,954	97,689
Fin Anlyst	60,875	70,914	62,275	72,545	63,708	74,214	65,173	75,921	66,672	77,667	2.30%	11.50%	38,536	44,891	55,226	64,333	77,626	90,428
Fin Anlyst Supv	72,264	84,201	73,926	86,138	75,626	88,119	77,365	90,145	79,145	92,219	2.30%	11.50%	45,746	53,302	65,557	76,387	92,148	107,370
Fin Anlyst,Asst	48,412	56,370	49,526	57,667	50,665	58,993	51,830	60,350	53,022	61,738	2.30%	11.50%	30,647	35,684	43,919	51,139	61,733	71,881
Fin Anlyst,Sr	67,050	78,072	68,592	79,868	70,169	81,705	71,783	83,584	73,434	85,506	2.30%	11.50%	42,445	49,423	60,827	70,827	85,499	99,555
Fire Capt-Dispatcher	95,909	100,026	98,115	102,326	100,372	104,680	102,681	107,087	105,042	109,550	2.30%	11.50%	60,714	63,320	87,009	90,743	122,300	127,549
Fire Capt-Prev Inspector I	100,712	105,034	103,028	107,450	105,398	109,921	107,822	112,449	110,302	115,036	2.30%	11.50%	63,754	66,490	91,365	95,286	128,424	133,935
Fire Chief,Asst	139,519	162,273	142,728	166,005	146,011	169,824	149,369	173,729	152,805	177,725	2.30%	11.50%	88,321	102,725	126,571	147,214	177,910	206,925
Fire Equip Tech	49,395	53,237	50,532	54,462	51,694	55,714	52,883	56,996	54,099	58,307	2.30%	11.50%	31,269	33,701	44,811	48,297	62,987	67,886
Fire Lieut-Prev Inspector I	88,317	92,068	90,348	94,185	92,427	96,351	94,552	98,567	96,727	100,835	2.30%	11.50%	55,908	58,282	80,121	83,523	112,619	117,401
Fire Marshal	139,519	162,273	142,728	166,005	146,011	169,824	149,369	173,729	152,805	177,725	2.30%	11.50%	88,321	102,725	126,571	147,214	177,910	206,925
Fire Prev Tech	67,050	78,072	68,592	79,868	70,169	81,705	71,783	83,584	73,434	85,506	2.30%	11.50%	42,445	49,423	60,827	70,827	85,499	99,555
Fire Protection Engr	65,838	76,609	67,352	78,371	68,901	80,173	70,486	82,017	72,107	83,904	2.30%	11.50%	41,678	48,496	59,728	69,499	83,954	97,689
Fire Protection Engr,Sr	75,168	87,402	76,897	89,413	78,665	91,469	80,475	93,573	82,326	95,725	2.30%	11.50%	47,584	55,329	68,192	79,291	95,851	111,452
Fire Svcs Spec	49,395	53,237	50,532	54,462	51,694	55,714	52,883	56,996	54,099	58,307	2.30%	11.50%	31,269	33,701	44,811	48,297	62,987	67,886
Fireftr-Prev Insp I	65,769	80,794	67,282	82,652	68,829	84,553	70,412	86,498	72,032	88,487	2.30%	11.50%	41,634	51,145	59,666	73,296	83,866	103,025
Fld Engrng Tech	45,279	49,007	46,321	50,134	47,386	51,287	48,476	52,467	49,591	53,673	2.30%	11.50%	28,663	31,023	41,077	44,459	57,738	62,492
Fleet Mgmt Anlyst	60,875	70,914	62,275	72,545	63,708	74,214	65,173	75,921	66,672	77,667	2.30%	11.50%	38,536	44,891	55,226	64,333	77,626	90,428
Fleet Mgmt Coord	60,875	70,914	62,275	72,545	63,708	74,214	65,173	75,921	66,672	77,667	2.30%	11.50%	38,536	44,891	55,226	64,333	77,626	90,428
Fncl Systs Anlyst	63,322	73,682	64,779	75,376	66,269	77,110	67,793	78,883	69,352	80,698	2.30%	11.50%	40,085	46,643	57,446	66,844	80,746	93,956
Forest Maint Wkr	50,013	53,878	51,163	55,117	52,340	56,384	53,544	57,681	54,775	59,008	2.30%	11.50%	31,660	34,107	45,372	48,878	63,775	68,703
Forest Maint Wkr,Sr	53,237	57,468	54,462	58,790	55,714	60,142	56,996	61,525	58,307	62,940	2.30%	11.50%	33,701	36,379	48,297	52,135	67,886	73,281
Gardener,Prin	53,237	55,364	54,462	56,637	55,714	57,940	56,996	59,273	58,307	60,636	2.30%	11.50%	33,701	35,047	48,297	50,226	67,886	70,598
Gardener,Sr	49,395	53,237	50,532	54,462	51,694	55,714	52,883	56,996	54,099	58,307	2.30%	11.50%	31,269	33,701	44,811	48,297	62,987	67,886
Hearing Examiner	91,930	192,139	94,045	196,558	96,208	201,079	98,421	205,704	100,684	210,435	2.30%	11.50%	58,195	121,631	83,399	174,308	117,226	245,009

Chart III - U.S. States & Cities - Job Titles - Salaries - Pension Estimates

WA-Seattle	2010 (Min)	2010 (Max)	2011 (Min)	2011 (Max)	2012 (Min)	2012 (Max)	2013 (Min)	2013 (Max)	2014 (Min)	2014 (Max)	5-Year Average % Raise	5-Year Cumulative Raise Estimate**	20-Year Annual Pension Benefit Estimate (Min.)***	20-Year Annual Pension Benefit Estimate (Max.)	25-Year Annual Pension Benefit Estimate (Min.)	25-Year Annual Pension Benefit Estimate (Max.)	30-Year Annual Pension Benefit Estimate (Min.)	30-Year Annual Pension Benefit Estimate (Max.)
Hearing Examiner,Dep	94,011	109,287	96,174	111,801	98,386	114,372	100,649	117,003	102,963	119,694	2.30%	11.50%	59,513	69,183	85,287	99,145	119,880	139,359
Housing Ordinance Spec	52,323	60,875	53,526	62,275	54,757	63,708	56,016	65,173	57,305	66,672	2.30%	11.50%	33,122	38,536	47,467	55,226	66,720	77,626
Housing Ordinance Supv	60,875	70,914	62,275	72,545	63,708	74,214	65,173	75,921	66,672	77,667	2.30%	11.50%	38,536	44,891	55,226	64,333	77,626	90,428
Housing/Zoning Inspector	57,468	67,050	58,790	68,592	60,142	70,169	61,525	71,783	62,940	73,434	2.30%	11.50%	36,379	42,445	52,135	60,827	73,281	85,499
Housing/Zoning Inspector Supv	67,050	78,072	68,592	79,868	70,169	81,705	71,783	83,584	73,434	85,506	2.30%	11.50%	42,445	49,423	60,827	70,827	85,499	99,555
Housing/Zoning Inspector,Sr	60,875	70,914	62,275	72,545	63,708	74,214	65,173	75,921	66,672	77,667	2.30%	11.50%	38,536	44,891	55,226	64,333	77,626	90,428
Human Svcs Anlyst	60,875	70,914	62,275	72,545	63,708	74,214	65,173	75,921	66,672	77,667	2.30%	11.50%	38,536	44,891	55,226	64,333	77,626	90,428
Human Svcs Anlyst,Sr	65,838	76,609	67,352	78,371	68,901	80,173	70,486	82,017	72,107	83,904	2.30%	11.50%	41,678	48,496	59,728	69,499	83,954	97,689
Human Svcs Coord	50,333	58,588	51,491	59,936	52,675	61,315	53,886	62,725	55,126	64,167	2.30%	11.50%	31,863	37,089	45,662	53,151	64,183	74,710
Human Svcs Prgm Supv	60,875	70,914	62,275	72,545	63,708	74,214	65,173	75,921	66,672	77,667	2.30%	11.50%	38,536	44,891	55,226	64,333	77,626	90,428
Human Svcs Prgm Supv,Sr	65,838	76,609	67,352	78,371	68,901	80,173	70,486	82,017	72,107	83,904	2.30%	11.50%	41,678	48,496	59,728	69,499	83,954	97,689
Info Technol Prgmmer Anlyst	60,875	70,914	62,275	72,545	63,708	74,214	65,173	75,921	66,672	77,667	2.30%	11.50%	38,536	44,891	55,226	64,333	77,626	90,428
Info Technol Prof A *	77,432	116,171	79,213	118,843	81,035	121,576	82,899	124,372	84,805	127,233	2.30%	11.50%	49,017	73,540	70,246	105,390	98,738	148,137
Info Technol Prof B	67,095	100,666	68,639	102,981	70,217	105,350	71,832	107,773	73,484	110,252	2.30%	11.50%	42,474	63,725	60,869	91,324	85,558	128,366
Info Technol Prof C	58,108	87,174	59,445	89,179	60,812	91,230	62,211	93,328	63,641	95,475	2.30%	11.50%	36,785	55,184	52,716	79,084	74,098	111,161
Info Technol Spec	53,237	62,064	54,462	63,492	55,714	64,952	56,996	66,446	58,307	67,974	2.30%	11.50%	33,701	39,289	48,297	56,305	67,886	79,142
Info Technol Systs Anlyst	64,649	75,168	66,135	76,897	67,657	78,665	69,213	80,475	70,805	82,326	2.30%	11.50%	40,925	47,584	58,649	68,192	82,438	95,851
Info Technol Tech	47,566	55,364	48,660	56,637	49,779	57,940	50,924	59,273	52,095	60,636	2.30%	11.50%	30,111	35,047	43,152	50,226	60,654	70,598
Info&Referral Spec	39,562	44,067	40,472	45,081	41,403	46,118	42,355	47,178	43,329	48,263	2.30%	11.50%	25,044	27,896	35,891	39,978	50,448	56,193
Inspection Support Anlyst	60,875	70,914	62,275	72,545	63,708	74,214	65,173	75,921	66,672	77,667	2.30%	11.50%	38,536	44,891	55,226	64,333	77,626	90,428
IT Prgmmer Anlyst-Spec	61,333	71,669	62,743	73,318	64,186	75,004	65,663	76,729	67,173	78,494	2.30%	11.50%	38,826	45,369	55,641	65,018	78,209	91,390
Labor Relations Coord	72,264	84,201	73,926	86,138	75,626	88,119	77,365	90,145	79,145	92,219	2.30%	11.50%	45,746	53,302	65,557	76,387	92,148	107,370
Labor Relations Spec	60,875	70,914	62,275	72,545	63,708	74,214	65,173	75,921	66,672	77,667	2.30%	11.50%	38,536	44,891	55,226	64,333	77,626	90,428
Labor Standards Tech Supv	56,370	65,838	57,667	67,352	58,993	68,901	60,350	70,486	61,738	72,107	2.30%	11.50%	35,684	41,678	51,139	59,728	71,881	83,954
Laboratory Tech I-II	38,693	60,875	39,583	62,275	40,493	63,708	41,425	65,173	42,378	66,672	2.30%	11.50%	24,494	38,536	35,102	55,226	49,340	77,626
Laborer	38,853	41,300	39,747	42,250	40,661	43,222	41,596	44,216	42,553	45,233	2.30%	11.50%	24,595	26,144	35,247	37,467	49,544	52,664
Land Use Plnr I-IV	62,064	87,402	63,492	89,413	64,952	91,469	66,446	93,573	67,974	95,725	2.30%	11.50%	39,289	55,329	56,305	79,291	79,142	111,452
Landscape Architect	67,050	78,072	68,592	79,868	70,169	81,705	71,783	83,584	73,434	85,506	2.30%	11.50%	42,445	49,423	60,827	70,827	85,499	99,555
Legal Advisor	82,554	95,818	84,453	98,022	86,396	100,276	88,383	102,583	90,415	104,942	2.30%	11.50%	52,260	60,656	74,893	86,926	105,270	122,184
Legal Asst	44,067	49,395	45,081	50,532	46,118	51,694	47,178	52,883	48,263	54,099	2.30%	11.50%	27,896	31,269	39,978	44,811	56,193	62,987
Legislative Anlyst	72,264	84,201	73,926	86,138	75,626	88,119	77,365	90,145	79,145	92,219	2.30%	11.50%	45,746	53,302	65,557	76,387	92,148	107,370
Lifeguard	29,637	35,880	30,319	36,706	31,016	37,550	31,730	38,413	32,459	39,297	2.30%	11.50%	18,761	22,714	26,887	32,550	37,792	45,753
Lifeguard,Sr	34,577	38,830	35,372	39,723	36,186	40,637	37,018	41,572	37,869	42,528	2.30%	11.50%	21,888	24,581	31,368	35,227	44,091	49,515
Magistrate	93,646	109,470	95,799	111,988	98,003	114,564	100,257	117,199	102,563	119,894	2.30%	11.50%	59,281	69,299	84,955	99,311	119,413	139,593
Maint Laborer	39,562	45,691	40,472	46,742	41,403	47,817	42,355	48,917	43,329	50,042	2.30%	11.50%	25,044	28,924	35,891	41,451	50,448	58,263
Mech Plans Engr	69,497	81,159	71,095	83,026	72,730	84,936	74,403	86,889	76,114	88,888	2.30%	11.50%	43,994	51,377	63,047	73,628	88,620	103,492
Mgmt Systs Anlyst	60,875	70,914	62,275	72,545	63,708	74,214	65,173	75,921	66,672	77,667	2.30%	11.50%	38,536	44,891	55,226	64,333	77,626	90,428
Mgmt Systs Anlyst Supv	79,582	92,319	81,412	94,442	83,284	96,615	85,200	98,837	87,160	101,110	2.30%	11.50%	50,378	58,441	72,196	83,752	101,480	117,722
Mgmt Systs Anlyst,Asst	53,237	62,064	54,462	63,492	55,714	64,952	56,996	66,446	58,307	67,974	2.30%	11.50%	33,701	39,289	48,297	56,305	67,886	79,142
Mgmt Systs Anlyst,Sr	72,264	84,201	73,926	86,138	75,626	88,119	77,365	90,145	79,145	92,219	2.30%	11.50%	45,746	53,302	65,557	76,387	92,148	107,370

Chart III - U.S. States & Cities - Job Titles - Salaries - Pension Estimates

WA-Seattle	2010 (Min)	2010 (Max)	2011 (Min)	2011 (Max)	2012 (Min)	2012 (Max)	2013 (Min)	2013 (Max)	2014 (Min)	2014 (Max)	5-Year Average % Raise	5-Year Cumulative Raise Estimate**	20-Year Annual Pension Benefit Estimate (Min.)***	20-Year Annual Pension Benefit Estimate (Max.)	25-Year Annual Pension Benefit Estimate (Min.)	25-Year Annual Pension Benefit Estimate (Max.)	30-Year Annual Pension Benefit Estimate (Min.)	30-Year Annual Pension Benefit Estimate (Max.)
Naturalist	46,651	54,266	47,724	55,514	48,822	56,791	49,945	58,098	51,094	59,434	2.30%	11.50%	29,532	34,353	42,322	49,230	59,488	69,199
Naturalist,Sr	50,333	58,588	51,491	59,936	52,675	61,315	53,886	62,725	55,126	64,167	2.30%	11.50%	31,863	37,089	45,662	53,151	64,183	74,710
Naturalist,Supv	64,649	75,168	66,135	76,897	67,657	78,665	69,213	80,475	70,805	82,326	2.30%	11.50%	40,925	47,584	58,649	68,192	82,438	95,851
Paralegal	52,323	60,875	53,526	62,275	54,757	63,708	56,016	65,173	57,305	66,672	2.30%	11.50%	33,122	38,536	47,467	55,226	66,720	77,626
Parking Enf Ofcr	45,462	51,980	46,508	53,175	47,577	54,398	48,672	55,649	49,791	56,929	2.30%	11.50%	28,779	32,905	41,243	47,156	57,972	66,282
Parking Enf Ofcr,Sr	47,566	55,364	48,660	56,637	49,779	57,940	50,924	59,273	52,095	60,636	2.30%	11.50%	30,111	35,047	43,152	50,226	60,654	70,598
Parking Facilities Coord	50,333	58,588	51,491	59,936	52,675	61,315	53,886	62,725	55,126	64,167	2.30%	11.50%	31,863	37,089	45,662	53,151	64,183	74,710
Parking Meter Collector	35,880	41,735	36,706	42,694	37,550	43,676	38,413	44,681	39,297	45,709	2.30%	11.50%	22,714	26,420	32,550	37,861	45,753	53,218
Permit Spec I-II	54,266	68,262	55,514	69,832	56,791	71,438	58,098	73,081	59,434	74,762	2.30%	11.50%	34,353	43,212	49,230	61,927	69,199	87,045
Personnel Anlyst	60,875	70,914	62,275	72,545	63,708	74,214	65,173	75,921	66,672	77,667	2.30%	11.50%	38,536	44,891	55,226	64,333	77,626	90,428
Personnel Anlyst Supv	72,264	84,201	73,926	86,138	75,626	88,119	77,365	90,145	79,145	92,219	2.30%	11.50%	45,746	53,302	65,557	76,387	92,148	107,37
Personnel Anlyst,Sr	67,050	78,072	68,592	79,868	70,169	81,705	71,783	83,584	73,434	85,506	2.30%	11.50%	42,445	49,423	60,827	70,827	85,499	99,555
Personnel Spec	56,370	65,838	57,667	67,352	58,993	68,901	60,350	70,486	61,738	72,107	2.30%	11.50%	35,684	41,678	51,139	59,728	71,881	83,954
Personnel Spec,Sr	60,875	70,914	62,275	72,545	63,708	74,214	65,173	75,921	66,672	77,667	2.30%	11.50%	38,536	44,891	55,226	64,333	77,626	90,428
Photographer	44,845	52,323	45,876	53,526	46,931	54,757	48,011	56,016	49,115	57,305	2.30%	11.50%	28,388	33,122	40,683	47,467	57,184	66,720
Photographer,Sr	50,333	58,588	51,491	59,936	52,675	61,315	53,886	62,725	55,126	64,167	2.30%	11.50%	31,863	37,089	45,662	53,151	64,183	74,710
Plng Anlyst,Asst	51,751	60,281	52,941	61,667	54,159	63,086	55,404	64,536	56,679	66,021	2.30%	11.50%	32,760	38,160	46,948	54,686	65,991	76,868
Plng Commis Anlyst	58,588	68,262	59,936	69,832	61,315	71,438	62,725	73,081	64,167	74,762	2.30%	11.50%	37,089	43,212	53,151	61,927	74,710	87,045
Plng Intern	37,618	38,853	38,484	39,747	39,369	40,661	40,274	41,596	41,200	42,553	2.30%	11.50%	23,814	24,595	34,127	35,247	47,969	49,544
Plng&Dev Spec I-II	58,588	73,682	59,936	75,376	61,315	77,110	62,725	78,883	64,167	80,698	2.30%	11.50%	37,089	46,643	53,151	66,844	74,710	93,956
Plng&Dev Spec,Sr	72,264	84,201	73,926	86,138	75,626	88,119	77,365	90,145	79,145	92,219	2.30%	11.50%	45,746	53,302	65,557	76,387	92,148	107,37
Plng&Dev Spec,Supvsng	78,072	90,695	79,868	92,781	81,705	94,915	83,584	97,099	85,506	99,332	2.30%	11.50%	49,423	57,414	70,827	82,279	99,555	115,65
Plnr,Asst I-II	51,751	66,387	52,941	67,913	54,159	69,475	55,404	71,073	56,679	72,708	2.30%	11.50%	32,760	42,025	46,948	60,226	65,991	84,654
Plumber	58,954	63,711	60,310	65,176	61,697	66,675	63,116	68,209	64,568	69,778	2.30%	11.50%	37,320	40,331	53,483	57,798	75,176	81,242
Plumber,Sr	62,682	65,289	64,124	66,791	65,598	68,327	67,107	69,898	68,651	71,506	2.30%	11.50%	39,680	41,330	56,865	59,230	79,930	83,254
Pol Chief,Dep	146,517	170,460	149,887	174,381	153,334	178,391	156,861	182,494	160,469	186,692	2.30%	11.50%	92,751	107,907	132,920	154,641	186,833	217,36
Pol Comms Anlyst	60,875	70,914	62,275	72,545	63,708	74,214	65,173	75,921	66,672	77,667	2.30%	11.50%	38,536	44,891	55,226	64,333	77,626	90,42
Pol Comms Dir	107,961	121,636	110,444	124,434	112,984	127,296	115,583	130,224	118,241	133,219	2.30%	11.50%	68,343	77,000	97,942	110,348	137,668	155,10
Pol Comms Dispatcher I-III	41,735	63,322	42,694	64,779	43,676	66,269	44,681	67,793	45,709	69,352	2.30%	11.50%	26,420	40,085	37,861	57,446	53,218	80,74
Pol Data Tech Supv	48,412	54,266	49,526	55,514	50,665	56,791	51,830	58,098	53,022	59,434	2.30%	11.50%	30,647	34,353	43,919	49,230	61,733	69,199
Pol Data Tech Trne	37,275	41,735	38,133	42,694	39,010	43,676	39,907	44,681	40,825	45,709	2.30%	11.50%	23,597	26,420	33,816	37,861	47,532	53,21
Pol Lieut	90,764	102,290	92,852	104,642	94,987	107,049	97,172	109,511	99,407	112,030	2.30%	11.50%	57,457	64,753	82,341	92,797	115,739	130,43
Pol Ofcr	51,842	73,430	53,035	75,119	54,255	76,847	55,502	78,614	56,779	80,422	2.30%	11.50%	32,818	46,484	47,031	66,615	66,107	93,63
Pol Sgt	75,580	84,452	77,318	86,395	79,096	88,382	80,915	90,415	82,776	92,494	2.30%	11.50%	47,845	53,462	68,566	76,615	96,376	107,69
Prob Counslr I-II	56,370	69,497	57,667	71,095	58,993	72,730	60,350	74,403	61,738	76,114	2.30%	11.50%	35,684	43,994	51,139	63,047	71,881	88,62
Prob Supv	68,262	79,582	69,832	81,412	71,438	83,284	73,081	85,200	74,762	87,160	2.30%	11.50%	43,212	50,378	61,927	72,196	87,045	101,48
Property Mgmt Spec	76,609	88,912	78,371	90,957	80,173	93,049	82,017	95,189	83,904	97,378	2.30%	11.50%	48,496	56,284	69,499	80,660	97,689	113,37
Property Rehab Spec	56,302	65,769	57,597	67,282	58,921	68,829	60,276	70,412	61,663	72,032	2.30%	11.50%	35,641	41,634	51,077	59,666	71,794	83,86
Publc Ed Prgm Spec	52,323	60,875	53,526	62,275	54,757	63,708	56,016	65,173	57,305	66,672	2.30%	11.50%	33,122	38,536	47,467	55,226	66,720	77,62
Publc Ed Prgm Supv	65,838	76,609	67,352	78,371	68,901	80,173	70,486	82,017	72,107	83,904	2.30%	11.50%	41,678	48,496	59,728	69,499	83,954	97,68
Pwr Anlyst	67,599	78,850	69,153	80,663	70,744	82,519	72,371	84,416	74,035	86,358	2.30%	11.50%	42,792	49,915	61,325	71,532	86,199	100,54
Pwr Anlyst,Sr	75,968	88,386	77,716	90,419	79,503	92,498	81,332	94,626	83,202	96,802	2.30%	11.50%	48,091	55,951	68,918	80,183	96,872	112,70
Rates Mgmt Anlyst	72,264	84,201	73,926	86,138	75,626	88,119	77,365	90,145	79,145	92,219	2.30%	11.50%	45,746	53,302	65,557	76,387	92,148	107,37
Rates Mgmt Anlyst,Sr	75,168	87,402	76,897	89,413	78,665	91,469	80,475	93,573	82,326	95,725	2.30%	11.50%	47,584	55,329	68,192	79,291	95,851	111,45

234

Chart III - U.S. States & Cities - Job Titles - Salaries - Pension Estimates

WA-Seattle	2010 (Min)	2010 (Max)	2011 (Min)	2011 (Max)	2012 (Min)	2012 (Max)	2013 (Min)	2013 (Max)	2014 (Min)	2014 (Max)	5-Year Average % Raise	5-Year Cumulative Raise Estimate**	20-Year Annual Pension Benefit Estimate (Min.)***	20-Year Annual Pension Benefit Estimate (Max.)	25-Year Annual Pension Benefit Estimate (Min.)	25-Year Annual Pension Benefit Estimate (Max.)	30-Year Annual Pension Benefit Estimate (Min.)	30-Year Annual Pension Benefit Estimate (Max.)
Real Property Agent	56,759	66,387	58,064	67,913	59,400	69,475	60,766	71,073	62,164	72,708	2.30%	11.50%	35,931	42,025	51,492	60,226	72,377	84,654
Real Property Agent,Sr	67,599	78,850	69,153	80,663	70,744	82,519	72,371	84,416	74,035	86,358	2.30%	11.50%	42,792	49,915	61,325	71,532	86,199	100,546
Real Property Supv	76,609	82,554	78,371	84,453	80,173	86,396	82,017	88,383	83,904	90,415	2.30%	11.50%	48,496	52,260	69,499	74,893	97,689	105,270
Rec Prgm Coord	56,370	65,838	57,667	67,352	58,993	68,901	60,350	70,486	61,738	72,107	2.30%	11.50%	35,684	41,678	51,139	59,728	71,881	83,954
Rec Prgm Coord,Sr	60,875	70,914	62,275	72,545	63,708	74,214	65,173	75,921	66,672	77,667	2.30%	11.50%	38,536	44,891	55,226	64,333	77,626	90,428
Rec Prgm Spec	48,412	56,370	49,526	57,667	50,665	58,993	51,830	60,350	53,022	61,738	2.30%	11.50%	30,647	35,684	43,919	51,139	61,733	71,881
Rec Prgm Spec,Sr	53,237	62,064	54,462	63,492	55,714	64,952	56,996	66,446	58,307	67,974	2.30%	11.50%	33,701	39,289	48,297	56,305	67,886	79,142
Rec Prgmmer	42,535	49,395	43,513	50,532	44,514	51,694	45,538	52,883	46,585	54,099	2.30%	11.50%	26,926	31,269	38,588	44,811	54,239	62,987
Retirement Spec	44,067	51,293	45,081	52,473	46,118	53,680	47,178	54,915	48,263	56,178	2.30%	11.50%	27,896	32,471	39,978	46,533	56,193	65,408
Retirement Spec,Asst	41,735	46,651	42,694	47,724	43,676	48,822	44,681	49,945	45,709	51,094	2.30%	11.50%	26,420	29,532	37,861	42,322	53,218	59,488
Risk Mgmt Anlyst	60,875	70,914	62,275	72,545	63,708	74,214	65,173	75,921	66,672	77,667	2.30%	11.50%	38,536	44,891	55,226	64,333	77,626	90,428
Security Ofcr	37,870	40,934	38,741	41,876	39,632	42,839	40,543	43,824	41,476	44,832	2.30%	11.50%	23,973	25,913	34,355	37,135	48,290	52,198
Security Ofcr,Sr	41,735	44,845	42,694	45,876	43,676	46,931	44,681	48,011	45,709	49,115	2.30%	11.50%	26,420	28,388	37,861	40,683	53,218	57,184
Security Ofcr,Supvsng	47,566	55,410	48,660	56,684	49,779	57,988	50,924	59,322	52,095	60,686	2.30%	11.50%	30,111	35,076	43,152	50,268	60,654	70,657
Security Prgms Spec	58,588	68,262	59,936	69,832	61,315	71,438	62,725	73,081	64,167	74,762	2.30%	11.50%	37,089	43,212	53,151	61,927	74,710	87,045
Sfty&Hlth Spec	63,322	73,682	64,779	75,376	66,269	77,110	67,793	78,883	69,352	80,698	2.30%	11.50%	40,085	46,643	57,446	66,844	80,746	93,956
Sfty&Hlth Spec,Sr	68,262	79,582	69,832	81,412	71,438	83,284	73,081	85,200	74,762	87,160	2.30%	11.50%	43,212	50,378	61,927	72,196	87,045	101,480
Strucl Plans Engr	69,497	81,159	71,095	83,026	72,730	84,936	74,403	86,889	76,114	88,888	2.30%	11.50%	43,994	51,377	63,047	73,628	88,620	103,492
Strucl Plans Engr Supv	79,582	92,319	81,412	94,442	83,284	96,615	85,200	98,837	87,160	101,110	2.30%	11.50%	50,378	58,441	72,196	83,752	101,480	117,722
Strucl Plans Engr,Sr	76,609	88,912	78,371	90,957	80,173	93,049	82,017	95,189	83,904	97,378	2.30%	11.50%	48,496	56,284	69,499	80,660	97,689	113,377
Surveyor,Asst	43,633	50,790	44,636	51,959	45,663	53,154	46,713	54,376	47,787	55,627	2.30%	11.50%	27,621	32,152	39,583	46,077	55,639	64,766
Surveyor,Chief	75,968	88,386	77,716	90,419	79,503	92,498	81,332	94,626	83,202	96,802	2.30%	11.50%	48,091	55,951	68,918	80,183	96,872	112,706
Systs Anlyst-Police	61,333	71,669	62,743	73,318	64,186	75,004	65,663	76,729	67,173	78,494	2.30%	11.50%	38,826	45,369	55,641	65,018	78,209	91,390
Tax Auditor	59,686	69,497	61,059	71,095	62,463	72,730	63,900	74,403	65,370	76,114	2.30%	11.50%	37,784	43,994	54,147	63,047	76,110	88,620
Tax Auditor,Sr	64,649	75,168	66,135	76,897	67,657	78,665	69,213	80,475	70,805	82,326	2.30%	11.50%	40,925	47,584	58,649	68,192	82,438	95,851
Telecom Syst Installer	54,678	63,528	55,936	64,989	57,222	66,484	58,538	68,013	59,885	69,577	2.30%	11.50%	34,613	40,216	49,604	57,632	69,723	81,009
Telecom Syst Installer,Sr	63,528	71,418	64,989	73,060	66,484	74,741	68,013	76,460	69,577	78,218	2.30%	11.50%	40,216	45,210	57,632	64,790	81,009	91,069
Telecom Systs Anlyst	72,264	84,201	73,926	86,138	75,626	88,119	77,365	90,145	79,145	92,219	2.30%	11.50%	45,746	53,302	65,557	76,387	92,148	107,370
Telecom Systs Anlyst,Sr	79,582	92,319	81,412	94,442	83,284	96,615	85,200	98,837	87,160	101,110	2.30%	11.50%	50,378	58,441	72,196	83,752	101,480	117,722
Wtr Equip Supv	65,838	76,609	67,352	78,371	68,901	80,173	70,486	82,017	72,107	83,904	2.30%	11.50%	41,678	48,496	59,728	69,499	83,954	97,689
Wtr Laboratory Tech	37,275	43,358	38,133	44,355	39,010	45,376	39,907	46,419	40,825	47,487	2.30%	11.50%	23,597	27,447	33,816	39,334	47,532	55,289
Wtr Maint Supv	79,582	85,802	81,412	87,775	83,284	89,794	85,200	91,859	87,160	93,972	2.30%	11.50%	50,378	54,316	72,196	77,839	101,480	109,411
Wtr Quality Anlyst	52,162	60,761	53,362	62,158	54,590	63,588	55,845	65,051	57,130	66,547	2.30%	11.50%	33,021	38,464	47,322	55,122	66,516	77,480
Wtr Quality Anlyst,Prin	60,875	70,914	62,275	72,545	63,708	74,214	65,173	75,921	66,672	77,667	2.30%	11.50%	38,536	44,891	55,226	64,333	77,626	90,428
Wtr Quality Anlyst,Sr	56,370	65,838	57,667	67,352	58,993	68,901	60,350	70,486	61,738	72,107	2.30%	11.50%	35,684	41,678	51,139	59,728	71,881	83,954
Wtr Quality Chemist	60,875	70,914	62,275	72,545	63,708	74,214	65,173	75,921	66,672	77,667	2.30%	11.50%	38,536	44,891	55,226	64,333	77,626	90,428
Wtr Quality Engr	75,168	87,402	76,897	89,413	78,665	91,469	80,475	93,573	82,326	95,725	2.30%	11.50%	47,584	55,329	68,192	79,291	95,851	111,452
Wtr Quality Engr,Sr	81,159	94,011	83,026	96,174	84,936	98,386	86,889	100,649	88,888	102,963	2.30%	11.50%	51,377	59,513	73,628	85,287	103,492	119,880
Wtr Quality Inspector	54,266	58,588	55,514	59,936	56,791	61,315	58,098	62,725	59,434	64,167	2.30%	11.50%	34,353	37,089	49,230	53,151	69,199	74,710
Wtr Quality Inspector,Chief	64,649	75,168	66,135	76,897	67,657	78,665	69,213	80,475	70,805	82,326	2.30%	11.50%	40,925	47,584	58,649	68,192	82,438	95,851
Wtr Quality Inspector,Sr	59,686	63,391	61,059	64,849	62,463	66,340	63,900	67,866	65,370	69,427	2.30%	11.50%	37,784	40,129	54,147	57,508	76,110	80,834
Wtr Quality Laboratory Supv	75,168	87,402	76,897	89,413	78,665	91,469	80,475	93,573	82,326	95,725	2.30%	11.50%	47,584	55,329	68,192	79,291	95,851	111,452

235

CHART IV: IT Skills Sets-IT Job Titles

Application Development, Programmer & Database Jobs

Programming Languages & Tools
>> AS/400 RPG
>> C,C,C++, Visual C++
>> CGI
>> Cobol
>> CICS
>> Extensile Markup Language (XML)
>> Groove (peer-to-peer development environment)
>> Java, Java Beans, Enterprise Java, JavaScript
>> Lotus Notes/Domino
>> Microsoft Exchange
>> Perl
>> PowerBuilder
>> Universal Modeling Language (UML)
>> Visual Basic (VB)
>> Wireless Applications Protocol (WAP)

Operating Systems
>> AS/400/OS
>> Linux
>> MVS
>> Novell NetWaree
>> PalmOS
>> Unix (including Sun Solaris, IBM AIX, Hewlett-Packard)
>> Windows 95/98/2000/XP
>> Windows CE
>> Windows NT

Database Languages
>> IBM DB2
>> Informix
>> Microsoft Access
>> Microsoft SQL Server
>> Oracle 8i
>> Sybase

Reporting Tools
>> Crystal Reports
>> Impromptu
>> Oracle Reports
>> SAS Enterprise Reporter

Online Analytical Processing Tools
>> IBM Intelligent Decision Server
>> Microsoft SQL Server OLAP Services
>> SAP Business Information Warehouse
>> SAS Software

Enterprise-Wide Application Suites
>> J.D. Edwards
>> Lawson
>> Oracle Enterprise Apps
>> PeopleSoft
>> SAP

Application Development, Programmer & Database Jobs

Data Warehouse & Data Mining Tools
>> Cognos Scenario
>> Cognos Visualizer
>> IBM Intelligent Miner
>> Oracle Darwin
>> SAS Enterprise Miner
>> GUI Interfaces

Systems Analysis Tools
>> CASE Management Software
>> Microsoft Project
>> Visio

Systems Analysis Work
>> Feasibility Studies
>> Hardware & Software Configuration
>> Requests for Proposals
>> Vendor Evaluation & Bid Analysis
>> Design System Programming Specifications

Application Development, Database Work
>> Customer Relationship Management System
>> Data Warehouse & Data Mining
>> Digital Libraries
>> E-Commerce Web
>> Electronic Data Interchange Systems
>> Financial Data Processing Systems
>> GIS Systems
>> Paperless Office Systems
>> Personnel Management Systems
>> Real-time Reservation Systems
>> SCM Systems
>> Supply Chain Management System
>> Web to Backend Integration
>> Wireless Real-Time Dispatch & Proof-of-Delivery Systems

PC Support & Help DeskCall Center Jobs

PC Support Work
>> HW/SW Installation
>> PC Operating System & Application Software Troubleshooting
>> Directory Mapping
>> HW/SW Inventory
>> HW/SW Licensing

Networking & Infrastructure Jobs

Hardware
>> Bridges
>> Brouters
>> Cables (Fiber optic, coaxial, twisted-pair)
>> Hubs
>> Modems

Networking & Infrastructure Jobs

>> Networked storage devices
>> Routers
>> Switches

LAN & WAN Technologies & Protocols
>> AppleTalk/AppleShare
>> Domain Name System (DNS)
>> Ethernet
>> File Transfer Protocol (FTP)
>> IBM's System Network Architecture (SNA)
>> Novell's Internetwork Packet Exchange
>> OSI Reference Model
>> Peer-to-peer networking
>> Simple Network Management Protocol (SNMP)
>> Storage area networks
>> Sun's Network Fine System (NFS)
>> TCP/IP
>> Token Ring
>> Virtual Private Network (VPN)
>> Wireless Application Protocol (WAP)
>> X-500 Directory Services, Directory Access Protocol (DAP), Lightweight Directory Access Protocol (LDAP)

Network Management Tools
>> IBM, HP, SUN Middleware
>> Veritas Network Management Software

Security
>> Antivirus Software
>> Data encryption/cryptography
>> Digital certificates
>> Firewalls (Checkpoint, Nokia, Symantec)
>> Internet Protocol Security (Ipsec)
>> Sniffer programs

Telecommunications Technologies
>> Asynchronous Transfer Mode (ATM)
>> Digital Subscriber Line (DSL)
>> Frame Relay
>> Hybrid Fiber Coaxial (HFC) networks
>> Integrated Services Digital Network (ISDN)
>> Inereactive Voice Response (IVR)
>> Private Branch Exchange (PBX)
>> Voice Over IP

Operations Jobs

Operations Hardware
>> DEC
>> HP
>> IBM
>> SUN
>> Unisys

Operations Jobs

Operating Systems
>> IBM MVS
>> IBM OS
>> Linux
>> Microsoft 95/98/2000/XP
>> Microsoft NT
>> Unix (HP, IBM, SUN)

Storage Management Systems
>> Computer Associates Unicenter
>> EMC
>> IBM
>> Microsoft
>> Storage Area Networks (SANs)

Disaster Recovery Planning Tools
>> Comdisco ComPAS
>> Strohl Business Impact Analysis (BIA)
>> Strohl Living Disaster Recovery (LDRPS)
>> SunGard Comprehensive Business Recovery
>> SunGard ePlanner
>> Tivoli Disaster Recovery Manager

Change Management & Capacity Planning Tools
>> Network Associates Sniffer/RMON
>> Peregrine
>> SAS/STAT Statistical Analysis Tools
>> Sniffer System

System Management Tools
>> Computer Associates Unicenter
>> Hewlett Packard OpenView
>> IBM
>> Veritas

Web Developer, e-Business & Internet Jobs

Web Development & DatabaseTools
>> Active Server Pages (ASP)
>> ATG Dynamic Server Suite
>> CGI
>> ColdFusion
>> Dynamic HTML (DHTML)
>> HTML E-mail Design
>> Java, JavaScript
>> Perl
>> Visual Basic
>> Wireless Application Protocol (WAP)
>> XML
>> Lotus Notes/Domino
>> Microsoft Exchange
>> Microsoft SQL Server
>> Oracle

Web Developer, e-Business & Internet Jobs

Operating Systems & Server Software
- Linux
- Microsoft Internet Information Server
- Sun Solaris, HP Unix
- Windows 95/98/2000/XP
- Windows NT

Website Design Tools & Standards
- IP Multicas
- Macromedia Dreamweaver
- Macromedia Fireworks
- Macromedia Flash
- Macromedia MX
- Microsoft FrontPage
- Real Networks Streaming Media
- Shockwave

-Business Platforms
- Ariba b2b Commerce Platform
- ATG Dynamo E-business Platform
- Blue Martini Software Customer Intereaction Software
- InterWorld Commerce Suite
- Vignette E-business Application Platform

Content Management Tools
- Artesia Technologies TEAMS Software Suite
- Vignette Content Management Server

-business Applications
- Chordiant Software Customer Relation Management
- i2 Supplier Relationship Management Suite
- Siebel Systems e-business Customer Relationship Management

Networking & Security Technologies & Protocols
- Cisco Routers & Switches
- Emerging Internet2 Standards
- Firewalls
- PCP Encryption
- Secure Socket Layer (SSL)
- TCP/IP

Web Development, E-commerce Work
- Ecommerce Website
- Flash Animation
- Flash MX
- HTML E-mail Design
- Internet Marketing
- Online Forms & Database Integration
- Search Engine Optimization (SEO)
- Web Design & Development
- Usability & Interface Design
- Web Hosting
- Web Programming

Graphic Design & Art Jobs

Graphic Design Software
- >> Adobe Illustrator
- >> Adobe Photoshop
- >> Adobe/Other
- >> Macromedia MX
- >> Macintosh Software
- >> Quark xPress

Graphic Design & Art Work
- >> 3D Graphics
- >> Annual Reports
- >> Art & Art Direction
- >> Banner Ads
- >> Billboards & Signage
- >> Brochures & Catalogs
- >> Computer Animation
- >> Datasheets & Press Kits
- >> Digital Imaging
- >> Direct Mail
- >> Graphic Design
- >> Illustration
- >> Logos
- >> Package Design
- >> Page & Book Layout
- >> Photo Retouching
- >> Photography
- >> Print Ads
- >> Printing
- >> Product Design

IT Management & Planning Jobs

IT Management & Planning Work
- >> Computer Center Planning
- >> Contract Management
- >> Contractor Management
- >> Enterprise Planning
- >> IT Personnel/Staffing/Human Resources
- >> IT Procedures & Policies
- >> IT Procurement
- >> IT Training & Development
- >> Project Management
- >> Requests for Proposals & Bid Analysis
- >> Vendors Relations

IT Planning Tools
- >> Microsoft Project
- >> Visio

Administrative Support Tech Jobs

Administrative Support Tools
- >> Custom Applications
- >> Microsoft Office
- >> Microsoft Word
- >> Microsoft Excel
- >> Microsoft Access
- >> Microsoft PowerPoint
- >> Microsoft Publisher

Administrative Support Tech Jobs

Administrative Support Tools
- >> Bulk Mailing
- >> Customer Response
- >> Data Entry
- >> Fact Checking
- >> Mailing List Development
- >> Office Management
- >> Research
- >> Transcription
- >> Travel Planning
- >> Word Processing

IT Training & Development
- >> Business Skills
- >> Business Software
- >> Media Training
- >> Policies & Manuals
- >> Programming Languages
- >> Technical Training

IT Certifications
- >> Certified Information Systems Auditor (CISA)
- >> Certified Network Professional (CNP)
- >> Cisco Certified Internetwork Expert (CCIE)
- >> Cisco Certified Network Associate (CCNA)
- >> Cisco Certified Network Professional (CCNP)
- >> Microsoft Certified Systems Engineer + Internet (MCSE+I)
- >> Microsoft Certified Trainer (MCT)
- >> Oracle Certified Professional (OCP)
- >> PMI Project Management Professional (PMP)

Sample IT Job Titles
- >> Applications Developer/ Programmer Mainframe
- >> Systems Manager Mainframe
- >> Applications Developer/ Programmer Mid Range
- >> Systems Manager Mid Range
- >> Applications Developer PC-Systems Manager PC
- >> Business Process Analyst (BPA) &
- >> Business Process Re-Engineering Analyst
- >> C++ Programmer
- >> Computer Aided Design & Drafting Specialist (CADD)
- >> Computer Animation Designer
- >> Computer Graphics Designer
- >> Computer Programmer
- >> Computer Software Engineer/ Computer Software Programmer
- >> Database Administrator/ Programmer/Specialist
- >> Data Conversion Specialist
- >> Desktop Asset Manager/Specialist
- >> Desktop Support Specialist
- >> Electronic Commerce (EC) & Electronic

Sample IT Job Titles
- >> Data Interchange (EDI) Developer
- >> Director of IT/IT Manager
- >> Documentation Specialist
- >> E-Commerce Manager/Director of E-Business
- >> Electronic Output Manager
- >> Electronic Output Manager
- >> Enterprise Resource Planning (ERP) Consultant
- >> Geographic Information Systems (GIS) Systems Analyst/Manager
- >> Help Desk Analyst/Manager
- >> Imaging Services Analyst/ Manager/Director
- >> Information Security Analyst/ Manager/Director
- >> Interactive Voice Response (IVR) Application Developer
- >> Internet/Intranet Applications Developer/Programmer
- >> IT Administrative Support Specialist
- >> IT Management & Planning: CIO/CTO/Development Director/
- >> IT Policies & Procedures Director/ Specialist/Analyst
- >> IT Procurement & Contracting Specialist/Manager
- >> IT Trainer
- >> Java Programmer
- >> JavaScript Programmer
- >> Local Area Network Services (LANs) Administrator/Technician
- >> Network Architect//Administrator
- >> Network Architect//Administrator
- >> Network Engineer
- >> Operations/Data Center Specialist/ Director
- >> Oracle Database Programmer
- >> PeopeSoft Programmer
- >> Point-Of-Sale Systems (POS)
- >> Quality Assurance Specialist
- >> Sales: Technical Sales Representative
- >> SAP Specialist
- >> Security Administrator/Specialist/ Technician
- >> Security Administrator/Specialist/ Technician
- >> Software Engineer
- >> Software Programmer
- >> Sun Solaris Systems Engineer
- >> Systems Integration Director/ Specialist
- >> Technical Trainer
- >> Tape Librarian
- >> Technical Writer
- >> Technology Procurement (Marketwatching) Specialist
- >> Telecommunications Engineer/ Director/Specialist/Analyst
- >> Web Designer/Site Designer
- >> Web Developer/Programmer/ Content Editor
- >> Webmaster
- >> Wide Area Network (WAN) Administrator/Specialist
- >> Workflow Management Services

Chart V - U.S. Postal Service Job Titles & Salaries

Chart V: U.S. Postal Service Job Titles & Salaries
5-Year Salary Projections & Pension Estimates

LEGEND:

*Salary minimum and maximum amounts are projected estimates, based on actual base published salaries, from base year in the U.S. Federal GS Schedule, plus the estimated raise percentage. The raise percentage used is based on a 5-year average of actual published raises for the U.S. Federal Government from over the most recent 5 years (USAOPM, GS Pay Schedule, 2006.).

** Cumulative 5-Year Raise Estimate, is based on 5-Year Average Raise Estimate, as determined from actual published raise figures from over the most recent 5 years. Compounded 5-Year Raise Estimate (not shown) is greater than Cumulative 5-Year Raise Estimate.

***Estimated Pension at 20-Years, 25-Years, and 30-Years is based on the Pension Formula for the U.S. Federal Government 3 part plan: 1) The Basic Benefit annual pension of Average of 3 Highest Years Salaries times Pension Percentage 1.1% times Number of Years. The Pension Benefit is based on a fixed formula. 2) Social Security Benefits are paid in addition to The Basic Plan Benefits. 3) The Thrift Savings Plan pays an Automatic Agency Contribution of 1% of base salary per year. Employees may make additional contributions to the Thrift Savings Plan; contributions will be matched by the Agency at a rate of $1.00 for $1.00 for the first 3% of base salary contributed, and $.50 for $1.00 for the second 2% of base salary contributed (USAOPM, FERS, 2006.)

****Retirement Benefit from Agency Thrift Savings Plan. The Retirement Benefit calculated here from The Thrift Savings Plan is calculated as 1% of base salary minimum or maximum per year, plus an estimated 4.5% estimated Interest accrued per year on the 1%. Employees may choose to save their Thrift Savings in any of a variety of investment savings vehicles; interest rates may vary. This calculation shown for demonstration purposes is made without any additional Employee Contributions (USAOPM, TSP, 2006.)

*****Senior Executive Service: The SES pay range has a minimum rate of basic pay equal to 120 percent of the rate for GS-15, step 1, and the maximum rate of basic pay is equal to the rate for level III of the Executive Schedule. For any agency certified as having a performance appraisal system, the maximum rate of basic pay will be the rate for level II of the Executive Schedule (USAOPM, SES, 2006.)

Disclaimer: The Salary & Pension performance data featured is based on past performance, which is no guarantee of future results. Current Salary & Pension may be higher or lower than the performance data quoted.

REFERENCEs:
U.S. Federal Government, Office of Personnel Management, Federal Employee Retirement System 2006, http://www.opm.gov/forms/pdfimage/RI90-1.pdf

U.S. Federal Government, Office of Personnel Administration, GS Pay Schedule, 2006, http://www.opm.gov/oca/06tables/pdf/gs.pdf;   http://www.opm.gov/oca/06tables/indexGS.asp.

U.S. Federal Government, Office of Personnel Administration, Senior Executive Service, 2006, http://www.opm.gov/oca/06tables/pdf/es.pdf   http://www.opm.gov/ses.

U.S. Federal Government, Office of Personnel Administration, Thrift Savings Plan, 2006, http://www.opm.gov/benefits/correction/faq/Thrift.htm

Chart V - U.S. Postal Service Job Titles & Salaries

U.S. Postal Service	GS Grade Range:	2010 Median Grade Min Salary (STEP 2)	2010 Maximum Grade Salary (STEP 2)	2011 Median Grade Min Salary (STEP 2)	2011 Maximum Grade Salary (STEP 2)	2012 Median Grade Min Salary (STEP 3)	2012 Maximum Grade Salary (STEP 3)	2013 Median Grade Min Salary (STEP 4)	2013 Maximum Grade Salary (STEP 4)	5-Year Average % Raise	20-Year Annual Pension Benefit Estimate (Min.)***	20-Year Annual Pension Benefit Estimate (Max.)	25-Year Annual Pension Benefit Estimate (Min.)	25-Year Annual Pension Benefit Estimate (Max.)	30-Year Annual Pension Benefit Estimate (Min.)	30-Year Annual Pension Benefit Estimate (Max.)	Agency Automatic Contributions 1% Thrift Savings Plan 20 Year Savings Plus 4.5% Interest (Min)*****	Agency Automatic Contributions 1% Thrift Savings Plan 20 Year Savings Plus 4.5% Interest (Max)	Agency Automatic Contributions 1% Thrift Savings Plan 25 Year Savings Plus 4.5% Interest (Min)	Agency Automatic Contributions 1% Thrift Savings Plan 25 Year Savings Plus 4.5% Interest (Max)*****
Mail Processing Jobs																				
MAIL CARRIER (www.NPMHU.org)	Level 4	#N/A	#N/A	#N/A	#N/A	#N/A	#N/A	#N/A	#N/A	1.70%	13,285	13,560	18,067	18,440	23,586	24,074	13,568	13,872	16,224	16,868
Management Services Jobs 2																				
OTHER GRADES (www.APWU.org)																				
Estimated Annual Salary	1	22,208	29,346	22,708	32,396	22,708	32,396	22,708	32,396	1.70%	10,051	18,689	14,236	26,789	19,252	36,230	9,024	15,477	11,088	20,083
	2	22,935	30,308	23,435	33,358	23,435	33,358	23,435	33,358	1.70%	10,339	19,069	14,640	27,325	19,800	36,954	9,295	15,835	11,417	20,530
	3	23,689	31,305	24,189	34,355	24,189	34,355	24,189	34,355	1.70%	10,637	19,463	15,060	27,880	20,367	37,705	9,576	16,206	11,758	20,992
	4	24,645	32,568	25,145	35,618	25,145	35,618	25,145	35,618	1.70%	11,015	19,962	15,593	28,583	21,087	38,656	9,932	16,676	12,192	21,578
	5	25,466	33,653	25,966	36,703	25,966	36,703	25,966	36,703	1.70%	11,339	20,391	16,050	29,187	21,706	39,473	10,237	17,080	12,563	22,082
	6	26,385	34,867	26,885	37,917	26,885	37,917	26,885	37,917	1.70%	11,702	20,871	16,561	29,863	22,398	40,387	10,579	17,532	12,980	22,645
	7	27,465	36,295	27,965	39,345	27,965	39,345	27,965	39,345	1.70%	12,129	21,435	17,163	30,658	23,211	41,462	10,981	18,064	13,469	23,307
	8	28,567	37,750	29,067	40,800	29,067	40,800	29,067	40,800	1.70%	12,565	22,010	17,776	31,469	24,041	42,558	11,392	18,606	13,968	23,982
	9	29,682	39,223	30,182	42,273	30,182	42,273	30,182	42,273	1.70%	13,006	22,593	18,397	32,289	24,880	43,667	11,807	19,154	14,473	24,666
	10	30,777	40,672	31,277	43,722	31,277	43,722	31,277	43,722	1.70%	13,438	23,165	19,007	33,096	25,705	44,758	12,214	19,693	14,969	25,338
	11	32,438	50,652	32,938	53,702	32,938	53,702	32,938	53,702	1.70%	14,095	27,110	19,932	38,653	26,956	52,274	12,833	23,409	15,722	29,968
	12	33,994	53,084	34,494	56,134	34,494	56,134	34,494	56,134	1.70%	14,710	28,071	20,798	40,007	28,128	54,105	13,412	24,314	16,426	31,096
	13	35,580	55,560	36,080	58,610	36,080	58,610	36,080	58,610	1.70%	15,337	29,050	21,681	41,386	29,322	55,970	14,002	25,236	17,145	32,245
	14	37,438	58,461	37,938	61,511	37,938	61,511	37,938	61,511	1.70%	16,071	30,197	22,716	43,001	30,721	58,154	14,694	26,316	17,987	33,591
	15	39,488	61,662	39,988	64,712	39,988	64,712	39,988	64,712	1.70%	16,881	31,462	23,857	44,783	32,265	60,565	15,457	27,507	18,915	35,076
	16	40,890	68,961	41,390	72,011	41,390	72,011	41,390	72,011	1.70%	17,436	34,347	24,638	48,847	33,321	66,061	15,979	30,225	19,550	38,462
	17	42,704	72,019	43,204	75,069	43,204	75,069	43,204	75,069	1.70%	18,153	35,555	25,648	50,550	34,687	68,364	16,654	31,363	20,372	39,881
	18	44,579	75,181	45,079	78,231	45,079	78,231	45,079	78,231	1.70%	18,894	36,805	26,692	52,311	36,099	70,745	17,352	32,540	21,221	41,348
	19	46,691	78,745	47,191	81,795	47,191	81,795	47,191	81,795	1.70%	19,729	38,214	27,868	54,295	37,689	73,429	18,139	33,867	22,178	43,002
	20	49,224	83,017	49,724	86,067	49,724	86,067	49,724	86,067	1.70%	20,730	39,903	29,279	56,674	39,596	76,646	19,082	35,457	23,325	44,984
	21	51,616	87,050	52,116	90,100	52,116	90,100	52,116	90,100	1.70%	21,675	41,497	30,611	58,920	41,398	79,683	19,972	36,959	24,409	46,855
	22	54,685	94,344	55,185	97,394	55,185	97,394	55,185	97,394	1.70%	22,888	44,380	32,319	62,981	43,709	85,176	21,115	39,674	25,799	50,239
	23	57,666	99,485	58,166	102,535	58,166	102,535	58,166	102,535	1.70%	24,066	46,412	33,979	65,844	45,954	89,047	22,224	41,588	27,149	52,624
	24	60,520	104,408	61,020	107,458	61,020	107,458	61,020	107,458	1.70%	25,195	48,357	35,568	68,585	48,103	92,754	23,287	43,420	28,442	54,908
	25	63,529	109,602	64,029	112,652	64,029	112,652	64,029	112,652	1.70%	26,384	50,410	37,244	71,477	50,369	96,666	24,407	45,354	29,805	57,317
	26	66,699	115,068	67,199	118,118	67,199	118,118	67,199	118,118	1.70%	27,637	52,571	39,009	74,521	52,756	100,782	25,587	47,389	31,241	59,853

NOTES:
1 NPMHU Base Published Salary from http://www.npmhu.org
2 APWU Estimated Annual Salary Base Published from http://www.APWU.org

Chart V - U.S. Postal Service Job Titles & Salaries

U.S. Postal Service	GS Grade Range:	2010 Median Grade Min Salary (STEP 2)	2010 Maximum Grade Salary (STEP 2)	2011 Median Grade Min Salary (STEP 2)	2011 Maximum Grade Salary (STEP 2)	2012 Median Grade Min Salary (STEP 3)	2012 Maximum Grade Salary (STEP 3)	2013 Median Grade Min Salary (STEP 4)	2013 Maximum Grade Salary (STEP 4)	5-Year Average % Raise	20-Year Annual Pension Benefit Estimate (Min.) ***	20-Year Annual Pension Benefit Estimate (Max.)	25-Year Annual Pension Benefit Estimate (Min.)	25-Year Annual Pension Benefit Estimate (Max.)	30-Year Annual Pension Benefit Estimate (Min.)	30-Year Annual Pension Benefit Estimate (Max.)	Agency Automatic Contributions 1% Thrift Savings Plan 20 Year Savings Plus 4.5% Interest (Min) *****	Agency Automatic Contributions 1% Thrift Savings Plan 20 Year Savings Plus 4.5% Interest (Max)	Agency Automatic Contributions 1% Thrift Savings Plan 25 Year Savings Plus 4.5% Interest (Min)	Agency Automatic Contributions 1% Thrift Savings Plan 25 Year Savings Plus 4.5% Interest (Max) *****
Corporate Jobs																				
ACCOUNTANT		62,817	106,560	64,837	112,188	66,406	114,903	68,013	117,684	1.70%	26,102	49,208	36,847	69,783	49,832	94,375	24,142	44,222	29,483	55,906
ASSOCIATE ACCOUNT MANAGER		39,826	61,150	41,290	65,680	42,289	67,270	43,312	68,897	1.70%	17,015	31,260	24,046	44,498	32,519	60,179	15,583	27,317	19,068	34,839
BUILDING SERVICES SPECIALIST		47,091	78,091	48,731	83,031	49,910	85,040	51,118	87,098	1.70%	19,887	37,955	28,091	53,931	37,990	72,936	18,288	33,623	22,359	42,698
BUSINESS EVALUATION ANALYST		61,037	103,542	63,014	109,097	64,539	111,738	66,101	114,442	1.70%	25,399	48,015	35,856	68,103	48,492	92,102	23,479	43,098	28,676	54,506
BUSINESS PROJECT LEADER		51,037	96,725	52,772	102,115	54,049	104,587	55,357	107,118	1.70%	21,446	45,321	30,288	64,307	40,962	86,969	19,756	40,560	24,146	51,343
BUSINESS SYSTEMS ANALYST		58,159	98,659	60,066	104,096	61,520	106,615	63,009	109,196	1.70%	24,261	46,085	34,254	65,384	46,325	88,425	22,408	41,280	27,373	52,240
BUSINESS SYSTEMS CONTRACT ANALYST		46,798	86,327	48,430	91,466	49,602	93,680	50,803	95,947	1.70%	19,771	41,211	27,928	58,517	37,769	79,139	18,178	36,689	22,226	46,519
COMMUNICATIONS EQUIPMENT SPECIALIST		57,019	96,725	58,899	102,115	60,324	104,587	61,784	107,118	1.70%	23,811	45,321	33,619	64,307	45,466	86,969	21,983	40,560	26,856	51,343
COMMUNICATIONS PROGRAMS SPECIALIST		54,071	91,726	55,880	96,996	57,232	99,343	58,617	101,747	1.70%	22,646	43,345	31,978	61,523	43,247	83,204	20,886	38,699	25,521	49,024
COMPUTER PROGRAMMER SOFTWARE SPEC		57,019	96,725	58,899	102,115	60,324	104,587	61,784	107,118	1.70%	23,811	45,321	33,619	64,307	45,466	86,969	21,983	40,560	26,856	51,343
COMPUTER SYSTEMS ADMINISTRATOR		58,159	98,659	60,066	104,096	61,520	106,615	63,009	109,196	1.70%	24,261	46,085	34,254	65,384	46,325	88,425	22,408	41,280	27,373	52,240
COMPUTER SYSTEMS ANALYST		62,817	106,560	64,837	112,188	66,406	114,903	68,013	117,684	1.70%	26,102	49,208	36,847	69,783	49,832	94,375	24,142	44,222	29,483	55,906
CUSTOMER CONTACT SOLUTIONS SPECIALIST		42,199	90,023	43,720	95,252	44,778	97,557	45,862	99,918	1.70%	17,953	42,672	25,367	60,575	34,306	81,922	16,466	38,066	20,143	48,234
DATABASE ADMINISTRATOR		62,817	106,560	64,837	112,188	66,406	114,903	68,013	117,684	1.70%	26,102	49,208	36,847	69,783	49,832	94,375	24,142	44,222	29,483	55,906
ELECTRONIC ENGINEER		57,019	96,725	58,899	102,115	60,324	104,587	61,784	107,118	1.70%	23,811	45,321	33,619	64,307	45,466	86,969	21,983	40,560	26,856	51,343
FINANCIAL SYSTEMS SPECIALIST		51,037	84,634	52,772	89,732	54,049	91,903	55,357	94,128	1.70%	21,446	40,542	30,288	57,574	40,962	77,864	19,756	36,059	24,146	45,734
FORENSIC DOCUMENT EXAMINER		52,057	86,327	53,817	91,466	55,119	93,680	56,453	95,947	1.70%	21,850	41,211	30,856	58,517	41,730	79,139	20,136	36,689	24,609	46,519
GLOBAL ACCOUNT MANAGER		52,057	86,327	53,817	91,466	55,119	93,680	56,453	95,947	1.70%	21,850	41,211	30,856	58,517	41,730	79,139	20,136	36,689	24,609	46,519
INDUSTRIAL ENGINEER		64,073	122,356	66,123	128,367	67,723	131,474	69,362	134,656	1.70%	26,599	55,452	37,547	78,579	50,778	106,270	24,609	50,102	30,051	63,235
INFORMATION SCIENCES SPECIALIST		62,817	106,560	64,837	112,188	66,406	114,903	68,013	117,684	1.70%	26,102	49,208	36,847	69,783	49,832	94,375	24,142	44,222	29,483	55,906
INFORMATION SYSTEMS SECURITY SPEC		64,073	122,356	66,123	128,367	67,723	131,474	69,362	134,656	1.70%	26,599	55,452	37,547	78,579	50,778	106,270	24,609	50,102	30,051	63,235
INFORMATION SYSTEMS SPECIALIST		44,079	73,095	45,645	77,914	46,750	79,800	47,881	81,731	1.70%	18,696	35,981	26,414	51,150	35,722	69,175	17,166	31,764	20,995	40,380
MAINTENANCE ENGINEERING ANALYST		54,071	91,726	55,880	96,996	57,232	99,343	58,617	101,747	1.70%	22,646	43,345	31,978	61,523	43,247	83,204	20,886	38,699	25,521	49,024
MANAGER, CONFLICT MGMT / DISPUTE RESOL SVS		62,817	106,746	64,837	112,379	66,406	115,099	68,013	117,884	1.70%	26,102	49,282	36,847	69,887	49,832	94,515	24,142	44,291	29,483	55,992

Chart V - U.S. Postal Service Job Titles & Salaries

U.S. Postal Service	GS Grade Range:	2010 Median Grade Min Salary (STEP 2)	2010 Maximum Grade Salary (STEP 2)	2011 Median Grade Min Salary (STEP 2)	2011 Maximum Grade Salary (STEP 2)	2012 Median Grade Min Salary (STEP 3)	2012 Maximum Grade Salary (STEP 3)	2013 Median Grade Min Salary (STEP 4)	2013 Maximum Grade Salary (STEP 4)	5-Year Average % Raise	20-Year Annual Pension Benefit Estimate (Min.) ***	20-Year Annual Pension Benefit Estimate (Max.)	25-Year Annual Pension Benefit Estimate (Min.)	25-Year Annual Pension Benefit Estimate (Max.)	30-Year Annual Pension Benefit Estimate (Min.)	30-Year Annual Pension Benefit Estimate (Max.)	Agency Automatic Contributions 1% Thrift Savings Plan 20 Year Savings Plus 4.5% Interest (Min) *****	Agency Automatic Contributions 1% Thrift Savings Plan 20 Year Savings Plus 4.5% Interest (Max)	Agency Automatic Contributions 1% Thrift Savings Plan 25 Year Savings Plus 4.5% Interest (Min)	Agency Automatic Contributions 1% Thrift Savings Plan 25 Year Savings Plus 4.5% Interest (Max)
MANAGER, GLOBAL TRANS CONTRACTS		64,073	122,356	66,123	128,367	67,723	131,474	69,362	134,656	1.70%	26,599	55,452	37,547	78,579	50,778	106,270	24,609	50,102	30,051	63,235
MANAGER, PRODUCTION OPERS BRANCH		58,159	98,659	60,066	104,096	61,520	106,615	63,009	109,196	1.70%	24,261	46,085	34,254	65,384	46,325	88,425	22,408	41,280	27,373	52,240
MARKETING SPECIALIST		58,159	98,659	60,066	104,096	61,520	106,615	63,009	109,196	1.70%	24,261	46,085	34,254	65,384	46,325	88,425	22,408	41,280	27,373	52,240
OCCUPATIONAL HEALTH NURSE ADMIN		62,817	119,978	64,837	125,931	66,406	128,979	68,013	132,100	1.70%	26,102	54,511	36,847	77,254	49,832	104,479	24,142	49,217	29,483	62,131
OPERATIONS SUPPORT SPECIALIST		59,840	101,511	61,788	107,018	63,283	109,608	64,815	112,260	1.70%	24,926	47,213	35,190	66,972	47,591	90,573	23,034	42,342	28,134	53,564
PROGRAM MANAGER INFORMATION TECH		32,715	50,231	34,007	54,497	34,830	55,816	35,673	57,166	1.70%	14,205	26,944	20,086	38,418	27,165	51,957	12,936	23,252	15,847	29,773
PURCHASING SPECIALIST		61,037	103,542	63,014	109,097	64,539	111,738	66,101	114,442	1.70%	25,399	48,015	35,856	68,103	48,492	92,102	23,479	43,098	28,676	54,506
REAL ESTATE SPECIALIST		51,037	84,634	52,772	89,732	54,049	91,903	55,357	94,128	1.70%	21,446	40,542	30,288	57,574	40,962	77,864	19,756	36,059	24,146	45,734
SALES MANAGER		60,913	105,088	61,413	108,138	61,413	108,138	61,413	108,138	1.70%	26,599	50,051	37,547	70,970	50,778	95,980	24,609	45,015	30,051	56,895
SALES PERFORMANCE ANALYST		48,520	81,828	49,020	84,878	49,020	84,878	49,020	84,878	1.70%	21,446	40,542	30,288	57,574	40,962	77,864	19,756	36,059	24,146	45,734
SALES SPECIALIST		51,405	88,685	51,905	91,735	51,905	91,735	51,905	91,735	1.70%	22,646	43,345	31,978	61,523	43,247	83,204	20,886	38,699	25,521	49,024
AP SYSTEMS SUPPORT SPECIALIST		56,889	98,146	57,389	101,196	57,389	101,196	57,389	101,196	1.70%	24,926	47,213	35,190	66,972	47,591	90,573	23,034	42,342	28,134	53,564
SECRETARY		31,102	48,566	31,602	51,616	31,602	51,616	31,602	51,616	1.70%	14,205	26,944	20,086	38,418	27,165	51,957	12,936	23,252	15,847	29,773
SENIOR ACCOUNT MANAGER		43,891	74,022	44,391	77,072	44,391	77,072	44,391	77,072	1.70%	19,522	37,350	27,577	53,079	37,295	71,784	17,944	33,053	21,941	41,988
SENIOR SYSTEMS ACCOUNTANT		51,405	88,685	51,905	91,735	51,905	91,735	51,905	91,735	1.70%	22,646	43,345	31,978	61,523	43,247	83,204	20,886	38,699	25,521	49,024
SOFTWARE SYSTEMS ADMINISTRATOR		58,027	100,109	58,527	103,159	58,527	103,159	58,527	103,159	1.70%	25,399	48,015	35,856	68,103	48,492	92,102	23,479	43,098	28,676	54,506
SYSTEMS ANALYST (MINI-MICRO)		58,027	100,109	58,527	103,159	58,527	103,159	58,527	103,159	1.70%	25,399	48,015	35,856	68,103	48,492	92,102	23,479	43,098	28,676	54,506

Appendix A:
General Service Salary Schedule

DRAFT SALARY TABLE 2008-GS

INCORPORATING THE 2.50% GENERAL SCHEDULE INCREASE

EFFECTIVE JANUARY 2008

Annual Rates by Grade and Step

Grade	Step 1	Step 2	Step 3	Step 4	Step 5	Step 6	Step 7	Step 8	Step 9	Step 10	WITHIN GRADE AMOUNTS
1	$ 17,046	$ 17,615	$ 18,182	S 18,746	S 19,313	S 19,646	S 20,208	$ 20,771	$ 20,793	S 21,324	VARIES
2	19,165	19,621	20,255	20,793	21,025	21,643	22,261	22,879	23,497	24,115	VARIES
3	20,911	21,608	22,305	23,002	23,699	24,396	25,093	25,790	26,487	27,184	697
4	23,475	24,258	25,041	25,824	26,607	27,390	28,173	28,956	29,739	30,522	783
5	26,264	27,139	28,014	28,889	29,764	30,639	31,514	32,389	33,264	34,139	875
6	29,276	30,252	31,228	32,204	33,180	34,156	35,132	36,108	37,084	38,060	976
7	32,534	33,618	34,702	35,786	36,870	37,954	39,038	40,122	41,206	42,290	1084
8	36,030	37,231	38,432	39,633	40,834	42,035	43,236	44,437	45,638	46,839	1201
9	39,795	41,122	42,449	43,776	45,103	46,430	47,757	49,084	50,411	51,738	1327
10	43,824	45,285	46,746	48,207	49,668	51,129	52,590	54,051	55,512	56,973	1461
11	48,148	49,753	51,358	52,963	54,568	56,173	57,778	59,383	60,988	62,593	1605
12	57,709	59,633	61,557	63,481	65,405	67,329	69,253	71,177	73,101	75,025	1924
13	68,625	70,913	73,201	75,489	77,777	80,065	82,353	84,641	86,929	89,217	2288
14	81,093	83,796	86,499	89,202	91,905	94,608	97,311	100,014	102,717	105,420	2703
15	95,390	98,570	101,750	104,930	108,110	111,290	114,470	117,650	120,830	124,010	3180

Appendix B:
U.S. Federal Government Definitions of Pay Grade Factors Determining Job Title Classification & Pay Grade

Knowledge Required by the Position:

This factor covers the nature and extent of the work; the nature and extent of information or facts that an employee must understand to do acceptable work (e.g., steps, procedures, practices, rules, policies, theories, principles, and concepts) and the nature and extent of the skills necessary to apply that knowledge.

The Role of Competencies:

Competencies are defined for each Job Family Group. They are specific to the nature of the work. For example, "Information technology as a field of work is finely attuned to the competencies it requires. By competency, it means an observable, measurable pattern of skills, knowledge, abilities, behaviors, and other characteristics that an individual needs to perform work roles or occupational functions successfully. The rapid pace of change in information technology results in constantly evolving competencies. This is true both in terms of the specific knowledge and skills that are changing and in terms of the way technological advances change the pattern of abilities and behaviors, as well as work and work roles," (USOPM, 2001, 2003). **(See Appendix B: Competencies Required for Federal IT Job Specialties).**

Supervisory Factors

This factor covers nature and extent of direct or indirect controls exercised by the supervisor or another individual over the work performed, the employee's responsibility, and the review of completed work will be considered. The supervisor determines how much information the employee needs to perform the assignments; e.g., instructions, priorities, deadlines, objectives, and boundaries. The employee's responsibility depends on the extent to which the supervisor expects the employee to develop the sequence and timing of the various aspects of the work, to modify or recommend modification of instructions, and to participate in establishing priorities and defining objectives. The degree of review of completed work depends upon the nature and extent of the review; e.g., close and detailed review of each phase of the assignment; detailed review of the completed assignment; spot check of finished work for accuracy; or review only for adherence to policy. The primary components of this factor are: How Work Is Assigned, Employee Responsibility, and How Work Is Reviewed.

Judgment Factors

This factor covers the nature of guidelines and the judgment employees need to apply them. Individual assignments may vary in the specificity, applicability, and availability of guidelines; thus, the judgment that employees use similarly varies. The existence of detailed plans and other instructions may make innovation in planning and conducting work unnecessary or undesirable. However, in the absence of guidance provided by prior agency experience with

the task at hand or when objectives are broadly stated, the employee may use considerable judgment in developing an approach or planning the work. Here are examples of guidelines used in administrative work in the Information Technology Group:

Policies and Guidance – Several policy and guidance statements influence and direct how the Government manages its information resources. The primary components of this factor are: **Guidelines Used** and **Judgment Needed**.

Nature of Assignment Factors

This factor covers the nature, number, variety, and intricacy of tasks, steps, processes, or methods in the work performed; the difficulty in identifying what needs to be done; and the difficulty and originality involved in performing the work. The primary components of this factor are: Nature of Assignment, What Needs To Be Done, and Difficulty and Originality Involved.

Scope of the Work

Effect of the Work Relationship between Nature of Work and Output
This factor covers the relationships between the nature of work, i.e., the purpose, breadth and depth of the assignment, and the effect of work products or services both within and outside the organization. Effect measures such things as whether the work output facilitates the work of others, provides timely services of a personal nature, or impacts on the adequacy of research conclusions. The primary components of this factor are: **Scope of the Work** and **Effect of the Work**.

Scope of Contacts – Purpose of Contacts

These factors include face-to-face and remote dialogue – e.g., telephone, email, and video conferences – with persons not in the supervisory chain. The levels of these factors consider and take into account what is necessary to make the initial contact, the difficulty of communicating with those contacted, the setting in which the contact takes place, and the nature of the discourse. The setting describes how well the employee and those contacted recognize their relative roles and authorities. The nature of the discourse defines the reason for the communication and the context or environment in which the communication takes place. For example, the reason for a communication may be to exchange factual information or to negotiate. The communication may take place in an environment of significant controversy and/or with people of differing viewpoints, goals, and objectives (U.S. Federal Government, Office of Personnel Management, "Job Family Position Classification Standard for Administrative Work in the Information Technology Group GS-2200", GS-2200, 2001, 2003; http://www.opm.gov/FEDCLASS/gs2200a.pdf).

Appendix C:
Sample Federal Job Announcements

CONTRACT SPECIALIST

Salary Range: 46,041.00 - 103,220.00 USD per year
Series & Grade: GS-1102-09/13
Position Information: Full-Time Permanent
Promotion Potential: 13
Duty Locations: Many vacancies - Emmitsburg, MD
Who May Be Considered: United States citizens and nationals.

 Job Summary:
Major Duties:

The incumbent will solicit, evaluate, negotiate, administer, award, analyze, advise on, and/or terminate contracts for the procurement of supplies and services to the Federal government. Perform work related to the contract pre-award, i.e., the work necessary to secure a contract to acquire goods and services. Perform contracting work using formal advertising procedures. Use a variety of contract types to procure items and/or services.

Utilize contract methods and types with nonstandard terms and conditions. Perform contracting work through use of negotiation techniques. Procure items and services through the negotiation process. Analyze sources for the products or services to be procured. Perform work related to the contract post-award process, i.e., the work accomplished after contact award. Perform contract administration work such as monitoring of contract performance and negotiation of necessary contract modifications to ensure satisfactory progress and completion of contract activities.

Monitor outstanding contracts to ensure satisfactory progress, to assure compliance with terms and conditions of the contract, and to identify problems that threaten contractor performance. Negotiate contract modifications and the terms and costs of contract changes.

Perform work related to the termination of contracts for either convenience of the government or default of the contractor. Negotiate the termination settlement with the contractor including equitable adjustments, change proposals, costs, profit, and other related matters.

Qualifications:

This position has a positive education requirement. Proof of successful completion of required course work MUST be provided to determine if you meet the basic qualification requirements for the position if you are not currently serving in a Contract Specialist series position. Without this proof, your application will be rated ineligible.

You must provide a copy of your school/college transcripts or a list of courses including course title, credit hours, and grade. You must submit your required proof as described in the Required Documentation section. Be sure to include the vacancy announcement number on your documents.

To qualify for this position you must meet the basic requirements below. Basic Requirements for GS-9 through GS-12 a) Completed a 4-year course of study leading to a bachelor's degree with a major in any field; OR at least 24 semester hours in any combination of the following fields: accounting, business, finance, law, contracts, purchasing, economics, industrial management, marketing, quantitative methods, or organization and management.

To qualify at the GS-9 level at least 1 year of experience must have been at or equivalent to GS-7. For GS-11 at least 1 year experience must have been specialized experience at or equivalent to GS-9. For GS-12 at least 1 year of experience must have been specialized experience at or equivalent to GS-11, and must have provided the knowledge, skills, and abilities to perform successfully the work of this position.

To be qualifying, this specialized experience is described as experience that has involved the application of contracting principles, laws, regulations and procedures in planning, developing, implementing, and maintaining all aspects of the administration of one or more major systems contracts; applying knowledge of a procurement functional area sufficient to provide expert technical leadership, staff coordination, and consultation; formulating guidelines, implementing new developments, and providing policy interpretation; performing in-depth evaluations of the financial and technical capabilities, or the performance, of the contractor. Substitution of Education for experience: GS-9 2 full academic years of progressively higher level graduate education or masters or equivalent graduate degree or LL.B. or J.D.

Graduate Education: Graduate education must be in one or a combination of the following fields is required: accounting business, finance, law, contracts, purchasing, economics, industrial management, marketing, quantitative methods, or organization and management. GS-11 3 full academic years of progressively higher level graduate education or Ph.D. or equivalent doctoral degree. GS-12 1 year specialized experience equivalent to at least the next lower grade level. There is no substitution of education at this grade level. Basic Qualifications for GS-13 level:GS-13 Basic Requirements for GS-13: 1 year specialized experience equivalent to at least the next lower grade level and completed at least 4 years experience in a contracting or related position. There is no substitution of education at this grade level;

A.   Completion of all mandatory training (listed below) prescribed by the head of the agency for progression to GS-13 or higher level contracting positions, including at least 4-years experience in contracting or related positions. At least 1 year of that experience must have been specialized experience at or equivalent to work at the next lower level of the position, and must have provided the knowledge, skills, and abilities to perform successfully the work of the position. AND

B.   A 4-year course of study leading to a bachelor's degree, that included or was supplemented by at least 24 semester hours in any combination of the following fields: accounting, business, finance, law, contracts, purchasing, economics, industrial management, marketing, quantitative methods, or organization and management.

C.   Exceptions: Applicants who have been in GS-1102 positions, at or above the GS-13 grade level will be considered to have met the qualification standard for positions they occupy on January 1, 2000 and held without a break in service. This also applies to positions at the same grade in the same agency or other agencies if the specialized experience requirements are met. However, they will have to meet the basic requirements and specialized experience requirements in order to qualify for promotion to a higher grade, unless granted a waiver described below.

D.   Waiver: When filling a specific vacant position at the GS-13 level, the senior procurement executive of the selecting agency, at his or her discretion, may waive any or all of the requirements of Paragraphs A and B above if the senior procurement executive certifies that the applicant possesses significant potential for advancement to levels of greater responsibility and authority, based on demonstrated analytical and decision making capabilities, job performance, and qualifying experience.

IN ADDITION TO THE EDUCATION AND EXPERIENCE REQUIREMENTS LISTED ABOVE, APPLICANTS MUST MEET THE DEPARTMENT OF HOMELAND SECURITY TRAINING REQUIREMENTS LISTED BELOW:

Defense Acquisition University: CON 110 Mission Support Planning (or equivalent) Defense Acquisition University: CON 111 Mission Strategy Execution (or equivalent) Defense Acquisition University: CON 112 Mission Performance Assessment (or equivalent) Defense Acquisition University: CON 120 Contracting for Mission Support (or equivalent) Targeted Elective – 16 hours Defense Acquisition University: CON 202 – Immediate Contracting (or equivalent) Defense Acquisition University: CON 204 – Intermediate Contract Pricing (or equivalent) Defense Acquisition University: CON 210 – Government Contract Law (or equivalent) Defense Acquisition University: CON 353 – Advanced Business Solutions for Mission Support (equivalent courses would be completion of both CON 301- and CON 333). Targeted Elective – 16 hours Targeted Elective – 16 hours Two Targeted Electives - each should be a minimum of 16 hours of assignment or individual specific learning identified as developmentally beneficial for the individual for career progression.

Electives can include formal training or education, seminars, conferences, special projects, or other developmental activities in the procurement field. Day-to-day work experience may not be used to fulfill elective requirements. Only courses offered by the Defense Acquisition University (DAU) or by a recognized equivalent provider may be used to meet the training requirements. Information on DAU equivalent providers may be found at http://www.dau.mil/learning/appg.asp. AND d) Completed at least 4 years of experience in a contracting or related position. You must be a U.S. citizen to qualify for this position.

SELECTIVE PLACEMENT FACTOR: None. In order to receive consideration at the GS-9/11 level, you must address the following KSA's:
1. Knowledge of Federal contracting and procurement policies and regulations, including performance-based acquisition.
2. Knowledge of commercial and government sources of supply for assigned requirements and knowledge of set aside and other socio-economic programs.
3. Knowledge of the contract administration process including contract closeout and proficiency in communication techniques.
4. Knowledge of and experience in costs and negotiation procedures and techniques.5. Ability to communicate, both orally and in writing.

In order to receive consideration at the GS-12/GS-13 level, you must address the following KSA's:
1. Knowledge of Federal contracting and procurement policies and regulations, including performance-based acquisition.
2. Knowledge of all phases of the procurement process (i.e., planning, solicitation, negotiations, pricing, administration, and termination).
3. Knowledge of commercial business and industry practices and market considerations, including various commodity areas; i.e., service, supplies, equipment, IT, and construction. 4. Skill in analyzing procurement situations, proposals, and market conditions.
5. Ability to communicate, both orally and in writing to represent and defend Agency Interest.

PUBLIC TRUST: This is a Public Trust position that requires a background investigation. Appointment to the position is subject to the applicant or appointee successfully completing essential security investigation forms, the applicant or appointee cooperating with the investigator, the completion of the investigation, and the favorable adjudication of the investigation.

CRIMINAL INVESTIGATOR
GS-1811-9 / 11 (GJ)

Salary Range: 47,407.00 - 72,164.00 USD per year
Series & Grade: GS-1811-09/11 Position Information: Full-time Permanent
Promotion Potential: 13 Duty Locations: 2 vacancies - Minneapolis, MN

Who May Be Considered: Current federal employees with competitive status; reinstatement eligibles; and candidates applying under the Interagency Career Transition Assistance Program.

MISSION STATEMENT
The Office of Criminal Enforcement, Forensics and Training is made up of Criminal Investigators, Environmental Scientists, Environmental Engineers, Attorneys, Financial Specialists and others, who work to ensure the protection of the lands, water and air of these United States.
Must be a U.S. citizen.   Security Clearance Required.
May be required to travel 6 to 10 days per month.

 Major Duties:
Independently plans and conducts complete criminal investigations of considerable difficulty and importance concerning violations of the environmental laws. In connection with the above investigations, develops sources of information, examines private and public records for the purpose of securing information or verifying data. Interrogates persons for the purpose of establishing facts and securing legal evidence, using technical and scientific devices in securing such evidence. Analyzes and assembles facts and evidence and incorporates them in criminal case reports. Submits reports to a Supervisory Criminal Investigator for review as to form, style, completeness, accuracy and fairness. Executes search warrants and arrests violators of the Federal environmental laws. Testifies in preliminary hearings and grand jury proceedings, and before the United States District Courts.

Qualifications:
Applicants must have general and/or specialized and/or experience as described below. This requirement is in accordance with the OPM'S Operating Manaual for Qualifications Standards for General Schedule Positions. When specified, applicant must also meet any Mandatory (Selective Placement) Factors listed. GS-9: Applicants must either possess a Master's degree, or 2 full years of progressively higher graduate education leading to a such a degree or a related LL.B. or J.D. degree OR 1 full year of specialized experience equivalent to the GS-7 grade level as described below.GS-11: Applicants must either possess a Ph.D or equivalent doctoral degree or 3 full years of progressively higher graduate education leading to such a degree; or LL.M., if related; OR 1 full year of specialized experience equivalent to the GS-9 grade level as described below.

EXPERIENCE REQUIREMENTS: At least one year of specialized experience comparable in difficulty and responsibility to the next lower grade level in the federal government is required. Specialized experience is that which has equipped the applicant with the experience to successfully perform the duties of this position. Examples of Specialized Experience: GS-9: Experience in assisting senior investigators in planning and conducting routine investigations, verifying and corroborating information, and preparing portions or investigative reports.GS-11: Experience in independently conducting routine investigations, conducting interviews, verifying and corroborating information, writing investigative reports, and testifying in court on criminal and/or civil matters.

KNOWLEDGE, SKILLS AND ABILITIES:1. Knowledge of Federal criminal statutes, Federal criminal and civil procedures, rules of evidence, and constitutional rights.2. Ability to investigate aspects of Federal environmental laws.3. Ability to research, analyze, monitor and make recommendations regarding complex investigations and administrative issues.4. Knowledge applicable to Federal and State laws; Constitutional laws related to search and seizure, and rights of individuals.5. Ability to effectively present information both orally and in writing. Federal employees must meet time in grade requirements within 30 days of the closing date of this announcement. Travel, transportation, and relocation expenses will not be paid by the Agency. Any

ENVIRONMENTAL ENGINEER/ ENVIRONMENTAL SCIENTIST/
LIFE SCIENTIST
GS-819/1301/401-11/12

Salary Range: 54,438.00 - 84,825.00 USD per year
Series & Grade: GS-0819,0401,1301-11/12 Position Information: Full-time Permanent
Promotion Potential: 13 Duty Locations: 1 vacancy - Atlanta, GA

Job Summary:
Major Duties:
Serves as a Remedial Project Manager responsible for managing site assessment, remedial and/or removal activities at assigned sites; e.g. conducts Preliminary Assessments, Site Investigations and Hazard Ranking System packages; Conducts Remedial Investigations and Feasibility Studies (RI/FS); Conducts negotiations with Potentially Responsible Parties (PRP) prior to RI/FS and RD/RA; Contract management for all work assignments associated with assigned sites. Responsible for assessing CERCLA hazardous waste sites for the purpose of identifying and measuring public health and welfare and environmental threats; identify remedial alternatives; and recommends and implements remedies.

Coordinates and oversees the contribution of other Federal, State and local officials and PRPs where appropriate. This includes organizing support teams to provide advice, counsel or other assistance; plans and conducts site-related meetings; coordinates with removal program officials in cases where removals are warranted; and oversees State and PRP O&M efforts. Provides advice to State and local agencies for various purposes; e.g. acquiring properties and easements necessary for remedial action, advising and assisting State Project Officers in preparing statements of work for State-lead sites, advising the states in the development of cooperative agreement and Superfund State Contracts (SSCs) for Fund-lead sites, monitoring State actions and expenditures for assigned sites.

Participates in, leads, or monitors enforcement activities related to assigned sites. Oversees or conducts PRP searches; reviews and evaluates PRP qualifications to perform the response activity; represents the Agency in conducting PRP technical negotiations for response actions; monitors compliance of PRPs with consent decrees and administrative orders; develops data bases to track and maintain PRP-specific data for document exchange; initiates and coordinates enforcement actions to rectify PRP non-compliance with administrative orders and consent decrees; provides technical information for cost recovery actions; develops and/or assists Regional Counsel in implementing case management plans; provides testimony, depositions and other assistance for site litigation.

Defines and prepares the scope of work for work assignments issued against the contract. Reviews and recommends approval/disapproval of the work plans issued by the contractor describing the approach necessary to implement the tasks in the work assignment. Monitors and oversees the performance of the work assignment. Reviews all vouchers submitted by the contractor for payment against the appropriate work assignment and recommends approval or disapproval through the Project Officer. Reviews all progress reports submitted by the contractor on the work assignment in order to properly monitor and control costs as well as ensure contractor performance.

Qualifications:
Applicants must have general and/or specialized experience and/or education as described below. This requirement is in accordance with the Office of Personnel Management's Operating Manual for Qualifications Standards for General Schedule Positions. When specified, applicants must also meet any Mandatory (Selective Placement) Factors listed.
EXPERIENCE REQUIREMENTS: To qualify for the GS-11 the specialized experience must be comparable in difficulty and responsibility to the GS-9 level and the GS-12 experience must be comparable in difficulty to the GS-11 level in the federal government. Specialized experience is that which has equipped the applicant with the experience to successfully perform the duties. of this

INFORMATION TECHNOLOGY SPECIALIST (APPLICATION SOFTWARE)

Salary Range: 74,074.00 - 96,292.00 USD per year Open Period: (Sample only)
Series & Grade: GS-2210-13 Position Information: Full Time Career/Career Conditional
Promotion Potential: 13 Duty Locations: 1 vacancy - Austin, TX
Who May Be Considered: U.S. Citizens

Job Announcement Number:
DS117475-BM

Job Summary:

The mission of the Department of Veterans Affairs, Austin Automation Center is to provide One-VA world-class service to veterans and their families by delivering results-oriented, secure, highly available, and cost effective IT services. *This position is located at the VA Austin Automation Center (AAC) Enterprise Systems Division, located in Austin, Texas. The division develops and maintain a application software to automate franchise fund business functions. The division serves internal customers and other federal agencies by analyzing customer's requests for information and implementing methods for customers to have easy access to the information they need.*

Full Performance Level: 13
Key Requirements: U.S. Citizenship

Major Duties:

Individuals within the Application Developer job family are responsible for the design, development, testing, documentation, maintenance, and integration of application software. Incumbents within the Application Developer job family obtain and refine business requirements through interaction with the Requirements Analysts and the customer. Application developer personnel are also required to provide Tier II and Tier III support for the Help Desk. In addition, the incumbents work as individual contributors, team members or serve as project task managers.

Qualifications:

Applicants must have one or more years of specialized experience as Information Technology Specialist (Application Software), completing computer project assignments that involve design, development, testing, documentation, maintenance and integration of application software; participation in technology planning, product evaluation and report development; and serving as a project manager. This experience must be equivalent to the GS-12 level in the Federal service, but could have been gained in the public or private sectors.

In addition, the following skills and experience is required: 1) Skill in administering a clustered BEA WebLogic Server environment in a RedHat Linux environment *and* 2) Skill in installing, configuring, tuning, troubleshooting, clustering, and deploying applications to WebLogic Server.

INFORMATION   TECHNOLOGY   SPECIALIST (NETWORK)

Salary Range: 74,074.00 - 100,554.00 USD per year Open Period: (Sample only)
Series & Grade: GS-2210-13 Position Information: Full Time Term NTE 2 years
Promotion Potential: 13 Duty Locations: 1 vacancy - St. Louis Metro area, 1
vacancy - Washington, DC
Who May Be Considered: U.S. Citizens

Job Announcement Number:
VZ119102TLC

Job Summary:
Be a member of a team providing compassionate healthcare to veterans.

THE FOLLOWING DOCUMENTS ARE REQUIRED TO APPLY FOR THIS
POSITION:
1. OF 306 – DECLARATION OF FEDERAL EMPLOYMENT (January 2001 or later version
required)
2. OF 612 – Optional Application for Federal Employment OR Resume
3. OPM 1203 FX – Occupational Questionnaire
4. Veterans Preference:
a. CPS, CP (10PT) – required documents: SF 15, DD214 – Member 4 copy which reflects
CHARACTER OF SERVICE (i.e. Honorable), VA disability letter dated 1991 or later
b. TP (5PT) – required documents: DD214 - Member 4 copy which reflects
CHARACTER OF SERVICE (i.e. Honorable)
c. XP OR XPP (10PT) – refer to SF 15 for required documents
5. College Transcripts (*see Qualifications/Evaluations section*)

Major Duties:
The VA Learning University (VALU) is a Department-wide, comprehensive, virtual, education-focused staff supporting VA continuing learning objectives through all-employee training, education, performance support, development and consultation. The incumbent will serve as the Senior Network Administrator responsible for technical support of live satellite-based Internet Protocol (IP) video to the desktop and Content Distribution Network (CDN) video on-demand across the entire Veterans Health Administration (VHA) healthcare system and other Department of Veterans Affairs offices as required. This support will frequently entail troubleshooting and direct customer support to assist clients with all aspects of video to the desktop including Content Library administration. In collaboration with the Employee Education System (EES) CDN Project Manager and the EES Media and Learning Technology Coordinator, plans, designs, and installs telecommunications hardware/software related to the design and implementation of IP desktop video and CDN within the VHA. This entails the selection, implementation and administration of telecommunications equipment inclusive of routers, hubs, switches, such as Cisco Content Engines. Incumbent serves as liaison to the (VISN) Chief Information Office (CIO) technical staff with regard to installation and the support of VALU IP video as well as other education support initiatives. Some examples include Internet Protocol Television, Content Distribution, Satellite uplink/downlink systems, Internet Protocol Multicast, and networking devices (LAN, WAN, and MAN). Supports and maintains telecommunications (WAN, LAN, MAN) operating systems, database management systems, programming languages, application software systems, programming utilities systems programming support, video communications

Qualifications:
GS-13 SPECIALIZED EXPERIENCE: One (1) year of specialized experience that equipped you with the knowledge, skills and ability to successfully perform, and that are related to the duties of this position. Specialized experience includes: Demonstrated accomplishment of computer project assignments that required a wide range of knowledge of computer requirements and techniques pertinent to this position. This knowledge is generally demonstrated by assignments where you

BASIC QUALIFICATION REQUIREMENTS FOR THE ENVIRONMENTAL ENGINEER:

A. Successful completion of a full 4-year course of study in an accredited college or university leading to a Bachelor's Degree in professional engineering from an ABET accredited school and/or the curriculum included differential and integral calculus and courses (beyond first-year physics and chemistry) in five of the following seven areas of engineering science; (a) statics, dynamics; (b) strength of materials (stress-strain relationships); (c) fluid mechanics, hydraulics; (d) thermodynamics; (e) electrical fields and circuits; (f) nature and properties of materials (relating particle and aggregate structure to properties); and (g) other comparable area of fundamental engineering science or physics, such as optics, heat transfer, soil mechanics, or electronics. OR

B. Have a combination of education and experience - college level education, training, and/or technical experience that furnished (1) a thorough knowledge of the physical and mathematical sciences underlying professional engineering, (2) a good understanding, both theoretical and practical, of the engineering sciences, and techniques and their applications to one of the branches of engineering. The adequacy of such background must be demonstrated by current registration as a professional engineer. OR

C. Have evidence of having successfully passed the Engineer-in-Training examination, and have completed all the requirements for either (a) a bachelor's degree in engineering technology (BET) from an accredited college or university that included 60 semester hours or courses in the physical, mathematical, and engineering sciences, or (b) a BET from a program accredited by the Accreditation Board for Engineering and Technology (ABET). OR

D. Have passed the written test required for professional registration. OR

E. Successful completion of at least 60 semester hours of courses in the physical, mathematical and engineering sciences and in engineering that included the courses specified in "A" above. OR

F. Successful completion of a curriculum leading to a bachelor's degree in engineering technology or in an appropriate professional field, e.g. physics, chemistry, architecture, computer science, mathematics, hydrology, or geology and one year of professional engineering experience under the guidance and supervision of a professional engineer.

BASIC QUALIFICATION REQUIREMENTS FOR THE ENVIRONMENTAL SCIENTIST:

A. Successful completion of a full 4-year course of study in an accredited college or university leading to a Bachelor's Degree in physical science, engineering, or mathematics that included 24 semester hours in physical science and/or related engineering science such as mechanics, dynamics, properties of materials, and electronics. OR

B. Have a combination of education and experience--education equivalent to one of the majors shown in A above that included at least 24 semester hours in physical science and/or relatedengineering coursework.

BASIC QUALIFICATION REQUIREMENTS FOR THE LIFE SCIENTIST:

A. Successful completion of a full 4-year course of study in an accredited college or university leading to a Bachelor's Degree in biological sciences, agriculture, natural resource management, chemistry, or related disciplines appropriate to the position. OR

B. Have a combination of education and experience--Courses equivalent to a major, as shown in A above, plus appropriate experience or additional education. If you are substituting education for experience, 3 full years of progressively higher level graduate education leading to a Ph.D. or equivalent doctoral degree, if related from an accredited college or university fully meets the requirements for the GS-11 grade level.

TRANSPORTATION SECURITY OFFICER (TSO) (Screener)

Salary Range: 23,836.00 - 35,754.00 USD per yearSalary Range does not include locality pay of 18.59%.
*This is the salary range for a full time position. Your salary will be pro-rated based on the actual number of hours you work.
Series & Grade: SV-1802-00/00

Position Information: Work Schedule: Work schedules will consist of part-time employment of 16-25 hours per week. Type of Appointment: Permanent – Part Time Positions. Under the TSA Health Benefit Incentive for Part-Time TSOs, all part-time TSOs will pay the same lower cost for federal health benefits as full-time employees. This is an Excepted Service Appointment.

Major Duties:
Principal Duties and Responsibilities: You will perform a variety of duties related to providing security and protection of air travelers, airports and aircraft. As a TSO, you may be required to perform passenger screening, baggage screening or both. You are expected to perform all of these duties in a courteous and professional manner. The principle duties and responsibilities include the following: • Performing security screening of persons, including tasks such as: hand-wanding (which includes the requirement to reach and wand the individual from the floor to over head), pat-down searches, and monitoring walk-through metal detector screening equipment; • Performing security screening of property, including the operation of x-ray machines to identify dangerous objects in baggage, cargo and on passengers; and preventing those objects from being transported onto aircraft; • Controlling entry and exit points; • Continuously improving security screening processes and; • Continuously improving own performance through training and development.TSOs MUST be willing and able to:• Repeatedly lift and carry up to 70 pounds;• Continuously stand between one (1) to four (4) hours without a break to carry out screening functions;• Walk up to two (2) miles during a shift; • Communicate with the public, giving directions and responding to inquiries in a professional and courteous manner;• Maintain focus and awareness and work within a stressful environment which includes noise from alarms, machinery, and people, distractions, time pressure, disruptive and angry passengers, and the requirement to identify and locate potentially life threatening devices and devices intended on creating massive destruction; and• Make effective decisions in both crisis and routine situations.

Qualifications:
• Be a U.S. Citizen or U.S. National (For further information concerning U.S. citizenship, please visit http://www.uscis.gov/; AND• Have a high school diploma, GED or equivalent; OR• Have at least one year of full-time work experience in security work, aviation screener work, or X-ray technician work.Possess the following job-related knowledge, skills, and abilities: • English Proficiency (e.g., reading, writing, speaking, listening);• Mental Abilities (e.g., visual observation, x-ray interpretation); • Personal Characteristics and Skills (e.g., customer service, dependability, integrity); and• Physical Abilities (e.g., repeatedly lifting and carrying baggage weighing up to 70 lbs, bending, reaching, stooping, squatting, standing, and walking) In addition, all TSOs must meet job-related medical standards that will be assessed in a pre-employment medical evaluation. This evaluation considers relevant aspects of all body systems (e.g., cardiovascular, respiratory, musculoskeletal, auditory, etc.). The medical standards include but are not limited to:• (various). The qualification requirements above comply with the Aviation and Transportation Security Act (ATSA) Public Law 107-71 (PDF* 174KB).. For more information and what it means to you please visit http://www.tsa.gov/research/laws/law_regulation_rule_0010.shtm.

Conditions of Employment:
To be considered for initial employment, you must be able to:• • Pass a pre-employment drug screening test • Pass a background investigation, including a criminal check and a credit check.

NOTE: This is a non-critical sensitive National Security position that requires you to be fingerprinted, photographed, and complete appropriate security paperwork, including a SF-86 Questionnaire for National Security Positions. The pre-employment background investigation must be completed with favorable results prior to a final offer of employment..If your credit check reveals any of the following, YOU WILL NOT BE ELIGIBLE FOR THIS POSITION:·Defaulted on $5,000 or more in debt (excluding certain circumstances of bankruptcy), or·Owe any delinquent Federal or State taxes, or· Owe any past due child support payments.•

• Pass initial hiring and all training requirements including 56-72 hours of classroom training, 112-128 hours of on-the-job training, and initial certification testing. NOTE: Initial training may require you to travel for up to two weeks on a full-time schedule.To maintain employment, you must meet all qualification requirements described above. In addition, you must be able to:• Demonstrate daily a fitness for duty without impairment due to illegal drugs, sleep deprivation, medication, or alcohol; • Work all of the following: Part-time (16-25) hours per week. Part-time work hours for this position consists of shift-work on any day from Sunday through Saturday, which may include irregular hours, nights, holidays, overtime, extended shifts and weekend shifts, changing shifts, and split shifts. A Split Shift schedule is defined as any two shifts, lasting at least two (2) hours each, in one 24-hour period with a break of at least two (2) hours between shifts. Exceptions include additional shifts to support morning, midday, and afternoon or evening operations. Specific work shifts and schedules will be determined by the airport. • Pass all recurrent and specialized training and re-certification tests on a periodic basis;• Pass random drug screening tests; and• Pass all recurrent background investigations, including a criminal check and credit check.

Appendix D:
Sample Knowledge, Skills Abilities Statement

INFORMATION TECHNOLOGY SPECIALIST (APPLICATION SOFTWARE)

See Appendix C: Sample Federal Jobs

Job Announcement #DS117475-BM

Duties: Individuals within the Application Developer job family are :

1. -Responsible for the design, development, testing, documentation, maintenance, and integration of application software

I have worked for 6 years, from 2001-2006, in Applications Development. In my position as Application Development Manager for Quad States Developers, from 2003-2006, I worked for 3 years in customized IT/IS applications development. As Applications Development Manager, I supervised a team of 3 application developers in the design of an application for a large Utility company. Strengths include programming knowledge, database knowledge, and experience with open architectures for application usage and growth.

Rresponsible for the design, development, testing, documentation, maintenance, and integration of application software for multiple clients with a variety of software tools. From 2001-2003, in my position as Application Developer with Quad States Developers, I worked as Project Leader of Application Development Team for Large Utility Company and managed 3 developers. Individual Contributor and Team Member on Application Development projects for U.S. mid-sized companies, using Oracle, Java in J2EE server environments, and with Linux and Windows. Part of a 6-member team from Quad States that enhanced and retooled financial applications for a Life Insurance company, a Bond Company, and an IT manufacturer, using Java.

Knowledge/Education:

Operating Systems: UNIX (AIX, HP-UX, Sun Solaris, RedHat Linux, BEA WebLogic); WINDOWS 2000 to Current; WINDOWS NT DBMS: Oracle 7/8/8i, , Java, Java Beans (Developer, Designer, DBA); MS SQL Server; MS Access; O2 (Object DBMS), J3EE, BEA WebLogic, Linux, Windows Operating System Training Languages/Tools: SQL, PL/SQL, SQL Server, ASP, Active X, VB Script, Jscript, HTML, XML   Specialty: Specialize in developing custom software applications to combine accounting, finance, and logistics, to process information on customer usage of product and services. Developed a reputation of making clients happy by completing projects easily, facilitating retrieval of information, and reducing costs.

Supervisory Controls & Leadership: For 6 years in Applications Development. In my position as Application Development Manager for Quad States Developers, from 2003-2006, ffor 3 years in customized IT/IS applications development. As Applications Development Manager from 2003-2006, I supervised a team of 3 application developers in the design of an application for a large Utility company. Strengths include programming knowledge, database knowledge, and experience with open architectures for application usage and growth. I have been responsible for the design, development, testing, documentation, maintenance, and integration of application software for multiple clients with a variety of software tools. From 2001-2003, in my position as Application Developer with Quad States Developers, I worked as Project Leader of Application Development Team for Large Utility Company and managed 3 developers. I have worked as Individual Contributor and Team Member on Application Development projects for U.S. mid-sized companies, using Oracle, Java in J2EE server environments, and with Linux and Windows. Part of a 6-member team from Quad States that enhanced and retooled financial applications for a Life Insurance company, a Bond Company, and an IT manufacturer, using Java.

Nature of Work & Scope of Difficulty: Responsible for analysis, design, and implementation of customized Application Software for Utility Company, Mid-Sized U.S. Manufacturer, and Bond Rating Company. References available on request.

>   2. -Obtain and refine business requirements through interaction with the
>   Requirements Analysts and the customer

I have worked for 6 years, from 2001-2006, in Applications Development. In my position as Application Development Manager for Quad States Developers, from 2003-2006, I worked for 3 years in customized IT/IS applications development. As Applications Development Manager, I supervised a team of 3 application developers in the design of an application for a large Utility company. Strengths include programming knowledge, database knowledge, and experience with open architectures for application usage and growth.

I have been responsible for the design, development, testing, documentation, maintenance, and integration of application software for multiple clients with a variety of software tools. From 2001-2003, in my position as Application Developer with Quad States Developers, I worked as Project Leader of Application Development Team for Large Utility Company and managed 3 developers. I have worked as Individual Contributor and Team Member on Application Development projects for U.S. mid-sized companies, using Oracle, Java in J2EE server environments, and with Linux and Windows. Part of a 6-member team from Quad States that enhanced and retooled financial applications for a Life Insurance company, a Bond Company, and an IT manufacturer, using Java.

Business requirements drove the design, development, testing, documentation, maintenance, and integration of application software with Oracle, Java Beans, MS Access, SQL Server and other software tools for business applications.

Knowledge/Education:
Supervisory Controls & Leadership: Part of a 3-member team from Quad States that enhanced and retooled financial applications for a Life Insurance company, a Bond Company, and an IT manufacturer, using Java.
Nature of Work & Scope of Difficulty: Analyzed existing systems, performance shortfalls, new module creation and migrations. Increased usability of existing database information.

>   3. Provide Tier II and Tier III support for the Help Desk.

In my position as Application Developer with Quad States Developers for multiple clients, from 2001-2002, I was responsible for the design, development, testing, documentation, maintenance, and integration of Help Desk software, including the installation of Network Solutions Support Magic and Peregrine Service Center. Installed and configured software on local machines. Supported desktop environment distributed in different buildings.
Knowledge/Education: Network Solutions Support Magic and Peregrine Service Center Training.
Specialty: 2+ Years experience in Help Desk application development and support. Management experience as Lead for the Help Desk team in initial phases, conducting training and support, productivity analysis, and performance assessments.
Supervisory Controls & Leadership: Managed and trained Help Desk supervisor in installation and use of Network Solutions Support Magic. Managed and trained a team of helpdesk analysts to provide first and second-level support to more than 350 end-users, explaining software components and escalation techniques.
Nature of Work & Scope of Difficulty: Implemented Help Desk application through system life-cycle, including Feasibility, System Design, Software Purchase and Customization, Installation and Use.

>   4. -Work as individual contributors, team members or serve as project task
>   managers.

I have worked for 6 years, from 2001-2006, in Applications Development. In my position as Application Development Manager for Quad States Developers, from 2003-2006, I worked for 3 years in customized IT/IS applications development. As Applications Development Manager, I supervised a team of 3 application developers in the design of an application for a large Utility company. Strengths include programming knowledge, database knowledge, and experience with open architectures for application usage and growth.

I have been responsible for the design, development, testing, documentation, maintenance, and integration of application software for multiple clients with a variety of software tools. From 2001-2003, in my position as Application Developer with Quad States Developers, I worked as Project Leader of Application Development Team for Large Utility Company and managed 3 developers. I have worked as Individual Contributor and Team Member on Application Development projects for U.S. mid-sized companies, using Oracle, Java in J2EE server environments, and with Linux and Windows. Part of a 6-member team from Quad States that enhanced and retooled financial applications for a Life Insurance company, a Bond Company, and an IT manufacturer, using Java.

Knowledge/Education:
Supervisory Controls & Leadership: Worked as Project Leader of Application Development Team for Large Utility Company. Worked as Individual Contributor and Team Member on Application Development projects for U.S. Mid-sized companies, using Oracle, Java in J2EE server environments, and with Linux and Windows operating systems.

Nature of Work & Scope of Difficulty: Application Development for Large Utility company, finance system; Mid-sized Manufacturing DBMS systems.

> *5. -Have a solid understanding of software, data structure, data management, and/or database design principles, system development life cycle, and prototyping methodology and techniques*

-Managed a team of 3 developers
-Managed the server team
-Installed and upgraded Oracle servers on several UNIX systems
-Created, configured, backed up, and tuned database instances
-Defined a common logical architecture for Oracle database and developed PL/SQL interfaces.
-Performed logical and physical data modeling
 -Project Leader with overall responsibility for defining business requirements (interviews and meetings with end-users), design, development and selection of software tools. Brought application to fruition in system life cycle from client-customer need, through design, development of database, population of database, migration of database, interfaces and end-user implementation

Knowledge/Education:
Specialty: Mid-sized Manufacturing DBMS systems
Supervisory Controls & Leadership:
-Project Leader with overall responsibility for defining business requirements (interviews and meetings with end-users), design, development and selection of software tools. Brought application to fruition in system life cycle from client-customer need, through design, development of database, population of database, migration of database, interfaces and end-user implementation
Nature of Work & Scope of Difficulty:
-Project Leader with overall responsibility for defining business requirements (interviews and meetings with end-users), design, development and selection of software tools. Brought application to fruition in system life cycle from client-customer need, through design, development of database, population of database, migration of database, interfaces and end-user implementation

> *6. -Responsible for applying project management principles to their individual project work*

-Demonstrated leadership and project management skills as Project Leader for design, development of database, population of database, migration of database, interfaces and end-user implementation
-Improved overall application performance on several applications, reducing the memory footprint over original specifications by applying object-oriented methodologies
-Utilized object-oriented design principles in ASPs, to create higher performance, improvements in speed, and easier code maintenance.
-Prepared and utilized Microsoft Project Management Timelines with Client-Customers for resource management and to estimate and carry out proper project management of development work
Knowledge/Education:
Supervisory Controls & Leadership:
-Project Leader with overall responsibility for defining business requirements (interviews and meetings with end-users), design, development and selection of software tools. Brought application to fruition in system life cycle from client-customer need, through design, development of database, population of database, migration of database, interfaces and end-user implementation
Nature of Work & Scope of Difficulty:
-Project Leader with overall responsibility for defining business requirements (interviews and meetings with end-users), design, development and selection of software tools. Brought application to fruition

in system life cycle from client-customer need, through design, development of database, population of database, migration of database, interfaces and end-user implementation

7. -Provide client support, consultation, and subject mater expertise for application development, maintenance and administration

I have worked for 6 years, from 2001-2006, in Applications Development. In my position as Application Development Manager for Quad States Developers, from 2003-2006, I worked for 3 years in customized IT/IS applications development. As Applications Development Manager, I supervised a team of 3 application developers in the design of an application for a large Utility company. Strengths include programming knowledge, database knowledge, and experience with open architectures for application usage and growth.

I have been responsible for the design, development, testing, documentation, maintenance, and integration of application software for multiple clients with a variety of software tools. From 2001-2003, in my position as Application Developer with Quad States Developers, I worked as Project Leader of Application Development Team for Large Utility Company and managed 3 developers. I have worked as Individual Contributor and Team Member on Application Development projects for U.S. mid-sized companies, using Oracle, Java in J2EE server environments, and with Linux and Windows. Part of a 6-member team from Quad States that enhanced and retooled financial applications for a Life Insurance company, a Bond Company, and an IT manufacturer, using Java.

Knowledge/Education:

Supervisory Controls & Leadership:

-Project Leader with overall responsibility for defining business requirements (interviews and meetings with end-users), design, development and selection of software tools. Brought application to fruition in system life cycle from client-customer need, through design, development of database, population of database, migration of database, interfaces and end-user implementation

Nature of Work & Scope of Difficulty:

-Project Leader with overall responsibility for defining business requirements (interviews and meetings with end-users), design, development and selection of software tools. Brought application to fruition in system life cycle from client-customer need, through design, development of database, population of database, migration of database, interfaces and end-user implementation

8. -Demonstrate autonomous work environment flexiblity in work assignments, and exhibit customer orientation skills.

Demonstrated autonomous work environment flexibility in work assignments with many clients, by making and meeting appointments at client-customer schedule, working with client support and technical teams on various schedules, adjusting work and work loads to accommodate timetables for required work.

Managed applications development team-member assignments to accommodate and account for required flexibility in work assignments, schedules, timetables for required work.

Knowledge/Education:

Supervisory Controls & Leadership:

-Project Leader with overall responsibility for defining business requirements (interviews and meetings with end-users), design, development and selection of software tools. Brought application to fruition in system life cycle from client-customer need, through design, development of database, population of database, migration of database, interfaces and end-user implementation

Nature of Work & Scope of Difficulty:

Demonstrated autonomous work environment flexibility in work assignments with many clients, by making and meeting appointments at client-customer schedule, working with client support and technical teams on various schedules; adjusting work and work loads to accommodate timetables for required work.

Managed applications development team-member assignments to accommodate and account for required flexibility in work assignments, schedules, timetables for required work.

<u>Qualifications for GS-13:</u>

1. -Applicants must have one or more years of specialized experience as Information Technology Specialist (Application Software), completing computer project assignments that involve design, development, testing, documentation, maintenance and integration of application software; participation in technology planning, product evaluation and report development; and serving as a project manager. This experience must be equivalent to the GS-12 level in the Federal service, but could have been gained in the public or private sectors.

I have worked for 6 years, from 2001-2006, in Applications Development. In my position as Application Development Manager for Quad States Developers, from 2003-2006, I worked for 3 years in customized IT/IS applications development. As Applications Development Manager, I supervised a team of 3 application developers in the design of an application for a large Utility company. Strengths include programming knowledge, database knowledge, and experience with open architectures for application usage and growth.

I have been responsible for the design, development, testing, documentation, maintenance, and integration of application software for multiple clients with a variety of software tools. From 2001-2003, in my position as Application Developer with Quad States Developers, I worked as Project Leader of Application Development Team for Large Utility Company and managed 3 developers. I have worked as Individual Contributor and Team Member on Application Development projects for U.S. mid-sized companies, using Oracle, Java in J2EE server environments, and with Linux and Windows. Part of a 6-member team from Quad States that enhanced and retooled financial applications for a Life Insurance company, a Bond Company, and an IT manufacturer, using Java.

Knowledge/Education:
Operating Systems: UNIX (A1X, HP-UX, Sun Solaris, RedHat Linux, BEA WebLogic); WINDOWS 2000 to Current; WINDOWS NT DBMS: Oracle 7/8/8i , Java, Java Beans (Developer, Designer, DBA); MS SQL Server; MS Access; O2 (Object DBMS), J3EE, BEA WebLogic, Linux, Windows Operating System Training. Languages/Tools: SQL, PL/SQL, SQL Server, ASP, Active X, VB Script, Jscript, HTML, XML. Specialty: Specialize in developing custom software applications to combine accounting, finance, and logistics, to process information on customer usage of product and services. Developed a reputation of making clients happy by completing projects easily, facilitating retrieval of information, and reducing costs.

Supervisory Controls & Leadership: I have worked for 6 years in Applications Development. In my position as Application Development Manager for Quad States Developers, from 2003-2006, I worked for 3 years in customized IT/IS applications development.
As Applications Development Manager from 2003-2006, I supervised a team of 3 application developers in the design of an application for a large Utility company. Strengths include programming knowledge, database knowledge, and experience with open architectures for application usage and growth.

I have been responsible for the design, development, testing, documentation, maintenance, and integration of application software for multiple clients with a variety of software tools. From 2001-2003, in my position as Application Developer with Quad States Developers, I worked as Project Leader of Application Development Team for Large Utility Company and managed 3 developers. I have worked as Individual Contributor and Team Member on Application Development projects for U.S. mid-sized companies, using Oracle, Java in J2EE server environments, and with Linux and Windows. Part of a 6-member team from Quad States that enhanced and retooled financial applications for a Life Insurance company, a Bond Company, and an IT manufacturer, using Java.

Nature of Work & Scope of Difficulty: Responsible for analysis, design, and implementation of customized Application Software for Utility Company, Mid-Sized U.S. Manufacturer, and Bond Rating Company. References available on request.
As Applications Development Manager from 2003-2006, I supervised a team of 3 application developers in the design of an application for a large Utility company. Strengths include programming knowledge, database knowledge, and experience with open architectures for application usage and growth.

2. -In addition, the following skills and experience is required: 1) Skill in administering a clustered BEA WebLogic Server environment in a RedHat Linux environment and 2) Skill in installing, configuring, tuning, troubleshooting, clustering, and deploying applications to WebLogic Server.

In my position as Application Developer, with Quad-State Developers for multiple clients, I worked from 2003-2006 in Linux environments and with BEA WebLogic Servers, and was responsible for the design, development, testing, documentation, maintenance, and integration of application software with BEA WebLogic software tools.
Knowledge: Knowledge of the fundamentals of distributed development using Enterprise JavaBeans 2.0. Knowledge of EJB deployment, and the general use of Java Message Service (JMS) and how to write messaging clients. In addition, knowledge of BEA WebLogic Administration Console.
Education: BEA WebLogic Server Training

Appendix E:
U.S. States & Major Cities
Sample Job Descriptions & Qualifications

STATE OF CALIFORNIA
http://www.my.ca.gov/
*See Charts for Salary & Pension Information

STAFF PROGRAMMER ANALYST (SPECIALIST)

Under general supervision, acts as a project leader on complex applications and/or on complex information technology system problems and works independently as a technical specialist. One year of experience in the California state service performing duties comparable to an Associate Programmer Analyst (Specialist) or Associate Programmer Analyst (Supervisor). Or Two years of progressively responsible experience in information technology systems study, design, and programming, which shall have included responsibility on a project for analyzing operational methods and developing computer programs to meet desired results. One year of experience in this pattern must include independent performance of programming and analysis work, lead of a programming team, or participation as a team member on projects of a very complex nature or broad scope. Or Thirty semester units or 45 quarter units of graduate work in information technology-related coursework from a recognized college or university.

STAFF PROGRAMMER ANALYST (SUPERVISOR)

Under general supervision, acts as a supervisor on complex applications. One year of experience in the California state service performing duties comparable to an Associate Programmer Analyst (Specialist) or Associate Programmer Analyst (Supervisor). Or two years of progressively responsible experience in information technology systems study, design, and programming, which shall have included responsibility on a project for analyzing operational methods and developing computer programs to meet desired results. One year of experience in this pattern must include independent performance of programming and analysis work, lead of a programming team, or participation as a team member on projects of a very complex nature or broad scope. Or thirty semester units or 45 quarter units of graduate work in information technology-related coursework from a recognized college or university.

TELECOMMUNICATIONS SYSTEMS ANALYST I-II

Education: The following education is required when non-State experience is used to qualify at any level: Equivalent to graduation from college, preferably with major specialization in electronics or related technical subject area. (Additional qualifying experience may be substituted for education on a year for year basis. Experience: One year of experience performing telecommunications systems or Four years' experience in the California state service coordinating, operating, and/or maintaining telecommunications systems, such as performed by incumbents in the classes of Supervising Telephone Operator, Radio Dispatch Supervisor, or Six months of experience performing the duties of a Management Services Technician, Range B, in a State service telecommunications operation; or Two years' experience in the California state service in a formal telecommunications training and development assignment to a class equivalent to Management Services Technician.

NEW YORK - NEW YORK CITY
http://www.nyc.gov

Residency: City residency is not required for this position.
English Requirement: Candidates must be able to understand and be understood in English.

COMPUTER ASSOCIATE (SOFTWARE LEVELS I-III)

Education and Experience Requirements:

(1) A baccalaureate degree from an accredited college, including or supplemented by twenty-four (24) semester credits in computer science or a related computer field and one (1) year of satisfactory fulltime computer software experience in computer systems development and analysis, applications programming, database administration, systems programming or data communications; or

(2) A four year high school diploma or its educational equivalent and five (5) years of full-time satisfactory computer software experience as described in "1" above; or

(3) A satisfactory combination of education and experience that is equivalent to "1" or "2" above. College education may be substituted for up to two years of the required experience in "2" above on the basis that sixty(60) semester credits from an accredited college is equated to one year of experience. In addition, twenty-four (24) semester credits from an accredited college or graduate school in computer science or a related field, or a certificate of at least 625 hours in computer programming from an accredited technical school (post high school), may be substituted for one year of experience. However, all candidates who attempt to qualify under option "3" must have at least a four year high school diploma or its educational equivalent .

COMPUTER SPECIALIST (SOFTWARE LEVELS I-IV)

Experience & Education Requirements:
(1) A baccalaureate degree from an accredited college, including or supplemented by twenty-four (24) semester credits in computer science or a related computer field and two (2) years of satisfactory full-time software experience in designing, programming, debugging, maintaining, implementing, and enhancing computer software applications, systems programming, systems analysis and design, data communication software, or database design and programming, including one year in a project leader capacity or as a major contributor on a complex project; or

(2) A four-year high school diploma or its educational equivalent and six   (6) years of full-time satisfactory software experience as described in "1" above, including one year in a project leader capacity or as a major contributor on a complex project; or
(3) A satisfactory combination of edu
cation and experience that is equivalent to (1) or (2) above. College education may be substituted for up to two years of the required experience in (2) above on the basis that sixty (60) semester credits from an accredited college is equated to one year of experience. A masters degree in computer science or a related computer field may be substituted for one year of the required experience in (1) or (2) above. However, all candidates must have a four year high school diploma or its educational equivalent, plus at least one (1) year of satisfactory full-time software experience in a project leader apacity or as a major contributor on a complex project.

Appendix F:
Locating Federal Jobs at Direct Hire Authority and Excepted Service Agencies

EXCEPTED SERVICE AGENCIES

Most Federal Government civilian positions are part of the competitive civil service. To obtain a Federal job, you must compete with other applicants in open competition.   Some agencies are excluded from the competitive civil service procedures. This means that these agencies have their own hiring system which establishes the evaluation criteria they use in filling their internal vacancies. These agencies are called **excepted service agencies**. If you are interested in employment with an **excepted service agency**, you should contact that agency directly. The U.S. Office of Personnel Management does not provide application forms or information on jobs in excepted service agencies or organizations. Below is a list of excepted service agencies, departments and public international organizations. This list is not all-inclusive and is subject to change.

MAJOR EXCEPTED SERVICE DEPARTMENTS AND AGENCIES

Federal Reserve System, Board of Governors
20th & C Street, NW.
Washington, DC 20551
www.federalreserve.gov
(202) 452-3038

Central Intelligence Agency
Office of Public Affairs
Washington, D.C. 20505
www.cia.gov; 703-82-0623

Defense Intelligence Agency
Civilian Personnel Office DAH-2
100 MacDill Blvd
Washington, DC 20340-5100
www.dia.mil; 202-231-8228

U.S. Department of State
2201 C Street NW
Washington, DC 20520
www.state.gov ; 202-647-4000

MAJOR EXCEPTED SERVICE
DEPARTMENTS AND AGENCIES

Federal Bureau of Investigation
J. Edgar Hoover Building
935 Pennsylvania Avenue, NW
Washington, D.C. 20535-0001
www.fbi.gov ; 202-324-3000

Government Accountability Office
441 G Street, NW., Room 1157
Washington, DC 20548
www.gao.gov; 202-512-6092

Agency for International Development
2401 E Street, NW., Room 1127
Washington, DC 20523
www.usaid.gov; 202-712-4810

National Security Agency
College Relations Branch
Fort Meade, MD 20750
www.nsa.gov; 1-866-672-4473

U.S. Nuclear Regulatory Commission
Division of Organization of Personnel
Resources and Employment Program
Washington, DC 20555
www.nrc.gov; 301-415-1534

Post Rate Commission
Administrative Office, Suite 300
Washington, DC 20268-0001
www.prc.gov ; (202) 789-6800

Postal Service
(Contact your local Postmaster) www.
usps.gov

Tennessee Valley Authority
Knoxville Office Complex
400 West Summit Hill Drive
Knoxville, TN 37902
www.tva.gov
865-632-2101

United States Mission to the United Nations
140 East 45th Street
New York, N.Y. 10017
www.un.int/usa
212-415-4050

U.S. Department of Veterans Affairs
810 Vermont Avenue, NW.
Washington, DC 20420
www.va.gov

JUDICIAL BRANCH

The Judicial Branch of the Federal
Government
includes all legal entities except the
U.S. Claims Court. For Judicial Branch
employment information contact:

United States Supreme Court Building
Personnel Office
1 First Street, NE.
Washington, DC 20543
202-479-3211

Office of Public Affairs
Administrative Office of the U.S. Courts
Washington, D.C. 20544
www.uscourts.gov
202-502-2600

United States Court of Federal Claims
717 Madison Place, NW.
Washington, DC 20005
www.uscfc.uscourts.gov
202-357-6400

LEGISLATIVE BRANCH

The Legislative Branch of the Federal
Government
includes Senators' and
Representatives' offices,
the Library of Congress and the U.S.
Capitol. For employment
information contact:

U.S. Senate
Senate Placement Office
Senate Hart Building, Room 142B
Washington, DC 20510
www.senate.gov
(202) 224-3121

U.S. House of Representatives
House Placement Office
House Office Building, Annex 2, Room 219
Third & D Street, SW.
Washington, DC 20515-6609
www.house.gov
202-224-3121

Library of Congress
Employment Office
Room 107, Madison Building
Washington, DC 20540
www.loc.gov
202-707-5627

PUBLIC INTERNATIONAL ORGANIZATIONS

The United States holds membership in numerous
international organizations which are not part of the Federal
Government. For employment information and application
procedures contact:

International Monetary Fund
Recruiting and Training Division
700 19th Street, NW.
Washington, DC 20431
www.imf.org
202-623-7000

Pan American Health Organization
Pan American Sanitary Bureau
Regional Office of the
World Health Organizations
525 23rd Street, NW.
Washington, DC 20037
www.paho.org
202- 974-3000

United Nations Children's Fund
333 East 38th Street
(Mail Code: GC-6)
New York, New York 10016
www.unicef.org
212-686-5522

United Nations Development Program
One United Nations Plaza
New York, NY 10017
www.undp.org
212-906-5000

United Nations Institute for Training and
Research
One United Nations Plaza
Room DC1-603,
New York, NY, 10017-3515
www.unitar.org
212-963-9196

United Nations Population Fund
220 East 42nd Street
New York, NY 10017
www.unfpa.org
212-297-5000

United Nations Secretariat
Office of Personnel Services
Recruitment Programs Section
New York, NY 10017
www.un.org/documents/st.htm

World Bank, IFC and MIGA*
Recruitment Division
International Recruitment
1818 H Street, NW.
Washington, DC 20433
www.worldbank.org
(202) 473-1000

Appendix G:
U.S. Federal Government,
Application for Employment OF-612

Form Approved
OMB No. 3206-0219

OPTIONAL APPLICATION FOR FEDERAL EMPLOYMENT - OF 612

You may apply for most jobs with a resume, this form, or other written format. If your resume or application does not provide all the information requested on this form and in the job vacancy announcement, you may lose consideration for a job.

1 Job title in announcement		2 Grade(s) applying for	3 Announcement number
4 Last name	First and middle names		5 Social Security Number - -
6 Mailing address			7 Phone numbers (include area code) Daytime ( )
City	State	ZIP Code -	Evening ( )

WORK EXPERIENCE

8 Describe your paid and nonpaid work experience related to the job for which you are applying. Do **not** attach job descriptions.

1) Job title (if Federal, include series and grade)

From (MM/YY)	To (MM/YY)	Salary $	per	Hours per week
Employer's name and address				Supervisor's name and phone number ( )

Describe your duties and accomplishments

2) Job title (if Federal, include series and grade)

From (MM/YY)	To (MM/YY)	Salary $	per	Hours per week
Employer's name and address				Supervisor's name and phone number ( )

Describe your duties and accomplishments

May we contact your current supervisor?

YES ☐   NO ☐ è   If we need to contact your current supervisor before making an offer, we will contact you first.

UCATION

Mark highest level completed.   Some HS ☐   HS/GED ☐   Associate ☐   Bachelor ☐   Master ☐   Doctoral ☐

Last high school (HS) or GED school. Give the school's name, city, State, ZIP Code (if known), and year diploma or GED received.

Colleges and universities attended. Do **not** attach a copy of your transcript unless requested.

Name			Total Credits Earned		Major(s)	Degree - Year
			Semester	Quarter		(if any) Received
City	State	ZIP Code -				
		-				
		-				

HER QUALIFICATIONS

Job-related training courses (give title and year). **Job-related** skills (other languages, computer software/hardware, tools, machinery, typing speed, etc. **Job-related** certificates and licenses (current only). **Job-related** honors, awards, and special accomplishments(publications, memberships in professional/honor societies, leadership activities, public speaking, and performance awards.) Give dates, but do **not** send documents unless requested.

NERAL

Are you a U.S. citizen?   YES ☐   NO ☐ è   Give the country of your citizenship.

Do you claim veterans' preference?   NO ☐   YES ☐ è   Mark your claim of 5 or 10 points below.

5 points ☐ è   Attach your DD 214 or other proof.   **10 points** ☐ è   Attach an *Application for 10-Point Veterans' Preference* (SF 15) and proof required.

Were you ever a Federal civilian employee?   Series Grade From (MM/YY) To (MM/YY)

NO ☐   YES ☐ è   For highest civilian grade give:

Are you eligible for reinstatement based on career or career-conditional Federal status?

NO ☐   YES ☐ è   If requested, attach SF 50 proof.

PLICANT CERTIFICATION

I certify that, to the best of my knowledge and belief, all of the information on and attached to this application is true, correct, complete and made in good faith. **I understand** that false or fraudulent information on or attached to this application may be grounds for not hiring me or firing me after I begin work, and may be punishable by fine or imprisonment. **I understand** that any information I give may be investigated.

SIGNATURE   **DATE SIGNED**

BIBLIOGRAPHY

AFSCME, CWA Local 1180, 2006, http://www.cwa1180.org/civil/civil.shtml

Americas Job Bank, http://www.ajb.org

Anderson Ross A., Security Engineering: A Guide to Building Dependable Distributed Systems, 2005.

Anderson, Ronald E., Ethics in Digital Government, in Digital Government, Principles and Best Practices, ed. Pavlichev, Alexei, and Garson, David, A., Idea Group Inc., 2004, 218-235
Association for Computing Machinery (ACM), http://www.acm.org/globalizationreport

Career One Stop Centers, http://www.careeronestop.org
Chabrow, Eric, Information Technology Hiring Hits an All-time High, Infromation Week, July 17, 2006

Corbett, Christopher, The Future of Digital Government, in Digital Government, Principles and Best Practices, ed. Pavlichev, Alexei, and Garson, David, A., Idea Group Inc., 2004, 344-367.

Crain's Business New York, Number of Vacant Computer Jobs Rises: Survey, Amanda Fung, March 29, 2006.

Fletcher, Patricia Diamond, Portals and policy: Implications of Electronic Access to U.S. Federal Government Information and Services, in Digital Government, Principles and Best Practices, ed. Pavlichev, Alexei, and Garson, David, A., Idea Group Inc., 2004, 52-62.

Franzel, Joshua M. and Coursey, David H., Government Web Portals: Management Issues and the Approaches of Five States, in Digital Government, Principles and Best Practices, ed. Pavlichev, Alexei, and Garson, David, A., Idea Group Inc., 2004, 63-77.

Friedman, Thomas, The World Is Flat, Farrar, Strauss and Giroux, 2006.

Gant, Jon and Ijams, Donald S., Digital Government and Geographic Information Systems, in Digital Government, Principles and Best Practices, ed. Pavlichev, Alexei, and Garson, David, A., Idea Group Inc., 2004, 248-262.

Garson, David A., The Promise of Digital Government, in Digital Government, Principles and Best Practices, ed. Pavlichev, Alexei, and Garson, David, A., Idea Group Inc., 2004, 2-15.

Gore, Al, quoted in Fletcher, Patricia Diamond, Portals and policy: Implications of Electronic Access to U.S. Federal Government Information and Services, in Digital Government, Principles and Best Practices, ed. Pavlichev, Alexei, and Garson, David, A., Idea Group Inc., 2004, 52-62.

Gross, Daniel, "Why 'Outsourcing' May Lost Its Power as a Scare Word," The New York Times, August 13, 2006.
Harper, Franklin Maxwell, Data Warehousing and the Organization of Governmental Databases, in Digital Government, Principles and Best Practices, ed. Pavlichev, Alexei, and Garson, David, A., Idea Group Inc., 2004, 236-247.

Hood, C., The Tools of Government, London, MacMillan, 1983.

Krysiak, Mark E.; Tucker, Carla; Spitzer, David; and Holland, Kevin, E-Procurement: State Government Learns from the Private Sector, in Digital Government, Principles and Best Practices, ed. Pavlichev, Alexei, and Garson, David, A., Idea Group Inc., 2004, 149-168.

Latchford, Michael, Lowry, Alexander, Roberts, Ian, PA Consulting Group, "Successful Program Management in a Complex Outsourcing Environment," quoted in CMP Global Services, July 24, 2006, http://www.globalservicesmedia.com/sections/sm/showArticle.jhtml?articleID=190500432

Lawson, Roy, InformationWeek, 2006, More U.S. Workers Have IT Jobs Than Ever Before, Eric Chabrow, InformationWeek, Apr 24, 2006

Levy, Frank and Murnane, Richard, The New Division of Labor: How Computers are Creating the Next Job Market, Princeton University Press, 2004.

Liston, Robert A., Your Career in Civil Service, Messner Publishers, 1967.

Margetts, Helen, Information Technology in Government: Britain and America, Routledge Press, 1999.

Marlin, John Tepper, City Economist, 2006, http://www.cityeconomist.com/pdf/CityEconomist06-04-01.pdf quoted in Crain's Business New York, February 2006, Number of Vacant Computer Jobs Rises: Survey, Amanda Fung, March 29, 2006.

McClure, C.R., Sprehe, T. and Eschenfelder, K. Performance Measures for Federal Agencies: Final Report. Retrieved December 13, 2001 from http://www.access.gpo.gov/su_docs/index.html

McDougall, Paul, U.S. Tech Workers In Hot Demand Despite More Outsourcing

Mullen, Patrick R., Digital Government and Individual Privacy, in Digital Government, Principles and Best Practices, ed. Pavlichev, Alexei, and Garson, David, A., Idea Group Inc., 2004, 134-148.

National Research Council (NRC), Funding a Revolution: Government Support for Computing Research, National Academy Press, 1999.

O'Looney, J.A., Wiring Governments, Challenges and Possibilities for Public Managers, Quorum Books, 2002.

Partnerships for Community Press, Info Tech Employment, "IT Federal Jobs Survey," 2007, http://www.infotechemployment.com.

Partnerships for Community Press, Info Tech Employment, "Survey of IT Job Titles in U.S. States & Major U.S. Cities," 2007,
http://www.infotechemployment.com.

Patterson, David A., Association for Computing Machinery, 2006, http://www.acm.org/globalizationreport; http://www.acm.org/pubs/cacm/

Registered Contract between 23 Companies and Client Company, 2006 from one Large U.S. Municipality, Published as Registered Contract in Municipal Government Public Records.

Relyea, Harold C. and Hogue, Henry B., A Brief History of the Emergence of Digital Government in the United States, in Digital Government, Principles and Best Practices, ed. Pavlichev, Alexei, and Garson, David, A., Idea Group Inc., 2004, 16-33.

Richardson, Ronald E., Digital Government: Balancing Risk and Reward through Public/Private Partnerships, in Digital Government, Principles and Best Practices, ed. Pavlichev, Alexei, and Garson, David, A., Idea Group Inc., 2004, 200-217.
Rose, Barbara, Tech Workers Plugging Back in to a Changed Job Marke, Chicago Tribune, July 2006

Society for Information Management, 2006, http://www.simnet.org

Stowers, Genie, Issues in E-Commerce and E-Government Service Delivery, in Digital Government, Principles and Best Practices, ed. Pavlichev, Alexei, and Garson, David, A., Idea Group Inc., 2004, 169-185.

Sun Microsystems, http://www.sunmicrosystems.com

U.S. Bureau of Labor Statistics, U.S. Government, 2006, 2007; http://www.bls.gov

U.S. Federal Government, Office of Personnel Management, 15 Executive Agencies & 101 Other Federal Agencies, 2006, http://www.loc.gov/rr/news/fedgov.html.
U.S. Federal Government, Office of Personnel Management, Administrative Careers with America -ACWA), http://www.opm.gov/qualifications/SEC-V/sec-v.asp
U.S. Federal Government, Office of Personnel Management, Career Transition Resources, 2006, http://www.careeronestop.org.
U.S. Federal Government, Office of Personnel Management, Detail and Transfer of Federal Employees to International Organizations, 2006, http://www.opm.gov/employ/internat/.
U.S. Federal Government, Office of Personnel Management, Direct Hiring Authority and by Excepted Agencies, http://www.apps.opm.gov
U.S. Federal Government, Office of Personnel Management, Federal Executive Boards, http://www.opm.gov
U.S. Federal Government, Office of Personnel Management, Form C Section C. Form C, it may be downloaded from_ http://www.opm.gov/forms/pdf_fill/OPM1203fx.pdf.
U.S. Federal Government, Office of Personnel Management, Form OF-612 may be downloaded and printed from http://www.opm.gov/forms/pdf_fill/of612.pdf.
U.S. Federal Government, Office of Personnel Management, General Services Salary Schedule, 2006, http://www.opm.gov.
U.S. Federal Government, Office of Personnel Management, Individual Development Plans (IDP), 2006, http://www.opm.gov/hcaaf_resource_center/assets/Lead_tool3.pdf.;
U.S. Federal Government, Office of Personnel Management, Intergovernmental Personnel Act Mobility Program, 2006, http://www.opm.gov/programs/ipa/.
U.S. Federal Government, Office of Personnel Management, Introduction to the Position Classifications Standard,1995, http://www.opm.gov/fedclass/gsintro.pdf.
U.S. Federal Government, Office of Personnel Management, Job Family Position Classification Standard for Administrative Work in the Information Technology Group GS-2200, GS-2200, 2001, 2003; http://www.opm.gov/FEDCLASS/gs2200a.pdf.
U.S. Federal Government, Office of Personnel Management, Leadership & Knowledge Management Programs, 2006, http://apps.opm.gov/HumanCapital/standards/lkmq5b.html
U.S. Federal Government, Office of Personnel Management, Student Employment; http://www.studentjobs.gov
U.S. Federal Government, Office of Personnel Management, The Classifier's Handbook, 1991, http://www.opm.gov/fedclass/clashnbk.pdf
U.S. Federal Government, Office of Personnel Management, The Executives in Residence Program, 2006, http://www.leadership.opm.gov/content.cfm?CAT=EIRP.
U.S. Federal Government, USAJOBS.gov, Official Jobs Web Portal, http://www.USAjobs.gov
U.S. Government, Department of Justice, U.S. Freedom of Information Act, 2006.

VARBusiness, March 2006.

Zieger, Robert H., American Workers, American Unions, Second Edition, Johns Hopkins University Press, 1994.

Index

A

Administrative , 59
AFSCME , 72

B

Benefits 18, 24–31, 36, 98, 133, 237
Business 19, 66–70, 19, 72, 97, 235, 236, 255–258, 265–267

C

Career 10, 23, 25, 31, 62, 14, 18, 24, 59, 67, 44, 46, 52, 57, 87, 249, 265, 266
Certifications 236
Civil Service 26-31
  U.S. Federal Government
    Benefits , 18, 36, 54, 98, 133, 237
    Completing the Application 12, 27, 42, 59, 65
    Federal Government Job Group, Job Title & Salary Grade Pay 42, 43
    General Services Salary Table 42, 81 (Appendix A)
    Information Technology Exchange Program (ITEP) 86
    Information Technology Main Job Titles 81
    No Written Civil Service Exam Required for IT Jobs 41
    Pension 11, 18, 97, 98, 133, 237, 259–260

Contract Labor 21
  Contract Specialist 96, (Appendix C)

Criminal Investigator 96, (Appendix C)

D

Database
  Database Jobs 235-236
Disabilities, Jobs for People With 45

E

Education 17, 19
    Entry-Level 21
        Environmental Protection, Department of 92

Environmental Engineer (Appendix C)

Environmental Scientist (Appendix C)

Experience 17
Experience as a Substitute for Education 17

F

Factors in Determining Job Grade Classification (Appendix B)

H

Homeland Security, Department of 88

I

Identifying Your Job Title 41
 Information Technology
    Information Technology - U.S. Federal 75-88
    Information Technology - U.S. Federal - 10 Job Specialties 82
    Information Technology - Sample Job Descriptions (Appendix C)
    Information Technology Specialist 88 (Appendix C)
    IT Certifications 236
    IT Exchange Program 82
    IT Job Titles-Skill Sets (Chart IV)
    IT Procedures & Policies 236
    IT Procurement 236
    IT Training & Development 236
    Project Management 236
    Internet and Intranets
    Internet 235, 236
Internships 19,

J

Jobs for People with Disabilities 45
Job Package, U.S. Federal 46
Job Package, U.S. States & Cities
Job Titles, Salaries, U.S. Federal (Chart II)
Job Titles, Salaries, U.S. States & Cities (Chart III)
Jobs
  Non-technical Technical Jobs
    Contract Management 236
    Contractor Management 236
    IT Personnel/Staffing/Human Resources 236
    IT Procedures & Policies 236
    IT Procurement 236
    IT Training & Development 236
    Media Training 236
    Policies & Manuals 236
    Project Management 236
    Requests for Proposals & Bid Analysis 236
    Training & Development 236
    Vendors Relations 236

K

Knowledge, Skills, Abilities Statement 42, (Appendix D)

L

M

Model Knowledge, Skills, Abilities Statement (Appendix D)

N

Network
  Networking & Infrastructure Skills 235
Non-technical Technical Jobs
  Contract Management 236
  Contractor Management 236
  IT Personnel/Staffing/Human Resources 236
  IT Procedures & Policies 236
  IT Procurement 236
  IT Training & Development 236
  Media Training 236
  Policies & Manuals 236
  Project Management 236
  Requests for Proposals & Bid Analysis 236
  Training & Development 236
  Vendors Relations 236

O

Outsourcing 13

P

Pensions 25, Chart II, III, V
Permanent, Career Civil Service 21, 71
Permanent Employee 21, 71
Programmer 235, 236
Public Unionism 26-31

Q

Qualifications 10-45
  Business Skills 236
  Certifications 236

R

S

Salaries 17, 18, Chart II, III, V, Appendix A,
Security 235-236
Skill Sets 235-236
Special Career Programs 19, 82-87, 88-91, 92-95

T

Technology in Fire, Police, EMS, 911 36
Technology in Government 32-38, 78, 88
Test, No Test Required 17, 41
Third-Party Vendors 39
Types of Technical & Non-Technical Jobs 79-82

U

U.S. Congress
U.S. Federal Government
  Administrative Careers with America (ACWA) 60
  Career One Stop Centers 62, 68
  Completing the Application and Hiring Process 59
  Direct Hiring Authority and by Excepted Agencies 60 (Appendix F)
  Form OF-612 62, (Appendix G)
  Factors in Determining GS Classification (Appendix B)
  Federal Career Intern Program 44
  General Services Salary Schedule (Appendix A)
  Knowledge, Skills, Abilities Statement (Appendix D)
  Information Technology Exchange Program (ITEP) 59, 86
  Internships 19, 61
  Interview, The 65
  Introduction to the Position Classifications 42, 64
  Learning about Available Jobs 59
  Official Federal Government Website Portal 59
  Outstanding Scholar Program 59, 60, 61
  Pensions 52
  Sample Job Announcements (Appendix C)
  Senior Executive Service 44, 66, 73, 86, 98, 133, 237
  Student Employment 60
  Supplemental Job Announcements

U.S. Postal Service Jobs 49-51, Chart V

U.S. State & Municipal Government 52
  Applying for a Posted or Advertised Provisional Position 68
  Completing a U.S. State or City Employment Application 69
  Civil Service Exam, The 70
  Filing the Application during an Open Filing Period 69
  Interview, The 71
  Job Hiring Pools 71
  Job Package 54
  Obtaining a Civil Service Exam Application 69
  Public Unionism 11, 26, 27
  Ranking by Score 70
  Sample Job Descriptions (Appendix E)
  Types of Employment Status 71

Unix 76, 235, 236

V

Veteran's Preference 45

W

Web , 85, 35, 44, 75, 76, 235, 236
Web Development 235, 236
Web Portal Model , 35
What Jobs Are Available 41 (Charts II, III, V)
Windows 76, 235, 236, 254, 255, 256, 257, 258
Wireless 235
World Wide Web (WWW) , 35